Lecture Notes in Computer Science 2449
Edited by G. Goos, J. Hartmanis, and J. van Leeuwen

Springer
Berlin
Heidelberg
New York
Hong Kong
London
Milan
Paris
Tokyo

Luc Van Gool (Ed.)

Pattern Recognition

24th DAGM Symposium
Zurich, Switzerland, September 16-18, 2002
Proceedings

 Springer

Series Editors

Gerhard Goos, Karlsruhe University, Germany
Juris Hartmanis, Cornell University, NY, USA
Jan van Leeuwen, Utrecht University, The Netherlands

Volume Editor

Luc Van Gool
Computer Vision Laboratory, ETH Zürich
Gloriastrasse 35, 8092 Zürich, Switzerland
E-mail: vangool@vision.ee.ethz.ch

Cataloging-in-Publication Data applied for

Die Deutsche Bibliothek - CIP-Einheitsaufnahme

Pattern recognition : ... DAGM Symposium .... - 23. 2001 -. - Berlin ;
Heidelberg ; New York ; Barcelona ; Hong Kong ; London ; Milan ; Paris ;
Tokyo : Springer, 2001
   (Lecture notes in computer science ; ...)
   Früher u.d.T.: Mustererkennung ...
24. 2002. Zurich, Switzerland, September 16-18, 2002 : proceedings. - 2002
   (Lecture notes in computer science ; 2449)
   ISBN 3-540-44209-X

CR Subject Classification (1998): I.5, I.4, I.3.5, I.2.10

ISSN 0302-9743
ISBN 3-540-44209-X Springer-Verlag Berlin Heidelberg New York

Springer-Verlag Berlin Heidelberg New York
a member of BertelsmannSpringer Science+Business Media GmbH

http://www.springer.de

© Springer-Verlag Berlin Heidelberg 2002

Typesetting: Camera-ready by author, data conversion by Steingräber Satztechnik GmbH, Heidelberg
Printed on acid-free paper   SPIN: 10871097   06/3142   5 4 3 2 1 0

Preface

We are proud to present the DAGM 2002 proceedings, which are the result of the efforts of many people.

First, there are the many authors, who have submitted so many excellent contributions. We received more than 140 papers, of which we could only accept about half in order not to overload the program. Only about one in seven submitted papers could be delivered as an oral presentation, for the same reason. But it needs to be said that almost all submissions were of a really high quality.

This strong program could not have been put together without the support of the Program Committee. They took their responsibility most seriously and we are very grateful for their reviewing work, which certainly took more time than anticipated, given the larger than usual number of submissions.

Our three invited speakers added a strong multidisciplinary component to the conference. Dr. Antonio Criminisi of Microsoft Research (Redmond, USA) demonstrated how computer vision can literally bring a new dimension to the appreciation of art. Prof. Philippe Schyns (Dept. of Psychology, Univ. of Glasgow, UK) presented intriguing insights into the human perception of patterns, e.g., the role of scale. Complementary to this presentation, Prof. Manabu Tanifuji of the Brain Science Institute in Japan (Riken) discussed novel neurophysiological findings on how the brain deals with the recognition of objects and their parts.

Last, but not least, I want to thank the many members of my research team who made DAGM 2002 possible: Jutta Spanzel, Vreni Vogt, and Corinna Jurr-Anderson for handling administrative issues such as the registration process; Petr Doubek handled the paper submissions; Petr Doubek, Andreas Griesser, and Andreas Turina took care of the websites; and Mattieu Bray and Jutta Spanzel took care of accommodation a and catering issues. As DAGM came closer several other members of our group contributed greatly as well. Thanks!

To the readers of these proceedings, enjoy!

June 2002   Luc Van Gool

Organization

DAGM e.V.: German Association for Pattern Recognition

General Chair

L. Van Gool   ETH Zürich

Program Committee

J. Buhmann	Univ. Bonn
H. Burkhardt	Univ. Freiburg
W. Förstner	Univ. Bonn
U. Franke	DaimlerChrysler
D. Gavrila	DaimlerChrysler
A. Grün	ETH Zürich
G. Hartmann	Univ. Paderborn
B. Jähne	Univ. Heidelberg
R. Koch	Univ. Kiel
W.-G. Kropatsch	TU Wien
F. Leberl	TU Graz
C.-E. Liedtke	Univ. Hannover
H. Mayer	Univ.-BW München
R. Mester	Univ. Frankfurt
H.-H. Nagel	Univ. Karlsruhe
B. Nebel	Univ. Freiburg
B. Neumann	Univ. Hamburg
H. Ney	RWTH Aachen
H. Niemann	FORWISS Erlangen
H. Ritter	Univ. Bielefeld
G. Sagerer	Univ. Bielefeld
D. Saupe	Univ. Konstanz
B. Schiele	ETH Zürich
C. Schnörr	Univ. Mannheim
G. Sommer	Univ. Kiel
G. Székely	ETH Zürich
T. Tolxdorff	Freie Universität Berlin
T. Vetter	Univ. Freiburg
F.M. Wahl	Univ. Braunschweig
J. Weickert	Univ. Saarland

Since 1978 the DAGM (German Association for Pattern Recognition) has staged annually at different venues a scientific symposium with the aim of considering conceptual formulations, ways of thinking, and research results from different areas in pattern recognition, to facilitate the exchange of experiences and ideas between the experts, and to stimulate the young generation.

The DAGM e.V. was founded as a registered society in September 1999. Until then the DAGM had been constituted from supporter societies which have since been honorary members of the DAGM e.V.:

DGaO   Deutsche Arbeitsgemeinschaft für angewandte Optik (German Society of Applied Optics)

GMDS   Deutsche Gesellschaft für Medizinische Informatik, Biometrie und Epidemiologie (German Society for Medical Informatics, Biometry, and Epidemiology)

GI   Gesellschaft für Informatik (German Informatics Society)

ITG   Informationstechnische Gesellschaft (Information Technology Society)

DGN   Deutsche Gesellschaft für Nuklearmedizin (German Society of Nuclear Medicine)

IEEE   Deutsche Sektion des IEEE (The Institute of Electrical and Electronics Engineers, German Section)

DGPF   Deutsche Gesellschaft für Photogrammetrie und Fernerkundung

VDMA   Fachabteilung industrielle Bildverarbeitung/Machine Vision im VMDA (Robotics + Automation Division within VDMA)

GNNS   German Chapter of the European Neural Network Society

DGR   Deutsche Gesellschaft für Robotik

The

DAGM Main Prize 2001

endowed with DEM 5000

was awarded to

R. Hanek,

TU Munich

for the following contribution:

Model-Based Image Segmentation with Local Self-Adapting Separation Criteria

and

S. Winkelbach and F.M. Wahl,

TU Braunschweig

for the following contribution:

Shape from 2D Edge Gradients

Further prizes endowed with DEM 1000 for the year 2001 were awarded to

F. Deinzer, J. Denzler, H. Niemann,
Univ. Erlangen-Nürnberg
On Fusion of Multiple Views for Active Object Recognition

J. Denzler, C.M. Brown, H. Niemann,
Univ. Erlangen-Nürnberg
Optimal Camera Parameter Selection for State Estimation
with Applications in Object Recognition

J. Keuchel, C. Schellewald, D. Cremers, C. Schnörr,
Univ. Mannheim
Convex Relaxations for Binary Image Partitioning and Perceptual Grouping

M. Luxen, W. Förstner,
Univ. Bonn
Optimal Camera Orientation from Observed Lines
(sponsored by ABW GmbH)

S. Siggelkow, M. Schael, H. Burkhardt,
Univ. Freiburg
SIMBA – Search IMages By Appearance

National Instruments Prize

A. Suppes, F. Suhling, M. Hötter,
FH Hannover
Robust Obstacle Detection from Stereoscopic Image Using Kalman Filtering

Table of Contents

Segmentation

Invited Talk

3D Shape

Posters II

Optical Flow

Recognition

Posters III

Spherical Images

Multimodal Shape Tracking
with Point Distribution Models

J. Giebel and D.M. Gavrila

Machine Perception, DaimlerChrysler Research,
Wilhelm Runge Str. 11, 89089 Ulm, Germany
{jan.giebel, dariu.gavrila}@daimlerchrysler.com

Abstract. This paper addresses the problem of multimodal shape-based
object tracking with learned spatio-temporal representations. Multimodality is considered both in terms of shape representation and in
terms of state propagation. Shape representation involves a set of distinct linear subspace models or Point Distribution Models (PDMs) which
correspond to clusters of similar shapes. This representation is learned
fully automatically from training data, without requiring prior feature
correspondence. Multimodality at the state propagation level is achieved
by particle filtering. The tracker uses a mixed-state: continuous parameters describe rigid transformations and shape variations within a PDM
whereas a discrete parameter covers the PDM membership; discontinuous shape changes are modeled as transitions between discrete states of
a Markov model. The observation density is derived from a well-behaved
matching criterion involving multi-feature distance transforms. We illustrate our approach on pedestrian tracking from a moving vehicle.

1 Introduction

For many real world tracking applications there are no explicit prior models
available to account for object appearance and motion. This paper presents a
technique to learn spatio-temporal shape models for complex deformable objects
from examples. See Figure 1. To capture the shape variation we derive a set of
distinct object parameterizations, corresponding to clusters of similar shapes,
based on the integrated registration and clustering approach introduced in [7].
For compactness a linear subspace decomposition reduces the dimensionality in
each cluster. To constrain the temporal changes in shape, these object parameterizations are treated as discrete states in a Markov model. The transition
probabilities for such a model can be derived from training sequences.

Tracking is performed using an adaption [9,12] of the stochastic framework
("Condensation") proposed by Isard and Blake [13], which can cope with the
mixed continuous/discrete state space of a spatio-temporal shape model. Due
to the stochastic nature and the ability to approximate multimodal probability
density functions, the algorithm is quite robust against cluttered backgrounds
and partial occlusions. The states of our tracker are propagated over time by
applying random noise assuming constant velocity of the 2D movement of the

L. Van Gool (Ed.): DAGM 2002, LNCS 2449, pp. 1–8, 2002.

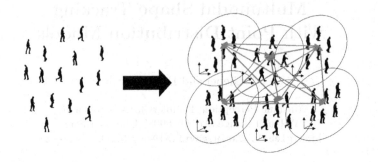

Fig. 1. Acquiring the proposed spatio-temporal shape representation

object. The observation density is computed from a matching criteria based on multi-feature distance transforms, which has previously been successfully applied to object detection [6].

The paper is organized as follows. Section 2 discusses previous work. Section 3 describes how the proposed spatio-temporal model can be learned from examples. Tracking with this representation is discussed in Section 4. Preliminary experiments are described in Section 5. Finally, the paper is concluded in Section 6.

2 Previous Work

Several representations have been proposed to cover the distribution of object appearance and motion.

Compact low-dimensional object parameterizations can be obtained by linear subspace techniques based on shape (PDMs) [4], texture [2,18], motion, or combinations [1,5] and are widely used in the computer vision community. However, these methods have some limitations. One concerns the global linearity assumption: nonlinear object deformations have to be approximated by linear combinations of the modes of variation. Therefore linear subspace models are not the most compact representations for objects undergoing complex (non-linear) deformations. They are also not specific, since implausible shapes can be generated, when invalid combinations of the modes are used.

To treat the problem of linearity, Bregler and Omohundro [3] developed a method to learn nonlinear surfaces from examples. The object manifold is approximated by the union of a set of locally-linear surface patches. Heap and Hogg used this idea to build their "Hierarchical Point Distribution Model" [8], which they extended to deal with discontinuous changes in shape for tracking [9].

Stochastic frameworks for object tracking are also frequently discussed in the computer vision literature. In particular particle filtering ("Condensation") has been popular recently [9,13,16]. It is conceptually simple and more general than the classical Kalman filter techniques since it does not rely on Gaussian noise or linearity assumptions and can even be applied when no closed-form solutions of the posterior are available. The algorithm simultaneously considers multiple hypothesis (without explicitly solving the correspondence problem), which makes it robust to escape from local maxima of the estimated probability density function. Several extensions to the original implementation have been proposed, for example to achieve real-time performance [11], to cope with high dimensional state spaces [16], to deal with mixed discrete/continuous state spaces [12], and multiple targets [14,17]. A rich variety of stochastic dynamical models were used in combination with particle filtering. In [15] the complex dynamics of an object are decomposed into several motion classes. The motion in each class is modeled by an auto-regressive process, while the class transitions are treated in Markov fashion. Unfortunately, it is not always straightforward to find distinct motion classes for complex objects.

Our approach, discussed in the next sections, builds upon previous work of Heap and Hogg [9] and is closely related to Isard and Blake [12]. We extended this work to deal with our spatio-temporal shape representation, which does not utilize a common object parameterization for all possible shapes. Instead a set of unconnected local parameterizations is used, which correspond to clusters of similar shapes. The learning scheme is more general since it does not assume prior feature correspondence among the training shapes. In contrast to single object parameterizations [4,12] an improved specificity of the model can be expected. During tracking we explicitly model the cluster membership as a discrete state of our samples. The observation density used in our experiments is based on multi-feature distance transforms. We demonstrate our system on difficult real world data, taken from a moving vehicle.

3   Spatio-temporal Shape Representation

This section describes how the spatio-temporal shape representation is obtained from examples. The algorithm passes a sequence of three successive steps. At first our integrated registration and clustering approach [7] partitions the shapes, establishes point correspondence between similar shapes, and aligns them with respect to similarity transform. For compactness, a separate linear subspace decomposition reduces the dimensionality in each cluster. Finally, the transition probabilities between the different parameterizations are determined for the Markov model. The learning scheme is illustrated in Figure 1. The shape distribution is represented by a set of linear subspace models, corresponding to clusters of similar shapes, with transition probabilities between them.

The next two paragraphs review the integrated registration and clustering approach, which is discussed in detail in [7].

Registration, which brings the points of two shapes into correspondence and aligns them with respect to similarity transform (ie. translation, scale and rotation), proceeds as follows. At first the shapes, represented by the sequence of their n x- and y-coordinates $s = (x_1, y_1, x_2, y_2, ..., x_n, y_n)$, are decomposed into segments locating the extrema of the curvature function. The segments on both shapes are characterized by their transformation invariant Fourier descriptors.

Since the ordering of the segments is known on the shapes, the optimal solution to the correspondence problem between them can be found by dynamic programming, using weighted Euclidean metrics on the low order Fourier coefficients as similarity measure. Dense point correspondence can then be derived by interpolation between the corresponding segments. Finally the shapes are aligned using a least squares fit [4].

The cluster algorithm has a k-means flavor and simultaneously embeds similar shapes into a common feature space. Iteratively a shape is chosen and registered to all existing prototypes. If the alignment error to the best matching prototype is below a user defined threshold, then the shape is assigned to the particular cluster and the corresponding prototype is updated to be the mean of the shape vectors inside this cluster. Otherwise, a new cluster is created with the chosen shape as prototype.

After the registration and clustering step we apply a principal component analysis in each cluster of registered shapes to obtain compact shape parameterizations known as "Point Distribution Models" [4]. From the N example shapes s_i of each cluster the mean shape $\bar{s}$ is calculated. The covariance matrix K is derived from the deviations of the mean

$$K = \frac{1}{N-1} \sum_{i=1}^{N} (s_i - \bar{s})(s_i - \bar{s})^T. \tag{1}$$

By solving the eigensystem $Ke_i = \lambda_i e_i$ one obtains the $2n$ orthonormal eigenvectors, corresponding to the "modes of variation". The k most significant "variation vectors" $E = (e_1 e_2 \ldots e_k)$ with the highest eigenvalues λ_i are chosen to capture a user-specified proportion of total variance contained in the cluster. Shapes can then be generated from the mean shape plus a weighted combination of the variation vectors $\tilde{s} = \bar{s} + Eb$. To ensure that the generated shapes are not outliers, we constrain the weight vector b to lie in a hyperellipsoid about the origin. Therefore b is scaled such that the weighted distance from the mean is less than a user-supplied threshold M_{max} [4]

$$\sum_{i=1}^{k} \frac{b_i^2}{\lambda_i} \leq M_{max}^2. \tag{2}$$

Finally, the transition probabilities between the different subspace models are determined and stored in a Markov state transition matrix T. An entry $T_{i,j}$ represents the probability of a discrete state transition from cluster i to j.

4   Tracking

Multimodal tracking is performed via an adaption of the "Condensation" algorithm [13], which can deal with "mixed" discrete/continuous state spaces. The "Condensation" algorithm approximates the probability density function $p(x_t|\mathcal{Z}_t)$ of the object's configuration x_t at times t conditioned by the observations $\mathcal{Z}_t = \{z_t, z_{t-1}, ..., z_1\}$ by a set of weighted samples. At each iteration the samples are predicted with a stochastic dynamical model $p(x_t|\mathcal{X}_{t-1})$ over time, where $\mathcal{X}_{t-1} = \{x_{t-1}, x_{t-2}, ..., x_1\}$. Usually the Markov-assumption is made so that $p(x_t|\mathcal{X}_{t-1})$ only depends on a predefined number of prior states, the order of the Markov model. When new measurements are available the samples are weighted according to an observation model $p(z_t|x_t)$. Proportional to these weights, they are chosen to approximate the prior for the next iteration using factored sampling.

In our implementation, the state vector $x = (c, d)$ of each sample consists of a discrete parameter d modeling the PDM membership and continuous parameters c corresponding to object translation, scale, rotation (similarity transform) velocity and the PDM shape parameters. Because the PDMs usually utilize a different number of parameters, the size of the state vector may vary in time.

The dynamical model of the tracker is decomposed, to account for discontinuous shape changes, corresponding to PDM transitions, during tracking [12]. They occur according to the transition probabilities $T_{i,j}$ of our spatio-temporal shape model. The decomposition is as follows:

$$p(x_t|x_{t-1}) = p(c_t|d_t, x_{t-1})p(d_t|x_{t-1}). \tag{3}$$

Since the transition probabilities $T_{i,j}$ of our shape model are assumed to be independent of the previous continuous shape and transformation parameters c_{t-1}

$$p(d_t = i|c_{t-1}, d_{t-1} = j) = T_{i,j}(c_{t-1}) = T_{i,j}. \tag{4}$$

In the case of $i = j$, when no PDM transition occurs, we assume

$$p(c_t|d_t = j, d_{t-1} = i, c_{t-1}) = p_{i,j}(c_t|c_{t-1}) \tag{5}$$

to be a Gaussian random walk. For $i \neq j$ the PDM membership is switched from i to j. In this case the transformation parameters are maintained with random displacement, while the shape parameters are assumed to be normally distributed about the mean shape of PDM j.

Our observation density, determining the "goodness" of a sample, is based on multi-feature distance transforms [6]. As features we use the position of directed edges in the experiments. If the image I is considered the observation z_t at time t and S is the projection of the shape parameters x_t into the image we assume that [16]

$$\log p(z_t|x_t) \equiv \log p(I|S) \propto -\frac{1}{|S|} \sum_{s \in S} D_I(s), \tag{6}$$

where $|S|$ denotes the number of features s in S and $D_I(s)$ is the distance of the closest feature in I to s. At this point we iterate the following algorithm [12]:

From the prior sample set $\{s_{t-1}^{(n)}, \pi_{t-1}^{(n)}, n \in \{1, .., N\}\}$ at time $t-1$ the nth sample $s_t^{(n)}$ with weight $\pi_t^{(n)}$ at time t is derived as follows to yield the posterior sample set $\{s_t^{(n)}, \pi_t^{(n)}, n \in \{1, .., N\}\}$:

Select a sample j of the prior population with probability $\pi_{t-1}^{(j)}$ and insert it into the new population $s'_t{}^{(n)} = s_{t-1}^{(j)}$

Predict (by sampling from $p(\boldsymbol{x_t}|\boldsymbol{x_{t-1}} = s_t'^{(n)})$ to find $s_t^{(n)}$)

- the transformation parameters assuming a Gaussian random walk and constant velocity.
- the discrete shape parameter by sampling the transition probabilities $T_{i,j}$. If $s_t'^{(n)}$ is in cluster a, this is done by generating a random number $r \in \{0, ..., 1\}$ and choosing the smallest b such that $C_{a,b} > r$, where $C_{r,c} = \sum_{i=1}^{c} T_{r,i}$ and r and c index the rows and columns of T and C.
- the continuous shape parameters. If $a = b$ the old parameters are maintained with random displacement, otherwise they are assumed to be normally distributed about the cluster mean of b.

Weight according to the observation density $\pi_t^{(n)} = p(\boldsymbol{z_t}|\boldsymbol{x_t} = s_t^{(n)})$.
Finally, the weights are normalized such that $\sum_n \pi_t^{(n)} = 1$.

5   Experiments

To demonstrate our system we performed preliminary experiments on tracking pedestrians from a moving vehicle. The different linear subspace models of the proposed spatio-temporal model were automatically learned from 500 pedestrian shapes of our database following the method described in section 3. Figure 2

Fig. 2. Varying the first mode of variation for three different clusters between $\pm 2\sigma$

illustrates the changes in shape while varying the first mode of variation for three different clusters between ± 2 standard deviations σ. For the moment the transition probabilities between the different subspace models were set to equal values. We are in the process of compiling them automatically from a large database of pedestrian sequences including thousands of images.

About 1000 samples per cluster were used to track the pedestrians in Figure 3 with that model. In both sequences we show the "modal" shape of each track in black or white, the one with the highest sample weight according to equation 6. Note that because of the discrete parameter in our state space and the different object parameterizations it is no longer possible to evaluate the mean properties of the posterior directly from the samples as in [10]. To illustrate the estimated probability density function of the first sequence we additionally show the sample set projected onto the edge image in black (second and fourth row of Figure 3). To initialize the tracks we generated a random population of shapes about a given starting position. The first part of the upper sequence is particularly difficult for the tracker (first row of Figure 3), because of the low contrast between the upper part of the body and the background. One observes that the sample set (approximating the probability density function) splits while the pedestrian passes the bushes behind him. The ambiguity is solved, because the "correct" mode of the estimated probability function dominates according to our observation density in time. In the second sequence the results of two different tracks are displayed. Although the scene is quite complex, the trackers correctly keep lock on the desired targets.

Fig. 3. Tracking results

6   Conclusions

This paper presented a general method to learn a spatio-temporal shape model from examples and showed how it can be used for tracking in a stochastic framework. A set of linear parameterizations was automatically learned from our training set to represent the shape distribution. A Markov model was applied to constrain the temporal changes in shape over time. For tracking we used an adaption of the "Condensation" algorithm, which can cope with mixed discrete/continuous state spaces. We obtained quite promising results on difficult image data using our proposed multi-modal shape tracking technique. Work in progress involves using more efficient sampling methods (we desire realtime performance), combining the tracker with hierarchical shape-based object detection using distance transforms, and testing our approach on a large database with several thousands of pedestrian images with given ground truth data.

References

1. A. Baumberg and D. Hogg. Learning flexible models from image sequences. *Proc. of the ECCV*, pages 299–308, 1999.
2. M.J. Black and A.D. Jepson. Eigentracking: Robust matching and tracking of articulated objects using a view-based representation. *Int. J. of Computer Vision*, 26(1):63–84, January 1998.
3. C. Bregler and S.M. Omohundro. Surface learning with applications to lipreading. In Jack D. Cowan, Gerald Tesauro, and Joshua Alspector, editors, *Advances in Neural Information Processing Systems*, volume 6, pages 43–50. Morgan Kaufmann Publishers, Inc., 1994.
4. T. Cootes, D. Cooper, C. Taylor, and J. Graham. Active shape models - their training and application. *CVIU*, pages 38–59, 1995.
5. T.F. Cootes, G.J. Edwards, and C.J. Taylor. Active appearance models. *IEEE Trans. on PAMI*, 23(6):681–684, June 2001.
6. D. M. Gavrila. Multi-feature hierarchical template matching using distance transforms. In *Proc. of the ICPR*, pages 439–444, Brisbane, 1998.
7. D. M. Gavrila, J. Giebel, and H. Neumann. Learning shape models from examples. In *Proc. of the Deutsche Arbeitsgemeinschaft für Mustererkennung*, pages pp. 369–376, Munich, Germany, 2001.
8. T. Heap and D. Hogg. Improving specificity in pdms using a hierarchical approach. In Adrian F. Clark, editor, *British Machine Vision Conference*, 1997.
9. T. Heap and D. Hogg. Wormholes in shape space: Tracking through discontinuous changes in shape. In *Proc. of the ICCV*, pages 344–349, 1998.
10. M. Isard and A. Blake. Contour tracking by stochastic propagation of conditional density. In *ECCV96*, pages I:343–356, 1996.
11. M. Isard and A. Blake. Icondensation: Unifying low-level and high-level tracking in a stochastic framework. In *Proc. of the ECCV*, pages I:893–908, 1998.
12. M. Isard and A. Blake. A mixed-state condensation tracker with automatic model-switching. In *Proc. of the ICCV*, pages 107–112, 1998.
13. Michael Isard and Andrew Blake. Contour tracking by stochastic propagation of conditional density. In *Proc. of the ECCV*, pages 343–356, 1996.
14. E.B. Meier and F. Ade. Tracking multiple objects using the condensation algorithm. *Journal of Robotics and Autonomous Systems*, pages 93–105, 2001.
15. B. North, A. Blake, M Isard, and J. Rittscher. Learning and classification of complex dynamics. *PAMI*, 22(8):781–796, August 2000.
16. V. Philomin, R. Duraiswami, and L.S. Davis. Quasi-random sampling for condensation. In *Proc. of the ECCV*, pages 134–149, 2000.
17. D. Schulz, W. Burgard, D. Fox, and A.B. Cremers. Tracking multiple moving objects with a mobile robot. In *Proc. of the IEEE CVPR Conf.*, 2001.
18. M. Turk and A. Pentland. Eigenfaces for recognition. *Journal of Cognitive Neuro Science*, 3(1):71–86, 1991.

Real-Time Tracking of Complex Objects Using Dynamic Interpretation Tree

Markus Brandner and Axel Pinz

Institute of Electrical Measurement and Measurement Signal Processing
Graz University of Technology, Austria
{brandner,pinz}@emt.tugraz.at

Abstract. Vision-based tracking for augmented reality (AR) applications requires highly accurate position and pose measurements at video frame rate. Typically several interaction devices have to be tracked simultaneously. While the geometry of all devices and the spatial layout of visual landmarks on the devices are well known, problems of occlusion as well as of prohibitively large search spaces remain to be solved. The main contribution of the paper is in high-level algorithms for real-time tracking. We describe a model-based tracking system which implements a dynamic extension of the structure of an interpretation tree for scene analysis. This structure is well suited to track multiple rigid objects in a dynamic environment. Independent of the class of low-level features being tracked, the algorithm is capable to handle occlusions due to a model-dependent recovery strategy. The proposed high-level algorithm has been applied to stereo-based outside-in optical tracking for AR. The results show the ability of the dynamic interpretation tree to cope with partial or full object occlusion and to deliver the required object pose parameters at a rate of 30 Hz.

1 Introduction

This paper presents a real-time vision-based tracking system for applications in Augmented Reality (AR). Our examples show devices for visualization and 3D human computer interaction in AR. From a more general point of view, this system is capable of the simultaneous tracking of several rigid objects in a scene at frame rate (i.e. 30 Hz). However, its specific characteristics are derived from the very stringent requirements AR applications demand from a tracking system: *Tracking* is defined as the precise measurement of position and orientation of all devices which are currently present in the 3D volume under inspection. *Six degrees of freedom (6 DoF)* (3 translational and 3 rotational parameters) have to be recovered for each device in 3D. The *accuracy* of the system should meet user's requirements, which are maximum errors of 1cm in position and 0.1 degrees in orientation of a device. *Real-time* operation at frame rate (30 Hz) is required. Temporal lags cannot be tolerated. *Recovery* strategies are needed in case of full or partial object occlusion. In summary, to meet the above requirements, both *consistency* of the provided data and *complexity* of the underlying algorithms

L. Van Gool (Ed.): DAGM 2002, LNCS 2449, pp. 9–16, 2002.
© Springer-Verlag Berlin Heidelberg 2002

are of relevance. We propose a dynamic extension of the well known interpretation tree data structure which has been successfully applied to static image analysis[6]. The *dynamic interpretation tree* allows to simultaneously track multiple objects and provides the basis for a model-dependent recovery strategy as it is used during partial or even full occlusion of the interaction devices. The proposed high-level algorithm is capable of handling different low-level image features such as corners, edges, and blobs. Thus, it can easily be adapted to track different types of landmarks.

The tracking performance of the dynamic interpretation tree algorithm for a typical AR application, especially the capability to reduce the search space and to deliver consistent interpretations even in ambiguous situations is shown in the experimental section.

1.1   Related Work in Vision-Based Tracking

Tracking for AR in complex environments has to focus on salient image features such as blobs, corners, edges or texture rather than processing the whole image. The type of the optimal low-level image feature to be used is closely related to the applied tracking algorithm [11]. For example Ferrari et al.[3] describe a combined tracking approach using corners and edges to improve accuracy.

Model-based tracking algorithms have to be used in order to deliver sufficiently accurate object pose information. In general, fitting a three-dimensional model onto two-dimensional image feature data is a computationally expensive task. The complexity of the correspondence search can be reduced for sequences of images once the object's approximate pose has been found. Lowe [10] has built as system based on line features and Kalman prediction. Various authors [8,1,9] combine model rendering with 1D feature detection which results in increased tracking speeds. The RAPID system as described in [8] is able to track 3D objects of known geometry using a standard video camera. The object model consists of a set of control points which are situated on high-contrast image features. Object motion is modeled using a Kalman filter approach. Armstrong and Zisserman [1] extend the RAPID idea using both line and conic features, a better object model, and additional redundant measurements which lead to robust tracking within an extended range of scene condition. Common to these approaches to model-based tracking is that they only support a single pose hypothesis at a time which is due to the fact that the prediction filter is based on unimodal Gaussian distributions. In contrast, the CONDENSATION tracker [9] is able to track parameterized curves over a sequence of frames using multi-modal distributions.

The tracking system presented in this paper has similarities with the RAPID tracker. However, we do not restrict the low-level features to be of any distinct type. Our tracker is based on a wire-frame model of the target geometry. Through the use of the interpretation tree structure the algorithm is able to initialize and recover after object occlusion without user interaction. As for the CONDENSATION algorithm, our tracker is able to handle multiple hypotheses simultaneously.

2   Dynamic Interpretation Tree

In trying to solve the model-based correspondence problem introduced above, object recognition is a basic building block for model-based visual tracking. The concept of interpretation tree for object recognition has been introduced by Grimson [6] in the context of static image analysis. This idea is briefly reviewed in the next subsection and subsequently being extended to the dynamic case.

Static Scene Analysis:

During tracker initialization or recovery, finding an initial correspondence of the model to be tracked within the search image can be formulated as a pattern matching problem: A set of features $\mathbf{F} = [F_1, F_2, \ldots, F_N]$ has to be computed for every tracker frame (i.e. the test features). These can be edgels, corners or other visual object features. Given this set and a set of model features $\mathbf{f} = [f_1, f_2, \ldots, f_M]$, the recognition task determines the transformation parameters that map the model features onto the data features while minimizing some means of fit-error. The interpretation tree algorithm applies local geometric consistency constraints during the tree building process which are a necessary condition for globally consistent matching. Possible *feasible interpretations* of the sensor and the model data are depicted by leaf nodes of the tree. However, local consistency is not a sufficient condition for global consistency which makes some additional testing necessary (cf.[6]). Several different geometric constraints have been applied to interpretation tree matching:

- **Unary Constraints:** Each pairing (f_i, F_j) is checked for consistency (e.g. corners match corners, a line can only match a line)
- **Binary Constraints:** A pair of model features (f_{i-1}, f_i) is checked against a pair of test features (F_1, F_j) (e.g. distances between point features)
- **Ternary Constraints:** A triple of model features (f_{i-1}, f_i, f_{i+1}) is checked against a triple of test features (F_1, F_j, F_m) as described in [2].

Simple constraints incorporate the geometric relations between features (e.g. the distance between blob features). These can be formulated as statistical hypotheses tests[5] with interval boundaries reflecting the accuracy of the tracker setup (e.g. the accuracy of the camera parameters). Subtrees can be omitted as soon as the corresponding root node fails to meet any of the local constraints. The use of heuristics and a search-cutoff threshold can decrease the matching time considerably[7]. In a final processing step the pose hypotheses as given by the list of feasible interpretations have to be verified. This can be accomplished during determination of the transformation parameters. The underlying numerics can be made robust to outliers through the use of advanced parameter estimation techniques such as the RANSAC method[4].

Dynamic Extensions – real-time tracking of position and pose:

A major drawback of object recognition algorithms is the computational complexity which makes it difficult to directly apply the methodologies to real-time tracking. However, depending on the frame rate the differences between two consecutive images in a video stream are relatively small. Tracking systems utilize this condition to increase the system performance. In the light of the *small differences* assumption as stated above we develop dynamic extensions to the interpretation tree. The *dynamic interpretation tree* (DITREE) allows for model-based tracking of complex objects in real time. Figure 1b depicts the basic structure of the DITREE. In addition to the static interpretation tree (cf. figure 1a) the following processing steps are required:

- **Dynamic Search Ordering:** Strong pose hypotheses are reflected in both a large number of model features being assigned to test features and a small residual fit-error. For a valid interpretation the expected location of each test feature will vary only little. Thus, we keep the interpretation tree structure from frame to frame and only update the test feature attributes. The order of both test and model features is rearranged to reflect the quality-of-fit of each interpretation. Thus, strong hypotheses will appear at the beginning of the interpretation tree processing. This, together with the search heuristic and the cutoff threshold, are powerful mechanisms to keep the residual tree complexity (i.e. the number of leaf nodes) small.
- **New Nodes:** New features are added to the interpretation tree as for the static case. If required, the resultant tree can adapt to the scene and grow.
- **Node Removal:** Feature pairings that fail to conform to the set of constraints (e.g. the attributes have changed too much between two consecutive tracker frames) have to be removed from the tree. As for the static case, subtrees starting at an invalid feature pairing will be removed. Thus, the tree is pruned whenever inconsistent features are detected.
- **Feature Recovery:** Apart from delivering a list of valid feature pairings for every feasible interpretation, the tree delivers some insight information about the current correspondence: the list of model features that have *not* been assigned successfully to a test feature can be used to recover those features. Assuming that missing features result from partial occlusion (which is true for simple features such as blobs), this information can be used to selectively search the subsequent input image at locations where the missing features are expected to be located.

The DITREE algorithm is capable of dealing with multiple hypotheses simultaneously through the use of a set of Kalman filters. The five strongest hypotheses are used to repeatedly update the corresponding filters. In a final processing step a Maximum Likelihood (ML) scheme is applied to identify the object pose for each tracker frame.

3   Experimental Setup

This paper is focused on *high-level* issues in the tracking of position and pose of rigid interaction devices for AR. Thus important low-level issues like calibration, features to track, interest operators, etc. are not discussed here. Our experiments were carried out using two different calibrated stereo vision systems. Figure 2a shows the two stereo rigs, one of them using infrared (IR) illumination and

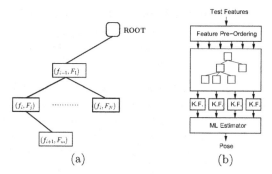

(a)   (b)

Fig. 1. Basic structure of the interpretation tree (a). Each node corresponds to a valid pairing of a model and a test feature. The DITREE system extends the basic tree structure and adds temporal constraints and a dynamic prediction scheme (b).

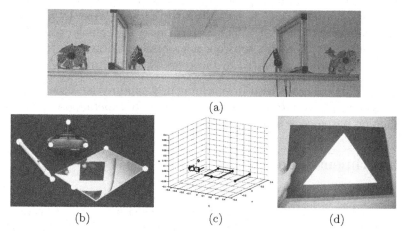

Fig. 2. The tracker hardware (a): both a visual and an IR stereo-setup have been used. Typical devices used during the experiments (b), and their wire-frame model (c). Target used for visible experiments (d).

filtering, the other working with visible light. The features which we track in the IR case are retroreflective spherical markers which can be easily located by simple thresholding and blob detection. The second setup is used to track visible passive targets like the pad shown in figure 2d using a corner detection algorithm. The stereo baseline is approximately $160cm$ for the IR setup and $120cm$ for the visible case. Each IR camera is equipped with an infrared filter and infrared illumination. All cameras are progressive scan cameras and provide a synchronous video stream at a rate of 30Hz.

Figures 2b,c depict some of the 'real-world' objects and the corresponding models that were used during our experiments. Note that only the HMD and the pad are required to be tracked with full 6 DoF while the pen can only be tracked with 5 DoF. An IR LED is attached to the pen to enable 'click-and-drop' interactions.

Each model consists of a list of features with associated attributes. The tracker was implemented in $C/C++$ and runs in real-time for 12 targets on a standard PC with 1GHz. Besides the interpretation tree algorithm there are other modules of the tracker used for our experiments:

- **Feature-Tracking** For each IR camera a 2D blob tracking algorithm is applied. Object segmentation is straight forward through the use of IR illumination and IR pass filters mounted at every camera. Simple linear motion prediction has shown to effectively decrease the search area needed to identify the corresponding blob in a sequence of images. Visible landmarks are tracked using a similar approach. The combination of a corner detector and a linear prediction module in 2D allows to reduce the search area.
- **Epipolar Geometry** Given the *intrinsic* and *extrinsic* parameters of the stereo setup the epipolar constraint can be applied to rule out invalid feature pairings between left and right images. After reconstruction of the points in 3D, a list of test features is passed on to the next layer. In practice the limited accuracy of the system parameters causes the epipolar constraints to be less effective. Therefore, subsequent processing blocks have to deal with a number of outliers generated by incorrect feature pairings.

A standard CCD camera is used to synchronously capture the scene during the IR experiments. The resultant video stream is used to superimpose model-data for evaluation purposes as shown in figure 3.

4   Experiments and Results

The setup as described in section 3 was used to perform experiments on the complexity of the high-level search algorithm in both the visual (corner features) and IR (blob features) case. Figure 3a depicts one frame out of a 365 frame video sequence used for evaluation of the DITREE complexity. The wire-frame models of PEN, PAD, and HMD are used to detect and track the test objects over the whole sequence of input images. The tracker successfully identifies the pen's LED and delivers the 'pick' information. In general, epipolar geometry can be applied to remove outliers from the list of point correspondences between the left and right camera images. However, situations occur when epipolar geometry fails to properly identify false correspondences. Figure 3b shows a situation where due to the weak epipolar constraint a large number of feasible hypotheses have to be verified by the correspondence module. We observed that such situations occur only during a limited number of tracking frames. However, for AR applications this would result in an unacceptable amount of pose jitter. The applications of temporal continuity constraints (ML estimation based on Kalman filter predictions) provides a suitable tool to identify the best-fit correspondence (see figure 3c) and results in stable pose information. The complexity of the DITREE is directly related to the number of feasible interpretations in the tree (i.e. the number of pose hypotheses to be verified). Figure 4 depicts the number of leaf nodes for a 366 frame sequence of stereo images. A set of different constraints ranging from standard geometric constraints (top figure) to dynamic constraints (bottom figure) has been applied. The average number of leaf nodes within the DITREE for this sequence is 21.57, 18.3, 6.2, and 1.3 for the static case, dynamic ordering, hypothesis candidates and pose estimates.

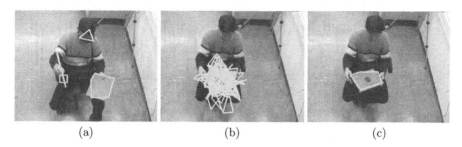

(a)   (b)   (c)

Fig. 3. 'Pick' operation performed using the PEN (a). All feasible interpretations of a given tracker frame (b). Due to the limited decision power of the epipolar geometry a number of *artificial* outliers is created. Interpretation tree processing and a prediction scheme identifies the correct interpretation (c).

Figure 4b indicates the Likelihood functions $L_i(n)$ for the second and third strongest interpretations. The ML estimation scheme selects the best-fit interpretation on a per-frame basis. The remaining interpretations are still being updated using the discrete-time Kalman filters. We found that only during short periods of time more than one interpretation is selected as a final candidate for pose determination. On average, the Likelihood function of the best-fit hypothesis is 60% larger than that of the remaining hypotheses ($\mathbf{L} = (1.0, 0.3899, 0.2693, 0.2210, 0.1895)^T$) which is sufficient for stable tracking.

5   Summary

Tracking of well-known geometric primitives in real-time is a basic building-block for many AR applications. Requirements are stringent as often complex objects have to be tracked over time in the presence of object occlusion and changing environments. In this paper we describe a model-based tracking system which implements a dynamic extension of the interpretation tree. The *dynamic interpretation tree* is able to meet the requirements posed by AR applications. Our experiments indicate that the complexity of the search tree can be reduced by at least a factor of 10 for both the IR setup (using simple blobs as features) and the visible setup (using corner features). Furthermore, our algorithm is able to cope with multiple simultaneous pose hypotheses. The combination of both geometric constraints – as for the static interpretation tree - and dynamic constraints is shown to be suitable to perform real-time model-based tracking.

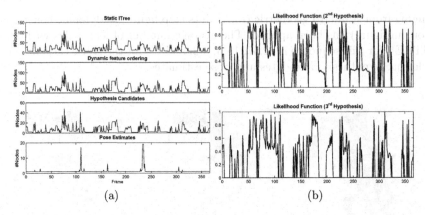

Fig. 4. Number of leaf nodes during the 366 frame sequence (a). The application of dynamic constraints greatly reduces the number of hypotheses to be verified. The DITREE algorithm lost track around frame 310 but was able to recover in the subsequent frame without violating the real-time constraint. The Likelihood functions L_2 and L_3 of the same sequence are shown in (b).

References

1. M. Armstrong and A. Zisserman. Robust object tracking. In *Asian Conference on Computer Vision*, volume 1, pages 58–61, 1995.
2. Markus Brandner, Miguel Ribo, Harald Ganster, and Axel Pinz. 3d optical tracking of retroreflective targets for ar applications. In 25th *Workshop of the Austrian Association for Pattern Recognition (ÖAGM/AAPR)*, pages 95–102, 2001.
3. V. Ferrari, T. Tuytelaars, and L. Van Gool. Markerless augmented reality with a real-time affine region tracker. In *Procs. of the IEEE and ACM Intl. Symposium on Augmented Reality*, pages 87–96. IEEE Computer Society, 2001.
4. M. A. Fischler and R. C. Bolles. Random sample consensus: A paradigm for model fitting with applications to image analysis and automated cartography. *Commun. ACM*, 24(6):381–395, 1981.
5. W. Förstner, A. Brunn, and S. Heuel. Statistically testing uncertain geometric relations. In *Proc. of the DAGM 2000 Kiel*, 2000.
6. W. E. L. Grimson. *Object Recognition by Computer: The Role of Geometric Constraints*. MIT Press, 1990.
7. W. E. L. Grimson. The combinatorics of heuristic search termination for object recognition in cluttered environmnets. *IEEE PAMI*, 13(9):920–935, 1991.
8. Chris Harris. Tracking with rigid models. In Andrew Blake and Alan Yuille, editors, *Active Vision*, pages 59–73. MIT Press, 1992.
9. Michael Isard and Andrew Blake. Condensation – conditional density propagation for visual tracking. *Int. J. of Computer Vision*, 29(1):5–28, 1998.
10. David G. Lowe. Robust model-based motion tracking through the integration of search and estimation. *Int. J. of Computer Vision*, 8(2):113–122, 1992.
11. Jianbo Shi and Carlo Tomasi. Good features to track. In *1994 IEEE Conference on Computer Vision and Pattern Recognition (CVPR'94)*, pages 593 – 600, 1994.

On Optimal Camera Parameter Selection in Kalman Filter Based Object Tracking

Joachim Denzler, Matthias Zobel*, and Heinrich Niemann

Lehrstuhl für Mustererkennung, Universität Erlangen–Nürnberg
91058 Erlangen, Germany
{denzler, zobel, niemann}@informatik.uni-erlangen.de

Abstract. In this paper we present an information theoretic framework that provides an optimality criterion for the selection of the best sensor data regarding state estimation of dynamic system. One relevant application in practice is tracking a moving object in 3–D using multiple sensors. Our approach extends previous and similar work in the area of active object recognition, i.e. state estimation of static systems. We derive a theoretically well founded metric based on the conditional entropy that is also close to intuition: select those camera parameters that result in sensor data containing most information for the following state estimation. In the case of state estimation with a non–linear Kalman filter we show how that metric can be evaluated in closed form.

The results of real–time experiments prove the benefits of our general approach in the case of active focal length adaption compared to fixed focal lengths. The main impact of the work consists in a uniform probabilistic description of sensor data selection, processing and fusion.

1 Introduction

In active vision it has been shown, also theoretically, that an active processing strategy that includes the image acquisition step can be superior to a passive one. The question of course is: how to figure out, which strategy is the best, i.e. how to actively control the image acquisition step in a theoretically optimal way? Answers to this question will have an enormous impact on broad areas in computer vision.

In recent work on active object recognition [2,5,11,12] it has already been shown that sensible selection of viewpoints improves recognition rate, especially in settings, where multiple ambiguities between the objects exist. The work of [8] is another example from robotics, where such ideas have been implemented for self–localization tasks.

Besides the success in the area of active object recognition no comparable work is known for selecting the right sensor data during object tracking. The advantages are quite obvious:

- For a single camera setting, i.e. one camera is used to track the moving object, the trade–off between a large and a small focal length can be resolved. Depending on the position, velocity, acceleration of the object, and on the associated uncertainty

---

* This work was partially funded by the German Science Foundation (DFG) under grant SFB 603/TP B2. Only the authors are responsible for the content.

L. Van Gool (Ed.): DAGM 2002, LNCS 2449, pp. 17–25, 2002.

in the estimation of these state values, a small focal length might be suited to ensure that the object is still in the image at the next time step. On the other hand, a large focal length can be advantageous for estimation of the class of an object in an high resolution image.

– For a setting with multiple cameras the possibility exists to focus with some cameras on dedicated areas in space, depending on the state estimation, while some other cameras keep on tracking using an overview image. Without mentioning the problems of sensor data fusion in such a setting and the weighting of the different sensors depending on the expected accuracy, the gain of dynamic focal length adjustment is expected to be relevant in a combined tracking and recognition scenario. Demonstrating this behavior is the focus of our ongoing research.

In this paper we make an important step toward active object tracking. The basis of our work is the information theoretic approach for iterative sensor data selection for state estimation in static systems presented in [4]. We extend this framework to have a metric for selecting that sensor data that yields most reduction of uncertainty in the state estimate of a dynamic system. We mainly differ to the work of [7,10] in how to select the optimal focal length. In [7] zooming is used to keep the size of the object constant during tracking, but it is not taken into account the uncertainty in the localization. The work of [10] demonstrates how corner based tracking can be done while zooming using affine transfer. However, the focus is not on how to find the best focal length.

Our framework is completely embedded in probabilistic estimation theory. The main advantage is that it can be combined with any probabilistic state estimator. Also sensor data fusion, which is important in multiple camera settings, can be done at no extra costs. We show the realization for a two–camera setting in the experimental part of the paper later on. Another side effect of the information theoretic metric is its intuitive interpretation with respect to state estimation.

The paper is structured as follows. In the next section the main contribution of our work can be found. The general framework for selecting optimal observation models during state estimation of dynamic systems is applied to the case of binocular object tracking. Real–time experiments with a mobile platform in an office environment, presented in Section 3, give us definite, quantitative results: first, our optimality criterion causes the expected behavior, second, adapting the focal length during tracking is better than using a fixed setting, and third, the theoretical framework also works in practice. Some problems and future extension of our approach are discussed in Section 4.

2   Selection of Optimal Observation Models

2.1   Review: Kalman Filter for Changing Observation Models

In the following we consider a dynamic system, whose state is summarized by an n–dimensional state vector x_t. The dynamic of the system is given by

$$x_{t+1} = f(x_t, t) + w \quad , \tag{1}$$

with $f(\cdot, \cdot) \in \mathbb{R}^n$ being a non–linear state transition function, and $w \in \mathbb{R}^n$ being additive Gaussian noise with zero mean and covariance matrix W. The observation o_t

is given by the observation equation

$$o_t = h(x_t, a_t, t) + r \quad , \tag{2}$$

which relates the state x_t to the observation $o_t \in \mathbb{R}^m$. The non–linear function $h \in \mathbb{R}^m$ is called observation function and might incorporate the observations made by k different sensors. Again, an additive noise process $r \in \mathbb{R}^m$ disturbs the ideal observation, having zero mean and covariance matrix R.

The main difference to the standard description of a dynamic system is the dependency of the observation function $h(x_t, a_t, t)$ on the parameter $a_t \in \mathbb{R}^l$. The vector a_t summarizes all parameters that influence the sensor data acquisition process. As a consequence the parameter also influences the observation o_t, or in other words: we allow changing observation models. In the following the parameter a_t is referred to as action, to express that the observation model (i.e. the sensor data) is actively selected. One example for the parameter a_t might be $a_t = (\alpha, \beta, f)^T$, with α and β denoting the pan and tilt angles, and f the motor controlled focal length of a multimedia camera.

State estimation of the dynamic system in (1) and (2) can be performed by applying the standard non–linear Kalman filter approach. Space limitations restrain us from giving an introduction to the Kalman filter algorithm. The reader is referred to [1]. In the non–linear case given by (1) and (2) usually a linearization is done by computing the Jacobian of the state transition and the observation function. As a consequence of the linearization the distributions of the following random vectors are Gaussian distributed:

- A priori distribution over the state x_t (and posterior, if no observation is made)

$$p(x_t | \mathcal{O}_{t-1}, \mathcal{A}_{t-1}) \sim \mathcal{N}(x_t^-, P_t^-) \quad ,$$

with the two sets $\mathcal{A}_t = \{a_t, a_{t-1}, \ldots, a_0\}$ and $\mathcal{O}_t = \{o_t, o_{t-1}, \ldots, o_0\}$ denoting the history of actions a_t and observations o_t respectively. The quantities x_t^- and P_t^- are the predicted state and error covariance matrix, respectively [1].
- Likelihood function, i.e. the likelihood of the observation o_t given the state x_t and the action a_t

$$p(o_t | x_t, a_t) \sim \mathcal{N}(h(x_t^-, a_t), R) \quad .$$

- A posteriori distribution over the state space (if an observation has been made)

$$p(x_t | \mathcal{O}_t, \mathcal{A}_t) \sim \mathcal{N}(x_t^+, P_t^+(a_t)) \quad . \tag{3}$$

The vector x_t^+ is the updated state estimate, the matrix $P_t^+(a_t)$ is the updated error covariance matrix. The matrix explicitly depends on the action a_t since the observation function in (2) depends on a_t. In the case, that no observation has been made, the quantities $P_t^+(a_t)$ and x_t^+ equal the corresponding predicted quantities P_t^- and x_t^-.

These three distributions are essential ingredients of our proposed optimality criterion, which is presented in the following. Note, that all quantities (i.e. $x_t^-, x_t^+, P_t^-, P_t^+$) are updated in the Kalman filter framework over time [1]. As a consequence, this information is available at no extra cost for our approach.

2.2 Optimal Observation Models

The goal is to find an optimal observation model, i.e. the best action a_t, that a priori most reduces the uncertainty in the state estimation with respect to the future observations. In order to find the optimal observation model the important quantity to inspect is the posterior distribution. After an observation is made we can figure out, how uncertain our state estimate is. Uncertainty in a distribution of a random vector x can be measured by the entropy $H(x) = -\int p(x) \log(p(x)) \, dx$. Entropy can also be calculated for a certain posterior distribution, for example for $p(x_t|\mathcal{O}_t, \mathcal{A}_t)$, resulting in

$$H(x_t^+) = -\int p(x_t|\mathcal{O}_t, \mathcal{A}_t) \log(p(x_t|\mathcal{O}_t, \mathcal{A}_t)) \, dx_t \quad . \tag{4}$$

This measure gives us *a posteriori* information about the uncertainty, if we took action a_t and observed o_t. Of more interest is of course to decide *a priori* about the expected uncertainty under a certain action a_t. This expected value can be calculated by

$$H(x_t|o_t, a_t) = -\int p(o_t|a_t) \int p(x_t|\mathcal{O}_t, \mathcal{A}_t) \log(p(x_t|\mathcal{O}_t, \mathcal{A}_t)) \, dx_t do_t \quad . \tag{5}$$

The quantity $H(x_t|o_t, a_t)$ is called *conditional entropy* [3], and depends in our case on the chosen action a_t. Having this quantity it is straight forward to ask the most important question for us: Which action yields the most reduction in uncertainty? The question is answered by minimizing the conditional entropy for a_t, i.e. the best action a_t^* is given by

$$\boxed{a_t^* = \operatorname*{argmin}_{a_t} H(x_t|o_t, a_t) \quad .} \tag{6}$$

Equation (6) defines in the case of arbitrary distributed state vectors the optimality criterion we have been seeking for. Unfortunately, in the general case of arbitrary distributions the evaluation of (6) is not straightforward. Therefore, in the next section we consider a special class of distributions of the state vector, namely Gaussian distributed state vectors. This specialization allows us to combine the selection of the best action with the Kalman filter framework. We will show, that this approach allows us to compute the best action *a priori*.

2.3 Optimal Observation Models for Gaussian Distributed State Vectors

We now continue with the posterior distribution in the Kalman filter framework. As a consequence of the linearization in the non–linear Kalman filter we know that the posterior distribution is Gaussian distributed (compare (3)). From information theory textbooks [3] we also know that the entropy of a Gaussian distributed random vector $x \in \mathbb{R}^n$ with $x \sim \mathcal{N}(\mu, \Sigma)$ is $H(x) = \frac{n}{2} + \frac{1}{2}\log((2\pi)^n|\Sigma|)$. Combining this knowledge we get for the conditional entropy $H(x_t|o_t, a_t)$ of the distribution in (3)

$$H(x_t|o_t, a_t) = \int p(o_t|a_t) \left(\frac{n}{2} + \frac{1}{2}\log((2\pi)^n|P_t^+(a_t)|) \right) do_t \quad . \tag{7}$$

Thus, neglecting the constant terms equation (6) becomes

$$a_t^* = \operatorname*{argmin}_{a_t} \int p(o_t|a_t) \log \left(|P_t^+(a_t)| \right) do_t \quad . \qquad (8)$$

From this equation we can conclude, that we have to select that action a_t that minimizes the determinant of $P_t^+(a_t)$. The key result is that $P_t^+(a_t)$ can be computed a priori, since the covariance matrix is independent of the observation o_t.

The criterion in (8) is only valid in any case if for the chosen action a_t an observation from the system can be made. Obviously, in practice the selected action (i.e. camera parameter) will affect observability. How to deal with this situation is considered in more detail in the next section.

2.4 Considering Visibility

Up to now we have assumed that at each time step an observation is made to perform the state estimation update in the Kalman filter cycle. Obviously, when changing the parameters of a sensor, depending on the state there is a certain a priori probability that no observation can be made that originates from the dynamic system. An intuitive example is the selection of the focal length of a camera to track a moving object in the image. For certain focal lengths (depending on the 3–D position of the moving object) the object will no longer be visible in the image. As a consequence no observation is possible. How are time steps treated, for which no observations can be made, and what is the consequence for the state estimate? If no observation can be made, no update of the state estimate is possible. The resulting final state estimate for such a time step is the predicted state estimate x_t^-, with the corresponding predicted covariance matrix P_t^-. The implication on the state estimate is significant: during the prediction step in the Kalman filter algorithm the covariance matrix of the state estimate is increased; thus, uncertainty is added to the state estimate. The increase in uncertainty depends on the dynamic of the system and the noise process w disturbing the state transition process.

Now, the task of optimal sensor parameter selection can be further substantiated by finding a balance between the reduction in uncertainty in the state estimate and the risk of not making an observation and thus getting an increase in the uncertainty. Considering this trade–off in terms of the Kalman filter state estimation the conditional entropy has to be rewritten as

$$H(x_t|o_t, a_t) = \underbrace{\int_{\{\text{visible}\}} p(o_t|a)do_t \, H_v(x_t^+)}_{w_1(a)} + \underbrace{\int_{\{\text{invisible}\}} p(o_t|a)do_t \, H_{\neg v}(x_t^-)}_{w_2(a)}, \qquad (9)$$

which is the weighted sum of $H_v(x_t^+)$ and $H_{\neg v}(x_t^-)$ where the weights are given by $w_1(a)$ and $w_2(a)$. The first integral in (9) summarizes the entropy of the a posteriori probability for observations that are generated by the system and that are *visible* in the image. The probability of such observations weight the entropy $H_v(x_t^+)$ of the corresponding a posteriori probability (for simplifications in the notation, we use here x_t^+ as synonym for the posterior). The observations that cannot be measured in the image (*invisible*) result in a Kalman filter cycle where no update of the state estimate is done and thus only a state prediction is possible. This state prediction is treated as a posteriori probability, without observation o_t. Again, the probability of such observations are used to weight the entropy $H_{\neg v}(x_t^-)$ of the a posteriori probability, when no observation has been made (again, we simplify notation by using x_t^- for the predicted state distribution). Now the conditional entropy can be rewritten similar to (7). Thus, for the minimization of $H(x_t|o_t, a_t)$ the optimization problem is given by

$$a_t^* = \underset{a_t}{\operatorname{argmin}} \left[w_1(a) \log \left(|P_t^+(a_t)| \right) + w_2(a) \log \left(|P_t^-| \right) \right] \quad . \tag{10}$$

The minimization in (10) is done by Monte Carlo evaluation of the conditional entropy and discrete optimization. For more details on the derivation of the approach, on the optimization, and some special cases in practice the reader is referred to [6].

3   Real–Time Experiments and Results

The following real–time experiments demonstrate the practicability of our proposed approach. It is shown that actively selecting the focal lengths significantly increases the accuracy of state estimation of a dynamic system.

For our experiments we used a calibrated binocular vision system (TRC Bisight/ Unisight) equipped with two computer controlled zoom cameras that are mounted on top of our mobile platform. In the following, tracking is done in a pure data driven manner, without an explicit object model. Thus, at least two cameras are necessary to estimate the state (position, velocity, and acceleration) of the object in 3–D.

In contrast to the usual setup for object tracking we did some kind of role reversal. Instead of a moving object with an unknown trajectory, we keep the object fixed at a certain position and track the object while moving the platform (with the mounted on cameras) on the floor in a defined manner. With this little trick, we obtain ground truth data from the odometry of the platform. It should be noted, that this information is not used for state estimation, but only for evaluation. For our experiments we decided to perform a circular motion with a radius of 300 mm. The object is located at a distance of about 2.7 m from the center of the circle in front of the platform. The optical axes of the two cameras are not parallel and lie not in the plane of the movement.

For the tracking itself, we used the region-based tracking algorithm proposed by [9], supplemented by a hierarchical approach to handle larger motions of the object between two successive frames. Given an initially defined reference template, the algorithm recursively estimates a transformation of the reference template to match the current appearance of the tracked object in the image. The appearance of the object might change due to motion of the object or due to changes in the imaging parameters. The advantage of this method for our demands is that it can directly handle scaling of the object's image region, as it will appear while zooming.

We conducted *three* real–time experiments that differ in the objects, in the backgrounds, and in the starting positions of the platform. We performed two runs for each

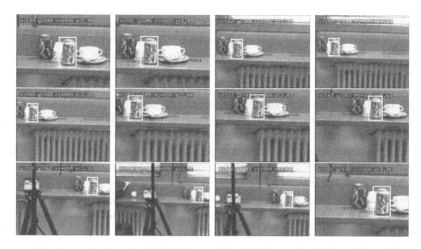

Fig. 1. Sample images from the left camera while tracking the cola can and actively adjusting the focal length. Note, that it centering of the object was not the criterion during tacking!

experiment, one with fixed focal lengths and one with active selection. For the fixed case we chose the largest possible focal length that guarantees the visibility of the object for the whole run.

In Fig. 1 images are shown from the left camera of the binocular camera system, taken during one of the experiments at approx. each twelfth planning step. The images give a visual impression of the planning results. As long as the uncertainty in the state estimate is high and the object is close to the border of the image the focal length is reduced (images 2 to 4, numbering line-by-line, starting top left). As soon as the uncertainty in the state estimate (i.e. not only position, but also velocity and acceleration in 3–D) is low, the approach follows intuition and increases focal length, even in the case that the object is close to the border of the image (6 and 12). The reader should take into account, that not 2–D centering of the object in the image was our criterion for success of tracking. The goal was estimation of the movement path in 3–D by selecting the best focal length setting of the two cameras.

The quantitative evaluation of the estimation error for the real–time experiments has been done by computing the Euclidean distance between the circular path and the estimated position. Averaged over all experiments, the mean distance in the case of fixed focal lengths is 206.63 mm (standard deviation: 76.08 mm) compared to an error of 154.93 mm (standard deviation: 44.17 mm) while actively selecting the optimal focal lengths. This results in a reduction in the error by 25%, as it has been similarly observed in simulations [6].

4   Conclusions and Future Work

In this paper we presented an original approach on how to select the right sensor data in order to improve state estimation of dynamic systems. For Gaussian distributed state vectors, a metric in closed form has been derived, that can be evaluated a priori. We showed how the whole approach fits into the Kalman filter framework and how to deal with the problem of visibility depending on the selected sensor parameters. Although not discussed in this paper, the theoretically well founded criterion can be formulated for the general case of k sensors [6].

The main difference to previous work is that the selected focal length depends not only on the state estimate but also on the uncertainty of the state estimate and on the reliability of the different sensors. Also, the special demands of the state estimator on the sensor data can be taken into account. This allows, for example, to solve the trade–off between large focal length for detailed inspection (for classification) and small focal length for tracking quickly moving objects. Experimental verification of this theoretical result are subject to future work.

The approach has been tested in real–time experiments for binocular object tracking. We tracked a static object while the cameras were moving. The estimated movement path of the camera is more accurate, when dynamically adapting the focal lengths. This result has been also verified in simulations, where the reduction in the estimation error was up to 43% [6].

Thanks to the Gaussian distributed state in the case of Kalman filter based tracking, the optimality criterion can be easily evaluated. However, for the general case of arbitrary distributed state vectors, the framework must be extended to allow the application of modern approaches like particle filters. In addition to that, we will verify the computational feasibility of our approach in applications, where frame–rate processing is necessary. One of the preliminaries to achieve frame–rate processing will be a smart and efficient way for the minimization in (6).

References

1. Y. Bar-Shalom and T.E. Fortmann. *Tracking and Data Association*. Academic Press, Boston, San Diego, New York, 1988.
2. H. Borotschnig, L. Paletta, M. Prantl, and A. Pinz. Appearance based active object recognition. *Image and Vision Computing*, (18):715–727, 2000.
3. T.M. Cover and J.A. Thomas. *Elements of Information Theory*. Wiley Series in Telecommunications. John Wiley and Sons, New York, 1991.
4. J. Denzler and C.M. Brown. Information theoretic sensor data selection for active object recognition and state estimation. *IEEE Transactions on Pattern Analysis and Machine Intelligence*, 24(2):145–157, 2002.
5. J. Denzler, C.M. Brown, and H. Niemann. Optimal Camera Parameter Selection for State Estimation with Applications in Object Recognition. In B. Radig and S. Florczyk, editors, *Pattern Recognition 2001*, pages 305–312, Berlin, September 2001. Springer.
6. J. Denzler and M. Zobel. On optimal observation models for kalman filter based tracking appoaches. Technical Report LME–TR–2001–03a, Lehrstuhl für Mustererkennung, Institut für Informatik, Universität Erlangen, 2001.
7. J. Fayman, O. Sudarsky, and E. Rivlin. Zoom tracking and its applications. Technical Report CIS9717, Center for Intelligent Systems, Technion - Israel Institute of Technology, 1997.
8. D. Fox, W. Burgard, and S. Thrun. Active markov localization for mobile robots. *Robotics and Autonomous Systems*, 25:195–207, 1998.
9. G.D. Hager and P.N. Belhumeur. Efficient region tracking with parametric models of geometry and illumination. *IEEE Transactions on Pattern Analysis and Machine Intelligence (PAMI)*, 20(10):1025–1039, 1998.

10. E. Hayman, I. Reid, and D. Murray. Zooming while tracking using affine transfer. In *Proceedings of the 7th British Machine Vision Conference*, pages 395–404. BMVA Press, 1996.
11. L. Paletta, M. Prantl, and A. Pinz. Learning temporal context in active object recognition using bayesian analysis. In *International Conference on Pattern Recognition*, volume 3, pages 695–699, Barcelona, 2000.
12. B. Schiele and J.L. Crowley. Transinformation for Active Object Recognition. In *Proceedings of the Sixth International Conference on Computer Vision*, Bombay, India, 1998.

Video-Based Handsign Recognition for Intuitive Human-Computer-Interaction

Stefan Funck

[1] Institute for Artificial Intelligence, Pattern Recognition Group, Prof. S. Fuchs,
Dresden University of Technology, Germany
http://www.inf.tu-dresden.de/~sf6/handsigns/
[2] Dr. Baldeweg AG, Bildanalytische Diagnosesysteme, Dresden, Germany

Abstract. In this paper we present a video-based HCI-system for the recognition of 10 different hand postures in real time. Automatic removal of the forearm from the segmented hand object garantees a consistent input to the feature calculation step. An extensive comparison of three different approaches to feature extraction (Hu moments, eigencoefficients, fourier descriptors) was carried out. The combination of classifiers using different methods of feature description leads to a recognition rate of 99.5%, requiring only 15-17 ms per frame on a normal PC. The main contribution of this paper is the thourough evaluation, selection and combination of known steps.

1 Introduction

With the increasing use of 3D-modelling in a variety of fields and the spatial presentation provided by auto-stereoscopic displays there is a need for intuitive interaction in virtual space by gesture, allowing free-hand drawing, moving or resizing objects etc. Using different hand postures as commands provides a convenient and intuitive method to control the interaction.

Vision-based systems for recognizing static hand postures can be categorized into 3D-model-based and appearance-based systems. 3D-model-based systems try to fit a 3D-hand model to the image input, providing a complete description of the hand configuration. Often these systems are somewhat restricted regarding the configuration, position or orientation of the hand and are computationally costly. Appearance-based methods rely on features describing the appearence of the 2D-projection of the hand into the image plane. They are applied if the exact configuration is not of interest but the input has to be classified into different postures. Appearance-based methods often follow the classical image processing pipeline: image acquisition - segmentation - feature extraction - classification.

As known for most pattern recognition problems, there exists no method to find the best feature description. Feature types used in the field of gesture recognition include moments [1], eigencoefficents [2], fourier descriptors [3], signatures [4] or geometric features [5]. Reported performance results vary significantly due to distinct problem settings and therefore are hardly comparable. Therefore, in this work the three most promising features were selected and investigated, permitting a well-founded comparison.

L. Van Gool (Ed.): DAGM 2002, LNCS 2449, pp. 26–33, 2002.

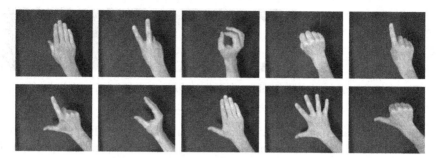

Fig. 1. Examples for each of the 10 postures to be recognized

2 Statement of Problem

Ten different hand postures were defined, as shown in Fig. 1. Using monocular imaging, the postures are to be classified independently of the person and regardless of the position, scale and orientation of the posture, whereby the orientation is naturally restricted to a sector of 180°. As the separation of the hand from the background has not been a focus of this work, dark background was used. Furthermore the handsigns are considered as being equally likely, therefore a symmetric cost function can be assumed for optimization of the classification. Due to the small number of postures appearance-based methods are used.

3 Sample Set and Testing Procedure

The selection of the best feature description by means of performance comparison requires a sample set adequately representing the variability of the classes.

In [2] two methods for estimating the required number of samples without knowledge about the underlying probability distribution were presented. The results indicate that 60 examples per posture class sufficiently describe the variability of the class. For our sample set a total of 966 images of hand postures, performed by 8 different persons, was captured so that at least 92 examples per class were available.

The design of a classifier is based on the presented training set; its performance has to be evaluated by a disjunct test set. Apart from the recognition rate also the required size of the training set is a subject of interest. Therefore the whole sample set has been separated into test- and training sets in different proportions (20/80, 30/70, 40/60, 50/50 percent).

4 Separating the Hand

The separation of objects from background is generally an extremely complicated problem, but due to the assumed conditions a simple thresholding technique can be applied. The present case of a dark background and a light object

Fig. 2. Segmentation from background and separation of hand and forearm

results in a bimodal distribution in the image histogram (see Fig. 2), where the optimal threshold value can easily be calculated. A subsequent morphological close-operation is applied for a smoother object boundary.

To prevent the forearm from influencing the feature calculation, it has to be removed from the image. An adapted version of the algorithm suggested in [6] is used. It is based on the observation that the maximum circular disk within a 2D-projection of a human hand always coincides with the palm. Therefore the centre of the largest circle inside the palm can serve as a stable reference point, it is determined by applying a *distance transformation* to the binarized image.

The enlarged palm circle consists of segments lying inside the object and segments being part of the background. Number, width and configuration of these segments are the features used to query a rule system which determines the object segment representing the forearm. The separation of hand and forearm is then defined by a tangent on the palm circle whose orientation is specified by the position of the forearm segment. An illustration is given in Fig. 2.

The algorithm failed in 4 cases, in which the maximum circular disk did not coincide with the palm. In all others of the 966 images the forearm segment was detected correctly.

5   Choice of Classifier

Before investigating the different feature types, a description of the classification method used will be given. This allows for an explanation of the variations applied to the classifier to suit the feature types described in the next section.

In the context of handsign recognition, a Gaussian density distribution of the features is assumed for most cases. To guarantee reliable classification results the validity of this assumption has to be verified. Using the χ^2-test for all three investigated feature types, approximately 50% of the features were found not to be normally distributed. Therefore the application of a normal distribution classifier is not appropriate.

Instead the *k-Nearest-Neighbour(kNN)*-classifier was choosen. The distance measure used to determine the nearest neighbours is the Euklidian distance, or alternatively, the normalized Euklidian distance:

$$\|\mathbf{v} - \mathbf{r}\|^* = \sqrt{\sum_i \left(\frac{v_i - r_i}{\sigma_i}\right)^2} \qquad \sigma_i - \text{std. deviation of } i\text{-th feature.} \qquad (1)$$

As a result, the bias due to the variability in the feature dimensions is reduced.

6 Feature Extraction and Experiments

6.1 Hu Moments

Hu moments, introduced in [7], are algebraic invariants based on the normalized central moments η_{pq}, additionally providing rotation invariance:

$$
\begin{aligned}
hu_1 &= \eta_{20} + \eta_{02} \\
hu_2 &= (\eta_{20} - \eta_{02})^2 + 4\eta_{11}^2 \\
hu_3 &= (\eta_{30} - 3\eta_{12})^2 + (3\eta_{21} - \eta_{03})^2 \\
hu_4 &= (\eta_{30} + \eta_{12})^2 + (\eta_{21} + \eta_{03})^2 \\
hu_5 &= (\eta_{30} - 3\eta_{12})(\eta_{30} + \eta_{12})\left[(\eta_{30} + \eta_{12})^2 - 3(\eta_{21} + \eta_{03})^2\right] + \\
&\quad (3\eta_{21} - \eta_{03})(\eta_{21} + \eta_{03})\left[3(\eta_{30} + \eta_{12})^2 - (\eta_{21} + \eta_{03})^2\right] \\
hu_6 &= (\eta_{20} - \eta_{02})\left[(\eta_{30} + \eta_{12})^2 - (\eta_{21} + \eta_{03})^2\right] + 4\eta_{11}(\eta_{30} + \eta_{12})(\eta_{21} + \eta_{03}) \\
hu_7 &= (3\eta_{21} - \eta_{03})(\eta_{30} + \eta_{12})\left[(\eta_{30} + \eta_{12})^2 - 3(\eta_{21} + \eta_{03})^2\right] - \\
&\quad (\eta_{30} - 3\eta_{12})(\eta_{21} + \eta_{03})\left[3(\eta_{30} + \eta_{12})^2 - (\eta_{21} + \eta_{03})^2\right] \ .
\end{aligned}
\tag{2}
$$

They are calculated from the binarized image. The maximum recognition rate of 93.8%, using the distance measure according to (1), is achieved when all 7 Hu moments are used. The variations of the results for different numbers k of nearest neighbours between 1 and 30 are within 1%, with the maximum at $k = 5$.

Figure 3 gives two examples for incorrect classifications. Many of them occur due to the similarity of the shapes, but even significantly different shapes result in similar Hu-Moments, as shown on the left of Fig. 3. This deficiency could be reduced by adding geometric features which represent the shapes compactness.

6.2 Hu Moments with Form Factor and Filling Grade

Features describing the compactness of an object are *form factor* and *filling grade*:

$$
V_{\text{form}} = \frac{p^2}{4\pi A} \ , \qquad\qquad V_{\text{fill}} = \frac{A}{w \cdot h} \ ,
\tag{3}
$$

with A being the area and p the perimeter of the object and w and h being width and height of the bounding rectangle. Both form factor and filling grade possess high discriminative power, by using only these two features more than 68% of the test set were classified correctly. Adding the filling grade as an additional feature to the Hu moments improves the recognition accuracy by 1%, the form factor by 2.5%, giving a total of 96.3%. Including both of them makes no difference.

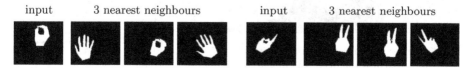

Fig. 3. Examples for incorrect classification when using Hu moments

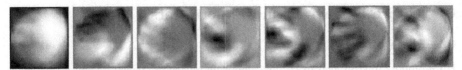

Fig. 4. The average image and the first six eigenvectors

6.3 Eigen Coefficients

Principal Component Analysis (PCA) is a method for de-correlation and compression of data. When applied to imagery, the image data is represented as a data vector by lexicographic ordering of the pixels. From a set of n training vectors $\mathbf{x}_i$ and the average vector $\boldsymbol{\mu}$ the *covariance matrix* C is calculated as

$$\mathbf{C} = \frac{1}{n-1} \sum_{i=1}^{n} (\mathbf{x}_i - \boldsymbol{\mu})(\mathbf{x}_i - \boldsymbol{\mu})^T \ . \tag{4}$$

Solving the eigenvalue problem $\lambda_i \, \mathbf{e}_i = \mathbf{C} \, \mathbf{e}_i$ yields the eigenvectors $\mathbf{e}_i$ and their corresponding eigenvalues λ_i, which are a measure of the data variance represented by the eigenvectors. They are ordered by decreasing variance, so $\lambda_1 \geq \ldots \geq \lambda_n$ holds. With the eigenmatrix $\mathbf{E} = (\mathbf{e}_1 \ldots \mathbf{e}_n)$ the mapping of an input image $\mathbf{x}_i$ to feature space is calculated by

$$\mathbf{v}_i = \mathbf{E}^T (\mathbf{x}_i - \boldsymbol{\mu}) \ , \tag{5}$$

where $\mathbf{v}_i$ is the vector of *eigencoefficients* to the input vector $\mathbf{x}_i$. The input can be reconstructed from the feature vector as a linear combination of the eigenvectors: $\mathbf{x}_i = \mathbf{E} \, \mathbf{v}_i + \boldsymbol{\mu}$. Fig. 4 shows an example for the average image and the first eigenvectors computed from the 80%-training set.

The input image has to be preprocessed as illustrated in Fig. 5 to obtain a definite position, orientation and size of the hand. For the final image various sizes have been tested. As can be seen from Fig. 7, an image size bigger than 32×32 pixels is of no advantage, even for a size of only 8×8 pixels a recognition rate of 96.7% is achieved. The best obtained result is 98.6% for $k = 1$ nearest neighbours, continuously decreasing for higher values of k, reaching 93.7% for $k = 30$ nearest neighbours. The scaling into the desired image size is done non-uniformly, since this was superior to uniform scaling.

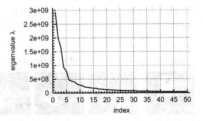

Fig. 5. Preprocessing: from the input image (*left*) the forearm is removed, the image rotated (*middle*) and scaled to a fixed size (*right*)

Fig. 6. Curve of eigenvalues

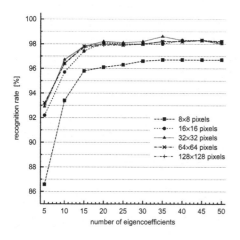
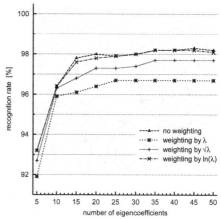

Fig. 7. Recognition rate depending on the number of eigencoefficients for different image sizes (20% test-, 80% training set; $k = 1$; no weighting)

Fig. 8. Recognition rate depending on the number of eigencoefficients for the different coefficient weightings (20% test-, 80% training set; $k = 1$; 64×64 pixels)

A typical curve of eigenvalues is shown in Fig. 6. With the idea being that the importance of an eigencoefficient for the object representation is correlated with the corresponding eigenvalue, it may be presumed that weighting of the eigencoefficients according to their corresponding eigenvalues may improve the recognition. Four different versions have been tested: weighting proportional to λ, $\sqrt{\lambda}$ or $\ln(\lambda)$, or no weighting at all. The outcomes are shown in Fig. 8. Obviously none of the weighting methods improves the recognition process.

The presented results are based on the Euklidian distance measure. Using the normalized Euklidian distance (1) instead leads to identical maximal recognition rates, with the difference being that only 20 instead of 35-45 coefficients are needed to obtain maximum accuracy.

6.4 Fourier Descriptors

The contour of an object can be written as a complex function $z(l) = x(l) + i\, y(l)$, with the parameter l as the arc length with respect to an arbitrary starting point $l = 0$. The transformation into a fourier series, with L as the total length of the contour and $\omega = \frac{2\pi}{L}$, yields

$$z(l) = \sum_{m=-\infty}^{\infty} C_m \, e^{im\omega l} \ , \qquad C_m = \frac{1}{L} \int_0^L z(l)\, e^{-im\omega l}\, dl \ . \qquad (6)$$

C_m is the *fourier descriptor* of frequency m and consists of two values - the real and the imaginary part. The fourier descriptors are used as features describing the shape of the hand. In our work only the outer contour is considered, inner

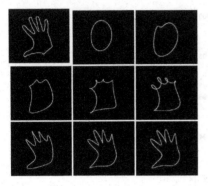

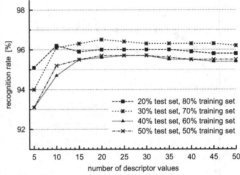

Fig. 9. Reconstruction of the original contour (*top left*) using 1, 3, 5, 7, 9, 11, 13 and 15 fourier descriptors

Fig. 10. Recognition rate depending on the number of descriptor values for different proportions of test and training sets

contours are ignored. The descriptors are normalized with respect to the position, scale and orientation of the contour and to the position of the starting point.

Using the left part of (6) the contour can be reconstructed from the fourier descriptors, thereby giving a good impression on how well the descriptors represent the shape. An illustration is given in Fig. 9.

The obtained recognition rate when using fourier descriptors is shown in Fig. 10. For the 20%-test, 80%-training set - combination a maximum recognition rate of 96.2% is reached with only 10 descriptor values and $k = 1$. The recognition rate is gradually decreasing for higher values of k, reaching 89% for $k = 30$. The vector distance calculation was performed using Euklidian distance, since this coincides with Parseval's theorem specifying the distance of two contours using their fourier descriptors. The variations among the different test and training set proportions are minimal. Surprisingly the 30%-70%-proportion is slightly better than the 20%-80%-proportion. From these results we conclude that a further increase of the number of training examples does not lead to any improvement. The same conclusion could be made for Hu moments and eigencoefficients.

7   Combination of Classifiers

The results obtained by the different feature descriptions are summarized in the following table:

feature description	k	distance measure	number of features	recognition rate
Hu moments	3-5	norm. Euklidian	7	93.8%
Hu moments, form factor	3-5	norm. Euklidian	8	96.3%
eigencoefficients	1	Euklidian	35	98.6%
fourier descriptors	1	Euklidian	10	96.2%

Further improvements can be achieved by combining classifiers using different feature types. If different classifiers recognize the same posture, it is accepted, otherwise the image frame is rejected. Thereby images representing an unspecified or intermediate state between two postures are reliably identified as invalid. The recognition rate now specifies the ratio of correct classifications to all classifications made (i.e. all inputs minus rejections). The results are as follows:

feature descriptions	recognition rate	rejection rate
eigencoefficients + Hu moments and form factor	99.4	4.3
eigencoefficients + fourier descriptors	99.5	5.0
fourier descriptors + Hu moments and form factor	99.2	5.0
eigenco. + fourier des. + Hu mom. and form factor	99.5	6.6

The rejection rates are acceptable since the system is to be used in a real-time application, where the rejection of a single frame does not obstruct the user.

8 Conclusions

We have introduced a recognition system reliably classifying 10 different handsigns in real time; requiring only 15-17 ms per frame on a normal PC running Linux or Windows, when two classifiers with different feature descriptions are combined. The high speed was achieved by downscaling the input image to a width of approximately 100 pixels.

The main contribution of this paper is the thourough evaluation, selection and combination of known steps. Three different feature types have been compared on a representative sample set, each of them was found to be applicable to the problem with recognition rates above 96%. Their combination leads to an extremely reliable system, also allowing to reject invalid postures.

References

1. J. Schlenzig, E. Hunter, R. Jain. Vision Based Hand Gesture Interpretation using Recursive Estimation. *28th Asilomar Conf. on Signals, Systems, and Comp.*, 1994.
2. H. Birk, T. B. Moeslund. Recognizing Gestures from the Hand Alphabet Using Principal Component Analysis. Master's Thesis, Aalborg University, 1996.
3. C. W. Ng, S. Ranganath. Gesture Recognition Via Pose Classification. *Proc. International Conference on Pattern Recognition (ICPR'00)*, Vol. III, 2000, pp. 703–708.
4. M. Stark, M. Kohler, u. a. ZYKLOP: Ein System für den gestenbasierten Dialog mit Anwendungsprogrammen. In "Modeling - Virtual Worlds - Distributed Graphics", W.D.-Fellner (Ed.), Infix-Verlag, 1995, pp. 69–82.
5. K.-H. Jo, Y. Kuno, Y. Shirai. Context-Based Recognition of Manipulative Hand Gestures for Human Computer Interaction. *Proc. 3rd Asian Conference on Computer Vision, Hong Kong, China, January 1998*, Vol. II, 1998.
6. B. Deimel, S. Schröter. Improving Hand-Gesture Recognition via Video Based Methods for the Separation of the Forearm from the Human Hand. *3rd Gesture Workshop, Gif-sur-Yvette, France, March 1999*.
7. M. K. Hu. Visual Pattern Recognition by Moment Invariants. *IRE Transactions on Information Theory IT-8*, January 1962, pp. 179–187.

Quality Enhancement of Reconstructed 3D Models Using Coplanarity and Constraints

H. Cantzler[1], R.B. Fisher[1], and M. Devy[2]

[1] Division of Informatics, University of Edinburgh,
Edinburgh, EH1 2QL, UK
{helmutc,rbf}@dai.ed.ac.uk
[2] LAAS-CNRS, 31077 Toulouse, France
michel@laas.fr

Abstract. We present a process to improve the structural quality of automatically acquired architectural 3D models. Common architectural features like orientations of walls are exploited. The location of these features is extracted by using a probabilistic technique (RANSAC). The relationships among the features are automatically obtained by labelling them using a semantic net of an architectural scene. An evolutionary algorithm is used to optimise the orientations of the planes. Small irregularities in the planes are removed by projecting the triangulation vertices onto the planes. Planes in the resulting model are aligned to each other. The technique produces models with improved appearance. It is validated on synthetic and real data.

Keywords: Surface geometry, Shape, Scene analysis, Constrained architectural reconstruction

1 Introduction

The process of 3D reconstruction is often affected by noise in the measurements. Furthermore, inaccuracies are created by view merging, segmentation and surface fitting. One way to improve the reconstruction is to use more sophisticated methods like photogrammetry techniques. Another way is to exploit properties of the scene. Architectural scenes are particularly suitable for the application of constraints since the geometry is typically very structured. Architectural constraints can be used for 3D reconstruction from single [15,7] or multiple [4,1] intensity images. Features used for architectural constraints are typically straight lines, large coplanar regions and the parallelism and orthogonality of lines or planes. These kinds of features can be easily found in architecture scenes. In [3] research is described that improves architectural 3D models by automatically straightening edges. The work presented in this paper concentrates on extracting planar regions and applying coplanar, parallelism and orthogonality constraints more comprehensive then in previous work to the full 3D model. We apply the constraints to the data following meshing. Zabrodsky concluded in [16] that corrections following meshing generally give a greater improvement. Our method is independent of the calculation of the 3D structure unlike the work presented in [15,7,4,1] where constraints are used in combination with reconstruction from intensity images.

L. Van Gool (Ed.): DAGM 2002, LNCS 2449, pp. 34–41, 2002.
© Springer-Verlag Berlin Heidelberg 2002

This work consists of three steps. First, architectural features are extracted from already triangulated 3D models (Section 2). We use a RANSAC technique [5] to find planes in the model (similar to [2]). The next step is the automatic extraction of the constraints out of the scene. Few papers have dealt with the automatic extraction leaving it to the user to specify them [11,14]. The interpretation of the scene is formalised as a constraint satisfaction problem [13]. Liedtke used a semantic net for interpretation of architectural scenes [8]. His interpretation is hypothesis driven. Hypotheses are verified or falsified by matching the 3D objects against the image. In our work we match the planes against a semantic net of a house by using a backtracking tree search (Section 3). The semantic net concentrates on the definition of the 3D objects and its relations. We check the interpretations only by verifying the relationships between the 3D objects. Constraints are assigned to almost-regularities like parallel or orthogonal walls. The last and final step consists of applying the constraints to the model (Section 4). The original model is fitted to the new constrained model. Optimising the model can be done in a number of ways (*e.g.* numerically [2,14] or evolutionary [11]). We use an evolutionary approach. The model and the constraints are passed to the GenoCop 5 algorithm, proposed by Michalewicz [9]. The vertices are projected onto the planes after finding the optimal parameters. The result is a model with fewer irregularities (*e.g.* edges on walls) and aligned walls.

2 Feature Detection

At all stages of the process, the model is a mesh consisting of vertices $V = \{(x, y, z)'\}$ and triangles $T = \{(v_1, v_2, v_3)\}$. The first step is to extract planes from the raw tri-angulated model. Before starting the extraction the model is normalised. It is mapped into an unit sphere at the origin. A robust RANSAC algorithm [5] is then used to obtain a set of planes. The algorithm generates a number of random plane hypothesis from the points in V. The distance of a triangle centroid to the hypothetical plane is calcu-lated by computing the difference between the distance of the plane to the origin D and the dot product between the triangle centroid $C = (c_x, c_y, c_z)'$ and the unit plane normal $N = (n_x, n_y, n_z)'$. Triangles that satisfy the following inequality belong to the hypothetical plane.

$$|C \cdot N - D| < tolerance \tag{1}$$

The size of a hypothetical plane is calculated by adding up its triangle sizes. The hypothesis that creates the largest plane is selected. The exact number of planes in a model is not known. So, we repeat the RANSAC algorithm until the size of the resulting plane falls under a certain threshold. (An EM algorithm could instead have been used to select the number of planes and fit them, but we chose a simpler technique to focus on the reconstruction issues.)

This technique gives reasonable results. However, it sometimes produces a plane that consists of small disconnected patches distributed over the scene. An architectural plane (*e.g.* a wall) is not usually separated by a large gap. However small gaps frequently occur for example due to the presence of pipes or decorations. Therefore, the planes are analysed by single linkage clustering [6] to ensure that the triangles of a plane are closely connected. The cluster technique starts with the individual triangles and groups them together to form larger and larger clusters (hierarchical clustering). The distance between two clusters is defined as the minimal Euclidean distance of any two triangles belonging to different clusters (nearest neighbor method). The clustering terminates after reaching a certain distance. This distance specifies how far apart parts of the plane can be.

3   Scene Interpretation

We interpret the scene using the features (planes) found previously. A model of an architectural scene is described in a semantic net (see figure 1). The model entities are represented as nodes in the net. The nodes are connected via different types of relationships. A semantically meaningful description is assigned to the scene features by matching them to the semantic net. A backtracking tree search is used to find the best match. The algorithm takes as input a set of features F, a set of possible model labels L and a set of binary model relationships R which limits the possible labelling. The tree search starts with the first feature from F and assigns all labels from L. A second feature is fetched from F and all labels are assigned. At this level some of the labels might be ruled out because they violate the given relationships. This process continues until all features have been labelled. A consistent labelling then exists if each feature is assigned a valid label that is also arc consistent with adjacent nodes. The relationships between features are used to select appropriate geometrical constraints for enforcing parallelism or orthogonality later in the optimisation step.

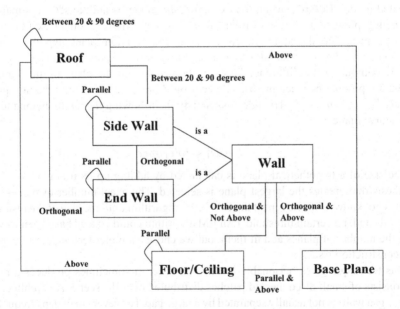

Fig. 1. The model of the architectural scene is represented by a semantic net. Nodes represent the model entities and are linked by architecturally meaningful relationships.

The model-entities (labels) and the relationships among the entities represent the knowledge of a typical architectural scene. Possible labels are L = {*Side Wall, End Wall, Base Plane, Ceiling/Floor, Roof, No Feature*}. The binary relationship functions check if the architectural relationship between two features and their labels is valid (*e.g.* horizontal and vertical walls are almost perpendicular). Angle relationships between two features are checked with a certain tolerance (3 degrees). The "Above" relationship is satisfied if 99% of the vertices of one plane are above a second plane defined by surface normal and distance. *No Feature* does not have any relation with a normal feature and can therefore be assigned everywhere. The final labelling is obtained by finding the solution that maximises the number of architectural labels.

The semantic net models a reasonable subset of all houses. It includes the interior and exterior structure of houses. The model can include an arbitrary number of walls. They can be on the same level or on different ones (then seperated by a *Floor/Ceiling*). The base plane is below all other parts of the building. It represents the ground on which the house stands. The roof is modelled as a typical sharp roof. Errors in the scene description are resolved by labelling them as *No Feature*. The semantic net can be easily extended with features like windows and doors. These features can be modelled as parallel and close to the actual walls. However, the previous plane detection concentrates on finding big planes. So, modelling windows and doors is not necessary at this step.

4   Model Optimisation

Optimising the model by enforcing the constraints found previously is formulated as a nonlinear programming problem. There are many algorithms which are designed to search spaces for an optimum solution. Some of them become ill-conditioned and fail with nonlinear problems. We use the GenoCop 5 algorithm developed by Michalewicz [9]. It is a genetic algorithm (GA) which uses real-value genes and includes methods to deal with linear, non-linear, inequality and domain constraints.

The GA uses the parameter vector p which concatenates all the parameters for the individual planes as the chromosome. The evaluation function consists of the squared residuals of the vertices and the constraint functions. The squared residual is the squared geometric distance from the mesh vertices $\{x_{i,j}\}$ to their planes $\{P_i\}$. The residual of every plane is normalised with its number of vertices N_i. Thus, model size does not affect results. Every constraint is represented by a constraint function c(). The values of these functions correspond to the degree that the constraints are satisfied. The constraint functions can be seen as a penalty functions. λ is a weight factor which scales the constraints to the residuals.

$$\sum_i \frac{1}{N_i} \sum_j dist(P_i(\boldsymbol{p}), x_{i,j})^2 + \lambda \sum_i c^{(i)}(\boldsymbol{p}) \tag{2}$$

Additionally, constraints are used to narrow the search space of the evolutionary algorithm. Domain constraints are applied to individual components of the surface normals and the distances. Each of the parameters can never be outside the range [-1,+1] since the 3D model is mapped into a normal sphere at the origin. Furthermore, unity constraints are applied to the surface normals N.

So far we have obtained the optimised model parameters. We now project the vertices of the planes onto their planes. We calculate the new coordinates $V_p = (x_p, y_p, z_p)'$ of the vertex with the original vertex $V = (x, y, z)'$, the unit surface normal of the plane $N = (n_x, n_y, n_z)'$ and the distance D of the plane to the origin as:

$$V_p = V - tN \tag{3}$$

where

$$t = \frac{V \cdot N - D}{N \cdot N} \tag{4}$$

5 Experimental Results

The proposed technique described above is general. It is independent of the way the 3D model was created (*i.e.* from range or intensity data) and of model properties like variance of the triangle size. It has been applied to several triangulated models. We will here present results for a synthetic model and for two reconstructed real models.

First, we applied the described technique to the synthetic model. The model consists of a perfect mesh of three walls at 90 degrees (1323 vertices & 2400 triangles). Two walls are parallel. A varying amount of Gaussian distributed 3D noise is added to the vertices. The first graph shows the angle error from plane extraction (top curve), improving the plane fit (middle curve) and application of constraints (bottom curve, near noise level axis). Improving the plane fit is done without using any constraints in the evaluation function. The angle error from plane extraction is a result of the random nature of RANSAC. Improving the fit using all data points from the planes gives much better results. Finally, using the constraints gives an angle error very close to zero. The second graph shows the mean squared residual after plane extraction (top curve), improving the fit (dashed curve) and constraining the model (solid curve). The parameters obtained from RANSAC show the biggest error. The mean residuals from improving the fit and from applying the constraints are fairly similar and are both significantly below the the RANSAC curve. The two graphs show that applying constraints improves the orientation of the walls without worsening the fit.

We show an experiment with the reconstructed model of Arenberg castle (in Belgium) reconstructed by the Catholic University of Leuven [10]. The model was reconstructed from an image sequence of 20 images (6292 vertices & 12263 triangles). The walls and the ground on the original solid model show clearly a lot of small irregularities (see figure 4). 5 planes are extracted (3 walls, 1 floor and 1 roof). The planes are constrained by 7 constraints. The angles between the planes vary from the optimum by 1.5 degrees on average before optimisation. After optimisation they differ less than 0.01 degrees. The result shows the model with removed irregularities and constrained planes. The average disparity of the moved vertices as a fraction of the model diameter is 0.33%. The optimisation step took 54 seconds on an Intel Celeron with 400MHz.

Next, we briefly describe results for a Bavarian farmhouse reconstructed by the European Commission Joint Research Centre (JRC) [12]. It was reconstructed from multiple range data scans (12504 vertices & 16589 triangles). This is a full 3D model.

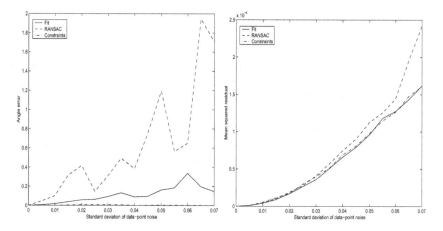

Fig. 2. Results for the synthetic model. The left graph shows the angle error in degrees versus the noise level. The graph on the right shows the mean squared residual versus the noise.

The plane extraction finds 4 walls and two planes for the roof. The orientations of the walls are already fairly good. The angles between the planes differ on average by 0.5 degrees in the original model. After optimisation they differ less than 0.01 degrees. The original solid model shows small edges on the walls. The result has these edges projected onto the wall (see figure 3 for a close view of a wall).

Fig. 3. A close view of a wall of the farmhouse. On the left is the unconstrained model. Surface ripples are most easily seen in the circled areas. On the right is the optimised model.

6   Conclusion and Future Work

Previous work used architectural constraints mainly for scene reconstruction from intensity images. This work shows how architectural constraints can be used for improving the reconstruction of full 3D models independent of the sensor data. Only 3D information is used. The constraints make architectural features more regular in terms of their architectural properties. We exploit common architectural features like walls and their relationships to each other.

Initially, a RANSAC technique obtains a set of planes from the 3D data. We automatically discover the graph of constraints between the planes by using a tree search strategy. Even conservatively loose thresholds on angles and position lead to a correct labelling of the planes in the scene. The model parameters are optimised with a robust evolutionary algorithm. A numerical normalisation of the model beforehand leads to

Fig. 4. The textured model (top/left), the original solid model (top/right), the extracted planes (bottom/left) and the resulting model after optimisation (bottom/right) from the castle. The extracted planes are displayed a bit darker than in the solid model.

domain constraints on the parameters which speeds up the search algorithm. The experimental results show how imperfections like small irregularities on planes and the orientations of walls are corrected. The visual appearance of the model is enhanced.

Future work aims at incorporating edges into the process of model optimisation. This includes extraction of edges in the model, straightening of edges and the use of parallelism or orthogonality constraints where applicable.

References

1. C. Baillard and A. Zisserman. A plane-sweep strategy for the 3d reconstruction of buildings from multiple images. *ISPRS Journal of Photogrammetry and Remote Sensing*, 33(B2):56–62, 2000.
2. A. Bartoli. Piecewise planar segmentation for automatic scene modeling. *Conference on Computer Vision and Pattern Recognition, Hawaii*, pages 283–289, 2001.
3. P. Dias, V. Sequeira, J.G.M. Goncalves, and F. Vaz. Combining intensity and range images for 3d architectural modelling. *International Symposium on Virtual and Augmented Architecture, Dublin*, pages 139–145, 2001.
4. A. Dick, P. Torr, and R. Cipolla. Automatic 3d modelling of architecture. *British Machine Vision Conference, Bristol*, pages 372–381, 2000.
5. M.A. Fischler and R.C. Bolles. Random sample consensus: A paradigm for model fitting with application to image analysis and automated cartography. *Communications of the ACM*, 24(6):381–395, 1981.
6. A.K. Jain and R.C. Dubes. *Algorithms for Clustering Data*. Prentice Hall, 1988.
7. D. Liebowitz, A. Criminisi, and A. Zisserman. Creating architectural models from images. *Eurographics*, 18(3):39–50, 1999.
8. C.-E. Liedtke, O. Grau, and S. Growe. Use of explicit knowledge for the reconstruction of 3d object geometry. *International Conference on Computer Analysis of Images and Patterns, Prague*, pages 580–587, 1995.
9. Z. Michalewicz. *Genetic Algorithms + Data Structures = Evolution Programs*. Springer, 1996.
10. M. Pollefeys. *Self-calibration and metric 3D reconstruction from uncalibrated image sequences*. PhD thesis, University of Loewen, 1999.
11. C. Robertson, R.B. Fisher, N. Werghi, and A. Ashbrook. Fitting of constrained feature models to poor 3d data. *Proceedings Adaptive Computing in Design and Manufacture, Plymouth*, pages 149–160, 2000.
12. V. Sequeira, K. Ng, E. Wolfart, J.G.M. Goncalves, and D.C. Hogg. Automated reconstruction of 3d models from real environments. *ISPRS Journal of Photogrammetry and Remote Sensing*, 54:1–22, 1999.
13. D.L. Waltz. *Generating Semantic Descriptions from Drawings of Scenes with Shadows*. PhD thesis, AI Lab, MIT, 1972.
14. N. Werghi, R.B. Fisher, A. Ashbrook, and C. Robertson. Shape reconstruction incorporating multiple non-linear geometric constraints. *Computer-Aided Design*, 31(6):363–399, 1999.
15. M. Wilczkowiak, E. Boyer, and P.F. Sturm. Camera calibration and 3d reconstruction from single images using parallelepipeds. *International Conference on Computer Vision, Vancouver*, pages 142–148, 2001.
16. H. Zabrodsky and D. Weinshall. Using bilateral symmetry to improve 3d reconstruction from image sequences. *Computer Vision and Image Understanding*, 67(1):48–57, 1997.

Multispectral Texture Analysis Using Interplane Sum- and Difference-Histograms

Christian Münzenmayer, Heiko Volk, Christian Küblbeck,
Klaus Spinnler, and Thomas Wittenberg

Fraunhofer Institut für Integrierte Schaltungen,
Am Wolfsmantel 33, D-91058 Erlangen
{mzn,volkho,kue,spk,wbg}@iis.fhg.de

Abstract. In this paper we present a new approach for color texture classification which extends the gray level sum- and difference histogram features [8]. Intra- and inter-plane second order features capture the spatial correlations between color bands. A powerful set of features is obtained by non-linear color space conversion to HSV and thresholding operation to eliminate the influence of sensor noise on color information. We present an evaluation of classification performance using four different image sets.

1 Introduction

Various solutions in industrial and medical applications make use of texture algorithms for classification of structured surfaces. Examples include microscopic images of cells (cytology), tissue (histology) and endoscopic images of mucous membranes of e.g. the larynx or intestine. Industrial applications are the decor of furniture or woodcut surfaces in the quality control of sawmills.

Many different approaches addressing the problem of texture classification have been published mainly based on gray scale images. In contrast, color histograms as a measure of the statistical distribution of colors have proven to be a powerful tool for classification. With more processing power at hand and new problems arising in industrial and medical applications, the fusion of color and texture approach is currently a new focus of interest and research.

Several different approaches have been under investigation so far. Panjwani and Healey extended the concept of Markov random fields in texture recognition for color images [6]. They used a Gaussian random field model for image segmentation and to capture dependencies between spatially neighbored pixels from different color planes. An approach by Lakmann is based on statistical dependencies between planes in color images [4]. The color covariance model is based on covariance matrices between color planes. Lakmann used matrices with dimension 11×11 on which 14 features similar to Haralick's co-occurrence features are defined.

Jain and Healey proposed the use of unicrome and opponent features based on Gabor filter outputs [3]. They used a filter bank of real circularly symmetric Gabor filters with three scales in octave distance and four orientations to

L. Van Gool (Ed.): DAGM 2002, LNCS 2449, pp. 42–49, 2002.
© Springer-Verlag Berlin Heidelberg 2002

compute features as mean energies within filter outputs. A similar approach was published by Van de Wouwer using biorthogonal spline wavelets for filtering [10]. This work also investigated the use of different linear color transformations.

One of the most common algorithms in gray level texture classification is the co-occurrence or spatial gray level dependence method (SGLDM) [1]. It estimates the joint probability function of pixels in certain spatial relationships which lead to the so-called co-occurrence matrices. For texture classification Haralick proposed 14 features which are calculated based on the normalized co-occurrence matrix of a gray level image. Hauta-Kasari et al. suggested a generalized co-occurrence approach not using gray levels but color classes [2]. Palm et al. proposed cross plane interactions modeled by co-occurrence matrices between color planes [5]. Features are calculated in the same way as for the SGLDM.

2 Unser Sum- and Difference-Histogram Features

Michael Unser used two one-dimensional histograms (sum- and difference-histogram) as an approximation for the two-dimensional co-occurrence matrix [8]. These histograms count the frequencies of sums respectively differences of pixel gray levels with a certain displacement (d_x, d_y) within a region of interest D. With G being the maximum gray level (here $G = 255$) these histograms are defined as:

$$h_s(i) = Card\{(x_1, y_1) \in D | g_{x_1,y_1} + g_{x_2,y_2} = i\}, i \in [0; 2(G-1)], \qquad (1)$$

$$h_d(j) = Card\{(x_1, y_1) \in D | g_{x_1,y_1} - g_{x_2,y_2} = j\}, j \in [-G+1; G-1]. \qquad (2)$$

Independence of image size is reached by normalization with the total number of pixels N in D:

$$N = \sum_{i=0}^{2(G-1)} h_s(i) = \sum_{j=-G+1}^{G-1} h_d(j), \qquad (3)$$

$$\hat{P}_s(i) = \frac{h_s(i)}{N}, \qquad (4)$$

$$\hat{P}_d(j) = \frac{h_d(j)}{N}. \qquad (5)$$

The displacement vector (d_x, d_y) can also be represented by (d, Θ) (Fig. 1 (a)). In general it is sufficient to use $\Theta \in \{0, \pi/4, \pi/2, 3\pi/4\}$ for a small radius d, and calculate features on each of the histograms separately. To introduce a certain degree of rotation invariance it is possible to accumulate histograms over all four directions and then calculate the features.

Unser showed how approximations of the Haralick co-occurrence features can be approximated based on the sum and difference histograms. The features used in the experiments described in section 6 are shown in Table 1.

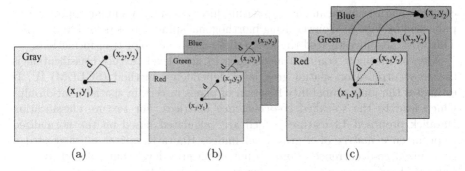

Fig. 1. Second order statistic in (a) Gray level image (b) Intra plane (c) Inter plane

Table 1. Unser sum-/difference-histogram features used in the experiments

Feature	Equation	Feature	Equation
sum-mean	$f_1 = \sum_i i \hat{P}_s(i) = \mu_s$	sum-variance	$f_2 = \sum_i (i - \mu_s)^2 \hat{P}_s(i)$
sum-energy	$f_3 = \sum_i \hat{P}_s^2(i)$	sum-entropy	$f_4 = -\sum_i \hat{P}_s(i) \log \hat{P}_s(i)$
diff-mean	$f_5 = \sum_j j \hat{P}_d(j) = \mu_d$	diff-variance	$f_6 = \sum_j (j - \mu_d)^2 \hat{P}_d(j)$
diff-energy	$f_7 = \sum_j \hat{P}_d^2(j)$	diff-entropy	$f_8 = -\sum_j \hat{P}_d(j) \log \hat{P}_d(j)$
shade	$f_9 = \sum_i (i - \mu_s)^3 \hat{P}_s(i)$	prominence	$f_{10} = \sum_i (i - \mu_s)^4 \hat{P}_s(i)$
contrast	$f_{11} = \sum_j j^2 \hat{P}_d(j)$	homogenity	$f_{12} = \sum_j \frac{1}{1+j^2} \hat{P}_d(j)$
correlation	$f_{13} = \sum_i (i - \mu_s)^2 \hat{P}_s(i) - \sum_j j^2 \hat{P}_d(j)$		
2nd ang moment	$f_{14} = f_3 * f_7$	entropy	$f_{15} = f_4 + f_8$

3   Inter-/Intra Plane Features

To extend a single plane algorithm to multiple image planes it is always possible to use each plane separately. The features are calculated on each plane in an RGB-image or any other multispectral image and concatenated to a feature vector having a size which is three times as long. For the Unser features this means that three pairs of sum- and difference-histograms $(h_{s,rr}, h_{d,rr})$, $(h_{s,gg}, h_{d,gg})$, $(h_{s,bb}, h_{d,bb})$ are calculated and from each of these pairs 15 features are derived:

$$h_{s,pp}(i) = Card\{(x_1, y_1) \in D | p_{x_1,y_1} + p_{x_2,y_2} = i\}, p \in \{r, g, b\}, \qquad (6)$$

$$h_{d,pp}(j) = Card\{(x_1, y_1) \in D | p_{x_1,y_1} - p_{x_2,y_2} = j\}, p \in \{r, g, b\}. \qquad (7)$$

In the following this will be called the *intra plane method* (Fig. 1 (b)). To cover statistical dependencies between planes the concept of co-occurrence can be extended to different planes. Palm [5] proposes inter plane co-occurrence for the Haralick feature extractor. This concept is applied to the Unser features here and called the *inter plane method* (Fig. 1 (c)):

$$h_{s,pq}(i) = Card\{(x_1, y_1) \in D | p_{x_1,y_1} + q_{x_2,y_2} = i\}, p, q \in \{r, g, b\}, p \neq q, \qquad (8)$$

$$h_{d,pq}(j) = Card\{(x_1, y_1) \in D | p_{x_1,y_1} - q_{x_2,y_2} = j\}, p, q \in \{r, g, b\}, p \neq q. \qquad (9)$$

Due to the associativity of summation and subtraction only three plane combinations $(h_{s,rg}, h_{d,rg})$, $(h_{s,rb}, h_{d,rb})$, $(h_{s,gb}, h_{d,gb})$ are needed. For both methods (intra- and inter-plane) the feature vector is three times longer as before. It should be noted that for inter-plane features a displacement of $d = 0$ can also be used as a way to express correlation between channels with no spatial displacement.

4   Color Distance Features

Another method of introducing color information into the Unser feature extractor is the use of a distance measure in color space (Fig. 3 (a)). The L2 metric (Euclidean distance) will be used to compute a scalar measure from the RGB-values of a pixel-pair. For the sum histogram the length of the sum vector is used:

$$s(x_1, y_1) = \sqrt{(r_{x_1,y_1} + r_{x_2,y_2})^2 + (g_{x_1,y_1} + g_{x_2,y_2})^2 + (b_{x_1,y_1} + b_{x_2,y_2})^2}, \qquad (10)$$

$$\hat{d}(x_1, y_1) = \sqrt{(r_{x_1,y_1} - r_{x_2,y_2})^2 + (g_{x_1,y_1} - g_{x_2,y_2})^2 + (b_{x_1,y_1} - b_{x_2,y_2})^2}, \qquad (11)$$

$$d(x_1, y_1) = \begin{cases} -\hat{d}(x_1, y_1) & \text{if } p_{x_1,y_1} - p_{x_2,y_2} < 0 \text{ for two or more } p \in \{r,g,b\}, \\ \hat{d}(x_1, y_1) & \text{otherwise} \end{cases}, \qquad (12)$$

$$h_s(i) = Card\{(x_1, y_1) \in D | s(x_1, y_1) = i\}, i \in [0; 2(G-1)\sqrt{3}], \qquad (13)$$

$$h_d(j) = Card\{(x_1, y_1) \in D | d(x_1, y_1) = j\}, j \in [-(G-1)\sqrt{3}; (G-1)\sqrt{3}]. \qquad (14)$$

The definition of $d(x_1, y_1)$ shown in (12) uses the direction of the distance vector which would be ignored if simply the L2-distance was used. This also has the effect that the total number of bins in the difference histogram becomes the same as in the sum histogram.

For an image with three channels of one byte each this corresponds to histograms of 883 bins. As the L2 norm leads in most cases to fractional numbers these are simply assigned to an integer bin by rounding.

Perceptually uniform color spaces are known for their property that distances in the color space are closely related to human perception. The Euclidean distance in the L*u*v* space is a measure for the perceptual distance perceived by the averarge human. So we use the L*u*v* representation for color distance features as well.

5   Non-linear HSV Features

Instead of the highly correlated and symmetric RGB color space the HSV (hue, saturation, value) color model can be useful in texture classification. An empirical evaluation by Paschos claims the superiority of the HSV space over RGB for color texture analysis [7].

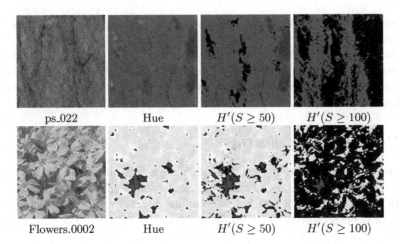

Fig. 2. Thresholding in hue channel of BarkTex (ps_022) and VisTex (Flowers.0002) images. Hue values are set to zero where saturation is below a certain threshold S_{min}

For small saturation values the hue H is highly sensible to sensor noise in the image. Therefore the idea for texture classification is to use the H channel only if a certain saturation threshold S_{min} is exceeded and otherwise set H to an arbitrary but constant value (here $H = 0$):

$$H' = \begin{cases} H & \text{if } S \geq S_{min} \\ 0 & \text{otherwise} \end{cases}. \tag{15}$$

Sample images of the hue channel after this thresholding-operation are shown in Fig. 2. Features can be calculated on the H' and the V plane individually and combined as inter-plane features. Further thoughts show that applying intra- and inter-plane distances to the HSV space is difficult because the hue channel is an angular representation. Hue values vary between 0 and 360° respectively 2π. Therefore a distance measure between the hue values H_1 and H_2 is proposed that is maximal for $\Delta h = \pi$:

$$d_H^0 = \sin\left(\frac{\Delta h}{2}\right) = \sin\left(\frac{H_1 - H_2}{2}\right). \tag{16}$$

For the summation the range of $[0; 2\pi]$ is exceeded but again a measure is proposed that is maximal for

$$H_1 + H_2 \mod 2\pi = \pi. \tag{17}$$

Note that the modulo operation is implicit in the computation of the sine:

$$s_H^0 = \sin\left(\frac{H_1 + H_2}{2} \mod \pi\right) = \sin\left(\frac{H_1 + H_2}{2}\right). \tag{18}$$

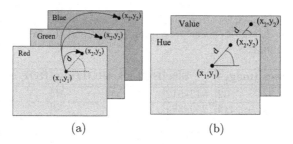

(a)   (b)

Fig. 3. Second order statistic (a) with color distance (b) in thresholded H'V space

To build discrete histograms these definitions are scaled to the same range as in the gray level case which is $[-255; 255]$ and $[0; 510]$ respectively:

$$s_H(x_1, y_1) = 510 \times \sin\left(\frac{h(x_1, y_1) + h(x_2, y_2)}{2}\right) \in [0; 510], \tag{19}$$

$$h_{s,H}(i) = Card\{(x_1, y_1) \in D | s_H(x_1, y_1) = i\}, \tag{20}$$

$$d_H(x_1, y_1) = 255 \times \sin\left(\frac{h(x_1, y_1) - h(x_2, y_2)}{2}\right) \in [-255; 255], \tag{21}$$

$$h_{d,H}(i) = Card\{(x_1, y_1) \in D | d_H(x_1, y_1) = i\}. \tag{22}$$

Features are then calculated with this distance and sum definition on the H' plane and with normal scalar sums and differences on the V plane (Fig. 3 (b)).

6   Experiments and Results

To validate our newly defined texture features we used four different color image sets. From the *VisTex* database we chose 32 images showing different color textures [9]. We selected 10 disjoint regions of interest (ROI) in each image for classification experiments. The *BarkTex* database contains 414 images of bark from 6 different types of trees [4]. A more practical image set was compiled from a project for cancer prevention by screening of cervical cells. Healthy cells can be discriminated from precancerous cells by their nuclues structure. It is known from biology that precancerous dysplasia cause changes in the chromatin structure of the nuclei. For this work 53 healthy reference and 53 dysplastic nuclei were used. A sample from industrial image processing is the *Wood* image database which contains images from wood cut surfaces with seven different classes. Among other these include normal wood, knotholes and bark margins.

Classification results were obtained by applying the leaving-one-out classification scheme with a nearest neighbor classifier using the L2-distance norm. All features were normalized to $\mu = 0$ and $\sigma = 1$. The proposed color texture features are evaluated in the context of their gray scale counterpart, so the color images were converted to gray scale using the weighted sum of RGB:

$$Y = 0.212671R + 0.715160G + 0.072169B. \tag{23}$$

Table 2. Validation image sets from the VisTex [9] and BarkTex [4] databases. The cell images are compiled from a cancer prevention project and the Wood images contains different wood cut images

Name	Classes	Images	Size	ROI-size	ROI/img	ROI/class	#ROIs
VisTex	32	32	512x512	64x64	10	10	320
BarkTex	6	414	256x384	64x64	4	272	1624
Cells	2	37	1000x700	32x32	-	53	106
Wood	7	208	128x128	128x128	1	-	208

Table 3. Classification results using leaving-one-out classification scheme. Recognition rates are shown in %. Displacement d and cumulation are shown which lead to best gray scale rate

Set	Cum.	d	Gray	Col-Histo	Intra	Inter	L2	L2 (L*u*v*)	HSV	S_{min}[1]
VisTex	no	1	86	95	89	**98**	85	83	97	0
BarkTex	no	1	73	77	83	**87**	75	74	85	25
Cervix	yes	2	96	90	93	92	**95**	85	91	100
Wood	no	2	66	58	67	69	65	65	**71**	50

For feature calculation the directions $\Theta \in \{0, \pi/4, \pi/2, 3\pi/4\}$ where used in distances $d = 1, 2$ as individual histograms leading to a feature vector of length $L = 60$. To obtain rotation invariance the histograms of these four directions were accumulated yielding $L = 15$ features. On each sample set four different gray scale settings were applied and the settings with best recognition rates were selected (see Table 3 column 4).

Using these parameters the proposed intra- and inter-plane features were applied. Classification results are shown in Table 3 with the best result marked in bold face. Different thresholds S_{min} were applied to the HSV image and the best results selected for the non-linear HSV features (see Table 3 column 10). Another reference classification rate was obtained by using color histogram features on the RGB image which do not take into account the spatial structure of the image (see Table 3 column 5).

7 Discussion

In this paper we presented four different approaches to extend sum- and difference histogram features for multispectral images. Classification results improved significantly for three of the used image sets as can be seen in Table 3. The inter-plane and thresholded HSV features outperformed intra-plane and color distance features as well as the gray level algorithm and color histograms.

---

[1] Thresholds S_{min} for HSV features which lead to best recognition rates. For each experiment values of $S_{min} \in \{0, 25, 50, 100, 150, 200\}$ were applied and the best setting selected.

In contrast recognition rates for the Cervix cell nuclei became worse. This might be the case because these images are quite gray in their appearance with strong camera noise. By using the weighted mean for a gray representation noise gets partially compensated and classification stabilized. Results obtained using the features from the Euclidean distance (L2) in the RGB- and the L*u*v*-space proved to be quite disappointing considering the computational cost involved.

On the VisTex image set color histograms with 95% recognition rate are nearly as powerful as the inter plane features but this surely has to do with the exceptional variance in colors between the images which is seldom found in practical applications. Here we propose the use of the inter-plane and the thresholded HSV features. Future work will focus on feature selection respectively reduction, multiscale analysis and the application to irregularly bounded regions.

References

1. Haralick R. M., Shanmugam K., and Dinstein I.: Textural Features for Image Classification. IEEE Transactions on Systems, Man, And Cybernetics, 3(6):610–621, 1973.
2. Hauta-Kasari M., Parkkinen J., Jaaskelainen T., and Lenz R.: Generalized Cooccurrence Matrix for Multispectral Texture Analysis Proceedings of the 13th International Conference on Pattern Recognition (ICPR), 785–789, 1996.
3. Jain A. and Healey G.: A Multiscale Representation Including Opponent Color Features for Texture Recognition. IEEE Transactions on Image Processing, 7(1):124–128, 1998.
4. Lakmann R.: Statistische Modellierung von Farbtexturen. Fölbach, Koblenz, 1998.
5. Palm C., Metzler V., Mohan B., Dieker O., Lehmann T., and Spitzer K.: Co-Occurrence Matrizen zur Texturklassifikation in Vektorbildern. Bildverarbeitung für die Medizin, Springer, 367–371, 1999.
6. Panjwani D. K. and Healey G.: Markov Random Field Models for Unsupervised Segmentation of Textured Color Images. IEEE Transactions on Pattern Analysis and Machine Intelligence, 17(10):939–954, 1995.
7. Paschos G.: Perceptually Uniform Color Spaces for Color Texture Analysis: An Empirical Evaluation. IEEE Transactions on Image Processing, 10(6):932–937, 2001.
8. Unser M.: Sum and Difference Histograms for Texture Analysis. IEEE Transactions on Pattern Analysis and Machine Intelligence, 8(1):118–125, 1986.
9. MIT Media Laboratory Vision and Modeling group: VisTex database. http://www-white.media.mit.edu/vismod/imagery/VisionTexture
10. Van de Wouwer G., Scheunders P., Livens S., and Van Dyck D.: Wavelet Correlation Signatures for Color Texture Characerization. Pattern Recognition 32(3):443–451, 1999.

Human Body Reconstruction from Image Sequences

Fabio Remondino

Institute of Geodesy and Photogrammetry, ETH Zurich, Switzerland
fabio@geod.baug.ethz.ch

Abstract. The generation of 3-D models from uncalibrated sequences is a challenging problem that has been investigated in many research activities in the last decade. In particular, a topic of great interest is the modeling of real humans. In this paper a method for the 3-D reconstruction of static human body shapes from images acquired with a video-camera is presented. The process includes the orientation and calibration of the sequence, the extraction of correspondences on the body using least squares matching technique and the reconstruction of the 3-D point cloud of the human body.

1. Introduction

The actual interests in 3-D object reconstruction are motivated by a wide spectrum of applications, such as object recognition, city modeling, video games, animations, surveillance and visualization. In the last years, great progress in creating and visualizing 3-D models of man-made and non-rigid objects from images has been made, with particular attention to the visual quality of the results. The existing systems are often built around specialized hardware (laser scanner), resulting in high costs. Other methods based on photogrammetry [12, 19] or computer vision [18], can instead obtain 3-D models of objects with low cost acquisition systems, using photo or video cameras. Since many years, photogrammetry deals with high accuracy measurements from image sequences, including 3-D object tracking [15], deformation measurements or motion analysis [7]; these applications requires very precise calibration, but automated and reliable procedures are available. In the last years many researchers have tried to increase the automation level for the production of 3-D models reducing the requirements and the accuracy of the calibration, with the goal of automatically extract a 3-D model "by freely moving a camera around an object" [18].

Concerning the reconstruction and modeling of human bodies, nowadays the demand for 3-D models has drastically increased. A complete model of human consists of both the shape and the movements of the body. Many available systems consider these two modeling processes as separate even if they are very close. A classical approach to build human shape models uses 3-D scanners [Cyberware]: they are expensive but simple to use and various modeling software are available. Other techniques use structured light methods [2], silhouette extraction [23] and multi-image photogrammetry [6]. These human models can be used for different purposes, like animation, manufacture or medical applications. For animation, only approximative measurements are necessary: the shape can be first defined (e.g. with 3D scanners or with meshsmooth or with volumetric primitives attached to a skeleton)

L. Van Gool (Ed.): DAGM 2002, LNCS 2449, pp. 50–57, 2002.
© Springer-Verlag Berlin Heidelberg 2002

and then animated using motion capture data. Both steps can also be joined fitting general body models to different image measurements [7]. For medical applications or in manufacturing industries, an exact three-dimensional measurement of the body is required [14] and usually performed with scanning devices [Tailor].

In this paper a photogrammetric reconstruction of 3-D shape of human bodies from uncalibrated image sequences is described. The recovered 3-D points can then be modeled with commercial software or used to fit 3-D model of humans. The reconstruction process mainly consists of four parts:
1. Acquisition and analysis of the images (section 2);
2. Calibration and orientation of the sequence (section 3);
3. Matching process on the human body between triplets of images and 3-D point cloud generation by forward intersection of the matched points (section 4).

This work belongs to a project called Characters Animation and Understanding from SEquence of images (CAUSE). Its goal is the extraction of complete 3-D animation models of characters from old movies or video sequences, where no information about the camera and the objects is available.

2. Image Acquisition

A still video camera or a standard camcorder can be used for the acquisition of the images. In our case, a Sony DCR-VX700E video camcorder is used. The acquisition lasted ca 45 seconds and requires no movements of the person: this could be considered a limit of the system, but faster acquisition can be realized. Nevertheless, the available commercial systems (3D scanners) require ca 20 seconds for the acquisition. For the process 12 frames are selected out of the sequence around the standing person (figure.1). The resolution of the acquired images is 576x720 pixel.

Fig. 1. Four frames (1, 5, 8, 12) of the twelve used for the reconstruction process

The artifacts created by the interlace effect during the digitization process are removed deleting one field of the frame and interpolating the remaining lines. A less smoothly sequence is obtained and the resolution in vertical direction is reduced by 50 per cent. Another possible approach would be to remove lines just in portions of the video where interlacing artifacts are present (adaptive deinterlacing).

The testfield in the background contains many similar targets (repeated pattern) but they are used just as features for the processing. No 3-D information is available.

3. Calibration and Orientation of the Image Sequence

Camera calibration and image orientation are prerequisites for accurate and reliable results for all those applications that rely on the extraction of precise 3-D information from imagery. With the calibration procedure, the geometric deviations of the physical reality from the ideal pinhole camera system are determined. The early theories and formulations of orientation procedures were developed more than 70 years ago and today there is a great number of procedures and algorithms available. A fundamental criterion for grouping these procedures is the used camera model, i.e. the projective camera or the perspective camera model. Camera models based on perspective collineation require stable optics, a minimum of 3 image correspondences and have high stability. On the other hand, projective approaches can deal with variable focal length, but are quite instables, need more parameters and a minimum of 6 image correspondences.

The calibration and orientation process used in this work is based on a photogrammetric bundle-adjustment (section 3.3); the required tie points (image correspondences) are found automatically (section 3.1) with the following steps:

- interest points extraction from each image;
- matching of potential feature pairs between adjacent images;
- false matches clearing using local filtering;
- epipolar geometry computation to refine the matching and remove outliers;
- correspondences tracking in all the image sequence.

In the following section these steps are described. The process is completely automatic; it is similar to [9] and [20], but some additional changes and extensions to these algorithms are presented and discussed.

3.1 Determination of Image Correspondences

The first step is to find a set of interest points or corners in each image of the sequence. Harris corners detector or Foerstner interest operator are used. The threshold on the number of corners extracted is based on the image size. A good point distribution is assured by subdividing the images in small patches and keeping only the points with the highest interest value in those patches.

The next step is to match points between adjacent images. At first cross-correlation is used and then the results are refined using adaptive least squares matching (ALSM) [10]. The cross-correlation process uses a small window around each point in the first image and tries to correlate it against all points that are inside a bigger window in the adjacent image. The point with biggest correlation coefficient is used as approximation for the ALS matching process. The process returns the best match in the second image for each interest point in the first image. The final number of possible matches between image pairs is usually around 40% of the extracted points.

The found matched pairs always contain outliers, due to the unguided matching process. Therefore a filtering of false correspondences has to be performed. A process based on disparity gradient concept is used [13]. If P_{LEFT} and P_{RIGHT} as well as Q_{LEFT} and Q_{RIGHT} are corresponding points in the left and right image, the disparity gradient of the pair (P,Q) is the vector G defined as:

$$G = \frac{|D(P) - D(Q)|}{D_{CS}(P, Q)} \tag{1}$$

where

$D(P) = (P_{LEFT,X} - P_{RIGHT,X}, P_{LEFT,Y} - P_{RIGHT,Y})$ is the parallax of P between the 2 images, also called disparity of P;

$D(Q) = (Q_{LEFT,X} - Q_{RIGHT,X}, Q_{LEFT,Y} - Q_{RIGHT,Y})$ is the parallax of Q between the 2 images, also called disparity of Q;

$D_{CS} = [(P_{LEFT} + P_{RIGHT})/2, (Q_{LEFT} + Q_{RIGHT})/2]$ is the cyclopean separator, e.g. the difference vector between the two midpoints of the straight line segment connecting a point in the left image to the corresponding in the right one.

If P and Q are close together in one image, they should have a similar disparity (and a small numerator in equation 1). Therefore, the smaller the disparity gradient G is, the more the two correspondences are in agreement. This filtering process is performed locally and not on the whole image: in fact, because of the presence of translation, rotation, shearing and scale in consecutive images, the algorithm achieves incorrect results due to very different disparity values. The sum of all disparity gradients of each match relative to all other neighborhood matches is computed. Then the median of this sum of disparity gradients is found, and those matches that have a disparity gradient sum greater than this median sum are removed. The process removes ca. 80% of the false correspondences. Other possible approaches to remove false matches are described in [17] and [22].

The next step performs a pairwise relative orientation and an outlier rejection using those matches that pass the filtering process. Based on the coplanarity condition, the process computes the projective singular correlation between two images [16], also called epipolar transformation (because it transforms an image point from the first image to an epipolar line in the second image) or fundamental matrix (in case the interior orientation parameters of both images are the same) [8]. The singular correlation condition between homologous image points of two images is:

$$\mathbf{x}_1^T \mathbf{M} \mathbf{x}_2 = 0 \quad \text{with} \quad \mathbf{x}_1^T = [x_1 \quad y_1 \quad 1], \quad \mathbf{x}_2 = [x_2 \quad y_2 \quad 1]^T \tag{2}$$

Many solutions have been published to compute the 3x3 singular matrix $\mathbf{M}$, but to cope with possible blunders, a robust method of estimation is required. In general least median estimators are very powerful in presence of outliers; so the Least Median of the Squares (LMedS) method is used to achieve a robust computation of the epipolar geometry and to reject possible outliers [21].

The computed epipolar geometry is then used to refine the matching process, which is now performed as guided matching along the epipolar lines. A maximal distance from the epipolar line is set as threshold to accept a point as potential match or as outlier. Then the filtering process and the relative orientation are performed again to get rid of possible blunders. However, while the computed epipolar geometry can be correct, not every correspondence that supports the orientation is necessarily valid. This because we are considering just the epipolar geometry between couple of images and a pair of correspondences can support the epipolar geometry by chance. An example can be a repeated pattern that is aligned with the epipolar line (fig.2, left). These kinds of ambiguity and blunders can be removed considering the epipolar geometry between three consecutive images (fig.2, right). A linear representation for the relative orientation of three images is represented by the trilinear tensor. For every triplet, a tensor is computed with a RANSAC algorithm using the correspondences that support two adjacent images and their epipolar geometry.

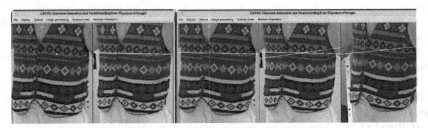

Fig. 2. Left: epipolar line aligns with a repeated pattern. Right: epipolar geometry between triplet of images used to remove ambiguities and outliers

As result, for each triplet of images, a set of corresponding points, supporting a trilinear tensor, is available. Then we consider all the overlapping tensors (T_{123}, T_{234}, T_{345},...) and we look for those correspondences which are present in consecutive tensors. That is, given two adjacent tensors T_{abc} and T_{bcd} with supporting points (x_a,y_b, x_b,y_b, x_c,y_c) and (x'_b,y'_b, x'_c,y'_c, x'_d,y'_d), if (x_b,y_b, x_c,y_c) in the first tensor is equal to (x'_b,y'_b, x'_c,y'_c) in the successive tensor, this means that the point in images a, b, c and d is the same and therefore this point must have the same identifier. Each point is tracked as long as possible in the sequence; the obtained correspondences are used as tie points in a photogrammetric bundle-adjustment.

3.2 Initial Approximations for the Unknown Orientation Parameters

Because of its non-linearity, the bundle-adjustment (section 3.3) needs initial approximations for the unknown interior and exterior parameters.

An approach based on vanishing point is used to compute the interior parameters of the camera (principal point and focal length). The vanishing point is the intersection of parallel lines in object space transformed to image space by a perspective transformation of the camera. Man-made objects are often present in the images; therefore geometric information of the captured scene can be derived from these features. The semi-automatic process to determine the approximations of the interior parameters consist of:

- edge extraction with Canny operator and merging of short segments taking into account segments slope and distance from the center of the image;
- interactive identification of three mutually orthogonal directions;
- classification of the extracted and aggregated lines according to their directions;
- computation of the vanishing point for each direction [5];
- determination of the principal point and the focal length of the camera [4].

The approximations of the exterior orientation are instead computed using spatial resection. In photogrammetry, spatial resection is defined as the process where the spatial position and orientation of an image is determined, based on image measurements and ground control points. If at least 3 object points are available, the exterior parameters can be determined without iterations; when a fourth point exists, a unique solution based on least squares can be achieved. In our case, 4 object points measured on the human body are used to compute the approximations of the external orientation of the cameras.

3.3 Self-calibration with Bundle-Adjustment

A versatile and accurate perspective calibration technique is the photogrammetric bundle adjustment with self-calibration [11]. It is a global minimization of the reprojection error, developed in the 50's and extended in the 70's. The mathematical basis of the bundle adjustment is the collinearity model, e.g. a point in object space, its corresponding point in the image plane and the projective center of the camera lie on a straight line. The standard form of the collinearity equations is:

$$x - x_0 = -c \cdot \frac{r_{11}(X - X_0) + r_{21}(Y - Y_0) + r_{31}(Z - Z_0)}{r_{13}(X - X_0) + r_{23}(Y - Y_0) + r_{33}(Z - Z_0)} = -c \cdot \frac{U}{W}$$

$$y - y_0 = -c \cdot \frac{r_{12}(X - X_0) + r_{22}(Y - Y_0) + r_{32}(Z - Z_0)}{r_{13}(X - X_0) + r_{23}(Y - Y_0) + r_{33}(Z - Z_0)} = -c \cdot \frac{V}{W}$$

(3)

where:

x, y are the point image coordinates;
x_0, y_0 are the image coordinates of the principal point PP;
c is the camera constant;
X, Y, Z are the point object coordinates;
X_0, Y_0, Z_0 are the coordinates in object space of the perspective center;
r_{ij} are the elements of the orthogonal rotation matrix R between image and object coordinate systems. R is a function of the three rotation angles of the camera.

The collinearity model needs to be extended in order to take into account systematic errors that may occur; these errors are described by correction terms for the image coordinates, which are functions of some additional parameters (APs). Usually a set of 10 APs is used [1,3] to model symmetric, radial and decentering distortion. Solving a self-calibrating bundle adjustment means to estimate the cameras exterior and interior parameters, the object coordinates of the tie points and the APs, starting from a set of observed correspondences in the images (and possible control points).

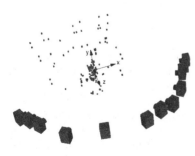

The tie points found with the process of section 3.1 are imported in the bundle. Two collinearity equations as in (3) are formed for each image point. Combining all equations of all points in all the images, a system of equations is built. These equations are non-linear with respect to the unknowns and, in order to solve them with a least squares method, must be linearized, thus requiring initial approximations (section 3.2). The resulting exterior orientation of the cameras and the used tie points are shown in figure 3.

Fig. 3. Recovered cameras poses and object points

4. Matching Process and 3-D Reconstruction of the Human Body

After the establishment of an adjusted image block, an automated matching process is performed [6], in order to produce a dense set of corresponding image points. It establishes correspondences between triplet of images starting from few seed points and is based on the adaptive least squares method. One image is used as template and the others as search image. The matcher searches the corresponding points in the two search images independently and at the end of the process, the data sets are merged to become triplets of matched points. For the process, all consecutive triplets are used. The 3-D coordinates of each matched triplet are then computed by forward intersection using the orientation parameters achieved in phototriangulation (section 3.3). At the end, all the points are joined together to create a unique point cloud of the human body. To reduce the noise in the 3-D data and get a more uniform density of the point cloud, a spatial filter is applied. After the filtering process, a uniform 3-D point cloud is obtained, as shown in figure 4 (left and central). For realistic visualization, each point of the cloud is back projected onto the central image of the sequence to get the related pixel color. The result is presented in figure 4 (right).

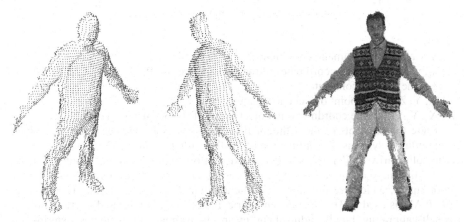

Fig. 4. Recovered 3-D point cloud of the human body and visualization with pixel intensity

5. Conclusions

In this paper a low cost system to create 3-D models of static human bodies from uncalibrated image sequence has been presented. The process is automatic; the obtained 3-D point cloud can be imported in commercial software to easily create a surface model of the person or 3-D human model can be fitted to the recovered data. The processes in [9] and [20] have been extended with ALSM and local filtering while LMedS has been used in relative orientation to remove outliers. As future work, the reconstruction of the body shape will also be extended to the back part of it. The process for the identification of image correspondences described in [17] could be included in our method, weighting the proximity matrix with the sigma of the ALSM process. Moreover, sequences where the camera is still and the person is moving or both camera and person are moving will be investigated.

References

1. Beyer, H.: Geometric and Radiometric Analysis of CCD-Cameras. Based Photogrammetric Close-Range system. Ph.D. thesis 51, IGP ETH Zurich (1992)
2. Bhatia G., Smith K. E., et al.: Design of a Multisensor Optical Surface Scanner. Sensor Fusion VII, SPIE Proc. 2355 (1994) 262-273
3. Brown, D.C.: Close-range Camera Calibration. PE&RS, Vol.37, No.8 (1971) 855-866
4. Caprile B., Torre, V.: Using vanishing point for camera calibration. International Journal of Computer Vision, Vol.4, No.2 (1990) 127-139
5. Collins, R.T.: Model acquisition using stochastic projective geometry. PhD thesis, Computer Science Dep., University of Massachusetts, 1993
6. D'Apuzzo, N.: Modeling human faces with multi-image photogrammetry. 3-Dimensional Image Capture and Applications V, SPIE Proc., Vol. 4661 (2002) 191-197
7. D'Apuzzo N., Plänkers R.: Human Body Modeling from Video Sequences. Int. Archives of Photogrammetry and Remote Sensing, Vol.32 (1999) 133-140
8. Faugeras O., Luong Q.T., et al.: Camera Self-calibration: Theory and Experiments. Lecture Notes in Computer Science 588, ECCV '92, Springer-Verlag (1992) 321-334
9. Fitzgibbon, A, Zisserman, A.: Automatic 3D model acquisition and generation of new images from video sequences. Proc. of ESP Confernce (1998), pp. 1261-1269
10. Grün A.: Adaptive least squares correlation: a powerful image matching technique. South African Journal of Photogrammetry, RS and Cartography Vol. 14, No. 3 (1985) 175-187
11. Grün A., Beyer, H.: System calibration through self-calibration. In: Grün, Huang (Eds.): Calibration and Orientation of Cameras in Computer Vision, Springer 34 (2001) 163-193
12. Gruen, A., Zhang, L., Visnovcova, J.: Automatic Reconstruction and Visualization of a Complex Buddha Tower of Bayon, Angkor, Cambodia. Proc. 21 DGPF (2001) 289-301
13. Klette R., Schlüns, K., Koschan, A.: Computer Vision: Three-dimensional data from images. Springer (1998)
14. McKenna P.: Measuring Up. Magazine of America's Air Force, Vol. XL, No.2 (1996)
15. Maas, H. G.: Digital Photogrammetry for determination of tracer particle coordinates in turbulent flow research. PE&RS, Vol.57, No.12 (1991), 1593-1597
16. Niini, I.: Relative Orientation of Multiple images using projective singular correlation. Int. Archives of Photogrammetry and Remote Sensing, Vol. 30, part 3/2 (1994), 615-621
17. Pilu, M: Uncalibrated stereo correspondences by singular value decomposition. Technical Report HPL-97-96, (1997), HP Bristol
18. Pollefeys, M.: Tutorial on 3-D modeling from images. Tutorial at ECCV 2000 (2000)
19. Remondino, F.: 3-D reconstruction of articulated objects from uncalibrated images. 3-Dimensional Image Capture and Applications V, SPIE Proc., Vol. 4661 (2002) 148-154
20. Roth, G., Whitehead, A.: Using projective vision to find camera positions in an image sequence. 13th Vision Interface Conference (2000)
21. Scaioni, M.: The use of least median squares for outlier rejection in automatic aerial triangulation. In: Carosio, Kutterer (Eds): Proc. of the 1st Int. Symposium on "Robust Statistics and Fuzzy Techniques in Geodesy and GIS", ETH Zurich (2001) 233-238.
22. Zhang, Z., Deriche, R, et al.: A robust technique for matching two uncalibrated images through the recovery of the unknown epipolar geometry. TR 2273, INRIA (1994)
23. Zheng, J. Y: Acquiring 3D models from sequences contours. IEEE Transaction on PAMI, 16 (2), pp 163-178 (1994)
24. Cyberware: http://www.cyberware.com; Taylor: http://www.taylor.com [June 2002]

A Knowledge-Based System for Context Dependent Evaluation of Remote Sensing Data

J. Bückner, M. Pahl, O. Stahlhut, and C.-E. Liedtke

Institut für Theoretische Nachrichtentechnik
und Informationsverarbeitung (TNT)
University of Hannover, Germany
http://www.tnt.uni-hannover.de
geoaida@tnt.uni-hannover.de

Abstract. Automatic interpretation of remote sensing data gathers more and more importance for surveillance tasks, reconnaissance and automatic generation and quality control of geographic maps. Methods and applications exist for structural analysis of image data as well as specialized segmentation algorithms for certain object classes. At the Institute of Communication Theory and Signal Processing focus is set on procedures that incorporate *a priori* knowledge into the interpretation process. Though many advanced image processing algorithms have been developed in the past, a disadvantage of earlier interpretation systems is the missing combination capability for the results of different - especially multisensor - image processing operators. The system GEOAIDA presented in this paper utilizes a semantic net to model *a priori* knowledge about the scene. The low-level, context dependent segmentation is accomplished by already existing, external image processing operators, which are integrated and controlled by GEOAIDA. Also the evaluation of the interpretation hypothesis is done by external operators, linked to the GEOAIDA system. As a result an interactive map with user selectable level-of-detail is generated.

1 Introduction

Knowledge-based image interpretation of remote sensing data offers a vast field of different applications, like automatic generation and quality control of geographic maps ([Gunst, 1996], [Englisch *et al.*, 1998]), environmental monitoring tasks like assessment of damage caused by clearing activities ([Hame *et al.*, 1998]) or natural disaster and also for surveillance of agricultural production. The rapidly growing number of multisensor remote sensing images enables several new applications, but also increases the labour-intensive manual evaluation of the data. This results in a growing demand for productive and robust techniques for (semi)automatic analysis and object extraction.

Previous analysis systems are often restricted to segmentation and classification of one or few different classes. They are highly specialized and optimised for a certain task or have difficulties processing large images. Especially methods which follow a strict structural approach ([Tönjes *et al.*, 1999],

L. Van Gool (Ed.): DAGM 2002, LNCS 2449, pp. 58–65, 2002.

[Niemann *et al.*, 1990], [Kummert *et al.*, 1993]), i.e. they work with primitive objects extracted from the image data, are not capable of handling large, high-detailed aerial images due to the great number of extracted primitives in such images. Another typical problem of such systems is the visualisation of the analysis results. High resolution input images contain lots of small objects which can lead to confusing interpretation result maps.

The analysis system described in the following integrates already existing image processing operators which are intelligently controlled by utilization of previous knowledge about the processed scene. The previous knowledge is modelled by a semantic net. The net handles properties and relationships of different nodes. One property of a node could be the assignment of an existing *holistic* image processing operator which will be used for the detection of a certain object class. If an image processing operator for a particular task isn't available, the node will be identified *structurally* by its components, i.e. the child nodes.

As GEOAIDA transfers the segmentation task to external operators there is no limitation to the type of input images. Therefore multisensor scene analysis is also possible. Results of the scene analysis are displayed in an interactive map, which allows the user to select a task-adapted level of detail. The hierarchic map covers all results gathered during scene interpretation.

2   Functionality of GeoAIDA

Figure 1 shows the design of GEOAIDA (Geo **A**utomatic **I**mage **D**ata **A**nalyser).

On the input side the system consists of the components *database* and *semantic net*. Data processing is handled by *top-down-* and *bottom-up operators* which are called by the system control unit. Results are shown in an *interactive map* which consists of a *symbolic scene description* and *thematic maps*. The core system control queries the image database, reads the semantic nets as well as project descriptions and generates hypotheses by calling top-down operators. The hypotheses are evaluated with bottom-up operators and once verified, stored as instance nets with corresponding label images, which describe the position of the instance nets' nodes.

2.1   Database

The database provides all input information available for the scene interpretation. This includes images of different sensors, like VIS, laserscan, IR or SAR, as well as GIS Information or results of an earlier scene interpretation for multi-temporal processing. GEOAIDA itself is not limited to any kind of input data - restrictions are only imposed by the attached external image processing operators, which work on their dedicated input data. Internally GEOAIDA manages two dimensional regions which are assigned to nodes of the hypothesis or instance net.

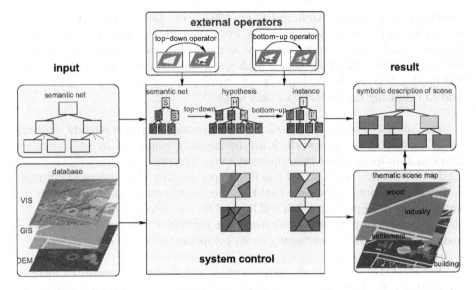

Fig. 1. GeoAIDA design

2.2   Semantic Net

The *a priori* knowledge about the scene under investigation is stored in a semantic net. The nodes of the net are ordered strictly hierarchical, i.e. each node has exactly one superior node. The topmost node is the scene node. Attributes can be assigned to each node. Common attributes are *name*, *class* and the associated *top-down* and *bottom-up* operators.

A *top-down* operator is capable of detecting objects of the node class in the given input data. For each detected objects a hypothesis node is generated. The *bottom-up* operator investigates the relationship between the subnodes and groups them into objects of the node class. These objects are represented by instance nodes. *Top-down* and *bottom-up* operators can also be configured by additional attributes, that are operator specific.

2.3   Top-Down Operators

Top-down operators (s. figure 2) are external image processing operators that run a segmentation on given input image data and assign the resulting objects to one or more classes. Additionally the operator is supplied with a binary mask which describes the areas of interest. If the native external operator doesn't handle masks, the masking is accomplished in a post processing step. Output of a *top-down* operator is a list of regions with a corresponding label image, which describes the position of the regions. Typical examples for such operators which are pre-registered with GeoAIDA are variance analysis for distinction of man-made and natural objects, supervised texture segmentation, building extraction from laserscan data, etc..

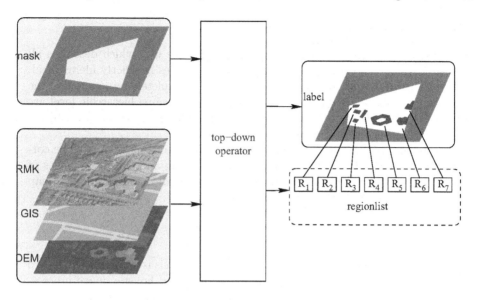

Fig. 2. Operation of a top-down operator

2.4 Bottom-Up Operators

Bottom-up operators are used to group a multitude of objects to a smaller quantity of superior objects, s. figure 3. These operators are also implemented as external programs. Input of a *bottom-up* operator is a list of hypothesis nodes together with the corresponding label images, which describe the geometric position of the objects in the scene. The output is a list of instance nodes resulting from the grouping process and a new label image describing the superior objects.

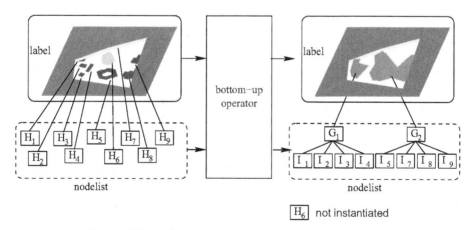

Fig. 3. Operation of a bottom-up operator

2.5   Interactive Map

The output of the GEOAIDA analysis is an instance net, which describes all verified objects of the scene. The ordering of the nodes is strictly hierarchical, i.e. the footprint of inferior (child) nodes is always completely represented in the superior (parent) node. Furthermore all nodes of the same hierarchic level are disjunctive. That means, that it is possible to describe the position of all objects of a whole instance tree in a two dimensional map.

Combination of the original semantic net with the instance net and the corresponding map leads to an interactive map. Opening and closing branches of the semantic or instance net changes the level of detail in the interactive map and improves the result evaluation for the user.

2.6   System Control

Main task of GEOAIDA itself is system control. Analysis is accomplished in two major steps. First a *top-down* pass calling the attached holistic image processing operators generates hypothesis about the objects detectable in the scene. According to the semantic net these hypothesis are structured in the hypothesis net. The second step is a *bottom-up* progression through the hypothesis net. During this pass an instance net is generated from the hypothesis nodes on the basis of object properties like size, structural relationship between neighbouring objects, etc. The instance net together with the object map is the result of the two pass analysis.

3   Analysis Example

In the following the functionality of GEOAIDA is illustrated with an example. Figure 4 shows a small excerpt of a multisensor aerial scene. Figure 4a is an orthophoto, figure is a 4b laserscan. Figure 4c to 4e are results of different holistic image processing operators, which were applied to the whole input image. Figure 4c was acquired by querying a geographic information system for street positions.

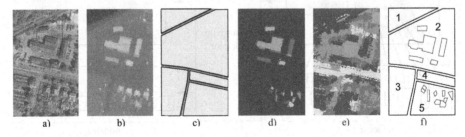

Fig. 4. a) ortho photo, b) laserscan, c) GIS segmentation, d) building extraction from laserscan data e) texture segmentation of ortho photo, f) final scene interpretation (1: forest, 2: industry, 3: forest, 4: unknown, 5: settlement)

With this information an initial region segmentation was executed. The laserscan image provides reliable data for building detection - the results are shown in figure 4d. Figure 4e shows the segmentation of a supervised texture analysis operator described by [Gimel'farb *et al.*, 1993].

All procedures deliver some special, detailed information about the investigated scene. However, none of them is capable of interpreting the scene in terms of land usage, as shown in figure 4f.

At first a model of the scene has to be designed. The scene knowledge is modelled in a semantic net, s. figure 5. The actual shape of the semantic net depends on the desired result but also on the available image processing operators. The topmost node of the model is always the scene. In this example the scene consists of regions. These regions are initially determined by a GIS query ([Grünreich, 1992]). Regions on the other hand contain inhabited and agricultural areas. The differentiation between those two object classes can be achieved by evaluation of laserscan data. Areas with buildings are assigned to inhabited area, areas without to agricultural land. Beyond this a discrimination of inhabited areas into the classes settlement and industry is impossible for a simple image processing operator. GEOAIDA solves the problem by generating hypotheses for both classes. Segmentation of the laserscan data ([Steinle 1999]) produces hypotheses for houses and buildings. In parallel the system searches for gardens and parking areas with the help of the texture segmentation operator. After creation of hypotheses for all these subnodes the *bottom-up* operators of settlement and industry create hypotheses for themselves which are then propagated to the superior node 'inhabited area'. That node finds a final decision for the region subdivision based on probability ([Dubois *et al.*, 1988]) and priority figures. The latter can be preset by the user or are generated during the analysis process respectively. In this example conflicts at the node 'inhabited area' are resolved by rating the objects in regard to size and compactness.

Due to the parallel execution of the semantic net branches, the agricultural areas have been segmented and classified as acreage, meadow or forest in the meantime. In this example the segmentation was carried out by one operator. Therefore the detected regions are already disjunctive. The *bottom-up* operator of the node 'region' gets the results of both branches and has to decide whether a region or part of a region is inhabited area or agricultural land. At this stage the initial region segmentation is verified. Existing regions can be splitted up or merged according to the analysis results. In the last step the new region partition is merged to the scene description.

Figure 4f shows the final scene interpretation result. Regions 1 and 3 have been identified as forest, area 2 is classified as industry because of the large buildings whereas area 5 is assigned to settlement. Area 4 is undetermined - no evidence for one of the modelled classes was found during the analysis course.

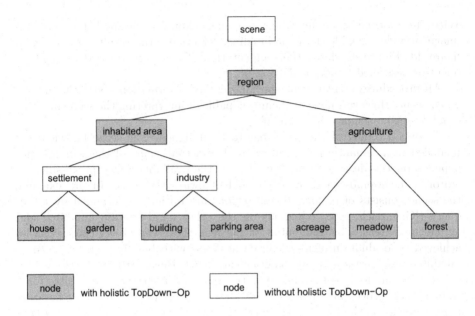

Fig. 5. Model of a scene represented by a semantic net

4   Conclusion

The knowledge-based, automatic image interpretation system GEOAIDA was presented. The functionality and features were demonstrated with an example application for land utilization. GEOAIDA uses *a priori* knowledge modelled by a semantic net together with two types of basic operators. *Top-down* operators segment and classify image data and produce probability and accuracy figures for the results. *Bottom-up* operators evaluate the hypothesis nodes generated by the *top-down* progression, solve classification conflicts and group the different object classes. The integration of external holistic image processing operators of different origin is easily accomplished. Due to the systems' capability of controlling holistic and structural analysis simultaneously it is predestined for the flexible classification of objects and regions in multisensor remote image data. A further extension of the application range of GEOAIDA is the possibility to incorporate previous knowledge of a geographic information system or earlier interpretation results of an investigated scene into the analysis process. Besides its flexible design for future research tasks GEOAIDA is a promising step towards productive use in image analysis and verification of geographic information systems.

References

Bückner *et al.*, 2000. J. Bückner, M. Pahl, O. Stahlhut, GEOAIDA - A Knowledge Based Automatic Image Data Analyser for Remote Sensing Data, CIMA 2001, Second International ICSC Symposium AIDA, June 19-22, Bangor, Wales, U.K., 2001

Dubois *et al.*, 1988. D. Dubois and H. Prade, Possibility Theory: An Approach to Computerized Processing of Uncertainty, Plenum Press, New York and London, p. 263, 1988

Englisch *et al.*, 1998. A. Englisch, C. Heipke, Erfassung und Aktualisierung topographischer Geo-Daten mit Hilfe analoger und digitaler Luftbilder, Photogrammetrie Fernerkundung Geoinformation, Vol. 3, pp. 133-149, DGPF, Stuttgart, 1998

Gimel'farb *et al.*, 1993. G.L. Gimel'farb, A.V. Zalesny, Probabilistic models of digital region maps based on Markov random fields with short and long-range interaction Pattern Recognition Letters, 14, pp. 789-797, 1993

Grünreich, 1992. D. Grünreich, ATKIS - A Topographic Information System as a Basis for a GIS and Digital Carthography in West Germany, Geol. Jb., Vol. A122, pp. 207-215, Hannover, 1992

Gunst, 1996. M. de Gunst, Knowledge Based Interpretation of Aerial Images for Updating of Road Maps, Dissertation, Delft University of Technology, Netherlands Geodetic Commission, Publications of Geodesy, New Series, Nr. 44, 1996

Hame *et al.*, 1998. T. Hame, I. Heiler, J. San Miguel-Ayanz, Unsupervised Change Detection and Recognition System for Forestry, International Journal of Remote Sensing, Vol. 19(6), pp. 1079-1099, 1998

Kummert *et al.*, 1993. F. Kummert, H. Niemann, R. Prechtel and G. Sagerer, Control and explanation in a signal understanding environment, Signal Processing, Vol. 32, No. 1-2, May, 1993

Niemann *et al.*, 1990. H. Niemann, G. Sagerer, S. Schröder, F. Kummert, ERNEST: A Semantic Network System for Pattern Understanding, IEEE Trans. on Pattern Analysis and Machine Intelligence, 12(9):883-905, 1990

Steinle 1999. E. Steinle, H.-P Bähr, Laserscanning for change detection in urban environment Altan & Gründig (eds.): Third Turkish-German Joint Geodetic Days 'Towards A Digital Age', Volume I, pp 147 - 156, Istanbul, Turkey, ISBN 975-561-159-2 (Vol. I), 1999

Tönjes *et al.*, 1999. R. Tönjes, S. Growe, J. Bückner and C.-E. Liedtke, Knowledge-Based Interpretation of Remote Sensing Images Using Semantic Nets, Photogrammetric Engineering and Remote Sensing, Vol. 65, No. 7, pp. 811-821, July 1999

Empirically Convergent Adaptive Estimation of Grayvalue Structure Tensors

Markus Middendorf and Hans-Hellmut Nagel

Institut für Algorithmen und Kognitive Systeme,
Universität Karlsruhe (TH), 76128 Karlsruhe, Germany
Phone: +49-721-608-4044/4323
Fax: +49-721-608-8481
markusm|nagel@ira.uka.de

Abstract. An iterative adaptation process for the estimation of a Grayvalue Structure Tensor (GST) is studied experimentally: alternative adaptation rules, different parameterizations, and two convergence criteria are compared. The basic adaptation process converges for both synthetic and real image sequences in most cases towards essentially the same results even if different parameters are used. Only two identifiable local grayvalue configurations have been encountered so far where adaptation variants do not converge according to the chosen criteria.

Keywords: Image features, Visual motion, Adaptive estimation, Grayvalue Structure Tensor, Anisotropic filtering, Optical flow.

1 Introduction

About ten years ago, Koenderink and van Doorn studied a family of generic *neighborhood* operators [6], taking into account aspects of many linear operators encountered for the extraction of *local* image properties. Based on what these authors take to be fundamental hypotheses, they consider a multivariate isotropic Gaussian kernel as the most elementary linear 'neighborhood' operator: it estimates the illuminance at each 'point' by a weighted average of grayvalues around the specified image position.

The *extent of the neighborhood* is quantified by the standard deviation of the Gaussian kernel. This standard deviation can be taken to represent the 'scale' of image properties considered to be relevant for a particular investigation of the illuminance distribution impinging onto the image plane. The *internal structure* of the grayvalue variation within such a neighborhood can be characterized by (functions of) more detailed local estimates obtained by the convolution of the image with partial derivatives of the Gaussian kernel.

Previous work, e.g. [11], shows, that it may be useful *not to fix a scale globally*, but to estimate the relevant scale in each dimension *locally* for each neighborhood, and, that the 'most appropriate scales' do not need to occur exactly along the axes of the initially chosen coordinate system. This procedure implies a 'hen-and-egg' problem: The neighborhood is specified by a chosen scale, whereas, at the same time, the scale has to be determined from the neighborhood properties.

L. Van Gool (Ed.): DAGM 2002, LNCS 2449, pp. 66–74, 2002.

This contribution studies a particular approach – the *adaptive estimation of a Grayvalue Structure Tensor (GST)* – in order to escape from this dilemma. The goal is to provide evidence that one can 'operationalize' the concept of an 'anisotropic neighborhood' in a *spatiotemporal* grayvalue distribution, provided certain boundary conditions are accepted.

2 On Related Publications

Since many years, 'anisotropic diffusion' constitutes an active research area – see, e.g., [17]. Originally, it has been studied for image enhancement by anisotropic smoothing and for edge extraction – see, e.g., [14,7]. Similar adaptive approaches have been used, too, in order to increase the robustness of structure extraction in cases where neighboring line structures have to be resolved, e. g., for automatic analysis of fingerprint images [1]. An early application of such ideas to Optical Flow (OF) estimation has been discussed in [4] – see, too, [5, Chapter 10 'Adaptive Filtering']. A kind of closed-form adaptive GST estimation approach for the estimation of OF-fields has been reported in [11], a more detailed study of adaptation effects for the same purpose in [12].

Recently, the aspect to reduce the influence of noise by a variant of anisotropic diffusion has been studied specifically in the context of GST-based OF estimation [15] where one can find additional references regarding this topic. Earlier publications about OF estimation have been surveyed in [3].

Usually, only one or two iterations are used for adaptation (see, too, [9,10]), although an adaptation algorithm 'naturally' raises a question regarding its convergence and its dependence on initial conditions or other parameters.

3 Adaptive Estimation of the GST

The GST is a weighted average (over a neighborhood of the current pixel) of the outer product of $\nabla g = (\frac{\partial g}{\partial x}, \frac{\partial g}{\partial y}, \frac{\partial g}{\partial t})^T$ with itself, where ∇g denotes the gradient of the greyvalue function $g(x, y, t)$ with respect to image plane coordinates (x, y) and time t. In both gradient computation and averageing, the extent of the Gaussian kernels involved is determined by their covariances Σ_G and Σ_A respectively. Inspired by [8], we use $\Sigma_A \simeq 2 \cdot \Sigma_G$.

In what follows, we basically use the same algorithms as proposed by [10], with some differences that will be pointed out in the sequel:

During the location-invariant 'initialisation step', the same fixed 'start covariance' matrices $\Sigma_{G0} = \mathrm{diag}(\sigma_{xy}, \sigma_{xy}, \sigma_t)$ and Σ_{A0} are used at every pixel position to determine GST_0 ("0-th iteration").

The subsequent GST *estimation phase adapts* Σ_G and thus Σ_A iteratively to the prevailing local grayvalue variation. During the i-th iteration ($i \geq 1$), Σ_{Gi} is basically set to the *inverse* of GST_{i-1}. GST_{i-1} is decomposed into a rotational matrix U and a diagonal matrix $E = \mathrm{diag}(\lambda_1, \lambda_2, \lambda_3)$, comprising the eigenvalues $\lambda_i, i = 1, 2, 3$. The extent of the Gaussian kernel is then derived from

E, its orientation from U. In contrast to [10], we shall compare two alternatives to compute the kernel's extent, namely the 'linear approach' proposed in [12]

$$\alpha_k = \tilde{\lambda}_k \cdot \sigma_{\min}{}^2 + (1 - \tilde{\lambda}_k) \cdot \sigma_{\max}{}^2 \tag{1}$$

and the 'inversion approach' first discussed by [10]

$$\alpha_k = \frac{\sigma_{\max}{}^2 \cdot \sigma_{\min}{}^2}{(1 - \tilde{\lambda}_k) \cdot \sigma_{\min}{}^2 + \tilde{\lambda}_k \cdot \sigma_{\max}{}^2} \ , \tag{2}$$

where $\tilde{\lambda}_k$ are the 'scaled eigenvalues' $\lambda_k/(\lambda_1 + \lambda_2 + \lambda_3)$, and α_k is the extent in the direction of the k-th eigenvector.

4   Experimental Setup

Although convergence is a well studied problem in mathematics, only experience can show whether the approach outlined above will converge under the additional constraints set by the algorithm, e.g. finite mask size, and – if so – which iteration alternatives and parameter settings lead to the desired result. We evaluated three image sequences with different characteristics (see Figure 1): A rendered, noise-less MARBLE BLOCK scene with known shift rate, used to check the implementation; the well known YOSEMITE sequence ([19]); and a real-world INTERSECTION scene ([18]), used to evaluate the algorithm's behaviour on noisy data.

MARBLE BLOCK scene   YOSEMITE scene   INTERSECTION scene

Fig. 1. Representative frames from the image sequences studied here (the rectangles mark the clipped image area used from each sequence).

The following questions are investigated in this context: Will the iterative approach (or at least some of the alternatives studied) 'converge' at all? Does the resulting GST-estimate depend on the initial conditions? And finally, which grayvalue configurations in an image sequence result in 'fast' convergence and which ones present greater obstacles?

An iterative GST estimation will be taken to converge if 'some scalar quantification' of the difference between GST_i and GST_{i-1} drops below a threshold.

A straightforward approach consists in using the Frobenius norm $\|\text{GST}_i - \text{GST}_{i-1}\|$, in our case with a threshold of 0.03 which corresponds to an average error of 0.01 in each matrix component.

In order to sharpen our intuition about what happens in case the iteration converges slowly or even fails to converge, we have chosen in addition an alternative, indirect convergence criterion, namely convergence of OF estimation associated with the GST. An OF-vector is treated as a three-dimensional spatiotemporal vector $\boldsymbol{u} = (u_1, u_2, 1)^T$. Based on a 'Total Least Squares (TLS)' approach, the OF-vector $\boldsymbol{u}(\boldsymbol{x})$ at position $\boldsymbol{x}$ will be determined from the eigenvector $\boldsymbol{e}_{\min}$ corresponding to the smallest eigenvalue $\lambda_{\min}$ of the GST (see, e. g., [16]). We consider the iterative GST estimation as convergent if the difference $\|\boldsymbol{u}_i(\boldsymbol{x}) - \boldsymbol{u}_{i-1}(\boldsymbol{x})\|_2$ between consecutive OF-estimates at image location $\boldsymbol{x}$ becomes smaller than $^1/_{1000}$ pixel per frame (ppf). Having in mind that ground truth of, e. g., the YOSEMITE sequence exhibits already a *quantisation uncertainty* of 0.0316 ppf, a convergence threshold of less than 0.0010 ppf appears acceptable.

Evidently, quantification of convergence based on the OF-difference and based on $\|\text{GST}_i - \text{GST}_{i-1}\|$ need not lead to convergence after the same number of iterations or may even yield different results regarding convergence in certain cases. Our experimental study showed, however, that both criteria are more or less equivalent.

5   Experimental Results

In a first series of experiments, we computed 100 adaption steps at each pixel position for each image sequence, thresholding the difference between consecutive OF-estimates as convergence criterion. The following alternatives have been compared:

- two different adaptation algorithms: linear vs. inversion (see Section 3);
- two different start covariances: $\sigma_{xy} = \sigma_t = 1.0$ vs. $\sigma_{xy} = 2.0, \sigma_t = 1.0$, and
- two different adaptation areas: $\left(\sigma_{\min}^2 = 1.0 \text{ pixel}^2 \text{ and } \sigma_{\max}^2 = 8.0 \text{ pixel}^2\right)$ vs. $\left(\sigma_{\min}^2 = 1.0 \text{ pixel}^2 \text{ and } \sigma_{\max}^2 = 16.0 \text{ pixel}^2\right)$;

except for the YOSEMITE sequence where we omitted the run with the large adaptation area due to the limited number (15) of frames, which would otherwise reduce the temporal extent of the convolution masks in an improper way.

Figure 2 plots the percentage of pixels for each of the three clippings as a function of the iteration count after convergence, when using the 'inversion' approach. The convergence threshold serves as curve parameter. The results for the 'linear' approach differ only by a few percent; the difference would hardly be visible in a plot like the one above. The results for the comparison between different *start* covariances are similar; neither of the two parameter sets exhibits obvious advantages.

The only significantly different results were observed when varying the range of admitted adaptation: For a larger adaptation area, the convergence rate was

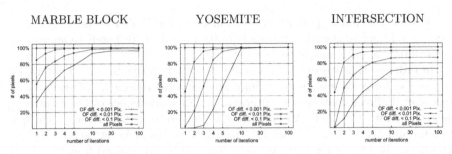

Fig. 2. Convergence for the 'inversion' approach, depending on convergence threshold.

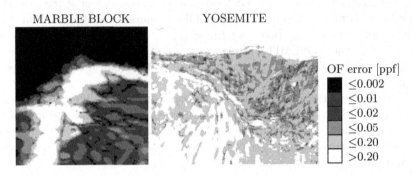

Fig. 3. Comparison of estimated Optical Flow with known ground truth. Experimental setup: inversion approach, iteration # 10, $\Sigma_G = \mathrm{diag}(2.0, 2.0, 1.0)$, $\sigma_{\max}^2 = 8.0$ pixel^2.

smaller. This observation is not surprising: a larger range of adaption leads to a higher number of configurations where convergence is prevented by special conditions (see later in this section).

As pointed out above, the determination of the eigenvector associated with the smallest eigenvalue of a convergent GST estimate provides a basis to estimate an OF-vector. Figure 3 compares estimates obtained in this manner for the two image sequences MARBLE BLOCK and YOSEMITE where the 'ground truth' is known: the color-coded difference between the 'true' value and the estimated one is superimposed to the clipping from the original image. As one can see immediately, discrepancies in the MARBLE BLOCK sequence are restricted to boundary curves where one expects discontinuities in the OF-field. In the YOSEMITE sequence, the discrepancies are much larger, but due to the quantization in the ground truth data, an average absolute error of about 0.02 ppf is to be expected even for 'perfectly' estimated OF vectors. The assumption of brightness constancy does not hold for the clouds, thus the large estimation error there is not surprising. The errors in the lower left part of the image may be explained by the restrictions on the mask size, which affect especially these areas with a high shift rate of up to 4.9 ppf.

Although the results on the YOSEMITE sequence do not look very good at first sight, they are better then almost every other OF estimation method so far.

MARBLE BLOCK   YOSEMITE   INTERSECTION

Fig. 4. Non-convergent cases after 10 iterations. The pixels are coloured according to their categorization: black – lack of image structure, results significantly influenced by noise; white – other categories. Experimental setup: inversion approach, $\Sigma_G = \text{diag}(2.0, 2.0, 1.0)$, $\sigma_{\max}{}^2 = 8.0$ pixel^2.

The average angular error observed in our experiments ranges from 3.16° (at 49.4% density) to 8.40° (at 71.6% density), depending on the parameterization, which is better than all results reported by [3]. Even newer approaches, e.g. [13], give worse results. The only approach – as far as we know – with comparable results was suggested by Alvarez et al. ([2]), which produces a slightly higher average error, but with a density of 100%.

In general, convergence is observed after 10 or at most 30 iterations. Pixel positions without convergence even after 70 additional iterations were scrutinized in search for identifiable grayvalue structures which could possibly explain the lack of convergence. Figure 4 illustrates the distribution of pixels without convergence after 10 adaptive iterations. Whereas most non-convergent estimates occur along the edges of the moving block in the MARBLE BLOCK sequence, non-convergent cases in the INTERSECTION sequence occur in the image background. These different distributions may be roughly assigned to one of two characteristic grayvalue configurations to be discussed in the sequel.

In the INTERSECTION sequence, most non-convergent pixels can be found in the image background (see right column of Fig. 4). In most cases (illustrated here by pixels painted black), trace(GST) is smaller than 5.0, indicating a lack of image structure: shape and extent of masks after adaptation are significantly influenced by noise. Small variations of the masks' extent may lead to significantly different derivatives, thus resulting in a different OF-estimate. Areas with low image structure occur only in the INTERSECTION sequence, and – consistently – non-convergent pixels with small trace(GST) are only observed in that sequence.

The MARBLE BLOCK sequence comprises only textured surfaces. Thus lack of image structure can not serve as an explanation for convergence failures.

Figure 5 shows a typical example for non-convergence in the MARBLE BLOCK sequence. After a few iterations, the mask extent oscillates between two states. The difference between iteration 18 and 19 – and between iteration

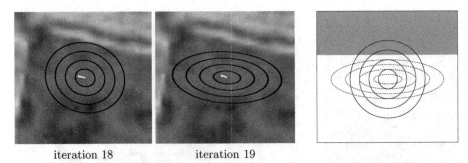

iteration 18   iteration 19

Fig. 5. Left and middle panel: Extent of the convolution masks, projected into the image plane. The black lines show the intersection of the ellipsoids containing 1, 2, 3, or 4 standard deviations, respectively, of a Gaussian with covariance matrix Σ_A. The example presented here shows one of those pixel locations where 'oscillation' can be observed most clearly. Right panel: Schematic explanation for the effect illustrated here. The initial mask (solid lines) with equal extents in both directions touches an edge. During adaptation, the mask is thus extended along the edge and compressed perpendicular to it. The resulting new mask (dashed lines) does no longer cover the edge, thus resulting – during the second iteration – in a mask with the same extent as the original, unadapted mask.

19 and 20 – is about $1/2$ ppf, whereas the OF-estimates differ only minimally ($\approx 1/1000$ ppf) between iteration 18 and 20.

6   Summary and Conclusions

It appears as a remarkable result that iterative adaptive GST-estimation converges at most image positions for all combinations of algorithmic alternatives, parameter selections, and test image sequences investigated. The degree of convergence differs somewhat in detail, depending on the image data: the convergence results for YOSEMITE ($\approx 99\%$ after 10 iterations) and MARBLE BLOCK ($\approx 95\%$ after 10 it.) are better than for INTERSECTION ($\approx 80\%$ after 10 it.). Given significant image areas in the INTERSECTION sequence with only minor grayvalue variations, but noticeable noise, this outcome does not really surprise. Generally, convergence seems to depend more on the properties of the image sequence than on the choice of parameter.

The right panel of Figure 5 explains the results in a simplified example where the masks in subsequent iterations alternately include and exclude an edge. The case in the left and middle panel is even more complicated: The elongated masks in iterations 17 and 19 include the edge on the lefthand side, but exclude the edge above, whereas in iteration 18, the edge above the pixel is covered and the edge on the left is excluded.

Based on the experience accumulated so far, our approach either converges towards a description of dominant local characteristics which can be represented by an anisotropic spatiotemporal 'Gaussian bell' or it points towards an *identifiable* grayvalue configuration which is incompatible with this representation.

Acknowledgements

Partial support by the Deutsche Forschungsgemeinschaft and the European Union (IST-2000-29404) for the investigations reported here is gratefully acknowledged.

References

1. A. Almansa and T. Lindeberg: Fingerprint Enhancement by Shape Adaptation of Scale-Space Operators with Automatic Scale Selection. IEEE Tr. on Image Processing **9**:12 (2000) 2027–2042.
2. L. Alvarez, J. Weickert, and J. Sanchez: Reliable estimation of dense optical flow fields with large displacement. International Journal on Computer Vision **39**:1 (2000) 41–56.
3. J. Barron, D. Fleet, and S. Beauchemin: Performance of Optical Flow Techniques. International Journal on Computer Vision **12**:1 (1994) 156–182.
4. J. Bigün, G.H. Granlund, and J. Wiklund: Multidimensional Orientation Estimation with Applications to Texture Analysis and Optical Flow. IEEE Tr. on Pattern Analysis and Machine Intelligence PAMI-**13**:8 (1991) 775–790.
5. G.H. Granlund and H. Knutsson: Signal Processing for Computer Vision. Kluwer Academic Publishers, Dordrecht Boston London 1995.
6. J.J. Koenderink and A. van Doorn: "Generic Neighborhood Operators". IEEE Tr. on Pattern Analysis and Machine Intelligence PAMI-**14**:6 (1992) 597-605.
7. T. Leung and J. Malik: Contour continuity in Region Based Image Segmentation. Proc. ECCV 1998, Vol. I, H. Burkhardt and B. Neumann (Eds.), LNCS 1406, pp. 544–559.
8. T. Lindeberg and J. Gårding: "Shape-Adapted Smoothing in Estimation of 3-D Depth Cues from Affine Distortions of Local 2-D Brightness Structure". Proc. ECCV 1994, J. O. Eklundh (Ed.), LNCS 800, pp. 389–400.
9. M. Middendorf and H.-H. Nagel: Vehicle Tracking Using Adaptive Optical Flow Estimation. Proc. First Int. Workshop on Performance Evaluation and Surveillance (PETS 2000), 31 March 2000, Grenoble, France. J. Ferryman (Ed.), The University of Reading, Reading, UK, 2000.
10. M. Middendorf and H.-H. Nagel: Estimation and Interpretation of Discontinuities in Optical Flow Fields. Proc. ICCV 2001, 9-12 July 2001, Vancouver/Canada; Vol. I, pp. 178–183.
11. H.-H. Nagel, A. Gehrke, M. Haag, and M. Otte: Space- and Time-Variant Estimation Approaches and the Segmentation of the Resulting Optical Flow Fields. Proc. ACCV 1995, 5-8 Dec. 1995, Singapore; In S.Z. Li, D.P. Mital, E.K. Teoh, and H. Wang (Eds.), Recent Developments in Computer Vision, LNCS 1035, pp. 81-90.
12. H.-H. Nagel and A. Gehrke: Spatiotemporally Adaptive Estimation and Segmentation of OF-Fields. Proc. ECCV 1998, 2-6 June 1998, Freiburg/Germany; H. Burkhardt and B. Neumann (Eds.), LNCS 1407 (Vol. II), pp. 86–102.
13. K. P. Pedersen and M. Nielsen: Computing Optic Flow by Scale-Space Integration of Normal Flow. In M. Kerckhove (Ed.) "Scale-Space and Morphology in Computer Vision", Proc. 3rd International Conference on Scale-Space, LNCS 2106, 2001.

14. P. Perona and J. Malik: Scale Space and Edge Detection Using Anisotropic Diffusion. IEEE Tr. on Pattern Analysis and Machine Intelligence PAMI-**12**:7 (1990) 629-639.
15. H. Spies and H. Scharr: Accurate Optical Flow in Noisy Image Sequences. In Proc. 8th International Conference on Computer Vision ICCV 2001, 9–12 July 2001, Vancouver, BC, Vol. I, pp. 587–592.
16. J. Weber and J. Malik: "Robust Computation of Optical Flow in a Multi-Scale Differential Framework.". Proc. ICCV-93, pp. 12–20; see, too, Intern. Journ. Computer Vision **14**:1 (1995) 67–81.
17. J. Weickert: Anisotropic Diffusion in Image Processing. B.G. Teubner, Stuttgart, Germany 1998.
18. Universität Karlsruhe: `http://i21www.ira.uka.de/image_sequences/` – the INTERSECTION scene is called "Karl-Wilhelm-Straße (normal conditions)" there.
19. Originally produced by Lynn Quam at SRI, available at the University of Western Ontario: `ftp://ftp.csd.uwo.ca/pub/vision/TESTDATA/YOSEMITE_DATA/`.

Real Time Fusion of Motion and Stereo
Using Flow/Depth Constraint for Fast Obstacle Detection

Stefan Heinrich

DaimlerChrylser Research, RIC/AP
Wilhelm-Runge-Str. 11, D-89089 Ulm, Germany
Stefan.Heinrich@DainlerChrysler.com

Abstract. Early detection of moving obstacles is an important goal for many vision based driver assistance systems. In order to protect pedestrians, in particular children, in inner city traffic, we are using stereo vision and motion analysis in order to manage those situations. The flow/depth constraint combines both methods in an elegant way and leads to a robust and powerful detection scheme. Pyramidal Opt. Flow computation together with compensation of rotational camera ego-motion expands the measurement range, enabling us to use the system also at higher speeds.

1 Intoduction

Within the DaimlerChrysler UTA (Urban Traffic Assistance) project, different vision modules for inner city traffic have been developed [1,2]. This includes fast stereo vision for Stop&Go, traffic sign and light recognition as well as pedestrian recognition and tracking. It is the goal of our current investigations to add collision avoidance capabilities to the existing system. In particular, we intend to recognize situations that implicate a high risk of accidents with pedestrians as shown in Fig. 1.

Fig. 1. (left) child running cross the street, (middle) color encoded disparity image, (right) computed gradient flow field

Stereo vision delivers three-dimensional measurements. Points above ground are grouped to objects. Detected objects are tracked over time to estimate their motion. Although very powerful, stereo analysis has some drawbacks with respect to the application that we have in mind. First, since object detection is done by clustering disparity features to gather 3D objects, objects with a close distance will merge to a

L. Van Gool (Ed.): DAGM 2002, LNCS 2449, pp. 75–82, 2002.
© Springer-Verlag Berlin Heidelberg 2002

single object even if velocities vary. Secondly, motion information included in the sequence is exploited for the detected objects only.

Motion analysis, on the other hand, allows to estimate the motion of any pixel based on the analysis over time and thus detection of any moving object. In vehicles, a precise recovery of the ego-motion is necessary in order to distinguish between static and moving objects. Unfortunately, the ego-motion estimation is a difficult problem which requires considerable computational power and usually lacks from robustness.

A proper combination of both techniques promises the optimal exploitation of the available information in space and time. In this paper, we present an elegant method which uses the fact that stereo disparity and optical flow are connected via real-world depth. The so called "flow/depth constraint" allows to test each motion vector directly against the stereo disparity to detect moving objects. The detection works within a few image frames with very low computational cost.

2   Stereo and Motion

2.1 Stereo Vision

Our stereo analysis [3] is based on a correlation-based approach. In order to reach real-time performance on a standard PC, design decisions need to be drawn carefully.

First of all, we use the sum-of-squared (SSD) or sum-of-absolute (SAD) differences criterion instead of expensive cross correlation to find the optimal fit along the epipolar line.

Secondly, in order to speed up the computation, we use a multi-resolution approach in combination with an interest operator. First, a gaussian pyramid is constructed for the left and right stereo image. Areas with sufficient contrast are extracted by means of a fast vertical Prewitt edge detector.

Pixels with sufficient gradient are marked, from which a binary pyramid is constructed. A non-maximum suppression is applied to the gradient image in order to further speed up the processing. Only those correlation windows with the central pixel marked in these interest images are considered during the disparity estimation procedure.If D is the maximum searched disparity at level zero, it reduces to

$(D/2)^n$ at level n. Furthermore, smaller correlation windows can be used at higher levels which again accelerates the computation.

The result of this correlation is then transferred to the next lower level. Here, only a fine adjustment has to be performed within a small horizontal search area of +/- 1 pixel. This process is repeated until the final level is reached. At this level, subpixel accuracy is achieved by fitting a parabolic curve through the computed correlation coefficients.

In order to eliminate bad matches we compute the normalized cross correlation coefficient for the best matches at the highest correlation level. The latter strategy avoids the erroneous detection of close obstacles caused by periodic structures. Fig. 1. shows the disparity image that we get by this scheme.

2.2 Motion Analysis

Based on performance comparison of a number of optical flow techniques, emphasizing the accuracy and density of measurements on realistic image sequences [6], we are using a basic differential (gradient based) optical flow method after Lukas and Kanade [13], where the two dimensional optical flow (Δu, Δv) is given by the temporal and spatial derivatives g_t and g_u within a small image region of N pixels.

$$
\begin{aligned}
G_{uu} &= \sum\nolimits_1^N g_u^2 & G_{ut} &= \sum\nolimits_1^N g_u g_t \\
G_{uv} &= \sum\nolimits_1^N g_u g_v & G_{vt} &= \sum\nolimits_1^N g_v g_t \\
G_{vv} &= \sum\nolimits_1^N g_v^2 & G_{uu}G_{vv} &- G_{uv}^2 \neq 0
\end{aligned}
\qquad
\binom{\Delta u}{\Delta v} =
\begin{bmatrix}
\dfrac{G_{vt}G_{uv} - G_{ut}G_{vv}}{G_{uu}G_{vv} - G_{uv}^2} \\[2ex]
\dfrac{G_{ut}G_{uv} - G_{vt}G_{uu}}{G_{uu}G_{vv} - G_{uv}^2}
\end{bmatrix}
\qquad (1)
$$

Applied to all layers of our gaussian pyramid, we are able to extend the basic gradient flow measurement range from the lowest layer up to 2^n at layer n. We also estimate the rotational component of the camera egomotion from the inertial vehicle sensory and use this predefined flow field to build the temporal derivatives for all layers. This in addition massively reduces the flow range which we have to cover.

Of course, many different methods for optical flow computation like region-based matching [8], energy-based [9] and phase based [10] methods are available. The basic gradient method can also be improved by using either second order derivatives or smoothness constraints for the flow field [11].

However, none of the above methods is capable to compute dense optical flow fields under real-time conditions. Usually, special hardware and parallel processing is needed in order to reach acceptable frame rates whereas the basic gradient flow can be computed in real-time on a standard PC. Furthermore, we will show that in combination with stereo the basic method is more than sufficient for our detection problem.

3   Fusion of Stereo and Motion

3.1 Flow/Depth Constraint

Let us assume a purely longitudinal moving camera and a stationary environment for the moment. For the transformations between the 3D world coordinate system (x, y, z) and the corresponding 2D image coordinate system (u, v), we are using a pinhole camera model with the focal length f and s_u as the size of a sensor element of the camera chip. With the pinhole camera model and the stereo base line b, we can derive the disparity D and the optical flow ($\dot{u}, \dot{v}$) from triangulation leading to the following equations:

$$D = \frac{f \cdot b}{s_u \cdot z} \quad , \quad \frac{\dot{u}}{u} = \frac{\dot{z}}{z} \quad , \quad \frac{\dot{v}}{v} = \frac{\dot{z}}{z} \tag{2}$$

Both, disparity and optical flow, depend on the real-world depth z. Therefore, the optical flow field can be computed from depth information and vice versa for stationary objects.

However, computation of the real-world depth is not necessary in our case. Switching variables for vehicle speed $\dot{z} = \Delta s$ and the horizontal and vertical components of the optical flow $\dot{u} = F_u$, $\dot{v} = F_v$, the depth factor is eliminated by building the quotient between the optical flow and the disparity. Separately applied to the horizontal and vertical components of the optical flow, this leads to the following constraints:

$$\frac{F_u}{D} = \frac{s_u \cdot \Delta s}{b \cdot f} \cdot u \qquad \frac{F_v}{D} = \frac{s_u \cdot \Delta s}{b \cdot f} \cdot v \tag{3}$$

Equations (3) can be illustrated by inclined planes over the image region (u, v). The gradient of the planes is determined by the stereo base line b, the size of a sensor element of the camera chip s_u, the focal length f and the vehicle speed Δs [m/frame].

Fig. 2. Deviation of flow/depth value (green) from the quotient plane (red) if a moving object is present

Fig. 2 shows three consecutive images of a test sequence. The flow/depth quotient is computed for one line in the image center only. The corresponding values are displayed in green. The value of the quotient plane is displayed in red. If stationary objects are present, the quotient measurements follow the predefined value of the plane. Quotient values corresponding to the moving object vary distinctively from the plane.

3.2 Quotient Noise

As we see from Fig. 2, there is measurement noise from the underlying stereo and optical flow within the flow/depth quotient which complicates segmentation of moving objects. But since the measurement noise for the disparity and optical flow preprocessing is well known, we can derive the maximum error of the quotient and use it as a threshold function for the segmentation. From:

$$Q + \Delta Q = \frac{F + \Delta F}{D + \Delta D} = \frac{F^*}{D^*} \tag{4}$$

we get the following function for the maximum quotient error for the horizontal and vertical flow, respectively:

$$\Delta Q = \frac{1}{D^*}(\Delta F - \Delta D Q) \tag{5}$$

where Q is the value of the flow/depth plane and D^* is the measurement value for the disparity. $\Delta D, \Delta F$ are the known maximum errors for the disparity and optical flow preprocessing. We will use this as the threshold function. Segmentation of moving objects now is a three step process:

1. Compute the horizontal and vertical quotients from the optical flow and the disparity for every pixel (u,v) for which depth and motion information is present.

2. Compare the computed quotient values with the reference values from the flow/depth plane at position (u,v).

3. Tag image position (u,v) as "moving object" if the difference between reference value and quotient is more than $|\Delta Q|$ in at least one direction.

3.3 Stabilization

So far, pure longitudinal camera motion was assumed. We use the above method within a demonstrator vehicle where the camera is mainly moving in longitudinal direction. Additionally, there are rotational components about all three axes.

There is a distinct flow pattern corresponding to rotation and translation along every camera axes. As the camera movement is a combination of camera translation and rotation, the optical flow is a linear combination of independent components.

In order to use the flow/depth constraint as described above, we have to stabilize the image so that all rotational components are zero and only the translational flow remains.

Our stabilization is estimating self-motion using a matched filter method [12]. Each filter is tuned to one flow pattern generated by either camera pitch, yaw or roll according rotation for the three camera axes. We assume that the flow preprocessing provides the optical flow as an input to the matched filters. The elimination of the rotational flow components is done in three steps:

1. Compute the filter output from the weighted sum of the scalar product between the optical flow and the matched filter pattern at each image position. This results in a single scalar which is the rotational speed for this axis.

2. An estimate for the rotational flow field is given by the product of the matched filter pattern and the rotational speed from the first step.

3. The compensated flow is given by the difference between the measured optical flow and the estimated rotational flow field from step 2.

The method is very well adapted to our stabilization task. Based on the optical flow which we take from the preprocessing stage there is only few extra computational power needed for the stabilization. The matched filter patterns for all three axes do not change over time, so they can be computed only once when the system is initialized. If we assume, that the optical flow is present for n pixels within the image, we only need $2n$ MUL, $2n$-1 SUM and 1 DIV operation to compute the rotational speed from step 1. The flow prediction from step 2 needs $2n$ MUL and the compensation from step 3 needs $2n$ SUB operations.

3.4 Results

The system has been tested on several inner city image sequences with pedestrians involved. As an example, one of these scenes is shown in Fig. 3.
The sequence has been taken from our in-vehicle stereo camera system. The vehicle speed is 18 km/h and the slight pitch and yaw movement of the camera has been compensated by the described matched filter method.

The result of the flow/depth constraint is overlaid onto the image. As can be seen, the algorithm is very sensitive to movements that don't match the motion of a static environment with respect to the moving camera, while background noise is very low.

The robust and fast detection can only be achieved because our fusion method is using the information from the stereo and the optical flow subsystems in an optimal way. The head of the child is detected within only three image frames after its first appearance behind the front window of the car. From stereo or optical flow alone this wouldn't be possible.

The detection is independent of size or shape of the object. Since everything is done on a small pixel based neighborhood, the detection even works for non-rigid motion from pedestrians where motion varies for different parts of the body. However, in Fig. 3, the motion of legs and arms with respect to their size is fairly high and can not be measured with the current approach.

The flow/depth constraint also works on areas where the flow is zero. Due to the fact that our camera is moving, a flow equals zero does not automatically mean a zero risk. The subimages in Fig. 3 have been cropped from the original video at a fixed position. Even though the child is moving with respect to world coordinates, there is almost zero optical flow for the child's head since its position within the image stays nearly constant. But as one can see there is no difference in detection even under this extreme conditions.

Using the rotational flow vector filed generated from the vehicle inertial sensory for generating the temporal derivatives for flow computation, the system has been tested at vehicle speeds up to 30km/h with yaw rates up to 25deg/s. The results show that even under these extreme driving conditions, the flow/depth constraint can be used for moving object detection.

Fig. 3. Fast detection of a child within an image sequence taken from a moving camera

4 Summary

The early detection of dangerous situations in urban traffic is a serious challenge for image understanding systems. Up to now, we had stereo vision to detect obstacles in front of the car only.

The presented fusion of stereo and motion analysis is a new powerful scheme that allows early detection of moving obstacles even if they are partially occluded and non-rigid. The disparity information is already available in our vehicle and the simple motion analysis runs in real-time, too. Since the fusion algorithm has to compare the flow/depth quotient against a threshold function at distinct points only, it is computationally highly efficient.

References

1. U.Franke, D.Gavrila, S.Görzig, F.Lindner, F.Paetzold, C.Wöhler: "Autonomous Driving Goes Downtown", *IEEE Intelligent Systems*, Vol.13, No.6, Nov./Dec.1998, pp.40-48
2. U.Franke, D.Gavrila, A.Gern, S.Goerzig, R.Janssen, F.Paetzold and C.Wöhler: "From door to door – principles and applications of computer Vision for driver assistant systems", in *Intelligent Vehicle Technologies: Theory and Applications*, Arnold, 2001
3. U.Franke: "Real-time Stereo Vision for Urban Traffic Scene Understanding", *IEEE Conference on Intelligent Vehicles 2000*, October, Detroit
4. C. Wöhler, J. K. Anlauf. An Adaptable Time Delay Neural Network Algorithm for Image Sequence Analysis. *IEEE Transactions on Neural Network*, vol. 10, no. 6, pp. 1531-1536, 1999.
5. U.Franke, A.Joos, B.Aguirre: "Early Detection of potentially harmful situations with children", *Intelligent Vehicles 2001*, Tokyo, Mai 2001
6. J.L. Barron, D.J.Fleet, S.S. Beauchemein: "Performance of Optical Flow Techniques", *International Journal of Computer Vision 1*, 1994

7.   W.B. Thompson and Ting-Chuen Pong: "Detecting Moving Objects", *Int. Journal of Comp. Vision 4*, 1990
8.   P. Anandan; "A computational framework and an algorithm for the measurement of visual motion", *Int. Journal of Comp. Vision 2*, 1989
9.   D.J. Heeger: "Optical flow using spatiotemporal filters", *Int. Journal of Comp. Vision 1*, 1988
10. D.J. Fleet and A.D. Jepson: "Computation of component image velocity from local phase information", *Int. Journal of Comp. Vision 5*, 1990.
11. H.H. Nagel: "Displacement vectors derived from second-order intensity variations in image sequences", *Comp. Graph. Image Processing 21*, 1983
12. M.O. Franz: "Minimalistic Visual Navigation", *VDI Reihe 8 Nr. 739*, 1999
13. B. Lucas and T. Kanade: "An iterative image registration technique with an application to stereo vision", *Proc. 7th Int. Conf. On Artificial Intelligence*, 1981

Polygon Partition into Stable Regions

Jairo Rocha

Departament de Matematiques i Informatica
University of the Balearic Islands,
E07071 Palma de Mallorca, Spain
jairo@uib.es

Abstract. Zou and Yan have recently developed a skeletonization algorithm of digital shapes based on a regularity/singularity analysis; they use the polygon whose vertices are the boundary pixels of the image to compute a constrained Delaunay triangulation in order to find local symmetries and stable regions. Their method has produced good results but it is slow since its complexity depends on the number of contour pixels. This paper presents an extension of their technique to handle arbitrary polygons, not only polygons of short edges. Consequently, not only can we achieve results as good as theirs for digital images but we can also compute skeletons of polygons of any number of edges. Since we can handle polygonal approximations of figures, the skeletons are more resilient to noise and faster to process.

1 Introduction

Decomposition into regular and singular regions and its application to skeletonization has been an important subject of research since the seminal papers (i.e.,[3]) of about 10 years ago. We present in this article the first method for regular/singular decomposition that works on any kind of polygon. Zou and Yan's method [4], that hereafter will be called ZYM, works only when the polygon nodes are very near each other so that they never have to be split to analyze the local symmetries. Rocha and Bernardino's method [2] works only when the edges are long so that a parallelism criterion can be robustly applied to characterize regular from singular regions. There are no other algorithms in the literature for polygon analysis that are rotationally invariant, that use no external parameters and that avoid protrusions in the skeleton. Our method gives as skeleton for a perfect rectangle only one axis, the longest one, in contrast with most methods.

Our method can be understood as a modification of the medial axis (calculated by the Voronoi diagram) of the polygon using the *perceptually stable* regions used by ZYM. However, since the proposed method works on any kind of polygons, the computational cost can be reduced since it depends on the number of edges in the polygon contour.

The basic idea of our method is to split the original polygon segments into subsegments according to the symmetries suggested by the Voronoi diagram of the polygon. The splitting points are the orthogonal projections of the branching

L. Van Gool (Ed.): DAGM 2002, LNCS 2449, pp. 83–90, 2002.

points onto the segments. The subsegments are related to only one polygon element: a subsegment or a vertex. After this, basically the same Constraint Delaunay Triangulation and the stable regions defined in ZYM are used to define the skeleton. Given the paper limitations, we suggest that the reader finds the details of the method in [4] and in the following, the differences.

2   Basic Definitions of Voronoi Diagrams of Polygons

Let us assume that we have a polygon possibly with polygonal holes. The polygon interior is assumed to be on the left side of the segments. We will briefly recall some notation of Voronoi diagrams for line segments. The polygon is assumed to be composed of open segments and vertex points, which are the elements of the polygon. Also, a polygon divides the plane into inside and outside points. If e is an element, the Voronoi region $V(e)$ is the locus of inside points closest to element e than to any other element (inside points whose distance to a segment e is the same as its distance to one of the vertices of e are considered closer to the vertex). The boundary edges of a Voronoi region are called *Voronoi edges*. The vertices of the region are called *Voronoi points*. The Voronoi edges shared by the Voronoi regions of two polygon segments are portions of a bisectrix of the lines that contain the segments, while the Voronoi edges shared by a vertex and a segment are portions of a parabola. The Voronoi edges shared by two vertices are also straight lines.

A Voronoi region of a segment s has as boundary s itself and some Voronoi edges. The following observation is simple but very useful. It is not proved due to paper limitations.

Remark 1 *Let P be a Voronoi point adjacent to $V(s)$, where s is a polygon segment. The orthogonal projection of P over s lies in s or in a vertex adjacent to s.*

Motivated by the previous statement, for each segment s, take the orthogonal projection over s of the Voronoi points adjacent to $V(s)$. Segments are naturally partitioned into subsegments according to their closest neighbor segments. In the rest of the paper, we will use the term polygon segments for the subsegments in which the original segments are divided according to the Voronoi diagram. Also, we will work only with the new Voronoi diagram, associated with the new segments, which has some additional edges that divide old Voronoi regions into new ones. In this way, each of the (new) polygon segments shares a Voronoi edge only with one element of the polygon. For an example, see Figure 1.

A (new) Voronoi region $V(s)$ of a segment s is bounded by s itself, two Voronoi rectilinear edges orthogonal to s and a Voronoi edge e_s that closes the boundary. Two open polygon segments s_1 and s_2 are *neighbors* if $e_{s_1} = e_{s_2}$. Notice that each Voronoi edge has two and only two polygon elements associated to it. Furthermore, each polygon segment s has a unique Voronoi edge e_s associated to it.

Fig. 1. (left) Voronoi edges of a polygon. (right) Projections of Voronoi points over their segments creating subsegments used for defining neighbor segments.

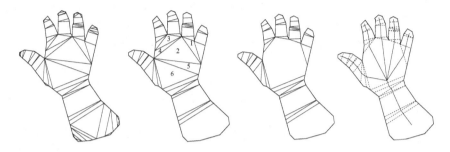

Fig. 2. Example of the process: partition, stabilization of end regions, of intersection regions and skeleton.

3   Original Polygon Partition

Hereafter, we find a partition of the polygon and merge the regions following the same ZYM idea. Each Voronoi edge has two polygon elements associated to it. For each pair of polygon elements associated to a Voronoi edge, we add the following interior segments: if the elements are two polygon segments AB and CD in the orientation given by the Voronoi edge, we add two new segments AC and BD (the segment AD is also added when we need to obtain a triangulation); if the elements are a vertex P and a polygon segment AB, we add the segments PA and PB; and, finally, if the elements are the vertices P and Q we add the segment PQ.

The interior segments form a partition of the polygon into triangles and trapezoids. Hereafter, we use the term *external* edges for the original polygon segments, and *internal* edges for the added segments. See Figure 2 for an example. A partition element has one of the following types: a *trapezoid* (generated by two neighbor segments and two internal edges), a *parabola triangle* (generated by an external edge and two internal edges from this to a polygon vertex), and a *totally internal triangle* (generated by three internal edges).

4   Unstable Regions

A *region* is a connected set of triangles. As in ZYM, we classify the regions according to the type of edges that make up their boundary. An *isolated* region has no internal edges in its boundary; an *end* region has one internal edge; a *regular* region has two internal edges, and an *intersection* region has more than two internal edges. A *singular* region is either an end or an intersection region.

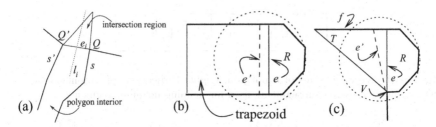

Fig. 3. (a) Orientation of an intersection region. (b) Merging of an end region with a trapezoid, and (c) with a parabola triangle.

The original regions defined above will be grouped to define the final regular and singular regions.

We now define when an end region and an intersection region are stable, modifying the criteria of ZYM to get very similar results at lower resolution level.

An end region R has one adjacent region S that shares the internal edge e with R. Let w be the maximum length among the internal edges of S, if S is an intersection region. Otherwise, w is the length of e. The circle centered in the mid-point of e and whose diameter is $\sqrt{2}w$ is called the *characteristic circle* of R. An end region is *unstable* if no part of it lies outside its characteristic circle.

An intersection region has n interior edges $e_1, \ldots e_n$, and it is adjacent to n regions (which are not intersection regions; otherwise, adjacent intersection regions are merged). The endings of an edge $e_i = QQ'$ lie on the polygon contour (that leaves the polygon interior on its left), and assume that QQ' leaves the intersection region on its right. (see Figure 3.a). Consider s the polygon segment adjacent to Q and before it in the contour order, and s' the polygon segment adjacent to Q' and after it. The bisectrix l_i of these two segments is defined to be the local orientation of the region adjacent to e_i. We define the *characteristic skeleton point* P of the intersection region as the point interior to the polygon that makes the distance to all l_i, $i = 1, \ldots, n$ a minimum. An intersection region is *unstable* if its characteristic skeleton point lies outside it.

An end region that is unstable is merged to some triangles of its adjacent region. An intersection region that is unstable is merged to a part of the adjacent region that is the nearest to its characteristic skeleton point. This merging process is called stabilization. After an end region is merged, it is possible that the new region is not an end region. However, during the merging process end regions are processed prior to intersection regions.

When an end region R is merged with an adjacent region S, there are three cases for the region S, according to the type of the triangle T in S adjacent to R: if T is singular, S is merged completely to R. If the triangle T is regular, let e be the internal edge common to R and S. If T is part of a trapezoid (see Figure 3.b), we find a new edge e' parallel to e with its extremes lying on the neighboring segments, as close as possible to e and that satisfies the following condition: the new region of R merged with the subregion between e and e'

is stable. If e' does not exist, the trapezoid is completely merged to R. If the triangle T is a parabola triangle with external edge f and vertex V (see Figure 3.c), we find a new segment e' from V to a point lying on f as close as possible to e and such that the new region of R merged to the subregion between e and e' be stable. If e' does not exist, T is completely merged to R.

For an intersection region R, the process is similar.

In the example shown in Figure 2, first, the internal triangles 1 and 2 are merged; second, the characteristic point of triangle 3 is outside it, so it is merged to triangle 4, which is then merged to the region of triangle 2; the region of triangles 1, 2, 3 and 4 is not stable so it is merged to triangle 5, which is again merged to its adjacent internal triangle 6. The whole region is stable.

Now, some words are needed on how to calculate the subregions described in the previous paragraphs. The subregion to be merged to an intersection region are completely defined by its characteristic skeleton point position. On the other hand, for an end region, the subregion to be merged should be taken as small as possible, so that the new region is stable. Below we explain a simple optimization problem to find it.

Let T be the triangle adjacent to the end region R. If T is part of a trapezoid, the distance that should be a minimum is the distance z between the two parallel edges e and e'. The diameter and the center of the new characteristic circle can be expressed linearly in terms of z; for each vertex of R, the constraint that it should be outside the circle is quadratic, so the whole problem is solved analyzing a quadratic polynomial in z for each vertex of R. If T is a parabola triangle, the distance that should be a minimum is the distance z between V and the point on f that defines the edge e'; again, the diameter and the center of the new characteristic circle can be expressed linearly in terms of z, although the constants are more complex; again, the quadratic polynomial roots solve the problem.

Table 1. Execution time for different number of segments in the polygon.

Shape	approx.	segments	time
	0	ZYM	12.50
	0	1232	132.50
human	2	117	3.43
	4	46	1.05
	0	1056	97.51
hand	2	77	1.81
	4	43	0.94
	0	1950	383.40
cow	2	152	5.40
	4	83	2.06
	0	789	68.90
spoon	2	50	1.08
	4	18	0.49
	0	889	81.50
sword	2	72	1.49
	4	29	0.71
	0	851	80.80
bottle	2	48	1.04
	4	21	0.66

5 Comparative Experiments

For simplicity, we use a slow but easy implementation of the Voronoi diagram calculation; for a new excellent implementation, the reader is referred to [1], which can handle thousands of segments per second with high precision with a comparable CPU. We extract the same unelongated images used by ZYM with a height of 500 pixels each. We use Pavlidis' polygonal approximation method that requires an error parameter: the maximum distance in pixels from a contour pixel to the polygon edge that approximates it.

The results are summarized in Table 1 (the second column is the parameter of the polygonal approximation; the third column is the number of segments in the polygonal approximation, except the first raw which is for the ZYM data; the fourth column is the CPU time in seconds), and the output is in Figures 4 and 5.

There is no visible difference between the original ZYM results and our results at our highest polygon resolution as shown in Figure 4. Our system is almost 10 times slower than ZYM's at the highest resolution. Nevertheless, the main point of the proposed method is that a large reduction is possible: for the second polygonal approximation level (a maximum distance of 2 pixels from a contour pixel to its corresponding segment) our method is 40 times faster than at the previous resolution; the differences in the skeleton are difficult to see. At the lowest approximation level, the proposed method is 3 times faster; at this level the skeleton segments are easier to see (bottom rows of Figure 5), so that the skeleton is not as smooth as the original one.

6 Conclusion

This paper extends the perceptual stability definitions of [4] to arbitrary polygons. The proposed method maintains the skeleton properties of its predecessor but it can be applied to arbitrary polygons. We draw to the reader's attention the good skeleton degradation and the big improvement in computational time caused by the polygon size reduction. More importantly, this paper shows a rotationally invariant, parameter free regular-singular analysis of arbitrary polygons, that inheres to the good results already proven by [4].

References

1. M. Held. VRONI: An engineering approach to the reliable and efficient computation of Voronoi diagrams of points and line segments. *Computational Geometry: Theory and Applications*, 18(2):95–123, 2001.
2. J. Rocha and R. Bernardino. Singularities and regularities via symmetrical trapezoids. *IEEE trans. on PAMI*, 20(4):391–395, April 1998.
3. J. C. Simon. A complementary approach to feature detection. In J. C. Simon, editor, *From Pixels to Features*, pages 229–236. North-Holland, 1989.
4. J. Zou and H. Yan. Skeletonization of ribbon-like shapes based on regularity and singularity analysis. *IEEE Trans. SMC, B:Cybernetics*, 31(3):401–407, 2001.

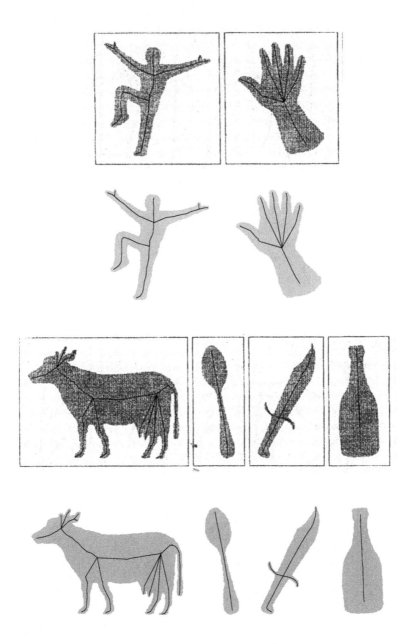

Fig. 4. (First and third rows) ZYM results. (Second and forth rows) Proposed method results for the highest resolution level.

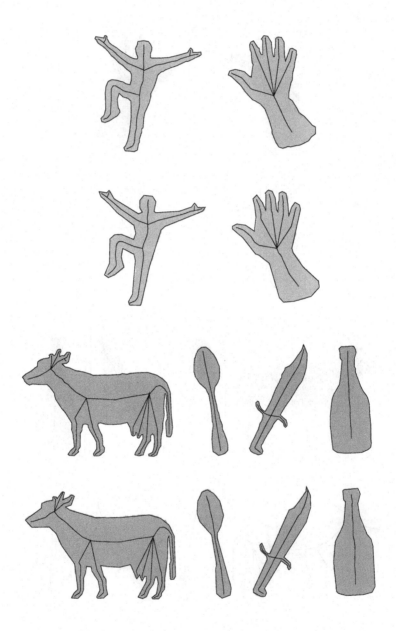

Fig. 5. Proposed method results for a medium resolution level (first and third rows) and for a low resolution level (second and forth rows).

Fast ICP Algorithms for Shape Registration

Timothée Jost and Heinz Hügli

Pattern Recognition Group, Institute of Microtechnology, University of Neuchâtel,
Breguet 2, CH-2000 Neuchâtel, Switzerland.
timothee.jost@unine.ch, heinz.hugli@unine.ch

Abstract. Shape registration plays an important role in applications such as 3D object modeling or object recognition. The iterative closest point (ICP) algorithm is widely used for the registration of geometric data. One of its main drawback is its time complexity $O(N^2)$, quadratic with the shape size N, which implies long processing time, especially when using high resolution data. Several methods were proposed to accelerate the process. One of the most effective one uses a tree search (k-D tree) to establish closest point relationships and reduces the complexity to $O(N \log N)$. This paper reviews several of the existing methods and proposes and analyses a new, even less complex ICP algorithm, that uses a heuristic approach to find the closest points. Based on a local search it permits to reduce the complexity to $O(N)$ and to greatly accelerate the process. A comprehensive analysis and a comparison of the considered algorithm with a tree search method are presented.

1 Introduction

Shape registration plays an important role in today's computer vision. It consists in finding the correct alignment of two or more sets of data. For example, 3D object modeling generally requires to assemble several complementary views into a single representation. Quality inspection and 3D object recognition are other examples of applications of the registration.

A common approach for shape registration uses techniques based on the intrinsic properties of measured surfaces, or geometric matching. One of the best known and widely used low level geometric matching algorithms is the iterative closest point (ICP) algorithm [3]. At each iteration, it first creates closest point correspondences between two sets of points P and X (or more generally geometric data) and then minimizes the average distance between both sets by finding an optimal rigid transformation. There exist several implementations and variations of it which mainly vary in the way they handle the point pairings. A recent overview and comparison of the different methods can be found in [7].

The main practical difficulty of the ICP algorithm is that it requires heavy computations. Its complexity is $O(N_p N_x)$, where N_p and N_x basically represent the number of points of the data sets. Matching detailed high resolution shapes (>20000 points) takes so much time on current computers that there is a real need for ways to reduce ICP computation time. Several solutions to speed up the algorithm have been proposed and can be divided into 3 categories: reduction of the number of iterations, reduction of the number of data points and acceleration of the closest point search.

L. Van Gool (Ed.): DAGM 2002, LNCS 2449, pp. 91–99, 2002.
© Springer-Verlag Berlin Heidelberg 2002

Besl [3] and later Simon [9] proposed variations named *"accelerated ICP"* which use a linear or quadratic extrapolation of the registration parameters to reduce the number of iterations. Typical results from these authors showed reductions of the computation time by a factor of 3 and 4 respectively.

Some authors proposed to use a *coarse to fine strategy* [11][10]. They execute the first iterations using a lower resolution, like 1/4 or 1/5 of the points, and finish with fine matching using full resolution. Zhang [11] found a reduction factor of about 2 to 4 using this strategy. Chen and Medioni [5] and Brett [4] proposed to use subsets of the surface points sitting respectively in smooth areas (for robust line plane intersections) and in high curvature areas (to keep significant features).

Benjemaa [1] proposed to project points into Z-buffers and then to perform local searches in them. This method reduces the complexity of closest point search to $O(N_p)$ but it needs a very good starting approximation of the matching and the Z-buffers need to be updated at each iteration. Finally, Besl [3] also suggested that using a k dimensional binary search tree, *k-D tree* [2], would greatly decrease closest point search time. Theoretically, searching the closest point in a k-D tree having N entries is of complexity $O(logN)$. Thus, using a balanced k-D tree in the case of ICP, the global complexity of the algorithm becomes $O(N_p logN_x)$. Practical results [9] showed gains of about 15 for meshes containing ≈ 2500 pts. and one can note here that the gain increases with the number of points, due to the reduction of the global complexity. Both theoretical and practical results confirm the importance of closest point search speedup to create fast ICP algorithms.

The "neighbor search" closest point algorithm is presented in this paper. It is designed to be adapted to the ICP algorithm and to optimally exploit, for speedup, the closest point neighborhoods of the two surfaces to be aligned. Specifically, it assumes that two neighbors on a surface possess closest points on the other surface that are neighbors and uses this property to obtain a first approximation of the closest point. It then refines the result with a local search. This method permits to avoid a global search for most points and leads to a closest points search (and ICP) algorithm that provides a complexity of $O(N_p)$. The neighborhood either exists a priori or can be built in range images, triangulated meshes and clouds of points, which are the common ways of obtaining and storing the 3D data measurements to be used in most applications that require registration.

Section 2 describes the "neighbor search" closest point algorithm. Some experiments and results using this new heuristic method are presented in section 3 as well as a comparison with a k-D tree search. Finally, conclusions and a future work discussion can be found in 4.

2   Neighbor Search Closest Point Algorithm

2.1 Neighborhood Relationship Hypothesis

The proposed algorithm assumes the existence of a neighborhood relationship between the two sets of points P and X. The relationship hypothesis is that two neighbors in a data set possess closest points that are neighbors in the other data set. Formally, the principle of this neighborhood relationship is exposed in figure 1: given a point p_k in data set P and its corresponding closest point x_k in data set X, the closest point x_i of p_i, if p_k belongs to neighborhood V of p_i, $V(p_i)$, is found in the neighborhood V' of x_k, $V'(x_k)$.

The proposed idea towards a faster search is to use good approximations of the closest points instead of exact closest points. The neighborhood relationship is used to get a first approximation of the closest point and, then, a local search can be performed to refine the result instead of an exhaustive one: if p_i possesses a neighbor p_k in data set P, with a known closest point x_k in data set X, finding the closest point of p_i can be reduced to searching the closest point in the neighborhood V' of x_k, $V'(x_k)$.

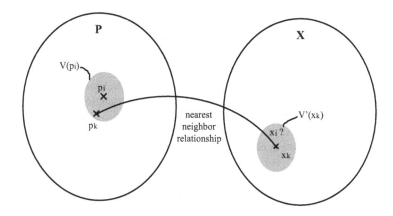

Fig. 1. The neighborhood relationship assumption

2.2 Basic Algorithm

The following procedure formulates the closest point search algorithm:

```
-input:        data sets P and X, with associated neighborhood,
               V(P) and V'(X)
-output:       for each pᵢ of P, an approximation xᵢ of its
               closest point in X
-procedure     neighbor_closest_point_search (P, X)
               for (each pᵢ of P) do:
               if (∃ xₖ closest point of pₖ ∈ V(pᵢ)) then:
                     xᵢ = search_closest_point (pᵢ, V'(xₖ) )
               else:
                     xᵢ = search_closest_point (pᵢ, X)
```

It appears that for each point p_i, the closest point search is performed either in the full set X or only in the neighborhood $V'(x_k)$, depending if at least one neighbor of p_i has already a known closest point. Formally, this closest point search algorithm has therefore a theoretical best case complexity of $O(N_p)$. This is better than the best case using k-D tree, $O(N_p \log N_x)$ and lets us expect an overall gain in speed over using a tree search.

The worst case complexity corresponds to the conventional full search discussed so far. A good suggestion here is to use a tree search, instead of an exhaustive search, when searching the full set X - other potential ideas would be to use a temporal cache or a heuristic method like 3 steps algorithm, in range images -. Using this method, it is interesting to note that the neighbor search algorithm acceleration worst case is basically equal to the tree search $O(N_p \log N_x)$, as long as the cost of the local search is smaller than a tree search of course.

2.3 Data Structure Considerations

Structured data sets are needed to have a defined neighborhood. In many cases, it already exists a priori or at least can be built. Generally, applications using 3D registration rely on either range images, clouds of points or triangle meshes as their input data. A neighborhood exists in a range image, where direct neighbors in the image are also neighbors on the surface. It also exists in the case of triangle meshes, where neighborhood is defined by belonging to the same triangle edge. In the case of a cloud of points, an existing triangulation algorithm (like the ball-pivoting algorithm for example) could be used to create a triangle mesh. Such a neighborhood is needed in both the P mesh, to obtain closest point approximation, and the X mesh, to make the local search.

Of course, the order in which points p_i of P are scanned is also important. Using a random method is a bad idea, as it would create a high number of global searches and pushes complexity toward the worst case. Consequently, the basic idea is to scan points using a diffusion method, such as the next point to be scanned is chosen in the neighborhood of the points that already have a known neighbor.

2.4 Algorithm Applied to Range Images

In a range image, each point generally possesses 8 direct neighbors (except points on borders). A very basic algorithm is considered here. Neighborhood V is 3x3 in P and neighborhood V' is nxn in X. We choose to scan the points of range image P *row by row, starting from upper left*. That way, the possible direct neighbors of p_i with a known closest point p_k can be found on the previous point in the same row and in the previous row (see image P on figure 2). Those 4 possible candidates are just checked sequentially and the first one that possesses a known closest point is chosen as p_k. Normally, any of the candidate neighbors possesses a known closest point, except for the first scanned point and in case of missing data points.

Once p_k. and its corresponding closest point x_k. are known, the local closest point search of p_i is done in a square neighborhood zone of size nxn, centered around the approximation x_k (see image X in figure 2). If no p_k can be found, a global search is performed in X, as suggested previously. Of course, the bigger the zone, the better the approximation, but the longer the search, so a compromise has to be found. Bigger search zone also implies a bigger neighborhood, which reduces the number of unconnected subsets in the range image.

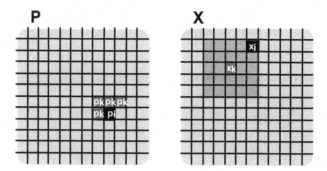

Fig. 2. Neighbor search using range images

3   Experiments and Results

In order to validate the proposed approach, the new neighbor search algorithm has been tested on different data sets and compared to an optimized ICP using a k-D tree search, similar to the one proposed by Zhang [11]. The comparison must focus on two things: computation speed and matching quality.

3.1 Matching Quality Comparison

Two measures can be considered to examine the quality of the matching procedure: the matching error and the domain of convergence. To compare the matching error, the algorithm must converge and the resulting alignment has to be the same or at least in the same error range as when matching using exact closest points.

To examine the domain of convergence, we use a method presented in [6] that permits to define and compare domains of successful initial configurations (SIC). A successful initial configuration is basically defined by a relative initial positioning of the two data sets that leads to a successful matching. The initial configuration space possesses 6 dimensions, so examining all of it isn't conceivable due to both heavy computations and difficulty to handle the results. The idea consists in examining a subset of "interesting" initial configurations that are liable to converge successfully. The different initial configurations are defined in a three-dimensional space by placing one surface on several points of the circumsphere of the other one. The results are plotted in 2D in a SIC-map. Each successful initial configuration is represented by a black sector (fig. 4). The higher the number of black sectors, the bigger the SIC domain is.

3.2 Matching Experiment

The presented experimental data consist in two different, partially overlapping data sets, which typically represents the problem of views registration for virtual modeling. The data are range images of the surface of an irregular substrate measured by an AFM and their overlap is approximately 30% of their total surface. Figure 3 shows a render of the two coarsely aligned sets. The considered meshes contain approximately 930 points.

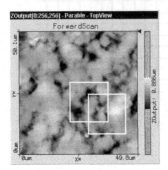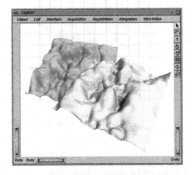

Fig. 3. Range image and surface rendering of two partially overlapping AFM data sets

Matching Quality. Trying to register both meshes using the sole point to point distance implies that the ICP algorithm practically never converges to the right positioning. Therefore, normals are added to the distance measurement, as shown by schütz [8], to improve the matching quality.

A comparison of the average errors show that they do not differ significantly in case of successful convergence. The registration error using k-D tree is about 1% in translation and 2° in rotation. There is a very small increase of the error in translation and respectively 0.2° to 0.8° in rotation when using 9x9 and 5x5 search zones.

The SIC-maps of figure 4 show that the range of successful initial configuration is practically reduced to nothing when using a 5x5 neighbor search zone but that it is even bigger when using a 9x9 zone than when using a tree search!

One can finally note that a small increase of the number of iterations of ICP can be observed when using neighbor search but the cost is negligible.

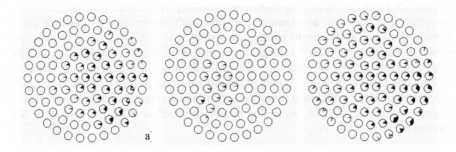

Fig. 4. SIC-maps of the AFM data, using point and normal distance (k=6):a) tree search b) neighbor search with a 5x5 zone c) neighbor search with a 9x9 zone

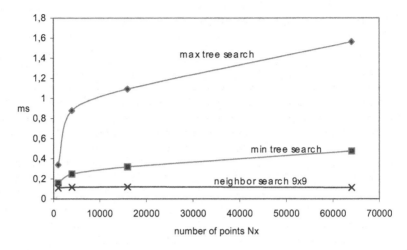

Fig. 5. Comparison of closest point computation time

Search Time. Figure 5 graphically presents the average closest point computation time per point of P, for the partially overlapping sets. The neighbor search method is compared with tree search at different resolutions. Two values of k-D tree are given at each resolution, a minimal time and a maximal time. This is to reflect the difference in the computation time depending on the distance between both data sets when using a k-D tree. Basically, the tree search is longer when data sets are farther from each other. The min / max values must be considered as a best case / worst case type of measure.

One can first observe on figure 5 that the theoretical complexity of $O(N_p)$ was practically reached for the neighbor search. The gain in speed lies typically between 2 and 5 over a best case k-D tree. Considering the worst case tree search values, the gain can go up to 13 times!

A complementary aspect of the speedup emerges when measuring the actual acceleration gain with respect to a practical implemented exhaustive search of theoretical complexity $O(N^2)$. Table 1 reports these gains of the closest point computation for a k-D tree, in best and worst cases, and for the presented neighbor search method. These results were obtained by matching partially overlapping data sets, with the setup of section 3.2, using point and normal distance. One can see that the acceleration gain can go up to 650 over an exhaustive search.

Table 1. Closest points search time gain for the best and worst k-D tree cases and neighbor search with a 9x9 zone over an exhaustive search, at different resolutions

number of points	1000	4000	16000	64000
max tree search	3.1	5.2	16.7	47
min tree search	6.6	18.3	57.4	153
local search, 9x9	9.5	39.8	154	650

4   Conclusion and Future Work

This paper presented a comparison of existing methods to speed up the ICP algorithm and proposed and analyzed a new algorithm for very fast ICP registration. It permits to reduce ICP complexity to $O(N_p)$ and differs from other approaches in that it uses a heuristic method to establish closest point correspondences. The method uses the assumption that two neighbors on a surface possess closest points that are neighbors on the other surface to easily obtain a first approximation of the closest point and then proceeds with a local search for refining the result.

Results from a series of registration experiments show that the proposed neighbor search algorithm performs significantly better than a tree search, the theoretical complexity of $O(N)$ being practically reached. Basically, the neighbor search algorithm ranges from 2 to 13 times faster than a tree search. Also, the method improves the computation speed of the ICP algorithm, without altering the matching error and the domain of convergence. The results show that, in nearly all cases, the ICP registration that uses the neighbor search still converges toward the same position as when using an exact closest points search. This confirms the good potential of the proposed method.

Furthermore, there is still place for improvement, in particular by using multiresolution and other local search strategy.

With respect to multiresolution, the analysis of the results and literature suggest that using a multiresolution adaptation of the neighbor search closest point algorithm will have several very positive factor on ICP and that it can be easily implemented in the case of range images.

With respect to the search strategy, it is clear that a local search method smarter than the square zone search could be used. A steepest descent or a local 3 steps algorithm could both diminish the number of local search and augment their exactness.

References

1. R. Benjemaa, F. Schmitt, "Fast Global Registration of 3D sampled Surfaces Using a Multi-Z-Buffer Technique", *Proceedings 3DIM,* Ottawa (1997) 113-119.
2. JL. Bentley, "Multidimensional Binary Search Tree Used for Associative Searching", *Communications of the ACM,* vol. 8(9) (1975) 509-517.
3. PJ. Besl, ND. McKay, "A Method for Registration of 3D Shapes", *IEEE Transactions on Pattern Analysis and Machine Intelligence,* vol. 14(2) (1992) 239-256.
4. AD. Brett, A. Hills, CJ. Taylor, "A Method of 3D Surface Correspondence and Inter-polation for Merging Shape", *Image and Vision Computing,* vol. 17(8) (1999) 635-642.
5. Y. Chen, G. Medioni, "Object modeling by registration of multiple range images", *International Journal of Image and Vision Computing,* vol. 10(3) (1992) 145-155.
6. H. Hügli, C. Schütz, "Geometric Matching of 3D Objects: Assessing the Range of Successful Initial Configurations", *Proceedings 3DIM,* Ottawa (1997) 101-106.
7. S. Rusinkiewicz, M. Levoy, "Efficient Variants of the ICP Algorithm", *Proc. 3DIM,* Quebec (2001) 145-152.
8. C. Schütz, T. Jost, H. Hügli, "Multi-Featured Matching Algorithm for Free-Form 3D Surface Registration", *Proceedings ICPR,* Brisbane (1998) 982-984.

9. DA. Simon, M. Hebert, T. Kanade, "Techniques for Fast and Accurate Intra Surgical Registration", *Journal of Image Guided Surgery*, vol. 1(1) (1995) 17-29.
10. G. Turk, M. Levoy, "Zippered Polygon Meshes from Range Images", *Proceedings of ACM Siggraph*, Orlando (1994) 311-318.
11. Z. Zhang, "Iterative Points Matching for Registration of Free Form Curves and Surfaces", *International Journal of Computer Vision*, vol. 13(2) (1994) 119-152.

Appearance Based Generic Object Modeling and Recognition Using Probabilistic Principal Component Analysis

Christopher Drexler*, Frank Mattern, and Joachim Denzler

Lehrstuhl für Mustererkennung
Universität Erlangen-Nürnberg, Martensstr. 3, 91058 Erlangen
Phone: +49 9131 8527826
Fax: +49 9131 303811
drexler@informatik.uni-erlangen.de

Abstract. Classifying unknown objects in familiar, general categories rather than trying to classify them into a certain known, but only similar class, or rejecting them at all is an important aspect in object recognition. Especially in tasks, where it is impossible to model all possibly appearing objects in advance, generic object modeling and recognition is crucial.

We present a novel approach to generic object modeling and classification based on probabilistic principal component analysis (PPCA). A data set can be separated into classes during an unsupervised learning step using the expectation–maximization algorithm. In contrast to principal component analysis the feature space is modeled in a *locally* linear manner. Additionally, Bayesian classification is possible thanks to the underlying probabilistic model.

The approach is applied to the COIL-20/100 databases. It shows that PPCA is well suited for appearance based generic object modeling and recognition. The automatic, unsupervised generation of categories matches in most cases the categorization done by humans. Improvements are expected if the categorization is performed in a supervised fashion.

1 Introduction

Object recognition ideally tackles the problem of identifying a certain set of objects under changing illumination, camera parameters, and viewpoints, as well as under partial occlusion. If the recognition is also unaffected by novel exemplars of a category, for which some different exemplars are already known, we call it *generic object recognition*. For example, given a generic object model (or category) of cars, the system should be able to classify never before seen cars into the category car. However, already known cars should get their individual class label, e.g. BMW. The motivation for such a coarse to fine strategy is that most tasks, for example in a service robot scenario, might be solved without exactly knowing the specific class of an object. In our work we are interested in categories that arise from appearance only and not from function.

---

* This work was funded by the German Science Foundation (DFG) under grant DE 735/2–1. Only the authors are responsible for the content.

L. Van Gool (Ed.): DAGM 2002, LNCS 2449, pp. 100–108, 2002.

Generic object modeling has been studied in the past (e.g. [8,10]). Our approach differs from segmentation based approaches followed by some sort of grouping mechanism [10,6] in that we use an appearance based approach. In contrast to image retrieval techniques we do not want to classify solely into generic categories but for known objects we would like to get the specific class label, as well. This demands for a hierarchical, from coarse (category level) to fine (class level), strategy.

Our work starts with the idea of appearance based recognition using principal component analysis (PCA). We review so called *factor analysis models* [1] that are a generative way of describing the images generated from a random vector (called factors), disturbed by an arbitrary noise source — in most cases Gaussian noise. Inherently uncertainty is modeled probabilistically. In Section 2 we will summarize the theory. Starting from factor analysis models we apply the approaches from [5,13] to the problem of generic object modeling and recognition: both introduce mixtures of factor analyzers, although in a slightly different manner. As a consequence the feature space is now approximated in a piecewise linear manner in contrast to the globally linear approximation of the PCA. In [13] restrictions on the statistical model results in the so called *probabilistic principal component analysis* (PPCA). The underlying statistical framework makes it possible to apply maximum likelihood or maximum a posteriori estimation for classification of objects. However, applying PPCA to image data for generic modeling needs some modification of the whole approach in practice (Section 3).

The benefits of the PPCA are shown in the experimental part of the paper in Section 4: using the expectation maximization algorithm (EM–Algorithm) [4] the PPCA can be estimated from a training set in an unsupervised manner, which results in categories of objects defined by similar appearance. Recognition rates for the COIL-100 database support the claim, that the approach is capable for hierarchical modeling and recognition.

2   From PCA to PPCA: Factor Analysis Models

Object models based on PCA have become a popular approach for appearance based object and face recognition in the past years [9,2]. With respect to generic object recognition the PCA has the advantage that — as a rule of thumb — eigenvectors belonging to larger eigenvalues model the coarse appearance of an object while others are responsible for finer details (see Fig. 1). Thus, generic object classes should summarize objects, whose features, when projected into the Eigenspace using eigenvectors belonging to large eigenvalues, are located close together.

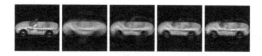

Fig. 1. Backprojection of an object using different numbers of Eigenvectors. From left to right: original image, backprojection using 5, 10, 15, 20 eigenvectors corresponding to the 5, 10, 15, 20 largest eigenvalues, respectively. Details are coded in the eigenvectors belonging to smaller eigenvalues.

Disadvantages of the PCA are its global linearity assumption in the feature space and a missing underlying statistical model that would allow soft decisions about the membership of a certain object using probabilities. In the following we present a new approach for appearance based recognition using factor analysis models, that — under certain assumptions — equals PCA.

2.1   Factor Analysis

In factor analysis [1] the assumption is that an observation (for example, an image) $t_i \in \mathbb{R}^d$ is generated by a q–dimensional random vector x_i (the elements of x_i are called factors) according to the following linear mapping

$$t_i = W x_i + \mu + \epsilon \ . \tag{1}$$

Like in PCA the vector t_i is built up from an image by concatenating the rows or columns of the image. The vector μ is a constant displacement vector and ϵ is a noise vector. The assumption is that $x_i \sim \mathcal{N}(0, I_q)$ as well as $\epsilon \sim \mathcal{N}(0, \Psi)$ are zero mean Gaussian distributed random vectors. The matrix I_q denotes the $q \times q$–dimensional identity matrix. The covariance matrix Ψ is assumed to be diagonal. As a consequence the observation t_i is also Gaussian distributed. Given a set of n observations t_i (i.e., for example images of a certain class; we will consider the unsupervised case in Section 4) the unknown parameters of the factor model W, μ, and Ψ can be estimated using the EM algorithm. Details for the computations during the E–step and the M–step can be found in [5].

2.2   Mixture of Factor Analyzers

The described factor analysis model in (1) can be extended to a mixture model of m Gaussian distributions. The observation vectors t_i are now modeled by

$$t_i = \sum_{k=1}^{m} \omega_k (W_k x_i + \mu_k + \epsilon_k) \tag{2}$$

with $x_i \sim \mathcal{N}(0, I_q)$ and $\epsilon_k \sim \mathcal{N}(0, \Psi_k)$. The quantity ω_k is the weight of the kth mixture component, Ψ_k again a diagonal covariance matrix of the observation noise. Similar to the factor analysis model, the EM–algorithm can be applied to estimate the unknown parameters of the mixture model, ω_k, W_k, μ_k, and Ψ_k. Due to lack of space we will not go into detail of the computations in the E–step and the M–step. The reader is referred to [5].

2.3   Probabilistic Principal Component Analysis

In [13] it has been shown that factor analysis and principal component analysis will coincide under special conditions. Coincidence means that the columns of the factor loadings matrix W contain the eigenvectors of the covariance matrix of the observations. Even if the exact correspondence is only guaranteed under specific conditions, practically there are no differences in the expression capabilities of the factor analyzer and the PCA models. However, the probabilistic approach by factor analysis has the advantage that soft decisions can be made based on probabilities. In the case of the mixture of factor analyzer, the feature space is approximated in a locally linear way, instead of a global linear one as in standard PCA.

In order to optimally approximate principal component analysis in practice without fulfilling the strict conditions, the diagonal covariance matrix $\boldsymbol{\Psi}$ is restricted to have identical diagonal elements, i.e. $\boldsymbol{\Psi} = \sigma^2 \boldsymbol{I}_d$ [13]. The log–likelihood function of the overall model

$$\mathcal{L} = \sum_{i=1}^{n} \ln p(t_i) \quad \text{where} \quad p(t_i) = \sum_{k=1}^{m} \omega_k p(t_i|k) \tag{3}$$

with n observations and m Gaussian distributions (submodels) will be maximized by a few EM–Iteration steps. The overall model can be divided into categories using a ML classifier with the likelihood distribution of the observation t_i given the submodel k

$$p(t_i|k) = (2\pi)^{-d/2}|C_k^{-1/2}| \exp\left(-\frac{1}{2}(t_i - \boldsymbol{\mu}_k)^T C_k^{-1}(t_i - \boldsymbol{\mu}_k)\right) \tag{4}$$

with $C_k := W_k W_k^T + \sigma^2 I_d$ or by a Bayes classifier with the a posteriori probability

$$p(k|t_i) = \frac{\omega_k p(t_i|k)}{p(t_i)} \tag{5}$$

of the submodel k given the observation t_i. These probabilities will be exploited for building a hierarchy from categories to specific classes and for performing generic object recognition (see Section 4).

3   PPCA for Generic Object Modeling and Recognition

Armed with the theory and estimation technique of the PPCA from the last section, we can now apply this framework to generic object modeling and recognition. First, some technical problems are discussed that occur when applying PPCA to large data sets of high–dimensional data. Then, we present an approach that applies first a standard dimensionality reduction by PCA, and then models the resulting features in the eigenspace by PPCA. The results of this approach with respect to generic object modeling are presented in Section 4.

Up to now, the PPCA has only been applied to observation vectors of a dimension less than 64. This prevents us from applying PPCA directly to images, since only images up to a size of 8×8 pixel could be processed.

The main reason for this restriction is that the computation of the determinant of the inverse covariance matrix depends on the dimension of the data. As a consequence, one gets numerical instabilities in the computation for large and/or small variances. For example, for an image size of 16×16 a variance larger than 16 will result in a determinant value that cannot longer be represented by a 64–bit $\mathtt{double}$ value on standard machines. Some solutions for these problems are discussed in [7].

To escape the curse of dimensionality we apply a normal PCA [9] in advance to reduce the input dimension for the PPCA algorithm to a maximum of 100, which is the maximum to be numerically manageable according to our experiments. In other words, the images are projected onto a lower dimensional space by PCA, on which a PPCA is performed in the following.

Besides the dimensionality reduction and the possibility to apply algorithms from standard eigenspace approaches one gets an additional degree of freedom in selecting features. Choosing different transformation matrixes of q successive eigenvectors, *not* starting with the first one, enables us to focus on different parts within the feature space and might be exploitable for generic object models. A systematic evaluation of such a procedure, especially on which eigenvectors to focus on, is under current investigation.

Fig. 2. Subset of 5 out of 20 categories of the automatic categorization of the COIL-20 database by PPCA using 20 mixture components. For each category a representative subset of views of the contained objects is presented

4   Experiments

We present results on experiments done with one of the standard database in the object recognition community: the COIL-20/100 databases (see [11], for the COIL-20), which contain images from 20 resp. 100 objects rotated on a turntable (72 images for each object, i.e. images taken every 5 degree). We performed the following experiments: unsupervised categorization, hierarchical model generation, and generic object recognition.

Unsupervised categorization. The objects in the COIL-20 database are modeled with mixtures of PPCA. In Fig. 2 a subset of the resulting categorization is shown. The number of mixture components has been set to 20. The expectations with respect to unsupervised categorization holds for most object classes, for example the cars and the pots. Interesting is the subsumption of dug and the wooden part, which have similar shapes from the given viewpoint. These results show that categorization based on appearance can be done automatically with the proposed approach. Similar results have been achieved for the COIL-100 database. The reader should note, that a pure vector quantization produces similar but marginally worse results. However, we get a complete probabilistic model out of the training data, that is optimized with respect to the likelihood. This gets more important in the case of generic object recognition, as a mere vector quantization can not provide adequate information for identifying previously unseen objects. This will be shown in the experiments on generic classification later on (Fig. 4 and 5).

Hierarchical model generation. We constructed up to three levels of mixtures of PPCA using all 20 objects of the COIL-20 database. For each level (0,1,2) a 5–dimensional

Eigenspace is used and the 5–dimensional feature vectors of the projected training data is used as input for the PPCA algorithm. Each mixture component of the PPCA at one level is used to select those views that are modeled at the next level by an individual mixture of PPCA. With these experiments we like to show, that a coarse (category level) to fine (class level) graduation can be realized by our approach in an unsupervised manner. In Table 1 the categorization at the first and second level is shown for one of the five formed categories. The entries in the table show the number of objects filled into one category at the first level and the split into five categories at the next level. One can see, that for this example already at the second level the objects are put into distinct categories. Another example is shown in Table 2. Here, at the second level still some visually similar objects from different classes are in the same category. The cream cheese box (cat1-2) and the cars in category cat1-3 are separated. The category cat1-0 contains the cars and the medication box (anacin) that look similar at that level of representation. At the third level (not shown in the table) category cat1-0 is subdivided into another five categories where finally the anacin box is separated from the cars into separate categories. One interesting aspect can be observed during generation of the hierarchies: as soon as the objects are separated into distinct categories the PPCA starts separating the different poses of the objects. This behavior is no surprise since the manifold of the images of one object is then approximated in a piecewise linear manner by the mixture components of the PPCA.

Table 1. Category 0 (cat0): The entries in the table show the number of objects from the training set, classified into that category at level 0 and into the five categories at level 1.

category	objects		
	"vaseline"	"wooden part3"	"piggy bank"
cat0	14	34	48
cat0-0			26
cat0-1			9
cat0-2		34	
cat0-3	14		
cat0-4			13

Table 2. Category 1 (cat1): The entries in the table show the number of objects from the training set, classified into that category at level 0 and into the five categories at level 1.

category	objects					
	"cup"	"cream cheese"	"car1"	"anacin"	"car2"	"tylenol"
cat1	48	48	41	37	39	33
cat1-0			3	24	3	
cat1-1				5		28
cat1-2		48				
cat1-3			27		25	
cat1-4	48		11	8	11	5

Although we can not generalize from these results that the different objects in a training set get separated as above, it can be seen, that the categorization is able to form meaningful visual classes. This is a prerequisite for the generic recognition shown in the next paragraph.

Generic object modeling and recognition. In order to test the ability of our models to classify previously unseen objects we also used the whole COIL-20 database but we completely omitted two objects during the training stage. Both objects leave similar objects in the training set (see Fig. 3). The "uncovered pot" has the "half covered pot" as a moderately similar object. The left out "car3" has two other similar cars in the training set. For these items we evaluated the ability of our models to classify seen and unseen objects.

UP   P1   UC   C1   C2

Fig. 3. The two unknown objects "car3" (UC) and "uncovered pot" (UP) omitted from the training set together with their visually most similar objects (according to the distance within the Eigenspace) "car1" (C1), "car2" (C2) and "half covered pot" (P1) contained in the training set.

For generic object recognition the PPCA mixture models have to provide two different kinds of information: to which visual class a test image is assigned to and how well the corresponding submodel is able to model the object in terms of visual class membership. As we descend the hierarchy levels from the categories to the distinct object classes the consistency with the submodel should increase for known objects, as the models get more specialized, and it should get worse for unknown objects, as the ability of modeling the unknown appearance decreases being closer to the class level.

Fig. 4 shows the log–likelihood for the hierarchy level 0 to 2 and Fig. 5 does the same for the "distance from feature space" function used as quality criteria for a nearest–neighbor classification. Both diagrams show the averaged curves over all test images for the two unknown objects "uncovered pot" and "car3" as well as for the three known objects "half covered pot", "car1" and "car2".

In Fig. 4 the two unknown objects can be easily identified with the "uncovered pot's" log–likelihood decreasing rapidly with each level. The unknown car fits as good to level 1 as the known cars, but the log–likelihood also decreases at the last level. The log–likelihood for the known objects increase or remain constant through all levels, as expected.

Fig. 5 demonstrates that an eigenspace approach with a nearest neighbor (NN) classification is not able to show similar behavior as the log–likelihood criteria. The distance gives no information on when to assign a given view to a category at a certain level and when to descend to the next level.

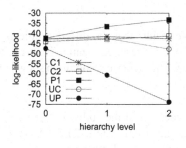

Fig. 4. PPCA

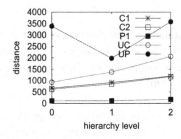

Fig. 5. NN

Log–likelihood (Fig. 4) and distance function plot (Fig. 5) for the two cars (C1,C2) and the pot (P1) which are part of the training set as well as for the unknown car (UC) and the unknown pot (UP).

Finally experiments were done to show how well PPCA is suited for classification of known object classes. We equally divided the COIL-100 dataset into training and test. The training set has been used for unsupervised construction of the hierarchy of categories. For all images put into the same category at the lowest level we performed a standard (supervised) PCA which is used for the actual assignment to a class. With a 3–dimensional PCA in the preprocessing step (compare Section 3), the recognition rate on the test set at level 0 of the hierarchy is 80.5%, at level 1 88.2% and at level 2 91.2%. With respect to the dimension of the feature space, this appears to be a reasonable result. In the case of a 15–dimensional PCA the recognition rate at level 0 is already 98.7%, slightly decreasing to 97.0% at level 2. This unwanted phenomenon is mainly due to small numbers of examples particularly falling into one category at level 2, thus preventing a reasonable 15-dimensional PCA.

5   Conclusions

In this paper we presented a novel way of using mixtures of PPCA (MPPCA) models for hierarchical generic object recognition, where the term "generic" aims at visually similar classes and not functional ones.

During the training step the MPPCA is computed for all input images of all different classes. The single mixture components define a disjunctive partition of the training set into visual classes according the maximum likelihood of each training vector. The elements of each partition are then used as input data for creating MPPCA models at the next, more specialized, hierarchy level.

Unlike in former publications we do not subsample the training data in order to reduce the input dimension but perform a Karhunen–Loève–Transformation into a low-dimensional Eigenspace. This preserves more information on high resolution input images than using a maximum input image size of 8×8 as done up to now.

The results of our experiments show that the unsupervised partition gives reasonable classes which are appropriate for building hierarchical MPPCA models suitable for generic recognition of previously unseen objects. Classification on large data sets (COIL-100) benefits from the hierarchical approach, as a recognition rate of up to 98.7% can be achieved already with low–dimensional feature vectors.

Further, experiments on other image databases with more objects and evaluations of the presented algorithm together with a robust feature calculation for handling partially occluded objects will be performed. Also, nonlinear PCA for generic object modeling, for example Kernel PCA introduced in [12], is one topic of our further investigation.

Although beyond the scope of generic object modeling a combination of the presented approach with a contour based representation of objects, introduced in [3], seems to be very promising for object representation and segmentation in general.

Acknowledgments

We thank C. Schnörr for stimulating discussions and pointing us to density estimation methods in Kernel space.

References

1. D. Bartholomew. *Latent Variable Models and Factor Analysis*. Charles Griffin & Co. Ltd., London, 1987.
2. N. Belhumeur, J. Hespanha, and D. Kriegman. Eigenfaces vs. Fisherfaces: Recognition using Class Specific Linear Projection. *IEEE Transactions on Pattern Analysis and Machine Intelligence*, 19(7):711–720, July 1997.
3. D. Cremers, T. Kohlberger, and C. Schnörr. Nonlinear Shape Statistics in Mumford–Shah based Segmentation. In *ECCV 2002*, to appear, 2002.
4. A.P. Dempster, N.M. Laird, and D.B. Rubin. Maximum Likelihood from Incomplete Data via the EM Algorithm. *Journal of the Royal Statistical Society, Series B (Methodological)*, 39(1):1–38, 1977.
5. Z. Ghahramani and G. Hinton. The EM algorithm for Mixtures of Factor Analyzers. Technical Report CFG–TR–96j–1, Dept. of Computer Science,University of Toronto, February 1997.
6. Y. Keselman and S. Dickinson. Generic Model Abstraction from Examples. In *Proceedings of the IEEE Conference on Computer Vision and Pattern Recognition*, 2001.
7. F. Mattern. Probabilistische Hauptachsentransformation zur generischen Objekterkennung. Technical report, Diploma thesis, Lehrstuhl für Mustererkennung (Informatik 5), Universität Erlangen–Nürnberg, 2001.
8. G.G. Medioni and A.R.J. Francois. 3–D Structure for Generic Object Recognition. In *Computer Vision and Image Analysis*, Volume 1, International Conference on Pattern Recognition, pages 30–37, 2000.
9. H. Murase and S. Nayar. Visual Learning and Recognition of 3–D Objects from Appearance. *International Journal of Computer Vision*, 14:5–24, 1995.
10. R. C. Nelson and A. Selinger. Large–Scale Tests of a Keyed, Appearance–Based 3-D Object Recognition System. *Vision Research*, 38(15–16), August 1998.
11. S. Nene, S. Nayar, and H. Murase. Columbia Object Image Library (COIL–20). Technical Report CUCS–005–96, Dept. fo Computer Science, Columbia University, 1996.
12. B. Schölkopf, A. Smola, and K.-R. Müller. Nonlinear Component Analysis as a Kernel Eigenvalue Problem. *Neural Computation*, 10:1299–1319, 1998.
13. M. E. Tipping and C. M. Bishop. Mixtures of Probabilistic Principal Component Analysers. *Neural Computation*, 11(2):443–482, 1999.

Skin Patch Detection in Real-World Images

Hannes Kruppa, Martin A. Bauer, and Bernt Schiele

Perceptual Computing and Computer Vision Group
ETH Zurich, Switzerland
http://www.vision.ethz.ch/pccv
{kruppa, bauerm, schiele}@inf.ethz.ch

Abstract. While human skin is relatively easy to detect in controlled environments, detection in uncontrolled settings such as in consumer digital photographs is generally hard. Algorithms need to robustly deal with variations in lighting, color resolution, and imaging noise. This paper proposes a simple generative skin patch model combining shape and color information. The model is parametric and represents the spatial arrangement of skin pixels as compact elliptical regions. Its parameters are estimated by maximizing the mutual information between the model-generated skin pixel distribution and the distribution of skin color as observed in the image. The core of this work is an empirical evaluation on a database of 653 consumer digital photographs. In addition, we investigate the potential of combining our skin detector with state-of-the-art appearance-based face detectors.

1 Introduction and Related Work

Skin detection plays an important role for example in tracking people, in filtering out adult web images, or in facilitating human-computer interaction. We are especially interested in skin detection as a cue for detecting people in real-world photographs. The main challenge is to make skin detection robust to the large variations in appearance that can occur. Skin appearance changes in color and shape and is often affected by occlusion (clothing, hair, eye glasses etc.). Moreover, changes in intensity, color and location of light sources affect skin appearance. Other objects within the scene may cast shadows or reflect additional light and so forth. Imaging noise can appear as speckles of skin-like color. Finally, there are many other objects in the world which are easily confused with skin: certain types of wood, copper, sand as well as clothes often have skin-like colors.

Physics-based approaches to skin color modeling [12] use spectrographic analysis to derive a physical reflectance model of skin. Skin reflectance is usually described by its thin surface layer, the epidermis, and a thicker layer underneath, the dermis. The light absorption in the dermis is mainly due to the ingredients in the blood such as haemoglobin, bilirubin and beta-carotene which are basically the same for all skin types. However, skin color is mainly determined by the epidermis transmittance which depends on the *dopa-melanin* concentration and hence varies among human races [12]. Skin color appearance can then be represented by using this model and by incorporating camera and light source parameters. In uncontrolled scenes, however, these parameters are not known.

Its rotation and scale invariance make skin color especially useful for real-time tracking systems. However, gesture trackers for human-computer interaction rely on

L. Van Gool (Ed.): DAGM 2002, LNCS 2449, pp. 109–116, 2002.

controlled lighting conditions [11]. In other scenarios like outdoor surveillance, potential illumination changes have to be addressed. Recently, approaches have been proposed which automatically adapt skin color model parameters by analyzing color differences of consecutive images [10]. Assuming motion continuity these approaches can deal with gradual changes in ambient light. They do not apply to still images though.

One of the most comprehensive accounts on skin color models for uncontrolled still images is due to Jones and Rehg [6]. In their case, a skin color model is learned from a huge collection of web images. A Bayesian classifier for skin color is then constructed which also incorporates a model of the non-skin class. The approach relies on color alone. Fleck and Forsyth [4] and Wang et al. [13] propose systems for filtering adult images by finding naked people. In the approach by Fleck and Forsyth a combination of low-level image filters is used combining skin color and texture features.

In this paper, we introduce a generative skin patch model combining color and shape information (section 2) and present results of a large empirical evaluation (section 3). As today's state-of-the-art face detectors do not make use of skin concepts, we also investigate the potential of combining skin and face detection in section 4. Finally, section 5 draws conclusions and outlines possible directions for future research.

2   Approach: A Generative Skin Patch Model

Rather than relying on skin color alone the proposed approach combines color information with shape constraints to locate skin patches. Allowable shapes of skin are embodied by a generative skin patch model. The shape parameters are estimated by maximizing the mutual information between the model-generated skin pixel distribution and the distribution of skin color as observed in the image. In the current implementation the skin patch model is represented as an unrotated ellipse with state variables $\gamma = (x_c, y_c, w, h)$ where (x_c, y_c) denotes the center and (w, h) the dimensions. Ellipses as shape primitives are frequently used for modeling the human body, in particular the head, arms and limbs [15]. The shape model is denoted by S and is employed by the algorithm for generating a distribution $p(\boldsymbol{x} = skin|\gamma)$, which for each image location $\boldsymbol{x} = (x, y)$ represents the probability that the corresponding pixel belongs to a skin patch. The model $p(\boldsymbol{x} = skin|\gamma)$ is represented by a piecewise constant function

$$S(\gamma) = S(x_c, y_c, w, h) = \begin{cases} \frac{1}{1+exp^{-a}} & : \frac{(x-x_c)^2}{w^2} \pm \frac{(y-y_c)^2}{h^2} \leq 1 \\ 0 & : \ else \end{cases}$$

where the parameter a in the logistic function (c.f. [1]) is increased towards the boundary to smooth out probabilities. Thus the proposed generative model embodies two intuitive properties about the spatial distribution of skin color: First, skin is distinguished as a contiguous region and second, skin often appears in oval shapes. Restricting the model to an unrotated oval introduces a bias for facial skin.

The core idea of the algorithm is to derive the parameters of S from a complementary cue, a skin color model C, thus combining shape and color information. We employ a Gaussian chrominance model with parameters θ which is trained from data using Maximum Likelihood Estimation. This color model has been shown to work for different skin complexions of the different human races [5]. At this stage one can also consider the use of color constancy techniques such as [3]. This implies the standard trade-off between discrimination and invariance. Even though not reported here our experience suggests that simple color models are well suited to the task especially when enough training data is available. Similar observations have been reported in [6]. For aligning shape and color information we now maximize the mutual information between $p(x = skin|\gamma)$ and $p(x = skin|\theta)$ searching the parameter space of γ:

$$\arg \max_{\gamma} I(S(\gamma), C(\theta)) \tag{1}$$

Maximizing mutual information is an alignment technique which maximizes statistical dependence. The concept has been used successfully in several vision and machine learning tasks e.g. for feature selection [2], for audio-visual data association [8] as well as for robust registration [14] which probably comes closest to the way it is used in this paper. In the following two section we will present qualitative and quantitative evidence that this alignment technique is robust to noise and discontinuities typical of real-world imaging. There is a direct relationship between mutual information and the Kullback-Leibler (KL) divergence. The KL-divergence between a probability mass function $p(u, v)$ and a distinct probability mass function $q(u, v)$ is defined as:

$$D(p(u,v)||q(u,v)) = \sum_{u_i, y_v} p(u_i, v_j) \cdot \log \frac{p(u_i, v_j)}{q(u_i, v_j)} \tag{2}$$

This relative entropy or information divergence measure is commonly used as a pseudo distance between two distributions. By defining $q(u, v) = p(u) \cdot p(v)$ the mutual information can be written as the KL-divergence between $p(u, v)$ and $p(u) \cdot p(v)$:

$$I(U; V) = D(p(u,v)||p(u) \cdot p(v)) \tag{3}$$

Mutual information therefore measures the "distance" between the joint distribution $p(u, v)$ and the product distribution $q(u, v) = p(u) \cdot p(v)$, which are identical if and only if they are independent.

Instead of resorting to stochastic parameter sampling as in [14] we derive a deterministic form of gradient ascent in mutual information space for efficiently estimating γ: The parameter space is traversed using an adaptive local grid which is succinctly centered over maxima of $p(x = skin|\theta)$ starting at the global maximum of this distribution and continuing at other maxima in descending order. At each iteration the algorithm follows the steepest gradient adapting the center point (x_c, y_c) or the dimensions (w, h). Typically, convergence is reached in about 5 to 10 iterations. Once the algorithm has converged γ represents a single computed skin region hypothesis.

For generating multiple skin patch hypotheses the skin distribution $p(x = skin|\theta)$ is then reshaped. More specifically, after a hypothesis has been formed the associated region is first excluded from the original distribution and after, the scheme is repeated. The value of mutual information is used to decide if a hypothesis is valid and if the search is to be continued. After a predefined number of examined hypotheses with a low mutual information value, the algorithm stops.

3   Experiments: Skin Detection

To evaluate the performance of the proposed skin detector we first examine retrieval and precision rates *on the pixel level* similar to [6]. In particular, the performance is compared to the naive approach using only color.

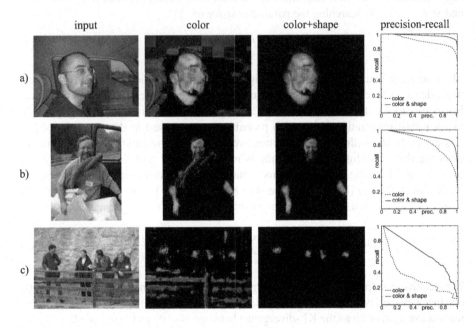

Fig. 1. The first two columns show input images and corresponding skin color distributions. Column three shows the hypotheses generated by the proposed skin detector combining color and shape information. The right column shows precision-recall curves, comparing the purely color based approach to the proposed scheme. See text for a detailed discussion of these examples.

The whole test database contains 653 color jpeg images. For skin detection these have been downsampled from a 3.3 megapixel resolution to 150 by 100 pixels. From a randomly chosen subset of 30 images, 53978 skin pixels where labeled manually. The fotos cover a wide range of real-world situations both indoor and outdoor (meetings, parties, ski-trips, beach scenes etc.). Figure 1 shows several representative example images. Input images are shown in the first column while the second column shows the distribution of skin color $p(x = skin|\theta)$. Column three shows the output of the proposed skin detector. Here only those color probabilities are shown which have been classified by the proposed detector as being part of a skin region. The last column in these figures shows precision-recall curves of skin pixel detection as a function over a detection threshold. Two curves are shown for each image: one is based on evaluating color alone (dotted line) the other (solid line) plots the results of the proposed detector.

Figure 1a) shows many false positives in color (car interior) as well as jpeg-artefacts which appear as block structures in the upper part of the image. As can be seen here, lossy compression used in image formats like jpeg cause discontinuities in $p(x = skin|\theta)$. Note that a connected-component approach would have difficulties to separate the full head from the car interior. With the proposed approach the equal error rate is improved from 85% to 95% in this example.

Figure 1b) shows a 15% increase in equal error rate. In this image the shape model separates out the skin portions from the red-colored hose which is wrapped around the person's shoulder. Note again that a connected-component approach would have difficulties to separate the hose from the person's face. The equal error rate is improved here from 70% to 85%. The advantages of the proposed detector become most evident as the amount of skin-like color in the image increases. In example 1c) the detector improves the equal error rate by 25%. In this image a wooden fence causes numerous false positive detections. Wood is a well-known distractor [6] which frequently occurs in both indoor and outdoor situations. The wooden fence and all remaining false positives are removed by the detector. Altogether, an equal error rate of 60% is reached while the color-based approach attains only 35%. A few false negatives occur from people's hands in the image because they hold directly on the wooden bars which makes hands and wood indiscernible for the algorithm.

While figure 1 shows only a small selection for lack of space, these images are representative for the obtained results on all images[1]. These results clearly demonstrate the advantage of integrating color and shape information. The shape constraints embodied by the skin patch model successfully eliminate a substantial amount of false positives which leads to improved detection performance. In particular, the detector proves to work robustly in unconstrained real-world photographs.

4   Experiments: Skin Detection vs. Face Detection

Unlike face recognition (i.e. subject identification), *face detection* is a classification problem concerned with locating all faces within arbitrary backgrounds. An extensive survey on face detection with more than 150 references appeared only recently [16]. Two state-of-the-art face detectors are due to Rowley et al. [7] and Schneiderman et al. [9]. Both approaches are appearance-based and only use intensity information. Rowley's neural network approach can handle in-plane rotations of faces but not out-of-plane rotations (profiles). However, profiles can be expected to occur much more often in photographs. To our knowledge Schneiderman's Bayesian face classifier is still one of the best systems in terms of detection performance. Since it is still the only system to support profile views it may even be *the* best face detector available today. Since both systems model only specific portions of the appearance space they are vulnerable to the many variations that occur in the real-world. Attempts to model the complete appearance space can be expected to fail because of degrading discriminance.

Although a face can be regarded as a special case of a skin patch, neither of the two face detectors makes use of skin concepts. Yet, from an algorithmic viewpoint, the proposed skin detector has at least three substantial advantages over face detectors: it is faster, it works at smaller resolutions and, most importantly, it is more robust to

---

[1] Results on the full data are available on the web (URL blinded to preserve anonimity of the authors)

Rowley   Schneiderman   Skin Detector

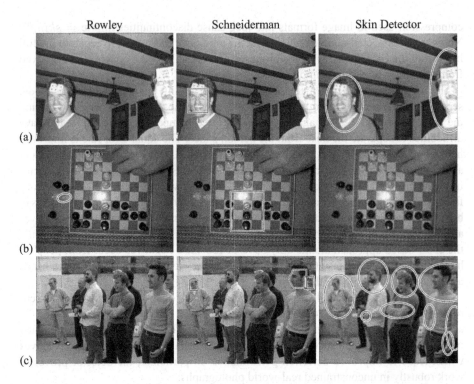

Fig. 2. Characterization of appearance-based face detection vs. skin detection. The first two columns show the face detection results of Rowley and Schneiderman, row three shows the skin finder's output. These examples illustrate characteristic effects of (a) occlusion and facial expression, (b) face-like distractors, (c) crowds

variation in appearance. In addition, this section also presents empirical evidence that the skin detector is robust to lighting changes.

Appearance based face detectors need to search all image locations at multiple scales. In contrast, the skin detector examines only skin colored regions at one scale which results in significantly faster execution. It also requires less image support allowing to detect very small skin patches. Figure 2 shows a few examples showing the outputs of the two face detectors and the proposed skin detector. Row 2(a) illustrates the effect of occlusion and rotational variation. Both face detectors fail on the right face since they model the appearance of a complete face only. Rowley's approach misses the other face, too, because the particular facial appearance is not part of the model. Both faces are detected by the skin-based approach. Since the proposed scheme allows for discontinuities, it also works when people wear beards, piercings or glasses. Face-like distractors pose additional challenges. For instance, checkered surfaces are likely to be confused with facial features like mouth, nose and eyes. This often occurs with shirts and other clothes, in figure 2(b) it occurs with a chess board. Note that in this example, the skin detector misses the chess player's hand. This is because the current implementation only allows for unrotated elliptical shapes. Row 2(c) shows a more complex scene with a crowd of

Table 1. A quantitative account of appearance-based face detection (Schneiderman, Rowley) and its combination with the proposed skin detector. Results are from a test set of 653 real-world consumer photographs containing 2243 faces. Here, Schneiderman's scheme compares favorably to Rowley's. When combining Schneiderman's face detector with the proposed skin finder, recall (OR-combination) or precision (AND-combination) is leveraged to above 90% in both cases.

	true positive	false negative	false positive	precision	recall
Schneiderman	387	305	165	70.1%	55.9%
skin detector OR Schneiderman	639	53	1458	30.5%	92.3%
skin detector AND Schneiderman	263	429	12	95.6%	38.0%
Rowley	150	542	94	60.5%	27.7%
skin detector OR Rowley	562	130	1397	40.2%	81.2%
skin detector AND Rowley	103	589	2	98.1%	14.9%

people. Faces are in profile view, some of them are only partially visible. Rowley has no detections, Schneiderman returns three faces. The skin detector retrieves all six faces and some additional skin regions.

Next we quantitatively compared the performance of the combined scheme to the individual face detectors on all 653 images containing 2243 faces. For evaluating Schneiderman's approach we uploaded our database to the on-line demo[2]. Rowley provided a copy of his system. The results are very promising. The skin finder returned 74.4% of all faces, whereas Schneiderman's face detector has a recall rate of 55.9% and Rowley's scheme 27.7%. That is, the skin detector's recall rate in detecting faces is almost 20% higher than Schneiderman's algorithm and 47% higher than Rowley's approach. As can be expected we found complementary results for precision. Since the proposed skin detector is designed to return skin region in general, not just faces, its precision is only 28.3%. Rowley's scheme reaches 60.5% and Schneiderman 70.1% on this data set. As performance of skin and face detectors turned out to be *complementary* we examined their combinations. When counting all faces found by either Rowley's scheme OR the skin detector the recall rate is boosted to 81.2% (versus an initial rate of 27.7%). Precision is raised to 98.1% (versus 60.5%) when counting only those faces found by both detectors. Results from combining the skin detector with Schneiderman's approach are equally encouraging: Precision is as high as 95.6% (versus 70.1%) which is comparable to the combined performance using Rowley's approach. Recall is raised to 92.3% using a logical OR combination. This is even higher than the combination with Rowley's scheme. These results indicate that the combination of skin and face concepts can lead to a substantially better face detection performance. Depending on the type of combination Schneiderman's face detector in combination with the proposed skin finder reaches precision or recall rates above 90%.

5   Conclusion and Future Work

This paper proposes a skin patch detector integrating color and shape information. An empirical evaluation of the detector on real-world photographs yields two main results:

---

[2] http://vasc.ri.cmu.edu/cgi-bin/demos/findface.cgi

First, there is a clear benefit in modeling skin as approximately contiguous regions of certain colors *and* shapes rather than relying on color alone. In particular, the proposed detector proves to work robustly in unconstrained real-world photographs. Second, appearance-based face detectors should be combined with skin detection for their *complementary* strengths and weaknesses. In future work we aim to analyze skin specific specularities and to encode this information within the generative model.

References

1. Christopher M. Bishop, editor. *Neural Networks for Pattern Recognition*. Oxford University Press, 1995.
2. A. Colmenrez and T. Huang. Face detection with informationbased maximum discrimination. In *CVPR*, pages 782–787, 1997., 1997.
3. G.D. Finlayson, B.V. Funt, and K. Barnard. Color constancy under varying illumination. In *ICCV'95*, pages 720–725, 1995.
4. Margaret M. Fleck, David A. Forsyth, and Chris Bregler. Finding naked people. In *ECCV (2)*, pages 593–602, 1996.
5. Hideo Fukamachi Jean-Christophe Terrillon, Mahdad Shirazi and Shigeru Akamatsu. Skin chrominance models and chrominance spaces for the automatic detection of human faces in color images. In *Proceedings of the Fourth IEEE International Conference on Automatic Face and Gesture Recognition*, March 2000.
6. Michael J. Jones and James M. Rehg. Statistical color models with application to skin detection. In *CVPR*, pages 274–280, 1999.
7. H. Rowley, S. Baluja, and T. Kanade. Neural network-based face detection. *PAMI*, 20(1):23–38, 1998.
8. D. Roy and A. Pentland. Learning words from natural audio-visual input. In *International Conference of Spoken Language Processing*, December 1998.
9. H. Schneiderman and T. Kanade. A statistical method for 3d object detection applied to faces and cars. In *CVPR*, June 2000.
10. Leonid Sigal and Stan Sclaroff. Estimation and prediction of evolving color distributions for skin segmentation under varying illumination. In *CVPR*, 2000.
11. T. Starner and A. Pentland. Real-time american sign language recognition from video using hidden markov models. In *SCV95*, page 5B Systems and Applications, 1995.
12. Moritz Stoerring, Hans J. Andersen, and Erik Granum. Skin colour detection under changing lighting conditions. In *7th International Symposium on Intelligent Robotic Systems '99*, pages 187–195, July 1999.
13. James Ze Wang, Jia Li, Gio Wiederhold, and Oscar Firschein. System for screening objectionable images using daubechies' wavelets. In *International Workshop on Interactiv Distributed Multimedia Systems and Telecommunication Services*, pages 20–30, 1997.
14. W.M. Wells III, P. Viola, H. Atsumi, S. Nakajima, and R. Kikinis. Multi–modal volume registration by maximization of mutual information. *Medical Image Analysis*, 1(1):35–52, march 1996.
15. Christopher Richard Wren, Ali Azarbayejani, Trevor Darrell, and Alex Pentland. Pfinder: Real-time tracking of the human body. *PAMI*, 19(7):780–785, 1997.
16. Ming-Hsuan Yang, David Kriegman, and Narendra Ahuja. Detecting faces in images: A survey. *PAMI*, 24(1):34–58, January 2002.

Logarithmic Tapering Graph Pyramid*

Yll Haxhimusa[1], Roland Glantz[2], Maamar Saib[1],
Georg Langs[1], and Walter G. Kropatsch[1]

[1] Pattern Recognition and Image Processing Group 183/2
Institute for Computer Aided Automation
Vienna University of Technology
Favoritenstrasse 9, A-1040 Vienna, Austria
[2] Dipartimento di Informatica
Università di Ca' Foscari di Venezia
Via Torino 155, 30172 Mestre (VE), Italy

Abstract. We present a new method to determine contraction kernels for the construction of graph pyramids. The new method works with undirected graphs and yields a reduction factor of at least 2.0. This means that with our method the number of vertices in the subgraph induced by any set of contractible edges is reduced to half or less by a single parallel contraction. Our method yields better reduction factors than the stochastic decimation algorithm, in all tests. The lower bound of the reduction factor becomes crucial with large images.

1 Introduction

In a regular image pyramid (for an overview see [KLB99]) the number of pixels at any level l, is r times higher than the number of pixels at the next reduced level $l + 1$. The so called reduction factor r is greater than one and it is the same for all levels l. If s denotes the number of pixels in an image I, the number of new levels on top of I amounts to $log_r(s)$. Thus, the regular image pyramid may be an efficient structure to access image objects in a top-down process.

However, regular image pyramids are confined to globally defined sampling grids and lack shift invariance [BCR90]. In [MMR91, JM92] it was shown how these drawbacks can be avoided by irregular image pyramids, the so called adaptive pyramids. Each level represents a partition of the pixel set into cells, i.e. connected subsets of pixels. The construction of an irregular image pyramid is iteratively local [Mee89, Jol02]:

- the cells have no information about their global position.
- the cells are connected only to (direct) neighbors.
- the cells cannot distinguish the spatial positions of the neighbors.

On the base level (level 0) of an irregular image pyramid the cells represent single pixels and the neighborhood of the cells is defined by the 4-connectivity of

---

* This paper has been supported by the Austrian Science Fund under grants P14445-MAT and P14662-INF

L. Van Gool (Ed.): DAGM 2002, LNCS 2449, pp. 117–124, 2002.

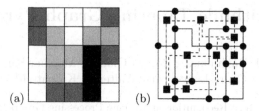

Fig. 1. (a) Partition of pixel set into cells. (b) Representation of the cells and their neighborhood relations by a dual pair $(\overline{G}, G)$ of plane graphs.

the pixels. A cell on level $l + 1$ (parent) is a union of neighboring cells on level l (children). This union is controlled by so called contraction kernels. Every parent computes its values independently of other cells on the same level. This implies that an image pyramid is built in $O[log(image\_diameter)]$ time. For more in depth on the subject see the book of Jolion [JR94]. Neighborhoods on level $l + 1$, are derived from neighborhoods on level l. Two cells c_1 and c_2 are neighbors if there exist pixels p_1 in c_1 and p_2 in c_2 such that p_1 and p_2 are 4-neighbors, Figure 1(a). We assume that on each level $l + 1$ ($l \geq 0$) there exists at least one cell not contained in level l. In particular, there exists a highest level h. Furthermore, we restrict ourselves to irregular pyramids with an apex, i.e. level h contains one cell.

In this paper we represent the levels as dual pairs $(\overline{G_l}, G_l)$ of plane graphs $\overline{G_l}$ and G_l, Figure 1(b). The vertices of $\overline{G_l}$ represent the cells on level l and the edges of $\overline{G_l}$ represent the neighborhood relations of the cells on level l, depicted with square vertices and dashed edges in Figure 1(b). The edges of G_l represent the borders of the cells on level l, depicted with solid lines in Figure 1(b), possibly including so called pseudo edges needed to represent the neighborhood relation to a cells completely surrounded by a cell. Finally, the vertices of G_l, the circles in Figure 1(b), represent meeting points of at least three edges from G_l, solid lines in Figure 1(b). The sequence $(\overline{G_l}, G_l)$, $0 \leq l \leq h$ is called (dual) graph pyramid.

The aim of this paper is to combine the advantage of regular pyramids (logarithmic tapering) with the advantages of irregular graph pyramids (their purely local construction and shift invariance). The aim is reached by exchanging the selection method for contraction kernels proposed in [Mee89] by another iteratively local method that now guarantees a reduction factor of 2.0. Experiments with both selection methods show that:

- the old method does not lead to logarithmic tapering graph pyramids, as opposed to our method, i.e. the reduction factors of graph pyramids built by the old method can get arbitrarily close to 1.0.
- the sizes of the receptive fields from the new method are much more uniform.

Not only stochastic decimation [Mee89], but also connected component analysis [KM95] gains from the new method.

The plan of the paper is as follows. In Section 2 we recall the main idea of the stochastic pyramid algorithm and in Section 2.2 we see that graph pyramids from maximal independent vertex sets may have a very small reduction factor. We propose a new method in Section 3, which guarantees a reduction factor of 2.0.

2   Maximal Independent Vertex Set

In the following the iterated local construction of the (stochastic) irregular image pyramid in [Mee89] is described in the language of graph pyramids. The main idea is to first calculate a so called *maximal independent vertex set*[1] [Chr75]. Let $\overline{V_l}$ and $\overline{E_l}$ denote the vertex set and the edge set of $\overline{G_l}$, respectively and let $\iota(\cdot)$ be the mapping from an edge to its set of end vertices. The neighborhood $\Gamma_l(\overline{v})$ of a vertex $\overline{v} \in \overline{V_l}$ is defined by

$$\Gamma_l(\overline{v}) = \{\overline{v}\} \cup \{\overline{w} \in \overline{V_l} \mid \exists \overline{e} \in \overline{E_l} \text{ such that } \overline{v}, \overline{w} \in \iota(\overline{e})\}.$$

A subset $\overline{W_l}$ of $\overline{V_l}$ is called maximal independent vertex set if:

1. $\overline{w_1} \notin \Gamma_l(\overline{w_2})$ for all $\overline{w_1}, \overline{w_2} \in \overline{W_l}$,
2. for all $\overline{v} \in \overline{V_l}$ there exists $\overline{w} \in \overline{W_l}$ such that $\overline{v} \in \Gamma_l(\overline{w})$.

An example of a maximal independent vertex set is shown with black vertices in Figure 2(a), the arrows indicate a corresponding collection of contraction kernels.

2.1   Maximal Independent Vertex Set Algorithm (MIS)

The maximal independent vertex set (MIS) problem was solved using heuristic in [Mee89]. The number of iterations to complete maximal independent set converges in most of the cases very fast, so called iterations for correction [Mee89]. MIS may be generated as follows.

1. Mark every element of $\overline{V_l}$ as *candidate*.
2. Iterate the following two steps as long as there are candidates:
   (a) Assign random numbers to the candidates of $\overline{V_l}$.
   (b) Determine the candidates whose random numbers are larger than the random numbers of all neighboring candidates and mark them as *member* (of the maximal independent set) and as *non-candidate*. Also mark every neighbor of every new member as *non-candidate*.
3. In each neighborhood of a vertex that is not a member there will now be a member. Let each non-member choose its neighboring member, say the one with the maximal random number (we assume that no two random numbers are equal).

---

[1] also called maximal stable set; we distinct maximal from maximum independent set, which construction is NP-complete.

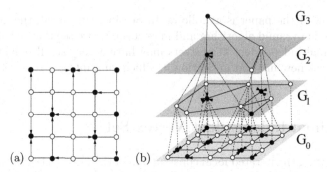

Fig. 2. (a) Maximal independent vertex set. (b) A graph pyramid from maximal independent vertex set.

The assignment of the non-members to their members determines a collection of *contraction kernels*: each non-member is contracted toward its member and all contractions can be done in a single parallel step. In Figure 2(a) the contractions are indicated by arrows. A graph pyramid from MIS can be seen in Figure 2(b), where G_0, G_1, etc. represent graphs on different levels of the pyramid. Note that we remove parallel edges and self-loops that emerge from the contractions, if they are not needed to encode inclusion of regions by other regions (in the example of Figure 2(b) we do not need loops nor parallel edges). This can be done by the dual graph contraction algorithm [Kro95].

2.2   Experiments with MIS

Uniformly distributed random numbers are given to vertices in the base graphs. We generated 1000 graphs, on top of which we built stochastic graph pyramids. In our experiments we used graphs of sizes 10000 and 40000 nodes, which correspond to image sizes 100×100 and 200×200 pixels, respectively. Figure 3 summarizes result of the first 100 of 1000 tests. Data in Table 1 were derived using graphs of size 200×200 nodes with 1000 experiments. We extract these parameters, the height of the pyramid, the maximum and the mean of the degree of vertices [2], and the number of iteration for correction to complete maximal independent set for any graph in the contraction process. We average these values on the whole data set. The degree of the vertex is of importance because directly related to the memory costs for the graph's representation [Jol02].

The number of levels needed to reduce the graph at the base level (level 0) to an apex (top of the pyramid) are given in Figure 3(a),(b). The vertical axis indicates the number of nodes on the levels indicated by the horizontal axis. The slopes of the lines correspond to the reduction factors. From Figure 3(a),(b) we see that the height of the pyramid cannot be guaranteed to be logarithmic, except for some good cases. In the worst case the pyramid had 22 levels for the 100×100, respectively 41 levels for the 200×200 node graph. In these

---

[2] the number of edges incident to a vertex

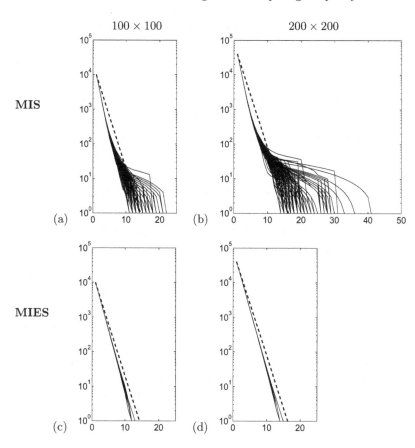

Fig. 3. Comparing MIS and MIES. Number of vertices in levels of MIS and MIES pyramids. The base levels are rectangular grid graphs containing 100×100 and 200×200 vertices . Dashed lines represent the theoretical reduction factor of 2.0.

cases we have a very poor reduction factor. A poor reduction factor is likely, as can be seen in Figure 3(a),(b), especially when the images are large. This is due to the evolution of larger and larger variations between the vertex degrees in the contracted graphs (Table 1). The absolute maximum vertex degree was 148. The *a priori* probability of a vertex being the local maximum dependents on its neighborhood. The larger the neighborhood the smaller is the *a priori* probability that a vertex will survive. The number of iterations necessary for correction are the same as reported by [Mee89](Table 1 $\mu(\#iter) = 2.95$)).

To summarize, a constant reduction factor cannot be guaranteed.

3   Maximum Independent Edge Set

In the following we aim at a collection C of contraction kernels in a plane graph $\overline{G}$ such that

- each vertex of $\overline{G}$ is contained in exactly one kernel of C, and
- each kernel C contains at least two vertices.

The contraction of all kernels in C will reduce the number of vertices to half or less.

3.1   Maximum Independent Edge Set Algorithm (MIES)

We start with independent *edge* sets or *matchings*, i.e. edge sets in which no pair of edges has a common end vertex. The maximal independent edge set (MIES), C is done in three steps.

1. Find a maximal matching M of edges in $\overline{G}$.
2. M is enlarged to a set M^+ that induces a spanning subgraph of $\overline{G}$.
3. M^+ is reduced to a subset defining C.

A maximal matching of $\overline{G}$ is equivalent to a maximal independent vertex set on the edge graph of $\overline{G}$ [Die97, Chr75] . Thus, a maximal matching may be determined by the iterated local process as used in MIS algorithm.

Note that M is only required to be maximal, i.e. the edge set M cannot be enlarged by another edge from $\overline{G}$ without loosing independence. A maximal matching M is not necessarily maximum: there may be a matching M' (Figure 4(b)) that contains more edges than M (Figure 4(a)). The collection of contraction kernels defined by a maximal matching M may include kernels with a single vertex. Let v denote such an isolated vertex (isolated from M) and choose a non-self-loop e that has v as an end vertex. Since M is maximal, the end vertex $w \neq v$ of e belongs to an edge that is contained in the matching. Let M^+ denote the set of edges that are in M or that are chosen to connect isolated vertices to M.

The subgraph of $\overline{G}$ that is induced by M^+ spans $\overline{G}$ and its connected components are trees of depth one or two (Figure 4(c)). In the second case, the tree can be separated in two trees of depths one by removing the central edge $\in M$, indicated by the crosses in Figure 4(c). Still, each vertex of $\overline{G}$ belongs to a tree, now of depth one. The arrows in Figure 4(d) indicate possible directions of contractions. Since each vertex of $\overline{G}$ is now contained in a non-trivial contraction kernel, we proved the following.

Proposition 1 (Reduction factor of MIES at least 2.0). *The MIES algorithm yields contraction kernels for parallel contractions with a reduction factor of at least 2.0.*

Note that in case of kernels with more than one edge the directions within the kernel cannot be chosen independently of one another. This is why the proposed method cannot be extended to applications in which there are a priori

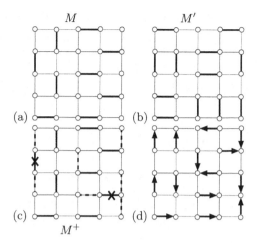

Fig. 4. (a) M: a maximal matching. (b) M': a matching with more edges than in (a). (c) M^+: the matching from (a) enlarged by connecting formerly isolated vertices to the maximal matching. (d) trees of depth two split into trees of depth one.

constraints on the directions of the contractions. However, the proposed method works for the stochastic case (no preconditions on edges to be contracted) and for connected component analysis, where the attributes of the end vertices are required to be identical.

3.2 Experiments with MIES

The same set of 1000 graphs was used to test MIES. The numbers of levels needed to reduce the graph on the base level to an apex of the pyramid are shown in Figure 3 (c),(d). Again the vertical axis indicates the number of vertices in the levels indicated by the horizontal axis. The experiments show that the reduction factor of MIES is indeed never smaller than the theoretical lower bound 2.0 (indicated by the dashed line in Figure 3(c),(d). MIES is more stable than MIS, as can be seen in Figure 3(c),(d) the variance of the slopes is smaller than in case of MIS, Figure 3(a),(b).

In Table 1 are given the height of the pyramid; the maximum vertex degree; the mean of vertex degree; and the number of iteration for correction averaged over the whole data set. The μ and σ of the height of the pyramid is smaller for MIES than for MIS. The same observation is also for maximal degree of vertices. The number of iterations for correction is higher for MIES (4.06) than for MIS (2.95). The two methods lead to almost the same mean vertex degree. The dependence of the data on this value seems to be little in both cases.

Table 1. Comparison of MIS and MIES.

Process	$\mu(height)$	$\sigma(height)$	$\mu(max)$	$\sigma(max)$	$\mu(mean)$	$\sigma(mean)$	$\mu(\#iter)$	$\sigma(\#iter)$
MIS	20.78	5.13	70.69	23.88	4.84	0.23	2.95	0.81
MIES	14.01	0.10	11.74	0.71	4.78	0.45	4.06	1.17

4 Conclusion and Outlook

Experiments with (stochastic) irregular image pyramids using maximal independent vertex sets (MIS) showed that reduction factor could not be bound as the image get larger. After an initial phase of strong reduction, the reduction decreases dramatically. This is due to the evolution of larger and larger variations between the vertex degrees in the contracted graphs. To overcome this problem we proposed a method (MIES) based on matchings which guarantees a reduction factor of 2.0. As in the case of independent vertex sets, the method based on matchings constrains the directions of the contractions. Future work will focus on improving the reduction factors also for the case of directional constraints i.e. directed edges. First experiments with a modification of the algorithm that addresses these constraints show comparable results to MIES.

References

BCR90.   M. Bister, J. Cornelis, and Azriel Rosenfeld. A critical view of pyramid segmentation algorithms. *Pattern Recognition Letters*, 11(9):605–617, 1990.

Chr75.   N. Christofides. *Graph theory - an algorithmic approach*. Academic Press, New York, 1975.

Die97.   Reinhard Diestel. *Graph Theory*. Springer, New York, 1997.

JM92.   Jean-Michel Jolion and Annick Montanvert. The adaptive pyramid, a framework for 2D image analysis. *Computer Vision, Graphics, and Image Processing: Image Understanding*, 55(3):pp.339–348, May 1992.

Jol02.   Jean-Michel Jolion. Stochastic pyramid revisited. *Pattern Recognition Letters. To appear*, 2002.

JR94.   J.M. Jolion and Azriel Rosenfeld. *A Pyramid Framework for Early Vision*. Kluwer Academic Publishers, Dordrecht, Netherlands, 1994.

KLB99.   Walter G. Kropatsch, Aleš Leonardis, and Horst Bischof. Hierarchical, Adaptive and Robust Methods for Image Understanding. *Surveys on Mathematics for Industry*, No.9:1–47, 1999.

KM95.   Walter G. Kropatsch and Herwig Macho. Finding the structure of connected components using dual irregular pyramids. In *Cinquième Colloque DGCI*, pages 147–158. LLAIC1, Université d'Auvergne, September 1995.

Kro95.   Walter G. Kropatsch. Building Irregular Pyramids by Dual Graph Contraction. *IEE-Proc. Vision, Image and Signal Processing*, 142(6):366 – 374, 1995.

Mee89.   Peter Meer. Stochastic image pyramids. *CVGIP*, 45:269 – 294, 1989.

MMR91.   Annick Montanvert, Peter Meer, and Azriel Rosenfeld. Hierarchical image analysis using irregular tesselations. *IEEE Transactions on Pattern Analysis and Machine Intelligence*, 13(4):pp.307–316, April 1991.

A New and Efficient Algorithm for Detecting the Corners in Digital Images

Eduard Sojka

Technical University of Ostrava, tr. 17. listopadu,
708 33 Ostrava-Poruba, Czech Republic
eduard.sojka@vsb.cz

Abstract. The corners and vertices are important features in images, which are frequently used for scene analysis, stereo matching and object tracking. Many algorithms for detecting the corners have been developed up to now. In this paper, a new and efficient algorithm is presented. The probability of the event that a point belongs to the approximation of the straight segment of the isoline of brightness containing the corner candidate being tested is determined using the technique of Bayesian estimations, and then used for computing the angle between the segments. The results of the tests show that, in the sense of the successfulness of detection, the new algorithm is better than the other known algorithms that are usually used for solving the problem.

1 Introduction

The problem of detecting the corners (feature points, significant points, points of interest) is well known in digital image processing. Corner detection is often an important step in various image-understanding and scene-reconstructing systems. The corner detectors should satisfy the following criteria. (1) All the true corners and no false corners should be detected. (2) The corners should be located precisely. (3) The detectors should not be sensitive to noise in images.

With respect to its numerous practical applications, the problem of corner detection is studied intensively for approximately three decades. Many algorithms for detecting the corners have been developed up to now. They may be divided into two groups. The first group contains the algorithms that work directly with the values of brightness of images (without segmenting the images in advance), the second includes the algorithms that extract the boundaries of objects first and analyse their shapes afterwards. The algorithms from the first group, called the direct corner detectors, seem to be more significant. The algorithm we propose falls into this category too.

The direct corner detectors proposed in [1]–[5] may be regarded as very popular and widely used. The difficulty of the task, however, causes that all of them have problems in practical applications if more complicated images are to be processed, which gives the motivation for further work in the area. Several algorithms have been presented recently. Let us mention at least the work [6] as an example. Let it be pointed out that several authors reported good experience with the algorithm described in [6].

L. Van Gool (Ed.): DAGM 2002, LNCS 2449, pp. 125–132, 2002.
© Springer-Verlag Berlin Heidelberg 2002

In this paper, we present a new algorithm for detecting the corners in grey-scale images. The probability of the event that a point belongs to the approximation of the straight segment of the isoline of brightness containing the corner candidate being tested is determined using the technique of Bayesian estimations, and then used for computing the angle between the segments. The paper is organised as follows. In Section 2, we present the theoretical background of the detector. The algorithm itself is described in Section 3. In Section 4, the results of testing and comparing with other known algorithms are presented.

2   Theoretical Foundations of the Detector

We first introduce a model of corner. Let $\psi(\xi)$ be a function describing the values of brightness across the edges (Fig. 1). Let its derivative be positive everywhere with a single maximum at $\xi=0$, which is regarded as a point at which the edge is located. The edge is oriented by the rule that the higher brightness lies to the left. The corner is an intersection of two noncolinear straight edges. Let $\varphi_1, \varphi_2 \in \langle 0, 2\pi \rangle$ be the directions of the gradient of brightness along the edge that comes into the corner and the edge that comes out from the corner, respectively. We set $\mathbf{n}_i = (\cos\varphi_i, \sin\varphi_i)$, $i=1,2$. The axis of corner is a line passing through the corner point in the direction of increasing brightness and halving the angle between both edges. The corner is convex if $\mathbf{n}_1 \times \mathbf{n}_2 > 0$ (i.e., $\cos\varphi_1 \sin\varphi_2 - \sin\varphi_1 \cos\varphi_2 > 0$). The brightness in the image containing a single corner at a point C is considered to be described by the function (Fig. 1)

$$b(X) = \begin{cases} \min\{\psi(\mathbf{n}_1 \cdot (X-C)), \psi(\mathbf{n}_2 \cdot (X-C))\}, & \mathbf{n}_1 \times \mathbf{n}_2 \geq 0 \\ \max\{\psi(\mathbf{n}_1 \cdot (X-C)), \psi(\mathbf{n}_2 \cdot (X-C))\}, & \text{otherwise} \end{cases} . \tag{1}$$

Let us say that the image described by Eq. (1) is infinite. The isolines of brightness are then formed by the pairs of half-lines (Fig. 1). Along every isoline, the size of the gradient of brightness remains constant. The two half-lines along which the size of the gradient of brightness is maximal are edges. Along each half-line that is a part of an isoline, the direction of the gradient of brightness remains constant. The directions of the gradient are different at the points lying to the left and to the right of the corner axis.

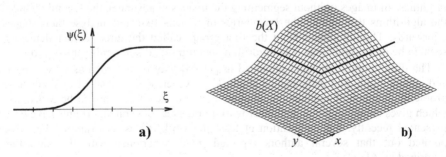

Fig. 1. The values of brightness across the edge (**a**), and the function of brightness defined by Eq. (1) at a convex corner (**b**). The *bold line* shows an isoline of brightness

Let $b(X)$, $g(X)$, $\varphi(X)$ denote the value of brightness, the size, and the direction of the gradient of brightness at X, respectively. The algorithm works with the samples of these functions. For the theoretical analysis, we assume that the value of the sample at X is equal to the value of the corresponding continuous theoretical function at X, which holds for all the mentioned functions, i.e., $b(X)$, $g(X)$, $\varphi(X)$.

Let Q be an image point, and let Ω be its certain neighbourhood. We suppose that Ω is homeomorphic to a disc. We take into account, however, that for the practical computation, Ω will be represented by a finite number of isolated points. Suppose that a certain curve is defined in Ω. With respect to the discrete representation of the image, we content ourselves with an approximation of the curve instead of its exact shape. We say that X is a point of the approximation if the curve passes through the pixel (area) that is represented by X. The point of approximation therefore lies in a certain distance from the theoretical curve. We use the term *deviation* for the distance provided with the sign indicating on which side of the curve X lies. We will denote the deviation of X by $d(X)$. The deviations of the points approximating a curve may be regarded as a random variable. Let $p_d(z)$ be its probability density.

Let the isolines of brightness be the curves of interest that are examined in Ω. Assume now that Ω contains one or more corners conforming to the model described earlier. The isolines of brightness are then formed by sequences of line segments (Fig. 2). Consider the isoline whose brightness is equal to the brightness of Q. Let X be a point of the approximation of this isoline. The difference of brightness at X (with respect to Q) is $\Delta b(X)=b(X)-b(Q)$ (we use the brief notation $\Delta b(X)$ for the difference, without stating Q explicitly). The deviation may be expressed in the form $d(X)=\psi^{-1}(b(X)) - \psi^{-1}(b(Q))$. The difference of brightness at the points approximating the isoline may be regarded as a random variable. Let $\mathrm{Br}Q$ denote the event that a point belongs to the approximation of the isoline whose brightness is $b(Q)$. We introduce the conditional probability density, denoted by $p_{\Delta b}(z|\mathrm{Br}Q)$, of the difference of brightness. In practical computation, the values of $p_{\Delta b}(z|\mathrm{Br}Q)$ will only be needed for $z=\Delta b(X)$. An easy computation [7] yields the result

$$p_{\Delta b}\left(\Delta b(X)|\ \mathrm{Br}Q\right)=\frac{p_d\left(d(X)\right)}{g(X)} \ . \tag{2}$$

Consider now an isoline segment lying on a straight line passing through Q (i.e., the segment aiming at Q, Fig. 2). The isoline itself containing the segment need not necessarily pass through Q. Let X be a point of the approximation of the segment being considered, let p_X denote the straight line perpendicular to the direction $\varphi(X)$ and passing through X (Fig. 2). We orient p_X by the same rule as that one used for the edges (the rule is applied at X). Let $h(X)$ be the deviation of Q from p_X. We define $h(X)$ to be negative for the points lying to the left of p_X. The deviation h determined for the approximation points of a segment of an isoline may be regarded as a random variable. We use $\mathrm{Dir}Q$ to denote the event that a segment of an isoline aims at the point Q, and we introduce the conditional probability density $p_h(z|\mathrm{Dir}Q)$ of the deviation h. For the model of corner and for the model of sampling introduced earlier, the deviation of Q from p_X is equal to the deviation of X form the theoretical isoline segment being considered (Fig. 2). This clearly forces $h(X)=d(X)$, $p_h(z|\mathrm{Dir}Q)=p_d(z)$.

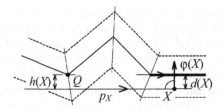

Fig. 2. The isoline of brightness passing through Q (*continuous line*), an isoline segment aiming at Q (*bold line*), a point X of the approximation of the segment, the deviation $d(X)$ of X from the segment, the deviation $h(X)$ of Q from p_X

We introduce the conditional probability $P(\mathrm{Br}Q|\Delta b(X))$ of the event that a point belongs to the approximation of the isoline whose brightness is $b(Q)$ providing that the difference of brightness is $\Delta b(X)$. Similarly, we introduce the probability $P(\mathrm{Dir}Q|h(X))$ of the event that a point belongs to the approximation of an isoline segment aiming at Q providing that the deviation of Q from p_X is $h(X)$. Using Bayes' formula yields the result

$$P(\mathrm{Br}Q \mid \Delta b(X)) = p_{\Delta b}(\Delta b(X) \mid \mathrm{Br}Q)\frac{P(\mathrm{Br}Q)}{p_{\Delta b}(\Delta b(X))} , \tag{3}$$

$$P(\mathrm{Dir}Q \mid h(X)) = p_d(h(X))\frac{P(\mathrm{Dir}Q)}{p_h(h(X))} . \tag{4}$$

To be able to apply the above equations, we carry out the estimations of the probabilities $P(\mathrm{Br}Q)$, $P(\mathrm{Dir}Q)$ and the probability densities $p_{\Delta b}(.)$, $p_h(.)$. Let A be the area of Ω, and let A_0 be the area of one pixel. We consider the linear size of Ω and the linear size of pixel by the values $\sqrt{A}$ and $\sqrt{A_0}$, respectively. Let l_Q be the length of the isoline in Ω whose brightness is $b(Q)$. Suppose that l_Q, at the same time, is the total length of all straight isoline segments in Ω (possibly belonging to different isolines) aiming at Q. Let the length of the isoline passing through X be l_X. We suppose that no other points with the same brightness, i.e. $b(X)$, exist in Ω except this isoline. Finally, we suppose that the deviation $h(X)$ varies in the range $-\frac{1}{2}\sqrt{A} \le h \le \frac{1}{2}\sqrt{A}$ and that the probability of its particular values is evenly distributed (the influence of the shape of Ω on $p_h(z)$ is thus neglected). A simple computation [7] yields the results

$$P(\mathrm{Br}Q) = P(\mathrm{Dir}Q) \approx \frac{l_Q\sqrt{A_0}}{A} , \qquad p_{\Delta b}(\Delta b(X)) \approx \frac{l_X}{g(X)A} , \qquad p_h(z) \approx \frac{1}{\sqrt{A}} . \tag{5}$$

Substituting the estimations from Eq. (5) into Eqs. (3), (4), taking into account Eq. (2), and letting $l_Q \approx l_X$, $\sqrt{A} \approx l_Q$, we obtain

$$P(\mathrm{Br}Q \mid \Delta b(X)) = \sqrt{A_0}\frac{l_Q}{l_X}p_d(d(X)) \approx \sqrt{A_0}p_d(d(X)) , \tag{6}$$

$$P(\mathrm{Dir}Q \mid h(X)) = l_Q\sqrt{\frac{A_0}{A}}p_d(h(X)) \approx \sqrt{A_0}p_d(h(X)) . \tag{7}$$

In the case of a continuous and error-free representation of image, X belongs to a straight isoline segment containing Q if the following three conditions are satisfied. (1) The brightness at X is equal to the brightness at Q, i.e., $\Delta b(X)=0$. (2) The line p_X passes through Q, i.e., $h(X)=0$. (3) The conditions (1), (2) are satisfied not only at X, but also at all other points of the line segment $\overline{QX}$. For the case of the discrete representation of image, we introduce the probability, denoted by $P_{SG}(X)$, of the event that X belongs to the approximation of a straight isoline segment containing Q. We set

$$P_{SG}(X)= \min_{Y\in \overline{QX}}\{P(\mathrm{Br}Q\,|\Delta b(Y))P(\mathrm{Dir}Q\,|h(Y))\} \cdot \tag{8}$$

The term $P(\mathrm{Br}Q|\Delta b(Y))$ expresses the probability of the event that Y is a point of the approximation of an isoline whose brightness is $b(Q)$ (Y is a point of the line segment $\overline{QX}$). The term $P(\mathrm{Dir}Q|h(Y))$ expresses the probability of the event that Y is a point of the approximation of an isoline segment (not necessarily with the same brightness as Q) that aims at Q. Both events are independent. Since Ω may contain more than one corner, the segments of the isoline whose brightness is $b(Q)$ need not generally aim at Q (Fig. 2). Conversely, an isoline segment aiming at Q may generally have an arbitrary brightness.

Let us say that X is a point lying on a straight isoline segment containing Q. It is clear that all the points of the line segment $\overline{QX}$ must lie on the segment too. Fig. 2 illustrates the fact that the conditions $\Delta b(X)=0$, $h(X)=0$ do not suffice to decide whether or not X belongs to an isoline segment containing Q. In other words: The probability of the event that Q, X are connected by a segment of isoline cannot be greater than the probability of the event that Q, Y are connected, where Y is an arbitrary point of the line segment $\overline{QX}$. This explains searching for the minimum in Eq. (8). Substituting the estimations form Eqs. (6), (7) into Eq. (8), we obtain

$$P_{SG}(X)= A_0 \min_{Y\in QX}\{p_d(d(Y))p_d(h(Y))\} \cdot \tag{9}$$

Let us determine at Q the "angle of break" of the isoline that passes through Q. For this purpose, we examine the values of $\varphi(X)$ in Ω. To take into account the notion that the relevance of the value of $\varphi(X)$ at X depends not only on the probability $P_{SG}(X)$, but also on the distance between the points Q and X, we introduce a positive weight function $w(r(X))$, where $r(X)$ stands for the distance between Q, X. We set $\sum_{X_i\in\Omega}P_{SG}(X_i)w(r(X_i))\equiv W$. For determining the angle of break at Q, we compute the quantities μ_φ and σ_φ^2 defined by the equations

$$\mu_\varphi = \frac{1}{W}\sum_{X_i\in\Omega}P_{SG}(X_i)w(r(X_i))\varphi(X_i),\quad \sigma_\varphi^2 =\frac{1}{W}\sum_{X_i\in\Omega}P_{SG}(X_i)w(r(X_i))[\varphi(X_i)-\mu_\varphi]^2 . \tag{10}$$

Let us now use $\mu_\varphi(Q)$, $\sigma_\varphi^2(Q)$ to express explicitly that we mean the values that were computed for a particular point (corner candidate) Q. We define the functions

$$Corr(Q)= g(Q)\sigma_\varphi^2(Q),\quad Appar(Q)= \sum_{X_i\in\Omega}P_{SG}(X_i)g(X_i)|\varphi(X_i)-\mu_\varphi| . \tag{11}$$

The function $Appar(Q)$ expresses the obviousness of the possible corner at Q. The algorithm is based on the following two theorems. Their proofs can be found in [7].

Theorem 1. Consider an image containing a corner conforming to the model introduced before. Assume that both the image and the neighbourhood Ω are infinite, that $p_d(z)$ is an arbitrary nonnegative symmetric function with a single maximum at $z=0$, and that $w(.)$ is an arbitrary positive decreasing function defined for nonnegative arguments. The following holds: The function $\sigma_\varphi^2(Q)$ has its maximum just at the points lying on the axis of the corner. At these points, the value $\mu_\varphi(Q)$ determines the direction of the corner axis, and the value $\pi - 2\sigma_\varphi(Q)$ is equal to the angle of corner.

Theorem 2. Under the assumptions of Theorem 1, the function $Corr(Q)$ has its maximum just at the corner point.

3   The Algorithm

The values of $g(Q)$ and $\varphi(Q)$ (the size and the direction of the gradient of brightness) for all image points are computed first. The derivatives $\partial b(x,y)/\partial x$, $\partial b(x,y)/\partial y$ are replaced by the differences. The image points at which the size of the gradient of brightness is greater than a predefined threshold are considered to be candidates for corners. The candidates are then examined by determining $\sigma_\varphi(Q)$, $Corr(Q)$ and $Appar(Q)$. The candidate at which the value of $Corr(Q)$ exhibits its local maximum and at which the values of $\sigma_\varphi(Q)$ and $Appar(Q)$ are greater than chosen thresholds is a corner. We choose p_d to be the normal distribution with a zero mean value and with σ varying typically from 0.5 to 1. As the weight function w, we use the Gaussian function too. In this case, the usual value of σ varies from 2 to 3. The neighbourhood $\Omega(Q)$ is square-shaped with Q at its centre. Its size is not critical since "the effective size" is always determined adaptively by the values of $P_{SG}(X)$. The sizes from 5×5 up to 11×11 pixels may be regarded as typical. Since ψ is an unknown function in practice, we determine the value of $d(Y)$ by the following estimation

$$d(Y) \approx \frac{2\Delta b(Y)}{g(Y) + g(Q)}. \tag{12}$$

We compute the values of $P_{SG}(X)$ in such a way that we proceed from Q (i.e., from the centre) to the borders of $\Omega(Q)$ and successively compute $P_{SG}(X)$ for all points of $\Omega(Q)$. Let us say that we have the points X_i, X_j, $X \in \Omega(Q)$ as depicted in Fig. 3. Suppose that the values of P_{SG} at X_i, X_j have already been computed and that the value of $P_{SG}(X)$ is to be computed now. Let us set $A_0 p_d(d(Y)) p_d(h(Y)) \equiv \tilde{P}_{SG}(Y)$ for brevity. We determine the sought value of $P_{SG}(X)$ by interpolating and choosing the minimum (λ is the length depicted in Fig. 3)

$$P_{SG}(X) \approx \min\left\{ (1-\lambda)\tilde{P}_{SG}(X_i) + \lambda\tilde{P}_{SG}(X_j), \ \tilde{P}_{SG}(X) \right\}. \tag{13}$$

Let the size of Ω be $M \times M$ pixels. The method descibed above enables to compute the values of $P_{SG}(X)$ for all $X \in \Omega(Q)$ in $\theta(M^2)$ time, which is also the overall time needed for processing one corner candidate. To speed up the computation, all X at which $g(X)$ is less than a predefined threshold or at which $|\varphi(X) - \varphi(Q)| > \pi/2$ are excluded from computing $\sigma_\varphi(Q)$, $Corr(Q)$ and $Appar(Q)$ [7].

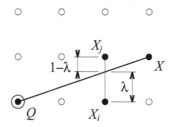

Fig. 3. On computing the value of $P_{SG}(X)$

4   The Results of Testing

The algorithm was implemented and tested. The tests included the comparison with several other recognised algorithms for corner detection [1]–[6] (Table 1). A synthetic image without noise, a synthetic image with an additive Gaussian noise (Fig. 4), and a real image obtained from a CCD camera were used for testing. We evaluated the number of corners detected correctly, the number of corners that were missed, the number of false detections, the number of multiple detections, and the localisation error. We define the *total error* of the detector to be the sum of the number of missed corners, false detections and superfluous multiple detections. For all the detectors, the values of all their parameters (e.g. thresholds) were set to the values giving the lowest possible total error. The values were found by searching in the space of parameters of each particular detector. For each test image, a separate set of optimal parameters was found. Moreover, the convolution of the input image with the Gaussian (σ=0.5, σ=0.75 or σ=1.0) was optionally carried out before finding the corners if it gave lower total error for the detector just being tested. The results of testing for the image from Fig. 4 are shown in Table 1. Similarly encouraging results were obtained also for other test images [7].

Table 1. The results of testing for the test image from Fig. 4

Detector	Correct detections[1]	Missed corners	False detections[2]	Multiple detections[3]	Total error	Localisation error
Beaudet [1]	363	107	54	24	185	1,62
Deriche–Giraudon [2]	190	280	10	13	303	1,24
Harris–Stephens [3]	431	39	14	9	62	0,73
Kitchen- Rosenfeld [4]	356	114	48	31	193	1,75
Noble [5]	206	264	71	38	373	1,72
SUSAN [6]	338	132	34	7	173	0,87
Proposed detector	**463**	**7**	**1**	**4**	**12**	**0,64**

[1] The test image contains 470 corners in total. [2] A corner is detected at a point at which (near which) no corner exists. [3] A single real corner is reported more than once.

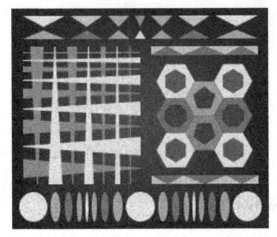

Fig. 4. An example of test image (a synthetic image with an additive Gaussian noise)

5 Conclusion

A new algorithm for detecting the corners in digital images has been presented. The algorithm was implemented and tested. The following was found out: (1) the detection of corners is highly reliable; (2) the localisation errors are small; (3) the sensitivity to noise is low; (4) the implementation of the algorithm is not complicated. The results of testing showed that, in the sense of the successfulness of detection, the new detector is better than the other known direct corner detectors that are usually used for solving the problem. Although the theoretical conclusions were obtained for L corners, the algoritm works also for the more complicated cases (T,Y,X junctions). Further details, including the source code of the algorithm, can be found in [7].

References

1. Beaudet, P.R.: Rotationally invariant image operators. In: Proc. Fourth Int. Joint Conf. on Pattern Recognition, Tokyo (1978) 579–583
2. Deriche, R., Giraudon, G.: A computational approach for corner and vertex detection. Int. J. Computer Vision 10 (1993) 101–124
3. Harris, C.G., Stephens, M.: A combined corner and edge detector. In: Proc. 4th Alvey Vision Conf., Manchester (1988) 189–192
4. Kitchen, L., Rosenfeld, A.: Gray-level corner detection. Pattern Recognition Letters 1 (1982) 95–102
5. Noble, J.A.: Finding corners. Image and Vision Computing 6 (1988) 121–128
6. Smith, S.M., Brady, J.M.: SUSAN - A new approach to low level image processing. Int. J. Computer Vision 23 (1997) 45–78
7. Sojka, E.: A new algorithm for detecting corners in digital images. Technical Report 2002-02, Dept. Comp. Science, TU Ostrava, Czech Rep. (2002) 29 pages, also available at http://www.cs.vsb.cz/~soj10/cordet/presentation.html

Fast Implicit Active Contour Models

Gerald Kühne[1], Joachim Weickert[2], Markus Beier[1], and Wolfgang Effelsberg[1]

[1] Praktische Informatik IV, Universität Mannheim,
L 15, 16, D-68131 Mannheim, Germany
{kuehne,beier,effelsberg}@informatik.uni-mannheim.de
[2] Fakultät für Mathematik und Informatik, Universität des Saarlandes,
Geb. 27.1, Postfach 15 11 50
D-66041 Saarbrücken, Germany
weickert@mia.uni-saarland.de

Abstract. Implicit active contour models are widely used in image processing and computer vision tasks. Most implementations, however, are based on explicit updating schemes and are therefore of limited computational efficiency. In this paper, we present fast algorithms based on the semi-implicit additive operator splitting (AOS) scheme for both the geometric and the geodesic active contour model. Our experimental results with synthetic and real-world images demonstrate that one can gain a speed up by one order of magnitude compared to the widely used explicit time discretization.

1 Introduction

Level-set-based or so-called implicit active contour models have been used in a variety of image processing and computer vision tasks [17]. Their main advantages over classical explicit snakes [6] are implicit handling of topological changes, numerical stability and independence of parametrization. However, their main drawback is the additional computational complexity. In their simplest implementation, most approaches are based on an explicit or forward Euler scheme which demands very small time steps.

To solve this problem, we provide a fast algorithm using an semi-implicit additive operator splitting (AOS) technique [9,20]. Our approach is suitable both for the geometric [3,10] and the geodesic active contour model [8,4].

The remainder of this paper is organized as follows: Section 2 introduces the geometric and the geodesic active contour model. Section 3 describes our numerical implementation of both models based on the AOS scheme. Section 4 presents results and computation times for the different implementations. Finally, Section 5 concludes the paper.

Related work. A number of fast implementations for implicit snakes have been proposed. However, most of them concentrate on narrow-band techniques and multi-scale computations [1,14,13]. In [5], Goldenberg et al. present for geodesic active contours an AOS strategy in combination with a narrow-band technique. However, in contrast to our implementation, each iteration in their approach requires a reinitialization step.

L. Van Gool (Ed.): DAGM 2002, LNCS 2449, pp. 133–140, 2002.
© Springer-Verlag Berlin Heidelberg 2002

2 Implicit Active Contour Models

Active contour models (deformable models) are used in a variety of image processing tasks, e. g., image segmentation or object tracking. The basic idea is that the user specifies an initial guess of an interesting contour (e. g. an organ, a tumour, or a person to be tracked). Then, this contour evolves under smoothness control (internal energy) and image-driven forces (external energy) to the boundaries of the desired object.

In the classical *explicit* snake model [6] the contour represented by a closed planar parametric curve $C_0(s) = (x(s), y(s))$, $s \in [0, 1]$, is embedded into an energy minimization framework. Apart from energy minimization the parametric curve can also evolve directly under motion equations derived from geometric considerations [16].

However, the parametrization of the curve causes difficulties with respect to topological changes and numerical implementations. Thus, to prevent these difficulties *implicit* active contour models have been developed. Here, the basic idea is to represent the inital curve $C_0(s)$ *implicitly* within a higher dimensional function, and to evolve this function under a partial differential equation. Usually, C_0 is embedded as a zero level set into a function $u_0 : I\!R^2 \to I\!R$ by using the *signed distance function*:

$$
u_0(x) = \begin{cases} d(x, C_0), & \text{if } x \text{ is inside } C_0 \\ 0, & \text{if } x \text{ is on } C_0 \\ -d(x, C_0), & \text{if } x \text{ is outside } C_0, \end{cases} \tag{1}
$$

where $d(x, C_0)$ denotes the distance from an arbitrary position to the curve.

The *implicit geometric active contour model* discovered by Caselles et al. [3] and later on by Malladi et al. [10] includes geometrical considerations similar to [16]. Let $\Omega := (0, a_x) \times (0, a_y)$ be our image domain in $I\!R^2$. We consider a scalar image on Ω. Then, using the level set technique [12] the model reads

$$
\frac{\partial u}{\partial t} = g(x)|\nabla u| \left(\text{div}\left(\frac{\nabla u}{|\nabla u|} \right) + k \right) \quad \text{on} \quad \Omega \times (0, \infty)
$$

$$
u(x, 0) = u_0(x) \quad \text{on} \quad \Omega. \tag{2}
$$

Here, k is a constant force term comparable to the balloon force known from explicit models and $g : I\!R^2 \to (0, 1]$ denotes a stopping function that slows down the snake as it approaches selected image features, e. g., edges. Note that normal and curvature to a level set are given by

$$
n = -\frac{\nabla u}{|\nabla u|}, \quad \kappa = \text{div}\left(\frac{\nabla u}{|\nabla u|} \right) = \frac{u_{xx}u_y^2 - 2u_x u_y u_{xy} + u_{yy}u_x^2}{(u_x^2 + u_y^2)^{3/2}}. \tag{3}
$$

In the *implicit geodesic active contour model* proposed simultaneously by Caselles et al. [4] and Kichenassamy et al. [8] the function u is embedded into an energy functional inspired by the explicit snake model:

$$\frac{\partial u}{\partial t} = |\nabla u| \left(\text{div} \left(g(x) \frac{\nabla u}{|\nabla u|} \right) + kg(x) \right) \quad \text{on} \quad \Omega \times (0, \infty)$$

$$u(x, 0) = u_0(x) \quad \text{on} \quad \Omega. \tag{4}$$

3   Numerical Implementation

While implicit active contour models avoid several of the difficulties known from explicit models, their main disadvantage is additional computational complexity. First, in their simplest implementation, the partial differential equation must be evaluated on the complete image domain. Second, most approaches are based on explicit updating schemes which demand very small time steps. While the first limitation can be addressed by narrow-band and/or multi-scale techniques [1,17,14], the latter requires different discretizations. In the following we focus on the second problem and develop semi-implicit schemes for both the geometric and the geodesic active contour model based on an additive operator splitting (AOS) technique [9,20]. Note that narrow-band and multi-scale techniques can be easily combined with our implementation.

Let us consider the following equation, which unifies the geometric and the geodesic model by introducing two additional functions a and b:

$$\frac{\partial u}{\partial t} = a(x)|\nabla u| \text{div} \left(\frac{b(x)}{|\nabla u|} \nabla u \right) + |\nabla u| kg(x). \tag{5}$$

Setting $a := g$, $b := 1$ yields the geometric model, while $a := 1$, $b := g$ results in the geodesic model. For the sake of clarity we assume a constant force $k = 0$ in the following and discuss the complete model later on. Interpreting the term $\frac{b(x)}{|\nabla u|}$ as "diffusivity" we can employ techniques similar to those as described in [20] in the context of nonlinear diffusion filtering.

To provide a numerical algorithm one has to consider discretizations of space and time. We employ discrete times $t_n := n\tau$, where $n \in \mathbb{N}_0$ and τ denotes the time step size. Additionally, an image is divided by a uniform mesh of spacing $h = 1$ into grid nodes x_i. To simplify the notation a discrete image is represented in the following by a vector $f \in \mathbb{R}^N$, whose components $f_i, i \in \{1, \ldots, N\}$, contain the pixel values. Consequently, pixel i corresponds to some grid node x_i. Thus, using standard notation, u_i^n denotes the approximation of $u(x_i, t_n)$. Hence, following [20], (5) with $k = 0$ reads in its semi-implicit formulation as

$$u_i^{n+1} = u_i^n + \tau \left(a_i |\nabla u|_i^n \sum_{j \in \mathcal{N}(i)} \frac{\left(\frac{b}{|\nabla u|} \right)_i^n + \left(\frac{b}{|\nabla u|} \right)_j^n}{2} \frac{u_j^{n+1} - u_i^{n+1}}{h^2} \right), \tag{6}$$

where $\mathcal{N}(i)$ denotes the 4-neighborhood of the pixel at position x_i. Here, straight-forward finite difference implementations would give rise to problems when $|\nabla u|$ vanishes in the 4-neighborhood. These problems do not appear if one uses a finite difference scheme with *harmonic* averaging [19], thus replacing $\frac{1}{2}\left(\left(\frac{b}{|\nabla u|}\right)_i^n + \left(\frac{b}{|\nabla u|}\right)_j^n\right)$ in (6) by its harmonic counterpart:

$$u_i^{n+1} = u_i^n + \tau \left(a_i |\nabla u|_i^n \sum_{j \in \mathcal{N}(i)} \frac{2}{\left(\frac{|\nabla u|}{b}\right)_i^n + \left(\frac{|\nabla u|}{b}\right)_j^n} \frac{u_j^{n+1} - u_i^{n+1}}{h^2} \right). \qquad (7)$$

Note that by evaluating only image positions with $|\nabla u|_i \neq 0$, the denominator in this scheme cannot vanish. In matrix-vector notation this becomes

$$u^{n+1} = u^n + \tau \left(\sum_{l \in \{x,y\}} A_l(u^n) \right) u^{n+1}, \qquad (8)$$

where A_l describes the interaction in l direction. In detail, the matrix $A_l(u^n) = (\hat{a}_{ijl}(u^n))$ is given by

$$\hat{a}_{ijl}(u^n) := \begin{cases} a_i |\nabla u|_i^n \frac{2}{\left(\frac{|\nabla u|}{b}\right)_i^n + \left(\frac{|\nabla u|}{b}\right)_j^n}, & j \in \mathcal{N}_l(i) \\ -a_i |\nabla u|_i^n \sum_{m \in \mathcal{N}_l(i)} \frac{2}{\left(\frac{|\nabla u|}{b}\right)_i^n + \left(\frac{|\nabla u|}{b}\right)_m^n}, & j = i \\ 0, \text{ else}, \end{cases} \qquad (9)$$

where $\mathcal{N}_l(i)$ represents the neighboring pixels with respect to direction $l \in \{x,y\}$. However, the solution u^{n+1} cannot be directly determined from this scheme. Instead, it requires to solve a linear system of equations. Its solution is formally given by

$$u^{n+1} = \left(I - \tau \sum_{l \in \{x,y\}} A_l(u^n) \right)^{-1} u^n \qquad (10)$$

where I denotes the unit matrix. Reformulating (10) using an AOS approximation yields

$$u^{n+1} = \frac{1}{2} \sum_{l \in \{x,y\}} (I - 2\tau A_l(u^n))^{-1} u^n. \qquad (11)$$

The operators $B_l(u^k) := I - 2\tau A_l(u^n)$ come down to strictly diagonally dominant tridiagonal linear systems which can be solved very efficiently [11]. Moreover, this scheme is unconditionally stable, thus, we can apply arbitrarily large time steps.

However, we have so far neglected the constant force term $|\nabla u|kg$ (cf. (5)). This term stems from the hyperbolic dilation/erosion equation $\partial_t u = \pm|\nabla u|$. Consequently, in a numerical implementation the gradient has to be approximated by an upwind scheme [12]:

$$|\nabla u|_i^n \approx \begin{cases} |\nabla^- u|_i^n = \left(\max(D^{-x}u_i^n,0)^2 + \min(D^{+x}u_i^n,0)^2 + \right. \\ \qquad\qquad \left. \max(D^{-y}u_i^n,0)^2 + \min(D^{+y}u_i^n,0)^2\right)^{1/2}, \text{ if } k \leq 0 \\ \\ |\nabla^+ u|_i^n = \left(\min(D^{-x}u_i^n,0)^2 + \max(D^{+x}u_i^n,0)^2 + \right. \\ \qquad\qquad \left. \min(D^{-y}u_i^n,0)^2 + \max(D^{+y}u_i^n,0)^2\right)^{1/2}, \text{ if } k > 0 \end{cases},$$

(12)

where D^{+x}, D^{+y}, D^{-x}, and D^{+y} denote forward and backward approximations of the spatial derivatives (see e. g. [17]). Integrating the constant force term into (11) is straightforward and yields for $k < 0$:

$$u^{n+1} = \frac{1}{2} \sum_{l \in \{x,y\}} (I - 2\tau A_l(u^n))^{-1} \left(u^n + \tau|\nabla^- u|^n kg\right).$$

(13)

Since the dilation/erosion equation approximated on a grid with $h = 1$ is stable only for $\tau \leq 0.5$ [12], the constant force term limits the applicable time step. Consequently, (13) is stable only for $|\tau kg| \leq 0.5$. However, since g is bounded by one, k is usually a small fraction of 1.0, and very large time steps ($\tau > 5.0$) degrade accuracy significantly [20,19], this constraint is not severe.

4   Experimental Results

With the AOS-based implementation it is possible to choose time steps much larger than in explicit updating schemes. Consequently, the evolution of the contour to its final location requires only a small number of iterations compared to explicit algorithms. However, a semi-implicit AOS iteration is more expensive than its explicit counterpart. In order to compare both approaches, we implemented the AOS-based models according to (13). For the explicit scheme we employed standard techniques [17,2]. In addition, we used a stopping criterion to indicate that the curve has reached a stable steady state. Every time a certain period Δt_k has elapsed, the average gray value of the evolving image u is calculated. E. g., when setting $\Delta t_k = 50$ and $\tau = 0.25$, the average gray value is computed every 200 iterations. The process stops if two consecutive measurements differ by less than an accuracy parameter α. In all experiments the parameters for the stopping criterion were set to $\Delta t_k = 50$ and $\alpha \in \{0.01, 0.1\}$.

To assess the final placement of the contour with regard to the underlying algorithm, a simple distance measure was developed. Given a result contour and a reference contour, we calculated for each pixel on the result contour the distance to the nearest pixel on the reference contour. Averaging these values yields the distance between the two contours. As reference contour we used in all cases the explicit implementation with a small time step $\tau = 0.1$.

We applied both algorithms to sample images (cf. Figures 1–3). A stopping function according to the Perona-Malik diffusivity [15] was used:

$$g(x) = \frac{1}{1 + |\nabla f_\sigma(x)|^2/\lambda^2},$$

(14)

 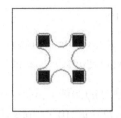 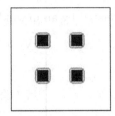

Fig. 1. AOS-based geometric active contour model on a synthetic image (size 128 × 128, $\tau = 5.0$, $k = -0.1$, $\sigma = 0.5$, $\lambda = 1$). From left to right: 10, 150, 250 iterations.

Fig. 2. AOS-based geodesic active contour model on hall-and-monitor image (size 352 × 240, $\tau = 5.0$, $k = -0.02$, $\sigma = 0.5$, $\lambda = 1$). From left to right: 100, 500, 1000 iterations.

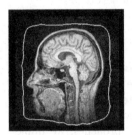 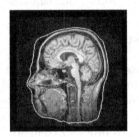 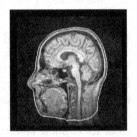

Fig. 3. AOS-based geometric active contour model on medical image (size 284 × 284, $\tau = 5.0$, $k = -0.1$, $\sigma = 1$, $\lambda = 1.5$). From left to right: 50, 150, 300 iterations.

where f_σ denotes the convolution of image f with a Gaussian kernel of standard deviation σ and λ is a contrast factor. While close to edges (high gradient magnitudes) of the image f, the stopping function approaches zero, it reaches one in flat image areas (low gradient magnitudes). To extract the person in the hall-and-monitor sequence we replaced the gradient term in the above equation by the results of a motion detector [7]. In each case the image u_0 was intialized to a signed distance function [18,14,17] from a mask that covered nearly the complete image domain. Table 1 summarizes the results calculated on a standard personal computer with 1.4 GHz. As expected, the AOS-based implementation reduced the number of iterations on the average by a factor of 20. Due to the coarse stopping criterion the reduction varies from 18 to 22. Furthermore, we observe that an AOS-based iteration is about twice as expensive, and in some cases three times as expensive as an explicit iteration. Combining those results, we observe that using AOS-based implementations of implicit active contour models yields

Table 1. Comparison of explicit and AOS-based schemes

geometric model (explicit scheme) image	τ	k	iterations	CPU time	distance (pixels)
synthetic image	0.25	-0.1	20200	49.0 s	0
hall-and-monitor image	0.25	-0.1	20000	324.5 s	0
medical image	0.25	-0.1	6600	126.3 s	0.01

geometric model (AOS scheme) image	τ	k	iterations	CPU time	distance (pixels)
synthetic image	5.0	-0.1	950	7.4 s	0.75
hall-and-monitor image	5.0	-0.1	1040	54.0 s	0.87
medical image	5.0	-0.1	370	25.0 s	0.48

geodesic model (explicit scheme) image	τ	k	iterations	CPU time	distance (pixels)
synthetic image	0.25	-0.02	10400	36.9 s	0
hall-and-monitor image	0.25	-0.02	30800	634.9 s	0
medical image	0.25	-0.05	12200	306.1 s	0.01

geodesic model (AOS scheme) image	τ	k	iterations	CPU time	distance (pixels)
synthetic image	5.0	-0.02	480	4.2 s	1
hall-and-monitor image	5.0	-0.02	1390	70.2 s	1.79
medical image	5.0	-0.05	640	36.8 s	1.32

a significant speedup. In our examples the speedup ranges from a factor of 5 to a factor of 9. Additionally, we applied the simple distance measure to the final contours of the AOS-based and the explicit algorithms. The distance column in Table 1 shows the average distance (in pixels) of the contours to the reference contour obtained by an explicit algorithm with $\tau = 0.1$. In all cases the results indicate that the accuracy of the final placement is sufficient with respect to the underlying segmentation task. We should note that the accuracy might be further improved by refining the simple stopping criterion.

5 Conclusions

We have presented fast algorithms for both the geometric and the geodesic active contour model. Our implementation based on the additive operator splitting scheme outperforms other widely used explicit updating schemes clearly. Future work will comprise the integration of narrow-band and multi-scale techniques and should further improve the computational efficiency.

References

1. D. Adalsteinsson and J. A. Sethian. A fast level set method for propagating interfaces. *Journal of Computational Physics*, 118(2):269–277, 1995.

2. G. Aubert and P. Kornprobst. *Mathematical Problems in Image Processing: Partial Differential Equations and the Calculus of Variations*, volume 147 of *Applied Mathematical Sciences*. Springer-Verlag, New York, 2002.
3. V. Caselles, F. Catt , T. Coll, and F. Dibois. A geometric model for active contours. *Numerische Mathematik*, 66:1–31, 1993.
4. V. Caselles, R. Kimmel, and G. Sapiro. Geodesic active contours. *International Journal of Computer Vision*, 22(1):61–79, 1997.
5. R. Goldenberg, R. Kimmel, E. Rivlin, and M. Rudzsky. Fast geodesic active contours. *IEEE Transactions on Image Processing*, 10(10):1467–1475, October 2001.
6. M. Kass, A. Witkin, and D. Terzopoulos. Snakes: Active contour models. *International Journal of Computer Vision*, 1:321–331, 1988.
7. G. K hne, J. Weickert, O. Schuster, and S. Richter. A tensor-driven active contour model for moving object segmentation. In *Proc. IEEE International Conference on Image Processing (ICIP)*, volume II, pages 73–76, October 2001.
8. S. Kichenassamy, A. Kumar, P. Olver, A. Tannenbaum, and A. Yezzi. Conformal curvature flows: from phase transitions to active vision. *Archive of Rational Mechanics and Analysis*, 134:275–301, 1996.
9. T. Lu, P. Neittaanm ki, and X.-C. Tai. A parallel splitting up method and its application to Navier-Stokes equations. *Applied Mathematics Letters*, 4(2):25–29, 1991.
10. R. Malladi, J. A. Sethian, and B. C. Vemuri. Shape modeling with front propagation: A level set approach. *IEEE Transactions on Pattern Analysis and Machine Intelligence*, 17(2):158–175, February 1995.
11. K. Morton and D. Mayers. *Numerical Solution of Partial Differential Equations : An Introduction*. Cambridge University Press, Cambridge, UK, 1994.
12. S. Osher and J. A. Sethian. Fronts propagating with curvature dependent speed: Algorithms based on Hamilton-Jacobi formulations. *Journal of Computational Physics*, 79:12–49, 1988.
13. N. Paragios and R. Deriche. Geodesic active contours and level sets for the detection and tracking of moving objects. *IEEE Transactions on Pattern Analysis and Machine Intelligence*, 22(3):266–280, March 2000.
14. D. Peng, B. Merriman, S. Osher, H. Zhao, and M. Kang. A PDE-based fast local level set method. *Journal of Computational Physics*, 155(2):410–438, 1999.
15. P. Perona and J. Malik. Scale-space and edge detection using anisotropic diffusion. *IEEE Transactions on Pattern Analysis and Machine Intelligence*, 12(7):629–639, July 1990.
16. J. A. Sethian. Curvature and the evolution of fronts. *Communications in Mathematical Physics*, 101:487–499, 1985.
17. J. A. Sethian. *Level Set Methods and Fast Marching Methods. Evolving Interfaces in Computational Geometry, Fluid Mechanics, Computer Vision, and Materials Science*. Cambridge Monograph on Applied and Computational Mathematics. Cambridge University Press, Cambridge, UK, 1999.
18. M. Sussman, P. Smereka, and S. Osher. A level-set approach for computing solutions to incompressible two-phase flow. *Journal of Computational Physics*, 114:146–159, 1994.
19. J. Weickert. Application of nonlinear diffusion in image processing and computer vision. *Acta Mathematica Universitatis Comenianae*, 70(1):33–50, 2001.
20. J. Weickert, B. M. ter Haar Romeny, and M. A. Viergever. Efficient and reliable schemes for nonlinear diffusion filtering. *IEEE Transactions on Image Processing*, 7(3):398–410, March 1998.

Unsupervised Image Partitioning with Semidefinite Programming

Jens Keuchel, Christoph Schnörr, Christian Schellewald, and Daniel Cremers

CVGPR-Group, Dept. Math. and Comp. Science
University of Mannheim, D-68131 Mannheim, Germany
{jkeuchel,schnoerr,cschelle,cremers}@ti.uni-mannheim.de
http://www.cvgpr.uni-mannheim.de

Abstract. We apply a novel optimization technique, semidefinite programming, to the unsupervised partitioning of images. Representing images by graphs which encode pairwise (dis)similarities of local image features, a partition of the image into coherent groups is computed by determining optimal balanced graph cuts. Unlike recent work in the literature, we do not make any assumption concerning the objective criterion like metric pairwise interactions, for example. Moreover, no tuning parameter is necessary to compute the solution. We prove that, from the optimization point of view, our approach cannot perform worse than spectral relaxation approaches which, conversely, may completely fail for the unsupervised choice of the eigenvector threshold.

1 Introduction

Partitioning images in an unsupervised way is a common goal of many low-level computer vision applications. Based on some locally computed features like color, texture, or motion, the image should be split into coherent groups whose members look "similar". As no prototypes for the different groups are given in advance, the "correct" partitioning cannot be easily defined. To this end, a hierarchical bi-partitioning approach is often pursued in practice: The image is split into two main parts, which could be split further in subsequent applications of the algorithm. Figure 1 shows two images taken from the VisTex-database [1] that should give you an impression of the difficulty of the partitioning task.

To guide the search for a "good" segmentation, an appropriate representation of the image is as well needed as optimization criteria which give measures of the quality of a segmentation. To this end, the representation of images by graph structures has recently attracted the interest of researchers [2,3,4]: An image is represented by a graph with locally extracted image features as vertices and pairwise (dis)similarity values as edge weights. The goal is to find a cut through this graph that divides it in two coherent parts. Several methods from spectral graph theory were proposed in the literature to solve this problem [5,6,2]. A major problem of these approaches concerns the appropriate choice of a threshold value to split the computed eigenvector in two reasonable parts.

L. Van Gool (Ed.): DAGM 2002, LNCS 2449, pp. 141–149, 2002.
© Springer-Verlag Berlin Heidelberg 2002

Fig. 1. A color scene (left) and a gray-value scene comprising some natural textures (right). How to partition such scenes into coherent groups in an *unsupervised* way based on pairwise (dis)similarities between local measurements?

In this paper, we investigate the application of a novel optimization technique, *semidefinite programming (SDP)*, to the field of unsupervised partitioning. Therefore, by using the graph representation, we derive a problem formulation that yields a quadratic functional defined over binary decision variables which has to be minimized subject to linear constraints. The combinatorial complexity of this optimization task is then dealt with in two steps: Firstly, the decision variables are lifted to a higher-dimensional space where the optimization problem is relaxed to a *convex* optimization problem [7]. Secondly, the decision variables are recovered from the global optimum of the relaxed problem by using a small set of randomly computed hyperplanes [8].

In contrast to related work [3,4], *no specific assumptions* are made with respect to the functional form apart from a symmetry condition. As a consequence, our approach can also be applied to other computer vision tasks like perceptual grouping or image restoration [9]. Other favourable properties of the semidefinite programming approach are:

- As the relaxed problem is convex, the global optimum can be computed.
- Interior-point algorithms [10] allow to find the optimum in polynomial time.
- No additional tuning parameters are necessary. This is a significant advantage over alternative optimization approaches [11].
- In contrast to spectral relaxation, no choice of a threshold value is necessary.

In the following, we will apply the semidefinite relaxation approach to binary partitioning problems, and compare the results to spectral relaxation methods.

2   Problem Statement: Binary Combinatorial Optimization for Unsupervised Partitioning

Consider a graph $G(V, E)$ with locally extracted image features as vertices V and pairwise similarity values as edge-weights $w : E \subseteq V \times V \to \mathbb{R}_0^+$. We wish to compute a partition of the set V into two coherent groups $V = S \cup \overline{S}$. Representing such a partition by an indicator vector $x \in \{-1, +1\}^n$, a measure for the partition can be defined as the weight of the corresponding cut:

$$w(S, \overline{S}) = \sum_{i \in S, j \in \overline{S}} w(i,j) = \frac{1}{8} \sum_{i,j \in V} w(i,j)(x_i - x_j)^2 = \frac{1}{4} x^\top L x \ . \tag{1}$$

Here, $L = D - W$ denotes the Laplacian matrix of the graph G, and D is the diagonal matrix with the entries $d(i,i) = \sum_{j \in V} w(i,j)$. As the weight function w encodes a similarity measure between pairs of features, coherent groups correspond to low values of $w(S, \overline{S})$.

In order to avoid unbalanced partitions which are likely when just minimizing $w(S, \overline{S})$, a classical partitioning approach is to demand that both groups contain the same number of vertices by adding the constraint $e^\top x = 0, e = (1, \dots, 1)^\top$, hence arriving at the following combinatorial minimization problem:

$$\inf_x x^\top L x \ , \quad e^\top x = 0 \ , \quad x \in \{-1, +1\}^n \ . \tag{2}$$

Since e is the eigenvector of the Laplacian matrix L with eigenvalue 0, a natural relaxation of this problem is to drop the integer constraint and compute the eigenvector corresponding to the second smallest eigenvalue of L (the so-called "Fiedler vector"; see, e.g. [5]). An approximate solution for (2) is then derived by thresholding this eigenvector. This raises the question for an appropriate choice of the threshold value. Two natural approaches seem to be promising: To threshold at 0 (because of the +1/–1-constraint on x) or at the median of the eigenvector (to meet the balancing constraint $e^\top x = 0$). However, we will show below that an unsupervised choice of the threshold value may fail completely.

In this paper, we focus on the semidefinite relaxation of (2), which *directly* takes into account the integer constraint with respect to x_i, $i = 1, \dots, n$, instead of just doing so by thresholding afterwards. We will show that this approach compares favorably to the computation of the Fiedler vector both in theory (Section 4) and in practice (Section 5).

Recently, Shi and Malik [2] suggested another successful approach, which is similar to (2): They use a normalized objective function which finally results in the following problem (*normalized cut*):

$$\inf_x \frac{x^\top L x}{x^\top D x} \ , \quad e^\top D x = 0 \ , \quad x \in \{-b, 1\}^n \ , \tag{3}$$

where the number b is not known beforehand. Dropping the integer constraint yields a relaxation of (3) which then can be solved by calculating the second smallest eigenvalue of the normalized Laplacian matrix $\tilde{L} = D^{-1/2} L D^{-1/2}$. A relation of this approach to the semidefinite relaxation approach can be derived by replacing the vector e in (2) by the vector De. As the details of this relation are not straightforward (due to the normalization of the objective function), they are beyond the scope of this paper and will be reported elsewhere [12].

Note that the positivity of the edge-weights w is essential for both spectral relaxation methods; however, the semidefinite relaxation described in the next section only requires the matrix L in (2) to be symmetric, and thus can also be applied in the case of *non-positive* edge-weigths!

3   Semidefinite Relaxation

To derive the semidefinite relaxation of (2), we first replace the linear and the integer constraint, respectively, by quadratic ones: $(e^\top x)^2 = 0$, $x_i^2 - 1 = 0, i = 1, \ldots, n$. Denoting the Lagrangian multiplier variables with $y_i, i = 0, \ldots, n$, the corresponding Lagrangian of (2) yields the following relaxed problem formulation of (2) after some standard transformations:

$$z_d := \sup_{y_0, y} e^\top y , \quad L - y_0 ee^\top - D(y) \in \mathcal{S}_+^n , \tag{4}$$

where $D(y)$ denotes the diagonal matrix with the vector y on its diagonal, and $\mathcal{S}_+^n$ is the set of positive semidefinite matrices. As this set is a cone (i.e. a special convex set), we arrive at a *convex* optimization problem. The relation to our original problem can be seen by deriving the dual problem of (4):

$$z_p := \inf_{X \in \mathcal{S}_+^n} L \bullet X , \quad ee^\top \bullet X = 0, \ D(X) = I . \tag{5}$$

Here $L \bullet X = \mathrm{Tr}\,[L^\top X]$ denotes the standard matrix inner product, and $D(X)$ is the matrix X with the off-diagonal elements set to zero. Notice that problem (5) again is convex!

If we rewrite the objective function of (2) as $\inf_x x^\top L x = \inf_x L \bullet xx^\top$, we immediately see the connection to the relaxed problem (5): The rank one matrix $xx^\top$ is replaced by an arbitrary matrix $X \in \mathcal{S}_+^n$, whereas the constraints are just lifted in the higher-dimensional space accordingly.

The elegant duality theory corresponding to the class of convex optimization problems [10] guarantees under mild conditions that optimal primal and dual solutions $X^*, (y_0^*, y^*)$ for (5) and (4) exist and that they yield no duality gap: $z_p - z_d = L \bullet X^* - e^t y^* = 0$.

For the problems considered in this paper, the constraint $ee^\top \bullet X = 0$ requires that the smallest eigenvalue of X is equal to 0, so that no strictly interior point for the primal problem (5) exists. Due to this observation we decided to use the dual-scaling algorithm from [13] for our experiments. This algorithm has the advantage that it does not need to calculate an interior solution for the primal problem during the iterations, but only for the dual problem.

To find a combinatorial solution x_S based on the solution matrix X^* to the convex optimization problem (5), we used the randomized-hyperplane technique proposed in [8]. As this technique does not take into account the constraint $e^\top x = 0$, the solution x_S does not need to be feasible for (2), and the resulting objective value $z_S = x_S^\top L x_S$ may be even smaller than the optimal value of the semidefinite relaxion z_d. Therefore, some modifications of the randomized-hyperplane technique have been proposed in the literature [14,15]. However, we decided to stick to it as for the applications considered in this paper, it is not mandatory to find a feasible solution: The constraint $e^\top x = 0$ only serves as a strong bias to guide the search to a solution that is balanced reasonably.

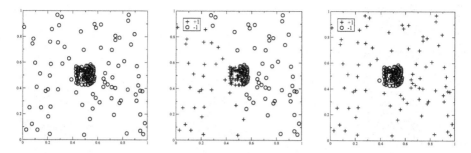

Fig. 2. Point set clustering. The corresponding graph contains a vertex for each point, and the edge weights are calculated from the Euclidian distances $d(i,j)$ between all points by $w(i,j) = \exp(-(\frac{d(i,j)}{0.05})^2)$. **Left:** Input data with 160 points. **Middle:** Solution computed with the Fiedler vector, thresholded at the median value: Spectral relaxation fails! **Right:** Solution computed with SDP.

4 Comparison to Spectral Relaxation

Poljak and Rendl [16] proved the following relation of the semidefinite relaxation (5) to an eigenvalue optimization problem:

$$z_d = \sup_{v \in \mathbb{R}^n} n\lambda_{\min}\left(V^\top\left(L + D(v)\right)V\right), \quad e^\top v = 0, \tag{6}$$

where $V \in \mathbb{R}^{n \times (n-1)}$ contains an orthonormal basis of the complement $e^\perp$, i.e. $V^\top e = 0$, $V^\top V = I$. An immediate consequence is the following lemma, which shows the connection between the semidefinite relaxation and the computation of the Fiedler vector:

Lemma 1. *The Fiedler vector yields a lower bound for (2) of $n\lambda_{\min}(V^\top LV)$, which is a **weaker** relaxation than (6): $n\lambda_{\min}(V^\top LV) \le z_d$.*

It is easy to construct examples where spectral relaxation is too weak and thus cannot compute a meaningful solution. In Figure 2, for example, the Fiedler vector is not able to seperate the dense cluster from the background, despite the fact that the balancing constraint is strictly enforced by the median threshold! In contrast to that, our approach finds two groups of nearly the same size (78 and 82 points).

5 Experiments

The results of the semidefinite relaxation approach for various binary partitioning problems are shown in Figures 3–5, and compared with segmentations obtained with the Fiedler vector. For all experiments, the edge weights $w(i,j)$ building the similarity matrix were computed from the distances $d(i,j)$ between the extracted image features i and j as $w(i,j) = \exp(-\frac{(d(i,j))^2}{\sigma})$, where $d(i,j)$ and σ were chosen application dependent. We studied two different approaches:

Fig. 3. Grayscale image partitioning. Each pixel is taken as a graph vertex, and the edge weigths are computed from the gray value differences $d(i,j)$ of adjacent pixels with method (b). **Left:** Input image (36×36 pixels) as part of a larger image. **Middle:** Segmentation computed with SDP: The hand is clearly separated from the ball. **Right:** Segmentation computed with the Fiedler vector: No clear separation is obtained by median thresholding. Thresholding at 0 just separates one pixel from the rest of the image.

(a) Compute $w(i,j)$ for all feature pairs (i,j) directly.
(b) Compute $w(i,j)$ only for neighboring features, and derive the other edge weights by calculation of a path connecting them. This was done by changing the similarity weights to dissimilarities, computing shortest paths, and transforming the weights back afterwards.

For a survey of numerous (dis)similarity measures, see [17].

The results approve the theoretical superiority of the semidefinite relaxation approach: Whereas even a supervised choice of the threshold value for the Fiedler vector does not necessarily yield satisfactory partitionings, the segmentations obtained with SDP are always very reasonable.

6   Conclusion

The results presented in this paper show that the semidefinite relaxation approach is well suited to perform unsupervised binary partitioning for a wide range of applications. It compares favorably both in theory and in practice to the computation of the Fiedler vector. In our further work we will study which other constraints are useful for unsupervised partitioning and could be incorporated into the semidefinite relaxation approach.

Acknowledgement

This work has been supported by the Deutsche Forschungsgemeinschaft (DFG; grant Schn457/3).

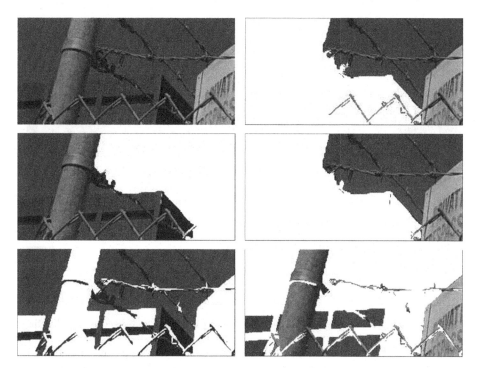

Fig. 4. Color image partitioning. We first compute an oversegmentation by applying the mean shift technique [18] at a fine spatial scale in order not to destroy any perceptually significant structure. Instead of thousands of pixels, the graph vertices are then formed by the obtained clusters, and $d(i,j)$ is computed as the color difference of two clusters in the perceptually uniform LUV space. **Top left:** Input image (298×141 pixels), yielding 209 clusters. **Top right:** Segmentation computed with the Fiedler vector thresholded at the median, using method (b). The requirement that both parts have the same size influences the result negatively. **Middle:** Segmentation computed with SDP, using method (b): Spatially coherent structures are favored. **Bottom:** Segmentation computed with SDP, using method (a): Similar colors are grouped together. Notice that for both methods, no choice of a threshold value is necessary for SDP!

References

1. Vision texture database. http://www-white.media.mit.edu/vismod/imagery/ VisionTexture/vistex.html.
2. J. Shi and J. Malik. Normalized cuts and image segmentation. *IEEE Trans. Patt. Anal. Mach. Intell.*, 22(8):888–905, 2000.
3. H. Ishikawa. *Global Optimization Using Embedded Graphs.* PhD thesis, Dept. Comp. Science, Courant Inst. Math. Sciences, New York University, 2000.
4. Y. Boykov, O. Veksler, and R. Zabih. Fast approximate energy minimization via graph cuts. *IEEE Trans. Patt. Anal. Mach. Intell.*, 23(11):1222–1239, 2001.
5. B. Mohar and S. Poljak. Eigenvalues in combinatorial optimization. In R.A. Brualdi et al., editors, *Combinatorial and Graph–Theoretical Problems in Linear Algebra*, volume 50 of *IMA Vol. Math. Appl.*, pages 107–151. Springer, 1993.

Fig. 5. Grayscale-texture partitioning. The texture measure is derived by subdividing the image into 24 × 24-pixel windows, and calculating local histograms for two texture features within these windows. Each window corresponds to a graph vertex, and $d(i,j)$ is computed as the χ^2-distance of the histograms using method (a). **Top left:** Input image (720 × 456 pixels), yielding 570 vertices. **Top right:** Segmentation computed with the Fiedler vector, using the threshold value 0. The median threshold does not make sense here, as the image does not contain two parts of the same size. **Bottom:** Segmentation computed with SDP: Considering the simplicity of this texture measure, the segmentation result is excellent.

6. Y. Weiss. Segmentation using eigenvectors: a unifying view. In *Proc. Int. Conf. Comp. Vision (ICCV'99)*, pages 975–982, 1999.

7. L. Lovász and A. Schrijver. Cones of matrices and set–functions and 0–1 optimization. *SIAM J. Optimization*, 1(2):166–190, 1991.

8. M.X. Goemans and D.P. Williamson. Improved approximation algorithms for maximum cut and satisfiability problems using semidefinite programming. *J. ACM*, 42:1115–1145, 1995.

9. C. Schellewald, J. Keuchel, and C. Schnörr. Image labeling and grouping by minimizing linear functionals over cones. In M. Figueiredo et al., editors, *Energy Minimization Methods in Computer Vision and Pattern Recognition*, volume 2134 of *Lect. Not. Comp. Sci.*, pages 235–250. Springer, 2001.

10. Y. Nesterov and A. Nemirovskii. *Interior Point Polynomial Methods in Convex Programming*. SIAM, 1994.

11. T. Hofmann and J. Buhmann. Pairwise data clustering by deterministic annealing. *IEEE Trans. Patt. Anal. Mach. Intell.*, 19(1):1–14, 1997.

12. J. Keuchel, C. Schnörr, C. Schellewald, and D. Cremers. Binary partitioning, perceptual grouping, and restoration with semidefinite programming. Technical Report 5/2002, Computer Science Series, CVGPR Group, Univ. Mannheim, 2002.

13. S.J. Benson, Y. Ye, and X. Zhang. Mixed linear and semidefinite programming for combinatorial and quadratic optimization. *Optimiz. Methods and Software*, 11&12:515–544, 1999.
14. A. Frieze and M. Jerrum. Improved approximation algorithms for max k-cut and max bisection. *Algorithmica*, 18:67–81, 1997.
15. Y. Ye. A .699-approximation algorithm for max-bisection. *Mathematical Programming*, 90:101–111, 2001.
16. S. Poljak and F. Rendl. Nonpolyhedral relaxations of graph-bisection problems. *SIAM Journal on Optimization*, 5:467–487, 1995.
17. J. Puzicha, J.M. Buhmann, Y. Rubner, and C. Tomasi. Empirical evaluation of dissimilarity measures for color and texture. In *7th Int. Conf. on Comp. Vision (ICCV'99)*, pages 1165–1172, 1999.
18. D. Comaniciu and P. Meer. Mean shift analysis and applications. In *7th Int. Conf. on Comp. Vision (ICCV'99)*, pages 1197–1203, 1999.

The Application of Genetic Algorithms
in Structural Seismic Image Interpretation

Melanie Aurnhammer and Klaus Tönnies

Computer Vision Group, Otto-von-Guericke University, Postfach 4120
39016 Magdeburg, Germany
{aurnhamm, klaus}@cs.uni-magdeburg.de

Abstract. In this paper, we examine the applicability and repeatability
of a genetic algorithm to automatically correlate horizons across faults in
seismic data images. This problem arises from geological sciences where
it is a subtask of structural interpretation of those images which has not
been automated before. Because of the small amount of local information
contained in seismic images, we developed a geological model in order to
reduce interpretation uncertainties. The key problem is an optimisation
task which cannot be solved exhaustively since it would cause exponential
computational cost. Among stochastic methods, a genetic algorithm has
been chosen to solve the application problem. Repeated application of
the algorithm to four different faults delivered an acceptable solution
in 94-100% of the experiments. The global optimum was equal to the
geologically most plausible solution in three of the four cases.

1 Geological Background

Seismic data are acquired using the seismic reflection method which explores the
subsurface by bouncing sound waves off the interfaces between rock layers with
differing physical properties. After several pre-processing steps, a rough estimate
of the underground structure can be obtained. By analysing the recorded and
processed signals, hypotheses about the underground structure can be developed
which should merge into a consistent subsurface model. All decisions in hydro-
carbon exploration and production are underpinned by such models obtained by
structural interpretation.

Structural interpretation comprises localisation and interpretation of faults,
tracking of uninterrupted horizon segments, and correlating these segments
across faults. Reflectors in seismic images usually correspond with horizons indicating boundaries between rocks of markedly different lithology. Faults are
discrete fractures across which there is measurable displacement of rock layer-
ing. On seismic sections, faults are usually identified where reflectors can be seen
to be displaced vertically. The amount of vertical displacement associated with
a fault at any location is termed the throw of the fault.

L. Van Gool (Ed.): DAGM 2002, LNCS 2449, pp. 150–157, 2002.
© Springer-Verlag Berlin Heidelberg 2002

2   Automated Structural Seismic Interpretation

Modern commercial interpretation software packages offer assistance for the interpretation of horizons and fault surfaces. The most commonly employed technique for horizon tracking is the so called autotracking or autopicking [2]. These algorithms require manually selected seed points and search for similar features on a neighbouring trace, but are not able to track horizons across discontinuities.

Computer-aided interpretation of fault surfaces is significantly less advanced than horizon interpretation [2]. Coherence measures such as cross correlation [3] or semblance [4] are applied to seismic data for imaging geological discontinuities like faults or stratigraphic features. However, they produce only potential fault pixels, but do not generate the actual fault lines or surfaces. There exist methods for fault autotracking which use the same basic approach as horizon trackers, but with limited success [5].

Previous attempts to solve the problem of correlating horizons across faults have been based on artificial neural networks [6,7]; however, these solutions use only similarities of the seismic patterns.

These automatic methods have in common that they are based only on local features. The tracking of horizons across faults is still done manually and therefore highly subjective and time-consuming. The difficulties of automating this task are due to the seismic images which contain only a small amount of local information, furthermore partially disturbed by vague or noisy signals. Therefore, more sophisticated methods have to be developed which impose geological and geometrical knowledge in order to reduce interpretation uncertainties.

3   The Geological Model

Our model consists of two components. The first component comprises the formation of horizon-pairs, consisting of one horizon from each side of the fault. The second component includes the combination of horizon-pairs to a global, geologically valid match for the complete area of interest. A-priori knowledge which is derived from the fault behaviour is introduced in each component in the following manner:

first component: horizon-pairs

- local measurement: similarity of reflector sequences
- constraint 1: consistent polarity
- constraint 2: restricted fault throw

second component: combinations of horizon-pairs

- global measurement: average displacement variation
- constraint 3: horizons must not cross
- constraint 4: sign of fault throw has to be consistent and correct
- constraint 5: throw function must not have more than one local maximum

A detailed description of these constraints can be found in[8]. In this work, we added a global measurement which is explained in the following.

Although the fault throw or the vertical displacement of corresponding horizon segments is not constant, the changes between left horizon differences to right horizon differences are small for geologically consistent correlations. The global measurement is calculated by comparing the vertical displacements of combined horizon segments. Horizon segments without counterpart on the other side are omitted. We calculate the average displacement variation of a combination i consisting of n horizon-pairs from

$$D_i = \frac{1}{n-1} \sum_{k=1}^{n-1} |(y_k^l - y_k^r) - (y_{k+1}^l - y_{k+1}^r)| \tag{1}$$

where y^l and y^r denote the averaged y-values (3 pixel) of left respectively right horizons at a fault. We define the global similarity G_i of a combination i as $G_i = D_{\max} - D_i$, where $D_{\max} = \max_i D_i$.

The result of the first component is a similarity value for each pair of left and right horizons. In the second step, the combination of those pairs, which is optimal according to all measurements and constraints, has to be found.

4   Optimisation Problem

The main problem regarding the optimisation task is the number of possible combinations of horizon-pairs. In order to simplify the calculation of the computational cost, we assume that the number of left horizons is equal to the number of right horizons. Every geometrically possible combination is considered, including those with missing connections.

Assuming that we have n left respectively right horizons, there is only one possibility to connect n pairs without violating constraint 3 (horizons must not cross). If we build arrangements consisting of $(n-1)$ pairs, we get $\binom{n}{n-1}$ different sets of left horizons. For each set of left horizons, there are $\binom{n}{n-1}$ possibilities to assign right horizons without violating constraint 3. The total number of arrangements for $(n-1)$ pairs is thus $\binom{n}{n-1}^2$. Similarly, for arrangements consisting of $(n-2)$ pairs, we get $\binom{n}{n-2}^2$ additional arrangements and so on.

The number of horizon-pair arrangements s_{max} follows therefore

$$s_{max} = \sum_{k=0}^{n} \binom{n}{k}^2 \tag{2}$$

This number increases exponentially with n since

$$\sum_{k=0}^{n} \binom{n}{k}^2 \geq \sum_{k=0}^{n} \binom{n}{k} = 2^n \tag{3}$$

which means that an exhaustive search strategy is not viable[1]. In order to find an appropriate optimisation method, it is necessary to consider not only the

---

[1] To express this relation in figures: even for the small data subset shown in figure 2(b) with 19 horizons on either side of the fault, already more than 35 billion different combinations are possible.

computational cost but also the nature of the search space and the type of constraints. Constraint 3 for instance disables us to use a more efficient strategy, which guarantees to find the global optimum, such as methods developed to solve the maximum-bipartite-matching problem. Besides, a dynamic programming approach is unsuitable since the total similarity of a combination does not follow directly from the similarity of its single pairs but comprises the global constraints (4,5).

Therefore, a random search method is required to solve the optimisation problem. Because undirected search techniques are extremely inefficient for large domains, we concentrate on directed random search techniques. Considering that our optimality function is discontinuous, hill climbing methods are inappropriate to the problem structure. Methods which can find the global optimum in discontinuous search spaces are e. g. Genetic Algorithms (GAs), Simulated Annealing (SA) or tabu search. Another characteristic of our problem is, that there is no adjacency relationship between solutions. While SA and tabu search work with such an adjacency relationship, this is not necessary for a GA. Additionally, compared with other heuristic methods such as neural networks, in GA it is more straightforward to precisely define the evaluation criteria.

5   Implementation

Genetic Algorithms (GAs), which were invented by Holland [9], are a robust and efficient directed random search technique for searching large spaces. They are based on drawing parallels between the mechanisms of biological evolution and mathematical modelling. GAs usually work with a population of individuals which are solutions to a problem, in order to enable a parallel search process. Each solution is represented by a string, called chromosome, which is composed of genes. A fitness function, as well as crossover, mutation, and selection operators determine on the development of the population.

5.1   Solution Representation

The solution representation we use is a 1D integer array where the index k represents the left horizon number and its allocated value $l(k)$ the right horizon number. If a left horizon has no counterpart, the value -1 is assigned. The two main advantages of this representation are a straightforward solution interpretation as well as simplifications regarding tests for geological validity (see 5.4).

5.2   Fitness Function

The fitness of a solution is composed of local and global measurement as well as local and global constraints. We calculate the fitness F_i of a solution i consisting of a number n of chromosomes, i. e. horizon-pairs, j from

$$F_i = \sum_{j=1}^{n} S_{k,l(k)}^2 + G_i - P_1 - P_2. \tag{4}$$

$S_{k,l(k)}$ denotes the local similarity which results from the cross-correlation co-efficient of the solution's chromosomes or horizon-pairs [8]. Using the square of $S_{k,l(k)}$ favours combinations with uneven distributed correlation values, while the summation encourages combinations consisting of a larger number of horizon-pairs. The latter can be considered as a reliability factor since the reliability of a global match decreases with a decreasing number of horizon-pairs; although a geologically valid solution may contain less horizon pairs than the maximum number of possible matches.

The global measurement G_i is calculated following equation 1 as described in section 3. Constraint 4 and 5 are represented by P_1 respectively P_2. If one of the constraints is violated, a penalty is subtracted from the fitness value which depends on the average fitness $\overline{f}$ at given generation t. The amount of the penalties $P_{1,2}$ is calculated by $P_{1,2} = \frac{1}{2} \cdot \overline{f}_{(t)}$. A combination, which violates both constraints but features an above average similarity value, has therefore still a chance to be selected for crossover, since it is possible that the offspring inherits a valid part with high similarity.

5.3   Initial Population

The initial population is created by randomly building combinations of horizon-pairs. However, we restrict the search space by applying constraints. First, the set of horizon-pairs is reduced by excluding those which do not follow the local constraints 1 and 2. Second, we avoid the generation of combinations within which horizon-pairs cross (constraint 3). This is achieved by restricting the random search in every step to the resulting possible horizon-pairs.

We set the population size I proportional to the product of left and right horizons in order to improve the exploring capabilities of the solution space for an increasing number of possible combinations.

5.4   Operators

As selection scheme, we adopted the usual *roulette wheel* procedure to pick r parents on the basis of their fitness [10]. Then $(I - r)$ distinct individuals are taken to survive unchanged into the next generation. I denotes the number of individuals in a generation. The remaining r individuals which are not selected as survivors will be automatically replaced by the r offspring produced in the breeding phase.

Offspring strings are generated by choosing two parent strings, randomly selecting a single crossing location and exchanging the substrings bounded by that crossing location. Before evaluating the fitness of a new solution obtained by crossover, its geometrical validity is verified and, as the case may be, discarded.

A classical mutation strategy which changes randomly chromosomes would generate an unreasonably high rate of combinations which are invalid regarding the constraint of non-crossing horizons. Thus, we use a revised strategy where we randomly choose between values denoting all those pairs which follow both local constraints, and additionally the value *no combination* (coded as -1). Mutations for a chromosome are produced repeatedly until constraint 3 is fulfilled.

6   Experimental Results

Experiments were performed with four examples of normal faults to assess the appropriateness of the fitness function. Crossover and mutation rates were chosen experimentally. We replaced 70% of the population at each iteration step and used a mutation rate of 0.01. Instead of using a fixed number of generations, we terminated the process if the number of distinct individuals is less than $(I - r) = 30\%$ (see 5.4).

The population size I was estimated by $I = C*n_l*n_r$, where n_l and n_r denote the number of left respectively right horizons. Figure 1 shows the number of unacceptable solutions for different values of C. Values larger than $C = 0.6$ give adequate results. The choice of C represent a compromise between computation time and stability of the algorithm. For $C = 1.1$, which we chose for our tests, the computation time was less than 60 s for all test cases. We used IDL (The Interactive Data Language) for our prototypical implementation on a PC with Pentium II, 266 MHz processor.

Figures 2(a) to 2(c) show results from three of those faults across which the displayed horizons were correlated by a typical run of the genetic algorithm. The solutions show the global optimum according to our fitness-function. To verify the correctness of the solutions, we compared them to those chosen by a human interpreter. In all three cases, the global optimum and the manual correlation were identical. Figure 2(d) shows the fourth case where those two solutions differ. The geologically most plausible solution has not been accepted as correct and therefore penalised by the fitness function because of the considerable decrease of throw in the upper part of the fault. The missing correlation is due to the high variation of fault throw between horizon-pairs 5 left - 5 right and 6 left - 6 right (numbering starts with 1 for the lowest horizon) which is increased by an inaccurate interpolation of the fault line.

In order to evaluate the repeatability of the results, 100 runs were carried out for each fault. The number of acceptable solutions ranged between 94 and 100% as shown in table 1.

Table 1. Repeatability of solutions. *Other acceptable solutions* are solutions where one pair at maximum is missing, *unacceptable solutions* are those with more than one missing pair and all geologically invalid solutions.

	Fault 1	Fault 2	Fault 3	Fault 4
Global optimum	92	84	73	78
Other acceptable solutions	2	13	25	22
$\sum$ **Acceptable solutions**	**94**	**98**	**98**	**100**
Unacceptable solutions	6	3	2	0

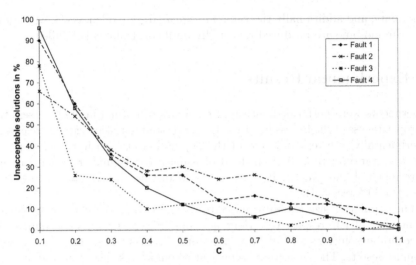

Fig. 1. Number of unacceptable solutions for different values of C

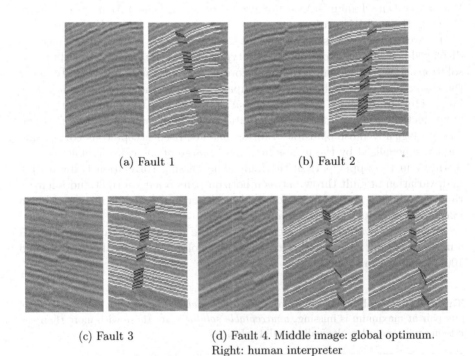

(a) Fault 1   (b) Fault 2

(c) Fault 3   (d) Fault 4. Middle image: global optimum.
                           Right: human interpreter

Fig. 2. Correlations of horizons found by the genetic algorithm

7   Conclusions

A genetic algorithm for correlating horizon segments across faults, which is based on a geological model, was introduced. It was shown that genetic algorithms are a suitable method to solve the optimisation problem. The results presented above indicate the appropriateness of the fitness function for geologically simple structures as well as a satisfactory repeatability of the genetic algorithm. Improvements of the fitness-function remain to be investigated, in order to enhance the applicability of the method to geologically more complicated structures. This might be done by implementing additional geological constraints and improving the local measurement. Additionally, the method will be tested on other data sets and different fault classes.

Acknowledgements

We would like to acknowledge Shell for the seismic data and stimulating discussions. Melanie Aurnhammer would like to thank Rafael Mayoral for his help regarding the test analysis and his careful revision.

References

1. L. C. Lawyer, From the Other Side, *The Leading Edge*, Vol. 17, No. 9, 1998, pp. 1190–1191.
2. G. A. Dorn, Modern 3-D Seismic Interpretation, *The Leading Edge*, Vol. 17, No. 9, 1998.
3. M. S. Bahorich, and S. L. Farmer, 3-D Seismic Discontinuity for Faults and Stratigraphic Features, *The Leading Edge*, Vol 14, No. 10, 1995, pp. 1053–1058.
4. K. J. Marfurt, R. L. Kirlin, S. L. Farmer, and M. S. Bahorich, 3-D Seismic Attributes Using a Semblance-Based Coherency Algorithm, *Geophysics*, Vol. 63, No. 4, 1998, pp. 1150–1165.
5. G. Fehmers, Shell Research, Netherlands, personal communications.
6. P. Alberts, M. Warner, and D. Lister, Artificial Neural Networks for simultaneous multi Horizon tracking across Discontinuities, *70th Annual International Meeting, SEG*, Calgary, Canada, 2000.
7. L. F. Kemp, J. R. Threet, and J. Veezhinathan, A neural net branch and bound seismic horizon tracker, Expanded Abstracts, *62nd Annual International Meeting, SEG*, Houston, USA, 1992.
8. M. Aurnhammer and K. Tönnies, Horizon Correlation across Faults Guided by Geological Constraints, Proceedings of SPIE, Vol. #4667, *Electronic Imaging 2002*, 21-23 January, San Jose, California USA. In press.
9. J. H. Holland, *Adaption in Natural and Artificial Systems* (MIT Press, 1975).
10. D. E. Goldberg, *Genetic Algorithms in Search, Optimization and Machine Learning* (Addison-Wesley, 1989).

Unsupervised Image Clustering
Using the Information Bottleneck Method

Jacob Goldberger[1], Hayit Greenspan[2], and Shiri Gordon[2]

[1] CUTe Systems Ltd. Tel-Aviv, Israel
jacob@cute.co.il
[2] Faculty of Engineering, Tel Aviv University, Tel Aviv 69978, Israel
hayit@eng.tau.ac.il

Abstract. A new method for unsupervised image category clustering is presented, based on a continuous version of a recently introduced information theoretic principle, the information bottleneck (IB). The clustering method is based on hierarchical grouping: Utilizing a Gaussian mixture model, each image in a given archive is first represented as a set of coherent regions in a selected feature space. Images are next grouped such that the mutual information between the clusters and the image content is maximally preserved. The appropriate number of clusters can be determined directly from the IB principle. Experimental results demonstrate the performance of the proposed clustering method on a real image database.

Keywords: Image Categories; Unsupervised Clustering; Image Grouping; Gaussian mixture modeling; Kullback-Leibler distance; Information bottleneck.

1 Introduction

Image clustering and categorization is a means for high-level description of image content. The goal is to find a mapping of the archive images into classes (clusters) such that the set of classes provide essentially the same prediction, or information, about the image archive as the entire image set collection. The generated classes provide a concise summarization and visualization of the image content. Image archive clustering is important for efficient handling (search and retrieval) in large image databases [6,2]. In the retrieval process, the query image is initially compared with all the cluster centers. The subset of clusters that has the largest similarity to the query image is chosen. The query image is next compared with all the images within the selected subset of clusters. Search efficiency is improved due to the fact that the query image is not compared exhaustively to all the images in the database.

In most clustering methods (e.g. K-means), a distance measure between two data points or between a data point and a class centroid is given a priori as part of the problem setup. The clustering task is to find a small number of classes with low intra-class variability. However in many clustering problems, e.g. image

L. Van Gool (Ed.): DAGM 2002, LNCS 2449, pp. 158–165, 2002.
© Springer-Verlag Berlin Heidelberg 2002

clustering, the objects we want to classify have a complicated high dimensional structure and choosing the right distance measure is not a straight-forward task. A choice of a specific distance measure can influence the clustering results.

The clustering framework presented in this work is based on hierarchical grouping: image pixels are first grouped into coherent regions in feature space; these are modelled via Gaussian mixture models (GMMs). Next, utilizing the information bottleneck (IB) method [7], the image models are grouped, bottom-up, into coherent clusters. Characteristics of the proposed method include: 1) Image *models* are clustered rather than raw image pixels. The clustering is thus done in a continuous domain. 2) The IB method provides a simultaneous construction of both the clusters and the distance measure between them. 3) A natural termination of the bottom-up clustering process can be determined as part of the IB principle. This provides an automated means for finding the relevant number of clusters per archive.

2 Grouping Pixels into GMMs

In the first layer of the grouping process we shift from image pixels to a mid-level representation of an image in which the image is represented as a set of coherent regions in feature space. In this work we model each image as a mixture of Gaussians in the color $(L * a * b)$ feature space. The representation model is a general one, and can incorporate any desired feature space (such as texture, shape, etc) or combination thereof. In order to include spatial information, the (x, y) position of the pixel is appended to the feature vector. Following the feature extraction stage, each pixel is represented with a five-dimensional feature vector, and the image as a whole is represented by a collection of feature vectors in the five-dimensional space.

Pixels are grouped into homogeneous regions, by grouping the feature vectors in the selected five-dimensional feature space. The underlying assumption is that the image colors and their spatial distribution in the image plane are generated by a mixture of Gaussians. The distribution of a d-dimensional random variable is a mixture of k Gaussians if its density function is:

$$f(y) = \sum_{j=1}^{k} \alpha_j \frac{1}{\sqrt{(2\pi)^d |\Sigma_j|}} \exp\{-\frac{1}{2}(y - \mu_j)^T \Sigma_j^{-1}(y - \mu_j)\} \tag{1}$$

Learning a Gaussian mixture model is in essence an unsupervised clustering task. The Expectation-Maximization (EM) algorithm is used [4], to determine the maximum likelihood parameters of a mixture of k Gaussians in the feature space (similar to [1]). The first step in applying the EM algorithm to the problem at hand is to initialize the mixture model parameters. The K-means algorithm is utilized to extract the data-driven initialization. The updating process is repeated until the log-likelihood is increased by less than a predefined threshold from one iteration to the next. In this work we choose to converge based on the log-likelihood measure and we use a 1% threshold. Using EM, the parameters

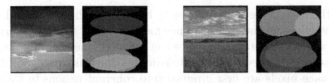

Fig. 1. Input image (left) Image modeling via Gaussian mixture (right).

representing the Gaussian mixture are found. K-Means and EM are calculated for $k \geq 1$, with k corresponding to the model size. The Minimum Description Length (MDL) principle [3] serves to select among values of k. In our experiments, k ranges from 3 to 6.

Figure 1[1] shows two examples of learning a GMM model for an input image . In this visualization each localized Gaussian mixture is shown as a set of ellipsoids. Each ellipsoid represents the support, mean color and spatial layout, of a particular Gaussian in the image plane.

3   The Agglomerative Information Bottleneck

The second layer of the image grouping process is based on information theoretic principle, the information bottleneck method (IB) [7]. Using the IB method, the extracted image models are grouped, bottom-up, into coherent clusters[2]. The IB principle states that among all the possible clusterings of the object set into a fixed number of clusters, the desired clustering is the one that minimizes the loss of mutual information between the objects and the features extracted from them. The IB method can be motivated from Shannon's rate distortion theory [3] which provides lower bounds on the number of classes we can divide a source given a distortion constraint. Given a random variable, X, and a distortion measure, $d(x_1, x_2)$, defined on the alphabet of X, we want to classify-quantize the symbols of X such that the average quantization error is less than a given number D. It is clear that we can reduce the average quantization error by enlarging the number of clusters. Shannon's rate distortion theorem states that the minimum log number of clusters needed to keep the average quantization error below D is given by the following rate-distortion function:

$$R(D) = \min_{p(\hat{x}|x)|Ed(x,\hat{x}) \leq D} I(X; \hat{X}) \qquad (2)$$

where the average distortion $Ed(x, \hat{x})$ is $\sum_{x,\hat{x}} p(x)p(\hat{x}|x)d(x, \hat{x})$ and $I(X; \hat{X})$ is the mutual information between X and $\hat{X}$ given by:

$$I(X; \hat{X}) = \sum_{x,\hat{x}} p(x)p(\hat{x}|x) \log \frac{p(\hat{x}|x)}{p(\hat{x})}$$

---

[1] A color version of the paper may be found in http://www.eng.tau.ac.il/~hayit

[2] Recent work using related information-theoretic concepts for within-image clustering, or segmentation, can be found in [5].

The random variable $\hat{X}$ can be viewed as a soft-probabilistic classification of X.

Unlike classical rate distortion theory, the IB method avoids the arbitrary choice of a distance or a distortion measure. Instead, clustering of the object space (denoted by X) is done by preserving the relevant information about another "feature" space (denoted by Y). In our case the objects are images and the feature space consists of local information we extract for each pixel (e.g. color, texture). We assume, as part of the IB approach, that $\hat{X} \to X \to Y$ is a markov chain, i.e. given X, the clustering $\hat{X}$ is independent of the feature space, Y. Consider the following distortion function:

$$d(x, \hat{x}) = D(\, p(y|X = x) \,||\, p(y|\hat{X} = \hat{x})\,) \tag{3}$$

where $D(f||g) = E_f \log \frac{f}{g}$ is the Kullback-Leibler divergence [3]. Note that $p(y|\hat{x}) = \sum_x p(x|\hat{x})p(y|x)$ is a function of $p(\hat{x}|x)$. Hence, $d(x, \hat{x})$ is not predetermined. Instead it depends on the clustering. Therefore, as we search for the best clustering we also search for the most suitable distance measure.

The loss in the mutual information between X and Y caused by the (probabilistic) clustering $\hat{X}$ is in fact the average of this distortion measure:

$$I(X;Y) - I(\hat{X};Y) = \sum_{x,\hat{x},y} p(x,\hat{x},y) \log \frac{p(x|y)}{p(x)} - \sum_{x,\hat{x},y} p(x,\hat{x},y) \log \frac{p(y|\hat{x})}{p(y)} =$$

$$= \sum_{x,\hat{x},y} p(x,\hat{x},y) \log \frac{p(y|x)}{p(y|\hat{x})} = \sum_{x,\hat{x}} p(x,\hat{x}) \sum_y p(y|x) \log \frac{p(y|x)}{p(y|\hat{x})} = E[D(p(y|x)||p(y|\hat{x}))] \tag{4}$$

Substituting distortion measure (3) in the rate distortion function we obtain:

$$R(D) = \min_{p(\hat{x}|x)|I(X;Y) - I(\hat{X};Y) \leq D} I(X; \hat{X}) \tag{5}$$

which is exactly the minimization criterion proposed by IB principle, namely, finding a clustering that causes minimum reduction of the mutual information between the objects and the features.

The minimization problem posed by the IB principle can be approximated by a greedy algorithm based on a bottom-up merging procedure [7]. The algorithm starts with the trivial clustering where each cluster consists of a single point. In every greedy step we merge the two classes such that the loss in the mutual information caused by merging them is the smallest. This ensures minimization of the overall information loss. Let c_1 and c_2 be two image clusters. The information loss due to the merging of c_1 and c_2 is:

$$d(c_1, c_2) = I(C_{before}, Y) - I(C_{after}, Y) = E[D(p(y|C_{before})||p(y|C_{after}))] \geq 0$$

where $I(C_{before}, Y)$ and $I(C_{after}, Y)$ are the mutual information between the classes and the feature space before and after c_1 and c_2 are merged into a single class. Standard information theory manipulation reveals:

$$d(c_1, c_2) = \sum_{y,i=1,2} p(c_i, y) \log \frac{p(c_i, y)}{p(c_i)p(y)} - \sum_y p(c_1 \cup c_2, y) \log \frac{p(c_1 \cup c_2, y)}{p(c_1 \cup c_2)p(y)} =$$

$$= \sum_{y,i=1,2} p(c_i,y) \log \frac{p(y|c_i)}{p(y|c_1 \cup c_2)} = \sum_{i=1,2} p(c_i) D(p(y|c_i)||p(y|c_1 \cup c_2)) \quad (6)$$

4   Using the IB Method for Clustering of Image GMMs

In this section we present the image clustering algorithm proposed, as defined from the IB principle. To apply the IB principle we have first to define a joint distribution on the images and the features. In the following we denote by X the set of images we want to classify. We assume uniform prior probability $p(x)$ of observing an image. Denote by Y the random variable associated with the feature vector extracted from a single pixel. The Gaussian mixture model we use to describe the feature distribution within an image x (section 2) is exactly the conditional density function $p(y|x)$. Thus we have a joint image-feature distribution $p(x,y)$. Note that since $p(y|x)$ is a GMM distribution, the density function per cluster c, $p(y|c) = \frac{1}{|c|} \sum_{x \in c} p(y|x)$, is a mixture of GMMs and therefore it is also a GMM. Let f_1, f_2 be the GMMs associated with image clusters c_1, c_2 respectively. The GMM of the merged cluster $c_1 \cup c_2$, denoted by f, is:

$$f(y) = \frac{|c_1|}{|c_1 \cup c_2|} f_1(y) + \frac{|c_2|}{|c_1 \cup c_2|} f_2(y)$$

According to expression (6), the distance between the two image clusters c_1 and c_2 is:

$$d(c_1,c_2) = \frac{|c_1|}{N} D(f_1(y)||f(y)) + \frac{|c_2|}{N} D(f_2(y)||f(y)) \quad (7)$$

where N is the size of the image database. Hence, to compute the distance between two image clusters c_1 and c_2 we need to compute the KL distance between two GMM distributions.

Since the KL distance between two GMMs can not be analytically computed, we can numerically approximate it through Monte-Carlo procedures. Denote the feature set extracted from the images, that belongs to cluster c_1, by $y_1 \ldots y_n$. The KL distance $D(f_1||f)$ can be approximated as follows:

$$D(f_1||f) \cong \frac{1}{n} \sum_{t=1}^{n} \log \frac{f_1(y_t)}{f(y_t)} \quad (8)$$

Another possible approximation is to use synthetic samples produced from the Gaussian mixture distribution f_1 instead of the image data. This enables us to compute the KL distance without referring to the images from which the models were built. Image categorization experiments show no significant difference between these two proposed approximations of the KL distance. The expression $D(f_2||f)$ can be approximated in a similar manner. The agglomerative IB algorithm for image clustering is the following:

1. Start with the trivial clustering where each image is a cluster.

2. In each step merge clusters c_1 and c_2 such that information loss $d(c_1, c_2)$ (equation 7) is minimal.
3. Continue the merging process until the information loss $d(c_1, c_2)$ is more than a predefined threshold, indicating that we attempt to merge two non-similar clusters.

5 Results

An image databases consists of 100 natural scenery images was randomly extracted from the COREL database. A Gaussian mixture model was built for each image as described in section 2. Next the bottom-up clustering method, described in section 4, was applied to the image models. We started with 100 clusters where each image is a cluster. After 99 steps all the images were merged into a single cluster.

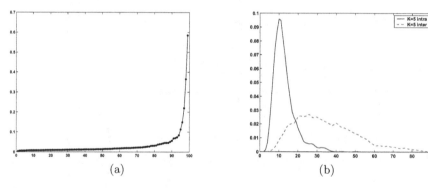

Fig. 2. (a) Loss of mutual information during the clustering process. (b) Statistical analysis: intra-class distance (solid) and inter-class distance (dashed).

The loss of mutual information during each merging step of the clustering process is presented in Figure 2(a). The x-axis indicates the steps of the algorithm. The y-axis shows the amount of mutual information loss (in bits) caused by merging the two clusters selected at the corresponding step. There is a gradual increase in information loss until a break point is reached indicating a significant loss of information. This point helps us to determine the "right" number of clusters that exist in the database. From that point on every merge causes a significant degradation of information and therefore leads to a worse clustering scenario. As can be seen from Figure 2(a) the break point is found in the transition from five clusters to four clusters, indicating that an appropriate number of clusters in this case is five. Figure 3 presents the grouping of the images database into the five clusters. The GMM model generated for each cluster is shown on the right. A clear distinction between the groups is evident in the Gaussian mixture characteristics, in blob color features and their spatial layouts. Progressing an

Fig. 3. Results: Clustering the database into 5 groups. A GMM model generated for each cluster is shown on the right.

additional step of the algorithm, towards four clusters, results in the merging of classes c_2 and c_3. We note that the two classes appear rather different. The visual inhomogeneity is consistent with the significant loss of information, as indicated via the information loss function.

To evaluate the quality of grouping presented in Figure 3, a histogram of the "intra-class" distances (symmetric KL-distances between all image pairs within the same cluster) is shown in Figure 2(b), and compared with the histogram of "inter-class" distances (distances between image pairs across clusters). The x-axis is the value of the KL distance and the y-axis is the frequency of occurrence of the respective distance in each of the two distance sets. We note that the "intra-class" distances are narrowly spread at the lower end of the axis (close to zero), as compared to the wide-spread and larger distance values of the "inter-class" set, showing that the image variability within clusters is much less than the variability across clusters.

In conclusion, we have presented an unsupervised clustering scheme that is based on information theoretic principles and provides image sets for a concise summarization and visualization of the image content within a given image archive. Several limitations that need to be addressed are the limited feature space (can be extended to include texture and shape) and the use of GMM for image representation that describes the image as a set of convex regions. Future work entails utilizing the extracted clusters for efficient search and retrieval and evaluating the performance by comparing with alternative clustering techniques.

References

1. S. Belongie, C. Carson, H. Greenspan, and J. Malik. Color and texture-based image segmentation using em and its application to content based image retrieval. In *Proc. of the Int. Conference on Computer Vision*, pages 675–82, 1998.
2. J. Chen, C.A. Bouman, and J.C. Dalton. Hierarchical browsing and search of large image databases. *IEEE transactions on Image Processing*, 9(3):442–455, March 2000.
3. T. M. Cover and J. A. Thomas. *Elements of Information Theory*. John Wiley and Sons, 1991.
4. A. Dempster, N. Laird, and D. Rubin. Maximum likelihood from incomplete data via the em algorithm. *J. Royal Statistical Soc. B*, 39(1):1–38, 1997.
5. L. Hermes, T. Zoller, and J. M. Buhmann. Parametric distributional clustering for image segmentation. In *Proceedings of ECCV02*, volume III, pages 577–591, 2002.
6. S. Krishnamachari and M. Abdel-Mottaleb. Hierarchical clustering algorithm for fast image retrieval. In *IS&T/SPIE Conference on Storage and Retrieval for Image and Video databases VII*, pages 427–435, San-Jose, CA, Jan 1999.
7. N. Slonim and N. Tishby. Agglomerative information bottleneck. In *In Proc. of Neural Information Processing Systems*, pages 617–623, 1999.

Efficient Modification of the Central
Weighted Vector Median Filter*

Bogdan Smolka*

Silesian University of Technology
Department of Automatic Control
Akademicka 16 Str, 44-101 Gliwice, Poland
bsmolka@ia.polsl.gliwice.pl

Abstract. A new filtering approach designed to eliminate impulsive noise in color images, while preserving fine image details is presented. The computational complexity of the new filter is significantly lower than that of the Central Weighted Vector Median Filter (CWVMF). The comparison shows that the new filter outperforms the CWVMF, as well as other standard procedures used in color image filtering for the removal of impulsive noise.

1 Standard Noise Reduction Filters

Multichannel signal processing has been the subject of extensive research during the last years, primarily due to its importance to color image processing. The amount of research published to date indicates a growing interest in the area of color image filtering and analysis. The most common image processing tasks are noise filtering and image enhancement. These tasks are an essential part of any image processing system, whether the final image is utilized for visual interpretation or for automatic analysis [9]. It has been widely recognized that the processing of color image data as vector fields is desirable due to the correlation that exists between the image channels, and that the nonlinear vector processing of color images is the most effective way to filter out noise. For this reasons, the new filtering technique presented in this paper is also nonlinear and utilizes the correlation among the color image channels.

A number of nonlinear, multichannel filters, which utilize correlation among multivariate vectors using various distance measures, have been proposed [1-16]. The most popular nonlinear, multichannel filters are based on the ordering of vectors in a predefined sliding window. The output of these filters is defined as the lowest ranked vector ac-cording to a specific ordering technique.

Let $\mathbf{F}(x)$ represent a multichannel image and let W be a window of finite size n. The noisy image vectors inside the window will be denoted as $\mathbf{F}_j$, $j=0,1,..,n-1$. If the distance between two vectors $\mathbf{F}_i, \mathbf{F}_j$ is $\rho(\mathbf{F}_i, \mathbf{F}_j)$ then the scalar quantity :

---

* Partially supported by KBN Grant PBZ-KBN-040/P04/08

L. Van Gool (Ed.): DAGM 2002, LNCS 2449, pp. 166–173, 2002.

$$R_i = \sum_{j=1}^{n} \rho(\mathbf{F}_i, \mathbf{F}_j) \tag{1}$$

is the distance associated with the noisy vector $\mathbf{F}_i$ in W. An ordering of the R_i's implies the same ordering to the corresponding vectors $\mathbf{F}_i$'s into a sequence $\mathbf{F}_{(0)}$, $\mathbf{F}_{(1)},\ldots,\mathbf{F}_{(n-1)}$. Nonlinear ranked type multichannel estimators define the vector $\mathbf{F}_{(0)}$ as the filter output. This selection is due to the fact that vectors that diverge greatly from the data population usually appear in higher indexed locations in the ordered sequence. However, the concept of input ordering, initially applied to scalar quantities is not easily extended to multichannel data, since there is no universal way to define ordering in vector spaces. To overcome this problem, different distance functions are often utilized to order vectors. As an example, the *Vector Median Filter* (VMF) makes use of the L_1 or $L2$ norm to order vectors according to their relative magnitude differences [1]. The output of the VMF is the pixel $\mathbf{F}_k \in W$ for which the following condition is satisfied:

$$\sum_{j=0}^{n-1} \rho(\mathbf{F}_k, \mathbf{F}_j) < \sum_{j=0}^{n-1} \rho(\mathbf{F}_i, \mathbf{F}_j), \ i = 0,\ldots,n-1. \tag{2}$$

In this way the VMF consists of computing and comparing the values of R_i and the output is the vector $\mathbf{F}_k$ for which R_k reaches its minimum. In other words if for some k the value: $R_k = \sum_{j=0}^{n-1} \rho(\mathbf{F}_k, \mathbf{F}_j)$ is smaller than $R_0 = \sum_{j=0}^{n-1} \rho(\mathbf{F}_0, \mathbf{F}_j)$, then the original pixel $\mathbf{F}_0$ in the filter window W is being replaced by $\mathbf{F}_k$ which satisfies the above condition, ($k = \arg\min_i R_i$).

The *Basic Vector Directional Filter* (BVDF) is a ranked-order, nonlinear filter which parallelizes the VMF operation [11]. The output of the BVDF is that vector from the input set, which minimizes the sum of the angles with the other vectors. To improve the efficiency of the directional filters, another method called *Directional-Distance Filter* (DDF) was proposed in [3]. This filter retains the structure of the BVDF but utilizes a new distance criterion to order the vectors inside the processing window.

Recently methods based on ansisotropic diffusion have been proposed, however they are not suitable for the reduction of impulsive noise, as they treat the impulsive pixels as edges and preserve them [14-16].

In [12] the vector median concept has been generalized and the so called weighted vector median has been proposed. Using the weighted vector median approach, the filter output is the vector $\mathbf{F}_k$, for which the following condition holds:

$$\sum_{j=0}^{n-1} w_j \rho(\mathbf{F}_k, \mathbf{F}_j) < \sum_{j=0}^{n-1} w_j \rho(\mathbf{F}_i, \mathbf{F}_j), \ i = 0,..,n-1, \tag{3}$$

where the w_j are the weights associated with vectors $\mathbf{F}_j$. In this paper we assume, that the only nonzero weighting coefficient is the w_0. In this way, we obtain the so called Central Weighted Vector Median Filter (CWVMF) [12].

2 Modified Central Weighted Vector Median Filter

The construction of the new filter is very similar to that of the Central Weighted VMF (CWVMF) proposed in [12], in which the filter output is the vector $\mathbf{F}_k \in W$, which-satisfies:

$$\sum_{j=0}^{n-1} w_j \rho(\mathbf{F}_k, \mathbf{F}_j) < \sum_{j=0}^{n-1} w_j \rho(\mathbf{F}_i, \mathbf{F}_j), \quad i = 0, \ldots, n-1. \tag{4}$$

where $w_j \neq 0$ for $j = 0$ and equals 0 otherwise. So the output of the CWVMF is $\mathbf{F}_0$ (Fig. 1), if the sum of distances between $\mathbf{F}_0$ and all its neighbors $R_0 = \sum_{j=0}^{n-1} \rho(\mathbf{F}_0, \mathbf{F}_j)$ is smaller than $R_k = \sum_{j=0}^{n-1} w_j(\mathbf{F}_k, \mathbf{F}_j)$ for k=1,2, ...,n-1, other-wise the CWVMF output is the vector $\mathbf{F}_k$ (Fig. 2), for which R_k is minimal. The difference between the VMF and CWVMF is that the distance between the central pixel $\mathbf{F}_0$ and its neighbors is multiplied by the weighting coefficient w_0, as shown in Fig. 2. The weighting privileges the central pixel $\mathbf{F}_0$ as the $w_0 \cdot \rho(\mathbf{F}_0, \mathbf{F}_0)$ is 0. However the weighting can be performed in a much simpler way which describes the new filtering approach.

Let the distance associated with the center pixel be :

$$R_0 = w_0 \sum_{j=0}^{n-1} \rho(\mathbf{F}_0, \mathbf{F}_j), \tag{5}$$

where $w_0 \leq 1$ is a weight assigned to the sum of distances between the central vector $\mathbf{F}_0$ and its neighbors. Then let the sum of distances associated with other pixels be like in VMF:

$$R_i = \sum_{j=0}^{n-1} \rho(\mathbf{F}_i, \mathbf{F}_j), \quad i = 1, \ldots, n-1. \tag{6}$$

If for some k, R_k is smaller than R_0

$$R_k = \sum_{j=0}^{n-1} \rho(\mathbf{F}_k, \mathbf{F}_j) < R_0, \tag{7}$$

then $\mathbf{F}_0$ is being replaced by $\mathbf{F}_k$. It happens when

$$\sum_{j=0}^{n-1} \rho(\mathbf{F}_k, \mathbf{F}_j) < w_0 \sum_{j=0}^{n-1} \rho(\mathbf{F}_0, \mathbf{F}_j), \tag{8}$$

which is the condition for the replacement of the central pixel by one of its neighbors.

The center pixel $\mathbf{F}_0$ will be replaced by its neighbor $\mathbf{F}_k$, if the distance R_k associated with $\mathbf{F}_k$ is smaller than R_0 and is the minimal distance associated with the vectors belonging to W. The weight w_0 is a design parameter. For $w_0 = 0$ no changes are introduced to the image, and for $w_0 = 1$ we obtain the standard vector median filter as proposed by Astola.

If $w_0 \in (0,1)$, then the new filter has the ability of noise removal, while preserving fine image details. It is easy to notice that the new filter is faster than the CWVMF, as the only weighting is applied to the sum of distances R_0. As a result the new filter needs only one additional multiplication compared with the VMF. The CWVMF needs 7 additional multiplications to perform the weighting of the distances between F_0 and all its neighbors. As a result the new filtering scheme is significantly faster than CWVMF and is more efficient as will be shown in the next section.

<table>
<tr><td></td><td>F_1</td><td></td></tr>
<tr><td>F_4</td><td>F_0</td><td>F_2</td></tr>
<tr><td></td><td>F_3</td><td></td></tr>
</table>
a)

<table>
<tr><td></td><td>F_1</td><td></td></tr>
<tr><td>F_4</td><td>F_2</td><td>F_0</td></tr>
<tr><td></td><td>F_3</td><td></td></tr>
</table>
b)

Fig. 1. In the vector median approach the sum of distances between the center pixel F_0 and its neighbors is computed. Then the neighbors of F_0 are being put to the center of the window W and the appropriate distances are being computed. Fig. **b)** shows the situation where the R_2 distance associated with the F_2 vector is determined.

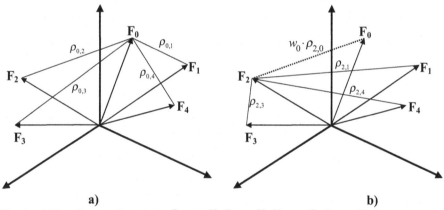

a)   b)

Fig. 2. a) The distance R_0 equals $R_0 = \rho(0,1) + \rho(0,2) + \rho(0,3) + \rho(0,4)$, **b)** the distance R_2 associated with F_2 equals $R_2 = \rho(2,0) + \rho(2,1) + \rho(2,3) + \rho(2,4)$ in the case of the VMF approach and $R_2 = w_0 \, \rho(2,0) + \rho(2,1) + \rho(2,3) + \rho(2,4)$ when applying the Central Weighted Vector Median Filter.

3   Efficiency of the New Filter

The color test image *LENA* has been contaminated by 4% impulsive noise (each RGB channel was distorted by impulsive *salt and pepper* noise with probability 0.04 so that the correlation of noise in each channel was equal to 0.5). The root of the mean squared error (RMSE), signal to noise ratio (SNR), peak signal to noise ratio (PSNR), normalized mean square error (NMSE) and normalized color difference (NCD) [9], were taken as measures of image quality. The comparison shows that the new filter outperforms significantly the standard Central Weighted Vector Median Filter, when the impulsive noise has to be eliminated. The efficiency of the new filtering technique is shown in Tables. 2 and 3.

Table 1. Filters taken for comparison with the new Modified Central Weighted Vector Median Filter (MCWVMF).

NOTATION	FILTER	REF.
AMF	Arithmetic Mean Filter	[5]
VMF	Vector Median Filter	[1]
BVDF	Basic Vector Directional Filter	[10]
GVDF	Generalized Vector Directional Filter	[10]
DDF	Directional-Distance Filter	[3]
HDF	Hybrid Directional Filter	[2]
AHDF	Adaptive Hybrid Directional Filter	[2]
FVDF	Fuzzy Vector Directional Filter	[8]
ANNF	Adaptive Nearest Neighbor Filter	[7]
ANP-EF	Adaptive Non Parametric (Exponential) Filter	[9]
ANP-GF	Adaptive Non Parametric (Gaussian) Filter	[9]
ANP-DF	Adaptive Non Parametric (Directional) Filter	[9]

Table 2. Comparison of the new algorithm with the standard techniques (Tab. 1), using the *LENA* standard image contaminated by 4% impulsive noise with 0.5 correlation between the RGB channels.

METHOD	NMSE $[10^{-3}]$	RMSE	SNR [dB]	PSNR [dB]	NCD $[10^{-4}]$
NONE	514.720	32.166	12.884	17.983	79.165
AMF	79.317	12.627	21.006	26.105	82.745
VMF	**18.766**	**6.142**	**27.266**	**32.365**	**40.467**
CWVMF	**12,105**	**4,933**	**29,170**	**34,269**	**19,019**
BVDF	24.587	7.030	26.093	31.192	41.151
GVDF	19.474	6.257	27.105	32.204	41.773
DDF	18.872	6.159	27.242	32.340	40.237
HDF	18.610	6.116	27.303	32.401	41.275
AHDF	18.310	6.067	27.373	32.472	41.166
FVDF	22.251	6.688	26.527	31.625	44.686
ANNF	26.800	7.340	25.719	30.817	48.009
ANP-E	78.601	12.570	21.046	26.144	82.457
ANP-G	78.623	12.571	21.045	26.143	82.478
ANP-D	24.178	6.971	26.166	31.264	46.070
NEW	8,095	4,034	30,918	36,017	10,753

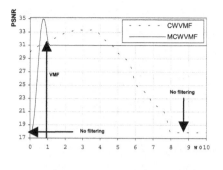

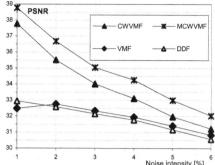

Fig. 3. PSNR dependency on w_0 value for the new filter and CWVMF (LENA image corrupted with 4% impulsive noise).

Fig. 4. Comparison of the efficiency of the standard central weighted vector median with the new modified filter and the vector median (LENA corrupted with 4% impulsive noise).

Figure 3 presents the PSNR value obtained with the CWVMF and with the new *Modified Central Weighted Vector Median Filter* (MCWVMF) in dependence on the w_0 weighting parameter when using the *PEPPERS* image contaminated by the 4% impulsive noise. Figure 4 shows the optimal (maximal possible) PSNR values for the new filter in comparison with the standard technique, when using the test color image *LENA* distorted by impulsive noise ranging from 1 to 6 % (each RGB channel was contaminated independently with *salt and pepper* impulsive noise with probability 0.0x, where x=1,2,..,6). Figure 5 shows the dependence of the PSNR on the weighting coefficient w_0 for images distorted by impulsive noise of different intensities. As can be seen the optimal value of the weighting coefficient is dependent on the noise intensity and increases toward 1 (VMF) with growing noise intensity. Figure 6 illustrates the efficiency of the modified CWVMF as compared with the standard VMF filter.

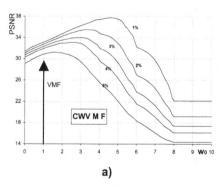

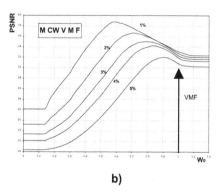

a)

b)

Fig. 5 Dependence of the central CWVMF and MCWVMF filter efficiency (**a)** and **b)** respectively) on the w_0 weighting coefficient for the *LENA* color image contaminated with impulsive noise (each RGB channel was distorted by salt and pepper noise with probability ranging from 1% to 5%).

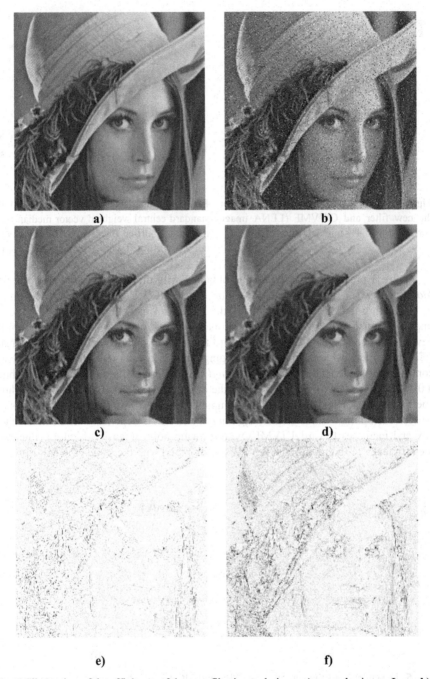

Fig. 6 Illustration of the efficiency of the new filtering technique: **a)** test color image Lena, **b)** image corrupted by impulsive noise process of 4%, **c)** the new technique, **d)** VMF, **e)** and **f)** the difference between the original image **a)** and images **c)** and **d)** respectively.

4 Conclusions

The new algorithm presented in this paper can be seen as a modification and improvement of the commonly used Vector Median Filter. The computational complexity of the new filter is lower than that of the Central Weighted Vector Median Filter. The comparison shows that the new filter outperforms the standard and central weighted VMF, as well as other basic procedures used in color image processing, when the impulse noise is to be eliminated. The future work will be focused on finding a way of automatic setting of the optimal weighting parameter, which should be adjusted to the intensity of the noise process, as clearly seen in Fig. 5. This could be achieved by first estimating the noise intensity [13] and then setting the appropriate value of the weighting parameter w_0.

References

1. Astola J., Haavisto P., Neuovo Y., (1990) Vector median filters, IEEE Proc., 78, 678-689
2. Gabbouj M., Cheickh F.A., (1996) Vector Median-Vector Directional hybrid filter for color image restoration, Proceedings of EUSIPCO-1996, 879-881
3. Karakos D.G., Trahanias P.E., (October 1995) Combining vector median and vector directional filters: The directional-distance filters, Proceedings of the IEEE Conf. on Image Processing, ICIP-95, 171-174
4. Pitas I., Tsakalides P., (1991) Multivariate ordering in color image processing, IEEE Trans. on Circuits and Systems for Video Technology, 1, 3, 247-256
5. Pitas I., Venetsanopoulos A. N, (1990) Nonlinear Digital Filters: Principles and Applications, Kluwer, Boston, MA.
6. Pitas I., Venetsanopoulos A.N., (1992) Order statistics in digital image processing, Proceedings of IEEE, 80, 12, 1893-1923
7. Plataniotis K.N., Androutsos D., Sri V., Venetsanopoulos A.N., (1995) A nearest neighbour multichannel filter, Electronic Letters, 1910-1911
8. Plataniotis K.N., Androutsos D., Venetsanopoulos A.N., (1995) Colour Image Processing Using Fuzzy Vector Directional Filters, Proc. of the IEEE Workshop on Nonlinear Signal/Image Processing, Greece, 535-538
9. Plataniotis K.N., Venetsanopoulos A.N., (June 2000) Color Image Processing and Applications, Springer Verlag.
10. Trahanias P.E., Venetsanopoulos A.N., (1993) Vector directional filters: A new class of multichannel image processing filters, IEEE Trans. on Image Processing, 2, 4, 528-534
11. Venetsanopoulos A.N., Plataniotis K.N, (1995) Multichannel image processing, Proceedings of the IEEE Workshop on Nonlinear Signal/Image Processing, 2-6
12. Viero T., Öistämö K., Neuvo Y., (1994) Three-Dimensional Median Related Filters for Color Image Sequence Filtering, IEEE Transactions on Circuits and Systems for Video Technology, 129-142, Vol. 4, No. 2, April
13. Förstner W., Image preprocessing for feature extraction in digital intensity, color and range images, in the Proceedings of Summer School on Data Analysis and the Statistical Foundations of Geomatics in Springer Lecture Notes on Earth Sciences, http://www.ipb.uni-bonn.de/Publications/
14. R. Whitaker R., Gerig G., (1994) Vector-Valued Diffusion, Ed. B.M. ter Haar Romeny, "Geomtry-Driven Diffusion in Computer Vision", Kluwer Academic Press, pp. 93-134
15. Blomgren P., Chan T., (March 1998 Color TV: Total variation methods for restoration of vector valued images, IEEE Transactions on Image Processing, , Special Issue on Geometry Driven Diffusion and PDEs in Image Processing

Fast Recovery of Piled Deformable Objects Using Superquadrics

Dimitrios Katsoulas[1] and Aleš Jaklič[2]

[1] Institute for Pattern Recognition and Image Processing, University of Freiburg,
Georges-Koehler-Allee 52, D-79110 Freiburg, Germany
dkats@informatik.uni-freiburg.de
[2] Computer Vision Laboratory, University of Ljubljana,
Tržaška cesta 25, SI-1000 Ljubljana, Slovenia
ales.jaklic@fri.uni-lj.si

Abstract. Fast robotic unloading of piled deformable box-like objects (e.g. box-like sacks), is undoubtedly of great importance to the industry. Existing systems although fast, can only deal with layered, neatly placed configurations of such objects. In this paper we discuss an approach which deals with both neatly placed and jumbled configurations of objects. We use a time of flight laser sensor mounted on the hand of a robot for data acquisition. Target objects are modeled with globally deformed superquadrics. Object vertices are detected and superquadric seeds are placed at these vertices. Seed refinement via region growing results in accurate object recovery. Our system exhibits a plethora of advantages the most important of which its speed. Experiments demonstrate that our system can be used for object unloading in real time, when a multi-processor computer is employed.

1 Introduction

This paper addresses the depalletizing problem (or robotic bin picking problem) in the context of which a number of objects of arbitrary dimensions, texture and type must be automatically located, grasped and transferred from a pallet (a rectangular platform), on which they reside, to a specific point defined by the user. The need for automated, robust and generic depalletizing systems, stems primarily from the car and food industries. Such systems are of great importance because they undertake a task that is very monotonous, strenuous and sometimes quite dangerous for humans. In this contribution we discuss the automatic recovery of piled deformable box-like objects (see Fig. 3), which are quite often encountered in distribution centers. These kind of objects tend to deform (usually bend) along their longer side, which renders their fast recovery a difficult task.

This is the reason why a multitude of systems aiming at depalletizing of rigid polyhedral objects or boxes have been reported ([1,5,7], etc.), while only a few systems which deal with depalletizing of non rigid objects exist. In [9,6] intensity imagery is employed for the recovery of neatly placed sacks. [9] is based

L. Van Gool (Ed.): DAGM 2002, LNCS 2449, pp. 174–181, 2002.
© Springer-Verlag Berlin Heidelberg 2002

on the detection of markers on the exposed surface of the objects, [6] on the detection of edges. These approaches although very fast, do not work when the objects are jumbled and inherit the major problem of the intensity based systems, that is, dependency on the lighting conditions. The system described in [6], additionally assumes that the number of objects on the pallet is known. This limits its application range even more. Approaches utilizing range imagery seem more promising. The system described in [4] employs range imagery and aims at the generic recognition of rigid, flat and "irregular" box like objects at the same time. However, no experimental results on the detection of "irregular" objects are shown and no efficiency measurements presented.

Our system employs a time of flight laser range finder mounted on the hand of an industrial robot to depalletize neatly placed and piled box-like objects. A vacuum gripper is used for object grasping. The system employs superquadrics for object modeling and is based on a hypothesis generation and refinement scheme. Object vertices are detected on the images acquired from the laser sensor, and superquadric seeds are placed on the vertices. These seeds are the initial object location hypotheses which are then refined in a region growing manner. In our application it is assumed that the objects contained in each platform are of the same kind and (known) dimensions and are full of material. We further assume that each object's length is longer than their width and both are much longer than their height, so that their largest surface is mainly exposed to the laser source. Despite these assumptions the application range of our system is vast. The advantages of our system are: Independence from lighting conditions since range imagery is used, computational efficiency due to fast region growing, accuracy and robustness due to the high quality initial hypotheses and the constant monitoring of their evolution via region growing, versatility since our system can deal with both jumbled and neatly placed configurations, low cost since a range finder is all we need, and last but not least simplicity.

2   Object Recovery

The problem we are dealing with, belongs to the category of model based range image segmentation problems and as stated in [3], interleaving model recovery with segmentation (segment-and-fit) is one of the best approaches for handling it. We use superquadrics for object modeling, since they exhibit a multitude of advantages. Among them, a small number of parameters with a large expressive power, and a fast method for their recovery from range images. The expressive power of superquadrics (SQs) can be further enhanced by the addition of a couple of global deformation parameters. We use global bending for modeling the bending of our objects along their longest side.

2.1   Object Modeling with Superquadrics

Superquadrics are a family of parametric shapes, the implicit form of which is given by Eq. 1. The parameters a_1, a_2, a_3 express the length of the SQ in the

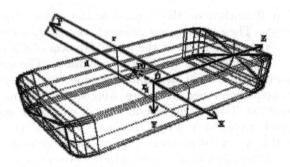

Fig. 1. Radial Euclidean distance from a superquadric

x, y, z axes respectively and ϵ_1, ϵ_2 its shape. The function F in Eq. 1, is called the inside-outside function, because it provides a simple test whether a given point lies inside or outside a SQ. If $F < 1$, then a given point lies inside the SQ. If $F = 1$, the point lies on the surface of the SQ, and if $F > 1$ the point lies outside the SQ.

$$F(x, y, z) = \left(\left(\frac{x}{a_1} \right)^{\frac{2}{\epsilon_2}} + \left(\frac{y}{a_2} \right)^{\frac{2}{\epsilon_2}} \right)^{\frac{\epsilon_2}{\epsilon_1}} + \left(\frac{z}{a_3} \right)^{\frac{2}{\epsilon_1}} \tag{1}$$

The radial Euclidean distance $|d|$ of a point $P(x, y, z)$ from a SQ (Fig. 1), is defined in terms of the inside-outside function, and is given in Eq. 2.

$$|d| = |\mathbf{r} - \mathbf{r_S}| = |\mathbf{r}||1 - F^{-\frac{\epsilon_1}{2}}(x, y, z)| = |\mathbf{r_S}||F^{\frac{\epsilon_1}{2}}(x, y, z) - 1| \tag{2}$$

We employ two global deformation parameters to model object bending and transform the z(elongated) axis of the SQ into a circular section. These are the curvature of the circular section k and the z axis bending plane angle a (see [3] for details).

Note that Eq.1, expresses a SQ placed at the origin of the model coordinate system. Six more parameters should be incorporated (three for translation and three for rotation) to allow for expressing the inside-outside function in the general position and two more for the global bending. This increases the number of our model parameters to 13. If we denote by $\mathbf{\Lambda}$ the set of model parameters, the inside-outside function takes the form $F(x, y, z; \mathbf{\Lambda})$.

We use the minimization approach of [10] to fit SQs to data points. This method minimizes the expression (3), where n is the number of points to fit.

$$\min_{\mathbf{\Lambda}} \sum_{i=1}^{n} \left(\sqrt{\lambda_1 \lambda_2 \lambda_3} (F^{\epsilon_1}(x_i, y_i, z_i; \lambda_1, \ldots, \lambda_{13}) - 1) \right)^2. \tag{3}$$

The method is very fast,but has the inherent problem of favoring the recovery of superquadrics which produce larger values for $\mathbf{r_s}$, since as pointed out in [11]:

$$F^{\epsilon_1}(x, y, z) - 1 = \frac{d}{|\mathbf{r_s}|} \left(\frac{d}{|\mathbf{r_s}|} + 2 \right). \tag{4}$$

2.2   Segmentation Approach

One of the most successful approaches for recovering SQs from range data is presented in [8,3]. The authors attempt recovery of multiple dissimilar occluded objects from range images using SQs, in a segment-and-fit framework. SQ seeds are placed in the image in a grid-like pattern of windows. Each seed encompasses a set of range data points. A SQ is fitted to this data set, and an initial set of SQ parameters is determined. The seeds are then allowed to grow by adding neighboring points to their point data set which have a small radial Euclidean distance from the already recovered models. The growing process continues until the average error of fit of a model to its data points is bigger than a threshold, no more points with a small distance from the recovered model exist (fully grown models), or at least one model reaches twice its original size. In the latter case, a model-selection procedure is initiated. This procedure retains a set of models which are determined to optimally (in the MDL sense) describe the data. In this way non-redundant models which accurately describe the data set are retained. The remaining models are then further grown and the whole process continues until no SQs can grow any more.

This system shows many advantages. Computational efficiency is achieved, because the fast fitting method of [10] is used. Furthermore, the fact that each seed grows independently, allows for parallel implementation of the algorithm. Accurate and robust object recovery is accomplished by the placement of numerous, redundant seeds in combination with the frequent invocations of the model selection procedure which allows only the best models to grow. However, even if the method is quite fast it is not appropriate for a real time implementation, due to the big number of seeds and the fact that the model-selection procedure is non-parallelisable. Algorithm acceleration requires reducing both the number of seeds as well as the number of invocations of the model-selection procedure. But this will inevitably reduce the recovery accuracy.

The solution to the problem lies in the experimental observation in [3], p. 135. It is there reported, that in the event of good quality of initial seeds, the output of the algorithm is equally satisfactory when the model-selection is invoked only once, after all seeds are fully grown. It is as well observed, that in this case no need for initializing many redundant seeds exists any more, since all the models would yield almost the same result at the end. Ideally one reliable seed per model would be enough to recover all the models in the image. This observation is the kernel of our approach. In [2] is stated that a three-dimensional visible vertex provides the strongest constraints for accurately determining the position of convex, three-dimensional objects and thus are very good approximations of the location of the objects in space. In [5] this principle has been employed for detecting boxes in piles. Since our objects are box-like, their vertices can still be used for generating accurate object location hypotheses. We therefore detect $3D$ object vertices in the scene, place SQ seeds to those vertices and let them grow to their full size. After all the seeds are fully grown the model-selection procedure is invoked only once and the best descriptions are retained. We thus reduce the number of seeds and minimize the number of model-selection

invocations without reducing the recovery accuracy. The high quality vertex
seeds result in fast region growing. The minimization of the number of model-
selection invocations accelerates the algorithm and renders it fully parallelisable.

Vertex detection and seed placement: $3D$ object vertices are detected
in the images in the way presented in [5] which is based on the joint use of
edge detection and a technique inspired by the fast dynamic generalized Hough
transform. A scene vertex is represented as a triplet which comprise the position
of the vertex point in the scene and the two normalized vectors pointing in the
direction of the edges joining at the vertex. The vertex is aligned with the xz
surface of the superquadric seeds. The alignment procedure is described in detail
in [5].

Region growing: We adopt the region growing method of [3,8], a description of which has already been presented. However the method as is has some
drawbacks which stem from the fitting function problem expressed by Eq.4.
Let's suppose that in the object configuration shown in Fig. 2 (a), the "black"
$3D$ range points correspond to the inclined object, while the white ones to the
horizontally placed. When using (3) to fit a model to the black points, the model
C_2 $(ABCD)$ depicted with dashed line in the figure is recovered, because then
the $|\mathbf{r_s}|$'s of all the black points are maximized (see Eq. 4). Actually in Fig. 2 (a)
$|\mathbf{r_{s12}}| > |\mathbf{r_{s11}}|$. In the next region growing operation, the point $\mathbf{P_2}$, will be added
to the set of data points of model C_2, although it belongs to another object. Due
to monotonic region growth, inclusion of outliers in a model's point set dete-
riorates the performance of the least square fitting and hinders its growth. A
solution to the problem could be the restriction of the size of the recovered
model along the y axis so as not to surpass its known maximum value. However,
it was observed in practice that this reduces the recovery speed. Another issue is
that the radial Euclidean distance function equally favors points which belong to
the model's growing direction (which is reliably defined by the $3D$ seed vertex)
and others which are probable outliers.

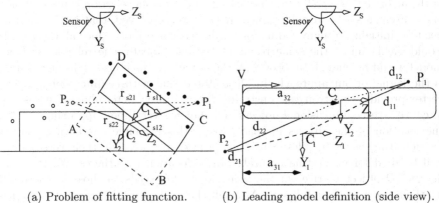

(a) Problem of fitting function.   (b) Leading model definition (side view).

Fig. 2.

(a) Box like packets   (b) Sacks

Fig. 3. Object configurations

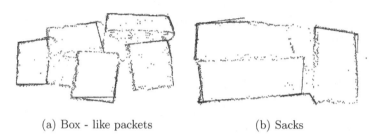

(a) Box - like packets   (b) Sacks

Fig. 4. Vertices

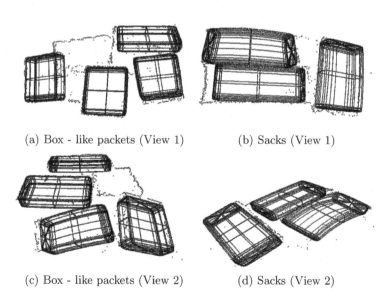

(a) Box - like packets (View 1)   (b) Sacks (View 1)

(c) Box - like packets (View 2)   (d) Sacks (View 2)

Fig. 5. Recovered superquadrics

In order to solve both problems, we exploit the fact that the growing direction is defined by the vertex with which the seed was aligned and thus the position of the inliers is grossly known. We include neighboring range points to a model's point data set only if they are close not to the growing model but to another model which is defined in this way so as to be near the probable inliers and away from the outliers. We name this model *Leading Model*, because it guides the region growing process. This model is aligned to the same vertex of the growing model which was fitted to the scene vertex. Its length along the y axis is kept to a small value, and the length along the x and z axes equals the corresponding lengths of the growing model increased by a user-defined small value. Fig. 2 (b) illustrates. The Leading Model (C_2) is aligned to the vertex V of the original model C_1. C_2 is bigger than C_1 along the z (and x) axis, but much smaller along the y axis. Points which lie in the growing direction (P_1) are favored because they have smaller radial Euclidean distance ($d_{12} < d_{11}$), while others (P_2) which are probably outliers are inhibited ($d_{22} > d_{21}$).

3   Experimental Results

For testing our system we used configurations of objects like the ones depicted in Fig. 3, more specifically box-like packets and sacks. For the configurations in Fig. 3, the detected vertices superimposed to the edge map are depicted in Fig. 4. Two views of the recovered superquadrics on the top of the edge map are presented in Fig. 5, where the reader can get an impression of the recovery accuracy. The time needed to process each of the range images was about 3 minutes while the time required for the recovery of a unique superquadric was about 30 seconds in a pentium *III* $650MHz$ PC. Since our algorithm is fully parallelisable the latter will approximately be the overall processing time required in a parallel architecture if one processor per seed is used. In terms of robustness, our experiments demonstrated that the system only occasionally fails to find at least one object in the pile.

Our system can as well deal with neatly placed object configurations, since a vertex is defined via only two direction vectors on the edges of the object's exposed surface. However, problems are encountered, if the objects are placed too close one after the other,when no edges and as a result no vertices can be detected. We expect that a sensor with a higher accuracy or an additional sensor could be used to overcome this problem. The alert reader may have already noticed that in Fig. 5 (b) the front sack has not been fully recovered but the length along the z axis is about 90 per cent of the actual length. This is due to the fact that the global bending we have used for modeling can not cover all the ways in which long objects may deform. We plan to solve this problem by introducing a few more global deformation parameters to our model.

4   Conclusions

We described a system for depalletizing piled deformable objects. Globally deformed superquadrics have been used for object modeling. We placed superquadric seeds to object vertices, the refinement of which via a region growing approach resulted in reliable object recovery. In the future we plan to continue experiments with the system so as to retrieve detailed accuracy measurements. In addition, we plan to introduce more deformation parameters to our model so as to be able to describe more accurately all possible target object deformations. Further target is the recovery of piled deformable objects of dissimilar dimensions.

References

1. A.J. Baerveldt. *Robust Singulation of Parcels with a Robot System using multiple sensors.* PhD thesis, Swiss federal institute of technology, 1993.
2. C. H. Chen and A. C. Kak. A robot vision system for recognizing 3-D objects in low-order polynomial time. *IEEE Transactions on Systems, Man, and Cybernetics,* 19(6):1535–1563, November-December 1989.
3. A. Jaklič, A. Leonardis, and F. Solina. *Segmentation and recovery of Superquadrics,* volume 20 of *Computational imaging and vision.* Kluwer Academic Publishers, Dordrecht, 2000.
4. A.C. Kak, A.J. Vayda, K.D. Smith, and C.H. Chen. Recognition strategies for 3-d objects in occluded environment. In T. C. Henderson, editor, *Traditional and Non-Traditional Robotic Sensors,* volume F 63 of *NATO Advanced Research Workshop Series,* pages 365–401. Springer-Verlag, Berlin, 1990.
5. D. Katsoulas, L. Bergen, and L. Tassakos. A versatile depalletizer of boxes based on range imagery. In *Proceedings of the IEEE International Conference on Robotics and Automation (ICRA-2002), Washington D.C.,* pages 4313–4319. IEEE Robotics and Automation Society, May 11–15 2002.
6. M. Kavoussanos and A. Pouliezos. Visionary automation of sack handling and emptying. *IEEE Robotics and Automation Magazine,* 2000.
7. S. Kristensen, S. Estable, M. Kossow, and R. Brosel. Bin-picking with a solid state range camera. *Robotics and autonomous systems,* 2001.
8. A. Leonardis, A. Jaklic, and F. Solina. Superquadrics for segmenting and modelling range data. *IEEE Transactions on PAMI,* 19(11):1289–1295, 1997.
9. D. Newcorn. Robot gains eyesight. *Packaging World,* 1998.
10. F. Solina and R. Bajcsy. Recovery of parametric models from range images: The case for superquadrics with global deformations. *IEEE Transactions on Pattern Analysis and Machine Intelligence,* 12(2):131–147, 1990.
11. P. Whaite and F. P. Ferrie. From uncertainty to visual exploration. *IEEE Transactions on Pattern Analysis and Machine Intelligence,* 13(10):1038–1049, October 1991.

Analysis of Amperometric Biosensor Curves Using Hidden-Markov-Models

Jörg Weitzenberg[1,*], Stefan Posch[1], and Manfred Rost[2]

[1] Martin-Luther-University Halle-Wittenberg, Institute of Computer Science
D-06099 Halle, Germany
{posch,weitzenb}@informatik.uni-halle.de
[2] Martin-Luther-University Halle-Wittenberg, Department of Physics
Friedemann-Bach-Platz 6, D-06099 Halle, Germany
rost@physik.uni-halle.de

Abstract. In this paper a HMM based method for analysing curves of amperometric biosensors is presented. In addition to our multi-HMM approach, we propose an enhanced single-HMM approach, which is used to detect the curve type, the end of the measurement and the correct measurement position. Besides, a problem-specific modified variant of the Baum-Welch algorithm is presented. The multi- and single-HMM approach yielded good accuracies and recognition rates. The modified Baum-Welch algorithm outperformed the standard Baum-Welch.

Key words: Hidden-Markov-Modells, Signal analysis, Biosensor

1   Introduction

Hidden-Markov-Modells (HMM) have been used already for automatic speech recognition for about 10 years. In the last years HMMs are increasingly applied for other problems, e.g. face- and handwriting recognition [1,2] or sequence analysis in bioinformatics [3].

In this article the application of HMMs for automatic analysis of signal curves of amperometric biosensors is proposed. Our system is adapted using statistical training data as well as specific expert knowledge.

Amperometric biosensors are used for measuring the concentration of analytes like glucose, lactate, alcohols or hydrogen peroxide. A biosensor is characterised by a combination of a biological receptor component (e.g. an enzyme) and a transducer [4]. Analogous to a lock and key, the analyte fits into the biological component of the sensor. This recognition reaction generates a signal, which is transformed to a detectable signal (e.g. an electrical current) by the transducer. Thus amperometric biosensors generate a current-time-curve $I_M(t, C_A)$ which contains the unknown analyte concentration. The current I_M is composed of an offset-current I_0 and a concentration-depending signal-current I_D. For each

---

* Supported by SensLab GmbH Leipzig, Germany, http://www.senslab.de

L. Van Gool (Ed.): DAGM 2002, LNCS 2449, pp. 182–189, 2002.
© Springer-Verlag Berlin Heidelberg 2002

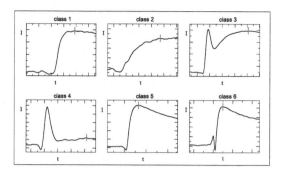

Fig. 1. Typical curves for different sensor handling and low (class 3,4) resp. high (class 1,2,5,6) analyte concentrations with marked measuring positions.

measurement I_0 and I_D have to be determined separately. In our work we concentrate on a specific procedure for single measurements with reusable amperometric biosensors. In this case, at first the sensor has to be dipped into a buffer solution to determine I_0. Thereafter the buffer solution has to be removed from the sensor. After dipping the sensor into the measurement solution, a characteristic signal-curve is observed. The shape of this curve depends on the sensor type, sensor handling and concentration of the sample solution. Figure 1 shows typical signal-curves for different sensor handling and different concentrations. While evaluating the shape of the curve, the end of the measurement is detected. Subsequently, the value of I_M is determined at a curve-specific position within the scanned curve, which has to be detected as well. The positions to end the measurement and for calculating the measurement value $I_D = I_M - I_0$ differ between curves significantly. In addition, there are variations in time flow and shape of the curves. Those variations are to be tolerated by the method presented in this article. Using I_D and a sensor depending calibration value the analyte concentration C_A can be calculated. In a former work [5,6] a simple method for analysing biosensor curves has been already proposed. This method is based on a fuzzy logic pattern recognition system and uses only sparse resources (memory and computing time) and therefore permits a straightforward implementation in microcontroller-based hand-held measuring devices. Besides the local processing of the curves, this method is unable to detect the end of the measurement.

A first approach for a significantly enhanced adaptive method, based on discrete HMMs has been proposed in [7]. In this approach, multiple discrete HMMs are used for classification of the curve types, for detection of the relevant measurement sections as well as for detection of the end of the measurement. For training and testing we used glucose biosensors, however our system is expected to work with other biosensor sensor types as well.

In this paper, we present an improved, more general approach, which permits simplification of the measurement procedure and propose a modified version of the Baum-Welch algorithm for improvement of accuracy. In addition, a variant, based on a semi-continuous HMM is presented. Finally, we compare the new approaches with each other.

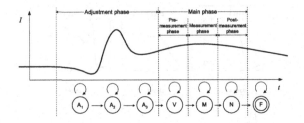

Fig. 2. Phases of a biosensor curve corresponding to the states of a HMM.

2   Multiple HMMs to Model Different Curve Classes

2.1   Modelling of the Measurement Process

As discussed in [7], a biosensor curve can be segmented into a number of relevant phases to find the measuring position and to detect the end of the measurement process. As stated in [7] we propose to assign every phase to one ore more internal states of a discrete HMM to facilitate global interpretation of the complete curve (Fig. 2). A typical biosensor curve starts with an adjustment phase. This phase is modelled using a number of n states $A_1, \ldots, A_n$, where n depends on the curve class. The following main phase is finer modelled with the measurement phase M and a pre- and post- measurement phase V and N respectively. The measurement value I_M is determined by maximisation over all current values $I(t)$ within the measurement phase. The shape and position of this phase depends on the curve class. After the measurement phase there is the post-measurement phase, modelled by the states N and F, where the signal remains constant or uniformly decreasing. Staying in this phase sufficiently long is a reliable indication to end the measurement. We use state N to model this period of time required, whereby state F operates as stop state.

2.2   Preprocessing and Feature Extraction

At first the sampled values are smoothed using a sliding average (window size of 30 samples). In the next step features to generate observation symbols are extracted. These features describe the local characteristics of the curve and are defined by the first and second derivation of the sensor curve. We use a window of 30 samples to approximate the curve using a quadratic function and calculate its derivatives. Finally a Self Organising Map (SOM) [8] is used to quantise the feature vectors into discrete observation symbols. In order to generate 16 different symbols we used a two dimensional SOM of 4×4 units. Initial experiments yielded no improvement using a larger set of symbols.

2.3   Training

Each different class of curves is modelled by an individual HMM, thus permitting classification during the measurement process as well. The transition and observation probabilities characterising the model are automatically learned from a set of sample curves using the Baum-Welch algorithm [9]. Due to the properties of the Baum-Welch algorithm the choice of suitable initial parameters is very important and are therefore estimated from the training curves: Besides the beginning and end of the measurement, only three relevant positions have to be marked manually using expert knowledge for each training sample. Subsequently the initial probabilities are estimated for each of the phases for all curves of a given class. In addition to the detection of the measurement position, an important problem is the detection of the end of the measurement. As stated in Sect. 2.1, the period of time required for reliable detection of the end of the measurement is modelled with state N and therefore with the transition probability from state N to F. The curve characteristics in the post-measurement phase, however are identical for states N and F. Thus the transition probability cannot be estimated by the Baum-Welch algorithm. Therefore we train the HMM up to state N using complete observation sequences. Subsequently the final state F is added with the same observation probabilities as state N. The state duration for state N is estimated using the average duration of the post-measurement phase as previously marked in the training data. Using this average durations, the transition probabilities from state N to state F are calculated.

2.4   Measurement Procedure

During analysis of a sequence of sampled values $I(t)$, we use this sequence to compute the most probable HMM (using the forward algorithm) and thus the class of the curve. In a next step the most probable state sequence for this class is determined with the Viterbi algorithm, which in turn is used to detect the end of the measurement and the position of the measurement phase. For this the following procedure is employed:

1. $t = 0$
2. Repeat steps (a) to (f),
   (a) $t = t + 1$
   (b) Fetch a new sample value $I(t)$.
   (c) Generate a new observation symbol o_t using feature extraction and vector quantisation using the SOM.
   (d) For $o_1, \ldots, o_t$ calculate the probability $P(o_1, \ldots, o_t | HMM_i)$ for each model i using the forward algorithm [9].
   (e) Choose the most probable model. This model is supposed to be the correct interpretation of the curve.
   (f) Calculate the most probable state sequence $q_1, \ldots, q_t$ for the given observation sequence and the chosen model using the Viterbi algorithm[9].
   until the last state q_t of the sequence $q_1, \ldots, q_t$ is a final state F, or the maximum specified time t_{max} is exceeded.
3. After reaching the final state F, the resulting measurement value is calculated: Using the determined state sequence $q_1, \ldots, q_t$, all current values $I(k), \ldots, I(k + n)$ associated to the measurement state M are utilized for calculating the measurement value. This is done using maximization. If the

maximum specified time $t_{\max}$ is exceeded and the final state F was not reached, it is checked, whether the measurement state M has been reached within $q_1, \ldots, q_t$. If so, the measurement value can be calculated as stated above, but a warning is given. If not, the measurement is rejected.

3   One Single HMM to Model Different Curve Classes

In order to derive a more general and more compact model for our problem we further developed our modelling approach. The main idea is to combine similar curve classes or curve phases in order to reduce the number of HMMs. This is motivated by the observation, that different curve classes considered so far, share a common shape of some phases. For example, the adjustment phase of class 3 and 4 (see Fig. 1) is virtually identical, while on the other hand the main phase is equivalent to classes 5 and 6 respectively. In addition we also included a preparation phase corresponding to the removal of buffer solution from the sensor (as described in Sect. 1). These considerations result in the structure of one single HMM as depicted in Fig. 3. The new state P models the preparation phase (removal of buffer solution). Subsequently, the observation sequence is interpreted to originate from one of m different parallel paths $\{A_1^1 \ldots A_n^1\}$, $\{A_1^2 \ldots A_n^2\}, \ldots, \{A_1^m \ldots A_n^m\}$ modelling the adjustment phase, followed by one of k different parallel paths $\{V^1 M^1 N^1 F^1\}, \ldots, \{V^k M^k N^k F^k\}$ for the main phase.

3.1   Modified Measurement Procedure

As an additional advantage, this compact representation also allows a simplification of the measurement procedure (see Sect. 2.4). Since only one single HMM is needed for modelling, the forward algorithm (step 2.d) for computing the most

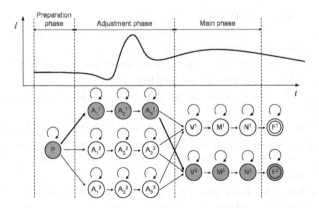

Fig. 3. Example of an enhanced HMM representing the actual data material for our glucose sensors.

probable model can be omitted (as well as step 2.e). Now, the analysis of an unknown curve is accomplished exclusively by the Viterbi algorithm, computing the most probable path (state sequence) for the given observation sequence (step 2.f). After reaching one of the final states $F^1, \ldots, F^k$ the end of the measurement is detected and the curve class (defined by the type of main phase) is given as the index of this final state. Step 3 of the measurement procedure to determine the measurement value (or reject the measurement) can performed exactly as in the first approach.

3.2   Modified Initialisation of Parameters

Due to the modified definition of curve classes using only the shape of the main phase, initialisation of parameters for the Baum-Welch training has to be adapted as well. According to this classification a set of representative sample curves is compiled and marked as stated in Sect. 2.3. The initialisation of the observation probabilities is treated differently for the preparation-, adjustment- and main phase: The observation probabilities of the preparation phase are initialised with the relative observation frequencies according to the marked sections in all sample curves. The observation probabilities for all m different adjustment phases are first identically initialised and subsequently random noise is added to allow adjustment of different curve types. For the main phases the observation probabilities of are initialised according to the curve types analogous to the technique employed in 2.3. The observation- and transition probabilities of the states N^i and F^i are estimated as stated in Sect. 2.3 as well. With this initialisation, parameters are again trained using the Baum-Welch algorithm.

3.3   Experimental Results

To compare the multi- and single-HMM approach, we used the same set of 205 sample curves, already utilised in [7]: The curves have been recorded using 5 glucose sensors of the same type at a sampling rate of 4 Hz. To get representative samples of curve types, different analyte concentrations and different types of sensor handling have been used. For the multi-HMM approach, as already stated in [7] the curves have been inspected visually and classified into 6 classes according to the general shape of the curve (Fig. 1). After setting the markers for the curve sections for each curve manually, one discrete HMM (DHMM) for each curve class has been trained using the Baum-Welch algorithm. For the single-HMM approach, we combined curve classes with virtually identical main phases, which results in two new classes with 165 (prior classes 1,2,3,4) resp. 40 (prior classes 5,6) members. For testing we used cross validation. In order to determine the accuracy of the measurement, we compared the manually evaluated current value I_{M_1} to the value I_{M_2} determined by the HMM. Results of both tests are shown in Tab. 1. For the application under consideration both tests yield satisfactory accuracies. The single-HMM approach achieved marginally better accuracies than the multi-HMM approach.

Table 1. Comparison between multi- and single-HMM approach with DHMM

	DHMM, multi			DHMM, single		
class	1	2	total	1	2	total
mean relative error in %	4.2	0.9	3.6	3.6	0.5	3.0
standard deviation in %	5.5	1.4	4.7	5.6	0.8	4.7

4   Modification of Baum-Welch Algorithm

In contrast to speech- or handwriting recognition, our main objective is to detect the correct measurement position. Thus, using the whole observation sequence $o_1, \ldots, o_T$ to estimate the probabilities of the phase-depending states during training is a disadvantage: When estimating the probabilities of states within a phase, observation symbols from other phases can adversely affect the resulting probabilities. To solve this problem, we propose the following modification: Instead of estimating the transition- and observation probabilities in the Baum-Welch formulas (for details see [9]) for the whole sequence $o_1, \ldots, o_T$, the probabilities are estimated only for the observation sequence sections $o_{t\_Start(Phase(S))}, \ldots, o_{t\_End(Phase(S))}$, manually assigned to the associated phase and thus state(s) of the HMM.

4.1   Experimental Results

The modified Baum-Welch algorithm has been tested using a set of 205 glucose curves and an extended set of 405 curves. Manual classification, marking and training of the curves has been conducted as stated above. For all further tests we chose the single-HMM approach.

In addition to the DHMM, we tested a semi-continuous HMM (SCHMM) for its potential to improve the measurement results. Therefore a semi-continuous codebook consisting of 16 probability density functions was used instead of a discrete codebook. For training and test we used the semi-continuous variants of the Baum-Welch and Viterbi algorithm [10]. The codebook was trained using feedback from the HMM estimation as stated in [10]. The results, displayed in Tab. 2, yield an improvement in accuracy for the modified Baum-Welch algorithm. With the set of 205 curves, the SCHMM performed marginally better with respect to accuracy than the DHMM, while with the set of 405 curves, the SCHMM obtains no improvement.

5   Conclusions

In this paper we presented a method for analysing curves of amperometric biosensors using Hidden-Markov-Models. We proposed a multi-HMM and an enhanced single-HMM approach, where the latter allows a more general and compact modelling of biosensor curves. Besides, the single-HMM approach permits a simplification of the measurement procedure. Both approaches yield good results in

Table 2. Comparison between unmodified Baum-Welch (DHMM), modified Baum-Welch (DHMM) and modified Baum-Welch (SCHMM).

205 curves	DHMM, unmod.			DHMM, mod.			SCHMM, mod.		
class	1	2	total	1	2	total	1	2	total
mean rel. error in %	3.6	0.5	3.0	3.0	0.2	2.5	2.4	0.7	2.1
std.- dev. in %	5.6	0.8	4.7	5.4	0.4	4.4	4.9	1.7	4.3
405 curves									
mean rel. error in %	2.7	1.2	2.6	1.4	1.1	1.4	1.5	0.9	1.4
std.- dev. in %	4.8	3.7	4.7	3.0	3.3	3.0	3.6	2.3	3.5

accuracy and recognition, while the single-HMM approach performed marginally better in accuracy than the multi-HMM approach. Due to these results, we decided to use the single-HMM approach for our planned micro-controller implementation in a biosensor hand-held measurement device. In addition a SCHMM was tested with our single-HMM approach, but the SCHMM variant obtained no significant improvement. Thus, we prefer a DHMM for our implementation, due to weaker requirements in resources (computing time, memory). For detection of defective sensors, special models resp. model structures are planned. Furthermore, we are going to do practical tests with different sensor types.

References

1. Eickeler, S., Müller, S., Rigoll, G.: Gesichtserkennung mit Hidden Markov Modellen. In Förster, W., Buhmann, J.M., Faber, A., eds.: Mustererkennung '99, 21. DAGM-Symposium Bonn, Berlin, Springer-Verlag (1999)
2. Bippus, R.D.: Pseudo zweidimensionale HMM zur Erkennung handgeschriebener Beiträge. In Paulus, E., Wahl, F.M., eds.: Mustererkennung '97, 19. DAGM-Symposium Braunschweig, Berlin, Springer-Verlag (1997) 245–253
3. Baldi, P.F., Brunak, S.: Bioinformatics: The machine learning approach. The MIT Press (1998)
4. Hall, E.A.: Biosensoren. Springer-Verlag, Berlin/Heidelberg (1995)
5. Weitzenberg, J.: Methoden der Fuzzy-Logik zur Auswertung von Meßkurven amperometrischer Biosensoren. Diplomarbeit, Martin-Luther-Universität Halle-Wittenberg (1998)
6. Weitzenberg, J., Posch, S., Bauer, C., Rost, M., Gründig, B.: Analysis of Amperometric Biosensor Data Using Fuzzy Logic and Discrete Hidden-Markov-Models. In Tränkler, H.R., ed.: SENSOR 2001 Proceedings, Volume II. (2001)
7. Weitzenberg, J., Posch, S., Rost, M.: Diskrete Hidden Markov Modelle zur Analyse von Meßkurven amperometrischer Biosensoren. In Sommer, G., Krüger, N., Perwass, C., eds.: Mustererkennung 2000, 22. DAGM Symposium Kiel, Berlin, Springer Verlag (2000) 317–324
8. Kohonen, T.: Self-Organizing Maps. Springer-Verlag, Heidelberg (1995)
9. Rabiner, L.R., Juang, B.H.: Fundamentals of Speech Recognition. Prentice Hall (1993)
10. Huang, X.D., Ariki, Y., Jack, M.A.: Hidden Markov Models for Speech Recognition. Edinburgh University Press (1990)

Unifying Registration and Segmentation for Multi-sensor Images

Boris Flach[1], Eeri Kask[1], Dmitrij Schlesinger[1], and Andriy Skulish[2]

[1] Dresden University of Technology,
bflach@inf.tu-dresden.de
[2] IRTCITS Cybernetics Center, Kiev

Abstract. We propose a method for unifying registration and segmentation of multi-modal images assuming that the hidden scene model is a Gibbs probability distribution.

1 Introduction

Obtaining a description of a complex scene by using multi-modal images of the scene (i.e. multi-sensor fusion) is a quite common task which arises for instance in medical diagnosis or in aerial surveying. Usually this task is split into interesting problems of their own: registration of multi-modal images, supervised or unsupervised learning of texture model parameters and segmentation of (registered) multi-modal images with respect to known texture models. The solution of the whole is approached then by solving these subtasks independently. The aim of our paper is to show, that the problem can be solved in a unified fashion (i.e. without splitting it into subtasks). The reasoning here is as follows: prior models are needed to solve each subtask, but in fact these rely on an unique model – the prior model of the scene itself.

Let us discuss this in a bit more depth considering at first the registration model. Usually it is not possible (or we don't want) to use artificial markers, so we have to use either fiducial points or some statistical similarity measures. But the first approach is usually prohibitive due to noise and lack of precise models for such fiducial points. The second approach needs to pose at least a statistical prior model of the scene (e.g. a probabilistic model for tissue segments in tomography). Common registration models are today quite simple. Often it is assumed that all voxels with a particular intensity value in one modality (say MRT) represent the same tissue type, so that values of corresponding voxels of the second modality (say PET) should also be similar to each other. This leads to a simple similarity measure for registration (see [7,4]), if the conditional probabilities for the intensities in each modality given the tissue class of the voxel are gaussians. Of course such a model is an oversimplification. Another way is to use the so called "normalized mutual information" (see e.g. [8]). Again behind the "scene" is a very simple model of the scene: the probability distribution for segment labels (e.g. tissue labels) is assumed to be voxelwise independent (see [3]). Again this model is too simple if we have in mind that we want to

L. Van Gool (Ed.): DAGM 2002, LNCS 2449, pp. 190–197, 2002.
© Springer-Verlag Berlin Heidelberg 2002

use the same prior model for registration and segmentation. We argue that it is necessary to use at least a Gibbs probability distribution in the prior model of possible scene segmentations, i.e. to assume that neighboring voxels are more likely to be of the same label class than to be of different label classes.

A second important point is, that we cannot assume to know all parameters of the prior model. Therefore it is necessary to include some kind of unsupervised parameter learning into simultaneous search for the best registration and segmentation. In general this means for instance an unsupervised learning of texture model parameters given some intermediate transform and some intermediate segmentation. Using the obtained texture models we can improve in turn the transform and the segmentation. Repeating this iteratively until a fixpoint is reached we obtain the registration and segmentation simultaneously.

2   The Model

Let us assume for simplicity a graph $\mathcal{G}(R, E)$, being a two or three dimensional lattice with a set of vertices R and edges E. We assume furthermore that we have two modalities (images) of the scene, and describe them by mappings $x \colon R \mapsto F$ and $y \colon R \mapsto F$ which associate intensity values to each vertex of the graph. Let y be additionally transformed by some (unknown) rigid body transform $T \colon R \mapsto R$. The third (unknown) mapping $z \colon R \mapsto K$ describes the segmentation of the scene, where K is the set of possible segment labels.

Posing a statistical model, we consider the tuples (x, y, z) as elementary events and choose the simplest nontrivial model of a probability distribution, i.e. a Gibbs distribution given by

$$p(x, y, z; T) = \frac{1}{Z} \prod_{(r,r')} g\big(z(r), z(r')\big) \prod_r q\big(x(r), z(r)\big) \prod_r h\big(y(Tr), z(r)\big), \quad (1)$$

where T, q, h are not known in advance. Let us discuss the assumptions in this formula in more detail. The á priori probability distribution $p(z)$ for possible segmentations is given by

$$p(z) = \frac{1}{Z} \prod_{(r,r')} g\big(z(r), z(r')\big),$$

i.e. a product over all edges of the lattice (Z is a normalizing constant). The function $g \colon K \times K \mapsto \mathbb{R}$ is chosen in advance according to the Potts model:

$$g(k, k') = \begin{cases} a & \text{if } k = k', \\ b & \text{otherwise} \end{cases}$$

where $a, b > 0$ and $a > b$, expressing the expectation that neighboring voxels tend to have the same label class. We assume furthermore that the intensity values in the modalities are conditionally independent given the segment label.

The functions $q, h\colon F \times K \mapsto \mathbb{R}$ represent conditional probabilities for intensities in modalities, given the segment label. Thats why we can assume without loss of generality, that

$$\sum_f q(f, k) = 1, \quad \sum_f h(f, k) = 1 \quad \forall k \in K$$

holds. Of course the used texture model is very simple here because we assume that the voxel intensities are generated independently.

Suppose for a moment that q, h, T are known. Then the segmentation task is a Bayes decision which depends on the chosen cost function for misclassification. If we choose simply $C(z, z^*) = \delta_{zz^*}$, where δ is the Kronecker symbol and z^* is the (unknown) "ground truth", then the minimal average cost is obtained by the maximum-á-posteriori decision. On the other hand this cost function is not very useful in structural recognition, because the cost of misclassification does not depend on the number of vertices classified incorrectly. A better choice for a cost function is

$$C(z, z^*) = \sum_r c\big(z(r), z^*(r)\big) \tag{2}$$

with some reasonable local function $c\colon K \times K \mapsto \mathbb{R}$. It is easy to see, that the Bayes decision for such a cost function is obtained as follows: first it is necessary to calculate the probabilities

$$p\big(z(r){=}k \mid x, y; T\big) \sim \sum_{z:\, z(r)=k} p(x, y, z; T) \tag{3}$$

for each vertex $r \in R$ and each label $k \in K$. Using these probabilities, the optimal segmentation is found by independent decisions for each vertex (see [5]). If the local cost function is as simple as $c(k, k^*) = 1 - \delta_{kk^*}$, the optimal decisions are

$$z^o(r) = \arg\max_k p\big(z(r){=}k \mid x, y; T\big).$$

Returning now to our problem, the question is, whether it is possible to learn the conditional probabilities q, h (unsupervised), to find T and to segment the registered images using the cost function (2)? To achieve this it is necessary to solve the problem

$$\ln \sum_z p(x, y, z; T) \to \max_{q, h, T} \tag{4}$$

and then to calculate the probablities (3). Both tasks are very hard computational problems.

3 Approximate Solution

To maximize (4) we use the EM-algorithm [6,1] and maximize iteratively

$$\sum_z \alpha(z) \ln p(x, y, z; T) - \sum_z \alpha(z) \ln \frac{p(x, y, z; T)}{\sum_{z'} p(x, y, z'; T)}$$

which coincides with (4) if $\alpha(z) \geq 0$ and $\sum_z \alpha(z) = 1$. Each iteration consists of two steps. In the first – usually called the E-step – choose α so that the second term reaches its maximum (with respect to $p(x, y, z; T)$) at the given actual $p^{(n)}(x, y, z; T)$:

$$\alpha^{(n)}(z) = p^{(n)}(z \mid x, y; T).$$

In the second step – usually called the M-step – the first term is maximized with respect to $p(x, y, z; T)$ for the fixed α obtained in the E-step:

$$\sum_z \alpha^{(n)}(z) \ln p(x, y, z; T) \to \max_{q, h, T}$$

Let us consider the M-step in detail. We substitute (1) for p. The function g and the normalizing constant Z are fixed. Thus we are interested only in those terms which depend on q and h. For those depending on q we obtain:

$$\sum_z p^{(n)}(z \mid x, y; T) \sum_r \ln q\big(x(r), z(r)\big) =$$
$$\sum_r \sum_k p^{(n)}\big(z(r){=}k \mid x, y; T\big) \ln q\big(x(r), k\big)$$

Analogously for h:

$$\sum_r \sum_k p^{(n)}\big(z(r){=}k \mid x, y; T\big) \ln h\big(y(Tr), k\big)$$

Therefore the problem of calculating the conditional probabilities $p\big(z(r){=}k \mid x, y; T\big)$ given q, h and T must be solved not only for the final segmentation but for each iteration of the EM-algorithm as well. Once these probabilities $p^{(n)}\big(z(r){=}k \mid x, y; T\big)$ are known, the subsequent evaluation of functions q and h and transform T for the next iteration is straightforward: denoting $X_f = \{r \in R \mid x(r){=}f\}$, the function $q^{(n+1)}$ is obtained as follows:

$$q^{(n+1)}(f, k) = \frac{1}{n(k)} \sum_{r \in X_f} p^{(n)}\big(z(r){=}k \mid x, y; T\big),$$

where $n(k)$ is a normalizing constant. The function $h^{(n+1)}$ is obtained in the same way, but here we have to vary also T. We use a small neighborhood centered at the actual $T^{(n)}$ (i.e. small translations and small rotations). Given the $q^{(n+1)}$, $h^{(n+1)}$ and $T^{(n+1)}$, we start the next iteration step. This is repeated until a fix-point is reached.

Therefore the remaining problem is to calculate $p\big(z(r){=}k \mid x, y; T\big)$ given the functions q and h and the transform T. Actually we don't know how to solve this problem in a closed fashion, except for simple graphs like trees and partial m-trees. Nevertheless it is possible to estimate these probabilities using a Gibbs sampler (see e.g. [2]): cycling through the vertices of the lattice many times and choosing in each step the label $z(r)$ in the vertex r according to the conditional probability distribution

$$p\big(z(r){=}k \mid z(R{\setminus}r), x, y; T\big) \sim q\big(x(r), k\big)\, h\big(y(Tr), k\big) \prod_{r':(r,r')\in E} g\big(k, z(r')\big) \quad (5)$$

we observe the labels k in each vertex r with probabilities $p\big(z(r){=}k \mid x, y; T\big)$. To be more precise, this holds in the limes of infinite sampling steps if all conditional probabilities in (5) are non-negative. Using the sampler with finite sampling steps, we estimate the probabilities $p\big(z(r){=}k \mid x, y; T\big)$ approximately. Hence we are able to perform the EM-algorithm and to obtain the final segmentation.

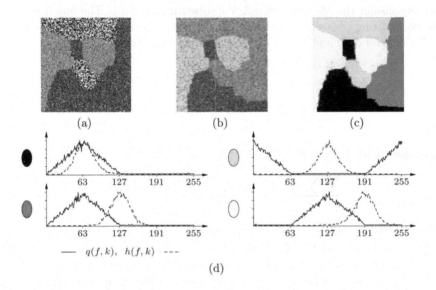

Fig. 1. Artificial test image pair 1(a) and 1(b). Registration and final labeling is in 1(c). In 1(d) the probability distributions $q(f, k)$ and $h(f, k)$ for each label colour k are shown.

4   Implementation and Experiments

The main iteration of the algorithm loops over all possible transforms T' around the "current" T (± 1 pixel, elementary rotations) while searching the overall "best" registration transform T. During this process one should consider the following. (1) As the EM-algorithm used for maximizing $p(x, y)$ converges into a local maximum one cannot take random values as initialisation for $q(f, k)$ and $h(f, k)$ for subsequent trials of T' – as the different intermediate optima then reached are not comparable – but use the $q(f, k)$ and $h(f, k)$ (as well as the z-label field) computed in the previous iteration of T. (Initially the $q(f, k)$

and $h(f,k)$ are uniform distributions and the z-field is sampled according to the á priori Gibbs model.) (2) This leads to a reduced number of steps the EM-routine has to execute for all but the first T' try in subsequent cycles. (3) As the T' now can have a better "quality" than T from the previous iteration, the current T quality has to be recalculated as well to avoid it from being neglected as a possible choice in this step.

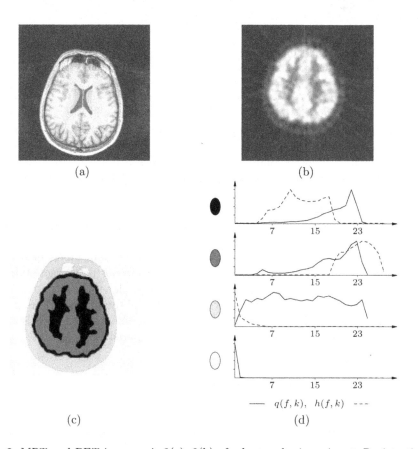

Fig. 2. MRT and PET image pair 2(a), 2(b) of a human brain as input. Registration and final labeling (with four colours) is in 2(c). Finally, 2(d) shows $q(f,k)$ and $h(f,k)$.

First, the theoretical model discussed in previous sections was tested with an artificial image pair as in Fig. 1(a) and 1(b). In 1(c) the result of registration and final labeling is shown. The statistical model used in generating the input pair can be recognised in 1(d) – the result of the EM-process applied to 1(a) and 1(b). One can observe the $q(f,k)$-distributions in 1(d) coloured ⬤ and ◕ are equal. The same is true for $h(f,k)$ in regions ◔ and ◯. This confirms the fact that there are *pairs* of label regions in the resulting segmentation 1(c) which correspond to the same texture parameters in 1(a) and 1(b) respectively.

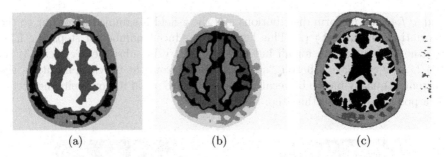

(a)   (b)   (c)

Fig. 3. Images of Fig. 2 labeled with five in 3(a) and six colours in 3(b). In 3(c) slightly different Potts parameters as in other experiments.

Next, the model was applied to MRT and PET images of Fig. 2(a) and 2(b). In 2(c) registration and final labeling with four labels is shown. Label regions ○ correspond to scene background, therefore in 2(d) $q(f, k)$ and $h(f, k)$ overlap. Further, label ○ corresponds to mostly disjunct regions in MRT and PET images in areas around and including cranium. In ● both $q(f, k)$ and $h(f, k)$ largely overlap according to the most interior of the brain structure in both images. Though, ● shows the effect of Potts model parameters suppressing thin geometrical elements, so PET image prevails in finegrained structural areas of MRT image.

As the label set in this experiment was restricted to four labels in advance, more detail about the structure in input images could not be extracted. In Fig. 3 labelings are shown using five labels in 3(a) and six labels in 3(b).

Figure 3(c) shows a result with six labels and slightly different Potts parameters (a/b=3, compared to a/b=9 in all other experiments) being not so strict in region boundary segmentation, particularly compared to 3(b).

5   Conclusions and Acknowledgements

We have shown how to unify registration and segmentation of multimodal images assuming hereby a Gibbs probability distribution for the hidden scene description. This includes unsupervised learning of at least simple texture models. We obtain an approximate solution mainly because we actually don't know how to calculate marginal probabilities for Gibbs distributions in a closed fashion. Though this problem is NP-complete in general it is therefore intriguing to search for solvable subclasses. A second interesting question is how to learn (unsupervised) the Gibbs distribution for the scene model in order to overcome the limitations of the Potts model.

At this point we are in dept to mention the great possibility we have had to work with Professor M.I. Schlesinger from Kiev, which – always a fruitful research – has lead us to a lot of invaluable knowledge.

One of us (B.F.) was supported during his work on this paper as fellow of the MIRACLE-Centre of Excellence (EC grant No. ICA1-CT-2000-70002) and wishes to thank all colleagues at the Center of Machine Perception Prague and especially Professor V. Hlaváč for interesting discussions and convenient conditions.

References

1. A. P. Dempster, N. M. Laird, and D. B. Durbin. Maximum likelihood from incomplete data via the EM algorithm. *Journal of the Royal Statistical Society*, 39:185–197, 1977.
2. Stuart Geman and Donald Geman. Stochastic relaxation, Gibbs distributions, and the Bayesian restoration of images. *IEEE Transactions on Pattern Analysis and Machine Intelligence*, 6(6):721–741, 1984.
3. Alexis Roche, Gregoire Malandain, and Nicholas Ayache. Unifying maximum likelihood approaches in medical image registration. Technical Report 3741, INRIA, 1999.
4. Alexis Roche, Gregoire Malandain, Xavier Pennec, and Nicholas Ayache. Multimodal image registration by maximization of the corralation ratio. Technical Report 3378, INRIA, 1998.
5. M. I. Schlesinger and V. Hlaváč. *Ten Lectures in Statistical and Structural Pattern Recognition*. Kluwer Academic Publishers, Dordrecht, 2002.
6. Michail I. Schlesinger. Connection between unsuprevised and supervised learning in pattern recognition. *Kibernetika*, 2:81–88, 1968. In Russian.
7. Milan Sonka and J. Michael Fitzpatrick, editors. *Handbook of Medical Imaging*, volume 2. SPIE Press, 2000.
8. C. Studholme, D. L. G. Hill, and D. J. Hawkes. An overlap invariant entropy measure of 3D medical image alignment. *Pattern Recognition*, 32:71–86, 1999.

Relations between Soft Wavelet Shrinkage and Total Variation Denoising

Gabriele Steidl[1] and Joachim Weickert[2]

[1] Faculty of Mathematics and Computer Science,
D7, 27, University of Mannheim, 68131 Mannheim, Germany,
steidl@math.uni-mannheim.de
[2] Faculty of Mathematics and Computer Science,
Building 27.1, Saarland University, 66041 Saarbrücken, Germany,
weickert@mia.uni-saarland.de

Abstract. Soft wavelet shrinkage and total variation (TV) denoising are two frequently used techniques for denoising signals and images, while preserving their discontinuities. In this paper we show that – under specific circumstances – both methods are equivalent. First we prove that 1-D Haar wavelet shrinkage on a single scale is equivalent to a single step of TV diffusion or regularisation of two-pixel pairs. Afterwards we show that wavelet shrinkage on multiple scales can be regarded as a single step diffusion filtering or regularisation of the Laplacian pyramid of the signal.

1 Introduction

Image denoising is a field where one is frequently interested in removing noise without sacrificing important structures such as edges. Since this is not possible with linear techniques many nonlinear strategies have been proposed in the last two decades. Two of these classes are wavelet methods [4,6,9] and techniques based on partial differential equations (PDEs) [10,11,14].

Although both classes serve the same purpose, not many results are available where their similarities and differences are juxtaposed and their mutual relations are analysed. However, such an analysis is highly desirable, since it will help to transfer results from one of these classes to the others. Moreover, a deeper understanding of the differences between these classes might be helpful for designing novel hybrid methods that combine the advantages of the different classes.

The goal of the present paper is to address this problem by analysing relations between two of the most popular wavelet and PDE based methods: soft wavelet shrinkage [6] and total variation (TV) denoising [11] in its formulation as a diffusion flow or a regularisation process. Figure 1 gives an illustration of the denoising properties of wavelet and TV methods. We observe that the results do not differ very much. Indeed, we shall prove in our paper that both methods are very closely related. In order to keep things as simple as possible we base our analysis on the 1-D case and consider only Haar wavelets. Generalisations and extensions will be considered in forthcoming publications.

L. Van Gool (Ed.): DAGM 2002, LNCS 2449, pp. 198–205, 2002.
© Springer-Verlag Berlin Heidelberg 2002

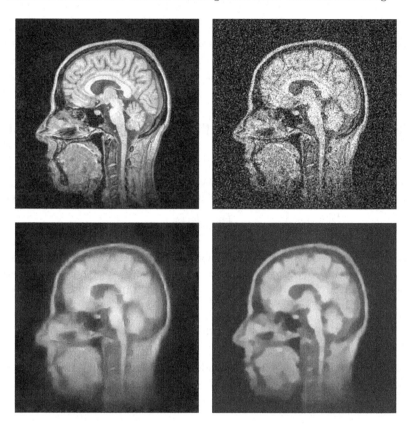

Fig. 1. (a) TOP LEFT: Original MR image. (b) TOP RIGHT: MR image degraded with Gaussian noise with standard deviation 50. (c) BOTTOM LEFT: Wavelet denoising of (b) using translation invariant soft shrinkage with Haar wavelets. (d) BOTTOM RIGHT: Total variation diffusion of (b).

Our paper is organised as follows. In Section 2 we prove a fundamental relation between soft wavelet shrinkage, nonlinear diffusion with TV diffusivity, and TV regularisation. While Section 2 is concerned with a single wavelet shrinkage step, Section 3 deals with the multiscale approach. Here we show the equivalence between multiscale wavelet shrinkage and TV diffusion / regularisation on a Laplacian pyramid. The paper is concluded with a summary in Section 4.

Related Work. Although we are not aware of any method in the literature that investigates the relations between discrete wavelet shrinkage and TV denoising, there are some interesting related techniques that should be mentioned in this context. Chambolle et al. [4] showed that one may interpret continuous wavelet shrinkage as regularisation processes in suitable Besov spaces. Durand and Froment [7] proposed to address the problem of pseudo-Gibbs artifacts in wavelet denoising by replacing the thresholded wavelet coefficients by coefficients that minimise the total variation. Their method is also close in spirit to an approach by Chan and Zhou [5] who postprocessed images obtained from wavelet shrinkage by a TV-like regularisation technique. Recently, Malgouyres [8] proposed a hybrid method that uses both wavelet packets and TV approaches. His experiments showed that it may restore textured regions without introducing ringing artifacts.

2   Soft Thresholding, TV Diffusion and TV Regularization

2.1   Soft Thresholding

We start by recalling a single Haar wavelet shrinkage step. Let $f = (f_i)_{i=0}^{N-1}$ be our initial signal, where $N = 2^n$. Then the *analysis step* produces the coefficients

$$c_i = \frac{f_{2i} + f_{2i+1}}{\sqrt{2}}, \quad d_i = \frac{f_{2i} - f_{2i+1}}{\sqrt{2}} \quad (i = 0, ..., N/2 - 1)$$

of the scaling functions and the wavelets on the next coarser grid. This step is followed by the *shrinkage operation* $S_\tau(d_i)$, where S_τ denotes in general a nonlinear function which depends on a threshold parameter τ. In this paper we are interested in the *soft thresholding*

$$S_\tau(\eta) = \begin{cases} \eta - \tau \operatorname{sgn} \eta & \text{if } |\eta| \geq \tau, \\ 0 & \text{if } |\eta| < \tau. \end{cases} \tag{1}$$

Other shrinkage functions will be considered in a forthcoming paper. After the *synthesis step*

$$u_{2i} = \frac{c_i + S_\tau(d_i)}{\sqrt{2}} = \frac{f_{2i} + f_{2i+1}}{2} - \frac{1}{\sqrt{2}} S_\tau \left(\frac{f_{2i+1} - f_{2i}}{\sqrt{2}} \right), \tag{2}$$

$$u_{2i+1} = \frac{c_i - S_\tau(d_i)}{\sqrt{2}} = \frac{f_{2i} + f_{2i+1}}{2} + \frac{1}{\sqrt{2}} S_\tau \left(\frac{f_{2i+1} - f_{2i}}{\sqrt{2}} \right)$$

we obtain a new signal u with smaller wavelet coefficients at the first decomposition level. The basic idea behind this procedure is that small wavelet coefficients mainly correspond to the noise contained in f while larger ones really signify basic features, e.g., edges, so that u can be considered as denoised version of f with preserved edges.

The Haar wavelet transform in (2) introduces a splitting of the signal f into successive two–pixel parts $(f_{2i} \; f_{2i+1}) \; (i = 0, ..., N/2)$. In the following we want to interpret a single wavelet shrinkage step as nonlinear diffusion of these successive two–pixel signals.

2.2   TV Diffusion

The basic idea behind nonlinear diffusion filtering is to obtain a family $u(x, t)$ of filtered versions of a signal $f(x)$ as the solution of a suitable diffusion process with $f(x)$ as initial condition [10]:

$$u_t = (g(u_x)u_x)_x, \tag{3}$$

$$u(x, 0) = f(x)$$

where subscripts denote partial derivatives and the time t is a simplification parameter: larger values correspond to stronger filtering.

Motivated by the wavelet splitting in the Haar basis, we are interested in space-discrete diffusion of two–pixel signals (f_0, f_1). We do not allow any flow over the signal boundary, i.e. we deal with the extended sequence f_0, f_0, f_1, f_1 where the boundary values have been mirrored. For this simple setting a space-discrete version of the diffusion equation (3) in both pixels can be written as

$$\dot{u}_0 = g(u_1 - u_0)(u_1 - u_0), \quad \dot{u}_1 = -g(u_1 - u_0)(u_1 - u_0), \tag{4}$$

where $u_0(0) = f_0$, $u_1(0) = f_1$, and the pixel size is assumed to be 1. Setting $w(t) := u_1(t) - u_0(t)$ and $\eta := f_1 - f_0$, we obtain the initial value problem

$$\dot{w} = -2\,g(w)w,$$
$$w(0) = \eta$$

by subtracting both equations in (4).

We are interested in the TV diffusivity $g(w) = 1/|w|$ since – unlike most other commonly used diffusivities – it does not require to specify additional contrast parameters. Moreover, it has a number of favourable qualitative properties [1,2]. By straightforward computation, the corresponding initial value problem

$$\dot{w} = -2\,\mathrm{sgn}\,w,$$
$$w(0) = \eta.$$

has the solution

$$w(t) = \begin{cases} \eta - 2t\,\mathrm{sgn}\,\eta & \text{if } t \le |\eta|/2, \\ 0 & \text{if } t > |\eta|/2. \end{cases}$$

Since $\dot{u}_0 + \dot{u}_1 = 0$ and $u_0(0) + u_1(0) = f_0 + f_1$, we see further that the average grey value is preserved:

$$u_0(t) + u_1(t) = f_0 + f_1.$$

By the definition of w it follows that

$$\begin{aligned} u_i(t) &= \frac{f_0 + f_1}{2} - (-1)^i\,\frac{w(t)}{2} & (i = 0, 1) \\ &= \frac{f_0 + f_1}{2} - (-1)^i \begin{cases} |\eta|/2 - t\,\mathrm{sgn}\,\eta & \text{if } t \le |\eta|/2, \\ 0 & \text{if } t > |\eta|/2. \end{cases} \end{aligned}$$

By (2) and (1) this coincides with the Haar wavelet shrinkage with soft thresholding, where the threshold parameter τ is related to the diffusion time t by $\tau = \sqrt{2}\,t$.

2.3   TV Regularization

Nonlinear diffusion filtering of signals is related to variational methods for signal restoration [12]. Here the basic idea is to use the minimiser u of

$$E_f(u) := ||f - u||_{L_2}^2 + \alpha \int \varphi(u_x)\,dx \tag{5}$$

as denoised version of the initial signal $f(x)$. Via the Euler–Lagrange equation it follows that this minimiser coincides with the solution of

$$\frac{u - f}{\alpha} = (g(u_x)u_x)_x,$$

where $g(s) = \frac{\varphi'(s)}{2s}$. This can be considered as a time discretisation of the diffusion filter (3), where the regularization parameter α approximates the stopping time of the diffusion process [12].

Again we are only interested in the two–pixel model (f_0, f_1). We consider a space-discrete variant of (5), namely

$$E_f(u_1, u_2) = (f_0 - u_0)^2 + (f_1 - u_1)^2 + \alpha\,\varphi(u_1 - u_0), \tag{6}$$

for the TV potential function $\varphi(s) = 2|s|$ corresponding to the TV diffusivity $g(s) = 1/|s|$. Straightforward computation results in the following minimiser of (6)

$$\begin{aligned}
u_i &= f_i + (-1)^i \alpha & (i = 0, 1)\\
&= \frac{f_0 + f_1}{2} - (-1)^i \begin{cases} |\eta|/2 - \alpha\,\mathrm{sgn}\,\eta & \text{if } \alpha \le |\eta|/2,\\ 0 & \text{if } \alpha > |\eta|/2. \end{cases}
\end{aligned}$$

By (2) and (1) this coincides with a single Haar wavelet shrinkage step on (f_0, f_1) with soft threshold S_τ, where the threshold parameter τ is related to the regularisation parameter by $\tau = \sqrt{2}\,\alpha$.

In summary, the nonlinear diffusion with TV diffusivity and the variational method (6) with TV regularisation applied to the successive two–pixel parts (f_{2i}, f_{2i+1}) of f coincide with a single step of Haar wavelet shrinkage with soft thresholding. The threshold parameter τ is related to the diffusion time t and to the regularisation parameter α by

$$\tau = \sqrt{2}\,t = \sqrt{2}\,\alpha.$$

It is remarkable that TV diffusion and TV regularisation give identical evolutions in the two-pixel case, if one identifies the diffusion time t with the regularisation parameter α. From the considerations in [12] one would only expect that the processes approximate each other.

3   Multiscale Approach

So far we have only considered soft wavelet shrinkage on a single scale. In this section, we interpret *multiscale* soft shrinkage with Haar wavelets as application of nonlinear TV based diffusion to two–pixel groups of *hierarchical* signals.

Let us start with wavelet shrinkage again. Two steps of Haar wavelet shrinkage are described by the filter bank in Figure 2. As usual we apply the z-transform notation $f(z) = \sum_{i=0}^{N-1} f_i z^{-i}$. Then $\boxed{H_i(z)}$ $(i = 0, 1)$ denotes the convolution of f with the low pass filter $(i = 0)$ and the high pass filter $(i = 1)$,

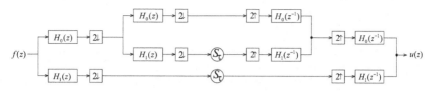

Fig. 2. Two steps of Haar wavelet shrinkage with $H_0(z) = \frac{1+z}{\sqrt{2}}$ and $H_1(z) = \frac{1-z}{\sqrt{2}}$.

i.e. $f(z)H_i(z)$, $\boxed{2\downarrow}$ and $\boxed{2\uparrow}$ downsampling and upsampling by 2, respectively, and the circle soft thresholding by S_τ. Finally • signifies addition; see also [13]. To obtain more scales we further split the upper branch of the inner filter bank cycle and so on.

We briefly recall the concept of *Gaussian* and *Laplacian pyramids* [3]. The Gaussian pyramid we are interested in is the sequence of H_0–smoothed and subsampled versions of an initial signal f given by

$$f = f^{(0)} \longrightarrow f^{(1)} \longrightarrow \ldots \longrightarrow f^{(n)},$$

where

$$f_i^{(j+1)} = (f_{2i}^j + f_{2i+1}^j)/\sqrt{2} \quad (j = 0, \ldots, n-1; \; i = 0, \ldots, N/2^{j+1} - 1).$$

Let $Pf^{(j)}$ denote the prolongated version of $f^{(j)}$ given by

$$Pf_{2i}^{(j)} = Pf_{2i+1}^{(j)} = f_i^{(j)}/\sqrt{2} \quad (j = 1, \ldots, n; \; i = 0, \ldots, N/2^j - 1). \qquad (7)$$

Then the corresponding Laplacian pyramid is the sequence

$$f - Pf^{(1)} \longrightarrow f^{(1)} - Pf^{(2)} \longrightarrow \ldots \longrightarrow f^{(n-1)} - Pf^{(n)} \longrightarrow f^{(n)}.$$

By

$$f^{(j)} = Pf^{(j+1)} + \left(f^{(j)} - Pf^{(j+1)} \right) \qquad (j = n-1, \ldots, 0)$$

we can reconstruct f from its Laplacian pyramid.

Let diff_t denote the operator of nonlinear diffusion with TV diffusivity and stopping time t, applied to the successive two–pixel parts of a signal. By Subsection 2.2 we know that diff_t performs like a single wavelet shrinkage step with soft threshold parameter $\tau = \sqrt{2}t$. Further, we see that the upper branch and the lower branch of the filter bank in Figure 2 are given by $Pf^{(1)}$ and $\text{diff}_t(f) - Pf^{(1)} = \text{diff}_t(f - Pf^{(1)})$, respectively, where the later equation follows (although diff_t is a nonlinear operator) by (7) and (2). Thus, one wavelet shrinkage step is given by

$$u = Pf^{(1)} + \text{diff}_t(f - Pf^{(1)}).$$

Now the multiscale Haar wavelet shrinkage up to scale n can be described by successive application of diff_t to the Laplacian pyramid:

$$u^{(n)} = f^{(n)} \qquad (8)$$
$$u^{(j)} = Pu^{(j+1)} + \text{diff}_t(f^{(j)} - Pf^{(j+1)}) \quad (j = n-1, \ldots, 0).$$

The result of the multiscale wavelet shrinkage is $u = u^{(0)}$.

4   Summary

In this paper we have seen that wavelet soft shrinkage on a single scale with Haar wavelets and threshold parameter τ is equivalent to TV-based nonlinear diffusion of two-pixel signal pairs with diffusion time $t = \tau/\sqrt{2}$. Moreover, it is also equivalent to TV regularisation of two-pixel pairs with regularisation parameter $\alpha = \tau/\sqrt{2}$. This might give rise to the conjecture that TV diffusion and regularisation yield identical results in general. Finally we showed that wavelet shrinkage on multiple scales is nothing but applying two-pixel TV diffusion or regularisation on the Laplacian pyramid of the signal.

These results are not only theoretically interesting, they may also have a number of practically relevant consequences. Firstly, they may help to make TV-based methods more popular for tasks such as image compression where wavelets constitute the state-of-the-art. Wavelet ideas may also help to make such PDE methods computationally more efficient. On the other hand, it is worth noting that PDE-based methods have no problems with translation and rotation invariance. Understanding their relation to wavelet methods might help to solve such well-known problems in the wavelet setting in a better way.

In our future work we intend to consider more advanced wavelet methods, to analyse the multidimensional case in detail, and to investigate possibilities to design hybrid methods that share the advantages of PDE-based techniques and wavelets.

Acknowledgements

Our joint research is partly funded by the project *Relations Between Nonlinear Filters in Digital Image Processing* within the the *DFG-Schwerpunktprogramm 1114: Mathematical Methods for Time Series Analysis and Digital Image Processing*. This is gratefully acknowledged.

References

1. F. Andreu, V. Caselles, J. I. Diaz, and J. M. Mazón. Qualitative properties of the total variation flow. *Journal of Functional Analysis*, 2002. To appear.
2. G. Bellettini, V. Caselles, and M. Novaga. The total variation flow in R^N. *Journal of Differential Equations*, 2002. To appear.
3. P. J. Burt and E. H. Adelson. The Laplacian pyramid as a compact image code. *IEEE Transactions on Communications*, 31:532–540, 1983.
4. A. Chambolle, R. A. DeVore, N. Lee, and B. L. Lucier. Nonlinear wavelet image processing: variational problems, compression, and noise removal through wavelet shrinkage. *IEEE Transactions on Image Processing*, 7(3):319–335, Mar. 1998.
5. T. F. Chan and H. M. Zhou. Total variation improved wavelet thresholding in image compression. In *Proc. Seventh International Conference on Image Processing*, Vancouver, Canada, Sept. 2000.
6. D. Donoho. De-noising by soft thresholding. *IEEE Transactions on Information Theory*, 41:613–627, 1995.

7. S. Durand and J. Froment. Reconstruction of wavelet coefficients using total-variation minimization. Technical Report 2001–18, Centre de Mathématiques et de Leurs Applications, ENS de Cachan, France, 2001.
8. F. Malgouyres. Combining total variation and wavelet packet approaches for image deblurring. In *Proc. First IEEE Workshop on Variational and Level Set Methods in Computer Vision*, pages 57–64, Vancouver, Canada, July 2001. IEEE Computer Society Press.
9. S. Mallat. *A Wavelet Tour of Signal Processing*. Academic Press, San Diego, 1998.
10. P. Perona and J. Malik. Scale space and edge detection using anisotropic diffusion. *IEEE Transactions on Pattern Analysis and Machine Intelligence*, 12:629–639, 1990.
11. L. I. Rudin, S. Osher, and E. Fatemi. Nonlinear total variation based noise removal algorithms. *Physica D*, 60:259–268, 1992.
12. O. Scherzer and J. Weickert. Relations between regularization and diffusion filtering. *Journal of Mathematical Imaging and Vision*, 12(1):43–63, Feb. 2000.
13. G. Strang and T. Nguyen. *Wavelets and Filter Banks*. Wellesley–Cambridge Press, Wellesley, 1996.
14. J. Weickert. *Anisotropic Diffusion in Image Processing*. Teubner, Stuttgart, 1998.

Data Resampling for Path Based Clustering

Bernd Fischer and Joachim M. Buhmann

Institut für Informatik III, Rheinische Friedrich-Wilhelms-Universität Bonn,
Römerstr. 164, 53117 Bonn, Germany,
{fischerb,jb}@cs.uni-bonn.de,
Phone: +49-228-73-4383/4380, Fax: +49-228-73-4382,
http://www-dbv.informatik.uni-bonn.de

Abstract. Path Based Clustering assigns two objects to the same cluster if they are connected by a path with high similarity between adjacent objects on the path. In this paper, we propose a fast agglomerative algorithm to minimize the Path Based Clustering cost function. To enhance the reliability of the clustering results a stochastic resampling method is used to generate candidate solutions which are merged to yield empirical assignment probabilities of objects to clusters. The resampling algorithm measures the reliability of the clustering solution and, based on their stability, determines the number of clusters.

Keywords: clustering, resampling, image segmentation

1 Introduction

Clustering objects into separated groups is an important topic in exploratory data analysis and pattern recognition. Many clustering methods group the data objects together to "compact" clusters with the assumption that all objects within one group are either mutually similar to each other or they are similar with respect to a common representative or centroid. The most prominent example of this concept is given for vectorial data by k-means, but pairwise clustering [3,4] and distributional clustering [6,7] are conceptually analogous methods for proximity and histogram data. An alternative principle to define clusters is the connectedness of data subsets which occupy elongated regions in feature space like spiral arms, circles or tube like data distributions. The spiral data set with the three arms in fig. 1(a) serves as an example of this type. k-means clustering and pairwise variants of it fail to extract the correct data patterns.

The well known single linkage algorithm, sometimes also called minimum spanning tree clustering algorithm [4] is able to find elongated (connected) structures in the data. A well-known problem of the minimum spanning tree algorithm is its extreme sensitivity against outliers as shows in figure 1(b). All but three objects are members of the same cluster. The two objects on the left (depicted by +) and the single object in the right part (depicted by □) form isolated clusters, since their minimal distance to all other objects is larger than the links between the other objects. The Path Based Clustering approach [1] is able to extract elongated structures from the data in a robust way. The intuitive picture

L. Van Gool (Ed.): DAGM 2002, LNCS 2449, pp. 206–214, 2002.
© Springer-Verlag Berlin Heidelberg 2002

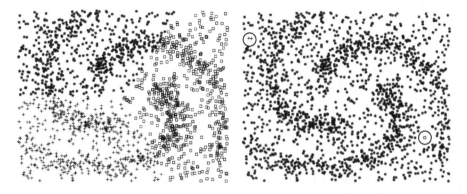

Fig. 1. (a) Pairwise Data Clustering is robust against outliers, but it prefers compact clusters. (b) Despite the fact that Minimum Spanning Tree Clustering can extract elongated structures, it is very sensitive to noise.

that two objects should be assigned to the same cluster if they can be connected by a mediating path of intermediate objects is modelled by a new cost function which is defined in section 2.

The new agglomerative optimization is achieved by a fast algorithm with satisfactory results. The agglomerative optimization is presented in section 3. For very noisy data, however, two clusters may be connected by small links or bridges which render the clustering results unreliable. We propose a resampling method based on bootstrap replications to avoid this detrimental effect (see sect. 4). Resampling is used to estimate probabilistic cluster assignments, thereby significantly enhancing the stability of the results. Resampling also allows us to measure the reliability of the resulting grouping. This approach is inspired by another important resampling method for clustering introduced in [2] which samples cuts on the basis of Karger's contraction algorithm [5].

The reliability measure provides us also with a statistical criterion to determine the number of clusters which is often not known a priori. Our criterion for model order selection chooses the number of clusters with the highest stability as the preferable solution. In section 5 we use the presented techniques for image segmentation. To show the generality of the clustering technique it is applied to segmentation on the basis of texture. The method has also been applied to grouping proteins and mircoarray data [8] in computational molecular biology.

2   Cost Function for Path Based Clustering

Assume the data objects are described by their pairwise dissimilarities. The matrix of dissimilarities is denoted by $\mathbf{D}$ and the set of objects by $\mathcal{O} = \{o_1, \ldots, o_n\}$. A mapping function $c : \mathcal{O} \rightarrow \{1, \ldots, k\}$ maps each object to one of the k labels. A cost function $\mathcal{H} : \mathcal{C} \rightarrow \mathbb{R}_+$ has to be defined, which ranks each possible mapping function c to the non-negative real numbers in such a way that the minimum of the cost function $\mathcal{H}(c)$ is the proper solution of the grouping problem. With $\mathcal{C}$ we denote the set of all possible mapping functions. In the sequel we denote by $\mathcal{O}_\nu(c)$ the set of objects, which are mapped to cluster ν by the current mapping function c.

The core of every clustering principle is given by a criterion to decide when two objects should belong to the same cluster. In pairwise clustering two similar objects o_i, o_j should be assigned to the same cluster, i.e., a small D_{ij} favors $c(i) = c(j)$. This concept can be generalized by assuming that object similarity behaves transitive in many applications. Therefore, we consider all paths $\mathcal{P}_{ij}(c)$ from object o_i to object o_j where all other objects on a connecting path belong to the same cluster as o_i and o_j. The dissimilarity mediated by a particular path $p \in \mathcal{P}_{ij}(c)$ is defined as the maximal dissimilarity on this path. The effective dissimilarity between two objects is calculated as the minimum over all path distances, i.e.,

$$D_{ij}^{\text{eff}} = \min_{p \in \mathcal{P}_{ij}(c)} \left\{ \max_{1 \leq h \leq |p|-1} D_{p[h]p[h+1]} \right\}. \tag{1}$$

With the definitions of the effective dissimilarity we are able to define the Path Based Clustering cost function. The costs for each cluster will be the mean effective dissimilarity multiplied by the number of objects within the cluster. The Path Based Clustering cost function is defined as

$$\mathcal{H}^{\text{pbc}}(c; \mathbf{D}) = \sum_{\nu \in \{1,\dots,k\}} \frac{1}{|\mathcal{O}_\nu(c)|} \sum_{o_i \in \mathcal{O}_\nu} \sum_{o_j \in \mathcal{O}_\nu} D_{ij}^{\text{eff}}(c; \mathbf{D}). \tag{2}$$

This cost function is invariant to additive shift and to scaling of dissimilarities.

3   Optimization

Many partitioning problems are known to be $\mathcal{NP}$-hard. It is unlikely to find an efficient algorithm which finds the global minimum of the partitioning function unless $\mathcal{P} = \mathcal{NP}$. To avoid an exhaustive search in the exponentially large space of all mapping functions, we suggest a fast agglomerative optimization heuristic.

Computing Cluster Costs: Before the agglomerative method is presented a fast algorithm to compute the Path Based Clustering function is given, which is needed for the agglomerative method. The cluster costs C_ν of a cluster ν are the sum over all effective dissimilarities within the cluster, i.e.,

$$C_\nu(c; \mathbf{D}) = \sum_{o_i \in \mathcal{O}_\nu} \sum_{o_j \in \mathcal{O}_\nu} \min_{p \in \mathcal{P}_{ij}(c)} \left\{ \max_{1 \leq h \leq |p|-1} D_{p[h]p[h+1]} \right\}. \tag{3}$$

The computation of C_ν can be solved with a variation of the Floyd-Warshall algorithm for the ALL-PAIRS-SHORTEST-PATH problem with $\mathcal{O}(n^3)$ running time.

The following observation helps to design a faster algorithm than the Floyd-Warshall version. Assume a partition of all objects of the cluster into ℓ subsets is given. For each subset all effective dissimilarities within the subset are known. Assume further that all links between the subsets are larger than all known effective dissimilarities within the subsets. In such a case the effective dissimilarity between the two subsets which are connected by the smallest link is equal to the dissimilarity of the smallest link. The smallest link describes the effective dissimilarity for each pair of objects between the two subsets.

This observation is used to create a recursive algorithm which is similar to Kruskal's MINIMUM SPANNING TREE algorithm. We start with a partitioning into n singletons, i.e., each subset contains exactly one object. The initial cluster costs vanish. All input dissimilarities are visited in increasing order. If a dissimilarity is found where the respective objects are in different subsets, this dissimilarity is the effective dissimilarity for each pair of objects from the two respective subsets. The multiplication of this dissimilarity value with the number of objects in the first subset and the number of objects in the second subset is added to the inner cluster costs. If only one subset remains, the inner cluster costs are computed. This algorithm computes the cluster costs of one cluster.

Agglomerative Optimization: The agglomerative optimization starts with n clusters, where exactly one object is assigned to each cluster. In each step two clusters are merged together. Assume a mapping function $c^\ell : \mathcal{O} \to \{1, \ldots, \ell\}$ for ℓ clusters is given. Each disjoined pair of clusters is a candidate for merging. This yields a set of candidate mapping functions $c^{\ell-1} : \mathcal{O} \to \{1, \ldots, \ell - 1\}$, with

$$\forall\, 1 \leq i < j \leq \ell : \; c_{i \cup j}^{\ell-1}(o) = \begin{cases} c^\ell(o) & \text{if } c(o) \notin \{i, j, \ell\} \\ i & \text{if } c(o) \in \{i, j\} \\ j & \text{if } c(o) = \ell \end{cases} \tag{4}$$

From all candidate mapping functions the mapping

$$c^{\ell-1} = \operatorname*{argmin}_{1 \leq i < j \leq \ell} \left\{ \mathcal{H}^{\text{pbc}} \left(c_{i \cup j}^{\ell-1} \right) \right\}, \tag{5}$$

is chosen which minimizes the Path Based Clustering cost function. The algorithm merges clusters until the desired cluster number is reached. On each level of the agglomerative clustering the Path Based Clustering function has to be recalculated ℓ^2 times. A naive implementation requires a running time of $\mathcal{O}\left(n^3(m+n)\log n\right)$, where n is the number of objects and m is the number of knwon dissimilarities. Using a priority queue to manage the pairs of clusters, which are candidates for merging, the running time is reduced to $\mathcal{O}(n^3 \log n)$.

4   Resampling

The agglomerative optimization yields satisfactory results and has a low running time, but we can not guarantee that the global minimum of the Path Based Clustering cost function is found. Furthermore, the result for two instances drawn from the same data distribution should be comparable.

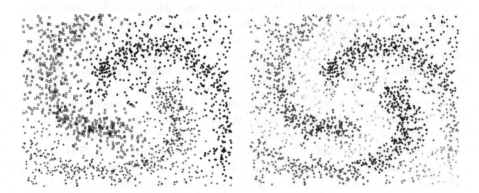

Fig. 2. Result of the resampling method. (a) The cluster assignments are chosen as the maximum likelihood of the cluster assignment probabilities. (b) The probability of the cluster assignments of the maximum likelihood assignments for each object. Dark color shows a high probability.

Maximum Likelihood Mapping: We suggest the following resampling scheme to get an empirical probability distribution over the cluster assignments for each object. Draw B different data sets by sampling n objects with replacements independent of the input instance. As in a bootstrap replications for error estimation some objects may occur multiple times in the resampled instance. The B multisets of objects on the resampled data set are denoted by $\mathcal{O}^b$ $(1 \leq b \leq B)$. The agglomerative optimization algorithm is used to get a mapping function c^b for each of the B replications. To estimate the probability of cluster assignments for each object, the B mapping solutions are brought into correspondance, thereby taking into account that a mapping is invariant to permutation of cluster labels. Let $h_o^b : \{1, \ldots, k\} \to \mathbb{N}$ be the histogram of cluster assignments for the first b mappings of each object o. The permutation $\pi_o^{b+1} : \{1, \ldots, k\} \to \{1, \ldots, k\}$, which optimally fits a new mapping c^{b+1} to the given histograms $\{h_o^b \,|\, o \in \mathcal{O}\}$ is

$$\pi^{b+1} = \underset{\pi \in \mathcal{S}_k}{\operatorname{argmax}} \left\{ \sum_{o \in \mathcal{O}^{b+1}} \frac{h_o^b\left(\pi\left(c^{b+1}(o)\right)\right)}{\sum_{1 \leq \ell \leq k} h_o^b(\ell)} \right\}, \tag{6}$$

where $\mathcal{S}_k$ is the symmetric group of k elements. The problem of finding the best permutation can be transformed to a maximum bipartite matching problem, for which fast flow algorithms are known.

With the help of the permutations we can estimate empirical cluster assignment distributions $\hat{p}_o(\ell)$ for each object. The maximum likelihood mapping function $\hat{c}(o) = \operatorname{argmax}_{1 \leq \ell \leq k} \hat{p}_o(\ell)$ is derived from these empirical distributions.

Figure 2(a) shows the maximum likelihood mapping for our example. The three noisy spiral arms are clearly found, but there are some unreliable assignments in the area of low density between the spiral arms. The empirical cluster assignment probability yields the information, how reliable the cluster assign-

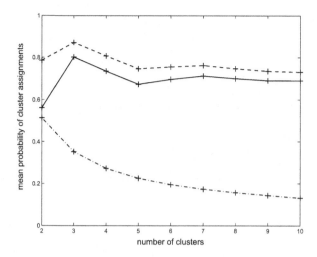

Fig. 3. The mean cluster assignment probability of the maximum likelihood estimation (dashed) and random assignments (dash-dotted) and the relative difference of both (solid).

ments are. In figure 2(b) the probabilities of the maximum likelihood assignments are drawn. Dark gray values denote high probabilities of the maximum likelihood assignment whereas a light gray value denotes low assignment probabilities. Note that the objects in the center of the spiral arms are almost assigned with certainty whereas assignments of objects between clusters are uncertain.

Estimated Number of Clusters: The mean cluster assignment probability $\bar{p} = \frac{1}{|\mathcal{O}|} \sum_{o \in \mathcal{O}} \hat{p}_o\left(\hat{c}(o)\right)$ can be used to indicate the number of clusters for which the maximum likelihood mapping $\hat{c}$ has the highest stability. In figure 3 the dashed line shows the mean cluster assignment probability of the given example for a differing number of clusters. In this example the solution with three clusters has the largest mean cluster assignment probability, but in general it is not enough only to consider the mean cluster assignment probability. For example for n clusters the cluster assignment probability is always 1 since we use the optimal permutation. The dotted line shows the mean cluster assignment probability of an algorithm which chooses the mapping function randomly. As an index to indicate the number of clusters for the given problem, which produces a solution with highest stability. According to [8] we use the number of clusters, which maximizes the difference between the mean cluster assignment probability of the maximum likelihood assignment $\bar{p}$ and the mean cluster assignment probability of random assignments $\bar{p}_0$ relative to the risk of the random cluster solution.

$$k^* = \underset{2 \leq i \leq n}{\operatorname{argmax}} \left\{ \frac{\bar{p} - \bar{p}_0}{1 - \bar{p}_0} \right\} \tag{7}$$

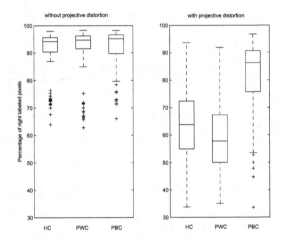

Fig. 4. Performance on a testbed of 100 Mondrian images: left without projective distortion and right with projective distortion. On the y-axis the percentage of correctly classified labels is drawn. The figure shows the boxplots for Histogram Clustering (HC), Pairwise Clustering (PWC) and Path Based Clustering (PBC). The boxes show the median, the first and second quartile.

The solid line in figure 3 shows the relative difference for a small number of clusters. The index reaches the maximum for three clusters.

5   Applications

Path Based Clustering is presented as a general clustering method independent of its application. To demonstrate its versatility, we have applied it to texture segmentation. In images which are projectively transformed, the clusters form elongated structures in features space, which renders conventional texture segmentation methods like Pairwise Clustering [3] or the Histogram Clustering [7] inappropriate, since they are based on compactness. Histogram Clustering can be regarded as a version k-means clustering in the histogram space.

To derive the dissimilarity matrix, a convolution with a multiscale family of Gabor wavelets is performed according to [1]. At each image position on a regular grid overlayed on the image an empirical distribution of the Gabor responses is estimated. The pairwise dissimilarities are derived as the result of a statistic $\mathcal{X}^2$ test for each pair of empirical distributions.

To demonstrate the performance of Path Based Clustering a testbed of 100 Texture Mondrians was created. The textures from the Brodatz album are projectively transformed. In each Mondrian image five textures are combined to one image. Figure 4 gives a statistical evaluation of the results on the testbed. The left part is the statistics for Mondrian images without projective distortion and the right part is a test with the described projective transformations. The results are compared to the ground truth assignments. For each clustering method

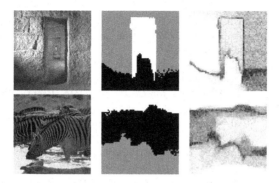

Fig. 6. Texture segmentation on real world images with Path Based Clustering: input image, segmentation result and cluster assignment probability.

a boxplot is drawn. The three lines of the boxes are the median, the first and third quartile of the percentage of matches. The two other lines show the rest of the data and the crosses are outliers. On the testbed without distortion the three methods are comparable, but on the testbed with projective distortion the Path Based Clustering performs best. The average running time for one 512×512 image is 10 minutes on a 1GHz-Pentium processor if the number of bootstrap replications is 100 for each image.

In a second test we applied the new Clustering approach to real world images. Figure 6 shows the input images, the resulting maximum likelihood assignments of Path Based Clustering and the assignment probabilities. The assignment probabilities are lower on the real world images than on the artificial Mondrian images, but one can clearly observe that the probability of assignment to the maximum likelihood solution is higher in the center of the different texture parts. Here again the assignment probability is very low only on the borders of the textures.

6   Conclusion

In this paper a fast agglomerative optimization algorithm for Path Based Clustering is presented, which yields satisfactory results in many cases. A bootstrap resampling method further increases the robustness of the results and it provides us with a measure for the reliability of cluster assignments. The reliability measure can be used to select the number of clusters, which has the highest stability. The applicability of the new clustering approach is shown for image segmentation of images with strong texture gradients.

References

1. B. Fischer, T. Zöller, and J. Buhmann. Path based pairwise data clustering with application to texture segmentation. In *Energy Minimization Methods in Computer Vision and Pattern Recognition*, LNCS 2134, pages 235–250, 2001.

2. Y. Gdalyahu, D. Weinshall, and M. Werman. Self organization in vision: Stochastic clustering for image segmentation, perceptual grouping and image database. *IEEE Tr. PAMI*, 23(10):1053–1074, 2001.
3. T. Hofmann and J. Buhmann. Pairwise data clustering by deterministic annealing. *IEEE Tr. PAMI*, 19(1):1–14, 1997.
4. A. Jain and R. Dubes. *Algorithms for Clustering Data*. Prentice Hall, Englewood Cliffs, NJ 07632, 1988.
5. D. Karger and C. Stein. A new appoach to the minimum cut problem. *Journal of the ACM*, 43:601–640, 1996.
6. F. Pereira, N. Tishby, and L. Lee. Distributional clustering for english words. In *IEEE Conf. on Computer Vision and Pattern Recognition*, pages 638–639, 1993.
7. J. Puzicha, T. Hofmann, and J. M. Buhmann. Histogram clustering for unsupervised segmentation and image retrieval. *Pattern Recognition Letters*, 20:899–909, 1999.
8. M. Braun V. Roth, T. Lange and J. Buhmann. A resampling approach to cluster validation. In *Int. Conf. on Computational Statistics*, 2002.

Statistical Image Sequence Processing for Temporal Change Detection

Martin Brocke

[1] Robert Bosch GmbH, FV/PLF2, P.O. Box 300240, 70442 Stuttgart*
[2] Interdisciplinary Center for Scientific Computing, INF 368, 69120 Heidelberg,
Martin.Brocke@iwr.uni-heidelberg.de

Abstract. The aim is to detect sudden temporal changes in image sequences, focusing on bright objects that appear in a few consecutive frames. The proposed algorithm detects such outliers by computing a variance weighted deviation from mean values for every pixel. On this result, an object segmentation based on 2D-moments and its invariants is done frame by frame at a $\approx 3\sigma$ threshold. The algorithm was designed for a wide range of tasks in pre-processing as a tool for detection of fast temporal changes such as suddenly appearing or moving objects. Two different applications on noisy sequence data were realized. The entire system proved to fulfill the requirements of industrial environments for online process control and scientific demands for data rejection.

Keywords: *change detection, outliers, image sequences, process control, automation*

1 Introduction

Our aim is to monitor noisy processes and give an alarm when sudden temporal changes (their intensity difference is not much larger than the noise) appear in the data (sensor drops, collapse of the process itself, illumination black-outs). For this, change detectors are an adequate tool – often hidden, but underlying all motion detection in image processing – and therefore play a key role in applications like surveillance, traffic flow, tracking, video indexing, gesture recognition. The most intuitive approach is thresholding the difference of two consecutive frames out of a sequence. As already stated in [1], the drawback is that threshold values are often empirically estimated and difficult to adapt. Furthermore, this strategy must fail when noise (uncorrelated sensor noise or normal distributed flicker from the observed scene) is of the same quantity as the temporal change. But what does temporal change distinguish from noise than? Change is not randomly distributed! While d follows a Gaussian $N(0, \sigma)$, temporal change as outcome of an event that happened during sequence acquisition does not so and change is connected in time-space into regions. So, we have to leverage this clustering property versus the over-all presence of noise

---

* The author thanks M.D. Schmidt and S. Hader for their comments and input.

L. Van Gool (Ed.): DAGM 2002, LNCS 2449, pp. 215–223, 2002.

to detect the change properly. From a statistician's point of view, we classify pixels into two populations $N_i(\overline{x}_i, \sigma_i)$ with unknown normal prior PDFs. Since $\sigma_i > |\overline{x}_1 - \overline{x}_2|$ the standard method using a critical value (threshold) and minimizing mis-classification costs is not applicable. Most change detectors in image processing and video coding operate on d or on frame-to-reference differences (surveillance). [1] is testing on several statistics of d the significance whether the questioned pixel comes from noise (H_0 null hypothesis) or from change regions. [7] does not operate on d, but compares Yakimovsky's likelihood ratio ([11] compares it to other statistical tests) of small windows of two consecutive frames. Similar [6] introduces temporal statistics at late stage on the level of selected block or region features. [3] considers the whole motion detection problem as a statistical classification in a Bayesian sense and operates on consecutive pairs of temporal derivatives instead of d formulating a MAP criterion on observations $\nabla_t g$ and Markov random fields for the change mask.

We group the content of a scene into: $\mathcal{A}$) objects (foreground) on a uniform background; $\mathcal{B}$) typical pixel noise due to quantum effects and sensor electronics; $\mathcal{C}$) known or expected changes to the foreground objects and the background implied by the process physics; $\mathcal{D}$) unexpected events or occurrences (objects move, appear or disappear). Restricted by $\mathcal{B}$), our goal is to detect $\mathcal{D}$), but not $\mathcal{C}$) (false positives). We limit our algorithm design to stationary sequences. This means a fixed camera observes the process and pixel intensities are at constant level in a mean sense. Noise or scene inherent changes are allowed, but no arbitrary moving of objects or sensor (wipes as in change detection in video indexing) occurs. However, we allow the data to be very noisy and of low resolution. Such sequence data is typical for surveillance tasks or image data consistency check we present in later sections. For normal distributed camera noise σ_c the distribution $p(d|H_0) \propto \exp\left(-\frac{d^2}{2\sigma_c}\right)$ suggests to make the decision pixel-wise on $\{g(\mathbf{x}, t) - g(\mathbf{x}, t-1)/2\sigma_c\}^2$. Doing so, only two pixels contribute while from our content concept much more stationary pixels would be available to compare with. Thus we suggest to construct $\mathcal{A}$) by statistical methods (knowing then how a sequence looks like in general). Hereby we suppress $\mathcal{B}$) at the same time. Variance based weights help to distinguish the statistically identified groups $\mathcal{C}) \cup \mathcal{D}$) which oppose $\mathcal{A}$). For construction of $\mathcal{A}$) we should exclude $\mathcal{D}$). That means that we have to know $\mathcal{D}$) already before. This problem is solved by an iterative computing of $\mathcal{A}$). In statistical domain *temporal change* is known as *outlier detection*. Good surveys are given by [9] and [2] that goes back to the work of Grubbs and Thompson [13] who proposed outlier tests very similar to the temporal change measure (2) presented herein.

2   Statistical Algorithm

Let us denote the gray value intensity of the n-th sequence $g(x, y, t, n)$ (we shorten $\mathbf{x} = (x, y)^T$) and $\langle \cdot \rangle_{i_s, \Delta i}$ the mean value regarding the dimension $i \in \{\mathbf{x}, t, n\}$ within the interval Δi (ΔI for the entire range available) starting at i_s. The idea for the proposed algorithm comes from the ability of the human visual system to detect an event (i.e. suddenly appearing objects) in a uniform background due to its size and the contrast ratio after having seen several frames. While the size of temporal changes is usually fixed by resolution, we gather information from the contrast measures by the *inverse contrast ratio* in spatial imagery

$$\frac{\langle g\left(\mathbf{x}\right)\rangle_{\mathbf{x},\varDelta\mathbf{x}}}{\left\langle\left(g\left(\mathbf{x}\right)-\langle g\left(\mathbf{x}\right)\rangle_{\mathbf{x},\varDelta\mathbf{x}}\right)^{2}\right\rangle_{\mathbf{x},\varDelta\mathbf{x}}^{\frac{1}{2}}} \tag{1}$$

This enhances weak edges; Gaussian white noise is reduced by the factor $(\varDelta X)^{-1}$ in a neighborhood of ideally constant intensity. The mean value $\langle\cdot\rangle$ corresponds to a spatial convolution with a uniform box window that reduces zero mean noise by the factor $(\varDelta x\varDelta y)^{-1}$ in a region constant over the window.

A special case of (1) is a transformation to unity variance, known as *statistical scaling*, by omitting the mean operation $\langle\cdot\rangle_{\mathbf{x},\varDelta\mathbf{x}}$ in the numerator. Beside the effects of both transformations to fine structure (weakening in both cases, smoothing in (1)), the visual image content is generally kept under these transformations. The difference of both transformations shows to what extend a pixel at given spacial position varies compared to the variance of its neighbors (in space $\varDelta\mathbf{x}$). Our algorithm brings these ideas now into temporal domain.

$$f\left(x,y,t,n\right)=\frac{g\left(x,y,t,n\right)-\langle g\left(x,y,t,n\right)\rangle_{t_{s},\varDelta t}}{\sqrt{\left\langle\left[g\left(x,y,t,n\right)-\langle g\left(x,y,t,n\right)\rangle_{t_{s},\varDelta t}\right]^{2}\right\rangle_{t_{s},\varDelta t}}}\begin{cases}\geq\theta\ temporal\ change\ \mathcal{D}\\\\<\theta\ no\ change\end{cases} \tag{2}$$

is the deviation of each pixel g from its mean $\langle g\left(x,y,t,n\right)\rangle_{t_{s},\varDelta t}$ normalized by its variance over the interval $\varDelta t$. By the statistics in temporal dimension (or small parts of it) we are able to distinguish the "typical scene" ($\mathcal{A}$) that we monitor from temporal changes that we aim to detect. Threshold values for θ are typically in the range $2.0\cdots4.0$. Pixels with temporal change have a large nominators in (2). This is weighted such that pixels of high variance do not contribute to the temporal change measure f that much as pixels with less variances in their intensity. The reader should note that we do not leverage the knowledge we could gain from $\langle\cdot\rangle_{n,\varDelta n}$. For both our applications learning over n-dimension doesn't make sense: sequences had to be analyzed independently from each other.

For fast decisions whether there was temporal change or not (no matter at which t) one can also sum up f or f^2. Because $\sum_{t}f^{2}\rightarrow T$ and $\sum_{t}f\rightarrow0$ it is not necessary to compute all f over t if we are only interested in that temporal change does not exceed a certain threshold. The events we seek leave a significant trace (fig. 1e) in the variance in (2), so that multiple detection of such events at the same position $\mathbf{x}$ but different t becomes difficult. An iterative detection (two or three iterations lead to sufficiently stable values in our data) avoids decreasing selectivity of the algorithm in the case of such multiple events: we compute f again and ignore thereby all pixels that belong to temporal changes.

For the iterative processing (iteration indices in parenthesis) of (2) we introduce a binary mask $b^{(i)}(x, y, t, n)$ and a modified normalization to update stepwise the mean value

$$f^{(i)} = \frac{g^{(i)} - \langle g \rangle_{t_s, \Delta t}^{(i)}}{\sqrt{\left\langle \left[g^{(i)} - \langle g \rangle_{t_s, \Delta t}^{(i)} \right]^2 \right\rangle_{t_s, \Delta t}}} \tag{3}$$

$$\langle g(x, y, t, n) \rangle_{t_s, \Delta t}^{(i)} = \frac{\sum\limits_{\Delta t} \left(g(x, y, t, n) \cdot \prod\limits_{j=0...i} b^{(j)}(x, y, t, n) \right)}{\sum\limits_{\Delta t} \prod\limits_{j=0...i} b^{(j)}(x, y, t, n)} \tag{4}$$

Initially, $\langle g \rangle^{(0)}$ and $f^{(0)}$ are the same as in (2) because $b^{(0)}(x, y, t, n) = 1$. The binary mask for higher iterations is $b^{(i+1)} = \mathcal{T}_\theta \left[f^{(i)} \right]$ which is a threshold operation at $\theta \approx 3.0$ that clips in $b^{(1)}$ all those pixels to zero that fulfill $f^{(0)}(x, y, t, n) > \theta$ and thus belong to a temporal change. The product $\prod$ gathers these pixels over all iteration steps. The updated mean value (4) enters in (3) and updates f. We improved our result $f^{(i)}$ and $b^{(i)}$ by segmentation of strong temporal changes before computing weaker changes with higher accuracy.

In case of a slow but continuous brightening of the entire scene, we pick up again an idea from image restoration in spatial domain and adapt it to the t-dimension. In (1) the window $\Delta\mathbf{x}$ that defines neighborhood rarely expands to the entire frame $\Delta\mathbf{X}$. Making the analogy in the t-domain this means introducing a window Δt smaller than the length of the sequence ΔT, that may also vary $\Delta t(t)$ along t or might even have other weights than uniform in $\langle \cdot \rangle$.

3   Classification of Detected Change Regions

We analyze the shape of the detected change regions $B = \prod_i b^{(i)}$ to discard those that do not have shape properties we look for. Therefor we label frame-wise all objects (denoted by o) in B using 8-connectivity. Morphological smoothing on B might be applied before object extraction. For object parameters, we used 2D central moment based invariants [12] of low order. The vector $\mathbf{m}_o(n, t) = (1, m_{o,2}, m_{o,3}, \ldots, m_{o,Q})^T$ contains for each object several parameter invariant under translation and rotation. These are for instance the volume of 2D objects $v_o = \sum_{\mathbf{x}} B_o(\mathbf{x}, t, n) \cdot f(\mathbf{x}, t, n)$ and their eccentricity

$$\epsilon = \frac{(\mu_{2,0} - \mu_{0,2})^2 + 4\mu_{1,1}^2}{(\mu_{2,0} + \mu_{0,2})^2}$$

$$\mu_{i,j} = \sum_{x,y} (x - x_c)^i (y - y_c)^j B(x, y, t, n) f(x, y, t, n) \tag{5}$$

where $(x_c, y_c)^T$ is the object's density center position. It is important that (5) is computed for each object individually; we suppressed the index o in (5) for better reading. In the application presented in section 4 we took $Q - 1 = 4$ different parameters $\mathbf{m}_o = (1, v, \mu_{2,0}, \mu_{0,2}, \epsilon)^T$ and combined $(P+Q)!/P!Q!$ monomials of grade up to $P = 5$ to enter $\mathbf{x}_0$. For a standard two-class (relevant vs. irrelevant temporal change) polynomial classifier (PC), the scalar $s(n, t)$ is the inner product of the vector of weights $\mathbf{a}$ (same for all objects) and vector $\mathbf{x}_o$

$$s(n, t) = \sum_o \mathbf{a}^T \mathbf{x}_o \quad \mathbf{x}_o = (1, \ldots, \prod_{q=1}^{Q} m_{o,q}^{p_q}, \ldots)^T \quad \text{with} \quad \sum_q p_q = P \quad (6)$$

We have chosen a PC because of its robustness and its analytical properties compared to other classifiers such as MLP. PCs lead directly to an optimal global solution due to the non-linear base functions [8]. Furthermore they are fast in both applying (6) and training of $\mathbf{a}$. PCs scale with the number of data sets in the training sample (t.s.), which is important for us, because both applications produce continuously new training data that we use to improve the weights $\mathbf{a}$. Also the PC allows successive update of its weights when new data is added to the t.s. For a t.s. with known class labels the weights are computed by minimizing $\min_{\mathbf{a}} \sum_{n \in t.s.} \sum_o (\mathbf{a}^T \mathbf{x}_o - l)^2$. We computed weights using polynomial grades $P = 4 \cdots 6$. The choice of the set of weights was made upon cross validation with 10%-sub-samples of the t.s. using an asymmetric loss function. It penalizes losses (existing relevant temporal change was not detected; false accept) 1000 times higher than false alarms (change was detected in processes without change).

We expect that $s(t, n)$ remains almost zero for frames with no other occurrences than from group $(\mathcal{B})$ and $(\mathcal{C})$. Ideally, s peaks up δ-like for temporal change (the value of s measures the event's markedness). When too much temporal change occurs in a sequence, we discard the sequence from further processing in our scientific application. In the industrial application, the change detector operates as tool for process quality control: too much temporal change within an observed process qualifies the dealt product as fault. This is the case when $s(n, t) > e$ for one or several consecutive frames. If there is no knowledge on the regions of change and their features (i.e. when starting from the scratch with detection of *"everything that is unusual"* in a sequence), we suggest to reduce (6) to the sum of the volume values v_o of all objects or even set $s(n, t)$ to the volume of the object with largest area μ_{00}. This turned out the best choice in order to gather enough data for a more accurate computation of $\mathbf{a}$, e and s. Using 3D moments is impossible for both our applications because object sizes are smaller than the displacement vectors between frames at t and $t + 1$. In that respect, objects are "too fast" compared with the frame rate we get from the camera. In none of our applications does an object appear in more than 6-8 consecutive frames.

4   Industry Application: Laser Welding Process Control

The aim is to control quality of a mass production laser welding process on metal parts. Defect parts are caused by irregular welding processes that show sputtering. These sputters and explosions cause weak but sudden temporal change in image sequences taken of the laser welding process. We have chosen an High-Dynamic-Resolution-CMOS (HDRC) imager to cover the demanding dynamic of the given scene (120 dB) and the required high speed frame rate of 1000 fps minimum at 64^2 pixels. The HDRC sensor ideally meets both criteria by providing log. compression and random access at 8 Mpix/s (10 bit depth) readout rate. For the system (laser beam light, filters, gain, ...) SNR is about 27dB for the relevant range of intensity levels. The entire image processing system is running on a PC (PIII, 750 MHz; frame grabber interface card; digital IO board for communication to the SPS control unit) using a sophisticated image processing library that is hidden behind a GUI. This allows easy and robust handling for local operators and remote service for software developers and engineers. Each sequence of 1500 frames observes the welding spot (fig. 1a); the scene consists of a bright spot in the center of a $10mm \times 10mm$ area. On its edges, variance over t reaches its highest values while the background is fairly illuminated. About 1 ‰ of the 3.9 TByte processed data (raw, ROI) show unusual effects. We especially aim to detect temporal change shown in fig.1b-d. Difficulties arise from the strong flicker of the center which is inherent to the scene and thus should

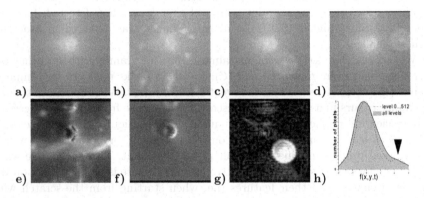

Fig. 1. a) The process should look like this in all frames. The central welding region shows strong flicker and variances in its shape. **b)** typical temporal change due to collapse of the energy transfer into the material to be welded. Small spots (sputtered metal) appear. **c)-d)** One big sputter or reflection crosses the frame ($\Delta t = 5$ms) from lower middle to upper right. Their shapes are blurry due to their out-of-focus position. **e)** std. dev. image as it enters (2) of the sequence where a)-d) were taken from. **f)** std. dev. image as in e) but after two iteration steps from (3). All effects from temporal change were removed, only the variances of the continuous flicker of the center region remain. This "cleaning effect" applies for the mean value $\langle g \rangle_t$ as well. **g)** temporal change measure f from (3) after two iterations for frame c). Sudden temporal change is found for the crossing object, but not for the center region. The algorithm can distinguish between sudden changes in single frames and regions that show strong variances over the entire process. Thus it is possible to separate scene content ($\mathcal{D}$) from the rest. **h)** Normalized histogram over f from (2) for this sequence. The center region flicker and the temporal change appear as shifted sub-set of a normal distr. at $f > 2$ especially in pixels with intensity levels < 50% of saturation (dotted line and ▼).

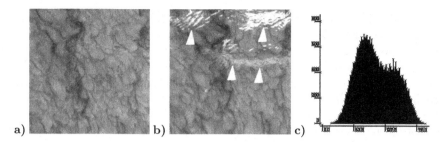

Fig. 2. **a)** Thermography image data of 5. Water surface shows structures of warm (bright) regions that move with the liquid flow and cool down (decrease gray value) **b)** Strong temporal changes are marked by white pointers ($\triangle$): sun-glitter appears on the ocean surface and crosses rapidly the frame while changing its shape ($\Delta t = 0.8$s). Intensity overflows (upper left and right corners) and a horizontal structure (right to the center) with weaker increase of intensity level disturb the temperature measurements significantly. **c)** Histogram for the image data sequence *a)* and *b)* are taken from. Due to additive temporal change, the theoretically expected distribution gets a shifted subset. There is no mean to separate temperature data and reflection by a simple threshold without cutting high temperatures of true data.

not to be detected as temporal change. At four phases of the process (totaling 30% of ΔT) the overall intensity of the frames $\langle g\,(x,y,t,n)\rangle_{\mathbf{X},\Delta\mathbf{X}}$ is at a significantly ($> 10\sigma$) higher level. Thus $\langle g\,(x,y,t,n)\rangle_{\mathbf{X},\Delta\mathbf{X}}$ switches between two levels, but once on such level, it remains stable. Hence the data requires the outlined modifications (transition from ΔT to $\Delta t\,(t)$).

For all produced parts we had access to the results of a 100% visual inspection. This allowed to validate the algorithm and to figure out a false-positives-rate. Parameters θ and e were adjusted such that the false-positives-rate was at 50% of all alarms. We would rather allow more pseudo errors than miss an event, which has proven not to be the case in the course of the six months while the system was tested, monitoring more than 1.5 million processes (cycle time available for processing: $1.7s$). Classification proved to be robust enough for mass production environments. As far as the technical side is concerned, a similar hardware set-up without using the HDRC high speed capabilities was tested by [10] to control laser welding processes and classifying on 4 parameters from run length coded 2D images. However, single frames (8 bit) were processed off-line while we classify parts from image sequence data into "good" or "defect". Since only few years ago online process control of laser welding is done camera based with spacial resolution. This allowed to patent [4] the herein described system recently.

5   Scientific Application: Outlier Rejection

This application uses the proposed algorithm as part of its pre-processing on recorded data (off-line, not limited by cycle times). Heat exchange at the ocean surface serves to trace gas exchange and thus gives insights to transport mechanisms which are of high interest in environmental physics, oceanography and climate modelling [5]. In IR image sequences (fig. 2a-b) from an ocean surface hot spots move with the liquid's general flow through the observed field, cool down and are then renewed by warm water from the depth. The camera (Galileo, $N_e \Delta t = 28$mK, 100 fps, SNR=30dB) looks under 60° to the ideal surface ($40cm \times 40cm$). The research interest lies on the the renewal rate and the radiative cool down process of the warm structures and thus needs to compute the flow field and decay of intensities at the same time. Sun-glitter on the liquid's surface appears as bright regions (fig. 2b) that move rapidly and under strong change of their shape across the frame. Difficulties in computing true flow field and temperature change can be avoided if such regions are detected properly in pre-processing. The temperature distribution is known theoretically and from laboratory experiments (fig. 2c). Sun-glitter adds to a randomly selected subsample of this distribution a constant.region. Our algorithm was able to detect sun-glitter in frames up to 32% covered by such contaminations and thus could lead to more robust estimation of the temperature flow field.

6   Conclusion

The proposed algorithm aims at detecting sudden temporal changes considering all available frames. We applied the described change detector to two samples of noisy, low-resolution data. The algorithm successfully operated on both and could be improved by iterations. Furthermore we showed that the algorithm meets industrial criteria such as robustness, speed, costs, and fulfills the needs of online quality control in mass production. We detected all bad processes (≈ 75ppm) for the application in industry. However, we accepted a relatively high rate of false positives (50% of all alarms). Nevertheless, the system shows significant better performance than other systems installed for online laser welding process control before. Future work will cover improvements of $\theta\,(x,y,t)$ and approximations of (3) and (2) that allow implementation on FPGA boards.

References

1. Aach, T., Kaup, A., Mester, R.: *Bayesian Algorithms for Change Detection in Image Sequ. Using Markov Random Fields*, Sig. Proc.-IC, vol. 7, no. 2, pp. 147-160, 1995
2. Beckman, R.J., Cook, R.D.: *Outlier....s*, Technometrics, vol. 25, pp. 119-149, 1983
3. Bouthemy, P., Lalande, P.: *Detection and tracking of moving objects based on a statistical regularization method in space and time*, Proc. ECCV, pp. 307-311, 1990
4. Brocke M., Schmidt, M. D. et al.: *Verfahren zur autom. Beurteilung von Laserverarbeitungsprozessen*, German Patent, DE 10103255, disclosure: 25.7.2002
5. Garbe, C., Jähne, B.: *Reliable estimates of the sea surface heatflux from image sequences*, In: B. Radig, Mustererkennung 2001, 23. DAGM-Symp., München
6. Hötter, M., Mester, R., Meyer, M.: *Detection of moving objects in natural scenes*, Proc. Carnahan Conf. on Security Technology, pp. 47-52, 1995

7. Hsu,Y. Z., Nagel, H.H. and Rekers, G.: *New likelihood test methods for change detection in image sequences*, CVGIP, vol. 26, pp. 73-106, 1984

8. Kreßel U. et al.: Polynomklassifikator vs. Multilayer-Perzeptron, In: R.E. Großkopf: Mustererkennung 1990, 12. DAGM-Symp. Oberkochen

9. Madalla, G. S., Yin Y.: *Outliers, unit roots and robust estimation*, In: G. S. Madalla et al: Handbook of Statistics, vol. 15, Elsevier, 1997

10. Nordbruch, S. et al.: *Analyse von HDRC-Bildern des Werkstoffübergangs des MSG-Schweißprozesses*, In: G. Sommer, Mustererkennung 2000, 22. DAGM-Symp., Kiel

11. Sethi, I., Patel, N.: *A Statistical Approach to Scene Change Detection*, SPIE Conf. Stor. and Retr. for Image and Video Database III, no. 2420, pp. 329-338

12. Teague,M. R.: *Image Analysis via the General Theory of Moments*, Opt. Soc. of America, vol. 70, no. 8, pp. 920-930, 1980

13. Thompson, W. R.: *On a criterion for the rejection of observations*, Ann. of Math. Stat., vol. 6, pp. 214-219, 1935

Single-View Metrology: Algorithms and Applications
(Invited Paper)

Antonio Criminisi

Microsoft Research, One Microsoft Way, Redmond, WA,
antcrim@microsoft.com

Abstract. This paper addresses the problem of extracting three-dimensional geometric information from a single, uncalibrated image of a scene.
This work, building upon [7], is divided into two parts. The first part describes, in simple steps, the basic algorithms to obtain partial or complete geometric reconstruction from single perspective images of a scene. The second part presents a panorama of applications of single-view metrology and discusses its relationship with different disciplines such as architecture, history of art and forensic science. Furthermore, techniques for increasing the level of automation of the reconstruction process are herein described.
Several examples on photographs and historical paintings demonstrate the power and flexibility of the proposed techniques.

1 Introduction

This paper aims at describing, in a coherent framework, simple and effective algorithms for extracting geometric information and constructing compelling three-dimensional models from single, uncalibrated perspective images of a scene. Furthermore, this paper discusses the relationship of single-view metrology tecnhiques with other disciplines such as architecture, forensic science and history of art.

When only one view of a scene (either real or imaginary) is available, multi-view geometry algorithms [11,16,19] cannot be applied to construct three-dimensional models of the oberved scene. Recently, novel techniques for the partial or complete reconstruction of scenes from single images have been developed [7,21,24,28,30,31,35]. The main challenge of such algorithms lies in correctly modeling the perspective distortions introduced by the imaging process from a single input image (fig. 1).

We are mainly concerned with two canonical types of measurement: (i) lenghts of segments on planar surfaces and (ii) distances of points from planes. In many cases, these two kinds of measurements are proved to be sufficient for a partial or complete three-dimensional reconstruction of the observed scene.

The proposed algorithms have been designed to work in an uncalibrated framework (i.e. no need for the camera pose or internal parameters to be known or computed). On the other hand, scene constraints such as orthogonality and parallelism of structures are exploited, thus making our algorithms especially suitable for scenes containing man-made structures such as architectural elements and geometric patterns.

The ideas in this paper can be seen as reversing the rules for drawing perspective images laid out for the first time by Leon Battista Alberti in his treatise on linear perspective [1].

L. Van Gool (Ed.): DAGM 2002, LNCS 2449, pp. 224–239, 2002.
© Springer-Verlag Berlin Heidelberg 2002

Fig. 1. Modeling perspective distortions in single images: **(a)** the four pillars have the same height in the world, although their images clearly are not of the same length because of perspective effects; **(b)** as shown, however, all pillars are correctly measured to have the same height. The perspective distortion has been removed.

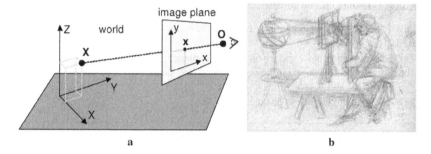

Fig. 2. The pinhole camera model. **(a)** A point **X** in the three-dimensional space is imaged as **x**. Euclidean coordinates X, Y, Z and x, y are used for the world and image reference systems, respectively. **O** is the centre of projection, i.e. the camera optical centre. **(b)** Leonardo's *Perspectograph* (detail), by Leonardo da Vinci (1452–1519), Codex Atlanticus c.5r. Property of the Ambrosian Library, Milano. The similarity between figure (a) and (b) is striking.

2   The Basic Algorithm

This section describes, in simple terms, the basic techniques for: (i) measuring lengths of segments on planar surfaces and (ii) distances of points from planar surfaces. Clear examples and step-by-step algorithms make the implementation of these techniques straightforward[1].

The camera model employed here is central projection (see fig. 2). Effects such as radial distortion, which corrupt the central projection model, can generally be removed [14] and are therefore not detrimental to these methods.

---

[1] The reader is referred to [7] for a more general and comprehensive description of the single-view techniques.

2.1 Planar Measurements

Given an image of a planar surface π, points on the image plane can be mapped into corresponding points in the world plane by means of a projective transformation called *homography* [19].

Points in one plane are mapped into the corresponding points in the other plane as follows:

$$\mathbf{X} = \mathtt{H}\mathbf{x} \qquad (1)$$

where $\mathbf{x}$ is an image point, $\mathbf{X}$ is the corresponding point on the world plane (both expressed in homogeneous coordinates) and $\mathtt{H}$ is the 3×3 matrix representing the homography transformation.

Therefore, once the homography matrix $\mathtt{H}$ is known (or has been computed), any image point can be mapped into the corresponding location on the world surface and distances between world points can be extracted as illustrated below.

Algorithm 1: planar measurements.

1. Given an image of a planar surface estimate the image-to-world homography matrix $\mathtt{H}$;
2. Repeat
   (a) Select two points $\mathbf{x}_1$ and $\mathbf{x}_2$ on the image plane;
   (b) Back-project each image point into the world plane via (1) to obtain the two world points $\mathbf{X}_1$ and $\mathbf{X}_2$;
   (c) Compute the Euclidean distance $d(\mathbf{X}_1, \mathbf{X}_2)$.

Thus, the only remaining problem is that of estimating the homography matrix $\mathtt{H}$ (point 1 in **Alg.1**). The homography may be computed directly from a set of at least four corresponding points as described in the appendix. A statistical analysis of the measurements accuracy may be found in [7]. Figure 3 shows an example where windows of a building wall are measured directly on the image. Furthermore, the computed homography may also be used to rectify images of slanted planar surfaces into front-on views as demonstrated in fig. 11d [9].

Fig. 3. Measuring distances on planar surfaces: **(Left)** A photograph of a wall of a building in Oxford. The position of four points have been manually measured in the world and the corresponding image points selected and marked in white on the image plane. **(Right)** Once the image-to-world homography has been computed (see appendix), measurements can be taken on the building wall as described in **Algorithm 1**.

2.2 Measuring Distances from Planes

This section addresses the problem of measuring distances of points *from* planes in the usual uncalibrated framework.

Figure 4a,b describes the problem in a schematic way. The aim is to compute the height of an object (the man in the figure) relative to a reference (the height of the column). Here, we assume that the vanishing line of the ground plane has been computed [2].

If $\mathbf{v}$ is the vanishing point for the vertical direction, l is the vanishing line of the ground plane, $\mathbf{t}_r$ and $\mathbf{b}_r$ are the top and base points of the reference, respectively and $\mathbf{t}_x$ and $\mathbf{b}_x$ are the top and base points of the object to be measured, then the following equation holds:

$$\alpha Z_i = -\frac{||\mathbf{b}_i \times \mathbf{t}_i||}{(\mathbf{l} \cdot \mathbf{b}_i)||\mathbf{v} \times \mathbf{t}_i||} \quad \forall i = r, x \tag{2}$$

where Z_x the height of the object we wish to measure, Z_r is the reference height and α a scalar quantity herein referred to as *metric factor*. Since αZ_i scales linearly we have obtained affine structure. If α is known, then a metric value for the height Z is obtained. Conversely, if the height Z is known then equation (2) provides a way of computing α and hence removing the affine ambiguity. Proof for (2) may be found in [7].

The complete algorithm for height computation from single images is described below, and examples of the computations are shown in fig. 4d.

Algorithm 2: computing heights of objects in single views.

1. Estimate the vanishing point $\mathbf{v}$ for the vertical direction;
2. Estimate the vanishing line l of the reference plane;
3. Select top and base points of the reference segment (points $\mathbf{t}_r$ and $\mathbf{b}_r$, respectively);
4. Compute the metric factor α by applying: $\alpha = -\frac{||\mathbf{b}_r \times \mathbf{t}_r||}{Z_r(\mathbf{l} \cdot \mathbf{b}_r)||\mathbf{v} \times \mathbf{t}_r||}$;
5. Repeat
   (a) Select top and base of the object to measure (points $\mathbf{t}_x$ and $\mathbf{b}_x$, respectively);
   (b) Compute the height Z_x by applying: $Z_x = -\frac{||\mathbf{b}_x \times \mathbf{t}_x||}{\alpha(\mathbf{l} \cdot \mathbf{b}_x)||\mathbf{v} \times \mathbf{t}_x||}$;

The key to the success of this algorithm is an accurate estimation of the vertical vanishing point $\mathbf{v}$ and the vanishing line l of the reference plane. The following section describes a simple technique for the automatic computation of vanishing points and lines as well as providing useful links to other techniques in the literature.

Estimating Vanishing Points and Lines. Given an uncalibrated input image, vanishing points and vanishing lines may be computed either from the image-to-world homography H (if known) or by applying automatic and semiautomatic techniques which work directly on the image plane [6,10,13,25,26,27,32,33,34].

Here a simple RANSAC-based algorithm is employed to automatically estimate dominant vanishing points and lines[3].

---

[2] For the purpose of this section the vanishing line of the ground plane suffices; i.e. a full metric calibration of the ground plane is not necessary.

[3] A more detailed and comprehensive description of this algorithm may be found in [32]

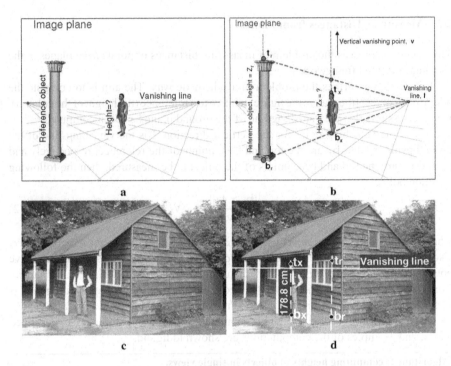

Fig. 4. Measuring heights in single images. **(a)** The aim is to compute the height of the human figure relative to the height of the column (reference). The vanishing line of the ground plane has been computed and is shown in white. **(b)** The unknown height ratio $\frac{Z_x}{Z_r}$ can be computed from image quantities only. See **Alg.2** for details. **(c)** A photograph of a garden shed in Oxford. **(d)** Once the height of the window top edge from the floor has been measured (reference), the height of the man is computed to be $178.8cm$; about $1cm$ off the ground truth.

The algorithm can be outlined as follows (*cf.* fig. 5):

1. Automatic Canny edge detection and straight line fitting to obtain the set of straight edge segments $\mathcal{E}$ (fig. 5b) [4];
2. Repeat
    (a) Randomly select two segments $\mathbf{s}_1, \mathbf{s}_2 \in \mathcal{E}$ and intersect them to give the point $\mathbf{p}$;
    (b) The support set $\mathcal{S}_p$ is the set of straight edges in $\mathcal{E}$ going through the point $\mathbf{p}$;
3. Set the dominant vanishing point as the point $\mathbf{p}$ with the largest support $\mathcal{S}_p$;
4. Remove all edges in $\mathcal{S}_p$ from $\mathcal{E}$ and goto 2 for the computation of the next vanishing point.

Different metrics may be used to decide when a straight line $\mathbf{s}$ goes through a given point $\mathbf{p}$. The Euclidean distance of a point from a line has been used herein; thus, $\mathbf{s} \in \mathcal{S}_p$ iff $d(\mathbf{p}, \mathbf{s}) < \sigma$, where σ is a fixed distance threshold ($\sigma = 2pix$ is used here)[4].

---

[4] Notice that this algorithm groups together lines which are parallel to each other in the scene (same vanishing point in the image), regardless of their coplanarity.

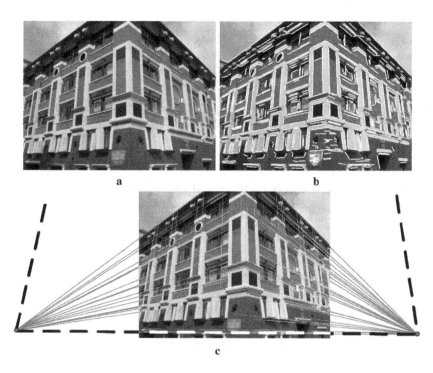

Fig. 5. Automatic computation of vanishing points and lines. (a) A photo of a building in Cambridge. (b) The automatically computed straight edges are superimposed (in white). (c) Automatic computation of the three dominant vanishing points. Edges of the same colour intersect in the same vanishing point. The three vanishing lines (thick dashed lines) are defined by joining the three pairs of automatically estimated vanishing points.

In fig. 5c vanishing lines are defined by joining pairs of vanishing points. Algorithms for the maximum likelihood estimation of vanishing points and lines are described in [32].

2.3 Constructing 3D Models

In the previous sections the basic algorithms to extract planar and off-plane distance measurements from single images have been described. In order to construct complete three-dimensional models two more ingredients are necessary: (i) segmentation of scene objects and (ii) filling of occluded areas.

Given an input image, meaningful objects, such as planar walls and human figures, need to be segmented, measured and placed in the output model consistently with the three-dimensional scene geometry.

Object Segmentation is achieved, here, by interactive silhouette cut-out.

Several techniques have been investigated in the past [2,5,29]. Amongst those, the dynamic programming-type algorithms cast the problem of estimating the contour between two user-specified points as one of finding the optimal path between them. The

Fig. 6. Interactive silhouette cut-out. **(a)** The original painting. **(b,c,d)** Three stages of the interactive silhouette cut-out process. The dots indicate the user clicks, the white curve indicates the automatically estimated best contour. **(e)** The extracted silhouette.

technique employed here, based on a Viterbi algorithm[5] [17], can be thought of as a simple variant on the dynamic-programming methods. The costs of the edges of the Viterbi diagram are defined in a typical minimum cumulative way where the incremental cost associated to each pair of points in consecutive columns is given by:

$$Cost = \frac{1 - Ncc}{2} * w; \text{ with } Ncc = \frac{\sum_\Omega (I(x, y) - \mu) * (I(x + u, y + v) - \mu')}{\sqrt{\sum_\Omega (I(x, y) - \mu)^2 \sum_\Omega (I(x + u, y + v) - \mu')^2}}$$

where Ncc is the normalized cross-correlation between two patches centred at (x, y) and $(x + u, y + v)$, respectively, μ and μ' are the average intensities for the two patches and w is a smoothing weight which tends to discourage very sharp changes in the contour curvature. The normalized cross-correlation is computed over patches Ω of fixed size (generally 3×3).

The use of normalized cross-correlation is justified by the observation that a contour can be thought of as a one dimensional curve that separates two dissimilar regions and such that points along the curve are "locally" similar in terms of the texture in their neighbourhood. The normalized cross-correlation measure in the costs of the Viterbi edges tends to constrain the extracted contour to follow peaks in the gradient map of an image, without the explicit computation of the image gradient.

This algorithm has the added benefit of being simple and easily implemented. Often, this technique is sufficient for a quick interactive silhouette cut-out (fig. 6), but does carry some drawbacks, namely: (i) as in most dynamic-programming approaches, incorporating dynamics and smoothness priors is not an easy task and (ii) the extracted silhouettes are restricted to pixel precision. These difficulties are overcome by the powerful particle-filtering technique described in [29].

Occlusion Filling. In order to achieve visually compelling 3D models it is also necessary to fill-in occluded areas in an "undetectable" way. Two main techniques exist: (i) Fill-in by exploiting symmetries and pattern regularities [8,32] and (ii) Non-parametric texture synthesis [15,20].

---

[5] http://www.sonic.net/~ejr/viterbi/viterbi.htm

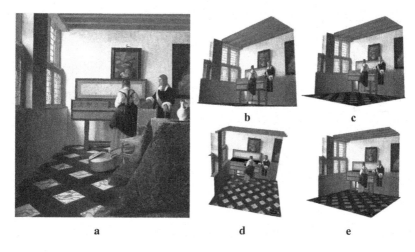

Fig. 7. Three-dimensional reconstruction of a painting. (**a**) *The Music Lesson* (1662-65), by J. Vermeer (1632-1675). (**b-e**) Snapshots of a virtual fly-through inside the reconstructed painting to show different views of the reconstructed room.

The first set of algorithms applies to regular geometric patterns and is used, in fig. 7d, to recover areas of the floor which where hidden in the original view.

Instead, non-parametric texture synthesis algorithms prove more useful for synthesizing stochastic (or generally less regular) textures. However, it is important to notice that these techniques cannot be applied directly to images showing strong perspective distortions, and a preliminary rectification of slanted planar surfaces is necessary.

The algorithm for the construction of complete three-dimensional models is outlined below and an example of complete reconstruction is shown in fig. 7.

Algorithm 3: complete 3D reconstruction

1. *Reference Plane Calibration:* select a reference plane and estimate the homography H (**Alg.1**);
2. *Height Calibration:* select a reference height and compute the metric factor α (**Alg.2**);
3. Repeat
   - Segment an object and measure its height and position on the reference plane;
   - Fill-in areas occluded by the selected object;
   - Insert the selected object in the output three-dimensional model.

---

3   Applications and Interdisciplinarity

The first part of this paper has described the basic algorithms for a partial or complete geometric reconstruction from single images. This second part discusses possible applications of single-view techniques and their relationships with other disciplines such as architecture, forensic science and history of art.

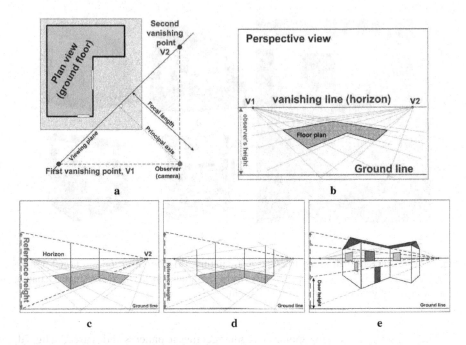

Fig. 8. Constructing a perspective image of a house. (a) Drawing the floor plan and defining the viewing conditions (observer position and image plane). (b) Constructing a perspective view of the floor. (c) A reference height (in this case the height of an external wall) is drawn from the ground line and the first wall is constructed in perspective by joining the reference end points to the horizontal vanishing point v_2. (d) All four external walls are constructed. (e) The elevations of all other objects (the door, windows and roofs) are first defined on the reference segment and then constructed in the rendered perspective view.

3.1   Architectural Drawing

Often architects need to create perspective views of three dimensional objects such as buildings or indoor environments on paper. This section describes the basic procedure for constructing perspective images (drawings) of three-dimensional objects[6] and its relationship to single-view metrology.

Figure 8 shows the process of constructing a perspective view of a house starting from its three-dimensional measurements. The basic steps of such procedure may be summarized as:

- **AD 1.** Draw a plan view of the ground floor (fig. 8a);
- **AD 2.** Set the viewing conditions: observer position and orientation, focal length, and viewing plane (fig. 8a);
- **AD 3.** Construct a perspective view of the ground plane (the reference plane, fig. 8b);
- **AD 4.** Draw a reference height and construct all elevations in perspective (fig. 8c,e).

---

[6] The interested reader may find useful reading material in any text book on technical drawing and descriptive geometry [3,18].

Fig. 9. Complete 3D reconstruction from single views. Two snapshots of the reconstructed three-dimensional model reconstructed from fig. 4c. The camera pose has, also, been estimated.

Instead, single-view metrology algorithms compute three-dimensional measurements from flat images. The procedure may be summarised as follows:

– **SVM 1.** Select a planar surface directly on the input perspective image (this can be viewed as the inverse of **AD 1**);
– **SVM 2.** Rectify the reference plane and take distance measurements (inverse of **AD 3**);
– **SVM 3.** Select a reference height on the image plane and estimate the height of any other object directly in the input image (inverse of **AD 4**);
– **SVM 4.** Estimate the camera pose and intrinsic parameters [35] (inverse of **AD 2**).

A comparison of the above procedures shows that single-view metrology can be seen as the technique inverting the long established rules of linear perspective and descriptive geometry through the powerful algebraic modeling provided by projective geometry. Notice that in general, architectural drawing assumes infinite vertical vanishing point and horizontal vanishing line of the reference plane. Such limitations do not exist in the single-view metrology framework. An example of three-dimensional reconstruction from a single photograph of an architectural structure is shown in fig. 9.

Nowadays, architectural rendering is no longer done manually. Sofisticated CAD programs have replaced the architect's drafting, but the underlying construction steps remain as before.

3.2 Forensic Investigation

Single-view metrology may also be used to analyse forensic imagery. A common requirement in surveillance images is to obtain measurements from the scene, such as the height of a suspect. Even when the suspect is no longer present in the scene, reference lengths can be measured from fixtures such as tables and windows.

An example of heights measurements is shown in fig. 10. Figure 10a is the input image, taken from a poor-quality security camera. In fig. 10b the input image has been corrected for radial distortion and the floor taken as the reference plane. After estimating the vertical vanishing point and the vanishing line of the ground plane, the height of the man has been computed from three known references. Details on the optimal use of multiple references may be found in [7].

Fig. 10. Measuring heights of people from single views. (**a**) Original photograph. (**b**) Image corrected for radial distortion and measurements superimposed. Three reference heights (marked with white segments) have been used and the man height has been measured to be $Z = 190.4 \pm 3.27$ cm. The uncertainty on the measurements has been estimated according to [7].

Single-view metrology techniques are currently used by forensic agencies in crime investigation applications.

3.3 Art History

Finally, in this section single-view metrology is used for analysing the geometry of paintings. Further details may be found in [8].

Comparing Heights of People in Paintings. Flagellation (in fig. 11a) by Piero della Francesca is one of the most studied paintings from the Italian Renaissance period. The "obsessive" accuracy of its geometry makes it one of the most mathematically rewarding paintings for detailed analysis purposes.

In fig. 11b the metrology algorithms described in the first part of this paper have been applied to compute the heights of the people in the painting. Due to the lack of an absolute reference the heights have been computed relative to a chosen unit reference, which in this case is the height of Christ. Therefore, height measurements are expressed as percentage variations from the height of Christ. Despite little variations, the measurements are all satisfactory consistent with each other, thus confirming the extreme accuracy and care in details for which Piero della Francesca has become famed [12].

Analysing Shapes and Patterns. This section demonstrates generation of new views of portions of paintings to better investigate the shape of patterns of interest.

The painting in figure 11a shows, an interesting black and white floor pattern viewed at a grazing angle (fig. 11c). Kemp in [22,23] has manually analysed the shape of the pattern and demonstrated that it follows the "square root of two" rule. Figure 11d shows the rectification achieved by applying our homography-based technique (section 2.1) to obtain a front-on view of the floor. The result of automatic rectification is strikingly similar to the manual rectification in [22] but has the added advantage of being much faster and allowing retention of the original colour and shading. Furthermore, our computer rectification reveals a second instance of the same geometric pattern (on the top part of fig. 11d). A complete 3D reconstruction of this painting may be found in [7].

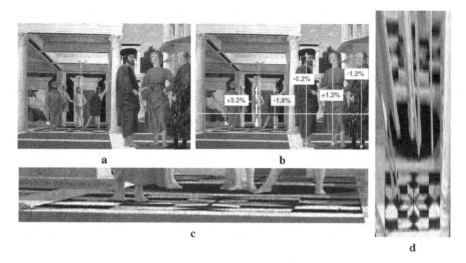

Fig. 11. Comparing heights of people in a Renaissance painting. (**a**) The original painting: *Flagellation* (approx. 1453), by Piero della Francesca (1416–92), Galleria Nazionale delle Marche, Urbino, Italia. (**b**) Heights of people have been measured relative to the height of Christ. They are expressed in percentage difference. (**c**) Enlarged image of the black and white floor pattern. (**d**) Automatic rectification of the floor into a front-to-parallel view. The rectified image has been obtained by applying our planar warping algorithm to the image of the painting directly. Note the striking similarity between the rectified pattern and that obtained by manual drafting by Kemp [8,22]. A complete 3D reconstruction of this painting may be found in [7].

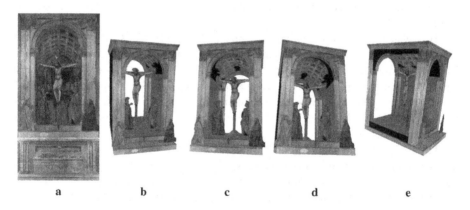

Fig. 12. Three-dimensional reconstruction of Masaccio's *Trinity*. (**a**) The original fresco: *The Trinity* (approx. 1426), by Masaccio (1401–1428), Santa Maria Novella, Florence. (**b-e**) Different views of the reconstructed three-dimensional model of the chapel in the Florentine fresco.

Analysing Geometric Ambiguities. The church of Santa Maria Novella, in Florence boasts one of Masaccio's best known frescoes, *The Trinity* (fig. 12a). The fresco is the first fully-developed perspectival painting from the Renaissance to use geometry to set up an illusion in relation to the spectator's viewpoint.

Reconstruction assuming **square ground plan** | *Reconstruction assuming* **square vault coffers**

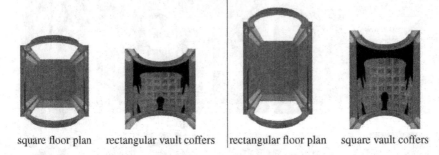

square floor plan   rectangular vault coffers | rectangular floor plan   square vault coffers

Fig. 13. Ambiguity in reconstructing the depth of the chapel in Masaccio's *Trinity*. Comparing two possible reconstructions from an infinite set of plausible ones. (**Left**) Assuming a square ground plan leads to rectangular vault coffers and (**Right**) Assuming square vault coffers leads to a rectangular ground plan, thus demonstrating that ground plan and coffers cannot be both square.

Single-view reconstruction algorithms were applied to an electronic image of the fresco to achieve a three-dimensional model of the chapel (fig. 12b,e) and to help art historians reach a consensus over debated disputes such as the relationship between the shape of the floor plan and the entabulatures of the chapel's vault.

In fact, since only one image is used and no scene metric information is available (the chapel is not real), an ambiguity arises in the reconstruction: it is not possible to uniquely recover the depth of the chapel without making some assumptions about the geometry of the scene.

Two plausible assumptions may be made: either the coffers on the vault of the chapel are square or the floor is square. The application of our single-view techniques has demonstrated that the two assumptions cannot coexist [8], i.e. square coffers imply a rectangular ground plan and vice-versa. Here the two models stemming from the two assumptions have been generated. Once the first model was constructed, the second one was obtained by applying a simple "affine transformation", a scaling in the direction orthogonal to the plane of the fresco.

The images of the chapel floor and that of the vault pattern shown in fig. 13 for both cases demonstrate that the square-ground-plan assumption yields rectangular angular coffers and the square-coffers assumption yields a rectangular ground plan. The advantage in terms of speed and accuracy over manual techniques is blatant.

Whatever the reason for Masaccio's ambiguity, the computer analysis performed has allowed both assumptions to be investigated in a rigorous and efficient manner.

The work in [8] shows further examples of analysing paintings using single-view techniques and presents an interactive virtual museum where the observer can not only move freely within the museum and look at the paintings, but even "dive" into the three-dimensional scenes reconstructed behind the plane of the canvas in a smooth and seemless way. This demonstrates the viability of our techniques in achieving compelling visual experiences which may be used to teach art students and art lovers about the power of linear perspective and its use in the Renaissance period.

4   Conclusion

This paper has presented easy-to-implement techniques to turn flat images into three-dimensional models and take distance measurements directly on the image plane.

The second part of this document has shown applications of our techniques to solve real problems such as meauring the height of a suspect in forensic images, or help resolve disputes over historical paintings. Furthermore, single-view metrology has been shown to be the inverse of the process of creating perspective architectural drawings.

Currently, we are planning to augment the flexibility and ease of use of single-view techniques by increasing the level of automation of the basic algorithms such as scene calibration and object segmentation.

Acknowledgments

The author is extremely grateful to A. Zisserman, M. Kemp, I. Reid, D. Liebowitz, L. van Gool, R. Szeliski, M. Uyttendaele, P. Anandan for contributing to the success of single-view metrology with interesting ideas, stimulating discussions, and their vast knowledge.

Appendix: Estimating the Image-to-World Homography

In the case of uncalibrated cameras, accurate estimation of the homography between the image and the world planes can be achieved directly from a set of known image-world correspondences (points or lines).

There are three standard methods for estimating the homography matrix H: (i) non-homogeneous linear solution; (ii) homogeneous solution; (iii) non-linear geometric solution. Only the second case is described herein. Details about the other cases may be found in [9].

Homogeneous Solution. From (1) each image-to-world point correspondence provides two equations which are linear in the elements of the matrix H. They are:

$$h_{11}x + h_{12}y + h_{13} = h_{31}xX + h_{32}yX + h_{33}X$$
$$h_{21}x + h_{22}y + h_{23} = h_{31}xY + h_{32}yY + h_{33}Y$$

For n correspondences we obtain a system of $2n$ equations in eight unknowns. If $n = 4$ (as in fig. 14) then an exact solution is obtained. Otherwise, if $n > 4$, the matrix is over-determined, and H is estimated by a suitable minimization scheme.

The solution is obtained using Singular Value Decomposition (SVD). This method minimizes an algebraic error which does not have a geometric meaning. It is good practice to employ this method to obtain a reliable initial solution and, then run a non-linear minimization step to refine the solution by minimizing a more meaningful geometric error.

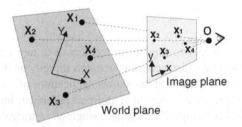

Fig. 14. Computing the plane-to-plane homography: at least four corresponding points (or lines) are necessary to determine the homography between two planes.

Writing the H matrix as a 9-vector $\mathbf{h} = (h_{11}, h_{12}, h_{13}, h_{21}, h_{22}, h_{23}, h_{31}, h_{32}, h_{33})^\top$ the homogeneous equation (1) for n points become $\mathbf{Ah} = \mathbf{0}$, with $\mathbf{A}$ the $2n \times 9$ matrix:

$$
\mathbf{A} = \begin{pmatrix}
x_1 & y_1 & 1 & 0 & 0 & 0 & -x_1 X_1 & -y_1 X_1 & -X_1 \\
0 & 0 & 0 & x_1 & y_1 & 1 & -x_1 Y_1 & -y_1 Y_1 & -Y_1 \\
\vdots & \vdots & \vdots & \vdots & \vdots & \vdots & \vdots & & \vdots \\
x_n & y_n & 1 & 0 & 0 & 0 & -x_n X_n & -y_n X_n & -X_n \\
0 & 0 & 0 & x_n & y_n & 1 & -x_n Y_n & -y_n Y_n & -Y_n
\end{pmatrix}
$$

The problem of computing the $\mathbf{h}$ vector is now reduced to the constrained minimization of the cost function $C = \mathbf{h}^\top \mathbf{A}^\top \mathbf{Ah}$ subject to the constraint that $||\mathbf{h}|| = 1$. The corresponding Lagrange function is: $\mathcal{L} = \mathbf{h}^\top \mathbf{A}^\top \mathbf{Ah} - \lambda(\mathbf{h}^\top \mathbf{h} - 1)$. Differentiating this with respect to $\mathbf{h}$ and setting these derivatives equal to zero we obtain $\mathbf{A}^\top \mathbf{Ah} = \lambda \mathbf{h}$. Therefore the solution $\mathbf{h}$ is a unit eigenvector of the matrix $\mathbf{A}^\top \mathbf{A}$ and $\lambda = \mathbf{h}^\top \mathbf{A}^\top \mathbf{Ah}$ is the corresponding eigenvalue. In order to minimize the C function, only the eigenvector $\tilde{\mathbf{h}}$ corresponding to the minimum eigenvalue $\tilde{\lambda}$ should be considered. This eigenvector can be obtained directly from the Singular Value Decomposition of $\mathbf{A}$. In the case of $n = 4$, $\mathbf{h}$ is the null-vector of $\mathbf{A}$ and the residuals are zero.

References

1. Leon Battista Alberti. *De Pictura*. 1435. Reproduced by Laterza (1980).
2. W. Barrett and Mortensen. Interactive live-wire boundary extraction. *Medical Image Analysis*, 1(4):331–341, 1997.
3. H. C. Browning. *The Principles of Architectural Drafting : A Sourcebook of Techniques and Graphic Standards*. Whitney Library of Design, Oct 1996.
4. J. F. Canny. A computational approach to edge detection. *IEEE T-PAMI*, 8(6), 1986.
5. L. Cohen and R. Kimmel. Global minimum for active contour models: A minimum path approach. *IJCV*, 24(1):57–78, 1997.
6. R. T. Collins and R. S. Weiss. Vanishing point calculation as a statistical inference on the unit sphere. In *Proc. ICCV*, pages 400–403, Dec 1990.
7. A. Criminisi. *Accurate Visual Metrology from Single and Multiple Uncalibrated Images*. Distinguished Dissertation Series. Springer-Verlag London Ltd., Sep 2001. ISBN: 1852334681.
8. A. Criminisi, M. Kemp, and A. Zisserman. Bringing pictorial space to life: computer techniques for the analysis of paintings. Technical report, Microsoft Research, 2002.

9. A. Criminisi, I. Reid, and A. Zisserman. A plane measuring device. *Image and Vision Computing*, 17(8):625–634, 1999.

10. A. Criminisi and A. Zisserman. Shape from texture: homogeneity revisited. In *Proc. BMVC*, pages 82–91, UK, Sep 2000.

11. P. E. Debevec, C. J. Taylor, and J. Malik. Modeling and rendering architecture from photographs: A hybrid geometry- and image- based approach. In *Proceedings, ACM SIGGRAPH*, pages 11–20, 1996.

12. Piero della Francesca. *De Prospectiva Pingendi*. Firenze, Italy, 1474. Reproduced by ed. Sansoni (1942), Edizione Critica.

13. J. Deutscher, M. Isard, and J. MacCormick. Automatic camera calibration from a single manhattan image. In *Proc. ECCV*, page 175ff, Copenhagen, 2002.

14. F. Devernay and O. D. Faugeras. Automatic calibration and removal of distortion from scenes of structured environments. In *Proc. of SPIE*, volume 2567, San Diego, CA, Jul 1995.

15. A. Efros and W.T. Freeman. Image quilting for texture synthesis and transfer. In *Proc. ACM SIGGRAPH*, pages 341–346, Eugene Fiume, August 2001.

16. O. D. Faugeras. *Three-Dimensional Computer Vision: a Geometric Viewpoint*. MIT Press, 1993.

17. G. D. Forney. The viterbi algorithm. *Proc. IEEE*, 61:268–278, Mar 1973.

18. R. W. Gill. *Basic Perspective*. W.W. Norton and Company, Feb 1980.

19. R. I. Hartley and A. Zisserman. *Multiple View Geometry in Computer Vision*. Cambridge University Press, ISBN: 0521623049, 2000.

20. A. Hertzman, C. E. Jacobs, N. Oliver, B. Curless, and D. H. Salesin. Image analogies. In *Proc. ACM SIGGRAPH*, pages 341–346, Eugene Fiume, August 2001.

21. Y. Horry, K. Anjyo, and K. Arai. Tour into the picture: Using a spidery mesh interface to make animation from a single image. In *Proc. ACM SIGGRAPH*, pages 225–232, 1997.

22. M. Kemp. *The Science of Art*. Yale University Press, New Haven and London, 1989. ISBN: 0-300-05241-3.

23. M. Kemp. *Visualizations: the nature book of art and science*. The University of California Press, Berkeley and Los Angeles, California, USA, 2000. ISBN: 0-520-22352-7.

24. T. Kim, Y. Seo, and K. Hong. Physics-based 3D position analysis of a soccer ball from monocular image sequences. *Proc. ICCV*, pages 721 – 726, 1998.

25. J. Koseka and W. Zhang. Video compass. In *Proc. ECCV*, page 476ff, Copenhagen, 2002.

26. D. Liebowitz and A. Zisserman. Metric rectification for perspective images of planes. In *Proc. CVPR*, pages 482–488, Jun 1998.

27. G. F. McLean and D. Kotturi. Vanishing point detection by line clustering. *IEEE T-PAMI*, 17(11):1090–1095, 1995.

28. MetaCreations. http://www.metacreations.com/products/canoma/.

29. P. Perez, A. Blake, and M. Gangnet. JetStream: Probabilistic contour extraction with particles. *Proc. Int. Conf. on Computer Vision (ICCV)*, II:524–531, Mar 2001.

30. M. Proesmans, T. Tuytelaars, and L. J. van Gool. Monocular image measurements. Technical Report Improofs-M12T21/1/P, K.U.Leuven, 1998.

31. I. Reid and A. Zisserman. Goal-directed video metrology. In R. Cipolla and B. Buxton, editors, *Proc. ECCV*, volume II, pages 647–658. Springer, Apr 1996.

32. F. Schaffalitzky and A. Zisserman. Planar grouping for automatic detection of vanishing lines and points. *Image and Vision Computing*, 18:647–658, 2000.

33. J. A. Shufelt. Performance and analysis of vanishing point detection techniques. *IEEE T-PAMI*, 21(3):282–288, Mar 1999.

34. T. Tuytelaars, L. van Gool, M. Proesmans, and T. Moons. The cascaded Hough transform as an aid in aerial image interpretation. In *Proc. ICCV*, pages 67–72, Jan 1998.

35. M. Wilczkowiak, E. Boyer, and P. Sturm. Camera calibration and 3D reconstruction from single images using parallelepipeds. In *Proc. ICCV*, Vancouver, 2001.

Shape from Single Stripe Pattern Illumination

S. Winkelbach and F. M. Wahl

Institute for Robotics and Process Control,
Technical University of Braunschweig
Mühlenpfordtstr. 23, D-38106 Braunschweig, Germany
{S. Winkelbach, F. Wahl}@tu-bs.de

Abstract. This paper presents a strategy for rapid reconstruction of surfaces in 3d which only uses a *single* camera shot of an object illuminated with a simple stripe pattern. With this respect, it is a meaningful extension of our 'shape from 2d edge gradient' method introduced earlier. The reconstruction is based on determining stripe directions and stripe widths in the camera image in order to estimate surface orientation. I.e., this method does not use triangulation for range data acquisition, but rather computes surface normals. These normals can be 2d integrated and thus yield the surface coordinates; in addition they can be used to compute robust 3d features of free-form surfaces for object recognition, pose estimation, etc. The method is straightforward and very efficient by processing only one image and using only simple image processing operations.

1   Introduction

3d shape recovery is an important field of research since many years. Many publications deal with shape reconstruction techniques, such as stereo vision [e.g.1] structured light [e.g.2,3,4], coded light [e.g.5] and one-shot systems projecting a local identification code [e.g.6,7]. All these systems are based on triangulation to compute range data. An other class of techniques estimate surface normals instead of absolute range data, such as shape from texture [e.g.8,9], shape from shading [e.g.10], shape from specularity [e.g.11],etc., as well as our 'shape from 2d edge gradients' approach published earlier in [12]. An advantage of the second class of systems is, that no correspondence problem has to be solved and, if surface properties are needed, they directly generate surface normals without the necessity to derive them subsequently from noisy range data. Surface normals are an important basis of robust 3d feature determination, as for example relative surface orientations, curvatures, local maxima of free-form surfaces. Moreover, they can be used to reconstruct the surface itself, or they can be utilized as basis for 3d segmentation, object recognition, pose estimation, calculation of an illumination independent model and recalculation of lighting from any desired direction, etc. The technique described here directly generates surface normals by acquiring only one shot of a single stripe pattern illumination. Thus, it even is able to retrieve the shape of moving objects! As instrumentation it requires one camera and one static light stripe projector (Figure 1). The reconstruction technique is based on the fact, that directions *and* widths of projected stripes in the cap-

L. Van Gool (Ed.): DAGM 2002, LNCS 2449, pp. 240–247, 2002.
© Springer-Verlag Berlin Heidelberg 2002

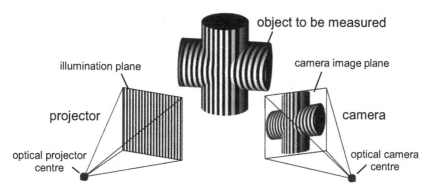

Fig. 1. Measurement setup with a static stripe pattern projector and a horizontally displaced camera

tured 2d image depend on the local orientation of the object's surface in 3d. Surface normals are obtained by analysing the local stripe edge directions and stripe widths of the deformed 2d stripe images. This approach is an alternative technique of our 'shape from 2d edge gradients' approach published earlier in [12], which employs local edge directions of two! stripe projections rotated relative to each other.

During the review process of this paper we became aware of two short papers of Asada, Ichikawa and Tsuji [13,14] which already described the possibility to use direction and width of stripe illumination for surface normal measurement. It appears to us, that these two papers have been forgotten by the computer vision community. In their work the authors describe only very briefly the essential image processing and calculation methods for surface normal calculation and then focus on usage of normals for segmentation of planar surface parts. The discussed results seem to be qualitative and quantitative poor; many advantages and applications of the 'one shot stripe illumination strategy' remain unconsidered. Maybe this is the reason why their work has been fallen into oblivion. In this paper we will give a more detailed discussion of the approach and answer some open questions of [13] and [14].

At a first glance, an almost similar method using a square grid has been presented in [15]; but in contrast to the approach discussed here it requires complex computation, e.g. for detection of lines and line crossings and for checking grid connectivity. Moreover, it achieves a lower density of measurement points yielding a lower lateral resolution.

The surface reconstruction described here can be subdivided into several functional steps. First, we take a grey level image of the scene illuminated with a stripe pattern. Subsequently, local edge directions and widths of stripes are measured (Section 2). Missing measure values between the stripes are augmented by simple linear 1d interpolation. On the basis of the local stripe directions and stripe widths we calculate the local surface normals (Section 3). Finally we present some experimental results and discuss the accuracy of this technique (Section 4).

2   Local Stripe Direction and Stripe Width Determination

If the object surface has an approximate homogeneous reflection characteristic, it is sufficient to analyse the stripe pattern of one camera image, for example by using a simple threshold to extract the illumination pattern from object colour. Object textures and other varying surface reflections may inhibit reliable detection and analysis of the projected illumination pattern in the camera image. For this case, we proposed a preprocessing procedure (see [12]), which separates the illumination pattern from the surface reflection characteristics of the object. By regarding real grey level edges rather than binary ones subsequent measurement of stripe widths and stripe directions becomes more precise and reaches sub-pixel precision.

Determination of local stripe directions already has been explained in detail in [12]. For reason of completeness we will give a short synopsis: Gradient directions can be calculated by well-known operators like Sobel, Canny, etc. Noisy angles arise mainly in homogenous areas where gradient magnitudes are low. Thus high gradient magnitudes can be used to mask reliable edge angles, i.e. eliminating erroneous ones. The masking of valid angles can be realized by simply using a threshold to separate high and low gradient magnitudes; but we even get better results by using only angles at local maxima of the gradient magnitudes for each 1d scan line. After elimination of erroneous angle values, they will be replaced by 1d interpolation.

Determination of local stripe widths should be performed on sub-pixel level in order to achieve high accuracy. Each scan line can be processed independently; thus only 1d signal processing operations are required. Our technique achieves slightly better results than the 'Linear Mixing Model' suggested in [13,14], but a detailed verification of these results needs more time and space and is a topic of further publications. To estimate the mean width of a stripe, we analyse a small region around each edge (see Fig. 2 left side), which can be found by using local maxima of edge gradient magnitudes.

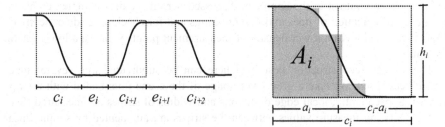

Fig. 2. Left side: Partitioning of a grey level profile into small regions around each edge Rigth side: Model of a stripe edge for sub-pixel estimation of the mean stripe width

The right side of Figure 2 shows a model of such a region around a stripe edge. The mean distance a_i between the left region margin and the edge can be calculated by

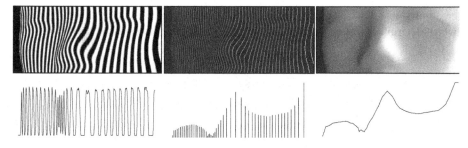

Fig. 3. Left: Normalized image of a stripe pattern illuminated surface and a profile line; Middle: Determined local stripe widths and corresponding profile line; Right: Linear interpolated stripe widths ('widths image') and corresponding profile line

the edge height h_i, the region width c_i and the area A_i below the sampled edge by using the width-area proportion

$$\frac{a_i}{c_i} = \frac{A_i}{c_i \cdot h_i} \qquad \Leftrightarrow \qquad a_i = \frac{A_i}{h_i} \tag{1}$$

After processing this calculation for every stripe edge, it is easy to compute the stripe widths d_i' of all stripes

$$d_i' = (c_i - a_i) + e_i + a_{i+1} \tag{2}$$

The mean width of two neighboured stripes can be stored into the 'width image' at the pixel location of the interior edge. By this method, we prevent errors if bright stripes are wider than dark stripes, which can result from camera white clipping or blooming. In a final step, missing values in the 'width image' are 1d interpolated. Figure 3 shows the result of this method applied to a normalized image of a stripe pattern illuminated surface.

3   Surface Normal Computation

After estimation of local stripe directions and stripe widths in 2d, the local surface normals can be computed. The model of Figure 4 illustrates the mathematical relation of surface slope and estimated local stripe direction (adapted from [12]). All vectors in the following are given with respect to the camera coordinate frame. Each image pixel defines a 'view vector' $\vec{s}$ which points from the camera coordinate origin of frame C (optical centre) to the pixel coordinate in the image plane. The stripe angle value ω at this image coordinate specifies a stripe direction vector $\vec{v}'$ lying in the viewing plane as well as in the image plane. The real tangential vector $\vec{v}_1$ of the projected stripe on the object's surface in 3d is a linear combination of $\vec{s}$ and $\vec{v}'$. Thus $\vec{v}_1$ is perpendicular to the normal $\vec{c} = \vec{v}' \times \vec{s}$. $\vec{v}_1$ is also perpendicular to the normal $\vec{p}$ of the stripe projection plane. Assuming that the projection planes of all stripes are parallel, all stripes have the same projection normal. This justifies the usage of the cross product $\vec{v}_1 = \vec{c} \times \vec{p}$ to calculate a tangential vector $\vec{v}_1$ of the local surface, which determines one degree of freedom of the corresponding surface normal in 3d.

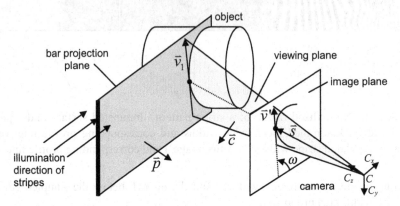

Fig. 4. Projection of a stripe edge onto an object's surface and its mapping into the image plane (adapted from [12])

This holds without using any correspondence information between stripes in the image and the illumination stripes of the projector.

In [12] we proposed to acquire a second image of the scene with a rotated stripe illumination relative to the first one, in order to get a second tangential vector $\vec{v}_2$; the surface normal in this case can be computed as $\vec{n} = \vec{v}_1 \times \vec{v}_2$. The approach described in this paper only uses one stripe illumination with one pattern orientation. In contrast to [12] we utilize the stripe widths to determine the remaining degree of freedom of the surface normals. This holds under the assumption of parallel projecting systems (camera and light projector). In practice we use telecentric lenses or systems with long focal lengths and small apex angles.

For calculation of surface gradients in 3d on the basis of stripe widths, we can use a simple 2d model. Figure 5 illustrates the 2d mathematical relation between the stripe widths in the image and the surface orientations. The stripe width d of the stripe pattern illumination and the constant angle γ between central stripe illumination direction and camera viewing direction can be derived from a simple preceding calibration. By using the stripe width d' of the stripe in the camera image we can calculate the surface gradient p as follows:

Regarding the triangles of the model in Figure 5, we get the simple trigonometrical equations

$$h + g = \frac{d}{\sin \gamma} \quad ; \quad g = \frac{d'}{\tan \gamma} \tag{3}$$

According to this, it follows that

$$h = \frac{d}{\sin \gamma} - \frac{d'}{\tan \gamma} = \frac{d - d' \cdot \cos \gamma}{\sin \gamma} \tag{4}$$

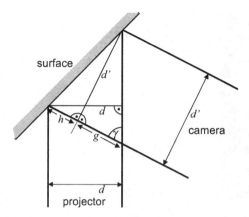

Fig. 5. Calculation of surface gradients on the basis of stripe widths

yielding the surface gradient p

$$p = \frac{h}{d'} = \frac{d/d' - \cos\gamma}{\sin\gamma} \tag{5}$$

The second tangential surface vector now is given by $\vec{v}_2 = (1 \quad 0 \quad -p)^\mathsf{T}$

To calculate the surface normal, we simply use the cross product of the two tangential surface vectors

$$\vec{n} = (n_x \quad n_y \quad n_z)^\mathsf{T} = \vec{v}_1 \times \vec{v}_2 \tag{6}$$

Instead of storing three values of the surface normals, we store the surface gradients p (in x-direction) and q (in y-direction). p is given by equation (5); for calculation of q we compute the y-z-ratio of the surface normal $q = -n_y / n_z$.

4   Experimental Results and Conclusion

For experimental evaluation we used an off-the-shelf CCD-camera and a conventional video beamer. For projection of only one simple stripe pattern it is also possible to use an ordinary slide projector or a low-cost static pattern projector. The method described above is totally unaffected by shifted patterns and only little affected by defocused pattern illumination or blurred camera images. In order to evaluate the new technique we conducted many experiments with varying setups and different test objects. Due to the limited space of this paper we only can show a few reconstruction results (Figure 6). Regarding accuracy we should mention, that the following experiments only use the angle γ between central stripe illumination direction and camera viewing direction as well as the stripe width d of the stripe pattern illumination from a simplified preceding calibration. Therefore inaccuracies also result from neglecting consideration of intrinsic camera and projector parameters. (a1) of Figure 6 shows a spherical surface, illuminated with a stripe pattern, which was the sole basis of our surface normal computation. (a2) shows a

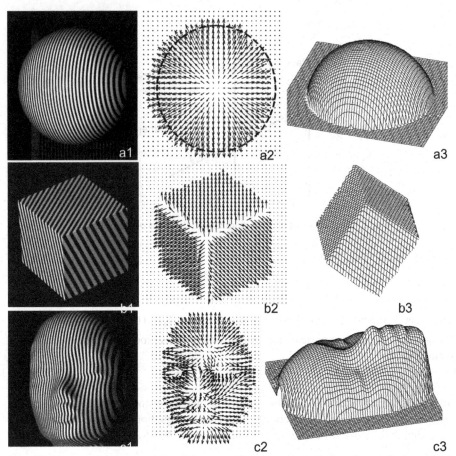

Fig. 6. Reconstruction results: (a1) stripe pattern illuminated spherical surface; (a2) determined surface normals; (a3) 3d plot of the reconstructed surface; (b1-b3) the same for a cube; (c1-c3) the same for a styrofoam head.

small fraction of the reconstructed surface normals (we compute normals at every pixel coordinate covered with a stripe edge and interpolate intermediate areas). Comparing the computed non-interpolated normals with the mathematical exact sphere normals we obtain a mean angular error between exact and reconstructed surface normals of 1.79 degrees with a standard deviation of 1.22 degrees. To compute range data from surface gradients, we applied the 2d integration method proposed by Frankot/Chellappa [16]. As a matter of fact, this integration technique only works for continuous surface parts and is only able to calculate relative range (shape) and not absolute distance information. Especially the discontinuous boundaries between object and background can cause problems and demand an adapted range estimation, which uses only valid gradients. For this purpose we develop a special iterative extension, which will be topic of a further publication. (a3) shows a 3d plot of the computed range map of the sphere. The next three images (b1-b3) show the same sequence for a solid cube. Comparing the computed cube normals with the mathematical exact ones we get an accuracy of 1.14 degree mean angular error with 0.58 degree standard deviation for the top cube face. The most inaccurate normals with 1.95 degree mean angular error and 2.12 degrees standard deviation are obtained for the lower left cube face. In this case the lower left surface has a high tilt angle and the stripes get very close together; thus measurement of stripe orientations and widths becomes more inaccurate. The last three images (c1-c3) show the same sequence with a styrofoam head as test object. As can be seen, shape acquisition with reasonable precision (sufficient for many applications) can be obtained with low cost equipment using just single camera shots. This makes the proposed technique attractive even in case of moving objects. The whole process (image acquisition, surface normals and range map reconstruction of a 512x512 image) only takes about two seconds on a 500 Mhz Pentium III. By acquiring several stripe illuminated scene images with same illumination direction but with phase shifted stripe patterns, the number of gradients with high magnitude can be increased, thus reducing the need for replacing erroneous stripe angles and stripe widths by interpolation.

References

1. D. C. Marr, T. Poggio: A computational theory of human stereo vision, Proc. Roy. Soc. London 204, 1979
2. T. Ueda, M. Matsuki: Time Sequential Coding for Three-Dimensional Measurement and Its Implementation, Denshi-Tsushin-Gakkai-Ronbunshi, 1981
3. M. Oshima, Y. Shirai: Object recognition using three dimensional information, IEEE Transact. on PAMI, vol. 5, July 1983
4. K. L. Boyer and A. C. Kak: Color-Encoded Structured Light for Rapid Active Ranging, IEEE Transact. on PAMI, vol. 9, no. 1, Januar 1987
5. F. M. Wahl: A Coded Light Approach for 3-Dimensional (3D) Vision, IBM Research Report RZ 1452, 1984
6. M. Maruyama, S. Abe: Range Sensing by Projection Multiple Slits with Random Cuts, IEEE PAMI 15(6), pp. 647-650, 1993.
7. P. Vuylsteke, A. Oosterlinck, Range Image Acquisition with a Single Binary-Encoded Light Pattern, IEEE Transact. on PAMI, vol. 12, no. 2, 1990.
8. J.J. Gibson, The Perception of the Visual World, MA: Reverside Press, Cambridge, 1950
9. J.R. Kender, Shape from texture, Proc. DARPA IU Workshop, November 1978
10. B. K. P. Horn and M. J. Brooks: Shape from Shading, M.I.T., Cambridge, 1989
11. G. Healey, T.O. Binford: Local Shape from Specularity, Proc. ICCV, London, June 1987
12. S. Winkelbach, F.M. Wahl: Shape from 2D Edge Gradients, Pattern Recognition, Lecture Notes in Computer Science 2191, Springer, 2001
13. M. Asada, H. Ichikawa, S. Tjuji: Determining of Surface Properties by Projecting a Stripe Pattern, IEEE Proc. of ICPR'86, 1986
14. M. Asada, H. Ichikawa, S. Tsuji: Determining Surface Orientation by Projecting a Stripe Pattern, IEEE Transact. on PAMI, vol. 10, no. 5, September 1988
15. M. Proesmans, L. Van Gool and A. Oosterlinck: One-Shot Active Shape Acquisition, IEEE Proc. of ICPR'96, 1996
16. Robert T. Frankot, R. Chellappa: A Method for Enforcing Integrability in Shape from Shading Algorithms, IEEE Transact. on PAMI, vol. 10, no. 4, July 1988

Disparity from Monogenic Phase*

Michael Felsberg

Department of Electrical Engineering, Linköping University,
SE-58183 Linköping, Sweden,
mfe@isy.liu.se, http://www.isy.liu.se/~mfe

Abstract. Disparity estimation is a fundamental problem of computer vision. Besides other approaches, disparity estimation from phase information is a quite wide-spread technique. In the present paper, we have considered the influence of the involved quadrature filters and we have replaced them with filters based on the monogenic signal. The implemented algorithm makes use of a scale-pyramid and applies channel encoding for the representation and fusion of the estimated data. The performed experiments show a significant improvement of the results.

1 Disparity Estimation

In this paper we introduce a new method for estimating the disparity between two images. Disparity typically occurs in a stereo camera setting. Due to the depth in space, the image plane position of an object point differs in the left and the right image. Knowing this displacement, it is possible to determine the depth of the object point and therefore its 3D position if the camera has been calibrated beforehand. Neglecting the problems of calibration and back-projection into 3D space, we solely focus on the problem of estimating the disparity.

1.1 Geometric Settings

The geometric setting of a stereo system is sketched in Fig. 1. This figure shows a simplified stereo configuration of two identical cameras with parallel optical axes and with a distance between the optical centers of $|\mathbf{o}^l - \mathbf{o}^r|$. The image planes are at a distance of z_0 from their optical centers and the object is located at a depth of z. Shifting the left optical center onto the right one yields the configuration in the right part of Fig. 1. The two projections of the house are shifted copies of each other with distance d, the *disparity*. From a simple geometric consideration it can be concluded that $|\mathbf{o}^l - \mathbf{o}^r|/z = d/z_0$, and hence $z = z_0 |\mathbf{o}^l - \mathbf{o}^r|/d$.

For a general camera configuration, the geometric setting is much more complicated. However, the depth increases always with decreasing disparity (see e.g. [1], page 211, and [2], page 87) and the relationship between disparity and depth can be computed using the calibrated matrices of the two cameras. The detailed analysis of these relationships is out of the scope of this paper.

---

* This work has been supported by DFG Grant FE 583/1-1.

L. Van Gool (Ed.): DAGM 2002, LNCS 2449, pp. 248–256, 2002.
© Springer-Verlag Berlin Heidelberg 2002

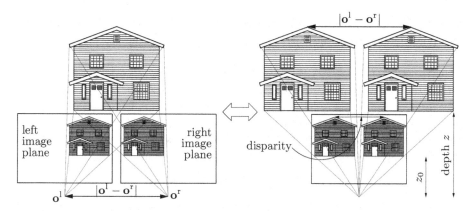

Fig. 1. Geometric setting of a stereo system. Left part: projection of 3D object (house) onto the left and right image plane. The left optical center is denoted by $\mathbf{o}^l$; the right optical center is denoted by $\mathbf{o}^r$. Right part: moving the left camera configuration onto the right one yields two projections of the house with a certain displacement, the disparity. The distance between the two back-projections into 3D space is given by the distance of the optical centers

1.2 Disparity from Phase

The disparity can be estimated by various methods, e.g. correlation based techniques, feature based techniques, and phase based techniques [3,4]. Phase based approaches are used for disparity estimation for the following reasons:

- Correlation based approaches are of a higher computational complexity.
- Feature based approaches do not yield unique correspondences between a left and a right image patch, since the data is projected onto a subspace.
- Phase based approaches yield sub-pixel accuracy without additional effort.
- Applying a phase based method in an appropriate multi-scale framework ensures to fulfill the constraint of a continuous disparity.

The phase based approach using classical quadrature filters can be found in various publications. In this paper we just refer to the more recent works in [5,6,3]. Further references can also be found in [2], Chap. 7.4.

The basic idea of disparity from phase is as follows. The disparity is estimated from the difference of the local phases obtained from quadrature filters applied to both images. In contrast to global shifts of the signal, the local phase is not linear to the shift parameter [7]. Hence, the shift theorem cannot be applied directly to estimate the disparity. However, by approximating the local phase in a first order Taylor series expansion, it is possible to estimate the disparity from the local phase difference and the local frequency.

Assume that the right image $I^r(\mathbf{x})$ (where $\mathbf{x} = (x, y)$) is obtained from the left one by the disparity map $\mathbf{d}(\mathbf{x})$, i.e., $I^r(\mathbf{x}) = I^l(\mathbf{x} - \mathbf{d}(\mathbf{x}))$. The map $\mathbf{d}(\mathbf{x})$ can be reduced to a scalar function, since the orientation of disparity is given by the camera geometry. For simplicity let us assume that $\mathbf{d}(\mathbf{x}) = (d(\mathbf{x}), 0)$, i.e., the disparity is constrained to be a horizontal displacement (we will return to this point later). From these assumptions, we conclude that

$$\varphi^{\mathrm{r}}(\mathbf{x}) = \varphi^{\mathrm{l}}(x - d(\mathbf{x}), y) \tag{1}$$

where $\varphi(\mathbf{x})$ is the local phase obtained from the response of a *horizontal* quadrature filter. Actually, (1) is an approximation which becomes worse with increasing gradient of d. Since there is no reason to prefer one of the two images, we will use the symmetric form of (1) in the following: $\varphi^{\mathrm{r}}(x + d(\mathbf{x})/2, y) = \varphi^{\mathrm{l}}(x - d(\mathbf{x})/2, y)$. The Taylor series expansions in $\mathbf{x}$ of these two terms read

$$\varphi^{\mathrm{r}/\mathrm{l}}(x \pm d(\mathbf{x})/2, y) = \varphi^{\mathrm{r}/\mathrm{l}}(\mathbf{x}) \pm d(\mathbf{x})/2 \, \partial_x \varphi^{\mathrm{r}/\mathrm{l}}(\mathbf{x}) + \mathcal{O}(d(\mathbf{x})^2) \ . \tag{2}$$

The partial derivative which occurs in this series expansion is the local frequency *in the horizontal orientation*. It is very important to note that the local frequency should be evaluated in the same orientation as the quadrature filter (see e.g. [1], page 396) and should not be mixed up with the magnitude of the gradient of the local phase, i.e., the isotropic local frequency (see e.g. [1], page 404). Plugging (2) into the symmetric version of (1) yields

$$d(\mathbf{x}) \approx 2 \frac{\varphi^{\mathrm{l}}(\mathbf{x}) - \varphi^{\mathrm{r}}(\mathbf{x})}{\partial_x \varphi^{\mathrm{l}}(\mathbf{x}) + \partial_x \varphi^{\mathrm{r}}(\mathbf{x})} \ . \tag{3}$$

Hence, the disparity can be estimated by the quotient of the local phase difference and the mean local frequency in horizontal orientation. If the disparity orientation is not horizontal but given by the unit vector $\mathbf{e}$, the corresponding terms in the previous considerations must be changed accordingly. The quadrature filter must be oriented according to $\mathbf{e}$ and the horizontal derivative is replaced by the directional derivative with respect to $\mathbf{e}$.

1.3   Reliability of the Estimate

The reliability of the disparity estimate depends on certain signal properties.

1. The approximation (1) becomes worse if the gradient of $d(\mathbf{x})$ becomes larger. Therefore, it must be assured that the disparity map is smooth to some degree. This will be done by a multi-scale approach, see below.
2. The influence of noise increases if the local amplitude of the filter response is low. If an additive noise model is assumed, the reliability is a linear function of the local amplitude.
3. The reliability depends on the local orientation and the local intrinsic dimension (iD). If the signal is locally i1D (or simple), the signal varies only in one orientation. The reliability of the displacement estimate along this orientation (the *normal displacement*) is independent of the absolute orientation. If the disparity orientation differs from the normal orientation by an angle θ, the former is obtained by projecting the displacement onto the disparity line, see Fig. 2. This projection increases the standard deviation of the measurement by $|\cos(\theta)|^{-1}$. Accordingly, the reliability is proportional to $|\cos(\theta)|$ which should be reflected by the measurement.

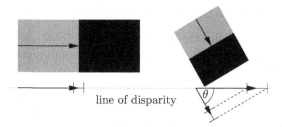

Fig. 2. Reliability of disparity estimates for different normal displacements. The standard deviation, indicated as small intervals at the tips of the displacement vectors, is increased if the displacement is projected onto the disparity line

The quadrature filters which are used in the literature so far are mostly Gabor filters (e.g. [7]) or polar separable quadrature filter (e.g. [5]). The former are clearly sub-optimal with respect to their angular behavior. Gabor filters only have a DC component close to zero if their standard deviation in the frequency domain is small compared to their center frequency. This implies that simple structures with orientations not being identical to the disparity orientation yield too little reliabilities for their disparity estimates. Furthermore, the orientation dependency differs with the local frequency. Polar separable filters according to [2] do not show this dependency on the local frequency. However, they also punish the orientation deviation too much ($\cos(\theta)^2$ instead of $|\cos(\theta)|$).

Hence, the optimal quadrature filter is a polar separable filter with an angular component of $|\cos(\theta)|$. However, any filter with an orientation dependent amplitude response mixes up the uncertainty of the measurement caused by noise (second point) and caused by the local orientation (third point). In order to obtain an optimal disparity estimate, it is necessary to keep the influence of noise and of the orientation separated. This is not possible with a classical quadrature filter but it is straightforward with a spherical quadrature filter (SQF) [8].

2   The New Approach

An SQF is the *monogenic signal* [9] of a radial bandpass filter. The monogenic signal and its phase approach have already been applied in other applications, see e.g. [10]. The monogenic signal generalizes the analytic signal to 2D by replacing the Hilbert transform with the Riesz transform. The latter is a vector valued LSI operator with the frequency response

$$\mathbf{H}(\mathbf{u}) = i\mathbf{u}/|\mathbf{u}| = i(\cos\psi, \sin\psi) \tag{4}$$

where $\mathbf{u} = q(\cos\psi, \sin\psi)$ is the frequency vector. Combining a signal $f(\mathbf{x})$ with its Riesz transform $\mathbf{f}_R(\mathbf{x}) = (f_{R1}(\mathbf{x}), f_{R2}(\mathbf{x}))$ yields a 3D-vector valued signal, the monogenic signal.

2.1   The Geometry of the Monogenic Phase

In [9] it has been shown that the appropriate phase approach for the monogenic signal is a vector valued phase. The phase vector is obtained as

$$\mathbf{r}(\mathbf{x}) = \frac{\mathbf{f}_R(\mathbf{x})}{|\mathbf{f}_R(\mathbf{x})|} \arctan\left(\frac{|\mathbf{f}_R(\mathbf{x})|}{f(\mathbf{x})}\right) . \tag{5}$$

According to [9] the *monogenic phase* $\mathbf{r}$ is identical to the classical phase multiplied by the orientation vector if the underlying signal is i1D. Hence, the local monogenic phase points in a direction perpendicular to a line or an edge.[1]

Under the presence of global shifts, the monogenic phase is linear to displacement *vectors* and not to their absolute values. It is thus straightforward to use the monogenic phase to estimate the normal displacements in a stereo image pair, generalizing the disparity estimation from local phase and local frequency. Assuming that the underlying signal is locally i1D, the normal displacement and the local phase vector are parallel, e.g., both have the orientation $\mathbf{e}$. The Taylor series expansion of $\mathbf{r}(\mathbf{x} \pm \mathbf{d}(\mathbf{x})/2) = \varphi(\mathbf{x} \pm d(\mathbf{x})\mathbf{e}/2)\mathbf{e}$ reads

$$\mathbf{r}\left(\mathbf{x} \pm \frac{\mathbf{d}(\mathbf{x})}{2}\right) = \mathbf{r}(\mathbf{x}) \pm \frac{d(\mathbf{x})}{2}\mathbf{e} \cdot \nabla \mathbf{r}(\mathbf{x}) + \mathcal{O}(d^2) = \mathbf{r}(\mathbf{x}) \pm \frac{d(\mathbf{x})}{2}\nabla \cdot \mathbf{r}(\mathbf{x}) + \mathcal{O}(d^2) \tag{6}$$

where ∇ is the gradient operator so that $\mathbf{e} \cdot \nabla$ is the derivative operator in the direction of $\mathbf{e}$. Hence, the normal displacement can be estimated by

$$\mathbf{d}(\mathbf{x}) \approx 2\frac{\mathbf{r}^l(\mathbf{x}) - \mathbf{r}^r(\mathbf{x})}{\nabla \cdot \mathbf{r}^l(\mathbf{x}) + \nabla \cdot \mathbf{r}^r(\mathbf{x})} . \tag{7}$$

Note that the local frequencies $\nabla \cdot \mathbf{r}(\mathbf{x})$ which occur in this equation are isotropic local frequencies, in contrast to those in (3). These isotropic local frequencies can be estimated by a similar method as described in [1], page 397, by

$$\nabla \cdot \mathbf{r}(\mathbf{x}) = \frac{\mathbf{f}_R(\mathbf{x}) \cdot (\nabla f(\mathbf{x})) - f(\mathbf{x})(\nabla \cdot \mathbf{f}_R(\mathbf{x}))}{f^2(\mathbf{x}) + |\mathbf{f}_R(\mathbf{x})|^2} . \tag{8}$$

In order to avoid phase wrappings in the enumerator of (7), the difference of the phase vectors is replaced by

$$\Delta\mathbf{r}(\mathbf{x}) = \frac{f^l(\mathbf{x})\mathbf{f}_R^r(\mathbf{x}) - f^r(\mathbf{x})\mathbf{f}_R^l(\mathbf{x})}{|f^l(\mathbf{x})\mathbf{f}_R^r(\mathbf{x}) - f^r(\mathbf{x})\mathbf{f}_R^l(\mathbf{x})|} \arctan\left(\frac{|f^l(\mathbf{x})\mathbf{f}_R^r(\mathbf{x}) - f^r(\mathbf{x})\mathbf{f}_R^l(\mathbf{x})|}{f^l(\mathbf{x})f^r + \mathbf{f}_R^l(\mathbf{x}) \cdot \mathbf{f}_R^r(\mathbf{x})}\right). \tag{9}$$

2.2   Disparity from Monogenic Phase

The reliability of the normal displacement estimate according to (7) is given by the local amplitudes of the two monogenic signals. In order to turn the displacement into a disparity measure, the former must be projected onto the disparity

---

[1] Whereas in [9] the phase vector is defined such that it points parallel to the structure, (5) lets it point in the perpendicular direction, i.e., it is rotated by $\pi/2$.

line as sketched in Fig. 2. Let $\mathbf{d}'(\mathbf{x})$ denote the disparity along the line given by $\mathbf{e}$, this projection is obtained as

$$\mathbf{d}'(\mathbf{x}) = |\mathbf{d}(\mathbf{x})|^2/(\mathbf{e} \cdot \mathbf{d}(\mathbf{x}))\,\mathbf{e} \ , \tag{10}$$

which yields an increase of the standard deviation by $\cos\theta = (\mathbf{e} \cdot \mathbf{d})/|\mathbf{d}(\mathbf{x})|$.

Thus, we have established a formalism for estimating the disparity which keeps track of the uncertainty due to noise and which treats the local geometry in an appropriate way. Furthermore, the disparity estimation from the monogenic phase is also more flexible with respect to the choice of the line of disparity. Whereas the classical method is more or less fixed to horizontal displacements, the new approach is *independent of the line of disparity* unless the projection (10) is performed. This can be used to estimate the actual line of disparity from displacement field. If, in another application, the disparity orientation is not constant but the cameras are calibrated, it is possible to project the displacement vector onto the epipolar line in order to get the disparity. Another possible setting are images from more than two cameras. The displacement vectors can then be combined to compute the most probable depth.

3 Implementation

3.1 The Disparity Estimation Algorithm

As stated above, the gradient of the disparity should not be too large for (1) being sufficiently accurate. This can be ensured by implementing the disparity estimation in a multi-scale algorithm. The two images are lowpass filtered and subsampled in order to obtain a resolution pyramid (see e.g. [11,12]). The disparity estimation starts at the coarsest scale, giving a coarse disparity map. This is then used to compensate large displacements on the next finer level. The modified images on this level are used to refine the disparity map. This procedure is repeated until the finest scale is reached. This multi-scale method, or hierarchical method, is illustrated in e.g. [2].

The filters which are applied to estimate the local phase and the local frequency are based on a radial bandpass filter given by $B(q) = \cos^2((5q - 3\pi)/4)$ if $q \in [\pi/5, \pi]$ and zero elsewhere. From this frequency response and its Riesz transform a 9×9 SQF is obtained by a weighted least square optimization (see e.g. [2]). The partial derivatives of the SQF, which are needed for (8), are obtained by a similar optimization as 11×11 filter masks. All optimized filters have a relative error of less than 5%.

Throughout the theoretic part, we have focused on having correct certainty measures. However, it is not trivial to propagate such measures through the multi-scale algorithm. An appropriate tool to represent data *and* its reliability is the *channel representation* [3,13]. Averaging information in the channel representation is similar to a normalized convolution (see e.g. [14]), i.e., the averaging is weighted by some certainty measure. Furthermore, the channel representation prevents edges from being blurred. Averaging in the channels does not imply that the decoded information itself will be blurred. The disparity estimates on each scale are stored *and added* as channels. Addition of channels yields a multiplication of the certainty measure, which is reasonable since the measurements are taken from disjunct frequency components and can therefore be considered as independent. In order to combine a coarser disparity map with a finer one, the former has to be interpolated. This is also done in the channel representation which yields a good noise suppression without blurring the disparity map.

3.2 Experiment

We have applied the described algorithm to a typical test image pair, showing the Pentagon, see Fig. 3. Compared to the result of a disparity algorithm based on classical quadrature filters and normalized convolution (see [5]), the noise is reduced while the steps in the disparity map are preserved better. Compared to the result from [3], the noise suppression and the preserving of edges are similar. However, the latter disparity map shows some less accurate estimates, see, e.g., the bridge in the upper right corner. Furthermore, the new approach is the fastest one and reduces the complexity by 40% compared to the simple approach based on classical quadrature filters (see Fig. 4).

Fig. 3. Upper row: left stereo image (left) and disparity obtained from the presented algorithm (right). Bottom row: disparities obtained from the approaches according to [5] (left) and according to [3] (right)

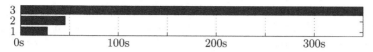

Fig. 4. Run-time comparison of Matlab-implementations on a Sun Ultra 60 for the methods according to [3] (3), according to [5] (2), and according to this paper (1)

4   Conclusion

We have presented a new method for disparity estimation, based on the monogenic phase. We have replaced the classical quadrature filters by spherical quadrature filters, motivated by some considerations of the measurement reliability. The resulting estimation formula is more flexible than the one based on horizontal quadrature filters. The implemented algorithm is based on a scale-pyramid and the channel representation in order to propagate the certainties through the hierarchy of the processing. The presented experiment shows that the disparity estimation from monogenic phase is less noise sensitive than the classical method. Furthermore, edges in the resulting disparity maps are preserved as good as for more complex methods like the one based on canonical correlation.

References

1. Jähne, B.: Digitale Bildverarbeitung. Springer-Verlag, Berlin (1997)
2. Granlund, G.H., Knutsson, H.: Signal Processing for Computer Vision. Kluwer Academic Publishers, Dordrecht (1995)
3. Borga, M.: Learning Multidimensional Signal Processing. PhD thesis, Linköping University, Sweden (1998)
4. Scharstein, D., Szelisky, R.: A taxonomy and evaluation of dense two-frame stereo correspondence algorithms. Int. Journal of Computer Vision **47** (2002) 7–42
5. Westelius, C.J.: Focus of Attention and Gaze Control for Robot Vision. PhD thesis, Linköping University, Sweden (1995)
6. Hansen, M.: Stereosehen - ein verhaltensbasierter Ansatz. PhD thesis, Inst. f. Inf. u. Prakt. Math. der Christian-Albrechts-Universität Kiel (1998)
7. Hansen, M., Daniilidis, K., Sommer, G.: Optimization of stereo disparity estimation using the instantaneous frequency. In: Proc. Computer Analysis of Images and Patterns. Volume 1296 of LNCS, Springer–Verlag (1997) 321–328
8. Felsberg, M.: Low-Level Image Processing with the Structure Multivector. PhD thesis, Inst. f. Inf. u. Prakt. Math. der Christian-Albrechts-Universität Kiel (2002)
9. Felsberg, M., Sommer, G.: The monogenic signal. IEEE Transactions on Signal Processing **49** (2001) 3136–3144
10. Felsberg, M., Sommer, G.: A new extension of linear signal processing for estimating local properties and detecting features. In: 22. DAGM Symposium Mustererkennung, Springer-Verlag (2000) 195–202
11. Burt, P.J., Adelson, E.H.: The Laplacian pyramid as a compact image code. IEEE Trans. Communications **31** (1983) 532–540
12. Granlund, G.H.: In search of a general picture processing operator. Computer Graphics and Image Processing **8** (1978) 155–173

13. Nordberg, K., Granlund, G., Knutsson, H.: Representation and Learning of Invariance. In: Proc. IEEE Int'l Conf. on Image Processing, Austin, Texas (1994)
14. Forssén, P.E., Granlund, G., Wiklund, J.: Channel representation of colour images. Technical Report LiTH-ISY-R-2418, Dept. EE, Linköping University (2002)

A Probabilistic Approach to Building Roof Reconstruction Using Semantic Labelling

Stephan Scholze[1], Theo Moons[2,3], and Luc Van Gool[1,2]

[1] ETH Zürich, Computer Vision Laboratory (BIWI), Zürich, Switzerland,
{scholze,vangool}@vision.ee.ethz.ch, http://www.vision.ee.ethz.ch/
[2] Katholieke Universiteit Leuven, Center for Processing Speech and Images
(ESAT/PSI), Leuven, Belgium
[3] Katholieke Universiteit Brussel, Group of Exact Sciences, Brussel, Belgium,
theo.moons@kubrussel.ac.be

Abstract. This paper investigates into model-based reconstruction of complex polyhedral building roofs. A roof is modelled as a structured ensemble of planar polygonal faces. The modelling is done in two different regimes. One focuses on geometry, whereas the other is ruled by semantics. Inside the geometric regime, 3D line segments are grouped into planes and further into faces using a Bayesian analysis. In the second regime, the preliminary geometric models are subject to a semantic interpretation. The knowledge gained in this step is used to infer missing parts of the roof model (by invoking the geometric regime once more) and to adjust the overall roof topology. Several successfully reconstructed complex roof structures corroborate the potential of the approach.

1 Introduction

In the advent of mega-cities the availability of cheap, reliable and up-to-date 3D city models for technical and environmental planning tasks becomes increasingly urgent. Although research in the field of fully automated building reconstruction has been conducted over the past decades, none of the developed systems made it into industrial production. However, very powerful systems have been proposed, able to work fully automatic in specific scenarios. Two key elements seem to be crucial to deal successfully with the complicated reconstruction task. Firstly, a balance between generic and detailed building models has to be found, in order to cope with the virtually infinite variability of roof types on one hand and with the need to support modelling with prior knowledge on the other. Secondly, a building reconstruction system, able to deal with missing or erroneous input data will need some sort of intelligent control to perform its task successfully.

1.1 Previous Work

Automated building reconstruction is still a challenging task. An overview of important developments and state-of-the-art in the field can be found in the Proceedings of the Ascona Workshops on Automatic Extraction of Man-Made

L. Van Gool (Ed.): DAGM 2002, LNCS 2449, pp. 257–264, 2002.
© Springer-Verlag Berlin Heidelberg 2002

Objects from Aerial and Space Images [1,2,3]. Some previous approaches, able to reconstruct complex buildings with minimal user interaction include [4,5,6,7].

The roof models used in the literature cover the range from very generic ones (polyhedral structures) up to very specific ones (parametrized models of different building types). For an overview see [8]. For handling uncertainty and imprecision of the input data, some building reconstruction systems already have a probabilistic underpinning [9,10,11].

1.2   A Geometric Model in a Probabilistic Setup

In this paper, a probabilistic formulation for geometric building reconstruction is presented. As a novelty, a semantic interpretation of generic roof parts is used to guide the geometric reconstruction. The conjunction of robust geometric reasoning in 3D space together with a semantic interpretation allows to reconstruct complex building roofs completely and with correct topology.

The organisation of this paper is as follows. In Sect. 2 the proposed roof model is presented. Sect. 3 briefly summarizes the processing steps from the image data up to a preliminary geometric model of the roof. In Sect. 4 the geometric model is augmented with semantic meaning, which is used to complete and refine the roof model. Finally, results of the approach are presented in Sect. 5.

2   Geometric Roof Model

A roof is geometrically modelled as an ensemble of planar polygonal faces (*patches*). It suffices to distinguish between triangular and quadrangular patches, since more complex patch shapes (e.g. L-shapes) are obtained by patch composition. Theoretically, it would suffice to use triangular patches only. However, since quadrangular patches are very common in building roofs, including them is advantageous for the practical application. The 3D line segments forming the border of a patch will be referred to as *patch segments*. The term edge is deliberately not used because of its widespread use in computer vision. Besides the collection of patches constituting the roof, the relations between the patches are of importance and will be integrated in the model as constraints.

2.1   Roof Atoms: Patches

In Fig. 1(a) the parametrization of a quadrangular patch is shown. The advantages of the chosen parametric representation are that the quantities involved have an obvious meaning. Probability distributions have been obtained from a test dataset. Additionally, this representation allows to incorporate symmetries between different patches of a roof model.

In parallel to the parametric representation, a representation based on the 3D world coordinates of the corner points $P_0, \ldots, P_3$ of the patch is kept. Although this dual representation is redundant, the coordinate based representation is especially useful when introducing coincidence constraints to ensure topological connectivity, as discussed in the next section.

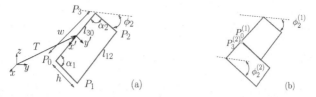

Fig. 1. (a): Quadrangular patch model. T is the transformation from world coordinates to the local 2D patch coordinate system. The slant of the patch plane is given by ϕ_2. The inclination of the bordering segments is denoted with α_1 and α_2 respectively. Given that l_{03} and l_{12} are parallel, the parametrization of the patch is completed by specifying the width w and the height h. (b): Illustration of the two different types of constraints. (Here $\alpha_1^{(1,2)} = \alpha_2^{(1,2)} = \pi/2$.) Further description in text.

2.2   Roof $= \sum$ Patches $+$ Constraints

A roof is described by its constituting patches and the relations between them. These relations are modelled as constraints between parameters or coordinates of different patches in a roof. As an example, consider the L-shaped patch in Fig. 1(b), constructed out of two quadrangular patches which have collinear upper borders. In order to compose the two patches to represent one L-shaped patch, two constraints are imposed. By making use of the parametric representation, a unique slant angle can be achieved by requiring $\phi_2^{(1)} = \phi_2^{(2)}$. Additionally, the coordinate based representation allows to glue corner points together by setting $P_0^{(1)} = P_3^{(2)}$.

3   Patch Reconstruction: The Geometric Regime

This section discusses the geometry based reconstruction of roof patches. From the raw input data, consisting of multiview, high resolution aerial imagery of densely built up urban areas, a set of 3D line segments is derived using feature based multiview correspondence analysis [12]. These line segments form the input data for the following reconstruction process.

3.1   Plane and Patch Hypotheses

Given a set of 3D line segments, planes which could correspond to roof structures, supported by these line segments, are now sought. The general approach is to rotate a half plane around some reference 3D line segment, e. g. a tentative ridge line. (For choosing the reference segments see Sec. 4.4.) For each inclination of the half plane, segments in its neighbourhood, which approximately lie in this plane are collected. To determine the number of planes and their positions, a Bayesian model selection procedure is applied. A detailed explanation of the procedure is available in [13]. The result is a set (usually 1-4) of plane hypotheses in the neighbourhood of a reference line together with their probabilities.

During the Bayesian plane selection procedure, 3D line segments are associated with different plane hypotheses. Now, the outlines of possible patches, containing the segments in the individual plane hypotheses, are to be determined. The outlines are found by computing the extremal points of the convex hull of the segments in a tentative plane. The extremal points correspond to the end points of the associated line segments, projected into the patch plane, with minimal/maximal coordinates. Then, the patch parameters are adjusted to contain the extremal points.

At this stage of the reconstruction, different patch and plane configurations exist in parallel. To select the optimal configuration Utility Theory is applied. The Utility Function used consists of two parts. One part quantifies the reliability of the patch hypothesis [14], whereas the second part takes into account the compatibility between different patches. Finally, the patch and plane configuration with Maximum Expected Utility is entered into a preliminary roof model. (A detailed description of plane and patch instantiation will be published elsewhere.)

Up to now, only geometric information conveyed by the 3D line segments has been used for reconstruction. Although the reconstructed patches capture the roof geometry, two aspects need to be improved. First of all, the pure geometric reconstruction fails to determine, if the entire roof structure has been retrieved or if patches are still missing. Secondly, small gaps appear between neighbouring segments which should be adjacent. Hence, the roof topology is not correct at this stage of reconstruction

4   Roof Reconstruction: The Semantic Regime

To obtain a complete and topological correct reconstruction of entire building roofs, the following reconstruction steps are driven by a semantic interpretation of the geometric patch models obtained so far.

4.1   Semantic Labels by Geometric Attributes, Test Dataset

Five different semantic labels for patch segments are distinguished. The five possible labels form the set Ω:

$$\Omega = \{\omega^{(1)} = \texttt{ridge}, \omega^{(2)} = \texttt{gutter}, \omega^{(3)} = \texttt{gable}, \omega^{(4)} = \texttt{convex}, \omega^{(5)} = \texttt{concave}\} \quad (1)$$

For convenience each semantic label (e. g. gutter) is represented by a variable $\omega^{(i)}$, where i encodes the actual label. The names of the labels are chosen to be coherent, although they should not be taken literally. For example, a gutter segment just corresponds to the lower boundary of a patch, no matter if there is a gutter in the scene or not. Fig. 2 gives an overview. In order to assign the semantic labels (later also referred to as *classes*) to the segments in a patch, geometric measurements are used. We distinguish measurements characterizing individual segments u_i (*unary attributes*) and measurements between adjacent

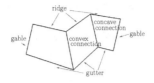

Fig. 2. Functional parts of a roof and their semantic labels. The label `ridge` is generally used for the upper boundary of a patch, `gutter` for the lower one. The boundaries of a patch are either labelled `gable`, `convex connection` or `concave connection` depending on the neighbourhood.

segments b_{ij} (*binary attributes*). The actual measurements of

$u_i^{(1)}$: length of segment i

$u_i^{(2)}$: slant angle of segment i relative to a horizontal plane

$b_{ij}^{(1)}$: angle enclosed by adjacent (coplanar) segments i and j

$b_{ij}^{(2)}$: (signed) mid point height difference of segments i and j (2)

are represented as attribute vectors $\mathbf{u}_i = (u_i^{(1)}, u_i^{(2)})$ and $\mathbf{b}_{ij} = (b_{ij}^{(1)}, b_{ij}^{(2)})$. Although the current set of measured attributes is complete in a sense that it reliably allows the assignment of correct labels, the system could be easily extended by introducing additional attributes in the future. Note that currently only intra patch relations are being used.

To learn the statistics of the geometric measurements at *test dataset* has been used. The dataset shows urban and sub-urban areas with four-fold overlap at an image scale of approximately 1:5000 [15]. Nearly 150 roofs, consisting of about 80 triangular and 270 quadrangular patches have been labelled manually using the semantic labels from Equation 1. Additionally to the semantic labels, the unary and binary attributes have been recorded.

4.2 Classification of New Measurements

We now concentrate on the problem of assigning semantic labels to the patch segments obtained from the geometry based reconstruction. In a first step, unary and binary attributes are computed for each patch individually. Using these measurements we want to assign semantic labels. For the unary attributes, the classes correspond to the semantic labels given in Equation 1. Since the binary attributes describe relations between pairs of line segments, their classes are given by compatible label combinations (e.g. `ridge;gable`).

A nonparametric classification technique, namely *Linear Discriminant Analysis* (LDA) is used to classify the unknown observations [16]. LDA is chosen because no restrictions on the number of classes are imposed (which would allow to use more attributes) and because the underlying distributions need not to be normal [17].

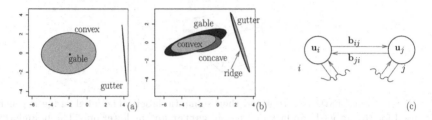

Fig. 3. (a,b): Schematic representation of unary attributes of the test dataset in the space of maximal separation (a: triangular patches, b: quadrangular patches). The clusters are shown as ellipses for visualization only – no normal distribution is assumed for classification. (c): Fragment of graph used in probabilistic relaxation labelling. The nodes i and j represent two adjacent patch segments. See description in text.

During LDA, the input data (unary and binary attributes) is transformed into a space, where the separation between the classes is maximal, allowing for better classification performance. Fig. 3(a,b) shows a schematic representation of the clusters formed by the unary attributes of triangular and quadrangular patches of the test dataset. Since the clusters are overlapping for both, unary and binary attributes (not shown), it is not possible to unambiguously assign labels using unary or binary attributes alone. This deficiency will be overcome in the next section.

4.3 Probabilistic Relaxation Labelling

The probability of patch segment i having label $\omega_i^{(l)} \in \Omega$ $(l = 1, \ldots, 5;$ cf. Eqn. 1) is known from LDA of the unary attributes. However, neither unary nor binary attributes alone allow an unambiguous labelling. This is overcome by an iterative procedure which determines the labels for all segments in a patch in such a way, that the *entire* label assignment (per patch) has maximal probability, exploiting unary and binary attributes *simultaneously*.

For this purpose, a probabilistic relaxation labelling algorithm is used [18]. The patch segments are represented as nodes in a cyclic graph (Fig. 3(c)). Each node i holds the conditional probabilities $P(\omega_i^{(l)}|\mathbf{u}_i)$. Between each two nodes of adjacent segments i and j, two edges are introduced in the graph, representing the binary attributes $\mathbf{b}_{ij}$ and $\mathbf{b}_{ji}$. Conditional probabilities of the form $p(\mathbf{b}_{ij}|\omega_i^{(l)}, \omega_j^{(m)})$ $(l, m = 1, \ldots, 5)$ are stored in the edges. These probabilities, obtained via LDA of the binary attributes, represent the compatibility of the labelling of two adjacent patch segments. Incompatible combinations have zero probability. In an iterative scheme the relaxation algorithm searches for a labelling which maximizes the overall patch probability. For all examples we have investigated, the algorithm converges rapidly ($\approx$ 10 iterations) to a stable and correct label assignment.

4.4   Semantic Model Completion

After having determined the semantic labels for all patch segments present in the geometric roof model, the roof is refined using a set of simple rules. The most important aspect is inference of missing patches. To locate these the outline of the reconstruction is scrutinized. The key idea is to identify patch segments on the outline which actually should correspond to an internal boundary of the roof – that is, a concave or convex joint of roof patches. If such segments could be identified (if present at all), these in turn form a set of seed segments which are fed into the reconstruction algorithm again. If no more missing patches can be inferred, the semantic labels are used to glue corresponding segments together, closing possible gaps and therefore ensuring a consistent roof topology. Thus, in this step, topological correctness is preferred over geometric precision.

5   Results and Conclusion

The presented results are obtained using a state-of-the-art dataset, produced by Eurosense Belfotop n.v. The image characteristics are 1:4000 image scale with a pixel size corresponding to 8×8 cm^2 on ground. The 3D line segments are obtained using three overlapping views. The precise sensor orientation is known. To emphasise the quality of the reconstructed roof geometry no texture mapping is applied.

For the presented set of experiments the initial reference line segments have been determined using the distribution of unary attributes only. Fig. 4(a) shows the reconstruction result for a building roof, which was completely reconstructed from its seed (here: ridge) line by one pass of the reconstruction algorithm. The reconstruction results are detailed and topologically correct. For instance the small difference in the slope of the two patches on the right side of the roof has been correctly detected. Fig. 4(b) shows the reconstruction of another building roof. The triangular patches on the front side do not lie in a plane given by the seed line. However, driven by the semantic labels attributed to the partially reconstructed roof (here: convex), the missing patches could be successfully found.

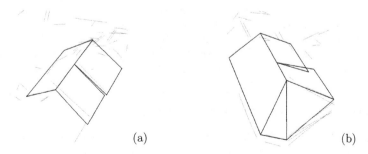

(a)   (b)

Fig. 4. (a,b): Three-dimensional view of reconstructed building roofs. The non trivial roof structures are captured to their full extent. Thin lines show the input 3D segments.

To conclude, we feel that the combination of probabilistic geometric and semantic reasoning presented in this paper leads to encouraging reconstruction results. The proposed roof model seems to meet a reasonable balance between being general and specific. Future work will focus on exploiting the knowledge available in form of test datasets to a broader extent, with the goal to initialize roof models with even less evidence in 3D space. Another research direction which is pursued at the moment is oriented toward the optimization of the geometric accuracy of the models using back-projection into the input images.

References

1. Grün, A., Kübler, O., Agouris, P.: Automatic Extraction of Man-Made Objects from Aerial and Space Images. Birkhäuser-Verlag, Basel (1995)
2. Grün, A., Baltsavias, E., Henricsson, O.: Automatic Extraction of Man-Made Objects from Aerial and Space Images. Birkhäuser-Verlag, Basel (1997)
3. Baltsavias, E., Grün, A., Van Gool, L.: Automatic Extraction of Man-Made Objects from Aerial and Space Images. Balkema Publishers, Rotterdam (2001)
4. Henricsson, O.: The Role of Color Attributes and Similarity Grouping in 3-D Building Reconstruction. CVIU **72** (1998) 163–184
5. Moons, T., Frere, D., Vandekerckhove, J., Van Gool, L.: Automatic Modelling and 3D Reconstruction of Urban House Roofs from High Resolution Aerial Imagery. In: ECCV. Volume 1. (1998) 410–425
6. Baillard, C., Zisserman, A.: A Plane-Sweep Strategy for the 3D Reconstruction of Buildings from Multiple Images. In: IAPRS. Volume 33 part B2. (2000) 56–62
7. Fischer, A., Kolbe, T., Lang, F., Cremers, A., Förstner, W., Plümer, L., Steinhage, V.: Extracting Buildings from Aerial Images Using Hierarchical Aggregation in 2D and 3D. CVIU **72** (1998) 185–203
8. Mayer, H.: Automatic Object Extraction from Aerial Imagery – A Survey Focusing on Buildings. CVIU **74** (1999) 138–149
9. Kulschewski, K.: Building Recognition with Bayesian Networks. In Förstner, W., Plümer, L., eds.: SMATI. (1997)
10. Cord, M., Jordan, M., Cocquerez, J.P.: Accurate Building Structure Recovery from High Resolution Aerial Imagery. CVIU **82** (2001) 138–173
11. Heuel, S., Förstner, W.: Topological and Geometrical Models for Building Reconstruction from Multiple Images. In: [3]. (2001)
12. Scholze, S., Moons, T., Ade, F., Van Gool, L.: Exploiting Color for Edge Extraction and Line Segment Stereo Matching. In: IAPRS. Volume 33. (2000) 815–822
13. Scholze, S.: Bayesian Model Selection for Plane Reconstruction. Technical Report BIWI–TR–259, Computer Vision Laboratory, ETH, Zürich, Switzerland (2002)
14. Scholze, S., Moons, T., Van Gool, L.: A Probabilistic Approach to Roof Patch Extraction and Reconstruction. In: [3]. (2001)
15. Institute of Geodesy and Photogrammetry: Dataset of Zürich Hoengg. Swiss Fed. Inst. of Technology (ETH) Zürich, CH-8093 Zurich, Switzerland (2001)
16. Fisher, R.A.: The Use of Multiple Measurements in Taxonometric Problems. Ann. Eugenics **7** (1936) 179–188
17. Hand, D.J.: Construction and Assessment of Classification Rules. John Wiley & Sons (1997)
18. Christmas, W.J., Kittler, J., Petrou, M.: Structural Matching in Computer Vision Using Probabilistic Relaxation. PAMI **17** (1995) 749–764

Adaptive Pose Estimation
for Different Corresponding Entities

Bodo Rosenhahn and Gerald Sommer

Institut für Informatik und Praktische Mathematik,
Christian-Albrechts-Universität zu Kiel, Preußerstrasse 1-9, 24105 Kiel, Germany,
{bro,gs}@ks.informatik.uni-kiel.de

Abstract. This paper concerns the 2D-3D pose estimation problem for different corresponding entities. Many articles concentrate on specific types of correspondences (mostly point, rarely line correspondences). Instead, in this work we are interested to relate the following image and model types simultaneously: 2D point/3D point, 2D line/3D point, 2D line/3D line, 2D conic/3D circle, 2D circle/3D sphere. Furthermore, to handle also articulated objects, we describe kinematic chains in this context in a similar manner. We further discuss the use of weighted constraint equations, and different numerical solution approaches.

1 Introduction

In this work we derive a solution approach for simultaneous 2D-3D pose estimation from different corresponding entities. Pose estimation itself is a basic visual task [3] and the first solution approaches were presented in the early eighties [7]. Monocular pose estimation means to relate the position of a 3D object to a reference camera coordinate system [14,10][1]. Nearly all papers concentrate on one specific type of correspondences. But many situations are conceivable in which a system has to gather information from different hints or has to consider different reliabilities of measurements. This is the main aspect of this work: We describe a scenario for adaptive pose estimation of simultaneously used different entities, without loosing linearity, good conditioned equations and real-time capability.

The Scenario of Pose Estimation

In the scenario of figure 1 we describe the following situation: We assume points, lines, spheres, circles or kinematic chain segments of an 3D object or reference model. Further, we extract corresponding 2D features in an image of a calibrated camera. The aim is to find the rotation R and translation t of the object, which lead to the best fit of the reference model with the actual projective reconstructed entities. This means, an image point is reconstructed to a *projection ray*, or an image line is reconstructed to a *projection plane*. Then constraints are build in the 3D space to compare the model features with the reconstructed image features.

---

[1] Many other scientists also concern this problem in several variations, but we can not quote them due to the space limits.

L. Van Gool (Ed.): DAGM 2002, LNCS 2449, pp. 265–273, 2002.

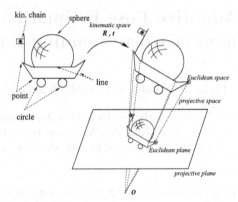

Fig. 1. The scenario. The solid lines describe the assumptions: the camera model, the model of the object (consisting of points, lines, circles, spheres and kinematic chains) and corresponding extracted entities on the image plane. The dashed lines describe the pose of the model, which leads to the best fit of the object with the actual extracted entities.

2   Geometric Algebras

We use geometric algebras to formalize the geometric scenario and the pose estimation process. The advantage of this language is its dense symbolic representations of higher order entities with linear operations acting on those. In this contribution we will not give a detailed introduction in geometric algebras. This can be found in [13]. The main idea of geometric algebras $\mathcal{G}$ is to define a product on basis vectors, which extends the linear vector space V of dimension n to a linear space of dimension 2^n. The elements are so-called multivectors as higher order algebraic entities in comparison to vectors of a vector space as first order entities. A geometric algebra is denoted as $\mathcal{G}_{p,q}$ with $n = p+q$. Here p and q indicate the numbers of basis vectors which square to $+1$ and -1, respectively. The product defining a geometric algebra is called *geometric product* and is denoted as uv for two multivectors u and v. Operations between multivectors can be expressed by special products, called *inner* $\cdot$, *outer* $\wedge$, *commutator* $\times$ and *anticommutator* $\overline{\times}$ product. The most powerful and only recently introduced algebra is the conformal geometric algebra $\mathcal{G}_{4,1}$ (ConfGA) [8]. Because it is suited to describe conformal geometry, it contains spheres as entities and a rich set of geometric manipulations. The point at infinity, $\mathbf{e}$, and the origin, $\mathbf{e}_0$, are special elements and define a null space in the conformal geometric algebra.

Rigid Transformations in ConfGA

Rotations are represented by rotors, $\boldsymbol{R} = \exp\left(\frac{\theta}{2}\boldsymbol{l}\right)$. The components of the rotor $\boldsymbol{R}$ are the unit bivector $\boldsymbol{l}$ which represents the dual of the rotation axis, and the angle θ which represents the amount of the rotation. The rotation of an entity can be performed by its spinor product $\underline{\boldsymbol{X}}' = \boldsymbol{R}\underline{\boldsymbol{X}}\widetilde{\boldsymbol{R}}$. A translation can be expressed by a translator, $\boldsymbol{T} = (1 + \frac{\mathbf{e}\boldsymbol{t}}{2}) = \exp\left(\frac{\mathbf{e}\boldsymbol{t}}{2}\right)$. To estimate the rigid body motion (containing a rotor $\boldsymbol{R}$ and translation vector $\boldsymbol{t}$), we follow e.g. [9]: A rigid body motion can be expressed by a rotation about a line in space. This results from the fact that for every $g \in SE(3)$ exists a $\xi \in se(3)$ and a $\theta \in \mathbb{R}$ such that $g = \exp(\xi\theta)$. The element ξ is also called a *twist*. The motor $\boldsymbol{M}$ describing a twist transformation has the general form $\boldsymbol{M} = \boldsymbol{T}\boldsymbol{R}\widetilde{\boldsymbol{T}}$, denoting the inverse translation, rotation and back translation, respectively. But whereas in Euclidean geometry, Lie algebras and Lie groups are only applied on point concepts, the motors and twists can also be applied on other entities, like lines, planes, circles, spheres, etc.

Constraint Equations for Pose Estimation

Now we express the 2D-3D pose estimation problem, *a transformed object entity has to lie on a spatial entity, projective reconstructed from an image entity*. Let $\underline{\boldsymbol{X}}$ be an object point and $\underline{\boldsymbol{L}}$ be an object line, given in ConfGA. The (unknown) transformations of the entities can be described as $\boldsymbol{M}\underline{\boldsymbol{X}}\widetilde{\boldsymbol{M}}$ and $\boldsymbol{M}\underline{\boldsymbol{L}}\widetilde{\boldsymbol{M}}$, respectively. Let $\boldsymbol{x}$ be an image point and $\boldsymbol{l}$ be an image line on a projective plane. The projective reconstruction of an image point in ConfGA can be written as $\underline{\boldsymbol{L}}_x = \mathbf{e} \wedge \boldsymbol{o} \wedge \boldsymbol{x}$. The entity $\underline{\boldsymbol{L}}_x$ is a circle, containing the vector $\boldsymbol{o}$ as the optical center of the camera, see e.g. figure 1, the image point $\boldsymbol{x}$ and the vector $\mathbf{e}$ as the point at infinity. This leads to a reconstructed projection ray. Similarly leads $\underline{\boldsymbol{P}}_l = \mathbf{e} \wedge \boldsymbol{o} \wedge \boldsymbol{l}$ to a reconstructed projection plane in ConfGA. Collinearity and coplanarity can be described by the commutator and anticommutator products. Thus, the constraint equations of pose estimation from image points read

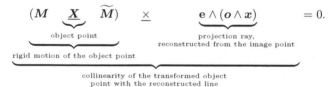

Constraint equations to relate 2D image lines to 3D object points, or 2D image lines to 3D object lines, can be expressed in a similar manner. Note: The constraint equations in the unknown motor $\boldsymbol{M}$ express a distance measure which has to be zero. But in contrast to other approaches, where the minimization of errors has to be computed directly on the geometric transformations [2], in our approach a distance in the Euclidean space constitutes the error measure.

3   Pose Estimation with Extended Object Concepts

This section concerns the derivation of constraint equations for kinematic chains, circles and spheres.

Kinematic Chains

With *kinematic chains* we mean linked rigid objects which can only change their pose in mutual dependence. Examples are tracked robot arms or human body movements, see e.g. figure 4. So far we have parameterized the 3D pose constraint equations of a rigid object. Assume that a second rigid body is attached to the first one by a joint. The joint can be formalized as an axis of rotation and/or translation in the object frame (*revolute* or *prismatic* joint respectively). Each joint defines a new coordinate system, and the coordinate transformations between joints can be described by suitable motors M_j. This means, an entity given in the coordinate system of the jth joint can be translated in an entity of the base coordinate system by transforming the entity with the motors $M_1, \ldots, M_j$. The points attached to the j-th joint are numbered as $\underline{X}_{j,1}, \ldots, \underline{X}_{j,i_j}$. The transformation of the points on the j-th joint in terms of the base coordinate system can be formalized as $\underline{X}^0_{j,i_j} = M_1 \ldots M_j \underline{X}_{j,i_j} \widetilde{M}_j \ldots \widetilde{M}_1$.

Now we will combine the introduced representation of a kinematic chain with the pose estimation constraints derived in the previous section. The pose of the base corresponds to a motor M. The constraint equation for a point at the j-th joint leads to

$$(M(M_1 \ldots M_j \underline{X}_{j,i_j} \widetilde{M}_j \ldots \widetilde{M}_1)\widetilde{M}) \underline{\times} \mathbf{e} \wedge (o \wedge x_{j,i_j}) = 0.$$

3.1 Circles and Spheres

We now explain, how to build constraint equations for 3D circles and 3D spheres. The key idea is to interpret circles and spheres as virtual kinematic chains: A circle can be described by a twist ξ and a point $\underline{X}_C$ on the circle. Let M_ϕ be a motor, describing a general rotation around the twist ξ. Then the circle is simply given by all points which result from the transformation of the point $\underline{X}_C$,

$$\underline{X}^\phi_C = (M_\phi \underline{X}_C \widetilde{M}_\phi) \quad : \quad \phi \in [0 \ldots 2\pi].$$

We can similarly proceed with spheres, just by rotating a point with two twists and gaining the points on a sphere:

$$\underline{X}^{\phi_1,\phi_2}_S = (M^1_{\phi_1} M^2_{\phi_2} \underline{X}_S \widetilde{M}^2_{\phi_2} \widetilde{M}^1_{\phi_1}) \quad : \quad \phi_1, \phi_2 \in [0 \ldots 2\pi].$$

The constraint equations for tangentiality of projection rays to circles or spheres can be summarized as

$$(M(M_\phi \underline{X}_C \widetilde{M}_\phi)\widetilde{M}) \underline{\times} \mathbf{e} \wedge (o \wedge x) = 0,$$
$$(M(M^1_{\phi_1} M^2_{\phi_2} \underline{X}_S \widetilde{M}^2_{\phi_2} \widetilde{M}^1_{\phi_1})\widetilde{M}) \underline{\times} \mathbf{e} \wedge (o \wedge x) = 0.$$

4 Experiments

In this section we will show experimental results of pose estimation.

4.1 Solving the Constraint Equations

In the last sections, several constraint equations to relate object informations to image informations are derived. In these equations, the object, camera and

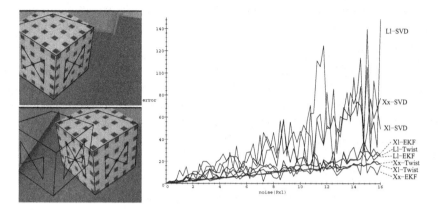

Fig. 2. The scenario of the first experiment. In the first image the calibration is performed and the 3D object model is projected on the image. Then the camera moved and corresponding line segments are extracted. For comparison reasons, the initial pose is overlaid. The diagram shows the performance comparison of different methods in case of noisy data.

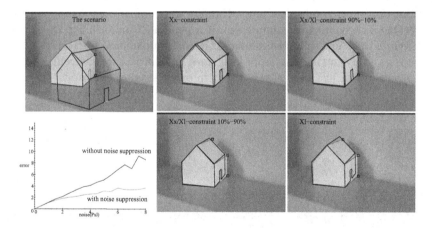

Fig. 3. Different weightings of constraints for pose estimation.

image data are assumed to be known and the motor M expressing the motion is assumed to be unknown. There exist several ways to estimate the motion parameters. In earlier works we concerned this problem and we estimated the motion parameters either on the Lie group $SE(3)$ itself (by using an SVD approach), or by using an extended Kalman filter (EKF) [12]. In [11] we presented a new method, which does not estimate the rigid body motion on the Lie group $SE(3)$, but the parameters which generate their Lie algebra $se(3)$ (*twist approach*), comparable to the ideas, presented in [1,7]. Note: Though the equations are expressed in a linear manner with respect to the group action, the equations in the unknown generators of the group action are non-linear and in the twist approach they will be linearized and iterated.

In our first experiment, we compare the noise sensitivity of these three methods, with respect to the three constraint equations, relating 3D points to 2D points (Xx), 3D points to 2D lines (Xl), or 3D lines to 2D lines (Ll). Therefore we add a Gaussian noise on extracted image points in a virtual scenario (see figure 2). Then we estimate the rigid body motion, and use the translational error between the ground truth and the disturbed values as error measure. The result is depicted in figure 2. It is easy to see, that the results, obtained with the SVD approach are the worst ones. Instead, the Kalman filter and the twist approach have a more stable and comparable error behavior. It is obvious, that the results of the experiments are not much affected by the used constraints themselves. This occurs because we selected certain points directly by hand and derived from these the line subspaces. So the quality of the line subspaces is directly connected to the quality of the point extraction. The result of this investigation is, that for noise corresponding to a distribution function, the Kalman filter or twist approach for pose estimation should be used. There are two main reasons, why we further prefer the twist approach for pose estimation instead of the EKF: Firstly, the Kalman filter is sensitive to outliers (see e.g. figure 4), leading to non-converging results. Secondly, Kalman filters must be designed for special situations or scenarios. So the design of a general Kalman filter, dealing with different entities in a weighted manner is hard to implement. Instead, this can be done very easily in the twist approach since the linearized constraint equations of any entity can just be scaled and put in one system of equations.

Fig. 4. Images of a tracked robot arm taken from a sequence of 40 images. The second row shows a stability example for disturbed color markers.

Adaptive Use of Pose Estimation Constraints

Image preprocessing algorithms sometimes enable a characterization of the quality of extracted image data. The idea to use these additional information in the context of pose estimation is the following: Every constraint equation describes a distance measure for the involved entities. These constraint equations can be scaled by a scalar $\lambda \in \mathbb{R}$ and so it is possible to individually scale the weighting of the equation to the whole equations system. Figure 3 shows an example: On the one hand we have three extracted image points and on the other hand three extracted image lines. We can use both information separately to evaluate the pose of the object. Since we have only few information for each type of correspondences, the object itself is not very well fitted to the image data (see e.g. the images with the Xx-constraint or Xl-constraint). On the other hand, we can put both constraint equations in one whole system of equations and solve the unknowns by using all image information at once. Furthermore, we are able to choose different weightings of the constraints. The change of the pose estimations is visualized in the other images of figure 3. To address the noise adaptive use of the pose estimation constraints, we add a Gaussian noise on some of the extracted image points. Then we solve the constraint equations with and without weighting the constraints, depending on the noise level. We call this method *noise suppression*. The result is visualized in the diagram of figure 3.

Pose Estimation of Kinematic Chains

In the next experiment (see figure 4), we use as object model a robot arm. We estimate the pose of the robot and the angles of the kinematic chain via tracked point markers. The errors we gain in these experiments are dependent on the calibration quality, lens distortion and accuracy of the point marker detection. They differ around 0.5 till 3 degree. The second row of figure 4 shows images of a second sequence. There we visualize the stability of our algorithm in the context of moved color markers and therewith resulting impossible kinematics: During the tracking, a student moves into the scenario and picks up a color marker and moves it around. The model will not be distorted. Instead, the algorithm leads to a spatial best fit of the model to the extracted image data.

4.2   Simultaneous Pose Estimation
with Different Kinds of Correspondences

In the last experiment we use a model which contains a prismatic and revolute joint, 3D points, 3D lines, 3D circles and a 3D sphere. Figure 5 shows some pose estimation results of the object model. Though we measured the size of the model by hand, the pose is accurate and also the joint parameters are good approximated. All information is accumulated in one linear system of equations. This leads to simultaneous solving of the pose parameters by using all features, without following the classical way of point based estimations of subspace concepts in vector space.

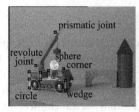

Fig. 5. Pose estimation by using different types of correspondences

5   Discussion

This contribution concerns the simultaneous estimation of 2D-3D pose for different kinds of correspondences. We present a new framework in the language of geometric algebra for pose estimation of object models, which consist of different types of entities, including points, lines, planes, circles, spheres and kinematic chains.

Compared with other algorithms, we are able to use a full perspective camera model in this context and not an orthographic one as e.g. in [1]. We also formulate the equations as differential approximation of the requested group actions and put them in one equations system. This enables an easy use of different entities in the same system. We also discuss different solution approaches for pose estimation and recommend the use of Kalman filters or twists for pose estimation, but not the estimation on the group manifold itself. This result is in contrast to the results presented in [6]. The noise adaptive use of the constraints is also interesting with respect to the design of behavior based or learning robot systems. Only sporadic work concerning this for stable running systems important topic exist so far (e.g. [5]). We implemented the sources in C++ and are able to estimate the motion (and kinematic chain) parameters in real-time with 15 frames per second on a SUN Ultra 10.

References

1. Bregler C. and Malik J. Tracking people with twists and exponential maps. *IEEE Computer Society Conference on Computer Vision and Pattern Recognition*, Santa Barbara, California, pp. 8-15, 1998.
2. Chiuso A. and G. Picci. Visual tracking of points as estimation on the unit sphere. In *The Confluence of Vision and Control*, pp. 90-105, Springer-Verlag, 1998.
3. Grimson W. E. L. Object Recognition by Computer. *The MIT Press, Cambridge, MA*, 1990.
4. Hel-Or Y. and Werman M. Pose estimation by fusing noisy data of different dimensions. *IEEE Transactions on Pattern Analysis and Machine Intelligence (PAMI)*, Vol. 17, No.2, February 1995.
5. Holt J.R. and Netravali A.N. Uniqueness of solutions to structure and motion from combinations of point and line correspondences. *Journal of Visual Communication and Image Representation*, Vol.7:2, pp. 126–136, 1996.

6. Lorusso A., Eggert D.W. and Fisher R.B. A comparison of four algorithms for estimating 3-d rigid transformations. In *British Machine Vision Conference*, Birmingham, pp. 237–246, England, 1995.
7. Lowe D.G. Three-dimensional object recognition from single two-dimensional images. *Artificial Intelligence*, Vol. 31 No. 3, pp. 355-395, 1987.
8. Li H. Generalized homogeneous coordinates for computational geometry. In [13], pp. 27-52, 2001.
9. Murray R.M., Li Z. and Sastry S.S. A Mathematical Introduction to Robotic Manipulation. *CRC Press*, Inc., 1994.
10. Horaud R., Phong T.Q. and Tao P.D. Object pose from 2d to 3d point and line correspondences. *International Journal of Computer Vision*, Vol. 15, pp. 225-243, 1995.
11. Rosenhahn B., Granert O., Sommer G. Monocular pose estimation of kinematic chains. *Applied Geometric Algebras for Computer Science and Engineering, Birkhäuser Verlag*, pp.371–381, 2002.
12. Sommer G., Rosenhahn B., and Zhang Y. Pose estimation using geometric constraints. *In R.Klette, Th. Huang, G.Gimmel'farb (eds.), Multi-Image Search and Analysis*, LNCS 2032, Springer-Verlag, Heidelberg, pp. 153–170, 2001.
13. Sommer G., editor. Geometric Computing with Clifford Algebra. *Springer-Verlag*, Heidelberg, 2001.
14. Walker M.W. and Shao L. Estimating 3-d location parameters using dual number quaternions. *CVGIP: Image Understanding*, Vol. 54:3, pp.358–367, 1991.

Properties of a Three-Dimensional Island Hierarchy for Segmentation of 3D Images with the Color Structure Code

Patrick Sturm and Lutz Priese

Universität Koblenz-Landau, Institute of Computational Visualistics,
Universitätsstraße 1, 56070 Koblenz, Germany,
{sturm,priese}@uni-koblenz.de

Abstract. The CSC a very robust and fast color segmentation method. To do a real 3d segmentation of voxel images with the CSC, we have to replace the hexagonal island hierarchy by a 3d island hierarchy with the same properties. The sphere island hierarchy which is defined on the most dense sphere package can be used for segmentation with the CSC algorithm. Unfortunately, the sphere island hierarchy cannot fulfill all properties of the hexagonal island hierarchy at the same time.

1 Introduction

The process of segmentation is essential to image processing. In our opinion the segmentation task can be described best by the detection of homogeneous and spatially connected regions in images (cf. [HP76]). The segmentation process should be independant of *a priori* knowledge and should also be applicable to as many applications as possible.

In this paper we want to present a 3d segmentation algorithm based on a very robust and fast (two-dimensional) color segmentation method – the Color Structure Code (CSC). The CSC is a hierarchical region growing algorithm developed by Rehrmann and Priese ([PR93],[RE98]) that works on a hexagonal island hierarchy originally proposed by Hartmann ([HA87]). The CSC combines local and global information to achieve a robust segmentation result. To develop a CSC algorithm for segmentation of 3d voxel images is not straight forward. The main problem is to find a 3d island hierarchy which has the same properties as the (2D) hexagonal island hierarchy. The properties of the hexagonal island hierarchy will be discussed later.

In section 2 and 3 we describe the construction of the hexagonal island hierarchy and how it is used to generate the CSC. In section 4 we show how a 3d island hierarchy that is comparable to the hexagonal island hierarchy could be constructed. Further we proove that our 3d island hierarchy could not hold all properties of the hexagonal island hierarchy at the same time.

L. Van Gool (Ed.): DAGM 2002, LNCS 2449, pp. 274–281, 2002.

2 The Hexagonal Island Hierarchy

The hexagonal island hierarchy is organized in different levels ([HA87], [RE98]). On the lowest hierarchy level a raster with hexagonal topology is divided into islands of level 0. The islands of level 0 consist of seven spatially connected pixels – one center pixel and its six neigbor pixels. Therefore a hexagonal island of level 0 is always completely defined by its center pixel and the neighborship of the pixels.

The hexagonal islands of level 0 are distributed in a certain way on the hexagonal raster (s. fig. 1), where every fourth pixel is a center pixel of an island of level 0. Each island of level 0 intersects with six other islands of level 0 in one common pixel. Each pixel of the raster is part of at least one island of level 0.

The islands of level $n > 0$ are constructed in an analog way. An island of level $n + 1$ consists of one center island of level n and its six neighbor islands. Two islands of level n are called neighbors, if and only if, they intersect each other. Each island (except the top most island) of level n is part of at least one island of level $n + 1$ (s. fig. 1).

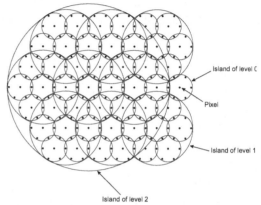

Island of level 0

Pixel

Island of level 1

Island of level 2

Fig. 1. The hexagonal island hierarchy

From one hierarchy level to the next one the number of islands decreases approximately by factor 4. The topmost hierarchy level consists of just one island that covers the entire raster.

3 Generation of the Color Structure Code

The CSC is generated in three steps: Coding, Linking and Splitting. In this paper we focus only on the first two steps of the CSC generation which show the usage of the hexagonal island hierarchy in the segmentation. For further information on the CSC refer to [PR93] and [RE98].

3.1 Coding

During the coding phase the image is devided into islands of level 0 (last section) consisting of 7 pixels. Each island of level 0 is divided into spatially connected regions which are homogenous in color. Each region should consist of at least two pixels. Therefore an island contains at most three disjoint color regions.

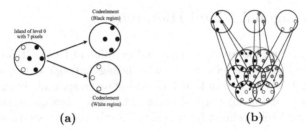

Fig. 2. a: Coding of an island of level 0 into two codeelements, b: Creation of codeelements of level 1 by linking codeelements of level 0 together.

Each detected region $R(c)$ (of level 0) is mapped to a codeelement c of level 0. A codeelement c of level 0 is a data object that stores information about the appearance and the average color of the region $R(c)$ (s. fig. 2a).

In the following processing steps regions are not considered anymore but only the codeelements.

3.2   Linking

In the coding step atomic regions of level 0 are detected. Now regions of level n are merged to new regions of level $n+1$. For that purpose, codeelements of level n are linked to a new codeelement of level $n+1$, if they are spatially connected, similar in color and are covered by a common island of level $n+1$. Each codeelement of level n represents a homogenous color region $R(c)$. Some codeelements $c_1, ..., c_m$ of a level n are connected and similar in color, if and only if the regions $R(c_1), ..., R(c_m)$ are spatially connected and similar in color. Because of the structure of the hexagonal island hierarchy, the regions $R(c_1), ..., R(c_m)$ are connected if they intersect each other, i.e.:

$$\forall 1 \le i \le m : \left(R(c_i) \cap \bigcup_{1 \le j \le m, j \ne i} R(c_j) \right) \ne \emptyset \tag{1}$$

By linking m codeelements $c_1, ..., c_m$ to a new codeelement c, the m regions $R(c_1), ..., R(c_m)$ are merged implicitly to a new region $R(c)$ that is spatially connected and homogenous in color. We call the codeelements $c_1, ..., c_m$ subcodeelements of c and the codeelement c the parent codeelement of $c_1, ..., c_m$. A codeelement can have at most two parent codeelements. Each codeelement represents a vertex in a directed graph where each subcodeelement is linked to its parent codeelement. Therefore all pixels of a region $R(c)$ can be obtained by traversing all links down to level 0 beginning at codeelement c.

3.3   Advantages of the CSC

Each segmentation step (coding, linking) works within islands. The segmentation result is independent of the order in which the islands are processed. Therefore the CSC is inherently parallel and can be accelerate on a multiprocessor system.

Although the CSC is a region growing algorithm, it does not lead to chaining mismatches. If two connected regions are not homogenous in color they will be separated in a additional splitting phase ([RE98]). Therefore the CSC generates disjoint regions which are homogenous in color.

4   A 3D Island Hierarchy and Its Properties

For 2D color image processing the CSC produces good segmentation results. The properties of the hexagonal island hierarchy guide the way towards a very simple and efficient segmentation algorithm. A 3d island hierarchy should therefore have the same properties as the hexagonal island hierarchy. In this case the segmentation algorithm could be used without any modifications. In this section we want to discuss the

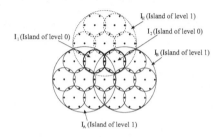

Fig. 3. Cover-of-neighborship

properties of the hexagonal island hierarchy in detail. After that, a construction of a 3d island hierarchy will be given.

4.1   Properties of the Hexagonal Island Hierarchy

The following list contains the essential properties of the hexagonal islands of level $n + 1$:

1. All islands of level $n+1$ comprise the same number of subislands. (Homogenity)
2. Two islands of level $n + 1$ intersect each other in at most one island of level n. (Plainness)
3. All subislands (except the center island) of an island of level $n+1$ are subislands of two different islands of level $n + 1$. (Saturation)
4. Each island of level n is subisland of at least one island of level $n+1$. (Cover)
5. Two neighboring islands I_1 and I_2 of level n are always subislands of a common island I of level $n + 1$, i.e. $I_1 \in I \wedge I_2 \in I$. (Cover-of-neighborship).

The first three properties are just good for the simple and elegant structure of the CSC algorithm. The last two properties, however, are relevant for good segmentation results.

What would happen, if the cover-of-neighborship property would not hold for the hexagonal island hierarchy? Let us consider the two neighboring islands I_1 and I_2 of level 0 in figure 3. Both islands are subislands of the common parent island I_H of level 1. Therefore, we say that the neighborship of the islands I_1 and I_2 is covered by the island I_H. Further, the two codeelements c_1 and c_2 of level 0 are given. We assume that the codeelement c_1 was generated in island I_1 and c_2 was generated in island I_2. Both regions $R(c_1)$ and $R(c_2)$ intersects each other, i.e. c_1 and c_2 are connected. If I_H would not exist the cover-of-neighborship property would not hold. Therefore the regions $R(c_1)$ and $R(c_2)$ could not be merged. The linking step works just within islands. In this case disjoint regions could not be guaranteed, because $R(c_1)$ and $R(c_2)$ have a common subregion.

4.2 An Island Hierarchy
Defined on the Most Dense Sphere Package

In this section we will present a 3d island hierarchy, that holds four properties of the hexagonal island hierarchy. Therefore, we have to define a 3d raster that is comparable to the hexagonal raster.

A 3d structure that is similar to the hexagonal raster is the most dense sphere package of sphere with uniform diameter d. For simplicity we will just consider spheres with a diameter $d = 1$. The most dense sphere package is a stack of (horizontal) sphere layers (s. figure 4). A sphere layer consists of spheres whose centers lie on a common plane. Two successive sphere layers are shifted towards one another. Each sphere of a sphere layer lies on three spheres belonging to the sphere layer below. There are several ways to build a most dense sphere package. It strongly depends on the chosen displacement. For definition of a 3d island hierarchy it does not matter which most dense sphere package is used.

We use a sphere package that is described by the set V. The set V contains all centers of spheres that belongs to the sphere package. Each center $C(i, j, k)$ of a sphere $(d = 1)$ can be written as a combination of three linear independent vectors.

$$V := \{C(i, j, k) \,|\, i, j, k \in \mathbb{Z}\} \tag{2}$$

$$C : \mathbb{Z} \times \mathbb{Z} \times \mathbb{Z} \ , \tag{3}$$
$$C(i, j, k) := i \cdot \left(1\ 0\ 0\right)^T$$
$$+ j \cdot \left(1/2\ \sqrt{3/4}\ 0\right)^T$$
$$+ k \cdot \left(1/2\ \sqrt{1/12}\ \sqrt{2/3}\right)^T$$

The most dense sphere package defined above can be considered as a 3d raster (sphere raster), where the spheres are the voxels (volume elements) of the

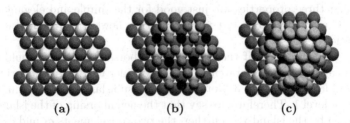

(a)   **(b)**   **(c)**

Fig. 4. Construction of the most dense sphere package. White spheres represent island centers of 3d-islands (of level 0). Black spheres represent holes in the hierarchy.

image. A sphere in the sphere raster has 12 neighbor spheres. Two spheres are called neighboring if they have a common point of contact.

A 3d island hierarchy that is similar to the hexagonal island hierarchy can now be built. A 3d-island of level 0 consists of an island center und its 12 neighbors (s. fig. 5a). In order to ensure that the saturation and plainness property hold for all 3d islands of level 0, we use each sphere with center $C(2i, 2j, 2k)$, $i, j, k \in \mathbb{Z}$ as an island center. Thus every eigth sphere of the raster is an island center.

On the first hierarchy level the homogenity, the plainness and the saturation property holds for all 3d islands. But does the cover property hold also? The following proof shows that this property *cannot* be valid for the sphere island hierarchy.

We assume, that our sphere raster consists of m ($m \to \infty$) spheres. Because of the chosen island distribution every eigth sphere must be an island center. Therefore, $\frac{1}{8} \cdot m$ islands of level 0 exist in our hierarchy. Further we know, that each island of level 0 consists of 13 spheres. 12 spheres are covered by two parent islands and 1 sphere is covered by only one parent island (Saturation). If we want to count the number of spheres that are covered by at least one island of level 0, we cannot just multiply the number of islands of level 0 with factor 13, because some spheres would be counted twice. Therefore, we say that each island of level 0 owns $1 + \frac{1}{2} \cdot 12$ spheres. The number of spheres that are part of at least one island of level 0 can now be computed as: $\frac{1}{8} \cdot m \left(1 + \frac{1}{2} \cdot 12\right) = \frac{7}{8} \cdot m$.

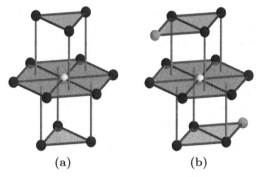

Fig. 5. (a) 3d islands of level 0 consisting of 13 voxels. (b) 3d island of level 0 consisting of 15 voxels (including two holes)

We see, that only $\frac{7}{8} \cdot m$ of all spheres can be covered by the island hierarchy. The remaining $\frac{1}{8} \cdot m$ spheres are called holes. If we want to use the sphere island hierarchy for segmentation the existence of holes could not be accepted. Every sphere should be covered by the sphere island hierarchy. A possible solution to this problem is the redefinition of the island structure. An enhanced island of level 0 (s. fig. 5b) consists of 15 spheres (1 island center, its 12 neighbors and two holes) and therefore gets two additional neighbors. With this modification the cover property holds for all islands of level 0 and the saturation, homogenity and plainness properties are still valid.

The remaining hierarchy levels can be constructed similarly. An island of level $n + 1$ consists of 15 neighboring islands of level n. The plainness, homogenity, saturation and cover properties holds for all hierarchy levels. From a hierarchy level to the next one the number of islands decreases approximately by factor 8.

4.3   Suitability of the Sphere Island Hierarchy for Segmentation

The sphere island hierarchy defined in the previous section fulfills the homogenity, plainness, saturation and cover property on all hierarchy levels. How about the cover-of-neighborship property? One can examine this property by looking at a very simple arithmetical example. First we compute the entire number of intersections between islands of level n and then we compute the number of intersections between islands of level n that are covered by islands of level $n+1$. If the island hierarchy holds the cover-of-neighborship property, both calculations should have the same result.

First we want to demonstrate the computations for the hexagonal island hierarchy:

We assume that m is the number of hexagonal islands of level n. Because every fourth island of level n is an island center of an island of level $n+1$, there must exist $\frac{1}{4} \cdot m$ islands of level $n+1$ in the hierarchy.

First we count the number of pairs (I_1, I_2) of neighboring hexagonal islands of level n. We call such pairs of islands *neighbor pairs*. Each hexagonal island of level n has 6 neighbors. Therefore $\frac{1}{2} \cdot 6 \cdot m = 3 \cdot m$ different neighbor pairs must exists on level n. The factor $\frac{1}{2}$ is important because there is no difference between the neighbor pairs (I_1, I_2) and (I_2, I_1). Without the factor all neighbor pairs would be counted twice.

The plainness property is valid in the hexagonal island hierarchy. Therefore there exists exactly one island of level $n+1$ that contains both islands (of level n) of a neighbor pair. In the hexagonal island hierarchy each neighbor pair of level n must be part of one island of level $n+1$ because the cover property is also valid. Now we count the number of different neighbor pairs of level n that are part of a common island of level $n+1$. Each hexagonal island of level $n+1$ contains 12 different neighbor pairs. We multiply the number of neighbor pairs within one island with the number of all islands of level $n+1$. In this way we get the whole number of neighbor pairs on level n: $12 \cdot \frac{1}{4} \cdot m = 3 \cdot m$. If the cover-of-neighborship property would not hold for the hexagonal island hierarchy the result of this second computation would be smaller than the result of the first. We see that each neighbor pair of level n is covered by just one island of level $n+1$.

Now we do the same computations for the sphere island hierarchy. We assume that m is the number of islands of level n. Therefore, $\frac{1}{8} \cdot m$ islands of level $n+1$ exist in the hierarchy. Remember, the construction of the sphere island hierarchy ensures the plainness, saturation and homogenity feature.

1. Each island of level n has 14 neighbor islands. The number of neighbor pairs of level n is therefore $\frac{1}{2} \cdot (14 \cdot m) = 7 \cdot m$, i.e. there exists $7 \cdot m$ different intersections between islands of leven n.

2. Each island of level $n+1$ contains 50 different neighbor pairs of level n. Because of the plainness property of the sphere hierarchy each neighbor pair is covered by at most one island. Therefore, only $\frac{1}{8} \cdot m \cdot 50 = 6.25 \cdot m$ different neighbor pairs could be covered by islands of level $n+1$.

The results of both computations are different. The conclusion is that not all $7 \cdot m$ neighbor pairs of level n could be covered by the islands of level $n + 1$. Therefore we can say that the sphere island hierarchy does not hold the cover-of-neighborship property. If we use the CSC algorithm (with the sphere island hierarchy) without modifications, the segmentation segmentation process does not result in a partition. Another problem is that two neighboring regions that are similar in color are not guaranteed to be merged together.

At the moment it seems as there is no sphere island hierarchy, that fulfills all five properties of the hexagonal island hierarchy at the same time.

5 Summary

We have shown how to implement a 3d sphere hierarchy that can be used in combination with the CSC algorithm. Although the sphere hierarchy could not cover all features of the hexagonal island hierarchy, it is possible to use it for segmentation purposes. We have to take in consideration that the segmentation could result in regions that are not disjoint. We presently investigate if there are possibilies to solve this problem. We already tried to use 3d island hierarchies that does not fulfil the plainness property but holds the cover-of-neighborship property. The segmentation results with such hierarchies does not meet the demands because of different problems.

References

HA87. G. Hartmann. Recognition of Hierarchically Encoded Images by Technincal and Biological Systems. In: Biological Cybernetics, 57:73-84, 1987.

HP76. S.L. Horowitz, T.Pavlidis. Picture Segmentation by a Traversal Algorithm. Journal of the ACM, 23:368-388, 1976.

PR93. L.Priese, V.Rehrmann. A Fast Hybrid Color Segmentation Method. In S.J. Pöppl and H.Handels, editors, Mustererkennung 1993, pages 297-304. Springer Verlag, 1993. 15. DAGM-Symposium, Lübeck, 27.-29.Sept. 1993.

RE98. V.Rehrmann, L.Priese. Fast and Robust Segmentation of Natural Color Scenes. 3rd Asian Conference on Computer Vision, Hongkong, 8-10th January 1998.

A Real Time Implementation
of the Saliency-Based Model of Visual Attention
on a SIMD Architecture

Nabil Ouerhani[1], Heinz Hügli[1], Pierre-Yves Burgi[2], and Pierre-François Ruedi[2]

[1] Institute of Microtechnology, University of Neuchâtel,
Rue A.-L. Breguet 2, CH-2000 Neuchâtel, Switzerland,
{Nabil.Ouerhani,Heinz.Hugli}@unine.ch
[2] Centre Suisse d'Electronique et de Microtechnique (CSEM),
Jaquet-Droz 7, CH-2007 Neuchâtel, Switzerland

Abstract. Visual attention is the ability to rapidly detect the visually salient parts of a given scene. Inspired by biological vision, the saliency-based algorithm efficiently models the visual attention process. Due to its complexity, the saliency-based model of visual attention needs, for a real time implementation, higher computation resources than available in conventional processors. This work reports a real time implementation of this attention model on a highly parallel Single Instruction Multiple Data (SIMD) architecture called ProtoEye. Tailored for low-level image processing, ProtoEye consists of a 2D array of mixed analog-digital processing elements (PE). The operations required for visual attention computation are optimally distributed on the analog and digital parts. The analog diffusion network is used to implement the spatial filtering-based transformations such as the conspicuity operator and the competitive normalization of conspicuity maps. Whereas the digital part of Proto-Eye allows the implementation of logical and arithmetical operations, for instance, the integration of the normalized conspicuity maps into the final saliency map. Using 64×64 gray level images, the on ProtoEye implemented attention process operates in real-time. It runs at a frequency of 14 images per second.

1 Introduction

Visual attention is the ability to rapidly detect visually-salient parts of a given scene. Using visual attention in a computer vision system permits a rapid selection of a subset of the available sensory information. The selected data represent the salient parts of the scene on which higher level computer vision tasks can focus. Thus, the computational modeling of visual attention has been a key issue in artificial vision during the last two decades. The saliency-based model of visual attention has been first reported in [1]. In a recent work [2], an efficient software implementation of this model has been presented. Using a variety of scene features, such as color, intensity and orientation, the reported bottom-up model

L. Van Gool (Ed.): DAGM 2002, LNCS 2449, pp. 282–289, 2002.
© Springer-Verlag Berlin Heidelberg 2002

computes a set of conspicuity maps. These maps are then combined, in a competitive manner, into the final saliency map. Finally, the most salient locations of the scene are detected by means of a winner-take-all (WTA) network.

Due to its complexity, the reported model needs, for a real time implementation, higher computation resources than available in conventional processors. To master the complexity issue, some previous works reported hardware models of visual attention implemented on fully analog VLSI chips [3,4]. The authors considered, however, simplified versions of the saliency-based algorithm of visual attention and implemented only small parts of the model. In both works emphasis has been put on the last stage of the attention model, namely, the winner-take-all (WTA) network.

A complete real time implementation of the saliency-based model of visual attention has been reported in [5]. The implementation has been carried out on a 16-CPU Beowulf cluster involving 10 interconnected personal computers, which might raise problems related to portability and power consumption.

This paper reports a real time implementation of the complete saliency-based model of visual attention on a low power, one board, highly parallel SIMD architecture, called ProtoEye (Fig. 1) [6]. ProtoEye consists of a 35 × 35 array of mixed analog-digital processing elements (PEs). The digital part of a PE, working on 4-bit words, contains an ALU, 6 registers and 2 flags. The analog part is composed of 9 analog multipliers and a diffusion network which efficiently performs the task of low and high-pass spatial filtering of images. Four ProtoEye chips are connected together to process 64 × 64 grey level images, provided by a CMOS imager. The complete architecture is controlled by a general purpose microcontroller running at a frequency of 4 MHz, yielding an effective performance of over 8 Giga operations per second.

The remainder of this paper is organized as follows. Section 2 presents the saliency-based model of visual attention. The architecture of the SIMD machine is reported in Section 3. The implementation of the visual attention model on ProtoEye is discussed in Section 4. Section 5 reports the experimental results. Finally, the conclusions are stated in Section 6.

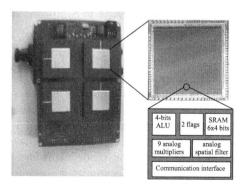

Fig. 1. ProtoEye platform.

2 Saliency-Based Model of Visual Attention

The original version of the saliency-based model of visual attention presented in [2] deals with static color images. It can be achieved in four main steps.

1) First, a number (n) of features are extracted from the scene by computing the so called feature maps (color, intensity, orientations).

2) In a second step, each feature map is transformed in its conspicuity map based on the center-surround mechanism. Each conspicuity map highlights the parts of the scene that strongly differ, according to a specific feature, from its surrounding. Multiscale *difference-of-Gaussians*-filters, which can be implemented using gaussian pyramids, are suitable means to implement the conspicuity operator.

3) In the third stage of the attention model, conspicuity maps are integrated together, in a competitive way, into a *saliency map*, which topographically codes for local conspicuity over the entire visual scene.

4) Finally, the most visually-salient locations are detected by applying a winner-take-all (WTA) network on the saliency map.

3 ProtoEye: SIMD Machine for Image Processing

The complete vision system is composed of a CMOS imager (352×288 pixel), a video output, a general purpose microcontroller (RISC processor) and 4 ProtoEye chips (Fig. 1). The 64×64 pixel images provided by the camera are transferred to the ProtoEye architecture by means of a DMA interface. Each ProtoEye chip then processes a 35×35 subimage. The same DMA interface is used to transfer the processing results from ProtoEye to the external memory, which is interfaced to the video output. The ProtoEye instructions are controlled by the microcontroller (sequencer) implemented on an FPGA.

It is obvious that the main component of this vision system is the SIMD machine ProtoEye. As mentioned above, it is composed of a 35×35 array of identical mixed analog-digital PEs. Each PE executes the same instruction on one element of an array of data and is connected to its 8 neighbors. The architecture of a PE is illustrated in Figure 2.

The digital part of a PE is organized around an internal 4-bit D-bus (D[3:0]). It contains a 4-bit ALU, which has as input the D-bus and the accumulator. The ALU operations include all logical functions, addition, subtraction, shifts of the accumulator content and comparison. The flag $F1$ can be set to mask conditional operations. The 6 registers can be used to keep temporary results within the processing element. In digital mode, transfers between neighboring PEs can be performed by shifting the accumulator content.

The analog part of each PE (shaded area on Fig. 2) is connected to the digital part through A/D and D/A converters. Its essential component is the analog

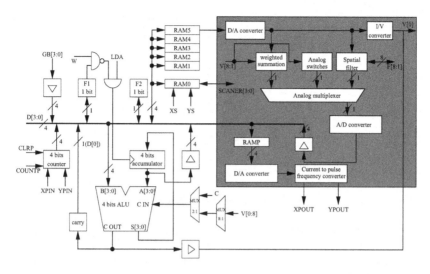

Fig. 2. ProtoEye: Architecture of a processing element (PE).

spatial filter, which is based on a diffusion network, made of pseudoconductances connecting the PEs [7]. The input of the spatial filter is the content of the register RAM5, converted to current by the D/A converter. Its output is a lowpass filtered version of the input image, which cut-off frequency is controlled by an external voltage.

4 Implementation Issues

This section reports some of the issues which have been considered in order to optimally implement the attention model on the described architecture.

4.1 Center-Surround Filter

The original version of the attention model realizes the center-surround mechanism using multiscale difference-of-gaussians filters ($\mathcal{D}o\mathcal{G}$). Practically, a gaussian pyramid is built from a given feature map. Center-surround is then implemented as the difference between fine and coarse scales of the pyramid. To take advantage of the analog diffusion network, the gaussian filtering of images is replaced by the spatial analog filter whose diffusion length is controlled by two external voltages V_R and V_G. It is generally admitted [7] that the behavior of the diffusion network corresponds to an exponential filter of the form:

$$h(x) = k \cdot e^{-\frac{x}{\lambda}} \tag{1}$$

Thus, the conspicuity transformation is implemented as a difference-of-exponentials filter $\mathcal{D}o\mathcal{E}$xp:

$$\mathcal{D}o\mathcal{E}\mathrm{xp}(x) = k_1 \cdot e^{-\frac{x}{\lambda_1}} - k_2 \cdot e^{-\frac{x}{\lambda_2}} \tag{2}$$

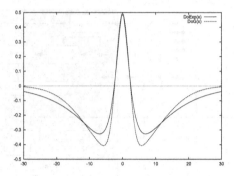

Fig. 3. $\mathcal{D}o\mathcal{E}$xp versus $\mathcal{D}o\mathcal{G}$.

For comparison purposes, Fig. 3 gives the shape of the $\mathcal{D}o\mathcal{E}$xp filter (solid line) and compares it to the $\mathcal{D}o\mathcal{G}$ filter (dashed line). The similarity of both filters guarantees the fidelity of the modified conspicuity operator to the original one.

Hence, a nine level exponential pyramid $\mathcal{P}$ is built by progressively lowpass filter the feature map by means of the analog spatial filter. Contrary to the original model, the nine level of the exponential pyramid have the same spatial resolution. This is due to the limited resolution of the images that ProtoEye can process (64×64).

Six intermediate conspicuity maps are then computed from the exponential pyramid:

$$C_1 = |\mathcal{P}(2) - \mathcal{P}(5)|, \; C_2 = |\mathcal{P}(2) - \mathcal{P}(6)|,$$
$$C_3 = |\mathcal{P}(3) - \mathcal{P}(6)|, \; C_4 = |\mathcal{P}(3) - \mathcal{P}(7)|,$$
$$C_5 = |\mathcal{P}(4) - \mathcal{P}(7)|, \; C_6 = |\mathcal{P}(4) - \mathcal{P}(8)|.$$

Where $\mathcal{P}(i)$ is the i-th level of the pyramid $\mathcal{P}$.

These conspicuity maps are sensitive to different spatial frequencies. Fine maps (e.g. C_1) detect high frequencies and thus small image regions, whereas coarse maps, such as C_6, detect low frequencies and thus large objects.

4.2   Conspicuity Maps

The computed maps have to be combined, in a competitive way, into a unique conspicuity map. A normalization strategy, called iterative localized interactions, is used in our implementation. This strategy relies on simulating local competition between neighboring conspicuous locations. Spatially grouped locations which have similar conspicuities are suppressed, whereas spatially isolated conspicuous locations are promoted. First, each map is normalized to values between 0 and 15, in order to remove modality-dependent amplitude differences. Each map is then convolved by a large 2D difference-of-exponentials filter $\mathcal{D}o\mathcal{E}$xp (the original version of the normalization strategy uses a $\mathcal{D}o\mathcal{G}$ filter). The negative results are clamped to zero after each iteration.

At each iteration of the normalization process, a given intermediate conspicuity map C is transformed as follows:

$$C \leftarrow \frac{|C + C * \mathcal{D}o\mathcal{E}\mathrm{xp}|_{\geq 0}}{2} \tag{3}$$

where $*$ is the convolution operator and $|.|_{\geq 0}$ discards negative values.

The final conspicuity map $\mathcal{C}$ is then computed in accordance with the following equation:

$$\mathcal{C} = \frac{C_1 + C_2 + C_3 + C_4 + C_5 + C_6}{8} \tag{4}$$

4.3   Saliency Map

For each considered scene feature, a conspicuity map is computed. Each of these conspicuity maps is iteratively normalized, according to **Eq. 3**. The saliency map is computed as the sum of the normalized conspicuity maps.

The final step of the task consists in selecting the most salient parts in the image. We implemented a k-Winner-Take-All (kWTA) network based on a large difference-of-exponential filter. The kWTA is iteratively applied on the saliency map. It separates the image locations into two categories, winners and losers, depending on their saliency activities.

5   Experimental Results

In this section we report experiments that assess the proposed implementation of the different steps of the visual attention model discussed in Section 4.

The first experiment (Fig. 4) refers to the operation of the multiscale channel. Two different scene images have been considered. For each image, the six conspicuity maps (C_1 .. C_6) are computed. The activity of the conspicuity maps is pseudo-colored according to the color palette of the same figure (top). The first image (left) consists of a small black disc on a white background. The conspicuity map C_2 has the highest response among the six maps. Due to the larger size of the disc on the second image (right), C_6 is the conspicuity map that contains the highest activity. To summarize, this experiment validates the implemented multiscale conspicuity transformation, since the different conspicuity maps are sensitive to different spatial frequencies.

The second experiment (Fig. 5) refers to the iterative normalization process. A conspicuity map is considered, which contains on one hand a set of spots spatially grouped and on the other hand a spot, which is spatially isolated. We then iteratively applied the normalization process on this map. The activity of the maps are pseudo-colored using the color palette on figure 4 (top). The spatially grouped activities are progressively suppressed compared to the isolated spot. This clearly shows the competition between neighboring conspicuous locations and thus validates the implemented normalization process.

The last experiment (Fig. 6) refers to the last stage of the attention model, namely, the kWTA network. Starting with a gray level real image (left), a saliency

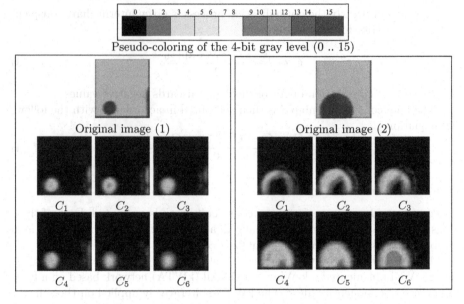

Fig. 4. Multiscale conspicuity transformation.

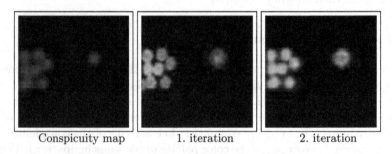

Fig. 5. Iterative normalization of conspicuity maps.

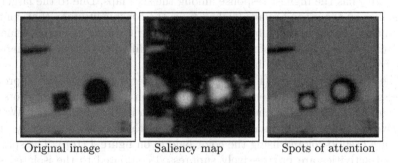

Fig. 6. Detecting the most salient locations in a grey-level image.

map (middle) is computed. The kWTA is then applied on it. The resulting spots (winners) are colored in red and are mapped onto the original image (right).

To conclude, these experiments clearly validate the on ProtoEye implemented saliency-based model of visual attention.

6   Conclusion

This paper reports a real time implementation of the saliency-based model of visual attention on a highly parallel SIMD architecture. Dedicated to low-level image processing, the fully-programmable SIMD machine consists of an array of mixed digital-analog processing elements that offers high-performance functionalities for implementing the various functions appearing in the model of visual attention. Practically, the results of visual attention does not suffer from the required adaptation of the original model to the available resources. They largely fulfill the theoretical expectations. Specifically, the on ProtoEye implemented attention algorithm processes 14 images per second, which allows the use of visual attention in practical real time applications related to computer vision.

Acknowledgment

This work was partially supported by the CSEM-IMT Common Research Program.

References

1. Ch. Koch and S. Ullman. Shifts in selective visual attention: Towards the underlying neural circuitry. *Human Neurobiology (1985) 4, pp. 219-227*, 1985.
2. L. Itti, Ch. Koch, and E. Niebur. A model of saliency-based visual attention for rapid scene analysis. *IEEE Transactions on Pattern Analysis and Machine Intelligence (PAMI), Vol. 20(11), pp. 1254-1259*, 1998.
3. V. Brajovic and T. Kanade. Computational sensor for visual tracking with attention. *IEEE Journal of Solid State Circuits, Vol. 33(8), pp. 1199-1207*, 1998.
4. G. Indiveri. Modeling selective attention using a neuromorphic VLSI device. *Neural Computation, 2000. Volume 12, pp.2857-2880*, 2000.
5. L. Itti. Real-time high-performance attention focusing in outdoors color video streams. *In: Proc. SPIE Human Vision and Electronic Imaging IV (HVEI'02), San Jose, CA, in press*, 2002.
6. P.-F. Ruedi, P.R. Marchal, and X. Arreguit. A mixed digital-analog SIMD chip tailored for image perception. *Proc. of International Conference on Image Processing 96, pp. 1011-1014, Vol. 2, Lausanne*, 1996.
7. E.A. Vittoz and X. Arreguit. Linear networks based on transistors. *Electronic Letters, Vol. 29, pp. 297-299*, 1993.

Designing 3-D Nonlinear Diffusion Filters for High Performance Cluster Computing

Andrés Bruhn[1], Tobias Jakob[2], Markus Fischer[2], Timo Kohlberger[3],
Joachim Weickert[1], Ulrich Brüning[2], and Christoph Schnörr[3]

[1] Mathematical Image Analysis Group,
Faculty of Mathematics and Computer Science,
Building 27.1, Saarland University, 66041 Saarbrücken, Germany,
{bruhn,weickert}@mia.uni-saarland.de
[2] Computer Architecture Group,
Department of Mathematics and Computer Science,
University of Mannheim, 68131 Mannheim, Germany,
{ulrich,mfischer,tjakob}@mufasa.informatik.uni-mannheim.de
[3] Computer Vision, Graphics, and Pattern Recognition Group,
Department of Mathematics and Computer Science,
University of Mannheim, 68131 Mannheim, Germany,
{schnoerr,tkohlber}@uni-mannheim.de

Abstract. This paper deals with parallelization and implementation aspects of PDE based image processing models for large cluster environments with distributed memory. As an example we focus on nonlinear isotropic diffusion filtering which we discretize by means of an additive operator splitting (AOS). We start by decomposing the algorithm into small modules that shall be parallelized separately. For this purpose image partitioning strategies are discussed and their impact on the communication pattern and volume is analyzed. Based on the results we develop an algorithmic implementation with excellent scaling properties on massively connected low latency networks. Test runs on a high–end Myrinet cluster yield almost linear speedup factors up to 209 for 256 processors. This results in typical denoising times of 0.5 seconds for five iterations on a $256 \times 256 \times 128$ data cube.

Keywords: diffusion filtering, additive operator splitting, cluster computing.

1 Introduction

In the last decade PDE based models have become very popular in the fields of image processing and computer vision. The efforts in this paper focus on non-linear isotropic diffusion models that allow to denoise images while preserving edges. This property makes them useful for restauration and segmentation purposes. Nonlinear diffusion models were first introduced by a work of Perona and Malik [5]. After some years their original model was improved by Catté et al. [1] from both a theoretical and practical viewpoint, and anisotropic extensions

L. Van Gool (Ed.): DAGM 2002, LNCS 2449, pp. 290–297, 2002.

with a diffusion tensor [7] followed. Efficient realizations include, among others, adaptive finite volume schemes [3], linearizations using auxiliary variables [2] or approximations in graphics hardware [6]. The use of fast additive operator splitting schemes [8] has triggered first parallel implementations for diffusion filtering [9]. These approaches have been generally restricted to systems based on *shared* memory. In recent years a rapid progress in this sector changed this situation completely. High performance cluster systems with massively connected low latency networks were built throughout the world. There are two reasons for this development: First cluster systems are much more attractive to customers, since they are less expensive. This increases their availability for research purposes. Moreover the number of processors is not limited by such severe hardware restrictions than in the case of shared memory systems, thus allowing larger scaling possibilities. In order to exploit this potential, parallelization approaches must fit the underlying network topology. This motivated us to show that a 3-D isotropic nonlinear diffusion process can be parallelized in such way, that it owns excellent scaling properties regarding both computation and communication on a *distributed* memory system.

The paper is organized as follows. In Section 2 a review on diffusion filtering and the AOS scheme is given. Furthermore a modular decomposition before parallelization is shown. In Section 3 partitioning and communication models are discussed. Relevant parallelization and implementation details of our approach are explained in Section 4. In Section 5 obtained results on a high performance cluster are presented. The summary in Section 6 concludes this paper.

2   Nonlinear Isotropic Diffusion Using AOS

In the following we give a very short review of the nonlinear diffusion model of Catté et al. [1]. A grey value image f is considered as a function from a given domain $\Omega_1 \subset \mathbb{R}^m$ into $\Omega_2 \subset \mathbb{R}$. In our case we have $m \in \{2, 3\}$, what corresponds to 2-D and 3-D images. The basic nonlinear diffusion problem then reads:
Find a function $u(x,t)\colon \Omega_1 \times \mathbb{R}_0^+ \to \Omega_2$ that solves the diffusion equation

$$\partial_t u = \operatorname{div}\Big(g(|\nabla u_\sigma|^2)\nabla u\Big) \quad \text{on} \quad \Omega_1 \times \mathbb{R}_0^+ \tag{1}$$

with f as initial value,

$$u(x,0) = f(x) \quad \text{on} \quad \Omega_1 \tag{2}$$

and reflecting boundary conditions:

$$\partial_n u = 0 \quad \text{on} \quad \partial\Omega_1 \times \mathbb{R}_0^+. \tag{3}$$

where σ is the standard deviation of the Gaussian kernel that is applied prior to differentiation, n is a normal vector perpendicular to $\partial\Omega_1$, and the diffusivity g is a nonnegative decreasing function with $g \in C^\infty[0, \infty)$. The solution $u(x,t)$ is a family of images over t, where the time t acts as a scale parameter. An example illustrating the performance of this diffusion filter is given in Figure 2.

Nonlinear diffusion filters require numerical approximations. In [8] a finite difference scheme based on an additive operator splitting (AOS) technique [4] is used for this purpose. This AOS technique is the basis for our parallelization efforts. It is an extension on the semi-implicit scheme for nonlinear diffusion filtering and can be described as

$$u^{k+1} = \frac{1}{m} \sum_{l=1}^{m} (I - m\tau A_l(u_\sigma^k))^{-1} u^k \qquad (4)$$

where u^k is a vector with the grey values at all pixels as components. The iteration index k refers to the diffusion time $t = k\tau$ where τ is the time step size. The tridiagonal matrix A_l is a discretization of the divergence expression along the l-th coordinate axis. Therefore, in each iteration step, the AOS method requires the solution of m tridiagonal linear systems of equations. Each system describes diffusion along one coordinate direction. It may even be decomposed into smaller tridiagonal systems. The final result at the next time level is obtained by averaging these 1-D diffusion results.

Typical AOS schemes are one order of magnitude more efficient than simple diffusion algorithms. Although they are stable for all time step sizes τ one usually limits the step size for accuracy reasons. Hence, the scheme is applied in an iterative way in order to reach some interesting stopping time.

2.1 Algorithmic Decomposition

The following algorithmic steps can easily be derived from the iteration instruction for the AOS Scheme (4).

1. Presmoothing of the image $u_\sigma^k = K_\sigma * u^k$
2. Computation of the derivatives $|\nabla u_\sigma^k|^2$ and the diffusivities $g(|\nabla u_\sigma^k|^2)$.
3. Resolution of the tridiagonal systems $(I - m\tau A_l(u_\sigma^k)) u_l^{k+1} = u^k$
   Averaging the results : $u^{k+1} = \frac{1}{m} \sum_{l=1}^{m} u_l^{k+1}$

3   Parallelization Models

The following parallelization models are based on image partitioning. This allows parallel execution of fast sequential algorithms instead of applying slower parallel variants to the complete image domain.

3.1   Communication Models

A large part of image processing algorithms consist of neighborhood operations. This raises problems at partition boundaries, since required information is missing. There are two communication models to handle this problem :

Repartitioning. The basic idea of the repartitioning strategy is to find an appropriate partitioning for each operation, such that the problem of missing neighborhood information does not occur. Therefore partitions have to be relocated and reshaped by means of communication. In many cases this communication involves data exchanges between all processes, the so called *all-to-all communication*. For large partition numbers such a connection–intensive communication pattern makes high demands to the network topology. Whether the network can satisfy these demands or not is reflected in a scaling of bandwith (pairwise disjunct communication) or a rise of communication time. For massively connected low latency networks the first case does apply.

Taking a look at the total communication volume the importance of this scaling property becomes obvious. Since non–overlapping partitions are used, each pixel is sent and received by no more than one process. Thus, the communication behavior imposes a limit to the total communication volume that is given by the image size. The number of processes and the required neighborhood can only affect the communication volume within this scope. Hence, each scaling of bandwith is passed on to the communication time.

Boundary Communication. Keeping existing partitions the second communication model simply exchanges the missing neighborhood information. One should note, that this implies a dependency of the total communication volume on two unknowns: The number of partitions as well as the boundary size.

For moderate values of both parameters, the communication is limited to its adjacent segments. In this case the total communication volume may drop significantly beyond that of a repartitioning strategy. Moreover such a simple communication pattern has a second advantage. Since it makes lesser demands to the network topology than the previously discussed all–to–all communication, also weakly connected cluster system do benefit from a bandwith scaling effect. Even for high latency networks this strategy is favorable due to its rather large message size that results from the limited communication pattern.

However, larger boundary sizes and partition numbers do change the situation completely. Then boundary–volume ratios deteriorate, communication patterns may require extensions to further partitions and finally an inefficient parallelization remains. This is reflected in the worst case communication volume that is only limited by $(n-1)$ times the image size, where n is the number of partitions.

Hence boundary exchange does only address operations that require information from a small neighborhood.

3.2 Partition Models

In addition to the communication models appropriate image partitioning strategies have to be chosen. In general cuboid partitions are preferred since they can be realized with commonly used data structures and are easier to handle. There are two partitioning models that result in such cuboid partitions.

Slice Partitioning. As the name anticipates the main idea of this strategy is to partition an image along one single direction. Thus no further boundaries arise. Operations that are separable or do not require neighborhood information from all directions can exploit this property.

However, there are two minor disadvantages of this strategy. First, the maximum number of partitions is limited by the number of pixels in the direction of partitioning, and secondly, slices have an evidently bad boundary–volume ratio. While the first drawback is only relevant for small image sizes, the second one has no relevance if repartitioning is applied.

Mesh Partitioning. This strategy focuses on partitioning an image along all directions. Thus the largest theoretical scalability is achieved, since the maximum number of partitions is only limited by the total number of pixels. Its main disadvantage is the occurrence of boundaries in all directions. In our case this drawback is quite severe, since the performance of certain operations lives on their separability property.

A special case of mesh partitioning is cube-like partitioning. Thereby an image is partitioned in such a way, that the sum of all partition boundaries is minimized. Obviously this partition strategy should be used when it comes to the exchange of boundary information.

4 Parallelization Details

Module 1: Gaussian Convolution. The Gaussian convolution is implemented exploiting separability and symmetry as well as optimizing the computational sequence for optimal cache use. The convolution masks are obtained by sampling the continuous function and truncate it at 3 times the standard deviation. Then the masks are renormalized such that its weight sum up to 1. In our approach the repartitioning strategy is used in combination with slice partitioning. Thus, Gaussian convolution in two out of three directions can be performed without communication effort. Only smoothing in the third direction requires a previous repartitioning step. Moreover, this implementation allows large values for the standard deviation σ, since no boundary exchange takes place.

Module 2: Derivatives and Diffusivity. Derivatives within the diffusivity are computed using central differences. Since this uses stencils of type $\frac{1}{2h}(-1,0,1)$, where h denotes the grid size, the boundary size is limited to 1. Besides, the computation diffusivity values demands matching partitions for all derivatives. Both aspects put a boundary exchange strategy in an advantageous position here. Although cube-like partitioning would be desirable, a change of the partition model at the cost of two repartitioning steps is obviously not profitable. Hence, slice partitioning combined with boundary communication is implemented. After the exchange of neighborhood information, the derivatives are computed sequentially for each direction. This can be done since parallelism is achieved via image partitioning. Finally the diffusivity values are computed based on

$$g(|\nabla u_\sigma^2|) := \frac{1}{1 + |\nabla u_\sigma^2|/\lambda^2} \tag{5}$$

where λ is a contrast parameter.

Module 3: Diffusion and AOS. As discussed before, AOS offers parallelism on two different levels. First, it allows to decouple the diffusion processes for each direction (coarse grain parallelism). For the same reason as in the case of the derivative computation, this property will not be exploited for parallelization purposes. Of major importance is the fact, that the huge linear tridiagonal equation systems for each diffusion direction can be decomposed into many small independent equation systems of same style (mid grain parallelism). Since each of these systems corresponds to the diffusion process along a complete image line in the diffusion direction, the use of a common boundary exchange approach makes no sense. Instead slice partitioning in combination with the repartitioning strategy seems desirable. Moreover, this implementation allows the application of fast sequential solvers such as the Thomas algorithm. It uses an LR decomposition, a forward substitution as well as a backward substitution step. Thus, special variants for a boundary exchange strategy could not have been developed without loss of parallelism and performance. However, even in the case of repartitioning the parallelization effort is large: In order to compute the diffusion process for one direction matching partitions for the original image *and* the diffusivity values are required. Therefore, not only the original image has to be repartitioned, but also the corresponding diffusivity data prior to computing the third diffusion direction. Finally combining the results of all three diffusion processes – the averaging step in the AOS scheme – requires a third repartitioning.

5 Results

Our test runs have been performed on the Score III cluster of the *RWCP* (Real World Computing Partnership) at the Tsukuba Research Center, Japan. Running a modified Linux 2.4 SMP Kernel it consists of 524 nodes with two PIII 933 MHz processors each. Focusing on distributed memory systems only one processor per node has been used at a time. The cluster is fully connected to a CLOS network using a Myrinet2000 network interface. Due to its performance it is ranked 40th in the last TOP 500 list of supercomputers.

As one can see from Figure 1 considerations regarding the parallelization for a specific network architecture do pay off. The obtained results demonstrate an excellent, almost linear scaling behavior up to 256 nodes with a top speedup of 209. This equals 82% of the theoretical maximum. The corresponding runtimes divided in computation and communication effort can be found in Table 1. For all test runs a 32-bit float data cube of size $256 \times 256 \times 128$ has been used resulting in communication volumes up to 1.83 Gbyte per second. These numbers show

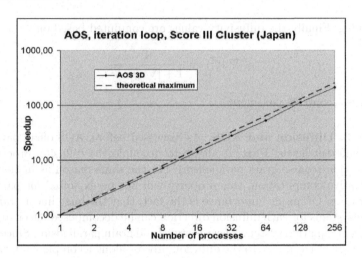

Fig. 1. Speedup Chart

Table 1. Runtimes for AOS 3-D , 10 iterations

Processors	1	2	4	8	16	32	64	128	256
Runtime [s]	212.741	114.625	57.534	29.401	15.065	7.731	4.029	1.894	1.017
Computation [s]	212.741	106.205	52.221	26.123	13.471	6.753	3.333	1.550	0.745
Communication [s]	0.000	8.420	5.313	3.278	1.594	0.978	0.696	0.344	0.272
Computation [%]	100.000	92.654	90.766	88.851	89.420	87.350	82.725	81.837	73.255
Communication [%]	0.000	7.346	9.234	11.149	10.580	12.650	17.275	18.163	26.745

the importance of a sophisticated algorithm design that allows bandwith scaling up to a large number of processors.

This scaling property is reflected in the percental distribution below, that shows only a moderate increase of the communication part. Even in the case of 256 processors this ratio does hardly exceed one quarter of the runtime.

6   Summary and Conclusions

The goal of this paper was to show how to design algorithms for high performance cluster systems. This was done by the example of nonlinear isotropic diffusion. Based on an AOS scheme we first performed a decomposition into modules. Then parallelization strategies suitable for a high performance low latency network were discussed. We saw that in this case a repartitioning approach is favorable for the majority of operations. Moreover, we noticed that this strategy should be combined with slice partitioning for optimal performance. Test runs with our implementation on a high end cluster system yielded speedup factors of up to 209 for 256 nodes, proving its excellent scalability.

Fig. 2. *From left to right:* (a) Test image with grey scale range $[0, 255]$ degraded by Gaussian noise with standard deviation $\sigma_n = 30$. (b) Image denoised by nonlinear isotropic diffusion filter, 5 iterations with $\sigma = 2.5$, $\lambda = 0.01$ and $\tau = 20$.

Acknowledgement

Our research has been partly funded by the *Deutsche Forschungsgemeinschaft (DFG)* under the project SCHN 457/4-1.

References

1. F. Catté, P.-L. Lions, J.-M. Morel, and T. Coll. Image selective smoothing and edge detection by nonlinear diffusion. *SIAM Journal on Numerical Analysis*, 32:1895–1909, 1992.
2. J. Heers, C. Schnörr, and H.-S. Stiehl. Investigation of parallel and globally convergent iterative schemes for nonlinear variational image smoothing and segmentation. In *Proc. 1998 IEEE International Conference on Image Processing*, volume 3, pages 279–283, Chicago, IL, Oct. 1998.
3. Z. Krivá and K. Mikula. An adaptive finite volume scheme for solving nonlinear diffusion equations in image processing. *Journal of Visual Communication and Image Representation*, 13(1/2):22–35, 2002.
4. T. Lu, P. Neittaanmäki, and X.-C. Tai. A parallel splitting up method and its application to Navier–Stokes equations. *Applied Mathematics Letters*, 4(2):25–29, 1991.
5. P. Perona and J. Malik. Scale space and edge detection using anisotropic diffusion. *IEEE Transactions on Pattern Analysis and Machine Intelligence*, 12:629–639, 1990.
6. M. Rumpf and R. Strzodka. Nonlinear diffusion in graphics hardware. In *Proc. Joint Eurographics – IEEE TCVG Symposium on Visualization*, Ascona, Switzerland, May 2001.
7. J. Weickert. *Anisotropic Diffusion in Image Processing*. Teubner, Stuttgart, 1998.
8. J. Weickert, B. M. ter Haar Romeny, and M. A. Viergever. Efficient and reliable schemes for nonlinear diffusion filtering. *IEEE Transactions on Image Processing*, 7(3):398–410, Mar. 1998.
9. J. Weickert, K. J. Zuiderveld, B. M. ter Haar Romeny, and W. J. Niessen. Parallel implementations of AOS schemes: A fast way of nonlinear diffusion filtering. In *Proc. 1997 IEEE International Conference on Image Processing*, volume 3, pages 396–399, Santa Barbara, CA, Oct. 1997.

Hierarchical Primitives Based Contour Matching

Xiaofeng Zhang[1] and Hans Burkhardt[2]

[1] Orbotech-Schuh GmbH Co. & KG, Bad Pyrmont, D-31812, Germany,
xiaofeng-z@orbotech.com,
[2] Chair of Pattern Recognition and Image Processing, Institute of Computer Science,
Faculty of Applied Science, Albert-Ludwigs-University, Freiburg, Germany
http://lmb.informatik.uni-freiburg.de

Abstract. An algorithm for contour matching is presented in this paper. It is implemented in two steps: firstly, bottom-up, corners are matched, the matched corner points guide line segment matching, and then the matched line segments guide contour matching. Line segments are grouped with the signature function defined in [10] from the extracted contours of image pairs. Secondly, top-down, with the computed signature functions of the matched contours, the contour points are corresponded by modifying the initial matching from line segments.

The novelty of our approach is that (1) features are incorporated, and the matching is implemented in two steps (bottom-up and top-down), thus dense correspondences along contours are acquired. Disadvantages such as the sparseness from only point correspondences, the inaccuracies from only line correspondences, and feature loss of correspondences along epipolar lines are avoided; (2) unlike the conventional way of matching along epipolar lines after rectification, signature functions developed in [10] are used to characterize the contours so that the matching is implemented along contours.

1 Introduction

An initial step, that is very important but difficult, in the reconstruction of 3D points in scenes is to identify the points through the frames of an image sequence, which correspond to the same physical points[8]. This is known as the *matching* or *correspondence problem*, i.e. given a token in image 1, what is its counterpart in image 2 [7] [4]? There are generally several possibilities for the choice of the corresponding tokens in the second image. So this is an ambiguous problem, which results in a number of questions concerning the selection of tokens, features and their constraints [4].

The tokens have to be reliably extracted from images. They can be pixels or edge pixels grouped to form different primitives like corner points, straight line segments and contours. These primitives are related to each other. It can be observed that corner points are usually the endpoints of line segments, line segments are some partitions of contours. Contours are an integration of the former two primitives and other irregular edges. Physically they are hierarchically correlated from point primitives (bottom level), line segments (middle level) to

L. Van Gool (Ed.): DAGM 2002, LNCS 2449, pp. 298–305, 2002.

contour primitives (high level). The higher the level, the richer the information they convey. As we move up in the hierarchy of these primitives, the regions containing the primitives get bigger and bigger. Therefore the higher the level, the more global the primitives.

Although the correspondence problem is inherently an ill-posed [7] or ill-defined [8] problem because of its ambiguity and uncertainty, great efforts have been taken and are still being taken to tackle the most challenging task in the photogrammetry and computer vision society. Many algorithms for the point matching [11], line segment matching [8] [2] and contour matching [5] have been developed. On the basis of these researches, we are inspired to develop a new method for contour matching.

In the next section, the hierarchical primitives, from corner points through line segments to contours and their relations, are addressed. Then in section 3 the two-step implementation mentioned above is presented in detail. Section 4 describes an experiment to demonstrate the functionality of the algorithm.

2   Hierarchical Primitives

2.1   Corners

Corners can be restrictively described as the junction of two homogeneous regions separated by a high-curvature boundary. They can be detected by the analysis of binary edge maps, from which chain codes are extracted in order to find high curvature points [3]. However, most techniques work directly at the image intensity level by defining a corner strength from local measurements in an image, e.g. Harris corner strength[6] and SUSAN (Smallest Univalue Segmentation Assimilating Nucleus) corner detector [9]

2.2   Line Segments

A line segment is a part of straight line with two ends. A straight line can be defined as $\rho = x \cos \theta + y \sin \theta$ with parameter ρ, θ. So a line segment can be represented by the analytical parameters ρ, θ or position parameters, end points (x_a, y_a) and (x_b, y_b) or the dimensional parameter, length l[2].

When a contour is from a polygonal object in an image, its points are well linear arranged and can be grouped and fitted accurately to line segments. But between the neighboring line segments there are turning points on contour, which are found out by our grouping algorithm as the separating points of groups along the contour. These points, corresponding to the variation of curvature, are where the slope changes as indicated by our signature function[10]. Because the detection of a corner with either the binary map or the brightness comparison is both from the high curvature of boundary, these turning points, or end points of neighboring line segments or corners of boundary should theoretically be in a small local region. In this way, the line segments for this part of a contour can be regarded as hinged together in the small region (see Fig. 1(b)). The test image designed in [9] is used to demonstrate the hinge relation of ends of line segments and corners, more details are shown in [10].

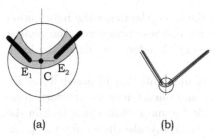

Fig. 1. neighboring line segments are hinged together (a) their hinge area including a corner point and two ends of these line segments (b) two neighboring line segments

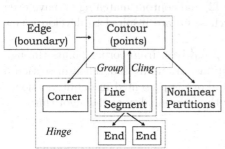

Fig. 2. Contour hierarchy: an edge is extracted and abstracted as a contour, which is separated into line segments and nonlinear partitions that hinge together. The ends of line segments and detected corners form a hinge region. Line segments are grouped from the contour points and cling to the contour.

2.3 Contours

A contour $\mathcal{C}$ with points P_i, $i = 1, \ldots, M$, is represented as

$$
\begin{aligned}
\mathcal{C} &= \{P_i, i = 1, \ldots, M\} \\
&= \{\text{grouped } \{P_k\}_{l_i}, l_i = 1, \ldots, m\} \cup \{\text{ungrouped } \{P_l\}_{l_j}\ l_j = 1, \ldots, n\} \\
&= \{\text{fitted line segment } L_{l_i}, l_i = 1, \ldots, m\} \cup \{\text{nonlinear } \{P_l\}_{l_j}\ l_j = 1, \ldots, n\}
\end{aligned}
$$

where $\{P_k\}_{l_i}$ is grouped into L_{l_i}, L_{l_i} cling to $\mathcal{C}$.

Thus a contour is related hierarchically downwards to the primitives, corners and line segments, as illustrated in Fig. 2.

3   Hierarchical Matching

3.1   Point Matching

This can be implemented by some software in the public domain, e.g. [12].

3.2   Line Matching Guided by Matched Points

The problem is stated as in Table 1.

Hinge Region Constraint. As already stated, in theory corners are almost hinge points of line segments. In practice they are in the hinge region of line segments.

Table 1.

given	(1)$\mathcal{P}_l = \{(x_{li}, y_{li})\}$ and $\mathcal{P}_r = \{(x_{ri}, y_{ri})\}$, $(i = 1, \ldots, n)$ are point sets extracted in the left and right image respectively, and $(x_{li}, y_{li}) \leftrightarrow (x_{ri}, y_{ri})$, both correspond to each other.
	(2) $\mathcal{L}_l = \{l_{lj}, j = 1, \ldots, N_l\}$ and $\mathcal{L}_r = \{l_{rj}, j = 1, \ldots, N_r\}$ are the sets of extracted line segments for an image pair. l is a vector composed of the parameters of the line segment.
find	line correspondence $l_{lk} \leftrightarrow l_{rk}, k = 1, \ldots, m, m \leq \min (N_l, N_r)$

When taking a pair of line segments in an image pair, the end points of the line segments can be checked to see if they are in the vicinity of a pair of matched corner points. Three cases, matched points at both ends or matched points at one of ends, are described in [10]. A difficulty in this process is the selection of a range around the corner. According to the SUSAN algorithm [9], the search range is chosen as a radius of 3.4 pixels around an end point, because the corner is found in such a circular mask by an optimization of the curvature along the contour in this region.

Supplemental Constraints. Now that we have a set of candidate correspondences of line segments, we must find some further constraints to determine the correct matching line segments between two images. Some criteria like similarity constraints from [2], intensity difference constraint and contour context constraint are supplied to make further matching.

Some Results In Fig. 3, guided by matched corner points, with the hinge region constraint, supplemented by similarity and intensity constraint, the line segments are matched.

3.3   Contour Matching Guided by Matched Line Segments

Contour Matching. Using the constraints presented in the previous sections, line segments grouped from contour tokens have been matched. The contour tokens, to which the matched line segments cling, are then considered matched.

Contour Points Matching. The problem is stated in Table 2.

Because the clues are matched line segments that cling to both contours, i.e. we have already the matching $\{L_{l_i}^1, l_i = 1, \ldots, m_1^1\} \iff \{L_{l_i}^2, l_i = 1, \ldots, m_1^2\}$, this method is thus called line segments guided contour matching.

Contour is a kind of 2D image primitive. The signature function described in [10] can be used to change the 2D characteristics of a contour into that of a

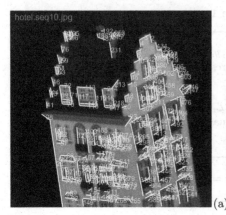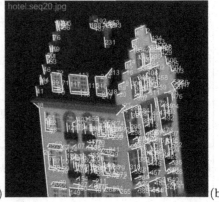

Fig. 3. Line segment matching guided by matched points for two frames (a)(b) from an image sequence

Table 2.

given	Suppose $\mathcal{C}^1$ and $\mathcal{C}^2$ are two contours (1) $\mathcal{C}^1 = \{\text{matched } L^1_{l_i}, l_i = 1, \ldots, m^1_1\} \cup \{\text{unmatched } L^1_{l_i}, l_i = 1, \ldots, m^1_2\}$ $\cup \{\text{ungrouped } \{P^1_{l_j}\} \ l_j = 1, \ldots, n^1\}$ (2) $\mathcal{C}^2 = \{\text{matched } L^2_{l_i}, l_i = 1, \ldots, m^2_1\} \cup \{\text{unmatched } L^2_{l_i}, l_i = 1, \ldots, m^2_2\}$ $\cup \{\text{ungrouped } \{P^2_{l_j}\} \ l_j = 1, \ldots, n^2\}$ (3) $\mathcal{C}^1 \Longleftrightarrow \mathcal{C}^2$, i.e. $\mathcal{C}^1$ and $\mathcal{C}^2$ are matched.
find	$\mathcal{C}^1 = \{P^{m_1}_i, i = 1, \ldots, N_m\} \cup \{P^1_i, l_i = 1, \ldots, M - N_m\}$, $\mathcal{C}^2 = \{P^{m_2}_j, j = 1, \ldots, N_m\} \cup \{P^2_j, l_j = 1, \ldots, N - N_m\}$, such that $\{P^{m_1}_i, i = 1, \ldots, N_m\} \Longleftrightarrow \{P^{m_2}_j, j = 1, \ldots, N_m\}$, i.e. points are matched.

1D function, with the points along the contour as the function argument. The behaviors of the signature functions for contours at the left and right image are similar, although they are not always exactly positioned. Matching points on contours can be converted to a comparison of two 1D signature functions of both contours. The point-to-point corresponding along signature function is implemented initially by referring the points, where a pair of matched line segments aligned and ends of both line segments are matched. More exact reference points are found by the cross-correlation of the 1D signature functions. For those that are from nonlinear partitions, this matching is implemented by extrapolating. The detail description of this algorithm can be found in [10].

4   Experiment

The images in our experiment are two frames of an image sequence from [1]. The perspective distortions among these frames are neglected because short intervals between neighoring frames. The line segments in both images are extracted with the algorithms described in [10]. They are matched hierarchically under the guidance of the matched points (as in section 3.1 and 3.2), and then the contours of both images are matched guided by the matched line segments as seen in section 3.3. With the algorithm of signature function in [10], the points on the matched contours in both images are matched and shown in Fig. 4. In (a) the matched points between both images are indicated by the motion of points on the contours of the image (the motion is indicated by *green* line segments connecting the points on contours of both images, every five points apart along contours), the homogeneity of the overall motion trend and the continuities along contours signify that the matches are almost all correct. The underlying line segments are found to be correctly matched with those in Fig. 4(b). Notice that in the figure the colored numbers with *light blue* in both graphs stand for contour numbers in both images, the black numbers are the grouped line segments from the contours they cling to. The black numbers on the both images are consistent. This indicates that the correspondences of line segments are successful.

To demonstrate more clearly our contour points matching, in Fig. 5(a) a pair of matched contours and their matched points are shown simultaneously (dots and circles indicate the contour points on different contours). More successful examples, closed and open contours, are found in [10].

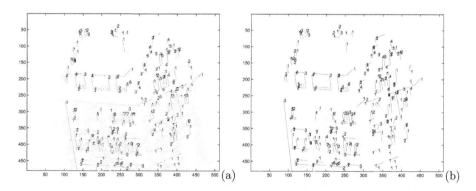

Fig. 4. Line segment guided contour point matching, (a) contours in one image and their point correspondences with underlying line segments. Line segments marked in *red* (*deep grey* if printed in black and white) are in the current image, line segments marked with *green* (*light grey*) dashes belong to another image. (b) contours, represented with *light blue* (*light grey*) color number, in another image and line segments, drawn in *red* (*dark*), grouped from these contours.

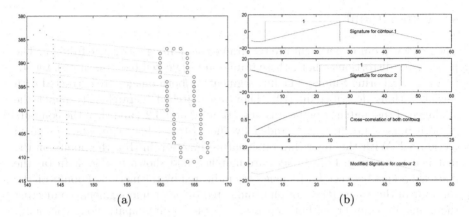

(a)   (b)

Fig. 5. (a) A pair of matched contours from two images (indicated by dots and circles respectively). The *light blue* (*grey* if printed in black and white) dashed lines are the grouped line segments from corresponding partitions of both contours. *Green* (*grey* dotted) line segments indicate the correspondences every five points along the contours. (b) Signature functions of both contours and determination of correspondence from them. The top two subgraphs are the signature functions of both contours. The partitions of the matched line segments are illustrated with *green* (*grey* dotted) line segments, from which the initial corresponding references are acquired. The third subgraph is the cross-correlation around the initially determined corresponding reference point. An exact corresponding reference will be found from the maximum of the cross-correlation. The bottom graph is the modified signature with the determined exact corresponding reference. Along the signature for contour 1 and the modified signature for contour 2 the contour points along the contours are corresponded.

5   Conclusions

In this paper we have presented a hierarchical primitive matching approach. The hierarchy of primitives consists of corner points, line segments and contours. Their relations are that: corners are approximately the hinge points between line segments, line segments cling to contours; contours consist of line segments, line segments have two ends. In the light of these relations, bottom-up, line segments can be matched on the basis of the matched corner points plus some supplementary constraints for line segments. Contours can then be matched by the matched line segments that cling to them. With the matched contours, top-down, the contour signature functions are computed, contour points are corresponded initially guided by the line segments that cling to them, then modified by the cross-correlation of signature functions. Experiments on the real images have been used to demonstrate the process, the results show that the matching is successful.

References

1. Image Database Carnegie-Mellon. *CMU/VASC Image Database.* World Wide Web, http://www.IUS.cs.cmu.edu/idb/html/motion/index.html, July, 1997. Last modified August 26, 2000.
2. Yuh-Lin Chang and J. K. Aggarwal. Line correspondences from cooperating spatial and temporal grouping processes for a sequence of images. In *Computer Vision and Image Understanding*, volume 67, No.2, 1997.
3. R. Deriche and O. D. Faugeras. 2d curve matching using high curvature points. In *Proc. of the 10th IAPR*, 1990.
4. Oliver Faugeras. *Three-Dimensional Computer Vision, A Geometric Viewpoint.* The MIT Press, 1996.
5. Joon Hee Han and Jong Seung Park. Contour matching using epipolar geometry. In *IEEE Trans. on PAMI*, volume 22, No. 4, April 2000.
6. C. Harris and M. Stephens. A combined corner and edge detector. In *Proc. of 4th Alvey Vision Conference*, 1988.
7. Christian Heipke. Overview of image matching techniques. In *OEEPE, Workshop on the Application of Digital Photogrammetric Workstations*, Lausanne, March 4-6 1996.
8. Jams H. McIntosh and Kathleen M. Mutch. Matching straight lines. In *Computer Vision, Graphics, and Image Processing*, volume 43, 1986.
9. S.M. Smith and J. M. Brady. Susan - a new approach to low level image processing. In *Int. Journal of Computer Vision, also Technical Report TR95SMS1c*, 1997.
10. X.-F. Zhang. Feature Based 3D Reconstruction of Man-made Scenes from Image Sequences. In *Ph. D Thesis, University of Freiburg*, Freiburg im Breisgau, Dec. 2001; ISBN 3-8322-0203-X, Shaker Verlag, Aachen 2002.
11. Z. Zhang, R. Deriche, O. Faugeras, and Q.-T. Luong. A robust technique for matching two uncalibrated images through the recovery of the unknown epipolar geometry. In *Artificial Intelligence Journal*, volume 78, October 1995. Also Technical Report No.2273, Inria Sophia-antipolis, also in Proc. 3rd Int. Conf. Automation Robotics Computer Vision, Singapore, Nov. 1994.
12. Zhengyou Zhang. *Software Image-Matching.* World Wide Web, http://www-sop.inria.fr/robotvis/personnel/zzhang/softwares.html.

Application of the Tensor Voting Technique for Perceptual Grouping to Grey-Level Images

Amin Massad, Martin Babós, and Bärbel Mertsching*

University of Hamburg, Dept. of Computer Science, IMA-Lab,
Vogt-Kölln-Str. 30, D-22527 Hamburg, Germany,
massad@informatik.uni-hamburg.de

Abstract. We show how the perceptual grouping method known as *tensor voting* can be applied to grey-level images by introducing the use of local orientation tensors computed from a set of Gabor filters. While inputs formerly consisted of binary images or sparse edgel maps, our extension yields oriented input tokens and the locations of junctions as input to the perceptual grouping. In order to handle dense input maps, the tensor voting framework is extended by the introduction of grouping fields with inhibitory regions. Results of the method are demonstrated on example images.

1 Motivation

The presence of perceptual grouping mechanisms in biological vision systems has been predicted by Gestalt theory and confirmed by several psychological studies (surveyed in [5,7]). These findings motivated the development of computational solutions (e. g. [12,13,14,16]) which seek a transition from local low-level features to more global high-level information, basically by the aggregation of low-level image features into lines, regions and surfaces. Among these techniques, we focus on the tensor voting (TV) approach introduced by [10], which has successfully been applied to different early vision problems. From a conceptual point of view, this method benefits from the simultaneous encoding of orientation and orientation uncertainty achieved by the use of tensor tokens – in contrast to other methods which are vector-based (e. g. [3,11,16]). Another advantage is the linearity of the method and its similarity to a convolution operation, hence computation does not involve iterative processing as required in other optimization-like approaches.

The input to TV in the 2-D domain so far only consisted of binary images or edgel maps (Sect. 2) – note that [4] reports the use of color images as input which is not applicable here because inputs with clearly separable color surfaces in RGB-space are required. Here, we introduce an extension to apply the method to grey-level images and camera images (Sect. 5). It is based on the local orientation tensor computed from a set of Gabor filters (Sect. 3) which naturally

---

* We gratefully acknowledge partial funding of this work by the Deutsche Forschungsgemeinschaft under grant Me1289/7-1 "KomForm".

L. Van Gool (Ed.): DAGM 2002, LNCS 2449, pp. 306–314, 2002.

extends the TV approach from input tokens to the use on images. As the method not only provides input with orientation information (similar to edgels) but also information about junctions, we discuss how this new information can be embedded into the framework. This paper focusses on the description of the proposed extension to the TV method. An investigation of a quantitative measure for the quality of the grouping results will be the topic of a follow-up paper.

2 Review of the Tensor Voting Technique

In [10], Medioni et al. describe a framework for grouping and segmentation called tensor voting which belongs to the class of perceptual saliency theories. It is based on the use of symmetric tensors as input and output tokens. The advantage of tensors over a vector representation is their ability to encode local image features as orientation and orientation uncertainty. In the 2D-case, a tensor over $\mathbb{R}^2$ can be denoted by a symmetric 2×2 matrix T with two perpendicular eigenvectors e_1, e_2 and two corresponding real eigenvalues $\lambda_1 > \lambda_2$. Depending on the eigenvalues, the points $x \in \mathbb{R}^2$, which satisfy the equation $x^\top T x = c$ for a constant c, give rise to three different interpretations: (1) If $\lambda_1 = \lambda_2$, the tensor corresponds to a circle and hence represents a region with high orientation uncertainty, i. e. a junction. (2) If $\lambda_2 = 0$, all points coincide with the first eigenvector, which is the case for high orientation certainty and thus a curve element in direction of e_1. (3) If $\lambda_1 > 0$ and $\lambda_2 > 0$, the equation corresponds to an ellipse, i. e. a case in between a junction and a curve.

Accordingly, the definition of saliency measures is deducted from the following decomposition of a tensor into $T = \lambda_1 e_1 e_1^\top + \lambda_2 e_2 e_2^\top$ or equivalently $T = (\lambda_1 - \lambda_2) e_1 e_1^\top + \lambda_2 (e_1 e_1^\top + e_2 e_2^\top)$. Then, the weighting factor $(\lambda_1 - \lambda_2)$ represents an orientation in the direction of the eigenvector e_1 and thus will be called *curve-* or *stick-saliency*. The second weight λ_2 is applied to a circle, hence we call it *junction-* or *ball-saliency* as its information about multiple orientations measures the confidence in the presence of a junction. As illustrated in Fig. 1a,

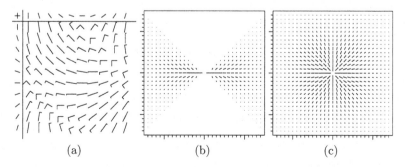

(a)   (b)   (c)

Fig. 1. (a) Tensor addition: The tensors are depicted by $\lambda_1 e_1 \perp \lambda_2 e_2$. (b) Stick-voting field. (c) Ball-voting field.

the tensor addition of similarly oriented tensors yields an increased stick-saliency whereas differently oriented tensors yield a high ball-saliency.

Grouping can now be formulated as the combination of elements according to their stick-saliency or ball-saliency. In stick-voting, for each oriented input token the stick-voting-field (Fig. 1b) is aligned to the eigenvector e_1 and weighted with $\lambda_1 - \lambda_2$. All fields are combined in a convolution-like manner by tensor addition. The field is designed to create groupings with neighboring tokens which fulfill the minimal curvature constraint. Thus, stick-voting strengthens locally collinear or co-circular structures and also infers virtual contours over gaps in the image data. Ball-voting is applied to locations for which an orientation is initially unknown. Hence, the field consists of radially aligned tensors (Fig. 1c) whose strength decays with distance from the center. This inference of orientation is usually applied as a preliminary step on sparse point data before stick-voting can be employed.

3   Computation of Input Tensors from Local Orientation

We use an approach similar to [2] for the computation of a tensor description from image data suitable as input to the TV technique. The responses of spherically separable directed quadrature filters are combined for each image location into a single representation by tensor addition. In contrast to [2], we apply two-dimensional Gabor filters for their known optimality with regards to the time-bandwidth product: $g(k) = K \exp\left(-\frac{1}{2}(k - k_0)^\top D(k - k_0)\right)$ where k denotes the frequency, K a normalization constant and D a 2×2 covariance matrix. The function describes a two-dimensional Gaussian centered around k_0 with variances σ_1^2, σ_2^2 as the eigenvalues of D. The parameters k_0, σ_1, σ_2 are chosen to give a good covering of the frequency plane by overlapping the filter bands at half of their maximal value. Here, we set $\|k_0\| = 0.8 \cdot k_{max}$ where k_{max} is the largest possible wave number in the image. Although the minimal number of filter bands needed is three [6], we use six bands as a compromise between orientation precision and computational effort.

Note that for a simple neighborhood with intensity variations only along one direction n, the transformation to the frequency domain yields elements different from zero only on a line with direction k_n, with $k_n \perp n$.

The response $g_i(x)$ of Gabor filter i, with the center frequency $k_{0,i}$ at image position x, is a measure for orientation certainty in the direction of that filter. We introduce the orientation tensor $T_i = e_i e_i^\top$, which represents an ideal orientation in the direction of the unit vector e_i perpendicular to $k_{0,i}$. By weighting T_i with $g_i(x)$ and summing over all i, the resulting tensor $T(x) = \sum_{i=1}^{n} g_i(x) T_i$ gives an estimate for the local orientation and orientation uncertainty at image position x. Figure 2b shows the tensors which result from applying this procedure to the image 2a, where the eigenvectors of the tensors multiplied by the corresponding eigenvalues are depicted.

The voting field has to be large enough to facilitate the inference of image features larger than the Gabor kernel size. As suggested by experiments in [1],

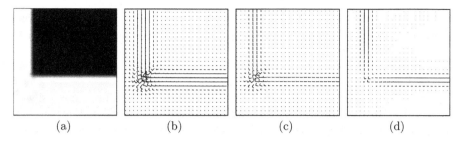

(a)   (b)   (c)   (d)

Fig. 2. Results on an ideal corner (a): The local orientation tensors from the Gabor transform (b) are refined by successive application of the inhibitory stick-field (c) and of the inhibitory ball-field (d).

the relation we use between voting field size σ_v and Gabor kernel size σ_g is $\sigma_v/\sigma_g = 6$.

4 Voting Fields with Inhibition

The voting field reviewed in Sect. 2 is designed to group m-D structures in n-D input space with $m < n$ (i. e. lines and points in 2-D space). However, with the method described in Sect. 3, for 0-D or 1-D image structures we get input tensors extending over regions due to the localization uncertainty of Gabor filters. In order to compensate for this blurring effect and to fit the input tokens better to the model of the voting field design, we propose to apply a non-maximum suppression method to the local orientation tensors prior to the grouping process. We can smoothly embed this thinning step into the TV framework by the introduction of inhibitory voting fields: Figure 3a shows that the excitatory stick-voting field developed by [10] is limited to the region F_+ and leaves out the region F_- with $\frac{\pi}{4} \leq \theta \leq \frac{3}{4}\pi$. All these points Q within F_- are excluded from excitatory grouping because the assumed circular connection with an *oriented* input token at P does not fulfill the minimal total curvature constraint (an elliptic connection would yield lower total curvature).

We define the inhibitory voting field (Fig. 3b) based on exactly these complementary positions F_-, which have previously been ignored in the grouping process. This newly defined field achieves edge thinning by suppressing orientations which are approximately parallel to an oriented input token P and have lower saliencies $sal(Q) < sal(P)$, as shown in Fig. 2c. Because non-maxima locations are assumed to lie perpendicular to the orientation of P, inhibition should be strongest at angles $\theta \approx \frac{\pi}{2}$ where $Q \parallel P$ and decrease to zero towards the two extremal cases along the circle $\theta \approx \frac{\pi}{4}$ and $\theta \approx \frac{3}{4}\pi$ where $Q \perp P$. Hence, the strength of the inhibition is defined as

$$
F_-(r,\theta) = \begin{cases} sal(P) \cdot \left(e^{-\frac{1}{2}\frac{r^2}{\sigma_1^2}} - e^{-\frac{1}{2}\frac{r^2}{\sigma_2^2}} \right) \cdot \cos^8(\theta) & \text{if } \frac{\pi}{4} \leq |\theta| \leq \frac{3}{4}\pi \\ 0 & \text{else} \end{cases}
$$

which is an adaptation of the formula by [3] overlaid with a difference of Gaussians (with $\sigma_1 > \sigma_2$ to model an off-surround behavior, while the on-center part consists of the excitatory field). The orientations $e(r, \theta)$ of the field tokens are defined by the normalized tangent vectors of the circles cotangent to P and encoded as stick-tensors $T = F_-(r, \theta) \cdot ee^\top$.

In analogy with excitatory fields, the inhibitory ball field for a non-oriented input token results from the rotation of the inhibitory stick-field about the center (Fig. 3c). The application of this field reduces orientation uncertainty in the vicinity of high ball-saliencies. As demonstrated in Fig. 2d, the region with blurred ball-saliencies is sharpened while stick-saliencies are strengthened near the corner.

Note that inhibitory grouping should not be performed simultaneously with excitatory grouping, but rather as a preceding step. Otherwise, non-suppressed non-maxima would create excitation spreading outside the boundaries of the cone covered by F_-, i.e. excitation which cannot be inhibited (see Q' in Fig. 3a).

Given a tensor $T = \lambda_1 e_1 e_1^\top + \lambda_2 e_2 e_2^\top$ from the input map and an inhibitory tensor $T^- = \lambda_1^- e_1^- e_1^{-\top} + \lambda_2^- e_2^- e_2^{-\top}$, we define the subtraction $T' = T \ominus T^-$ as $T' := \lambda_1' e_1 e_1^\top + \lambda_2' e_2 e_2^\top$ with the same eigenvectors as T and new eigenvalues

$$(\lambda_1', \lambda_2') := \begin{cases} (\lambda_1 - d_1, \lambda_2) & \text{if } |e_1 e_1^-| > |e_2 e_1^-| \\ (\lambda_1 - d_2, \lambda_2 - d_2) & \text{else} \end{cases}$$

which results in a reduced stick-saliency in the first case, where e_1^- and e_1 are oriented similarly, and in a reduced ball-saliency in the second case, where e_1^- is closer to the direction of e_2. The saliencies subtracted result from projection of $\lambda_1^- e_1^-$ onto the nearest eigenvector of T and by clipping at the boundaries (zero stick-saliency or zero ball-saliency resp.): $d_1 := \min(|\lambda_1^- e_1^- e_1|, \lambda_1 - \lambda_2)$ and $d_2 := \min(|\lambda_1^- e_1^- e_2|, \lambda_2)$.

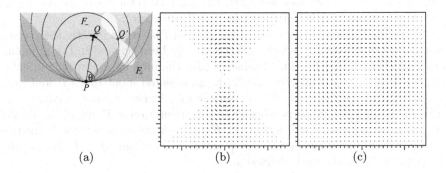

(a)   (b)   (c)

Fig. 3. Inhibitory voting field: (a) Construction deducted from the excitatory field definition (see text). Only the upper half is depicted, the lower part results from mirroring about the x-axis. (b) Inhibitory stick-field. (c) Inhibitory ball-field.

5   System Overview

Figure 4 shows an approach which extends TV to the application to grey-level images. Step (1) computes the local orientation tensors by combining the Gabor filter set responses (Sect. 3). In step (2), inhibitory followed by excitatory stick-voting is applied to the stick components of the tensor data in order to close gaps in the possibly disconnected contours extracted by Gabor filtering. Furthermore, stick voting results in a reduction of ball saliencies which have previously been located at gaps.

While step (1) yields candidates for junctions with higher positional precision than from grouping over larger regions, some of these locations could correspond to isolated points or endpoints at gaps. The junction candidates from step (2) result from grouping of larger contexts. Hence, they carry higher confidence in the presence of junctions in exchange for a reduced positional precision. Therefore, in step (3) we combine both saliencies into one refined ball saliency map.

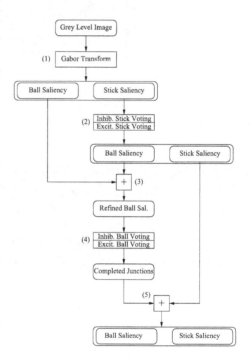

Generally, the stick saliency in the vicinity of junctions is diminished due to the overlap of different incoming orientations. To compensate for this effect, the gaps in the stick saliency map are closed by growing the incoming edge in the direction of the junction – already accomplished by step (2) – and simultaneously the junction towards the neighboring edges by application of an isotropic ball field to the junctions in step (4). The outcomes

Fig. 4. System overview

of both processes are combined in step (5) which yields results similar to the feature integration method by [15] but without the need to delete curve information around junctions.

The final output contains refined orientation certainty in the proximity of junctions while preserving locations with orientation discontinuities as shown in Fig. 2.

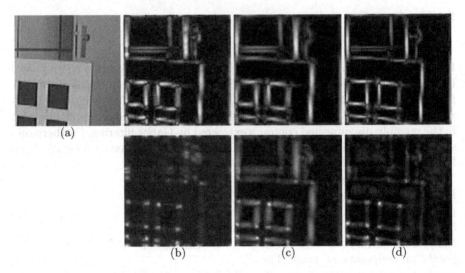

Fig. 5. Results on an indoor scene: (a) Input image, (b) stick-saliency (top) and ball-saliency (bottom) of Gabor responses, (c) stick- and ball-saliency with excitatory voting only, as in [9] , (d) stick- and ball-saliency from combination of inhibitory and excitatory voting.

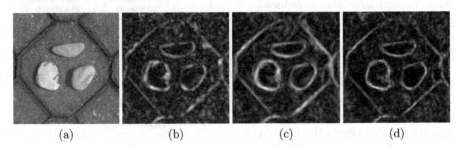

Fig. 6. Results on an natural scene: (a) Input image from [8], (b) stick-saliency of Gabor responses, (c) stick-saliency with excitatory voting only, as in [9], (d) stick-saliency from combination of inhibitory and excitatory voting.

6   Results

Figure 5 depicts the application of the technique described in Sect. 5 to a scene showing parts of a calibration pattern in front of an indoor background. The comparison of the different ball-saliencies reveals a reduction of the orientation uncertainty resulting from combined inhibitory and excitatory voting: high ball-saliencies are concentrated at locations of junctions and blurring parallel to lines is reduced significantly.

Although the application of Gabor filters may be sufficient to extract salient structures in this simple environment, Fig. 6b gives an example of an image where grouping is needed to infer structures beyond the size of a Gabor kernel in order to bridge gaps and compensate for considerably high noise.

Compared to the approach in [8], our approach infers salient structures without the incorporation of an edge detector, which hypothesizes step-edges, and by local operations only instead of considering global connections between all image features. Additionally, we require no further assumptions about the objects' geometry than good continuation and proximity.

7   Conclusion

We have shown that the combination of Gabor filtering and tensor voting robustly infers salient contours and junctions in grey-level images. For the extraction of edges from these saliency maps, a marching algorithm according to [10] can be applied in order to trace curves along the maximal saliencies. The extension of stick saliencies beyond junctions should be handled by the inclusion of end-stopped cells which is subject to further development.

Ongoing research deals with quantitative evaluations intended to measure positional precision of junctions and contours as well as to achieve a comparison measure to other grouping techniques.

References

1. D. Field, A. Hayes, and R. Hess. Contour integration by the human visual system: Evidence for a local association field. *Vision Research*, 33:173–193, 1993.
2. Gösta Granlund and Hans Knutsson. *Signal Processing for Computer Vision*. Kluwer Academic Press, 1995.
3. F. Heitger and R. von der Heydt. A computational model of neural contour processing: Figure-ground segregation and illusory contours. In *ICCV*, pages 32–40, 1993.
4. E. Kang and G. Medioni. Color image segmentation based on tensor voting. In *3rd Workshop on Perceptual Organization in Computer Vision (POCV'2001)*, 2001.
5. P. Kellman and T. Shipley. A theory of visual interpolation in object perception. *Cognitive Psychology*, 23:141–221, 1991.
6. H. Knutsson. *Filtering and Reconstruction in Image Processing*. PhD thesis, Linköping University, Sweden, 1982. Dissertation No. 88.
7. I. Kovacs. Gestalten of today: Early processing of visual contours and surfaces. *Behav. Brain Res.*, 82:1–11, 1996.
8. S. Mahamud, K. Thornber, and L. Williams. Segmentation of salient closed contours from real images. In *ICCV*, volume 2, pages 891–897, 1999.
9. A. Massad, M. Babos, and B. Mertsching. Perceptual grouping in grey level images by combination of gabor filtering and tensor voting. In *ICPR*, 2002.
10. G. Medioni, M. Lee, and C. Tang. *A Computational Framework for Segmentation and Grouping*. Elsevier, 2000.
11. M. Nitzberg and D. Mumford. The 2.1-D sketch. In *ICCV*, pages 138–144, 1990.
12. S. Sarkar and K. Boyer. Integration, inference, and managment of spatial information using bayesian networks: Perceptual organization. *PAMI*, 15:256–274, 1993.
13. E. Saund. Perceptual organization of occluding contours of opaque surfaces. *CVIU*, 76:70–82, 1999.
14. A. Sha'ashua and S. Ullman. Structural saliency: the detection of globally salient structures using a locally connected network. In *ICCV*, pages 312–327, 1998.
15. C. Tang and G. Medioni. Inferring integrated surface, curve, and junction description from sparse 3-D data sets. *PAMI*, 20:1206–1223, 1998.
16. K. Thornber and L. Williams. Analytic solution of stochastic completion fields. *Biol. Cybern.*, 75:141–151, 1996.

Combined Forward and Backward Anisotropic
Diffusion Filtering of Color Images

Bogdan Smolka*

Silesian University of Technology, Department of Automatic Control,
Akademicka 16 Str, 44-101 Gliwice, Poland,
bsmolka@ia.polsl.gliwice.pl

Abstract. In this paper a novel approach to the problem of edge preserving noise reduction in color images is proposed and evaluated. The new algorithm is based on the combined forward and backward anisotropic diffusion with incorporated time dependent cooling process. This method is able to efficiently remove image noise while preserving and even enhancing image edges. The proposed algorithm can be used as a first step of different techniques, which are based on color, shape and spatial location information.

1 Anisotropic Diffusion

Perona and Malik [3] formulate the anisotropic diffusion filter as a process that encourages intraregional smoothing, while inhibiting interregional denoising. The Perona-Malik (P-M) nonlinear diffusion equation is of the form [1-7,11] :

$$\frac{\partial}{\partial t} \mathbf{I}(x, y, t) = \nabla \left[c(x, y, t) \nabla \mathbf{I}(x, y, t) \right],\tag{1}$$

where $\mathbf{I}(x, y, t)$ denotes the color image pixel at position (x, y), t refers to time or iteration step in the discrete case and $c(x, y, t)$ is a monotonically decreasing conductivity function, dependent on the image gradient magnitude: $c(x, y, t) = f\left(||\nabla \mathbf{I}(x, y, t||\,|\right)$ such as :

$$c_1(x, y, t) = \exp \left\{ -\left(\frac{||\nabla \mathbf{I}(x, y, t)||}{\beta} \right)^2 \right\}, c_2(x, y, t) = \left\{ 1 + \left(\frac{||\nabla \mathbf{I}(x, y, t)|\,|}{\beta} \right)^2 \right\}^{-1},\tag{2}$$

which were introduced in the original paper of Perona and Malik [3]. The parameter β is a threshold value, which influences the anisotropic smoothing process. Adopting the notation $g = ||\nabla \mathbf{I}(x, y, t)||$, $s = g/\beta$, where $||\cdot||$ denotes the vector norm, we obtain following formulas for the conductivity functions: $c_1(x, y, t) = \exp\left(-s^2\right)$, $c_2(x, y, t) = 1/(1 + s^2)$. In order to simplify the whole scheme, it is helpful to define a flux function $\Phi(x, y, t) = c(x, y, t) ||\nabla \mathbf{I}(x, y, t)||$. With the flux function defined above, Eq. (1) can be rewritten as: $\frac{\partial}{\partial t} \mathbf{I}(x, y, t) = \nabla \Phi(x, y, t)$.

* This work was partially supported by KBN grant PBZ-KBN-040/P04/08

L. Van Gool (Ed.): DAGM 2002, LNCS 2449, pp. 314–320, 2002.

2   Discrete Implementation

Although not obvious from Eq. (1), the discrete implementation of the nonlinear aniso-tropic diffusion filter is straightforward. In one dimension, the gradient and divergence expressions reduce to derivatives:

$$\frac{\partial}{\partial t} I(x,t) = \frac{\partial}{\partial x} \left[c(x,t) \frac{\partial}{\partial x} I(x,t) \right].$$
(3)

Substituting discrete approximations for the derivatives and introducing the flow functions we get:

$$\frac{\partial}{\partial t} I(x,t) \approx \frac{\partial}{\partial x} \left\{ c(x,t) \frac{1}{\Delta x} \left[I\left(x + \frac{\Delta x}{2}, t\right) - I\left(x - \frac{\Delta x}{2}, t\right) \right] \right\} \approx$$

$$\approx \frac{1}{(\Delta x)^2} \left[c\left(x + \frac{\Delta x}{2}, t\right) (I(x + \Delta x, t) - I(x,t)) \right.$$

$$\left. - c\left(x - \frac{\Delta x}{2}, t\right) (I(x,t) - I(x - \Delta x, t)) \right].$$

The conductivity values $c(x + \frac{\Delta x}{2}, t)$ and $c(x - \frac{\Delta x}{2}, t)$ are easily computed by substituting the discrete approximation of the gradient :

$$c(x,t) \approx f\left(\frac{1}{\Delta x} \left| I\left(x + \frac{\Delta x}{2}, t\right) - I\left(x - \frac{\Delta x}{2}, t\right) \right| \right),$$

$$c\left(x + \frac{\Delta x}{2}, t\right) \approx f\left(\frac{1}{\Delta x} |I(x + \Delta x, t) - I(x,t)| \right),$$

$$c\left(x - \frac{\Delta x}{2}, t\right) \approx f\left(\frac{1}{\Delta x} |I(x,t) - I(x - \Delta x, t)| \right).$$

Introducing the notation:

$$c_R = c(x + \tfrac{\Delta x}{2}, t) \cdot \tfrac{1}{\Delta x^2}, \quad c_L = c(x - \tfrac{\Delta x}{2}, t) \cdot \tfrac{1}{\Delta x^2},$$

$$\nabla_R I(x,t) = I(x + \Delta x, t) - I(x,t); \quad \nabla_L I(x,t) = I(x - \Delta x, t) - I(x,t),$$

we obtain:

$$\frac{\partial}{\partial t} I(x,t) = c_L \cdot \nabla_L I(x,t) + c_R \cdot \nabla_R I(x,t) = \Phi_L + \Phi_R,$$

$$I(x, t + \Delta t) \approx I(x,t) + \Delta t \cdot \frac{\partial}{\partial t} I(x,t) = I(x,t) + \Phi_L + \Phi_R.$$

The 1-D discrete formulation of the diffusion process is straightforwardly extended to the 2-D case:

$$\frac{\partial}{\partial t} I(x,y,t) = \frac{\partial}{\partial x} \left[c(x,y,t) \cdot \frac{\partial}{\partial x} I(x,y,t) \right] + \frac{\partial}{\partial y} \left[c(x,y,t) \cdot \frac{\partial}{\partial y} I(x,y,t) \right] \approx$$

$$\approx \frac{1}{(\Delta x)^2} \left[\begin{array}{l} c\left(x + \frac{\Delta x}{2}, y, t\right) \cdot \left(I\left(x + \Delta x, y, t\right) - I\left(x, y, t\right)\right) + \\ -c\left(x - \frac{\Delta x}{2}, y, t\right) \cdot \left(I\left(x, y, t\right) - I\left(x - \Delta x, y, t\right)\right) \end{array} \right] +$$

$$+ \frac{1}{(\Delta y)^2} \left[\begin{array}{l} c\left(x, y + \frac{\Delta y}{2}, t\right) \cdot \left(I\left(x, y + \Delta y, t\right) - I\left(x, y, t\right)\right) + \\ -c\left(x, y - \frac{\Delta y}{2}, t\right) \cdot \left(I\left(x, y, t\right) - I\left(x, y - \Delta y, t\right)\right) \end{array} \right] =$$

$$= c_N(x, y, t) \cdot \nabla_N I(x, y, t) + c_S(x, y, t) \cdot \nabla_S I(x, y, t) + c_W(x, y, t) \cdot \nabla_W I(x, y, t) +$$

$$+ c_E(x, y, t) \cdot \nabla_E I(x, y, t) = \Phi_N + \Phi_S + \Phi_W + \Phi_E \,,$$

where

$$c_N = c(x, y + \tfrac{\Delta y}{2}, t) \cdot \tfrac{1}{\Delta y^2}, \quad c_S = c(x, y - \tfrac{\Delta y}{2}, t) \cdot \tfrac{1}{\Delta y^2},$$
$$c_E = c(x + \tfrac{\Delta x}{2}, y, t) \cdot \tfrac{1}{\Delta x^2}, \quad c_W = c(x - \tfrac{\Delta x}{2}, y, t) \cdot \tfrac{1}{\Delta x^2},$$

$$\nabla_N I(x, y, t) = I(x, y + \Delta y, t) - I(x, y, t),$$
$$\nabla_S I(x, y, t) = I(x, y - \Delta y, t) - I(x, y, t),$$
$$\nabla_E I(x, y, t) = I(x + \Delta x, y, t) - I(x, y, t),$$
$$\nabla_W I(x, y, t) = I(x - \Delta x, y, t) - I(x, y, t).$$

$$I(x, y, t + \Delta t) \approx I(x, y, t) + \Delta t \cdot (\Phi_N + \Phi_S + \Phi_W + \Phi_E)\,.$$

The filtering process consists of updating each pixel in the image by an amount equal to the flow contributed by its nearest neighbors, (we assume 4-neighborhood system, the extension to 8-neighborhood is a trivial task). The parameter Δt should be less than $1/4$ for the 4-neighbourhood and less than $1/8$ for the 4-neighbourhood case to ensure the stability of the process.

3   Forward-and-Backward Diffusion

The conductance coefficients in the P-M process are chosen to be a decreasing function of the signal gradient. This operation selectively smoothes regions that do not contain large gradients. In the Forward-and-Backward diffusion (FAB), a different approach is taken. Its goal is to emphasize the extrema, if they indeed represent singularities and do not come as a result of noise. As we want to emphasize large gradients, we would like to move "mass" from the lower part of a "slope" upwards. This process can be viewed as moving back in time along the scale space, or reversing the diffusion process. Mathematically, we can change the sign of the conductance coefficient to negative: $\frac{\partial}{\partial t} \mathbf{I}(x, y, t) = \nabla \left[-c(x, y, t) \nabla \mathbf{I}(x, y, t) \right]$, $c(x, y, t) > 0$. However, we cannot simply use an inverse linear diffusion process, because it is highly unstable. Three major problems associated with the linear backward diffusion process must be addressed: explosive instability, noise amplification and oscillations.

One way to avoid instability explosion is to diminish the value of the inverse diffusion coefficient at high gradients. In this way, when the singularity exceeds a certain gradient threshold it does not continue to affect the process any longer. The diffusion process can be also terminated after a limited number of iterations. In order not to amplify noise, which after some pre-smoothing, can be regarded as having mainly medium to low gradients, the inverse diffusion force at low gradients should also be eliminated. The oscillations should be suppressed the moment they are introduced. For this, a forward diffusion force that smoothes low gradient regions can be introduced to the diffusion scheme.

The result of this analysis is that two forces of diffusion working simultaneously on the signal are needed - one backward force (at medium gradients, where singularities are expected), and the other, forward one, used for stabilizing oscillations and reducing noise. These two forces can actually be combined to one coupled forward-and-backward diffusion force with a conductance coefficient possessing both positive and negative values. In [8-10] a conductivity function that controls the FAB diffusion process has been proposed

$$c_{FAB}(g) = \begin{cases} 1 - (g/k_f)^n & , \quad 0 \le g \le k_f \\ \alpha \left[((g - k_b)/w)^{2m} - 1 \right] & , \quad k_b - w \le g \le k_b + w \\ 0 & , \quad \text{otherwise} \end{cases} \qquad (4)$$

where g is an edge indicator (gradient magnitude or the value of the gradient convolved with the Gaussian smoothing operator), k_f, k_b, w are design parameters and $\alpha = k_f/(2k_b)$, $(k_f \le k_b)$ controls the ratio between the forward and backward diffusion.

In this study we propose two more natural conduction coefficients directly based on the P-M approach:

$$c_{1_{FAB}}(s) = 2\exp\left(-s_1^2\right) - \exp\left(-s_2^2\right), \quad c_{2_{FAB}}(s) = \frac{2}{1 + s_1^2} - \frac{1}{1 + s_2^2}. \qquad (5)$$

The plots of the $c_{1_{FAB}}$ and $c_{2_{FAB}}$ diffusion coefficients are shown in Fig. 2. In the diffusion process smoothing is performed when the conductivity function is positive and sharpening takes place for negative conduction coefficient values.

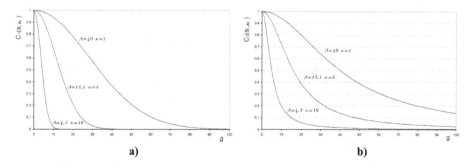

a)   b)

Fig. 1. Dependence of the conductivity functions on the iteration step and the image gradient g for the c_1 and c_2 conductivity functions, (forward diffusion, $\beta_1 = 40$, $\gamma = 0.8$).

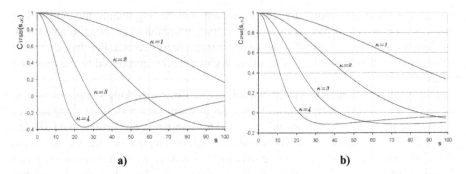

Fig. 2. Dependence of the conductivity functions on the iteration number κ and the normalized image gradient s for the c_{1FAB} and c_{2FAB} conductivity functions, (forward and backward diffusion), for $\beta_1(1) = 40$, $\beta_2(1) = 80$ and $\gamma = 0.5$. Note, that because of low $\gamma = 0.5$ already in the second iteration, the conductivity functions have negative values for large enough gradients.

4   Cooling Down of the Diffusion Process

Various modifications of the original diffusion scheme were attempted in order to overcome stability problems. Yet, most schemes still converge to a trivial solution (the average value of the image gray values) and therefore require the implementation of an appropriate stopping mechanism in practical image processing. In case of images contaminated by Gaussian noise, a common way of denoising is the usage of nonlinear cooling, which depends on the gradient, where large gradients cool faster and are preserved [12]. In this study the standard time-dependent conductivity functions were used:

$$c_1(g,t) = \exp\left[-\frac{g}{\beta(t)}\right]^2, \quad c_2(g,t) = \frac{1}{1 + \left(\frac{g}{\beta(t)}\right)^2}, \tag{6}$$

to obtain new forward and backward conductivity functions, derived from the unsharp masking procedure :

$$c_{1_{FAB}}(s,t) = 2\exp\left[-\frac{g}{\beta_1(t)}\right]^2 - \exp\left[-\frac{g}{\beta_2(t)}\right]^2, \tag{7}$$

$$c_{2_{FAB}}(s,t) = \frac{2}{1 + \left(\frac{g}{\beta_1(t)}\right)^2} - \frac{1}{1 + \left(\frac{g}{\beta_2(t)}\right)^2}. \tag{8}$$

where $g = ||\nabla\mathbf{I}(x,y,t)||$ is the L_1 or L_2 norm of the color image vector in the RGB space, $\beta_i(t+1) = \beta_i(t)\cdot\gamma$, $\gamma \in (0,1]$, $\beta_i(1)$ is the starting parameter, $i = 1,2$, $\beta_1(t) < \beta_2(t)$.

The scheme depends only on two (in case of forward or backward diffusion) or three (in case of FAB diffusion) parameters: initial values of starting β_i parameters and the cooling rate γ. Setting γ to 1 means, that there is no cooling in the system. As γ decreases, the cooling is faster, less noise is being filtered but edges are better preserved. Figure 1 illustrates the dependence of diffusion coefficients $c_1(s,t)$ and $c_2(s,t)$ on iteration step t. The behaviour of the diffusion coefficients $c_{1_{FAB}}(s,t)$ and $c_{1_{FAB}}(s,t)$ are compared in Fig. 2.

If the cooling coefficient γ is lower than 1, then the gradient threshold $\beta(t)$ decreases with time, allowing lower and lower gradients to take part in the smoothing process. As time advances, only smoother and smoother regions are being filtered, whereas large gradients can get enhanced due to local inverse diffusion. The scheme converges to a steady state for $\beta \to 0$, which means that no diffusion is taking place.

5 Experimentations and Results

In this paper a novel approach to the problem of edge preserving smoothing is proposed. The experiments revealed that better results of noise suppression using the FAB scheme were achieved using the conductivity function c_2 from the original P-M approach.

The efficiency of the proposed technique is presented in Fig. 3, where three color images are enhanced using the purely backward and FAB anisotropic techniques. The ability of the new algorithm to filter out noise and sharpen the color images is shown in Fig. 4, where two color test images were contaminated with Gaussian noise ($\sigma = 30$) and restored with the FAB anisotropic diffusion scheme.

The results confirm excellent performance of the new method, which could be used for the enhancement of noisy images in different techniques which are based on color, shape and spatial location information.

References

1. L. Alvarez, F. Guichard, P.L. Lions, J.M. Morel, Image selective smoothing and edge detection by nonlinear diffusion, SIAM J. Numer. Anal., 29, 845-866, 1993
2. F. Catté, F. Dibos, G. Koepfler, Image selective smoothing and edge detection by nonlinear diffusion, SIAM J. Numer. Anal., 29, 182–193, 1992
3. P. Perona, J. Malik, Scale space and edge detection using anisotropic diffusion, IEEE PAMI, Vol. 12, No. 7 pp. 629-639, July 1990
4. R. Whitaker, G. Gerig, Vector-Valued Diffusion, Ed. B.M. ter Haar Romeny, "Geometry-Driven Diffusion in Computer Vision", Kluwer Academic Press, pp. 93-134, 1994
5. M.J. Black, G. Sapiro, D.H. Marimont and D. Heeger, Robust anisotropic diffusion, IEEE Transactions on Image Processing, Vol. 7 (3), pp. 421-432, March 1998
6. J. Weickert, "Anisotropic Diffusion in Image Processing", Stuttgart-Germany: Teubner-Verlag, 1998
7. P. Blomgren, T. Chan, Color TV: Total variation methods for restoration of vector valued images, IEEE Transactions on Image Processing, March 1998, Special issue on Geometry Driven Diffusion and PDEs in Image Processing
8. G. Gilboa, Y. Zeevi, N. Sochen, Anisotropic selective inverse diffusion for signal enhancement in the presence of noise, Proc. IEEE ICASSP-2000, Istanbul, Turkey, vol. I, pp. 211-224, June 2000
9. G. Gilboa, Y. Zeevi, N. Sochen, Resolution enhancement by forward-and-backward nonlinear diffusion process, Nonlinear Signal and Image Processing, Baltimore, Maryland, June 2001
10. G. Gilboa, Y. Zeevi, N. Sochen, Signal and image enhancement by a generalized forward-and-backward adaptive diffusion process, EUSIPCO-2000, Tampere, Finland, September 2000
11. G. Gerig, R. Kikinis, F.A. Jolesz, Nonlinear anisotropic filtering of MRI data, IEEE Trans. Medical Imaging, 11, 221-232, 1992
12. X. Li, T. Chen, Nonlinear diffusion with multiple edginess thresholds, Pattern Recognition 27, 1029-1037, 1994

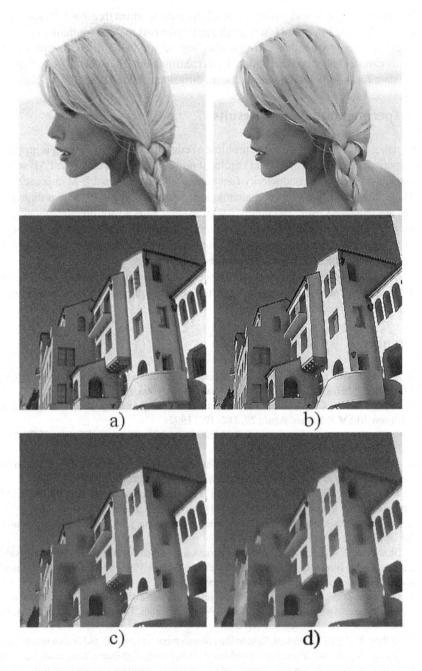

Fig. 3. Illustration of the efficiency of the new combined forward and backward anisotropic diffusion scheme. **a)** color test images, **b)** images enhanced with the new FAB diffusion scheme. To enable the visual evaluation of the proposed method, Figs. **c)** and **d)** depict the results obtained with the P-M approach without the cooling process, using the functions c_1 and c_2 from (2) respectively.

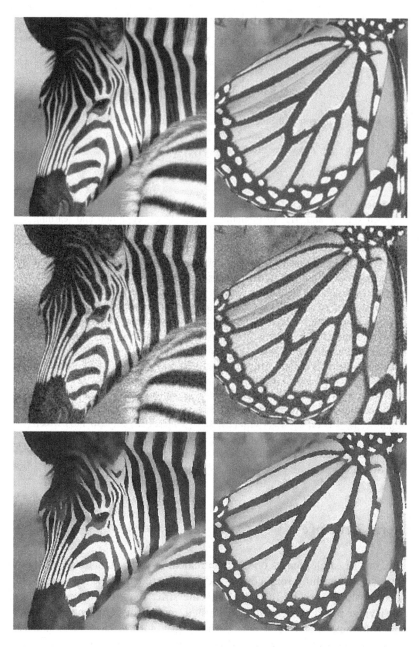

Fig. 4. Efectivness of the new coupled forward and backward anisotropic diffusion scheme. Top row: two color test images, below images contaminated with additive Gaussian noise ($\sigma = 30$ added independently on each RGB channel), bottom row shows the images enhanced with the new FAB anisotropic diffusion scheme.

Reinforcement Learning to Drive a Car
by Pattern Matching

Michael Krödel and Klaus-Dieter Kuhnert

University of Siegen, Institute for Real-Time-Systems,
Hölderlinstrasse 3, D-57068 Siegen / Germany
http://www.kuhnert@pd.et-inf.uni-siegen.de

Abstract. This research focuses on vision guided autonomous steering of a wheeled vehicle and tries to implement elementary recognition and learning abilities. While other researchers mainly focussed on using neural networks (e.g. [1], [2], [3], [4]) or explicit modelling of vehicle and environment (e.g. [5],[6],[7]) we established a system which classifies the video information and the vehicle behaviour into patterns and uses a very quick Pattern Matching Algorithm to decide on the required interactions with the environment (i.e. issuance of steering commands) in order to autonomously steer a vehicle

Within our research, such capabilities of driving by Pattern Matching got successfully implemented but the quality of the driving behaviour is strongly dependant on knowledge on how to react in certain driving situations. Any feedback on the appropriateness of the driving behaviour is delayed and unspecific in relation to single issued steering commands.

Therefore, a further central element in this research is a machine learning algorithm learning by reinforcement based on noisy and delayed rewards. An initial Reinforcement Learning algorithm (e.g. [8], [9]) has been implemented which shows very promising results for creating a system which autonomously steers a car purely based on visual information and even self-improves driving behaviour over time.

1 General Structure

In specific, this research focuses on the requirement to steer a simulated autonomous car along a curvy and hilly road course with no intersections and no other vehicles respectively obstacles on the road but with the strict requirement to self-improve driving behaviour based on delayed, self-created rewards or punishments. The structure of the autonomous driving system is shown in Figure 1. The system consists of three subsystems: INTELLIGENT IMAGE PROCESSING (IIP), PATTERN MATCHING (PM) and REINFORCEMENT LEARNING (RL).

The subsystem INTELLIGENT IMAGE PROCESSING is responsible for processing the incoming video stream and the real-time calculation of reduced parametric descriptions of the scene called Abstract Complete Situation Descriptions (ACSD's).

L. Van Gool (Ed.): DAGM 2002, LNCS 2449, pp. 322–329, 2002.

The Subsystem PATTERN MATCHING has the task to retrieve similar situations in comparison to the actual situation the vehicle is in. A large number of previously recorded situations, respectively their ACSD's, is being stored in a pattern database which is being accessed by the subsystem PATTERN MATCHING in two ways: Firstly, the Subsystem PM "scans" the pattern database for similar situations in comparison to the actual one; secondly, it also stores the ACSD of the actual situation together with the actual steering commands for further reference.

The subsystem REINFORCEMENT LEARING is responsible for determining a suitable behaviour in terms of steering commands for the current situation. This determination is based on the actual situation in conjunction with previously recorded, similar situations and their issued steering commands. For such task it is crucial to rate the appropriateness of any previously issued steering command, otherwise optimisation of behaviour would not be possible. Therefore, this subsystem is also responsible for weighting the success, respectively the appropriateness of any calculated steering command and also copes with the difficulty that such appropriateness can often only be determined after a quite long time delay.

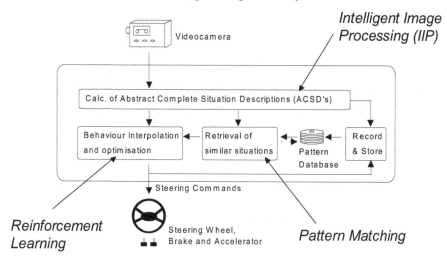

Fig. 1: Structure of the research

2 Related Work

Up to now the visual control of systems for autonomous vehicle driving with learning components have been implemented in several ways. [1] describes a short direct connection between image processing and one soft computing learning method using a neural network. This approach provides good results but only for as long as input pictures of the scene are similar to the training pattern. In [2] this approach got enhanced by a multiple neural network but could not completely solve the dependency problem of the taught training patterns. Further improvements have been tried e.g. [3], [4].

A completely different approach is being followed by using explicit modelling. [5] describes an early success with international attention of a vehicle system using a real-time vision system BVV2 [6]. Further developments stayed with the aspect of modelling (e.g. [7]), thus always in need for loading the system with many parameters for the modelling process.

The presented approach is a study of avoiding both neuronal networks or similar approximation methods as well as explicit models It derives a Situation Description of the scene and develops driving behaviour by a optimisation technique. With reference to the need for machine learning capabilities the current research follows the basic principles of Reinforcement Learning (e.g.[8], [9]) and focuses on a way of combining such area of research with pattern recognition algorithms.

3   Subsystem Intelligent Image Processing

A single connected camera is being used as the basis to build an abstract complete situation description (ACSD) of the situation the vehicle is currently in. This part combines traditional edge finding operators in order to locate contrast differences with a new technique of Bayes prediction for each part of the video image in order to predict whether a contrast difference results from a road mark edge or not.

During runtime the System, first scans for horizontal contrast differences and memorises all locations of possible candidates of a Road Mark Edge. In a second pass, all those candidates may be connected to chains. The probability density function for connected edge candidates is estimated by a quantized approximation indicating the expected orientation of the road course. Further details are described in [10] and [11].

4   Subsystem Pattern Matching

The major requirements of this subsystem are to identify similar situations as recorded before as well as to estimate the position within already driven road courses.

After performing the image processing, the current situation is described by the ACSD's but not explicitly modelled. By utilising a very fast pattern matching algorithm (ANN [12], [13]) approximately 10.000 Patterns can be searched in several milliseconds.

A proposition for the generation of reward signals the system needs the capability to at least identify a certain type of curve or even better to be able to estimate the position along a certain road course. These abilities deliver two basic pieces of information: first how the Situation Descriptions of the further road *might look like* and second the possibility for *time measurement* as a basis for any performance determination.

The postion can be quite reliably estimated by observing mainly the lateral steering commands. Of course also the longitudinal commands contain some information but it is not really necessary to evaluate them for this purpose.

5   Subsystem Reinforcement Learning

The base requirement for this subsystem is to provide machine learning functionality within the overall system.

In detail, the current subsystem needs to be able to optimize the quality of the Steering Commands (longitudinal and lateral) over time. The paradigm of this research is to avoid implicit learning (e.g. by a neuronal network) as well as explicit modeling. Instead, the system learns how to act in certain situations by gradual reinforcement and builds itself a set of Behavioural Patterns over time. A Behavioural Pattern (i.e. policy) is constituted by the recorded ACSD as explained before, the generated Steering Commands from that time and a factor indicating the success or failure of this combination. Thus, the System tries to learn explicitly the relation between certain states in configuration space and the reaction appropriate for the task. The system works in real time with continuous feedback from the environment and any such Behavioural Pattern is being continuously optimized. A complete protocol of all the Behavioural Pattern generated during a round course delivers the knowledge base for further actions.

The difficulty of optimising such Behavioural Pattern stems from the fact, that the success or failure of any generated Steering Command may not be calculated immediately. Almost no situation in the environment delivers directly a response about the value of the actual behaviour. Our optimisation criterion is the time needed to drive a specific route; i.e. we try to learn to drive as fast as possible. With this criterion in mind only after a completed round or time stop evaluation of the Behavioural Pattern used in between can be performed. Such characteristic of delayed rewarding or punishing makes learning much more difficult. Speaking in general terms, the learning methodology being used for this research can be referred to as Reinforcement Learning.

Reinforcement Learning (RL) is a machine learning method which copes with different requirements.

Firstly, RL copes with delayed rewards. In specific this means that a system receives rewards or punishments long after a series of actions has been performed. This makes it difficult to judge which of all chosen actions were especially good or bad and finally led to the received reward. In our case a vehicle drives along a course and the driving system needs to issue Steering Commands in real-time, therefore 10 to 20 Steering Commands per second. The quickest (negative) rewards come if the vehicle produces any accident; this might happen after a few seconds of driving and therefore after e.g. 100 issued Steering Commands. In other cases rewards come only after a whole section of the course has been driven or in maximum after the whole course is completed. If the latter results in around 5 minutes overall driving time, the reward comes only after having issued a few thousand Steering Commands.

Secondly, RL balances between exploration and exploitation. Once a system has learned how to drive a course it is reasonable for the system to exploit the knowledge and use it for proper driving. However, how does the system know the knowledge of driving can't be optimised? Basically, since there is no supervision or other external feedback it can't and so it is required to always explore new actions, monitor the (delayed) rewards and update the built-up knowledge.

Due to the fact that in our case rewards may come after having issued several thousand Steering Commands, we need one variant which converges as quick as possible. Therefore the TD-Reinforcement Learning method was choosen.

The concept of using RL methods in our system works that way that for each ACSD's the set of actions are being stored which ever have been issued at the corresponding situation and a value each representing the appropriateness of this action at this situation. While driving along the course the system keeps track of which ACSD's have been stored in which sequence. Once a reward is being received the reward value is being used to update the value of the current action of the current ACSD according to Formula 1. Within this formula V represents the Value of a action/situation combination, w represents the action (the Steering Command), x the situation (the ACSD) and gamma a discount factor.

$$V(x_t, w_t) = r(x_t) + \gamma \cdot V(x_{t+1}, w_t) \tag{1}$$

Since the system kept track of the previous ACSD's and issued Steering Commands, their action values are being updated as well, however, with r(x) being exponentially decreased by gamma.

6 Experimental Results

6.1 Pattern Matching

The results regarding Intelligent Image Processing can be found in [10][11].

The quality of the subsystem Pattern Matching can be shown twofold. Firstly, Figure 2 shows a series of images where the first image on the top is the incoming Single Image stemming from the attached video camera. All remaining images are the ones classified by the Pattern Matching algorithm as similar ones. If considered that those classified images are only some out of a pattern database with several thousand record entries which contain all various types of images it can be seen that all images classified as similar are truly similar to the first image.Even if they look very similar they stem from different runs and locations.

From a pure image comparison point of view this might not be astonishing but in our case it needs to be noted that this has been achieved in addition to speed optimisation and adaptation to road situations. The search time for finding those 8 similar images out of a database of around 5.000 images was done in less than 5 ms on an ordinary PC.

The second way to demonstrate the results of the Subsystem Pattern Matching is to compute the confusion matrix. Table 1 displays such matrix indicating the statistics of finding the proper local course type (e.g. a left curve).

It can be seen that in average 61,0 % of all classifications were correct and even the hit-rates for curves are up to 45.3, respectively 50.5%. At a first glance this result looks not very impressing but is has to be considered that almost all errors stem from quantisation e.g. a confusion matrix with slight left/right curve would present even better results.

Incoming Singe Image

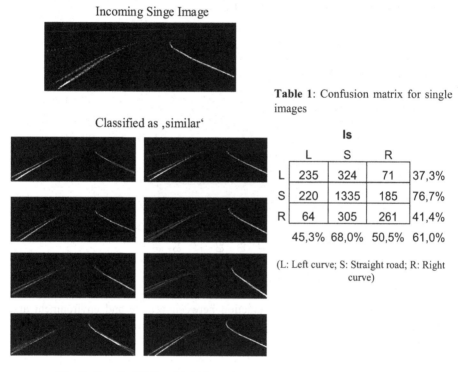

Table 1: Confusion matrix for single images

	Is			
	L	S	R	
L	235	324	71	37,3%
S	220	1335	185	76,7%
R	64	305	261	41,4%
	45,3%	68,0%	50,5%	61,0%

(L: Left curve; S: Straight road; R: Right curve)

Classified as ‚similar'

Fig. 2.: Result of Pattern Matching

6.2 Driving by Pattern Matching

In order to test first driving skills based only on the pattern matching algorithm a pattern database (approx. 5.4000 patterns) for different situations has been build up.

The tests then let the vehicle drive each time for approx. 5 minutes along a curvy and partial unknown road course. Average results of tests are shown below:

- Time of autonomous driving : 300 sec
- Calculated Steering Commands: 3000 (10 per second)
- Number of major errors (road course left completely): 1
- Number of errors (crash barrier scratched): 4

6.3 Reinforcement Learning

Prior to any combination of Reinforcement Learning (RL) with Pattern Matching methods, several RL methods with different parameter sets have been studied before. In order to have RL separated from the rest of the research, another virtual Race Track simulator got implemented with the goal to find the shortest path. The environmental input is fed to a simulated vehicle and also receives and processes steering commands. Even though both environment and vehicle are being rebuild in a rather simple manner, the kind of interfaces to and from the RL system are very similar to the interfaces of the main research and its RL system.

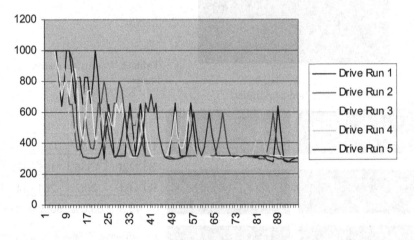

Fig 3: Number of steps to reach end point over run through episodes of learning

Those interfaces simulate the interaction between vehicle and environment and lastly calculate in parallel, rewards for the RL system: a small punishment for simply driving along the course (usage of resources), a big punishment for bumping or scratching any obstacle and a big reward for reaching a defined goal. With those interfaces the RL system has been established according to paragraph 5.

With such separate RL system, several runs through episodes were performed. Within each episode the RL system starts 100 times from a given starting point and steps along the race track while counting the number of steps until a given goal point or a maximum number of 1000 steps got reached.

Figure 3 displays the average number of steps needed to reach the goal point during each episode over a series of 100 episodes. Such curve is been displayed for 5 different Drive Runs and shows the improvement over time. All 5 Drive Runs start with 1000 steps each at the beginning and slowly oscillate their way down to a range of around 290 after 100 episodes. The absolute minimum of 274 steps for the shortest path is never been achieved. This, however, is reasonable since the RL issues random (new) steering commands with probability ε in order to further explore it's environment.

7 Summary

In the paper the actual state of a System is presented that is aimed to *LEARN* driving autonomously different vehicles on different courses exclusively by visual input.

The Subsystem INTELLIGENT IMAGE PROCESSING allows, as required, to locate the Road Mark Edges of each Single Image. A trained search algorithm allows optimal search speed and high recognition rate and consequently efficiently converts Road Mark Edges into Abstract Complete Situation Descriptions (ACSD's) capturing in a storage-efficient way the current situation the vehicle is in.

The Subsystem PATTERN MATCHING successfully retrieves similar situations to the current one based on a pattern matching algorithm

The Subsystem REINFORCEMENT LEARNING is still under implementation. However, a simple approach implemented so far allows already autonomous driving on a learning-by-knowledge-transfer basis promising further positive results in the area of autonomous driving based on pattern matching.

References

1. Pommerleau, D.A.: Efficient Training of Artificial Neural Networks for Autonomous Navigation, Neural Computation 3, 1991
2. Jochem, T.M., Pomerleau, D.A., Thorpe, C.E.: MANIAC: A Next Generation Neurally Based Autonomous Road Follower, IAS-3, Int. Conference on Intelligent autonomous Systems, February 15-18, 1993, Pittsburgh/PA, USA, F.C.A. Groen, S.Hirose, C.E.Thorpe (eds), IOS Press, Washington, Oxford, Amsterdam, Tokyo, 1993
3. Jochem, T.M., Pomerleau, D.A., Thorpe, C.E.: Vision Guided Lane Transition, Intelligent Vehicles '95 Symposium, September 25-26, 1995, Detroit/MI, USA
4. Baluja, S., Pomerleau, D.A.: Expectation-based selective attention for visual monitoring and control of a robot vehicle, , Robotics and Autonomous System, Vol.22, No.3-4, December, 1997
5. Dickmanns, E.D., Zapp, A.: Autonomous High Speed Road Vehicle Guidance by Computer Vision, Preprints of the 10th World Congress on Automatic Control, Vol.4, International Federation of Automatic Control, Munich, Germany, July 27-31, 1987
6. Kuhnert, K.-D.: A Vision System for Real Time Road and Object Recognition for Vehicle Guidance, Proc. Mobile Robots, Oct 30-31, 1986, Cambridge, Massachusetts, Society of Photo-Optical Instrumentation Engineers, SPIE Volume 727
7. Dickmanns, E.D., Behringer, R., Hildebrandt, T., Maurer, M., Thomanek, F., Schiehlen, J.: The Seeing Passenger Car 'VaMoRs-P', Intelligent Vehicles '94 Symposium, October 24-26, 1994, Paris, France
8. Sutton, R., Reinforcement Learning: An introduction, MIT-Press, 1998, Cambridge (USA)
9. Baird III, L., Reinforcement Learning through Gradient Descent, Dissertation, Carnegie Mellon University, 1999 Pittsburgh, USA
10. Krödel, M., Kuhnert K.-D.: Towards a Learning Autonomous Driver System, IEEE International Conference on Industrial Electronics, Control and Instrumentation, October 22-28, 2000, Nagoya, Japan
11. Krödel, M., Kuhnert, K.-D.: Autonomous Driving through Intelligent Image Processing and Machine Learning, Int'l Conference on Computational Intelligence, October 1-3, Dortmund, Germany
12. Mount, D. M.: ANN Programming Manual, Department of Computer Science and Institute for Advance Computer Studies, University of Maryland, 1998
13. Langenhangen, J.: Nearly nearest Neighbour search with principal components, Student Thesis, Siegen, 2001

Robust Point Correspondence for Image Registration Using Optimization with Extremal Dynamics

Souham Meshoul and Mohamed Batouche

Computer Vision Group, LIRE Laboratory
Computer Science Department, Mentouri University
25000 Constantine, Algeria
{meshoul, batouche}@wissal.dz

Abstract. Robust Point Correspondence for image registration is still a challenging problem in computer vision and many of its related applications. It is a computationally intensive task which requires an expensive search process especially when issues of noisy and outlying data have to be considered. In this paper, we cast the problem as a combinatorial optimization task and we solve it using extremal optimization, a new general purpose heuristic recently proposed by Boettcher and colleagues. We show how this heuristic has been tailored to the point correspondence problem and resulted in an efficient outlier removal scheme. Experimental results are very encouraging and demonstrate the ability of the proposed method in identifying outliers and achieving robust matching.

1   Introduction

In the quest of finding high quality solutions to NP-hard discrete combinatorial optimization problems like the Traveling Salesman and Quadratic Assignment problems, non-deterministic heuristic methods have been derived from nature by taking inspiration from biology (Genetic Algorithms), physics (Simulated Annealing) and ethnology (Ant Colony Optimization). Extremal Optimization (EO) is a general-purpose method recently proposed as a powerful addition to the canon of stochastic optimization methods [1]. Unlike simulated annealing which is inspired by equilibrium statistical physics, EO is based on models used to simulate far-from equilibrium dynamics. Precisely, it is inspired by the concept of Self-Organized Criticality (SOC). EO heuristic has been successfully applied to some benchmark problems and its performance has been proven to be competitive with more elaborate stochastic optimization procedures [1]. This is one of the reasons which explain our motivation in the use of EO heuristic to address a core problem in image analysis field that is point correspondence applied to image registration.

Image registration is the process that attempts to bring into the best possible spatial correspondence two or more images with respect to each other. Its aim is to find the best transform relating the two images and making them match. Many tasks in computer vision and related areas rely heavily on image registration. These include stereo matching to recover shape for autonomous navigation, fusion of images acquired from different imagery systems like in medical imaging, motion tracking by relating time-separated images and content-based retrieval of image data. Image

L. Van Gool (Ed.): DAGM 2002, LNCS 2449, pp. 330–337, 2002.
© Springer-Verlag Berlin Heidelberg 2002

registration acts to determine the transformation between a newly sensed image and a reference image.

In [2], Brown proposed a good review of a broad range of methods for image registration and a framework to classify them with respect to four criteria : the search space, the feature space, the similarity metric and the search strategy. Point correspondence or matching is a problematic part of a point-based image registration method because it requires an expensive search process. Its complexity is computationally intensive and becomes even more critical with the increase of the number of points to be matched, the presence of outlying and noisy data and the complexity of the registering transformation. It still remains the focus of a great deal of research effort [3-7].

This paper outlines an efficient outlier removal framework based on optimization with extremal dynamics to solve the problem of point correspondence for image registration purpose. In order to be self-contained, the remainder of the paper is organized as follows. In section 2, we introduce Extremal Optimization heuristic. The framework proposed to solve point correspondence is formulated and described in section 3. Then some experimental results are presented in section 4. Finally conclusions and future work are drawn.

2   Extremal Optimization

EO is a newly proposed meta-heuristic which is added to the canon of the stochastic optimization methods. EO is based on the Bak-Sneppen model of evolution [8] which uses the principle of Self-Organized Criticality (SOC). SOC is a new concept proposed in [9] to describe the dynamics with emergent complexity.

The key idea underlying this new concept consists in the fact that emergence of complex structures is often the result of the elimination of their bad components. Bak and Sneppen used this principle to describe their model of evolution where a species is characterized by a fitness value $\lambda_i \in [0, 1]$ and the weakest species (smallest λ) and its closest dependent species are successively selected for adaptive changes by assigning them new fitness values. The main characteristic of this model is its simplicity, no control parameter is needed and it reproduces non trivial features of paleontological data including broadly distributed lifetimes of species, large extinction events and punctuated equilibrium [1, 10].

EO has been introduced recently by Stefan Boettcher [1, 10] as the result of the application of the Bak-Sneppen mechanism to hard optimization problems yielding a new dynamic optimization procedure free of selection parameters. When using EO, extremely undesirable components of a sub-optimal solution are successively eliminated according to a stochastic rule.

Given an optimization problem, it is question to find the best solution S_{best} in the search space, Ω, minimizing a predefined cost function $C(S)$. Each solution $S \in \Omega$ consists of a large number of variables x_i. Unlike Genetic Algorithms and Simulated Annealing, EO requires the definition of local cost contributions for each variable instead of merely a global cost. To solve the problem, EO performs a search starting from a single configuration $S \in \Omega$ and proceeds as follows [10]:

1.   Initialize configuration S at will; set $S_{best} := S$.

2.   For the current configuration S,

    a)   Evaluate λ_i for each variable x_i

    b)   Find j satisfying $\lambda_j \le \lambda_i$ for all i , *i.e.*, x_j has the "worst fitness."

    c)   Choose $S' \in$ *Neighborhood of S* so that x_j must change.

    d)   Accept S := S' *unconditionally*

    e)   If $C(S) < C(S_{best})$ then set $S_{best} := S$.

3.   Repeat at step (2) as long as desired.

4.   Return S_{best} and $C(S_{best})$

This version of EO algorithm focuses only on the worst undesirable components of a solution. This may lead to a deterministic process (premature convergence). To improve the results, a new variant called τ-Extremal Optimization has been introduced by adding a single adjustable parameter τ and updating components randomly according to a probability distribution over the ranks k obtained by using fitness values as the ranking criterion. EO has been successfully used to solve some generic combinatorial optimization problems like graph partitioning and TSP [1, 11].

3   Point Correspondence Using Extremal Optimization

In this section, we formulate the problem of point correspondence followed by the description of our iterative algorithm based on optimization with extremal dynamics applied to image registration.

3.1 Problem Statement

Given two images to be registered namely I_1 and I_2 where I_1 is the sensed image and I_2 is the reference image, an appropriate point of interest extraction procedure is applied to these images to obtain two sets P_1 and P_2 containing respectively n_1 and n_2 points. The problem is then to find the state of correct point-to-point correspondences taking into account the presence of noise and outliers. An outlier is a point in one image that has not its homologous point in the other image. When n_1 and n_2 are equal and no outlier is present, the number of matching configurations to be checked is about $n_1!$, however in the other case ($n_1 \ne n_2$), the number of matching configurations is even more critical. This is obviously a combinatorial optimization problem. To solve this problem, we need to define a cost function defining the quality of each solution. A straightforward representation of a feasible solution is a match-matrix representing the point-to-point correspondences from which an affine transformation $A=(L,T)$ can be determined. An extra row and an extra column are added to handle the case of outliers. Each element m_{ij} of M is set to 1 if the point i is matched to the point j and 0 otherwise. As each point in each image must be matched to at most one point in the other image. Two constraints have to be satisfied :

$$\sum_{k=1}^{n_2+1} m_{ik} = 1 \quad \text{for } i \in [1..n_1] \quad \text{and} \quad \sum_{k=1}^{n_1+1} m_{kj} = 1 \quad \text{for } j \in [1..n_2]$$

The mapping transformation $A=(L,T)$ is such that :

$$Y_j = L X_i + T + \varepsilon_{ij}$$

where L is a linear transformation, T is a translation vector, ε_{ij} is a residual term which represents some white noise, and Y_j and X_i are the matched points. Therefrom, the cost function to be minimized may be defined as :

$$E(M,T,L) = \sum_{i=1}^{n_1} \sum_{j=1}^{n_2} m_{ij} (Y_j - LX_i - T)^2 + \alpha \left(\sum_{i=1}^{n_1} m_{i(n_2+1)} + \sum_{j=1}^{n_2} m_{(n_1+1)j} \right)$$

The first term represents the sum of the squares of residuals ε_{ij}. The second term is used to reinforce all correct matches while rejecting outliers. Thus, the process consists of finding the match matrix M which provides the best mapping function through the minimization of the energy function $E(M, T, L)$. This cost function is highly non-linear, non convex and exhibits many local minima. A stochastic optimization method is then needed for its minimization.

3.2 Algorithm Description

We now describe how EO has been tailored to point correspondence problem in order to achieve the registration of two images. As formulated in the previous section, a solution S of the problem to be solved consists of a pair (M, A) where M is a match-matrix representing the point-to-point correspondence and A is the affine transformation defined by the parameters of L and T which are estimated using a least of squares methods over the matches in M.

The cost function $E(M, T, L)$ to be minimized in order to find a good quality solution S_{best} is in fact the sum of individual contributions that is the contribution of each match (i, j), instead to say match (X_i, Y_j), and also the contributions of outliers. Thus, the main requirement for the application of EO heuristic for our problem is fulfilled knowing that the need to define local cost contributions instead of merely a global cost is the most apparent distinction between EO and other heuristics. The key idea underlying our EO-based framework is the following. Given a current solution $S=(M,A)$, each match (i, j) in M has some contribution with regard to the quality of the current transformation A. This contribution is evaluated by its corresponding residual given by : $\varepsilon_{ij} = j - A(i)$. The less is the residual ε_{ij} the better and more desirable is the match (i, j) for the current solution. Larger residual indicates larger deviation from the underlying model. Therefrom, one way to improve the quality of the solution is either to discard bad matches or to match an outlier with a close neighbor according to the current affine transformation. EO is a dynamic stochastic heuristic which enable us to perform such updates among the bad solution components. To apply EO to our problem, we need to define two measures : the fitness of individuals and the closeness between pairs of matched points. Consider each point i as a degree of freedom. Its fitness value λ_i is based on the correspondence emerging from it. The values of λ_i should be normalized to the range [0, 1]. Let us define the fitness of a point $i \in P_1$ to be :

$$\lambda_i = \begin{cases} 0 & \text{if the point } i \text{ is an outlier} \\ 1 - \dfrac{r_i}{\max\limits_{j}\{r_j\}} & \text{otherwise} \end{cases}$$

where r_i is the residual ε_{ij} corresponding to the match (i, j), so that $\lambda_i \rightarrow 1$ for good matches (with small residual) whereas $\lambda_i \rightarrow 0$ for bad matches and outliers.

The closeness measure is defined in terms of proximity and similarity between points. Given a point $i \in P_1$, the closeness measure is used to determine a close neighbor $j \in P_2$ with regard to the current transformation A and may be expressed as follows :

$$closeness(i, j) = d(A(i), j) * \frac{(1 + \rho(i, j))}{2}$$

where d is the Euclidean distance and ρ is the correlation coefficient between a neighborhoods around the point i and a neighborhood around the point j.

Starting from an initial solution, the algorithm evolves through an iterative process and proceeds as follows. At each iteration, the current solution $S_i = (M_i, A_i)$ is modified by perturbing hypothetical bad correspondences and outliers. It would not be sufficient to focus only on bad matches and outliers, instead we use a selection mechanism which gives them higher probability to be chosen. So, let us select a point $i \in P_1$ according to its fitness rank n_i, using the distribution $P(n) \sim n^{-\tau}$. Then, two situations may be encountered. The selected point i is either an outlier or consists of a part of a match pair (i, j) in the current match matrix M_i. When the selected point i is an outlier, a new correspondence (i, j) emerging from the point i has to be established by selecting a close neighbor $j \in P_2$ using the same distribution $P(n)$ as for the rank list of fitnesses, but now applied instead to a rank list of closenesses. In this manner, a deterministic choice process is avoided because the selected point j is not necessarily always the best candidate with regard to the closeness measure. On the other hand, when the selected point i belongs to a match pair (i, j) in the current match matrix M_i, the change consists simply in breaking this "bad" match (i, j) yielding two new outliers which may be, at ulterior stages of the search process, matched to other points so that to obtain "better" matches. Finally, the match matrix is updated in a way to maintain its consistency. From the matches of the updated match-matrix M, a new affine transformation A is determined. Then, the cost of the new solution is evaluated and the best solution obtained from the beginning of the search is updated. This process is repeated for the new solution until a termination criterion is reached (a maximum number of iterations). More formally, the general scheme of our algorithm can be summarized as follows :

Input : Two sets of points P_1 and P_2 extracted from the sensed and the reference image respectively.

- Generate an initial solution $S = (M, A)$ where M is the initial match_matrix and A its corresponding affine transformation; Set $S_{best} := S$;

Repeat
- Rank each point $i \in P_1$ according to its fitness λ_i
- Select a point i from P_1 according to its fitness rank n_i using the distribution function $P(n_i) \sim n_i^{-\tau}$

If the selected point i is an outlier **Then**
- Rank each point $j \in P_2$ according to its closeness to $A(i)$
- Select a point j from P_2 according to its closeness rank n_j using the distribution function $P(n_j) \sim n_j^{-\tau}$ in order to create a new match pair (i, j). When the selected neighbor j is already matched as part of a pair (k, j), the point k becomes an outlier.

Else
- The match pair of points (i, j) is broken into two new outliers i and j

End if

- Update M and compute the new affine transformation A. Set $S' := (M, A)$;
- Accept $S := S'$ *unconditionally*

If $C(S) < C(S_{best})$ **Then** $S_{best} := S$; **End if**

Until a *termination-criterion* is achieved;

Output : $S_{best} = (M_{best}, A_{best})$

Two important remarks must be outlined at this stage. By ranking the points, we keep some memory about good components of solutions. This memory directs the search to the neighborhoods of increasingly better solutions. In an other word, it favors the intensification of the search around good solution components. By another way, the updates we have described impact the fitness of neighboring points and cause large fluctuations of the search. This results in significant hill climbing ability and favors good exploration of the search space by visiting new configurations. Consequently, we expect achieving in this manner better balance between the exploration and intensification processes.

4   Experimental Results

We have conducted a wide range of experiments on the algorithm presented above. Both real and synthetic images have been used to assess its performance. Several questions have been investigated in these experiments : the convergence of the search process, the behavior of the algorithm under varying values of the tunable parameter τ and the effect of the starting solution on the convergence of the algorithm. In figure 1, we show the results of our experiments on real world images. The sensed and reference images contain more than 70 points of interest extracted using Harris' detector [12]. To evaluate the accuracy of the results, we computed the RMSE statistic. It was equal to 0.361 which reveals that reliable correspondences have been established and sub-pixel accuracy has been achieved.

Fig. 1. Image registration using EO Algorithm : The sensed image (left) the reference image (middle) The transformed sensed image using the best registering transformation (right).

In figure 2 (on the left), we show the behavior of the cost function through iterations. It is apparent that the algorithm converges rapidly to near optimal solutions, then large fluctuations ensue which allow to explore efficiently many local minima. Figure 2 (on the right) shows the best values of the cost function recorded during the search with the parameter τ set to 2.0. Using $\tau \rightarrow 0$ would lead to a random walk through the search space while using τ too large would lead to a deterministic local search. We have found that the values ranging from 2.0 to 2.5 seem to give the best results. Furthermore, during the experiments, we have observed that the performance of the algorithm is much improved when starting from a good initial guess.

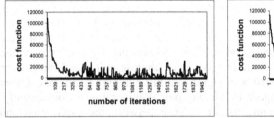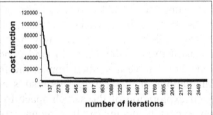

Fig. 2. Convergence behaviors of the proposed algorithm : The cost function values as a function of the iteration number (left), The best cost function values through iterations (right)

5   Conclusion

We have described a new framework based on Extremal Optimization (EO) heuristic to handle the problem of point correspondence. The developed algorithm is remarkably simple to implement and uses only one adjustable parameter τ. Thanks to its ranking mechanism and the fluctuations caused by the defined updates on the solution components, the algorithm is expected to achieve better balance between the intensification and diversification of the search process. Experiments have shown that the proposed algorithm is able to establish reliable correspondences and to achieve robust pose estimation. Furthermore, the algorithm performance is improved when using a clever startup routine.

References

1. S. Boetthcher and A. G. Percus. Nature's way of optimizing. Artificial Intelligence, 119:275—286, 2000.
2. L. G. Brown. A survey of image registration techniques. ACM surveys, 24(4) : 325-376, December 1992.
3. S. Banerjee and D. Dutta Majumdar. Shape matching in multimodal medical images using point landmarks with Hopfield net. Neurocomputing, 30(2000) : 103-116, 2000.
4. S. Gold and al. New algorithms for 2D and 3D point matching : Pose estimation and Correspondence. Pattern Recognition, 31(8) : 1019-1031, 1998.
5. D. M. Mount, N. S. Netanyahu and J. Le Moigne. Efficient algorithms for robust feature matching. Pattern Recognition, 32(1) : 17-38, January 1999.
6. X. Dai and S. Khorram. A Feature-Based Image Registration Algorithm Using Improved Chain-Code Representation Combined with Invariant Moments. IEEE Transactions on Geoscience and Remote Sensing, 37(5):2351—2362, Septembre 1999.
7. E. Guest, E. Berry, R. A. Baldock, M. Fidrich and M. A. Smith. Robust Point Correspondence Applied to Two- and Three-Dimensional Image Registration. IEEE Transactions on PAMI, 23(2):165—179 , February 2001.
8. P. Bak and K. Sneppen. Punctuated equilibrium and criticality in a simple model of evolution. Physical Review letters, 71:4083—4086, 1993.
9. P. Bak. How nature works : The science of Self-Organized Criticality. New York, NY : Copernicus Press, 1996.
10. S. Boetthcher and A. G. Percus. Optimization with extremal dynamics. Physical Review letters, 86:5211—5214, June 2001.
11. S. Boetthcher and A. G. Percus. Extremal optimization for graph partitioning. Physical Review E, 64(026114):1—13, July 2001.
12. C. Harris and M. Stephens. A combined corner and edge detector, Proceedings of the Fourth Alvey Vision Conference, pp. 147—151, 1988.

Extending Active Shape Models to Incorporate a-priori Knowledge about Structural Variability

Stephan Al-Zubi and Klaus Tönnies

Institut für Simulation und Graphik
39016 Magdeburg
[stephan, klaus] @isg.cs.uni-magdeburg.de

Abstract. A new deformable shape model is defined with the following properties: (1) A-priori knowledge describes shapes not only by statistical variation of a fixed structure like active shape/appearance model but also by variability of structure using a production system. (2) Multi-resolution description of shape structures enable more constrained statistical variation of shape as the model evolves in fitting the data. (3) It enables comparison between different shapes as well as characterizing and reconstructing instances of the same shape. Experiments on simulated 2D shapes demonstrate the ability of the algorithm to find structures of different shapes and also to characterize the statistical variability between instances of the same shape.

1 Introduction

Shape representation, recognition and classification is used for analyzing 2-d and 3-d data as well as to analyze 3-d data from 2-d projections. This work is interested in the former. Various deformable shape models have been developed in recent years and used for segmentation, motion tracking, reconstruction and comparison between shapes. These models can be broadly classified into three classes:

1. Statistical models that use a-priori knowledge about how the shape varies to reconstruct that shape.
2. Dynamic models that fit the shape data that use built-in smoothness constraints to maintain an optimal solution.
3. Structural models that extract structural features from shapes to compare and classify them.

Examples of the first class are: (1) Active Shape/Appearance Models developed by Cootes et. al [1] that utilize principal component analysis in order to describe variations of landmarks and textures. (2) The Active Appearance Motion Model by Mitchell et. al [2] that extends active appearance models to fit a time varying shape like the heart. (3) Probabilistic registration by Chen [3] that uses the per-voxel gray level and shift vector distributions to guide a better fit between the atlas and the data. Smoothness constraints between neighboring shift vectors results in improved results.

The main restriction in statistical models is that they describe the statistical variations of a *fixed-structure shape* and not structural differences between different shapes.

L. Van Gool (Ed.): DAGM 2002, LNCS 2449, pp. 338–344, 2002.
© Springer-Verlag Berlin Heidelberg 2002

Examples of the second class are: (1) Front propagation methods by Malladi et. al [4] that simulate an expanding closed curve that eventually fits the shape. (2) Dynamic particles by Szeliski et. al [5] that simulate a system of dynamic oriented particles that expand into the object surface guided by internal forces that maintain an even and smooth distribution between them. (3) T-snakes / surfaces by McInerny et. al [6] that use the ACID grid (a triangular decomposition of space) that enable traditional snakes to become adaptive to complex object topologies.

The above deformable models are able to segment/sample objects of complex topology like blood vessels. Their restriction is that they *cannot characterize the shapes* they segment either statistically or structurally.

Examples of the third class are: (1) Shock grammar by Siddiqi et. al [7]. This model defines four types of shocks, which are evolving medial axes formed from colliding propagating fronts that originate at shape boundaries. This model defines a shock grammar that restricts how the shock types can combine to form a shape. The grammar is used to eliminate invalid shock combinations. The shock graphs that describe a shape facilitate comparison between shapes. (2) Finite element methods by Pentland et. al [8] define a dynamic finite element model that fits the shape. The low order modal coordinates describes the object structure under its free vibration modes. A simple dot product of the modal vectors of two shapes is a strong discriminator of their structural differences. (3) Super quadrics by Terzopoulos et. al [9] can describe shape in a multi-resolution fashion both globally and locally. The global superquadric facilitates comparison between shapes and the local displacements enable object reconstruction. (4) Shape blending by DeCarlo et. al [10] is used to fit an ellipsoid to the object model. The fitting process tears the surface into two blended surface patches at points where the object has protrusions or holes. The importance of blended surfaces is that we can construct a graph of protrusion / hole structures of these shapes.

The models of this class are data driven in that they have *no prior knowledge* about the structures of the shapes they fit. They can not describe the shapes they fit statistically.

The model we propose defines a multi-resolution a-priori knowledge about the shape both at the structural and the statistical level. This extends the ability of statistical models to handle structural variability and structural models to include a-priori information about shape.

2 Method

The following definitions apply to 2-D shapes. A *shape system* is a tuple (S, P) where: (1) S is the *set of shape units*. (2) P is the *set of productions*.

A *shape unit* $(S_i \in S)$ is a translation/rotation invariant polygonal mesh. It is characterized by a multivariate edge-length distribution. It is defined by the tuple $(V, E, \mu, \Sigma, \Phi)$ where:

1. V is a set of vertices.
2. E is a list of directed edges $(e_1, e_2 ... e_n)$ defined over V.
3. μ is the vector of mean edge-lengths.
4. Σ is the covariance matrix of edge lengths.

5. $\Phi = \lfloor \phi_1, \phi_2 ... \phi_t \rfloor$ is the matrix of the first t eigen vectors derived from Σ by principal component analysis.

A *shape unit instance* s_j of a shape unit S_i is a tuple $(\mathbf{b}, \theta, t_x, t_y)$ where $\mathbf{b} = (b_1, b_2 ... b_t)$ is a vector of valid eigen coordinates such that the edge lengths can be calculated by $\mathbf{l} = \mu + \Phi \mathbf{b}$, θ is the orientation of the mesh defined by the angle between the first edge in E (call it e_j) and the x axis and (t_x, t_y) are the coordinates of the first vertex in e_j. A *shape instance SI* is the set of all shape unit instances which constitute the working memory of the system. We define a function $f_{graph}(s_j)$ that returns the graph $G_j=(V_j, E_j)$ of the shape instance.

The edge list E is defined over V such that it always satisfies the following geometric constraints: (1) As long as triangular inequality is not violated, each edge length can be changed without affecting the lengths of the other edges. (2) All vertex coordinates can be computed by iterating a triangulation procedure beginning with at least two known vertex-coordinates connected by an edge and a valid list of all other edge lengths.

Because triangulation from two vertex coordinates has two solutions we use the following procedure to select a unique solution (see Fig. 1):

1. If more than three vertex-coordinates have been computed select the triangulation coordinate that maximizes the distance from the centroid of known vertices. This has the effect of preventing the polygonal mesh from folding onto itself.
2. If only two vertices are known we use the direction of the edge connecting them to select a unique solution (e.g. right solution to the edge).

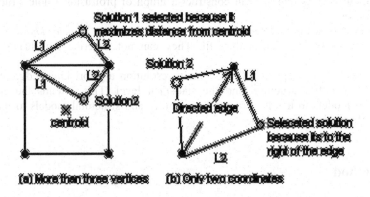

Fig. 1. Selecting a unique solution for triangulation.

The *set of productions* $(P=P_g \cup P_m)$ are rules that specify how shape units connect to each other. P consists of two types of productions (see Fig. 2): (1) *Generating productions* (P_g) that use current context to generate likely shape candidates. This is where structural a-priori knowledge is specified. (2) *Merging productions* (P_m) specify which neighboring groups of shape units can be merged into a bigger shape unit. This is where multi-resolution is specified. When a bigger shape unit is formed, a more *constrained* joint multivariate distribution of its components units is specified accordingly.

To define generating and merging productions we must define *shape configuration*. A *shape configuration* is a set of connected shape-instance graphs $\{f_{graph}(s_j): s_j \in S \wedge S$ is connected$\}$. A set of shape instance graphs S is connected iff $\forall s_j \in S, \exists s_k \in S$ such that $V_j \cap V_k \neq \varnothing$ where V_j, V_k are the set of vertices for s_j, s_k respectively. *SC* is the set of all shape configurations. We define $V(A)$ as the set of all vertices in the shape configuration A.

P_g is a relation between two shape configurations: $\{(A, B): A,B \in SC \wedge A \subseteq B\}$. When applying a generation rule on *SI*, we match and replace a shape configuration A with a shape configuration B specified by P_g. We define the set of vertices that are generated as a result of applying a generating production as *free vertices*: $V(B)-V(A)$ and the original vertices before applying the production as *bound vertices*: $V(A)$.

The vertex coordinates of a generated shape instance s_j are initialized such that *bound vertices* are left unchanged and *free vertices* are set to minimize $f_{deformation}(s_j)$ (see eq. 1).

Pm is a *function* between two shape configurations: $\{(A, B): A,B \in SC \wedge A \subseteq B \wedge V(A)=V(B)\}$. After applying a merging production (A, B), new shape unit instances in B-A constitute a grouping of the original sub-shapes into bigger shape units with a more specific joint distribution. The super shapes of B-A are then optimized using the new multivariate distribution. We still retain the original sub-shapes in set A because they may generate potential new shapes but they are not statistically optimized further.

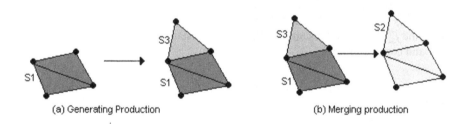

(a) Generating Production   (b) Merging production

Fig. 2. Productions.

Shapes are associated with images by two fitness measures between a mesh instance (s_j) and an image: The image force f_{image}, which is a suitably defined measure between vertices and the image and a deformation force, which is the Mahalanobis distance of the edge-length vector l from the mean μ.

$$f_{deformation}(s_j) = (l-\mu)'\Sigma^{-1}(l-\mu) \tag{1}$$

The shape reconstruction algorithm (see Fig. 3) is a production system which begins from an initial shape instance. It generates a conflict set of candidate instances using generating shape productions. Each candidate is statistically optimized to fit the data. The best matching candidate is selected and generated. As shape groups are formed they are merged into bigger units using the merging productions. These groups are then statistically re-optimized using the new super shape. The output is a reconstructed shape described both statistically and structurally. The following is the pseudo code:

```
1 Initialize SI={s₀} where s₀ is the initial shape.

2 Generate all candidate shapes (CS) from SI using P.

3 For each sᵢ∈ CS that merges shape units do

        3.1 Minimize (bi, θi, txi, tyi) fimage(sᵢ).

        3.2 SI:=SI ∪{sᵢ. Re-compute CS.

4 For each sᵢ∈ CS that generates new shapes do

        4.1 Minimize (bi, θi, txi, tyi) fimage(sᵢ).

5 Select sₖ∈ CS with minimum fₖ=fimage(sₖ)+αfdeformation(sₖ).

6 If fₖ> β then Stop. Else add Add sₖ to SI.

7 Goto 2
```

3 Experiments

We demonstrate the deformable model on simulated 2D images of polygonal silhouettes (see Fig. 3). The silhouettes corner points (C) are the image features used to define f_{image}. f_{image} is the sum of the minimum distance between the instance-vertices $\{v_i\}$ and corner points C.

$$f_{image}(s_k) = \frac{1}{n}\sum_{i=1}^{n} \min_{c_j \in C}\left(\left\|v_i - c_j\right\|\right)$$

(2)

Fig. 3. A polygonal silhouette and its corner features.

Given a predetermined set of shape units and productions, the purpose of this demonstration is to show the ability of the algorithm to reconstruct the shapes such that we can differentiate between shapes that have different structures and characterize statistically the variability of shapes that have the same structure.

For the sake of brevity, we denote adjacent shape unit instances S_i, S_j used in the productions by a string S_iS_j. Three shape units are used to construct the images as shown in Fig. 4. Four generating productions are defined: Pg= {S1→S₁S₃ mapped as shown in Fig. 2(a), $S_1 \to S_1 S_2$, $S_2 \to S_2 S_3$, $S_3 \to S_3 S_1$}. One merging production is defined: Pm= {$S_1 S_3 \to S_2$} mapped as shown in Fig. 2(b).

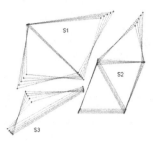

Fig. 4. Shapes units used to construct the silhouettes with their first mode of variation.

Fig. 5 demonstrates the ability of the algorithm to recognize and reconstruct shapes for three silhouettes. The left and middle figures are two variations of the same shape. The algorithm is able to recognize their structure: $S_1 — S_2 — S_3$. The modal coordinates are reconstructed using the first two coordinates per shape unit: {S_1(0.09, 0.12), S_2(-0.0024, 0.21), S_3(0.0064, 0.12)} for the left and {S_1(0.057, 0.091), S_2(0.090, 0.12), S_3(0.44, 0.056)} for the middle. The right figure is reconstructed as:

$$S_2(0.076,\ 0.023) - \overbrace{S_1(0.17,0.12)}^{S_2(0.5145,0.3884)} - S_3(0.044,-0.031)$$

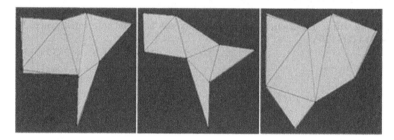

Fig. 5. Three silhouettes with optimized mesh instances overlaid.

4   Conclusions and Future Work

Using prior knowledge about structures and there deformations, we demonstrated a new shape model that is able to reconstruct and represent shapes in a form suitable for recognition, reconstruction and comparison.

The shape model has potential applications in several fields such as: (1) Classifying an image database of shapes into several categories. (2) Hierarchical segmentation of a shape into sub shapes that have some meaning in terms of the image. (3) Using prior knowledge to search for and recognize instances of a certain shape in an image. We plan to test the ability of the model on recognizing database of 2D images and then on recognizing structures in medical images.

References

1. Cootes, T., Taylor, C.: Statistical Models of Appearance for Medical Image Analysis and Computer Vision. Proceedings of SPIE in Medical Imaging: ImageProcessiong, Vol. 4322 (2001) 236-248.
2. Mitchell, S., Lelieveldt, B., van der Geest, R., Bosch, H., Reiber, J., Sonka, M.: Time Continuous Segmentation of Cardiac MR Image Sequences using Active Appearance Motion Models. Proceedings of SPIE in Medical Imaging: ImageProcessiong, Vol. 4322 (2001) 249-256.
3. Chen M.: 3-D Deformable Registration Using a Statistical Atlas with Applications in Medicine. MICCAI (1999) 621-630.
4. Malladi, R., Sethian, J., Vemuri, B.: Shape Modeling with Front Propagation: A Level Set Approach. IEEE Transactions on Pattern Analysis and Machine Intelligence, Vol. 17(2). (1995) 158-175.
5. Szeliski, R., Tonnesen, D., Terzopoulos, D.: Modeling Surfaces of Arbitrary Topology with Dynamic particles. Proc. Computer Vision and Vision Recognition (CVPR) (1993) 82-87.
6. McInerney, T., Terzopoulos, D.: Topology Adaptive Deformable Surfaces for Medical Image Volume Segmentation. IEEE Transactions on Medical Imaging, Vol. 18(9). (1999) 100-111.
7. Siddiqi, K., Kimia, B.: Toward a Shock Grammar for Recognition. IEEE Conf. on Computer Vision and Pattern Recognition, 1996.
8. Pentland, A., Sclaroff, S.: Closed-Form Solutions for Physically Based Shape Modeling and Recognition. IEEE Transactions on Pattern Analysis and Machine Intelligence, Vol. 13(7). (1991) 715-729.
9. Terzopoulos, D., Metaxas, D.: Dyanamic 3D Models with Local and Global Deformations: Deformable Superquadrics. IEEE Transactions on Pattern Analysis and Machine Intelligence, Vol. 13(7). (1991) 703-714.
10. DeCarlo, D., Metaxas, D.: Shape Evolution with Structural and Topological Changes using Blending. IEEE Transactions on Pattern Analysis and Machine Intelligence, Vol. 20(11). (1998) 1186-1205.

A New Approach for Defect Detection in X-ray CT Images

H. Eisele[1] and F.A. Hamprecht[2]

[1] Robert Bosch GmbH,
P.O. Box 300240, 70442 Stuttgart, Germany,
Heiko.Eisele@bosch.com

[2] Interdisciplinary Center for Scientific Computing, University of Heidelberg,
69120 Heidelberg, Germany,
Fred.Hamprecht@iwr.uni-heidelberg.de

Abstract. We introduce a novel method to automatically evaluate X-ray computed tomography (CT) images for the purpose of detecting material defects by evaluating the significance of features extracted by first order derivative filters. We estimate the noise of the original image and compute the noise of the filtered image via error propagation. The significance of these features can then be evaluated based on the signal-to-noise ratio in the filtered image. The major benefit of that procedure is, that a sample-independent threshold on the signal-to-noise ratio can be chosen. The results are demonstrated on parts drawn from an industrial manufacturing line.

1 Introduction

X-ray computed tomography (CT) enjoys a growing interest in industrial quality control as it can be used on a wide range of products and provides detailed information about otherwise unaccessible features. Major application areas are the inspection of castings, the detection of gas bubbles or inclusions and cracks. Image processing algorithms should be robust to cope with the noise and poor contrast characteristic of X-ray images.

1.1 Review of Related Work

An overview of methods for flaw detection in castings is given in [1]. In early methods, the image data are compared to data obtained from a reference object. This approach requires either exact repositioning of the probes or a matching of the image data, which is non-trivial and computationally expensive. Also, these methods cannot allow for tolerances in the manufacturing process. In the case of castings, it is not even possible to produce a reference part that is totally free of defects. Here, the question is rather whether or not these defects are critical. An alternative strategy is to generate a reference object from the image data themselves. Several such methods have been proposed, most of which are based on modifications of median filtering techniques [2–6]. They basically differ in the

L. Van Gool (Ed.): DAGM 2002, LNCS 2449, pp. 345–352, 2002.

way the filter masks are adapted to the structure of the object and the choice of threshold value for fault detection. However, these methods have difficulty in detecting small low-contrast defects such as cracks. Also, the threshold values are chosen either empirically or based on rarely justified assumptions such as two-mode histograms.

In another approach, local areas are analyzed for defects based on their Fourier transform [7]. This technique, however, does not distinguish between defects and noise. Multi-resolution image analysis [8] has similar drawbacks, i.e. poor performance on low-contrast noisy images.

This paper suggests a solution to both, the challenge to detect coherent structures in noisy images, and the issue of systematically choosing the proper threshold for detection.

2   Modeling and Descriptive Statistics of the Image

We model the absorption $g(x)$ of an intact object as locally homogeneous with added correlated isotropic normal noise. In other words, we interpret the data as realization of a stochastic process with drift (the mean is only locally constant). The covariance structure is assumed constant throughout the random field (homoscedasticity), and it is estimated based on a homogeneous training region (see fig. 2). The probability of a voxel being intact can then be estimated using statistical tests at a chosen significance level. If a moderate significance level is chosen to reduce errors of the second kind[1], a large number of pseudo errors result – at a significance level of 95%, for instance, $(1 - 0.95) \cdot 10^3 = 50$ pixels will be marked as defect in an intact cube with a length of 10 pixels. We therefore need to apply techniques that smooth out the noise and enhance the defects (section 3). If we still wish to calculate probabilities, we need to see what happens to the noise under the filtering operations, see section 4.

3   Defect Enhancement

The key to defect enhancement is to detect oriented structures within the image. Commonly used techniques are tensorial approaches, which are discussed in [9–12]. These methods require eigenvalue computation for each pixel, which results in a computationally expensive procedure. In addition, they respond to both edges and to noise. As an alternative, we suggest to simply take the square of locally averaged derivates as an edge detector. This suppresses the noise and – at the same time – enhances pixels within areas of coherent grey value structure. The corresponding operator looks like this:

$$F\{g(x)\} = \sum_{p=1}^{3} \left(\int w(x - x') \frac{\partial g(x')}{\partial x_p} dx' \right)^2 \tag{1}$$

---

[1] In this context, an error of the second kind means classifying a defect voxel as intact.

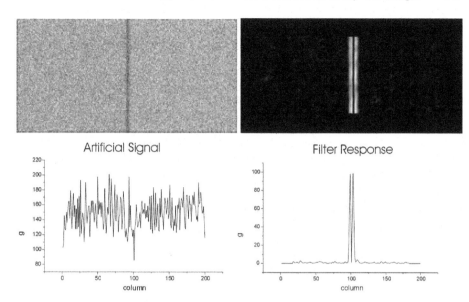

Fig. 1: Artificial test image. Upper left: XY cross section through artificial volume data with a planar crack parallel to the YZ plane. We added uncorrelated normal noise (with standard deviation $\sigma = 20$) to the image and finally convolved it with a binomial mask of size 5 to obtain correlated noise. Upper right: test image after filtering according to (1). Lower left: horizontal cross section through the upper left image displayed as a signal. Lower right: horizontal cross section through the processed image.

where p runs over the spatial directions. Fig. 1 shows the result obtained on an artificial image with a defect simulated as a vertical crack in the center. The crack appears as a signal in front of the noisy background. The transformations can be implemented discretely by applying x-,y- and z-derivative and smoothing filters to the image $g(x)$ and summing the square of these terms.

4   Error Propagation

This section details how the transformation in (1) affects the noise. Differentiation and smoothing are performed by a single filter f. This can be expressed as

$$g'_{(i,j,k)} = \sum_{\{l,m,n\}=-r}^{r} f_{(l,m,n)}g_{(i-l,j-m,k-n)} \tag{2}$$

If the image is modeled as a random field as described in section 2, the variance of $g'_{(i,j,k)}$ is

$$\sigma^2_{(i,j,k)} = E\left[\left(g'_{(i,j,k)} - E\left[g'_{(i,j,k)}\right]\right)^2\right], \tag{3}$$

where E denotes expectation. We substitute (2) into (3), rearrange terms and compute the expectation value term by term in order to obtain

$$\sigma^2_{(i,j,k)} = \sum_{\{l,m,n,o,p,q\}=-r}^{r} f_{(l,m,n)} f_{(o,p,q)}$$
$$E\left[\left(g_{(i-l,j-m,k-n)} - E\left[g_{(i-l,j-m,k-n)}\right]\right)\right.$$
$$\left.\left(g_{(i-o,j-p,k-q)} - E\left[g_{(i-o,j-p,k-q)}\right]\right)\right] \qquad (4)$$

Eq. 4 can be rewritten as

$$\sigma^2_{(i,j,k)} = \sum_{\{l,m,n,o,p,q\}=-r}^{r} f_{(l,m,n)} f_{(o,p,q)} Cov(i-l, j-m, k-n, i-o, j-p, k-q).$$
$$(5)$$

As mentioned above, we assume the covariance function to be constant over space so that the variance at a pixel becomes

$$\sigma^2 = \sum_{\{l,m,n,o,p,q=-r\}}^{r} f_{(l,m,n)} f_{(o,p,q)} Cov(l-o, n-p, n-q). \qquad (6)$$

The value of σ^2 is determined based on a training region as shown in Fig. 2. The size of that region has to be at least 2 times the filter size in each direction, so that all covariances in (6) can be accounted for. It might be larger for the benefit of statistically more precise results at the cost of execution time. The average grey value used in the covariance matrix corresponds to the arithmetic mean within the training region. Fig. 2 illustrates that it is indeed necessary

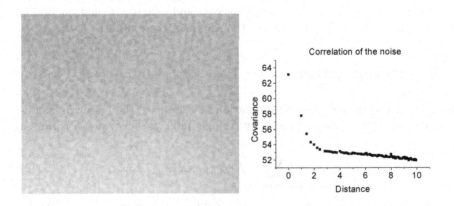

Fig. 2: Analyzing the correlation of the noise in real data. Left: homogeneous region within a real object; right: autocovariance vs. distance for the image to the left. The noise within that region is highly correlated, as can be seen from the slowly decaying autocovariance function (note the scale on the vertical axis).

to include the off-diagonal terms of the covariance function in (6): The noise is highly correlated.

To compute the square of the random variables in (1), consider a Gaussian random variable y with zero mean and variance σ_y^2. The variance of y^2 is by definition

$$\sigma_{y^2}^2 = E[y^4] - E[y^2]^2 \tag{7}$$

and

$$E[y^2]^2 = \sigma_y^4 \tag{8}$$

$$E[y^4] = 3\sigma_y^4 \tag{9}$$

Substituting (8) and (9) in (7) yields

$$\sigma_{y^2}^2 = 2\sigma_y^4 \tag{10}$$

The last step of (1) consists in taking the sum of random variables. Even though the derivatives of a random field are spatially correlated, the derivatives with respect to different spatial directions taken at the *same* point are *un*correlated in an isotropic random field. Assuming isotropy, the variance of the sum in (1) is equal to the sum of the individual variances. Using that and equations (6) and (10) we note that the variance σ_F^2 of the filtered image becomes

$$\sigma_F^2 = 6\sigma^4 \tag{11}$$

where σ^2 is given by (6). We finally compute the signal-to- noise ratio:

$$SNR_F = \frac{F\{g(\boldsymbol{x})\}}{\sigma_F} \tag{12}$$

There is one drawback of this operator with respect to the purpose of detecting cracks: Since it yields the strongest response in areas where there is a predominating gradient direction across a local neighborhood, it will yield a stronger response to edges than to cracks. We attempted to work around this problem by subtracting the original image from the image obtained after a closing operation. While defects disappear after the closing, edges should remain relatively unchanged. This worked on some data, but did not prove to be a reliable method in general. At this point, therefore, we merely exclude regions close to the object boundary from consideration. In other words: We only detect defects in the interior of the object and label the remaining part of the image as invalid. To determine the valid region, we choose a global threshold which we determine dynamically from the histogram as described in the following section.

5 Excluding the Boundary Region

Fig. 3 shows a histogram typical for one-component CT-images with strong X-ray absorption: It actually contains two major peaks, the right one coming from the material itself and the other one arising due to artefacts in the spherial

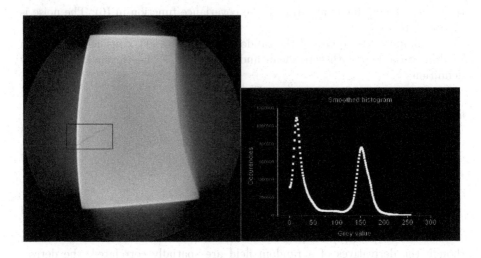

Fig. 3: Approximate segmentation of the data. Left: cross-section through a CT- image of a massive steel part with a crack; right: typical histogram of a one- component object after smoothing. The threshold value is placed at the minimum between the two peaks

region close to the object. Based on this grey value distribution, we perform an approximate segmentation by choosing the minimum between the two major peaks as a threshold. To ensure the uniqueness of this minimum, we apply an iterative smoothing algorithm to the histogram, which works as follows: Smooth the histogram with a (3×1) binomial mask, count the total number of maxima and repeat this procedure until left with exactly two maxima. This strategy allows an approximate distinction between object and background for one- as well as for multi-component images. We then define the interior region of the object by eroding the binarized image. Defect detection will only be meaningful within the region thus obtained.

6   Experimental Results

Fig. 4 summarizes the defect detection algorithm and quantifies the parameters used. We apply the operator described by (12) to the original image and detect defects by applying a threshold on the region of interest, which excludes areas close to the object boundaries. The left picture of Fig. 5 shows the original image processed according to (12). The center and right figures show the processed image binarized at a threshold value of 1 and 13 respectively. The filter f is generated by convolving a $(5 \times 5 \times 5)$ Gaussian with a $(3 \times 3 \times 3)$ derivative operator that has been optimized for isotropy [13]. The image is filtered accordingly, where we take advantage of filter separability. The other parameters are the number of components – one in the example – and the size of the mask used for eroding the region that has been determined to be the object region according

Fig. 4: Schematic summary of the image processing procedure. Parameters: f: $(5 \times 5 \times 5)$ Gaussian convolved with a $(3 \times 3 \times 3)$ derivative operator; number of components: 1; mask size used for erosion: (5×1) applied in each direction.

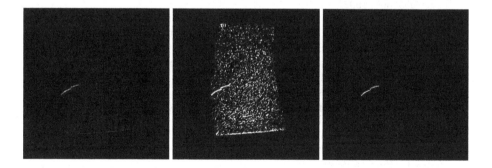

Fig. 5: Left: Data set shown in fig. 3 after filtering with f. 3D Image size: $511 \times 511 \times 280$ pixels; center and right: the left image binarized at thresholds of 1 and 13.

to the histogram-based thresholding explained in the previous section. For faster processing, it is desirable to process the image at a lower-than-original resolution if the feature size permits. In the example, the crack could still be safely detected at half the original resolution.

7 Conclusion

We proposed a rather general method to detect defects in CT-images as structural deviations from the local background. We demonstrated its effectiveness on cracks, which are difficult to detect with other methods. We used linear filters together with neighborhood information to emphasize the defects, and outlined a procedure for a systematic rather than heuristic choice of the detection threshold. We intend to apply the framework to other types of faults by adapting the linear filter used for defect enhancement.

References

1. D. Mery et. al. Automated quality control of castings: state of the art (German). *Technisches Messen*, 68, 2001.
2. D. Filbert et al. Computer aided inspection of castings. In *IEEE-IAS Annual Meeting*, pages 1087–1095, 1987.
3. W. Heinrich. A speed optimized rank ordering operator for the automation of the radiological inspection of castings. Technical Report 123, Institute for Electrical Engineering, Technical University of Berlin, 1987.
4. W.Heinrich. *Automated X-ray inspection of castings in series*. PhD thesis, Institute for Electrical Engineering, Technical University of Berlin, 1988.
5. H. Hecker und D. Filbert. X-ray inspection: Automatic adaption of an inspection system to inspection tasks (in German). In *DGZfP Annual Meeting*, volume 33.2, pages 655–660, 1992.
6. H. Hecker. *A new method for the evaluation of X-ray images for the automated inspection of castings (In German)*. PhD thesis, Institute for Electrical Engineering, Technical University of Berlin, 1995.
7. A. Gayer et al. Automatic recognition of welding defects in real-time radiography. *NDT International*, 23(4):131–136, 1990.
8. Y. Chitti. Detection of small intensity changes in CCD images with non-uniform illumination and large signal dependent noise. *CVGIP: Graph. Models and Image Processing*, 59(3):139–148, 1997.
9. J. Bigün and G.H. Granlund. Optimal detection of linear symmetry. In *Proceedings ICCV'87, London 1987*, pages 433–438, Washington,DC, 1987. IEEE, IEEE Computer Society Press.
10. H. Knutsson. Representing local structure using tensors. In *The 6th Scandinavian Conference on Image Analysis*, Oulu, Finland, June 19-22 1989.
11. A.R. Rao and B.G. Schunk. Computing oriented texture fields. In *Proceedings CVPR'89, San Diego, CA*, pages 61–68, Washington, DC, 1989. IEEE, IEEE Computer Society Press.
12. A.R. Rao. *A taxonomy for texture description and identification*. Springer, New York, 1990.
13. H. Scharr. *Optimal operators in Digital Image Processing*. PhD thesis, University of Heidelberg, 2000.

Object Tracking
with an Adaptive Color-Based Particle Filter

Katja Nummiaro[1], Esther Koller-Meier[2], and Luc Van Gool[1,2]

[1] Katholieke Universiteit Leuven, ESAT/VISICS, Belgium,
{knummiar,vangool}@esat.kuleuven.ac.be
[2] Swiss Federal Institute of Technology (ETH), D-ITET/BIWI, Switzerland,
{ebmeier,vangool}@vision.ee.ethz.ch

Abstract. Color can provide an efficient visual feature for tracking non-rigid objects in real-time. However, the color of an object can vary over time dependent on the illumination, the visual angle and the camera parameters. To handle these appearance changes a color-based target model must be adapted during temporally stable image observations. This paper presents the integration of color distributions into particle filtering and shows how these distributions can be adapted over time. A particle filter tracks several hypotheses simultaneously and weights them according to their similarity to the target model. As similarity measure between two color distributions the popular Bhattacharyya coefficient is applied. In order to update the target model to slowly varying image conditions, frames where the object is occluded or too noisy must be discarded.

1 Introduction

Object tracking is required by many vision applications, but especially in video technology [2,5,7,12]. Tracking methods can be divided into two main classes specified as *bottom-up* or *top-down* approaches. In a *bottom-up* approach the image is generally segmented into objects which are then used for the tracking. For example blob detection [12] can be used for the object extraction. In contrast, a *top-down* approach generates object hypotheses and tries to verify them using the image. Typically, model-based [5,7] or template matching approaches [2] comprise this class. The proposed particle filter with color-based image features belongs to the *top-down* approaches as the image content is only evaluated at the hypothetical object positions.

The idea of a particle filter – to apply a recursive Bayesian filter based on sample sets – was independently proposed by several research groups [3,5,7,11]. These filters provide robust tracking frameworks as they are neither limited to linear systems nor require the noise to be Gaussian. In this paper we present the integration of color distributions into particle filtering, which has typically used edge-based image features [4,5,7,13]. Color histograms have many advantages for tracking non-rigid objects as they are robust to partial occlusion, are rotation and scale invariant and are calculated efficiently. In [8] color information has

L. Van Gool (Ed.): DAGM 2002, LNCS 2449, pp. 353–360, 2002.
© Springer-Verlag Berlin Heidelberg 2002

already been employed in particle filtering for foreground and background model using Gaussian mixtures. Our target model has the advantage of matching only objects that have a similar histogram, whereas for Gaussian mixtures objects that contain one of the colors of the mixture will already match.

The color of an object can vary over time dependent on the illumination, the visual angle and the camera parameters. To handle these appearance changes the color model must be adapted during temporally stable image observations. Particle filtering has already been used with several static target models [4], but to the best of our knowledge it has not yet been applied with an adaptive model.

A related tracking approach which also uses color histograms is the mean shift tracker [2]. In comparison, our proposal employs multiple hypotheses and a model of the system dynamics which results in a more reliably tracking in cases of clutter and occlusions. Adaptive models have been discussed in [9,14], but both approaches employ Gaussian mixture models while we use color histograms together with multiple hypotheses.

The outline of this paper is as follows. In Section 2 we briefly describe particle filtering and in Section 3 we indicate how color distributions are used as object models. The integration of the color information into the particle filter is explained in Section 4 and Section 5 describes the model update. Finally, some experimental results are presented in Section 6.

2   Particle Filtering

Particle filtering [5,7] was developed to track objects in clutter, in which the posterior density $p(X_t|Z_t)$ and the observation density $p(Z_t|X_t)$ are often non-Gaussian. The quantities of a tracked object are described in the state vector X_t while the vector Z_t denotes all the observations $\{z_1, \ldots, z_t\}$ up to time t.

The key idea of particle filtering is to approximate the probability distribution of the object state by a weighted sample set $S = \{s^{(n)}, \pi^{(n)})|n = 1 \ldots N\}$. Each sample consists of an element s which represents the hypothetical state of the object and a corresponding discrete sampling probability π where $\sum_{n=1}^{N} \pi^{(n)} = 1$.

The evolution of the sample set is calculated by propagating each sample according to a system model. Each element of the set is then weighted in terms of the observations and N samples are drawn with replacement, by choosing a particular sample with probability $\pi^{(n)} = p(z_t|X_t = s_t^{(n)})$. The mean state of the object is estimated at each time step by

$$E[S] = \sum_{n=1}^{N} \pi^{(n)} s^{(n)}. \tag{1}$$

Particle filtering provides a robust tracking framework, as it models uncertainty. It can keep its options open and consider multiple state hypotheses simultaneously. Since less likely object states have a chance to temporarily remain in the tracking process, particle filters can deal well with short-lived occlusions.

3   Color Distributions

We want to apply such a particle filter in a color-based context. To achieve robustness against non-rigidity, rotation and partial occlusion we focus on color distributions as target models. These are represented by histograms which are typically calculated in the RGB space using 8x8x8 bins.

Not all pixels in a region are equally important to describe an object. For example, pixels that are further away from the region center can be assigned smaller weights by employing a weighting function

$$k(r) = \begin{cases} 1 - r^2 & : \quad r < 1 \\ 0 & : \quad \text{otherwise} \end{cases} \tag{2}$$

where r is the distance from the region center. Thus, we increase the reliability of the color distribution when these boundary pixels belong to the background or get occluded. It is also possible to use a different weighting function for example the Epanechnikov kernel [2].

The color distribution $p_{\mathbf{y}} = \{p_{\mathbf{y}}^{(u)}\}_{u=1...m}$ of a region R at location $\mathbf{y}$ is calculated as

$$p_{\mathbf{y}}^{(u)} = f \sum_{\mathbf{x}_i \in R} k\left(\frac{\|\mathbf{y} - \mathbf{x}_i\|}{a}\right) \delta[h(\mathbf{x}_i) - u] \tag{3}$$

where δ is the Kronecker delta function and $h(\mathbf{x}_i)$ assigns one of the m-bins of the histogram to a given color at location $\mathbf{x}_i$. The variable a provides invariance against scaling of the region and the normalization factor f ensures that $\sum_{u=1}^{m} p_{\mathbf{y}}^{(u)} = 1$.

In a tracking approach the estimated state is updated at each time step by incorporating the new observations. Therefore, a similarity measure is needed between the color distributions of a region in the newly observed image and the target model. A popular measure between two distributions is the Bhattacharyya coefficient [1,10]. Considering discrete densities such as two color histograms $p = \{p^{(u)}\}_{u=1...m}$ and $q = \{q^{(u)}\}_{u=1...m}$ the coefficient is defined as

$$\rho[p, q] = \sum_{u=1}^{m} \sqrt{p^{(u)} q^{(u)}}. \tag{4}$$

The larger ρ is, the more similar the distributions are. For two identical histograms we obtain $\rho = 1$, indicating a perfect match. As distance between two distributions we define the measure

$$d = \sqrt{1 - \rho[p, q]} \tag{5}$$

which is called the Bhattacharyya distance.

4   Color-Based Particle Filtering

The proposed tracker employs the Bhattacharyya distance to update the a priori distribution calculated by the particle filter. The target regions are represented by ellipses, so that a sample is given as

$$\mathbf{s} = \{x, y, \dot{x}, \dot{y}, H_x, H_y, \dot{H}_x, \dot{H}_y\} \tag{6}$$

where x, y represent the location of the ellipse, $\dot{x}$, $\dot{y}$ the motion, H_x, H_y the length of the half axes and $\dot{H}_x$, $\dot{H}_y$ the corresponding scale changes.

The sample set is propagated through the application of a dynamic model

$$\mathbf{s}_t = A\,\mathbf{s}_{t-1} + \mathbf{w}_{t-1} \tag{7}$$

where A defines the deterministic system model and $\mathbf{w}_{t-1}$ a random vector drawn from the noise distribution of the system. In our application we currently use a first order model for A describing an object moving with constant velocity for x, y, H_x and H_y. Expanding this model to second order is straightforward.

To weigh the sample set, the Bhattacharyya coefficients are computed between the target distribution and the distributions at the locations of the hypotheses. Each hypothetical region is specified by its state vector $\mathbf{s}^{(n)}$. Both the target q and the candidate histogram $p_{\mathbf{s}^{(n)}}$ are calculated from Eq. 3 where the target is centered in the origin and $a = \sqrt{H_x^2 + H_y^2}$.

The observation probability of each sample

$$\pi^{(n)} = \frac{1}{\sqrt{2\pi}\sigma}\, e^{-\frac{d^2}{2\,\sigma^2}} = \frac{1}{\sqrt{2\pi}\sigma}\, e^{-\frac{(1-\rho[p_{\mathbf{s}^{(n)}},q])}{2\,\sigma^2}} \tag{8}$$

is specified by a Gaussian with variance σ. During filtering, samples with a high weight may be chosen several times, leading to identical copies, while others with relatively low weights may not be chosen at all.

A comparison of this approach to the mean shift tracker [2] and different methods for the initialization respectively re-initialization of the color-based particle filter are described in [15]. An extension for multiple objects and the usage of more than one histogram per sample can be found in [16].

5   Model Update

Illumination conditions, the visual angle as well as the camera parameters can influence the quality of the color-based particle filter. To overcome these appearance changes we update the target model during slowly changing image observations. By discarding image outliers – where the object is occluded or too noisy – the tracker can be protected against updating the model when the object has been lost. So, we use the update rule

$$\pi_{E[S]} > \pi_T \tag{9}$$

where $\pi_{E[S]}$ is the observation probability in terms of the mean state $E[S]$ and π_T is a threshold.

The update of the target model is implemented by the equation

$$q_t^{(u)} = (1 - \alpha)\, q_{t-1}^{(u)} + \alpha\, p_{E[S_t]}^{(u)} \tag{10}$$

for each bin u where α weighs the contribution of the mean state histogram $p_{E[S_t]}$ to the target model q_{t-1}. Thus, we evoke a forgetting process in the sense that the contribution of a specific frame decreases exponentially the further it lies in the past.

6   Results

To illustrate the adaptive color-based particle filter and its behavior, we applied the proposed method to a *traffic* and a *face* sequence and show the tracking results. The experiments have been processed with a 800 MHz Pentium3 PC under Linux, using the RGB color space with 8x8x8 bins and images of size 360x288 pixels. The goal of the experiments has been to track a manually initialized object region (car, human) during the sequence until it has disappeared.

To show the importance of the model update we regard the *traffic* sequence of 234 frames recorded by a highway monitoring system. There is an evident scale change during this sequence as the camera was placed towards the traffic flow. Furthermore, different viewing angles of the car and partial occlusions make the experiment more difficult. In the top row of Figure 1 no model update is performed and the resulting region gets stuck on the left front side of the car. In contrast, the bottom row shows the effectiveness of the model update.

frame 1   frame 100   frame 200

Fig. 1. The *traffic* sequence illustrates the importance of an adaptive target model in cases of occlusions and large scale changes. The white ellipses represent the mean states of the underlying sample distribution of $N = 100$ elements. In the top row the tracking results without a model update are presented while in the bottom row an update is applied.

frame 1   frame 120   frame 320

frame 400   frame 470   frame 600

Fig. 2. The *face* sequence shows the tracking performance with an adaptive model. The tracker handles a large object motion and illumination changes using $N = 100$ samples.

In Figure 2 the *face* sequence of 600 frames is shown which has been captured with a strong sun/shadow effect. At the beginning of the sequence the face is situated in the shadow for the initialization and at the end of the sequence it is moved into the sun. The tracked face is affected by changing illumination conditions and facial expressions as well as a full turn of the person and large scale changes. In frame 400, the tracked position is not very exact as the model does not match the back of the head very well. Nevertheless, the person can still be tracked and the positions improves rapidly once the person has turned around.

The target model of our tracker is only updated according to Eq. 9 as outliers must be discarded, for example when the person is turning. A related update rule is given by the maximization of the log-likelihood [9] over the last M frames: $L = \sum_{t=1}^{M} log\, \pi_{E[S]}^{(t)}$. In Figure 3 both update possibilities are plotted for the *face* sequence. The two update approaches behave similarly in the sense that a model update is only performed under slowly varying image conditions. As the history of samples through the log-likelihood does not significantly improve the results, we use our more efficient method.

Finally, Figure 4 illustrates the running times of the adaptive color-based particle filter for the *face* sequence for two different image sizes. The proposed approach has real-time capability but the processing time is dependent on the region size and the number of samples.

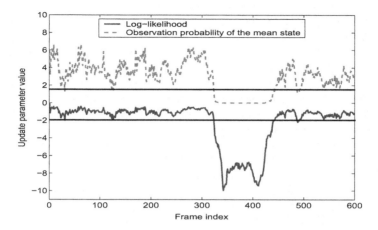

Fig. 3. The log-likelihood L and the observation probability $\pi_{E[S]}$ (here scaled with factor 10) can be both applied as an update rule with an appropriate threshold.

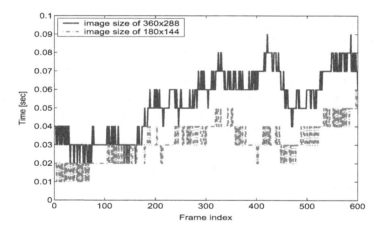

Fig. 4. Running times for the *face* sequence for two different image sizes using $N = 100$ samples.

7   Conclusion

The proposed tracking method adds an adaptive appearance model based on color distributions to particle filtering. The color-based tracker can efficiently and successfully handle non-rigid and fast moving objects under different appearance changes. Moreover, as multiple hypotheses are processed, objects can be well tracked in cases of occlusion or clutter. As a limitation of the proposed approach the tracker might loose an object when it changes appearance quickly – for example through occlusion – and makes a rapid movement at the same time. The application of an adaptive model comprises always a trade-off between an increasing sensitivity to extended occlusions and a more reliable tracking under appearance changes.

Acknowledgment

The authors acknowledge the support by STAR (IST-2000-28764) which is a project of the European Commission and by the GOA/VHS+ project financed by the Research Fund KUL.

References

1. F. Aherne, N. Thacker and P. Rockett, *The Bhattacharyya Metric as an Absolute Similarity Measure for Frequency Coded Data*, Kybernetika, pp. 1-7, Vol. 32(4), 1997.
2. D. Comaniciu, V. Ramesh and P. Meer, *Real-Time Tracking of Non-Rigid Objects using Mean Shift*, CVPR, pp. 142-149, Vol. 2, 2000.
3. N. Gordon and D. Salmond, *Bayesian State Estimation for Tracking and Guidance Using the Bootstrap Filter*, Journal of Guidance, Control and Dynamics, pp. 1434-1443, Vol. 18(6), November-December, 1995.
4. T. Heap and D. Hogg, *Wormholes in Shape Space: Tracking through Discontinuous Changes in Shape*, ICCV, pp. 344-349, 1998.
5. M. Isard and A. Blake, *Contour Tracking by Stochastic Propagation of Conditional Density*, ECCV, pp. 343-356, Vol. 1, 1996.
6. M. Isard and A. Blake, *ICONDENSATION: Unifying Low-Level and High-Level Tracking in a Stochastic Framework*, ECCV, pp. 893-908, Vol. 1, 1998.
7. M. Isard and A. Blake, *CONDENSATION – Conditional Density Propagation for Visual Tracking*, International Journal on Computer Vision, pp. 5-28, Vol. 1(29), 1998.
8. M. Isard and J. MacCormick, *BraMBLe: A Bayesian Multiple-Blob Tracker*, ICCV, pp. 34-41, 2001.
9. A. Jepson, D. Fleet and T. El-Maraghi, *Robust Online Appearance Models for Visual Tracking*, CVPR, pp. 415-422, Vol. 1, 2001.
10. T. Kailath, *The Divergence and Bhattacharyya Distance Measures in Signal Selection*, IEEE Transactions on Communication Technology, pp. 52-60, Vol. COM-15(1), 1967.
11. G. Kitagawa, *Monte Carlo Filter and Smoother for Non-Gaussian Nonlinear State Space Models*, Journal of Computational and Graphical Statistics, pp. 1-25, Vol. 5(1), 1996.
12. D. Koller, J. Weber and J. Malik, *Robust Multiple Car Tracking with Occlusion Reasoning*, ECCV, pp. 189-196, 1994.
13. J. MacCormick and A. Blake, *A Probabilistic Exclusion Principle for Tracking Multiple Objects*, ICCV, pp. 572-587, Vol. 1, 1999.
14. S. McKenna, Y. Raja and S. Gong, *Tracking Colour Objects Using Adaptive Mixture Models*, Journal of Image and Vision Computing, pp. 225-231, Vol. 17, 1999.
15. K. Nummiaro, E. Koller-Meier and L. Van Gool, *A Color-Based Particle Filter*, First International Workshop on Generative-Model-Based Vision, in conjunction with ECCV'02, pp. 53-60, 2002.
16. P. Pérez, C. Hue, J. Vermaak and M. Gangnet, *Color-Based Probabilistic Tracking*, ECCV, pp. 661-675, Vol. 1, 2002.

Analysis of Object Interactions
in Dynamic Scenes*

Birgit Möller[1] and Stefan Posch[2]

[1] Technical Faculty, Applied Computer Science, University of Bielefeld
[2] Institute of Computer Science, University of Halle,
Von-Seckendorff-Platz 1, 06099 Halle/Saale,
posch@informatik.uni-halle.de

Abstract. One important source of information in scene understanding
is given by actions performed either by human actors or robots. In this
paper an approach to recognition and low-level interpretation of actions
is presented. Since actions are characterized by specific motion patterns
of moving objects, recognition is done by detecting such motion patterns
as specific constellations of interactions between moving objects. First
of all, motion detection and tracking algorithms are applied to extract
correspondences between moving objects in consecutive images of a sequence. Subsequently these are represented with a graph data-structure
for further analysis. To detect interactions of moving objects robustly a
short history of motion of objects is traced using a finite-state automaton.
Finally activities are segmented based on detected interactions. Since robust motion data are required consistency checks and corrections of the
acquired motion data are performed in parallel.

1 Introduction

The analysis of dynamic scenes is of growing interest in todays computer vision
research. Especially interacting systems often rely on the analysis and interpretation of motions and actions taking place in their work space. Since this analysis
is based on image sequences, a large amount of data has to be analyzed to extract
relevant information. To simplify this task one might, on the one hand, reduce
the data representing image sequences by one single mosaic image [5,8]. On the
other hand, one can focus on preselected, potentially interesting parts of the
scene. Often such parts are characterized by actions in the scene projected into
the image. In this paper we present an approach to detect events and activities
in order to determine such regions of interest.

In the literature events or actions are often defined by physical data of mon-
itored objects such as velocities and motion directions [3] or spatial relations [4].
Mann et al [7] suggest to use dynamic and kinematic models to understand objects' behaviors and interactions. Since the computation of physical features requires highly accurate segmentation data, we in contrast define events as changes

---

* This work has been supported by the German Research Foundation (DFG) within
SFB 360.

L. Van Gool (Ed.): DAGM 2002, LNCS 2449, pp. 361–369, 2002.
© Springer-Verlag Berlin Heidelberg 2002

in the motion characteristics of moving objects originating from object interactions, e.g. merging, splitting, and start or end of motion. Activities are defined as specific constellations of such events. Similar to [1], we assume that these activities, and thus as well underlying actions, can be detected to a large degree based on interactions of moving objects and without exploitation of high level or scene knowledge [3]. Our analysis is therefore focused on blob constellations and interactions (e.g. in contrast to [1], where blob shapes or orientations are explored), solely based on motion detection and tracking results presented in [8].

Actions are usually characterized by varying temporal scales. To achieve a robust and flexible recognition, this temporal variance has to be considered. Often this is done using HMM- or parser-based approaches [10,6]. Since the usage of HMMs usually requires large amounts of training data, we use a training-free graph-based approach, similar to the one in [2]. All detected temporal correspondences between moving objects are represented within a graph data-structure. Interactions and activities can then be defined and recognized as specific subgraph constellations. To achieve robust recognition, additionally a finite-state automaton is used to process a short history of detected moving objects and thus verify recognized interactions. According to the states and transitions of the automaton, events are hypothesized, consistency checks on the motion data performed and further analysis steps invoked.

In the following section the basics of motion detection and tracking are outlined as well as the graph data-structure used. The graph-based annotation and correction of motion data using a finite-state automaton is described in section 3, subsequent activity detection in section 4. Results are presented in section 5 and we conclude with some final remarks.

2   Motion Data Extraction and Representation

To detect moving objects[1] within a scene and to track them over time the two-step strategy outlined in [8] is used, which is briefly summarized in the following paragraph. Subsequently the graph data-structure is described in detail.

In a first step intensity residuals between the current image and a reference image[2] are calculated. Since often only small displacements occur between two consecutive images there is the tendency to detect only parts of the moving object, especially in case of objects with homogeneous surfaces. Therefore we use a continuously updated representation of the static scene background as reference image for motion detection. This background representation is generated by integrating static parts of all sequence data into one single (mosaic) image. Given these motion data, subsequent binarization and region segmentation yields moving regions, which are grouped into connected components with regard to spatial

---

[1] Using 2D image sequences, only projections of moving objects can be detected and tracked, obviously. However, for simplification we use the terms objects and their projections synonymously.

[2] For active cameras images are first aligned using projective transformations, see [8].

neighborhood. These connected components are tracked over time using their intensity histograms as well as the distance of their centroids and difference of size as matching criteria. Tracking connected components instead of single regions in isolation yields more robust tracking data despite variance in segmentation. To handle also cases where connected components could not be matched as a whole, all subsets of their constituting regions are calculated and matched against each other. Thus splitting and merging of connected components can easily be detected and serves as a basis for recognition of object interactions.

Resulting temporal correspondences between moving connected components are represented using a graph data-structure, in the following referred to as *correspondence graph*. For every frame and each connected component a node of this graph is created while matches are represented by edges in between. Matches of region subsets are represented by inserting and connecting the connected components the subsets belong to. The associated match information is stored using a list of the corresponding edge. In this way, we not just link connected components in case they match as a whole, but also if matched only partially. Hence it is possible to detect events like splitting and merging as graph nodes with multiple incoming or outgoing edges.

3 Graph-Based Data Annotation and Correction

Based on our assumption that interesting parts of a scene (i.e. parts where actions are expected to occur) can be detected analyzing motion-based activities, we propose a two-step strategy to locate such activities.

In the first step of our approach we detect interactions (events) between moving connected components or region subsets based on the above mentioned correspondence graph. Since matches of connected components as well as region subsets are represented by the graph representation we will in the following refer to both as *components*. Each sequence of linearly linked nodes in the graph where all nodes have in-degree and out-degree equal to one, except the first with in-degree and the last with out-degree larger one, represents a period of continuous[3] motion of a component. Thus to detect events it is sufficient to analyze the first and last node of such a sequence with respect to the number of incoming and outgoing edges. However, due to inaccurate tracking data or variance in segmentation, events like splitting or merging might occur even if no real object interaction takes place. To cope with such situations a short history of motion of components is used as temporal context which is analyzed using a finite-state automaton. This automaton currently consists of ten states and an alphabet of five possible input symbols, listed in the tables below. The transition diagram is shown in figure 1.

---

[3] In this context we do not consider continuity as continuous velocity or acceleration but periods of motion without any interaction.

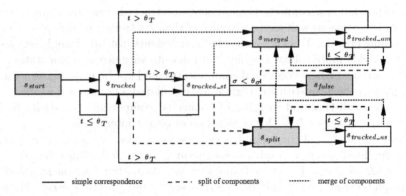

Fig. 1. The finite-state automaton for tracing the short history of motion of objects. For clearness reasons some self-transitions and the state $s_{stopped}$ have been omitted.

State	Description
s_{start}	start of motion
$s_{tracked}$	simple tracked, $T \leq \theta_T$
$s_{tracked\_st}$	simple tracked, $T > \theta_T$
$s_{tracked\_am}$	tracked after merge
$s_{tracked\_as}$	tracked after split
s_{merged}	merge
s_{split}	split
s_{false}	detected, but not in motion
$s_{stopped}$	not detected

Symbol	Edge Constellation	Line Code
t_{match}	1 in - 1 out	solid
t_{split}	1 in - multi out	dashed
t_{merge}	multi in - 1 out	dotted
$t_{mergesplit}$[6]	multi in - multi out	
t_{stop}	not matched	

Each state of the automaton codes either a certain event (gray boxes) or a specific phase of continuous motion (white boxes). If a state coding an event is reached, the corresponding event is hypothesized for further analysis in the activity detection step. In case a state coding a specific phase of motion is reached special procedures are invoked to perform e.g. consistency checks or to detect components incorrectly classified as moving. The input alphabet of the automaton is defined based on possible constellations of incoming and outgoing edges of graph nodes (see table above). When analyzing an image sequence, the correspondence graph is annotated based on the automaton. In this way each graph node, respectively the corresponding component, is associated with one state of the automaton. Edges between graph nodes are labeled with symbols of the input alphabet where the edge constellation of the source node is evaluated. This analysis of the correspondence graph is now discussed in some detail.

With each frame processed the correspondence graph is updated by inserting the detected matches. Nodes associated with components detected for the first time are labeled with the state s_{start}. However, if a component at a nearby position has been detected a few frames previously, an undetected correspondence is assumed. Hence the graph is corrected accordingly by inserting an additional edge.

Each newly detected component is subsequently associated with the state $s_{tracked}$ for a total of θ_T (typically five to eight) frames. If it is further tracked,

---

[6] This constellation is currently only recognized but not explicitly handled.

state $s_{tracked\_st}$ is entered. In this state the component is assumed to have been stably tracked and additional analysis steps are invoked. As an example, the variance σ of its centroid positions during the last frames yields the possibility to identify incorrectly classified moving regions, which have ceased moving and thus show little variance ($\sigma < \theta_\sigma$). If such an incorrectly classified component is detected, the state s_{false} is assigned and it is removed from the set of moving components. Furthermore this observation provides the opportunity for top-down verification and update of the background representation, since these classification errors are due to an inconsistency between the static mosaic image and the current state of the scene: If e.g. an initially static objects starts to move, intensity residuals result at its former position and a seemingly moving region is detected. However, integrating data of the current image to this area the representation can be corrected.

If an interaction is detected during continuous tracking the state of the involved components switches to s_{merged} or s_{split}. Thus, merge or split events are hypothesized, however not accepted straight away. Rather checks for spurious splitting and merging due to segmentation errors are performed first. To this end for subsequent frames the components originating from a split or merge enter the state $s_{tracked\_as}$ ('tracked after split') or $s_{tracked\_am}$ ('tracked after merge'). Only if no further events occur until they are stably tracked again the hypothesized event is accepted and the state $s_{tracked}$ is assigned. If further events are recognized the previously hypothesized event is assumed to be incorrect, probably due to very large variance in segmentation. Therefore these events are rejected and the graph representation is corrected accordingly: In case of a spurious split we directly link the two nodes where the split respectively the merge event had been detected. The subgraph in between is not considered any longer. However, in the future one could merge components of this subgraph which share the same time stamp and thus interpolate the trajectory of the moving object. Similarly spurious merges of components can be amended. As outlined above, the annotation and analysis of the correspondence graph is performed simultaneously to motion detection and tracking. Thus consistency checks and if necessary corrections are continuously performed on the acquired motion data.

4   Activity Detection

In the construction scenario of the SFB 360 [9] under consideration a human and a robot in cooperation are supposed to perform an assembly task. Activities are given by more or less complex steps of such tasks, e.g. to add objects to the scene, to remove objects, to move objects from one position to another and to manipulate, assemble or disassemble them. According to our basic assumption that each single activity can be coded as a constellation of previously defined interaction events, the final step in our approach consists of evaluating the formerly generated event constellations as described below.

In the following diagram two activity definitions are shown. Since adding objects to the scene and removing them share the same event constellation, they share the same definition as well and therefore can only be distinguished analyzing the image data directly.

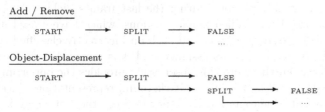

Obviously, to recognize such an activity, the start of a motion has to be detected first. In case of a 'Remove'-activity, which is explained in detail now, an actor, e.g. the arm of a human, starts moving, grasps an object and leaves the workspace (see figure 3). During monitoring this activity, initially only one single moving region is detected since the object to be removed is still part of the static scene background. When contact has been established between actor and object this moving region grows since actor and object are now moving simultaneously. With growing distance between the moving actor and the former object position, the moving component splits up: One resulting component corresponds to the moving actor including the object, the second one results from intensity differences at the initial object position (see section 3). After this split the actor is tracked further while the second component is detected as incorrectly classified and eliminated. Summarizing resulting event constellations one can conclude that initially a new motion is recognized, then the component splits up. One of the components resulting from the split keeps moving, while the second one is classified as non-moving a short period of time later. As a result a 'Remove'-activity is hypothesized to have taken place.

These explanations show that the proposed activity detection is based on interactions of tracked components exclusively. World or context knowledge is used only to interpret the different activities with regard to the scenario under consideration. Thus it is easy to transfer this approach to other scenarios as well, where activities can be identified by moving entities and their interactions.

5   Results

To evaluate the presented algorithms we have chosen image sequences from the the above mentioned scenario where assembly tasks are performed. In this section we present three examples. The first one illustrates results of the graph-based consistency checks, the two others show activity detection results. In each figure the first row contains several images of the underlying image sequence, the second row segmented moving regions/components and in the bottom row the development of the correspondence graph over time is visualized.

Figure 2 shows several images of a hand passing through the scene. Due to low contrast between the bright background and the moving hand it is not possible to completely detect it. Instead multiple moving regions result from the

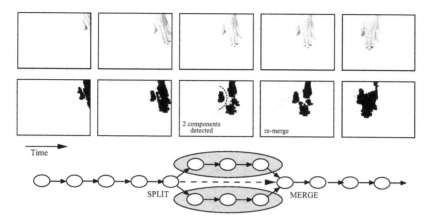

Fig. 2. Robust tracking: Due to a leak of contrast the moving hand is only partially detectable, but graph correction enables tracking of the hand as one object.

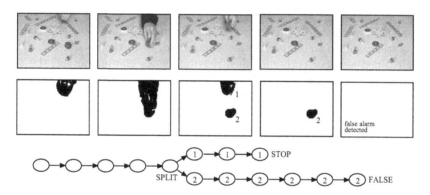

Fig. 3. 'Remove'-activity: The hand grasps the cube and removes it.

segmentation process. At the beginning of tracking, these regions are correctly grouped into one component which is easily tracked. However, after some frames, more than one component results, caused by segmentation errors, and two independent components are tracked in the following. This error can not be detected until both merge again into one component only a few frames ($t < \theta_T$) later. Therefore, the events detected are assumed to be due to variance in segmentation and the graph is corrected as shown: The split and merge events are removed (marked gray in figure 2) and the associated graph nodes are connected directly (dashed line).

In the second sequence (see figure 3) a hand enters the scene removing a cube. As shown, initially one single moving component is detected correctly. After grasping took place, the hand starts to leave the scene and still one component consisting of two regions is detected. This component finally splits into two components, where the second one (id 2) results from intensity differences

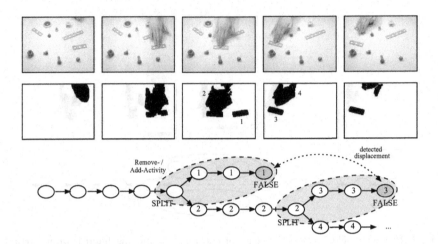

Fig. 4. 'Object Displacement'-activity: The 3-hole-bar is moved from right to left.

between the background representation and the current image since the removed cube is still assumed to be part of the background. Nevertheless, after θ_T frames it is identified as incorrectly classified moving, hence eliminated and the background representation is updated accordingly.

The last example in figure 4 illustrates results from a more complex activity. The 3-hole-bar is moved from right to left. Due to interactions of moving components one can deduce that the moving region appearing initially belongs to an acting entity. The first split and subsequent false alarm indicates adding or removing of an object. Since the same sequence of events is observed some frames later again, either a second object has been removed or the first object has been moved to this new position. To decide for one of the two cases is currently not possible since to this end image data has to be scrutinized directly with respect to e.g. significant gradient norms or object contours in the region of interest. Nevertheless one might hypothesize that an 'Object-displacement'-activity has taken place which could be verified by high-level analysis.

6   Conclusion and Future Work

In this paper we presented an approach to detect activities within arbitrary scenes. Based on motion detection and tracking, resulting interactions between moving objects in the scene, called events, are analyzed. Since activities are assumed to consist of specific constellations of events, typical activities of the construction scenario under consideration can be segmented. In conclusion the proposed strategy to scene analysis and event detection provides an opportunity for robust pre-selection of scene parts where more detailed and elaborate analysis steps can be performed. Thus scene understanding and high-level interpretation is possible without the need for analyzing large amounts of data by focussing on interesting regions where activities have been recognized.

This approach might in the future be extended to recognize more complex activities, e.g. complete assemblies, where multiple objects are involved. Further on more work is necessary to extract additional details from analysis steps performed, e.g. to decide whether an object has been added or removed, since both tasks currently share the same event constellation. At last the graph consistency checks should be developed further.

References

1. Matthew Brand. Understanding Manipulation in Video. Proc. of 2nd International Conference on Face and Gesture Recognition (1996)
2. Isaac Cohen and Gérard Medioni. Detection and Tracking of Objects in Airborne Video Imagery. CVPR Workshop on Interpretation of Visual Motion (1998)
3. Gérard Medioni, Ram Nevatia and Isaac Cohen. Event Detection and Analysis from Video Streams. DARPA Image Understanding Workshop (1998), Monterey
4. J. Fernyhough, A.G. Cohn and D.C. Hogg. Building Qualitative Event Models Automatically from Visual Input. ICCV (1998) 350-355
5. M. Irani, P. Anandan. Robust multi-sensor image alignment. PIEEE (1998) 905-921
6. Y. Ivanov, C. Stauffer, A. Bobick and E. Grimson. Video Surveillance of Interactions. Proc. of the CVPR Workshop on Visual Surveillance (1998), Fort Collins, Colorado
7. Richard Mann, Allan Jepson and Jeffrey Mark Siskind. Computational Perception of Scene Dynamics. Computer Vision and Image Understanding (1997) 65(2):113-128
8. Birgit Möller, Stefan Posch. Detection and Tracking of Moving Objects for Mosaic Image Generation. LNCS 2191, Proc. of 23rd DAGM Symposium (2001) 208-215
9. Gert Rickheit and Ipke Wachsmuth. Collaborative Research Centre "Situated Artificial Communicators" at the University of Bielefeld, Germany, Integration of Natural Language and Vision Processing (1996) IV:11-16
10. Junji Yamato, Jun Ohya and Kenichiro Ishii. Recognizing Human Action in Time-Sequential Images using Hidden Markov Models. Proc. of CVPR (1992) 379-385

Automatic Monocular 3D-Reconstruction of Indoor Environments Using Mobile Vehicles

Christian Bräuer-Burchardt

Friedrich Schiller University Jena, Dept. of Computer Science,
Digital Image Processing Group, D-07740 Jena, Germany
cbb@pandora.inf.uni-jena.de

Abstract. A new methodology to realise automatic exploration of an indoor environment using single view sequences from a camera mounted on an autonomously moving vehicle is presented. The method includes geometric reconstruction and acquisition of texture information using image rectification. The algorithm of wall edge detection and position determination is given as the heart of the methodology. Navigation planing and self localisation by the moving vehicle are realised whereas obstacles are neglected. Examples for 3D models and accuracy results are presented and discussed.

1   Introduction

The goal of this work was to design a robust method of monocular 3D reconstruction of an unknown indoor environment. The resulting model could be used for example for architectural purpose or to produce maps for autonomous moving vehicles. In order to simplify the general task the following assumptions are made:

- the ground of the region to be explored should be planar
- the height of the rooms is constant
- the resulting model should be a straight prism a with polygonal ground surface
- the walls have rectangular shape (walls are vertical)
- the used camera is calibrated
- parallel and orthogonal lines can be found in the images

Additionally, it is assumed that no map of the area to be explored is available, static obstacles may occur and moving obstacles can appear.

In order to realise automatism and low effort the camera is mounted on a mobile robot. Using a mobile robot requires the knowledge of the position and orientation of the robot, static and moving obstacles must be recognised, collisions must be avoided, and navigation must be realised. Several techniques to control moveable robots have been established, e.g. [14]. There are often used landmarks to achieve localisation and to control navigation in known environments [10]. However, a plan of the environment is often not available. Therefore 3D reconstruction or mapping of an unknown environment is an important task of may applications of robotics (see e.g. [19]).

L. Van Gool (Ed.): DAGM 2002, LNCS 2449, pp. 370–378, 2002.

Recent work has been dealt with model acquisition under these conditions. Shah and Aggarwal [17] propose a stereo fish-eye system. Whereas Armstrong [1] and Faugeras [12] used three, and Beardsley and Zisserman [2] used two views for reconstruction, Montiel [16] proposed a monocular approach. Our goal is a monocular method too, but is should not be restricted to orthogonal ground plan lines.

Our situation is the following. A camera with known intrinsic parameters and known radial lens distortion function is mounted on a mobile robot. When a zoom lens is used the actual focal length must be determined from two vanishing points of orthogonal directions [4], and the radial lens distortion function must be considered depending on the actual focal length. The height of the projection centre of the camera over the ground and the tilt angle between ground plane and optical axis of the camera are known. With known robot position and orientation also the exterior camera parameters are available which are necessary for the image rectification.

2   General Approach

The goal is the final 3D-model of the environment, and the general approach of the 3D reconstruction can be outlined as follows:

- initialisation (finding an edge of the ground polygon, insertion into the model)
- finding of succeeding edges of the ground polygon and the corresponding rectangular wall surfaces simultaneously in a loop, insertion into the model
- identification and matching of the last with the first edge of the ground polygon
- ground plan equalisation
- finding and modelling of holes in the ground surface

3   Image Acquisition and 3D-Modeling

3.1 3D Model Description

The 3D model of the indoor environment contains a prismatic polyhedron to describe the geometry, a set of images to describe the surface (texture) of the polyhedron, and a set of relationships between 3D-points of the polyhedron and 2D-points in the images.

Let the polyhedron Π consist of a polygonal ground surface with n outer nodes. If the polygon has holes this should be considered, but without loss of generality we assume that there are no holes. Thus we have two identical polygonal surfaces s_g (the ground surface) and s_c (the ceiling surface). Let the rectified (see section 3.4) images $I_1, \ldots, I_n$ of all n rectangular surfaces $s_1, \ldots, s_n$ be given. The 3D-model is defined as a tupel $\mathcal{M} = [\mathbf{P}, \mathbf{S}, \mathbf{I}, \mathbf{R}]$ where $\mathbf{P} = \{P_i\}$ is a set of 3D point co-ordinates, $\mathbf{S} = \{s_j\}$ is the set of the two polygonal and the n rectangular facets, $\mathbf{I} = \{I_k\}$ a set of rectified images and $\mathbf{R} = \{R_j\}$ the relationships $R_j = (k, p_1, p_2, p_3, \ldots)$ between the facets and the 2D point co-ordinates $p_j = (x_j, y_j)$ in the I_k.

3.2 Model Construction Approach

The idea to construct the searched 3D-model is the following. Initially the robot position is at the origin of the world co-ordinate system Σ_W. A first image is recorded, and a rectangular surface of the polyhedron is searched by image processing. This search may be assisted by the robot sensor data. The algorithm of rectangular surface detection and insertion into the model works as follows:

- image recording
- wall existence recognition and confirmation
- wall border detection and image rectification
- determination of the 3D co-ordinates of the corner points
- insertion into the model

After the first insertion the next consecutive rectangle should be found and connected in the model and so on. Here self localisation and navigation planning is necessary. The whole procedure stops when an edge is found to be identical to the initial edge. Then an equalisation of the word co-ordinates should be performed.

3.3 Vanishing Points and Orientation

In order to determine the orientation of the wall surfaces and rectify the images the determination of horizontal vanishing point plays an important role. If the rotation angle κ around the optical axis is $\kappa = 0$ (can be initially realised by fixation or camera or image rotation) and the tilt angle ω of the camera is fixed the vanishing point $Q_v=(x_v,y_v)$ of the vertical lines depends only on the camera constant f (also denoted as effective focal length) which is a-priori known using lenses with fix focal length. The orientation of the wall in the 3D scene can be described by the angle φ between the optical axis and the normal of the planar wall. Rotation κ, tilt ω, and orientation φ correspond to the vanishing point $Q_h=(x_h,y_h)$ of horizontal lines on the walls surface by

$$\kappa = \arctan\frac{X - x_v}{Y - y_v} \ , \qquad \omega = \arctan\frac{f \cos(\kappa)}{Y - y_v} \ , \qquad \varphi = \arctan\frac{f \cos(\kappa)}{(x_h - X)\cos(\omega)} \qquad (1)$$

with the principal point $P=(X,Y)$. For further description see [20, 4].

Hence, the orientation angle φ can be easily obtained when a calibrated camera is used and the tilt angle ω is known. The remaining problem is the robust vanishing point determination in the image with corrected radial lens distortion. This is realised as follows. The original image is searched for a number of edge segments. If the lens distortion is too strong (this is a-priori known) the image itself should be corrected, and the segments should be found in the corrected image. Otherwise the segment end points can be corrected using the distortion function. From the corrected segment list all vertical segments can be removed (the vertical vanishing point is a-priori known). The remaining segments are the input to a vanishing point calculation algorithm described in [3] yielding the searched horizontal vanishing point Q. Because the y-coordinate of Q is also known a-priori by the fix ω the result can be easily controlled.

3.4 Image Rectification

The transformation of the original camera image into a similarity mapping of the planar surface of the wall should be called image rectification. This includes first the removal of the radial lens distortion and then the inversion of the projective mapping. The first part is realised by the application of the inverse distortion function to the image and the second one by the principal point determination proposed by Kanatani [13]. These transformations are detailed described in [4, 5] and lead to rectified images (see Fig.1 upper and lower row).

3.5 Wall Detection

The wall detection should be reduced to the detection of the four bordering edges of the rectangular surface in the image. This should be obtained according to the following approach.

- edge detection
- classification and reduction of edges (vertical and horizontal wall edges)
- calculation and correction of the 3D position of the wall corners
- image rectification and model insertion

    Assuming that the wall edges are not occluded there should be long edge segments to be found in the image. Thus an edge detection algorithm [9] should be applied to the original or corrected image (Fig.1 upper right). Long vertical segments are candidates for vertical wall edges and other segments are those for the horizontal ones.

3.5.1 Finding Horizontal Wall Edge Candidates

First, two cases are to be distinguished. The first case includes the assumption of a perpendicular ground polygon, i.e. all horizontal wall edges are in one of only two directions. This is the easier case and leads to simplifications. The second one assumes arbitrary directions for the horizontal wall edges. Let us consider the first one without loss of generality. Using the vanishing point detection algorithm two classes of horizontal segments can be formed. From these two classes all segments in the same direction behind others are removed. Thereafter the two classes are merged getting an ordered list of ground wall edge candidates (see Fig.1 middle row). If the edge candidates coming from the ground of the 3D scene their actual position can be determined directly using the a-priori knowledge about the camera parameters as described in [6]. Thus the 3D position of any ground point can be calculated from the camera parameters (intrinsic parameters, vertical vanishing point, and height of the projection centre over the ground) and the image co-ordinates.

    However, the assumption that the detected points are truly in the ground may fail. That's why the distance obtained from image analysis should be confirmed using the robots sensor data. If there arises a considerable deviation an alternative hypothesis concerning the corner position is stated using the sensor data and the assumption of parallelism of the false edge with the actual one. If parallelism can be detected the wall edge candidate is parallel shifted towards the camera position.

3.5.2 Wall Position Calculation

The two lists of ordered vertical and horizontal segments, respectively, are used for detection of wall corners on the ground. The algorithm works as follows

- take the first segments from both lists (from left to right)
- compare the positions, test if they are candidates to have a common corner
- if a left corner is found → set flag
- if a right corner is found → look if the corresponding left corner is present
- select one or two new edges (at most one from each list)
- stop if all edges are processed

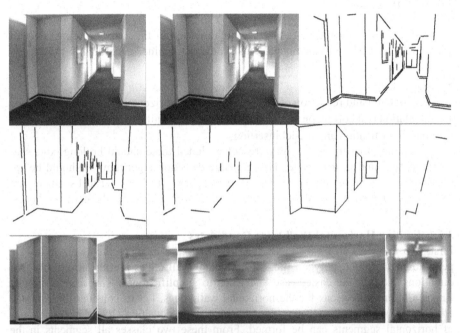

Fig. 1. Original and corrected image, segments (upper), reduced segments, wall edges, detected walls, partial map (middle), and rectified wall images from the original image (lower)

3.6 Ground Polygon Equalisation

In result of the consecutive edge insertion one get a ground plan of the region to be explored. Typically, the starting point and the end point of the ground plane, which should be equal, will differ because of measuring and reconstructing errors (gap between the two left upper edges in Fig.2). A compensation of these errors is achieved by correcting the co-ordinates (x_i, y_i) of the points p_i, $i = 1, ..., n$ of the ground plan edges by

$$x'_i = x_i + c_x \sum_{j=2}^{i} |x_j - x_{j-1}| \qquad\qquad y'_i = y_i + c_y \sum_{j=2}^{i} |y_j - y_{j-1}| \qquad (2)$$

with
$$c_x = \frac{x_1 - x_n}{\sum_{j=2}^{n} |x_j - x_{j-1}|} \qquad\qquad c_y = \frac{y_1 - y_n}{\sum_{j=2}^{n} |y_j - y_{j-1}|}$$

getting new point co-ordinates $p_i' = (x_i', y_i')$.

Note, that the general error is distributed to the single edges according to their length. This procedure does not necessarily imply a reduction of the single errors. As a result of our example we get the corrected ground plan (see Figure 2). Note, that there are still small errors due to the equalisation process. These errors, recognised by a-priori knowledge or image information, may be reduced after the production of the whole model. Of course, all points connected to the polygons with corrected points have to be corrected in the same manner.

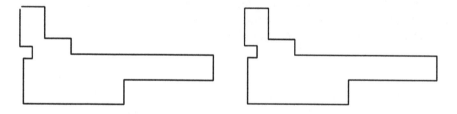

Fig. 2. Ground polygon equalisation: original (left) and corrected ground plan (right)

4   Self-localisation and Navigation

The task of self localisation of the mobile robot is a nontrivial problem (see [15]), especially in unknown environment. Following the strategy of consecutive completion of the ground polygon the most important is the prevention of error accumulation.

This problem was solved in the following way. Every newly explored corner is used as a landmark. After controlled robot movement the new position is theoretically known by the controlled navigation. For position correction the odometric data as well as the landmarks are used. Another image based assistance can be given by the use of the SDR method [18]. For orientation correction after turns also vanishing points are used. Additional correcting mechanisms should be applied in the case of large areas to be mapped, e.g. as proposed by Gutmann [11].

Considering navigation two aspects have to be analysed. First, the exploration area should be visited completely and second, the robot movements should be efficient. The following navigation strategy is expected to allow an efficient and complete reconstruction.

- start with the first edge of the ground polygon, if only a part of such an edge is detectable, start with this part and try to complete by a suitable movement
- find a connecting edge
- move along the border of the ground polygon inside the moveable region, take and rectify images, complete the ground polygon
- after ground polygon equalisation: if there are holes in the inner of the polygon then insert the holes into the model by surrounding these regions (if necessary)
- if the final completion of the model by the texture of the ground plane is desired: calculate the best image recording positions, move there, take and rectify images

The size of the navigation step depends on the validity of the recent result and the viewing field of the camera. It must be sure how a new calculated position can be achieved without any collision. Therefore common navigation techniques, e.g. [10, 14] can be used. The production of an occupancy grid [8] may be useful to obtain this. If the next robot position is calculated the sensor data should make sure that no collision with a wall happens. In order to improve the currently available data (8 sensors) the robot may turn around itself taking as much sensor data as necessary.

The use of certain obstacle prevention techniques [7] would reduce the risk of collisions, but this is not yet implemented in our system.

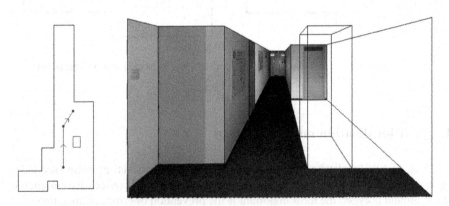

Fig. 3. Ground plan with robot positions (left), partial model with texture information obtained from the hallway views from the marked positions

5   Summary and Outlook

A method for automatic 3D reconstruction of unknown indoor environments using a mobile robot and single image sequences was outlined.

First experiments in the rooms of our department have been performed. We produced a 3D model of a part of a hallway with an extension of about 12 x 5 m. A video camera with a wide angle 4.8 mm lens with strong radial distortion was used. The height of the projection centre was about 1.2 m, and the mean length of one navigation step was about 1 m. Figure 3 shows the way of the robot in a map (actual known geometry), the positions of image recording (circles) and a wire-frame representation with additional texture information of a part of the obtained model.

Unsolved problems so far are the detection of not compact obstacles, finding an optimal navigation strategy, and unsupervised automatic error treatment. Experiences from further experiments should improve the methodology in the next time. Future work should also include more detailed comparison to other systems, e.g. [11, 16].

References

1. Armstrong, M., Zisserman, A., and Hartley, R.: Self-calibration from image triplets. Proc. ECCV 1996, Springer (1996) 3-16
2. Beardsley, P. and Zisserman, A.: Affine calibration of mobile vehicles. Proc. Europe-China workshop on geometrical modelling and invariants for computer vision. (1995) 214-221
3. Bräuer-Burchardt, C. and Voss, K.: Robust vanishing point determination in noisy images. Proc.15th ICPR, vol. I, IEEE Computer Society, 2000, 559-562
4. Bräuer-Burchardt, C. and Voss, K.: Image rectification for reconstruction of destroyed buildings using single views. Proc VAA'01, Springer, 2001, 159-170
5. Bräuer-Burchardt, C. and Voss, K.: Automatic lens distortion calibration using single views. In Mustererkennung 2000, Springer, 187-194
6. Bräuer-Burchardt, C. and Voss, K.: Mapping of indoor environments using mobile robots and single image sequences. Proc. TIARP 2001, Mexico-City, 119-129
7. Branca, A., Stella, E., and Distante, A.: Ground plane obstacle detection using projective geometry. Proc IEEE Int Conf on Intelligent Vehicles, 587-592
8. Burgard, W., Fox, D., Hennig, D., and Schmidt, T.: Estimating the absolute position of a mobile robotusing position probability grids. Proc AAAI-96, 1996, 896-901
9. Burns, J.B., Hansen, A.R., and Riseman, E.M.: Extracting straight lines. IEEE Trans PAMI (8), 1986, 425-455
10. Dulimarta, H.S. and Jain, A.K.: Mobile robot localization in indoor environment. Pattern Recognition 30(1), 1997, 99-111
11. Gutmann, J.-S. and Konolige, K.: Incremental mapping of large cyclic environments. Proc CIRA'99, Monterey, November 1999
12. Faugeras, O.D., Quan, L., and Sturm, P.: Self-calibration of a 1d projective camera and its application to the self-calibration of a 2d projective camera. Proc. ECCV 1998, 36-52
13. Kanatani, K.: Constraints on length and angle. CVGIP 41, 1988, 28-42
14. Kosaka, A. and Kak, C.: Fast vision-guided robot navigation using model-based reasoning and prediction of uncertainties. CVGIP Image Understanding 56(3), 1992, 271-329
15. Lee, W.H., Roh, K.S., and Kweon, I.S.: Self-localization of a mobile robot without camera calibration using projective invariants. PRL 21, 2000, 45-60

16. Montiel, J.M.M. and Zisserman, A: Automated architectural acquisition from a camera undregoing planar motion. Proc. VAA'01, Springer (2001) 207-218
17. Shah, S. and Aggarwal, J.K.: Mobile robot navigation and scene modeling using stereo fish-eye lens system. Machine Vision and Applications (10), 1997, 159-173
18. Suesse, H., Voss, K., Ortmann, W., Baumbach, T.: Shift detection by restoration. Proc CAIP, 1999, 33-40
19. Thrun, S., Burgard, W., and Fox, D.: A probabilistic approach to concurrent mapping and localizationfor mobile robots. Mach Learn and Auton Robots 31/5, Kluwer, 1998, 1-25
20. Wolf, P.R.: Elements of Photogrammetry. McGraw-Hill, 1983, 588ff

Dense Parameter Fields
from Total Least Squares

Hagen Spies[1] and Christoph S. Garbe[2]

[1] ICG-III: Phytosphere, Research Center Jülich, 52425 Jülich, Germany,
h.spies@fz-juelich.de
[2] Interdisciplinary Center for Scientific Computing, University of Heidelberg,
INF 368, 69120 Heidelberg, Germany,
Christoph.Garbe@iwr.uni-heidelberg.de

Abstract. A method for the interpolation of parameter fields estimated by total least squares is presented. This is applied to the study of dynamic processes where the motion and further values such as divergence or brightness changes are parameterised in a partial differential equation. For the regularisation we introduce a constraint that restricts the solution only in the subspace determined by the total least squares procedure. The performance is illustrated on both synthetic and real test data.

1 Introduction

The parameters governing the changes in an image sequence can be estimated locally by means of a total least squares technique [1; 2]. For the simple case of movement alone, i.e. optical flow, it is known that in areas with one dominant gradient direction only the component of the velocity in that direction can be computed. This is the well known aperture problem [3]. When there are more parameters to be estimated there might be even more such linear dependencies between them. We show how such cases can be detected and how an appropriate minimum norm solution can be obtained.

In many applications we are nevertheless interested in dense parameter fields and thus there is the need for an interpolation procedure. Clearly it is desirable to utilise the available information from the minimum norm solutions. Towards this end we present a regularisation framework that restricts the interpolated solution only in the subspace in which a solution is available. This is in contrast to variational methods that directly seek to minimise the constraint over the entire data set [4; 5]. The main idea of the presented regularisation has been introduced for the special case of 3D velocity (range flow) estimation in [6]. Here this is extended and applied to more general dynamic processes.

2 Dynamic Processes in Image Sequences

In scientific image processing one often encounters a linear equation for a set of model parameters $\boldsymbol{m}$ at each data point (pixel) of type: $\boldsymbol{a}^T \boldsymbol{m} = b$; $\boldsymbol{a}, \boldsymbol{m} \in \mathbb{R}^m$.

L. Van Gool (Ed.): DAGM 2002, LNCS 2449, pp. 379–386, 2002.
© Springer-Verlag Berlin Heidelberg 2002

An ordinary least squares estimate implies that only b is erroneous while a is exact. This assumption certainly does not hold for the cases discussed below where a contains derivatives. Therefore we introduce a new parameter vector p of dimension $n = m + 1$ and rewrite the constraint as:

$$d^T p = 0 \quad \text{with} \quad d = (a^T, -b)^T \quad \text{and} \quad p = (m^T, 1)^T . \tag{1}$$

This concept is very general in the sense that the parameters of any dynamic process that can be modeled by a linear partial differential equation falls into this scheme [2; 7]. Prominent physical examples are source terms, relaxation and diffusion processes. If there is no such model available a Taylor series expansion up to the desired order may be used [7]. A few examples that are used in the later experiments (Sect. 5) are:

Optical Flow. The assumption that all temporal variation in the image brightness $g(x, y, t)$ is caused by movements implies [4]: $\frac{dg}{dt} = g_x \frac{dx}{dt} + g_y \frac{dy}{dt} + g_t = 0$. With indices denoting partial derivatives. This *brightness change constraint equation* forms the basis of many algorithms to compute the optical flow $[u, v]^T = [\frac{dx}{dt}, \frac{dy}{dt}]^T$ [3; 1]. This is readily expressed in the form of (1) using $d = [g_x \, g_y \, g_t]^T$ and $p = [u \, v \, 1]^T$.

Source Terms. Source terms cause first-order temporal changes in the image sequence proportional to a source strength q: ($\frac{dg}{dt} = q$) yielding $d = [g_x \, g_y \, 1 \, g_t]^T$ and $p = [u \, v \, q \, 1]^T$. Source terms occur for example in infrared images if an object is heated or cooled or if the global illumination of a scene changes [8]. The same equation is obtained in the study of the three-dimensional movement of surfaces from sequences of depth maps: $z_x u + z_y v + z_t = w$. Here $[u \, v \, w]^T$ denotes the 3D-movement also called range flow [6].

Divergent Velocity. The proposed concept can also model spatial variations in the velocity field, e.g. an affine velocity field [1]. If we are interested in a particular aspect of the flow field, such as its divergence or rotation, we can only include this in our estimation. For divergence d this reads as: $d = [g_x \, g_y \, (xg_x + yg_y) \, g_t]^T$; $p = [u \, v \, d \, 1]^T$. Here x, y denote local coordinates with respect to the computed location. Examples include camera movement along the optical axis or local growth rates in biological experiments.

3   TLS Estimation

The presented estimation framework extends previous work on total least squares optical flow estimation [2]. For an estimation we pool the constraints (1) over a local neighbourhood and assume the parameters to be constant within:

$$\hat{p} = \arg \min \int_{-\infty}^{\infty} w(x - x', t - t')(d^T \hat{p})^2 dx' dt' \quad \text{subject to} \quad \hat{p}^T \hat{p} = 1 . \tag{2}$$

Here $w(x - x', t - t')$ is a weighting function that defines the spatio-temporal neighbourhood where the parameters are estimated. In order to avoid the trivial solution we require the solution vector $\hat{p}$ to be normalised. Minimisation leads to an eigenvalue equation of the extended structure tensor J:

$$J\hat{p} = \lambda\hat{p} \quad \text{with} \quad J(x) = \int_{-\infty}^{\infty} w\,(x - x', t - t')\,(d\,d^T)\,\mathrm{d}x'\mathrm{d}t' \ . \qquad (3)$$

It follows that the solution to (2) is given by the nullspace of J [9]. Section 3.2 describes how to recover the parameters. For an unbiased and optimal TLS estimate the errors in all data terms need to be independent random variables with zero mean and equal variance [9; 10]. This implies a scaling with respect to the absolute error values.

3.1   Type and Confidence Values

The spectrum of J can be used to detect linear dependencies in the data. In the following we assume the eigenvalues of J to be sorted in descending order: $\lambda_1 \geq \lambda_2 \geq \ldots \geq \lambda_{n-1} \geq \lambda_n$. The trace of J is used to determine if there is enough variation (texture) in the data for the computation to make sense. Thus we only proceed where $tr(J) > \tau_1$.

The smallest eigenvalue directly yields the residual of the parameter fit. Thus we reject unreliable estimates if $\lambda_n > \tau_2$, with a threshold τ_2 corresponding to the noise level. This occurs at discontinuities where a single set of parameters is not sufficient or when no coherent motion is present.

A small λ_n does not ensure that all the parameters can be estimated independently from each other. More than one eigenvalue may be close to zero ($< \tau_2$) and we can no longer uniquely pick a solution. Any vector in the nullspace of J is a possible solution, see Sect. 3.2. A type measure that indicates how well the dimensionality of the nullspace of J has been determined can be obtained by examining how much the first relevant eigenvalue λ_q is above the threshold:

$$\omega_t = \left(\frac{\lambda_q - \tau_2}{\lambda_q}\right)^2 \ , \qquad \lambda_1 \geq \ldots \geq \lambda_q > \lambda_{q+1} \approx \ldots \approx \lambda_n < \tau_2 \ . \qquad (4)$$

For a simple optical flow example of a moving square (Fig. 1) a map indicating which type of flow can be computed is given in Fig. 1b.

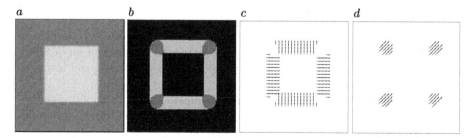

Fig. 1: *Moving square example: **a** image data, **b** type of flow (black: trace to small, light grey: linear dependency and dark grey: full estimate possible), **c** normal flow and **d** full flow.*

3.2   Minimum Norm Solutions

As stated above any vector in the nullspace of J is a possible solution. A sensible choice is that resulting in an estimate with minimal norm. This solution is given in terms of the eigenvectors $\hat{e}_i$ $(i > q)$ to the vanishing eigenvalues [9]:

$$p_k = \frac{\sum_{i=q+1}^{n} e_{ik} e_{in}}{\sum_{i=q+1}^{n} e_{in}^2} \; ; \quad k = 1 \ldots n . \tag{5}$$

The parameter vector $m = [p_1 \ldots p_{n-1}]^T$ can be expressed in a vector equation:

$$m = \frac{\sum_{i=q+1}^{n} e_{in}[e_{i1}, \ldots, e_{i(n-1)}]^T}{\sum_{i=q+1}^{n} e_{in}^2} . \tag{6}$$

Thus the solution can be expressed as a linear combination of the "reduced" eigenvectors: $\hat{b}_k = \frac{1}{\sqrt{\sum_{i=1}^{n-1} e_{ki}^2}} [e_{k1} \ldots e_{k(n-1)}]^T$. The resulting solutions for normal and full flow on the moving square sequence are given in Fig. 1b and c.

However when we are estimating parameters that are of greatly different magnitude some caution is advisable. A scaling procedure will lead to different relative errors of the estimated parameters. Moreover, being a linear combination for $q < n-1$, the minimum norm solution is dominated by the larger parameters. For pure velocity [6] this does not occur but here it has to be taken into account in further processing steps such as the regularisation procedure described next.

4   Parameter Field Regularisation

We now present a framework that allows to compute dense parameter fields from the previously computed minimum norm solutions. From the structure of the TLS solution given by (6) we can use the reduced eigenvectors $\hat{b}_k$ to the non-vanishing eigenvalues to define a projection matrix which projects onto the subspace determined by the TLS algorithm:

$$P = B_q B_q^T \quad \text{where} \quad B_q = [\hat{b}_1 \ \ldots \ \hat{b}_q] . \tag{7}$$

Each estimated parameter vector m restricts the solution within this subspace. We require the regularised solution r to be close in a least squares sense. A zero weight ω reflects locations where no solution could be found. A conceptually similar data term using the orthogonal projection on a subspace of an ordinary least squares solution based on multiple constraints at the same pixel has been given by [11].

Combining such a data constraint with a simple membrane smoothness constraint, as used by [4], in the the considered area A yields the following minimisation problem (we set $\omega = \omega_t$ in the following):

$$\int_A \left\{ \omega \left(Pr - m \right)^2 + \alpha \sum_{i=1}^{m} (\nabla r_i)^2 \right\} dxdy \rightarrow \min . \tag{8}$$

Here α is a regularisation parameter that controls the influence of the smoothness term. Evaluating the Euler-Lagrange equations yields:

$$2\omega P(Pr - m) - 2\alpha \left[\frac{d}{dx}(r_x) + \frac{d}{dy}(r_y) \right] = 0 . \tag{9}$$

The Laplacian $\Delta r = r_{xx} + r_{yy}$ can be approximated as $\Delta r = \bar{r} - r$, where $\bar{r}$ denotes a local average [12]. Thus we arrive at:

$$(\omega P + \alpha \mathbb{1}) \, r = \alpha \bar{r} + \omega Pm . \tag{10}$$

This now enables an iterative solution to the minimisation problem. Let $A = \omega P + \alpha \mathbb{1}$, then an update r^{k+1} from the solution at step k is given by:

$$r^{k+1} = \alpha A^{-1} \bar{r}^k + \omega A^{-1} Pm . \tag{11}$$

Initialisation could be done with zero. However, in order to speed up the convergence we use an interpolation of the available full parameter field by normalised averaging. The matrix A^{-1} can be found to be:

$$A^{-1} = \alpha^{-1} \left(\mathbb{1}_m - \frac{\omega}{\alpha + \omega} P \right) . \tag{12}$$

In order to verify that $A^{-1}A = \mathbb{1}$ only the idempotence of the projection matrix is needed. Inserting (12) into (11) yields:

$$r^{k+1} = \bar{r}^k - \frac{\omega}{\alpha + \omega} P \bar{r}^k + \frac{\omega}{\alpha + \omega} Pm . \tag{13}$$

Using $\mathbb{1} = P + P^\perp$ we can separate the two subspaces:

$$p^{k+1} = P^\perp \bar{r}^k + \frac{1}{\alpha + \omega} P(\alpha \bar{r}^k + \omega m) . \tag{14}$$

In the orthogonal subspace, where no initial TLS solution is available, the local average is used. In the TLS subspace the iterative update is given by a weighted mean of the local average and the originally available solution. The weights are determined by the regularisation constant α and the confidence measure ω respectively. Notice that the choice of α only regulates the amount of smoothing in the TLS subspace and has no effect in the orthogonal subspace.

The effect of this regularisation on the example of Fig. 1 is shown in Fig. 2 ($\alpha = 10$). Initially the flow field is dominated by the normal flows. With increasing iterations the full flow information spreads out until a dense full flow field is obtained. Here the trace is used to mask the area A.

As stated above some of the minimum norm parameters can be unreliable when there is a difference in magnitude between the parameters. This can be accounted for by choosing different confidence values ω_i for each parameter r_i in (13):

$$\omega_i = \begin{cases} c_i \, \omega & \text{if } q < n - 1 \\ \omega & \text{else} \end{cases} . \tag{15}$$

a   b   c   d

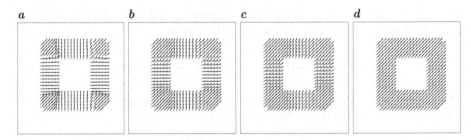

Fig. 2: Moving square optical flow after: **a** *10,* **b** *100,* **c** *200 and* **d** *500 iterations.*

a   b   c   d

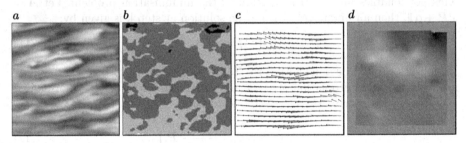

Fig. 3: IR sequence of the water surface: **a** *original image,* **b** *map indicating the type of flow (see Fig. 4),* **c** *velocity field and* **d** *source term (temperature change)* $[-0.5, 0.5]K/frame$.

Where c_i is a factor reflecting the confidence that the parameter r_i is reliably computed in the minimum norm solutions. In the same way we can also choose a different smoothing strength α_i for the different parameters.

5 Experiments

We are now ready to demonstrate the proposed algorithm on a few examples.

Heat Flux. Using IR cameras to view the water surface gives a direct way to study the heat exchange [8]. Here a linear source term is used to capture the rate of change. An example is given in Fig. 3 where we find that the temperature change (Fig. 3d) does not seem to be correlated to either the original temperature distribution (Fig. 3a) nor the velocity field (Fig. 3c).

Diverging Tree. Frame 20 of the diverging tree sequence is shown in Fig. 4a [3]. Because we are estimating a second order process we have chosen the following weight and smoothness factors in this case: $\alpha_{1,2} = 1$, $\alpha_3 = 10$, $c_{1,2} = 1$ and $c_3 = 0.01$. When the divergence of the optical flow field is modeled we obtain a type map as given in Fig. 4b. There is a large region where all parameters can be estimated that corresponds to the tree. Around this area some dependencies occur. The velocity part of the estimated parameter field at these locations is shown in Fig. 4c and d. The correct and the regularised velocity are shown in Fig. 4e and f, the only noticeable difference occurs at the image boundaries

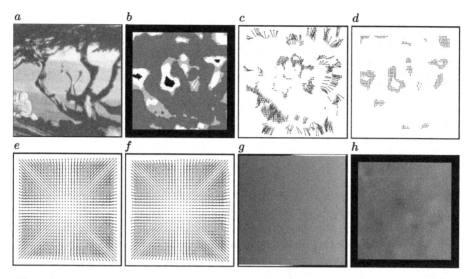

Fig. 4: *Diverging tree sequence:* **a** *original image,* **b** *map indicating the type of flow, black:* $tr(\boldsymbol{J}) < \tau_1$, *white:* $q = n - 3$, *light grey:* $q = n - 2$, *dark grey:* $q = n - 1$. **c** *velocity corresponding to the first normal flow* $q = n - 2$, **d** *velocity corresponding to the second normal flow* $q = n - 3$. **e** *correct optical flow and* **f** *estimated dense optical flow,* **g** *correct divergence map and* **h** *estimated divergence map* $[0, 0.04]$ *1/frame.*

where the averaging is problematic. The computed divergence (Fig. 4h) is much less accurate, compare to Fig. 4g. However the following numbers indicate that the estimated optical flow does indeed improve when the divergence is modeled, here the angular error E_a is reported [3]:

model	full flow density	initial E_a	final E_a at 100%
only motion $\boldsymbol{p} = [u\,v\,1]^T$	50.2%	2.4 ± 1.6	1.8 ± 1.3
with div $\boldsymbol{p} = [u\,v\,d\,1]^T$	73.5%	1.0 ± 0.8	1.0 ± 0.8

When the divergence is included the density of full parameter estimates greatly increases as well as the error drops substantially. The regularisation fills the parameter field without decreasing the optical flow accuracy.

Growing Maize Root. The study of growing plants presents another application where a direct estimation of the divergence (= local growth rate) is useful. As we know that negative growth rates do not make sense we can improve the result by removing the few occurring negative values by setting the confidence to zero. The result obtained by applying our technique to a sequence of a growing maize root is shown in Fig. 5. In the growth map (Fig. 5d) we observe two zones of increased growth: directly at the tip and about 3mm behind the tip.

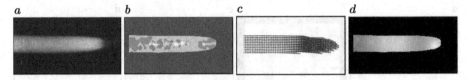

*Fig. 5: Growing maize root: **a** original image, **b** map indicating the type of flow (see Fig. 4), **c** movement and **d** divergence (growth rate) $[0, 36]\%/h$.*

6 Conclusion

We introduced a framework that allows to compute dense parameter fields using all the available information from a previous TLS estimation. Besides optical flow this can be used for the extraction of the parameters governing dynamic processes that can be expressed in a linear partial differential equation. The proposed regularisation uses a data constraint that restricts the solution within the subspace determined by the TLS algorithm. Currently a simple membrane smoother is used but we intend to extend this to anisotropic smoothers as well.

References

[1] Haußecker, H., Spies, H.: Motion. In: Handbook of Computer Vision and Applications. Academic Press (1999)

[2] Haußecker, H., Garbe, C., Spies, H., Jähne, B.: A total least squares for low-level analysis of dynamic scenes and processes. In: DAGM, Bonn, Germany (1999) 240–249

[3] Barron, J.L., Fleet, D.J., Beauchemin, S.: Performance of optical flow techniques. International Journal of Computer Vision **12** (1994) 43–77

[4] Horn, B.K.P., Schunk, B.: Determining optical flow. Artificial Intelligence **17** (1981) 185–204

[5] Schnörr, C., Weickert, J.: Variational image motion computation: Theoretical framework, problems and perspectives. In: DAGM, Kiel. Germany (2000) 476–487

[6] Spies, H., Jähne, B., Barron, J.L.: Regularised range flow. In: ECCV, Dublin, Ireland (2000) 785–799

[7] Haußecker, H., Fleet, D.J.: Computing optical flow with physical models of brightness variation. PAMI **23** (2001) 661–673

[8] Garbe, C. S., Jähne, B.: Reliable estimates of the sea surface heat flux from image sequences. In: DAGM, Munich, Germany (2001) 194–201

[9] Van Huffel, S., Vandewalle, J.: The Total Least Squares Problem: Computational Aspects and Analysis. SIAM, Philadelphia (1991)

[10] Mühlich, M., Mester, R.: The role of total least squares in motion analysis. In: ECCV, Freiburg, Germany (1998) 305–321

[11] Schnörr, C.: On functionals with greyvalue-controlled smoothness terms for determining optical flow. PAMI **15** (1993) 1074–1079

[12] Jähne, B.: Digital Image Processing. 3 edn. Springer, Germany (1995)

A Factorization-Based Method
for Projective Reconstruction
with Minimization of 2-D Reprojection Errors

W.K. Tang and Y.S. Hung

Department of Electrical and Electronic Engineering, The University of Hong Kong,
Pokfulam Road, Hong Kong,
{wktang,yshung}@eee.hku.hk

Abstract. In this paper, we consider the problem of projective reconstruction based on the factorization method. Unlike existing factorization based methods which minimize the SVD reprojection error, we propose to estimate the projective depths by minimizing the 2-D reprojection errors. An iterative algorithm is developed to minimize 2-D reprojection errors. This algorithm reconstructs the projective depths robustly and does not rely on any geometric knowledge, such as epipolar geometry. Simulation results using synthetic data are given to illustrate the performance of the algorithm.

1 Introduction

In the area of computer vision, there are many existing approaches [1][2][3][4][5] to reconstruct the 3-D Euclidean structure from multiple views. One of the popular strategies is 'stratification' [1]. It decomposes the reconstruction process into different procedures that recover the projective space first and then upgrade it to Euclidean space by applying metric constraints. One of the main benefits of this approach is that each procedure can be considered and developed independently. Projective reconstruction is the first step of the stratification strategy to reconstruct the 3-D shape and the projection matrices in projective space from correspondences between 2-D planar images.

Some existing methods [6][7] reconstruct the 3-D structure by solving the geometric properties between two views, three views or even four views with multilinear constraints. All of them are linear methods but they can relate only two to four views at the same time. Since there is no general representation for multiple (more than four) views based on geometric properties, the advantages of multiple views cannot be fully applied. The well-known projective factorization method [8], proposed by Tomasi and Kanade, generalizes projective reconstruction for multiple-view configuration. However, one set of parameters, the projective depths, need to be estimated in the reconstruction. Han and Kanade [2] use an iterative method to solve for the depths in a decomposition process iteratively without calculating the fundamental matrices. Poelman and Kanade [9] also propose other methods to estimate the depths in paraperspective or orthogonal projection as the starting points for the iterative method [2]. Triggs [10]

L. Van Gool (Ed.): DAGM 2002, LNCS 2449, pp. 387–394, 2002.
© Springer-Verlag Berlin Heidelberg 2002

proposes a method to solve for the depths by calculating fundamental matrices between any two views. It provides a very accurate result and fast converging on noise-free situations. However, it has the same problems as the above geometric methods since the fundamental matrices are calculated in advance.

There exist several projective reconstruction methods [11][12][13] for missing data. The sequential updating method by Beardsley [11] is able to deal with missing data but it does not optimize all the views at the same time. Jacobs [12] proposes a method that is good in noise-free situations and the result can be the starting points for iterative methods. Shum, Ikeuchi and Reddy [13] parameterize the minimization problem of factorization method as weighted least squares (WLS) minimization problems. The minimizations are set up by existing data only. The problem is stated as minimizing the sum of squares of the SVD reprojection errors [14]. Unlike 2-D reprojection errors which represent the distance between the input point and the reprojected point on a 2-D image plane, SVD reprojection errors lack physical meaning. Most of the factorization-based methods minimize the SVD reprojection errors rather than 2-D reprojection errors. A difficulty of minimizing 2-D reprojection errors is that the minimization problem [3] becomes non-linear.

In this paper, we propose an algorithm for projective reconstruction and it is based on the factorization method and WLS minimization. The proposed algorithm can deal with missing data and projective depth estimation and it minimizes 2D reprojection errors from all views at the same time.

This paper describes all the background and existing methods first. Our algorithm is developed in Sections 2, 3 and 4. In Section 5, simulation results using synthetic data are given to illustrate the performance of our algorithm in comparison with an existing method. Section 6 contains some concluding remarks.

2   Problem Formulation

For a 3-D point $X_j = \begin{bmatrix} x_j \ y_j \ z_j \ 1 \end{bmatrix}^T$, let its projection in the ith view be the image point $x_{ij} = \begin{bmatrix} u_{ij} \ v_{ij} \ 1 \end{bmatrix}^T$ in homogenous coordinates. The *perspective projection equation* relates these two sets of coordinates as:

$$\lambda_{ij} x_{ij} = P_i X_j \tag{1}$$

where λ_{ij} is the *real depth* of the point and P_i is a 3×4 projection matrix. The *Joint projection matrix* P combines all the m projection matrices P_i as $P = \begin{bmatrix} P_1^T, P_2^T, ..., P_m^T \end{bmatrix}^T \in \Re^{3m \times 4}$. Similarly, *projective shape* X combines all the n 3-D projective points X_j as $X = [X_1, X_2, ..., X_n] \in \Re^{4 \times n}$. The product of P and X represents the projection of all the 3-D points to all the cameras, giving rise to a *scaled measurement matrix*:

$$PX = \{\lambda_{ij} x_{ij}\} \in \Re^{3m \times n} \tag{2}$$

Since P and X are at most rank 4, the scaled measurement matrix $\{\lambda_{ij} x_{ij}\}$ is *at most rank 4* too. If we know the projective depths λ_{ij}, it is possible to factorize the scaled measurement matrix into two rank-4 matrices, $\hat{P}$ and $\hat{X}$. This decomposition reverses the perspective projection process and is the basis for the factorization method [8]. However, the decomposition is not unique since it is possible to insert an 4×4 invertible matrix and its inverse between $\hat{P}$ and $\hat{X}$ without changing the product.

In general, the true projective depths λ_{ij} are unknown and we need to estimate *projective depths* $\tilde{\lambda}_{ij}$ such that the scaled measurement matrix $\left\{ \tilde{\lambda}_{ij} x_{ij} \right\}$ becomes close to rank 4 so that it can be factorized approximately as:

$$\left\{ \tilde{\lambda}_{ij} x_{ij} \right\} \simeq \hat{P} \hat{X} \tag{3}$$

where $\hat{P} = \left[\hat{P}_1^T, \hat{P}_2^T, ..., \hat{P}_m^T \right]^T$ is a rank-4 projective joint projection matrix, and $\hat{X} = \left[\hat{X}_1, \hat{X}_2, ..., \hat{X}_n \right]$ is a rank-4 projective shape matrix. The recovered $\hat{X}$ can be reprojected back to 2-D images by $\hat{P}$ as:

$$\hat{P} \hat{X} \equiv \left\{ \hat{\lambda}_{ij} \hat{x}_{ij} \right\} \tag{4}$$

where $\hat{x}_{ij}$ is the 2-D reprojected point and $\hat{\lambda}_{ij}$ is its reconstructed projective depth.

Existing factorization methods [8][10] minimize

$$\left\| \left\{ \tilde{\lambda}_{ij} x_{ij} \right\} - \hat{P} \hat{X} \right\|_F^2 \tag{5}$$

$$= \sum_{1 \le i \le m, 1 \le j \le n} \left\| \tilde{\lambda}_{ij} x_{ij} - \hat{P}_i \hat{X}_j \right\|_F^2 \tag{6}$$

The Singular Value Decomposition (SVD) is used to obtain the rank 4 matrices $\hat{P}$ and $\hat{X}$ which minimize (5). The error achieved in the minimization problem (5) is called the *SVD reprojection error*. However, the SVD reprojection error does not represent a physically meaningful quantity. In this paper, we propose to minimize the *2-D reprojection errors*,

$$\sum_{1 \le i \le m, 1 \le j \le n} \left\| x_{ij} - \hat{x}_{ij} \right\|_F^2 \tag{7}$$

We also want to formulate (3) as a minimization that can deal with *missing data*. Since missing data produces 'holes' inside the scaled measurement matrix, it poses problems for the SVD approach.

3   Minimization of 2-D Reprojection Errors

We will show that the 2-D reprojection errors can be approximated by weighting each term of SVD reprojection errors by an appropriate weighting factor γ_{ij}. The

SVD reprojection error (5) weighted by $\{\gamma_{ij}\}$ can be related to *2-D reprojection error* (7) [14]:

$$\sum_{1\leq i\leq m,1\leq j\leq n} \gamma_{ij}\left\|\tilde{\lambda}_{ij}x_{i,j} - \hat{P}_i\hat{X}_j\right\|_F^2 = \sum_{1\leq i\leq m,1\leq j\leq n} \gamma_{ij}\left\|\tilde{\lambda}_{ij}x_{ij} - \hat{\lambda}_{ij}\hat{x}_{ij}\right\|_F^2$$

$$= \sum_{1\leq i\leq m,1\leq j\leq n} \gamma_{ij}\tilde{\lambda}_{ij}^2\left\|x_{ij} - \frac{\hat{\lambda}_{ij}}{\tilde{\lambda}_{ij}}\hat{x}_{ij}\right\|_F^2$$

$$= \sum_{1\leq i\leq m,1\leq j\leq n} \gamma_{ij}\underbrace{\tilde{\lambda}_{ij}^2}_{\text{projective-depth weight}}\left\|\underbrace{(x_{ij} - \hat{x}_{ij})}_{\text{2D reprojection error}} + \underbrace{\left(1 - \frac{\hat{\lambda}_{ij}}{\tilde{\lambda}_{ij}}\right)\hat{x}_{ij}}_{\text{truncation error}}\right\|_F^2 \tag{8}$$

We wish to choose the weighting factor γ_{ij} such that (8) becomes the 2-D reprojection error. The weighting factor γ_{ij} is defined as:

$$\gamma_{ij} = \frac{1}{\left(\tilde{\lambda}_{ij}\right)^2}\left[\begin{array}{c} 1 \\ 1 \\ \max\left(|u_{ij}|,|v_{ij}|\right) \end{array}\right] \tag{9}$$

From (8), each individual norm is weighted by its own projective depth $\tilde{\lambda}_{ij}$. Hence, points further away from the camera will have a heavier weighting in the minimization, which is undesirable. The first factor $\tilde{\lambda}_{ij}^{-2}$ in (9) is to cancel out the projective-depth weight so that the 2-D reprojection errors are minimized uniformly over all points.

The purpose of the factor $\left[1\ 1\ \max\left(|u_{ij}|,|v_{ij}|\right)\right]^T$ in (9) is to reduce the truncation error such that the minimization of (8) approximates the problem of minimizing the 2-D reprojection error.

4   A Novel WLS Algorithm

4.1   Formulations

Estimating Projective Depths $\tilde{\lambda}_{ij}$ Consider minimizing (8) as:

$$\min_{\hat{P},\hat{X},\tilde{\lambda}} \sum_{1\leq i\leq m,1\leq j\leq n} \gamma_{ij}\left\|\tilde{\lambda}_{ij}x_{i,j} - \hat{P}_i\hat{X}_j\right\|_F^2 \tag{10}$$

Since (10) is a non-linear minimization problem on $\hat{P},\hat{X}$ and $\tilde{\lambda}$, (10) is expressed as three different WLS problems [13] where $\hat{P},\hat{X}$ and $\tilde{\lambda}$ are evaluated one by one iteratively while keeping the others unchanged. The superscript k indicates that the variables are updated in k^{th} iteration. The minimization problems for each unknown are as follows:

1. To find $\hat{X}^{k+1}$: fix $\hat{P}^k$ and $\tilde{\lambda}_{ij}^k$ and solve

$$\min_{\hat{X}} \sum_{1 \leq i \leq m, 1 \leq j \leq n} \gamma_{ij}^k \left\| \tilde{\lambda}_{ij}^k x_{i,j} - \hat{P}_i^k \hat{X}_j \right\|_F^2 \tag{11}$$

2. To find $\hat{P}^{k+1}$: fix $\hat{X}^{k+1}$ and $\tilde{\lambda}_{ij}^k$ and solve

$$\min_{\hat{P}} \sum_{1 \leq i \leq m, 1 \leq j \leq n} \gamma_{ij}^k \left\| \tilde{\lambda}_{ij}^k x_{i,j} - \hat{P}_i \hat{X}_j^{k+1} \right\|_F^2 \tag{12}$$

3. To find $\tilde{\lambda}_{ij}^{k+1}$: fix $\hat{P}^{k+1}$ and $\hat{X}^{k+1}$ and solve

$$\varepsilon = \min_{\tilde{\lambda}} \sum_{1 \leq i \leq m, 1 \leq j \leq n} \gamma_{ij}^k \left\| \tilde{\lambda}_{ij} x_{i,j} - \hat{P}_i^{k+1} \hat{X}_j^{k+1} \right\|_F^2 \tag{13}$$

Missing Data. From the above parameterization, handling missing data can be treated simply by skipping those missing data in the minimization, so that (10) becomes

$$\min_{\hat{P}, \hat{X}, \tilde{\lambda}} \sum_{(i,j) \in E} \gamma_{ij}^k \left\| \tilde{\lambda}_{ij}^k x_{i,j} - \hat{P}_i^k \hat{X}_j^k \right\|_F^2 \tag{14}$$

where E is the set of all the observed 2-D points,

$$E = \left\{ \begin{array}{l} (i,j) \in \Re^2 | x_{ij} \text{ is observed as} \\ j^{th} \text{ corresponding point in } i^{th} \text{ view} \end{array} \right\} \tag{15}$$

4.2   Algorithm

The algorithm can be implemented as follows:

1. Initialization: if $\hat{P}^o$ and $\hat{X}^o$ are not provided as initial guesses, they are initialized by the rank 4 approximation of $\left\{ \tilde{\lambda}_{ij}^o x_{ij} \right\}$. $\tilde{\lambda}_{ij}^o$ are set to 1. k is set to 1 to start the algorithm.
2. Evaluate γ_{ij}^k by (9).
3. Minimize (11) by fixing $\hat{P}^k$ and γ_{ij}^k to find $\hat{X}^{k+1}$.
4. Minimize (12) by fixing $\hat{X}^{k+1}$ and γ_{ij}^k to find $\hat{P}^{k+1}$.
5. Minimize (13) by fixing $\hat{P}^{k+1}$ and $\hat{X}^{k+1}$ to find $\tilde{\lambda}_{ij}^{k+1}$ and ε.
6. If ε is bigger than or equal to a set threshold value, go to step 2 and $k = k+1$.
7. Stop

5   Evaluation by Synthetic Data

Two simulations on synthetic data have been done for evaluating the performance of the algorithm.

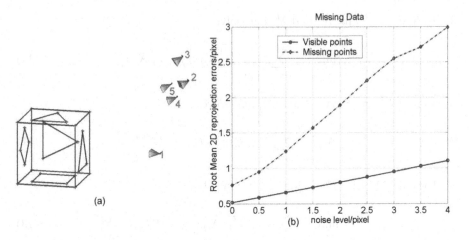

Fig. 1. (a) A synthetic view of a 3D box and cameras and (b) Estimating Missing data

5.1   Scene Configuration

In fig.(1a), a box is defined in a 3-D world with a set of cameras. The size of the box is $60cm \times 60cm \times 60cm$ and it contains 25 3-D points. The box is placed with its centroid at 1.1m from the first camera. There are 5 cameras with the same intrinsic parameters and the sizes of all the images are 1080×720. The cameras are pointed towards the centroid of the box and such that the box appears with maximum size in each image. The location of the cameras are otherwise random.

We apply the algorithms repeatedly for the noise levels from 0 to 4 pixels and the increment is 0.5 pixels. The initial guess of λ_{ij} is 1. There are 50 trials for each noise level and the figures show the mean values.

5.2   Results of Two Simulations

Missing Data Simulation. The purpose of this simulation is to evaluate the performance of the proposed algorithm for estimating missing points in the 2-D images. In this simulation, there are 17 image points missing in the measurement matrix. The root-mean-squared 2-D reprojection errors for visible points and missing points are shown in fig.(1b). The RMS 2-D reprojection error for the visible points are measured relative to the noisy data whereas the error for the missing points are measured relative to the ground truth as noisy data for these points do not exist. The errors of the estimated missing points are comparable with the noise level corrupting the visible points.

Comparison Simulation. In this simulation, we compare the results of our algorithm with Triggs' algorithm [10]. All the 3-D points are visible in all the cameras.

Performance on Estimating Projective Depths. Since the projective depths cannot be uniquely recovered, in order to compare how good the estimated projective depths are, we make use of the cross ratio of projective depths defined as:

$$cr\left(\lambda_{ij}\right) = \frac{\lambda_{ij}\lambda_{i+1,j+1}}{\lambda_{i,j+1}\lambda_{i+1,j}}, \begin{cases} 1 \le i \le m-1 \\ 1 \le j \le n-1 \end{cases} \tag{16}$$

A *cross ratio matrix* is formed as $\left\{cr\left(\lambda_{ij}\right)\right\} \in \Re^{(m-1)\times(n-1)}$. The mean-squared cross-ratio error (MSCRE) is then defined as

$$\frac{1}{(m-1)(n-1)} \left\| \left\{cr\left(\tilde{\lambda}_{ij}\right)\right\} - \left\{cr\left(\lambda_{ij}\right)\right\} \right\|_F^2 \tag{17}$$

The MSCRE of the two algorithms are plotted in fig.(2a). The MSCRE of our algorithm is much smaller than that obtained with Triggs' Algorithm.

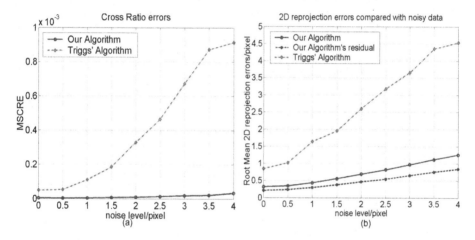

Fig. 2. Performance on (a) Projective Depth Estimation and (b) 2-D Reprojection Errors

Performance on 2-D Reprojection Error. Fig.(2b) plots the 2-D reprojection errors of the two algorithms. As expected the 2-D reprojection error of our algorithm is better than that of Trigg's algorithm as our method is designed to minimize the 2-D reprojection error. The residual ε of our algorithm against different noise levels is also plotted in fig.(2b). The trend of the 2-D reprojection error closely follows that of the residual ε in different noise levels.

6   Conclusion

In this paper, a projective reconstruction algorithm has been developed to estimate the projective depths, missing data while minimizing the 2-D reprojection error. The algorithm is robust to noisy images. The errors of the estimated missing points are comparable with the noise levels corrupting the visible points. The cross-ratios of the estimated projective depths are almost the same as the cross-ratios of the ground truth. It can be shown that the residual ε in the algorithm is monotonic decreasing and therefore the algorithm is guaranteed to converge.

References

[1] O. Faugeras, "Stratification of 3-dimensional vision: Projective, affine, and metric representations," *JOSA-A*, vol. 12, pp. 465–484, March 1995.

[2] M. Han and T. Kanade, "Scene reconstruction from multiple uncalibrated views," tech. rep., January 2000.

[3] B. Triggs, P. McLauchlan, R. Hartley, and A. Fitzgibbon, "Bundle adjustment – A modern synthesis," in *Vision Algorithms: Theory and Practice* (W. Triggs, A. Zisserman, and R. Szeliski, eds.), LNCS, pp. 298–375, Springer Verlag, 2000.

[4] R. I. Hartley, "Euclidean reconstruction from uncalibrated views," vol. 825, pp. 237–256, Springer-Verlag, 1993.

[5] M. Pollefeys and L. V. Gool, "Stratified self-calibration with the modulus constraint," *IEEE Transactions on Pattern Analysis and Machine Intelligence*, vol. 21, pp. 707–724, August 1999.

[6] Q. T. Luong and O. Faugeras, "The fundamental matrix: Theory, algorithms, and stability analysis," *International Journal of Computer Vision*, vol. 17(1), pp. 43–76, 1996.

[7] R. I. Hartley, "A linear method for reconstruction from lines and points," in *Fifth International Conference on Computer Vision*, (Cambridge, MA, USA), pp. 882–887, IEEE, 1995.

[8] C. Tomasi and T. Kanade, "Shape and motion from image streams under orthography: A factorization method," *International Journal of Computer Vision*, vol. 9(2), pp. 137–154, 1992.

[9] C. Poelman and T. Kanade, "A paraperspective factorization method for shape and motion recovery," in *Proc. of the ECCV, LNCS Vol 810, Springer Verlag*, 1994.

[10] B. Triggs, "Factorization methods for projective structure and motion," in *IEEE Conf. on Computer Vision and Pattern Recognition*, pp. 845–851, 1995.

[11] P. Beardsley, A. Zisserman, and D. Murray, "Sequential updating of projective and affine structure from motion," *International Journal of Computer Vision*, vol. 23, pp. 235–259, June-July 1997.

[12] D. W. Jacobs, "Linear fitting with missing data for structure-from-motion," *Computer Vision and Image Understanding*, vol. 82, pp. 57–81, 2001.

[13] H. Y. Shum, K. Ikeuchi, and R. Reddy, "Principal component analysis with missing data and its application to polyhedral object modeling," *IEEE Transactions on Pattern Analysis and Machine Intelligence*, vol. 17(9), pp. 854–867, Sept. 1995.

[14] B. Triggs, "Some notes on factorization methods for projective structure and motion." unpublished, 1998.

Head Detection and Localization from Sparse 3D Data

Markus Clabian [1], Harald Rötzer [1], Horst Bischof [2], and Walter Kropatsch [3]

[1] Advanced Computer Vision GmbH, Donau City Str.1, A-1220 Vienna, Austria
{markus.clabian, harald.roetzer}@acv.ac.at
[2] Institute for Computer Graphics and Vision,
Graz University of Technology, Inffeldgasse 16 , A-8010 Graz, Austria
bischof@icg.tu-graz.ac.at
[3] Pattern Recognition and Image Processing Group
Institute of Computer Aided Automation, Computer Science Department,
Vienna University of Technology, Favoritenstr. 9, A-1040 Vienna, Austria
krw@prip.tuwien.ac.at

Abstract. Head detection is an important, but difficult task, if no restrictions such as static illumination, frontal face appearance or uniform background can be assumed. We present a system that is able to perform head detection under very general conditions by employing a 3D measurement system namely a structured light distance measurement. An algorithm of head detection from sparse 3D data (19x19 data points) is developed that reconstructs a 3D surface over the image plane and detects head hypotheses of ellipsoidal shape. We demonstrate that detection and rough localization is possible in up to 90% of the images.

1 Introduction

Head detection is the starting point of several methods that are elaborated in the fields of face recognition, gesture recognition and man machine interaction. Usually the detection can be done based on the robust detection of an outline (shape) [3] or based on general appearance [10]. The outline of the head can only be obtained reliably when a uniform background and non varying illumination is assumed. Appearance based methods perform well in case of frontal face appearance but show high false detection rates, when the head of a person shall be detected in arbitrary pose e.g. [11].

Some authors have proposed to use 3D information for head detection [3,4,6,8]. All these approaches either use a pre-selected set of data points that are known to lie at the person, or they use a very dense data set coming from stereo/disparity imaging. In this paper we present a novel system that performs fast detection of head hypotheses using sparse 3D information derived by a simple structured light technique (19x19 points). The head search is performed by surface reconstruction and an ellipse search within equidistant planar cuts parallel to the image plane.

The paper is organized as follows: First the acquisition system similar to [2] is presented. Improvements of the technique are summarized and a new method to solve the correspondence problem is presented in section 2. Section 3 explains the head detection method that comprises surface reconstruction, ellipse search using planar surface cuts and ellipse hypothesis selection. Section 4 presents the results based on 2 real

L. Van Gool (Ed.): DAGM 2002, LNCS 2449, pp. 395–402, 2002.
© Springer-Verlag Berlin Heidelberg 2002

sequences, section 5 gives a summary and draws conclusions for future algorithms and applications.

2 Acquisition System

The acquisition system is based on the well known technique of structured light projection [e.g. 7] and acquires a 3D point cloud of 361 points at maximum. It consists of the four steps: (i) projection of a dot matrix pattern (ii) dots detection (iii) dot labeling (iv) distance calculation.

2.1 Structured Light Technique to Acquire Distance Points

Structured light is a well known technique for obtaining 3D information in various applications [e.g. 12]. It is used to measure distances by projecting artificial feature points (patterns) onto a scene of interest. These points are emitted from a light projector and therefore lie on a line (epipolar line) in the image. The location of the point on the line (disparity) measures the position of the projected point in 3D space. The 3D coordinates can then be calculated via triangulation using the known positions of the calibrated camera and the projector.

Our implementation of the structured light system comprises two main devices: a camera and a pattern generation unit. The camera is a CCD-video camera with 752(H) x 582(V) picture elements and a chip size of 4.9mm (H) x 3.7mm (V). The pattern generation unit consists of a laser light source (LASIRIS-model: 670 nm, 10 mW), and a changeable beam shaping optics to generate the projection pattern (19x19 dot matrix). Both devices are mounted on a stable board at same height, without any horizontal tilt. From a top view the camera is pointed inwards at a distance of 12.5mm to the projector. The camera was calibrated by using the techniques presented by [5] and [15]. The projected dot pattern was rotated against the horizontal line to achieve a near-degenerate epipolar alignment [1].

2.2 Dot Detection

To segment the projected dots from the rest of the image the simple thresholding procedure [2] was improved by applying a difference of Gaussian (DoG) filter operation to the Image I, which gives I_F. This filter checks the property that projected dots can be found as a small area of pixels that have higher intensity as the pixels in its surrounding. After filtering I_F is thresholded to get a binary output I_T that is used to determine the central point of each dot by calculating the center of gravity (CoG).

2.3 Dot Labeling

Dot labeling is the task of assigning the detected dots to the corresponding epipolar line, defined by the projector and camera positions. This is necessary to allow a proper distance calculation and can be accomplished by using spatial and temporal constraints as discussed in [2]. To improve the speed of the initialization procedure surfaces on which the dots are projected are assumed locally approximately planar. Therefore the projected dot pattern of rectangular shape is transformed by an affine transformation. The algorithm has two major steps:

First every four epipolar lines that belong to a rectangular part of the projected dot pattern are tested, whether their corresponding dots satisfy the affine transformation condition. This is tested by calculating the parameters of an affine transformation in a least square sense. If the error of the transformation is less than a limit •, the dots are assigned to the corresponding epipolar lines.

In the second step all lines are labeled that are close to already assigned lines. Again neighboring dots have to satisfy the affine transformation condition. The allowed deviation limit • is increased, if the number of assigned dots per iteration step is low (<5). This guarantees that the region grows in planar region first. After that discontinuities are overleaped due to the increase of allowed deviation limit •. The two main assumptions of rectangular shaped pattern and projection on a planar surface may be violated to a limited degree which is given by the size of the deviation limit •.

If the dots are detected and labeled correctly and if the camera is calibrated, distance calculation can be done by triangulation using the distance between camera and projector.

3   Head Detection Module

The structured light system measures surface points in 3D. The described system yields 361 (maximal) or fewer points (usually 20 to 70 points are occluded). The critical information that should be extracted from the point cloud is:

- Foreground/background separation: The background can be an arbitrary scene; the foreground is the head/thorax region of a human. This separation is simple, if the background can be modeled very accurate. All points that do not lie on the background model belong to the foreground.
- Localization of the head region: To localize the head, a model is fitted to the point cloud. This can be done either directly or by determining several parameters of the surface that is spanned by the given points.

In the following it is assumed that the background model is not available. Therefore the foreground/background separation can either be determined by searching for the relevant depth discontinuities in the point cloud which is a non-trivial problem for sparse (19x19) depth measurements, or by fitting a foreground (head/thorax) model onto the data. Trying to fit e.g. an ellipsoid model to the data points was not robust, because of the usually small amount of points (10-15) that lie on the head surface.

3.1 Depth Surface Reconstruction

The depth of the surface is a function that arises over the image plane (x,y). The given data points $P(x,y,z)$ define this surface $z=f(x,y)$. The surface reconstruction can therefore be seen as an approximation problem. The data points define a function z that shall be approximated. The approximation shall exhibit following properties:

- Robust approximation: outliers should have no influence on the approximation.

- Strong separation: different objects should appear separated in the representation. Therefore depth discontinuities should be preserved.
- Correct extrapolation: as data points are defined in a certain area, the behavior of the function at the borders should not influence its behavior in the defined area.

A surface can be approximated by a sum of basis functions $B(x,y)$

$$z = \sum_{n=1}^{m} c_n B_n(x, y) \tag{1}$$

The coefficients c_n are determined by solving the system of linear equations given in a least square sense. The choice of the basis function B_n influences the properties of the approximation. In a set of experiments (using different types of multiquadrics and Gaussians functions) it turned out that

$$B(x,y) = \sqrt{x^2 + y^2 + 1} \tag{2}$$

has for head detection purposes advantages over other basis functions. Especially head regions that lie at the border of the projected grid stay convex.

3.2 Planar Surface Cuts (Isodistance Lines)

To analyze the resulting surface z, different representations can be used. For the specific task of finding the head region, the surface was represented by its planar cuts at equal distances. Therefore the surface was cut by parallel planes of equal distances and the resulting polygons were analyzed.

By taking the polygons stepwise from the nearest cut to the furthest, the centers of gravity of *closed* polygons are close to the extrema of the function. Growing confocal polygons are minima (convex, from camera perspective), shrinking polygons (concave) are maxima. Minima can be marked as head/thorax-hypotheses. Every closed polygon that surrounds a minimum is marked as supporting the corresponding hypothesis. Therefore each hypothesis consists of a sequence of growing polygons.

Open polygons must be handled differently (Fig.1). As they cannot be assigned to a certain hypothesis, they are cut into parts, where at least one polygon part has the following properties: (i) it is of elliptical shape (ii) it surrounds and therefore supports an existing hypothesis. If such a cut is not possible, the open polygon is not used. After considering all polygons usually a small number (~5) of elliptical hypotheses remain.

3.3 Ellipse Search and Hypothesis Analysis

When a hypothesis is found, this represents a convex surface part of the overall surface. Every hypothesis is tested, whether it is a head region or not. Following tests are applied:

(i)   Area limits: A head must have a certain minimum and maximum size. Hypotheses that violate those limits can be removed.

(ii)   Curvature limits: The head can be approximated by an ellipsoid. Therefore planar cuts are ellipses that have same focus and have increasing area. The

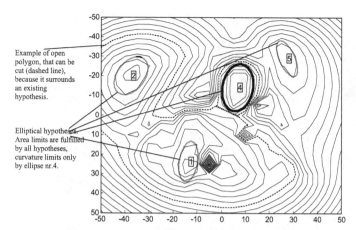

Fig.1.: Contour plot of reconstructed surface with ellipse hypotheses. Darker lines are contours that are close to the camera. Dashed line shows an example of an open polygon and a cut of an elliptical part of the polygon. Ellipses show hypothesis, dark ellipse fulfils all head conditions, bright ellipses violates curvature condition.

      increase from one slice of the ellipsoid to the next can be used to calculate the curvature of the ellipsoid. If this curvature is beyond a certain interval, the corresponding hypothesis can be removed.

(iii)   Shape limits: The polygon must be of elliptical shape. Additionally the ratio of the axis of the ellipse must be in a certain range, as very narrow ellipses are not allowed. Hypotheses that violate this condition are removed.

All remaining hypotheses are assumed to be head regions.

4 Results

We have tested the reconstruction and ellipsoid finding algorithm on 2 sequences of 50 image frames each. The sequences show one sitting person (46 frames each), some frames show an empty seat (4 each). Sequence 1 had no hand movements, whereas in Sequence 2 the hands were moved strongly, partly occluding the head or regions close to the head. Both sequences can be seen as representative for applications in the fields of man-machine interaction and face detection, particular for close range surveillance applications, where initial head detection is required. The results can be summarized as follows: Sequ.1.: In all images showing a person the head location is found as elliptical hypotheses (46 out of 46). In 37 cases the head was found without any ambiguity. Sequ.2: From the 46 images showing a person the head location is found as elliptical hypothesis in 41 cases. In 13 cases the head was found correctly, in 18 cases more than one hypothesis was selected and in 3 cases no hypothesis was selected.

As demonstrated in Fig. 2 the head is found robustly as ellipsoid hypothesis. Two errors occur in frames 4 and 7, due to the facts that the surface reconstruction is not perfect in small parts of the image (frame 4) and the curvature constraint is violated (frame 7). However seven frames show exact head ellipse detection from which the distance to the camera can be calculated correctly.

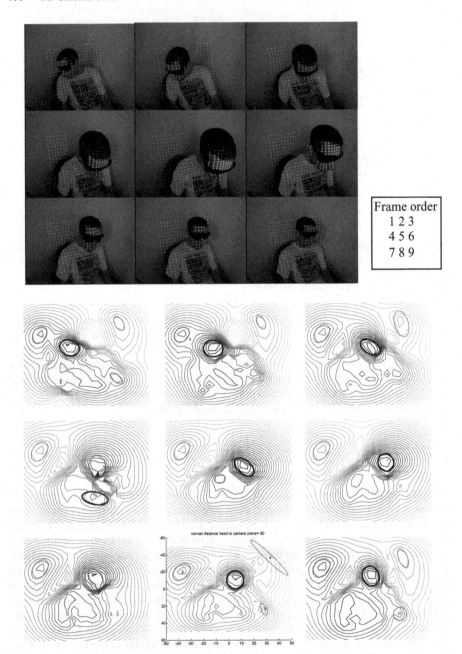

Fig.2.: Nine consecutive frames of a sequence showing a moving person. Upper part: control images. Lower part: contour plot of the reconstruction surface. The ellipse hypotheses and the selected head hypotheses are shown. The estimated distance to the camera is given. Seven (nr.1,2,3,5,6,8,9) show correct head detection, nr.4 shows a wrong head detection due to bad reconstruction in the area between ellipse 2 and 4, nr. 7 shows a non-detection due to the fact that ellipse 1 violates the curvature constraint.

Table 1.: Result of head detection process of two sequences. In most frames the head was detected as elliptical hypotheses. The selection of the correct hypothesis as head is ambiguous or fails, if hands are occluding the head or are in regions close to the head.

	total	showing		head detected as ell. hyp.		head selection from ell. hyp.			
				Yes	no	correct without amb.	correct with amb.	wrong	not done
Sequ 1	50	head	46	46		37	1	3	5
		no head	4						4
Sequ 2	50	head	46	41	5	13	18	7	3
		no head	4						4

The head is not detected in the following cases: (i) The head is not fully within the dot projection area or rather close to the border of that area.(ii) The head does not separate enough from its background. This is only the case if the background is concave in the way that the head fits well into it and forms a rather planar surface. Other possible errors occur, if close objects influence the surface in the way that it does not separate the head. This can occur e.g. if hands are close to the head. Objects are detected as heads if they form surfaces that are similar to that of heads. These cases cannot be detected from the 3D information of the region alone.

5   Summary and Conclusions

We have presented a fast method based on a simple structured light system that performs head hypotheses detection in situations, where methods using shape or appearance fail. The overall computing time is low as it is spent almost exclusively on the DoG calculated over the whole image and the labeling process of a low (361) number of points. Using sparse 3D data up to 100% location detection and up to 80% correct hypothesis selection is possible. Ambiguities occur only in very specific cases (see section 4). To avoid these situations, the following improvements are proposed:

- using model information: in this work the underlying head model is very simple. It assumes that the head is an ellipsoid of a certain size, defined by all possible human head sizes. If specific properties of the person are known, this could lead to a more exact description of the person's head. Additionally information about the body size and position can be included to remove wrong hypothesis.
- using sequence information (tracking): as each frame is treated independently, we expect significant improvements, if frame-to-frame dependencies are considered.
- using 2D (gray value) information: each hypothesis can be tested by applying facial feature detection algorithms to the 2D part of the image that corresponds to the detected head area. If facial features are found, the hypothesis is confirmed.

The 3D range information is the main information that is used by our head detection method. As our proposed rule based system is not limited to 3D information derived from a structured light system, the results can be transferred to other systems such as systems based on stereo or multiple cameras. The algorithm of finding the suitable ellipsoids in the 3D view can be applied to any 3D range data that can be described as a function arising from the image plane.

Acknowledgements

This work has been carried out within the K plus Competence Center ADVANCED COMPUTER VISION. This work was funded from the K plus Program. We would like to thank M. Peternell for many helpful discussions.

References

1. Blake A., McCowen D., Lo H. R., Lindsey P. J.: Trinoculuar active range-sensing. IEEE Trans. on Pattern Analysis and Machine Intelligence 15, (1993) 477-483.
2. Clabian M., Rötzer H., Bischof H.: Tracking structured light pattern. SPIE – Conf. Intelligent Robots and Computer Vision XX: Algorithms, Techniques and Active Vision (2001) 183-192.
3. Gavrila D. M., Davis L.S.: 3-D model-based tracking of human upper body movement: a multi-view approach. (1995) 253-258.
4. Grammalidis N., Strintzis M.G.: Head detection and tracking by 2-D and 3-D ellipsoid fitting. IEEE Proc. Int. Conf. Computer Graphics (2000) 221-226.
5. Heikkilä J., Silven O.: A four-step camera calibration procedure with implicit image correction. Proc. of Int. Conf. on Computer Vision and Pattern Recognition (1997) 1106-1112.
6. Iwasawa S., Ohya J., Takahashi K., Sakaguchi T., Kawato S., Ebihara K., Morishima S.: Real-time, 3D-estimation of human body postures from trinocular images. Proc. Int. Workshop on Modelling People (1999) 3-10.
7. Jarvis R.: A perspective on range finding techniques for computer vision, IEEE Trans. on Pattern Analysis and Machine Intelligence 5 (1983) 122-139
8. Luo R., Guo Y.: Tracking of moving heads in cluttered scenes from stereo vision. Robot Vision (2001) 148-156.
9. Le Moigne J., Waxman, A.M.: Structured light patterns for robot mobility. IEEE J. of Robotics and Automation 4 (1988) 541-548.
10. Papageorgiou C., Poggio T.: A trainable system for object detection. Int. J. of Computer Vision 38(1) (2000) 15-33.
11. Reyna R., Giralt A., Esteve D.: Head detection inside vehicles with a modified SVM for safer airbags. IEEE Proc. Int. Transp. Systems (2001) 268-272.
12. Stockman G. C., Chen S.-W., Gongzhu H., Shrikhande N.: Sensing and recognition of rigid objects using structured light. IEEE Control System Magazine 8 (1988) 14-22
13. Trobina M., Leonardis A.: An application of a structured light sensor system to robotics: Grasping arbitrarily shaped 3-D objects from a pile. Proc. IEEE Int. Conf. on Robotics and Automation 1 (1995) 241-246.
14. Zhang L., Lenders P.: A New Head Detection Method Based on the Region Shield Segmentation in Complex Background. Proc. Int. Symp. on Intell. Multimedia, Video and Speech Processing (2001) 328-331.
15. Zhang Z.: Flexible camera calibration by viewing a plane from unknown orientations. Proc. of 7th IEEE Int. Conf. on Computer Vision 1 (1999) 666-673.

Segmentation of the Date
in Entries of Historical Church Registers

M. Feldbach and K.D. Tönnies

Computer Vision Group, Department of Simulation and Graphics,
Otto-von-Guericke University, P.O. Box 4120, D-39016 Magdeburg, Germany,
{feldbach,klaus}@isg.cs.uni-magdeburg.de

Abstract. Handwriting recognition requires a prior segmentation of
text lines which is a challenging task, especially for historical scripts. Ex-
emplary for the date in entries of historical church registers, we present
an approach which enables a segmentation by using additional knowledge about the word sequence. The algorithm is based on probability
distribution curves and a neural network, which assesses local features of
potential word boundaries. Our database consists of 298 different date
entries from the 18th and 19th century which contain 674 word boundaries. The algorithm generates hypotheses for the expected date type,
ordered by their probability. Tests resulted in an accuracy of 97% for the
best four hypotheses.

Keywords: Handwriting recognition, word segmentation, document image processing

1 Introduction

Automatic reading of historical documents such as church registers would provide historians or sociologists with an efficient tool for extracting information.
Vast amounts of such documents are stored unread in churches and archives. If
automatic methods cannot be provided, most of those documents will never be
transcripted. Apparently, automatic recognition of historical documents cannot
be achieved at once but requires several preprocessing steps. We introduce an
interactive system which provides new findings about detecting word boundaries
as well as support for users regarding the identification of date entries.

Since the positions of word boundaries cannot be reliably found by analysing
geometrical attributes only, we generate a list of hypotheses, sorted by their
probability. Those hypotheses enable a specialised word respectively cipher rec-
ognizer, to process and recognise the isolated script objects. Essential preprocessing steps are the reconstruction and separation of text lines which have been
described in [1] and [2].

If information about the characters is available, the analysis of character sequences leads to reliable predictions about word boundaries [3]. However, we
don't have this information. In order to find word gaps, several distance measuring methods have been investigated, such as run-length Euclidean heuristic

L. Van Gool (Ed.): DAGM 2002, LNCS 2449, pp. 403–410, 2002.
© Springer-Verlag Berlin Heidelberg 2002

distance [10], convex hull [7] etc. These methods analyse relations between adjacent connected components and find gap metrics to cope with various spacing styles [9,10]. Manmatha et al. [8] analyses characteristics of old scripts and segments words consisting of isolated and connected characters. Nonetheless, the examined scripts show straight text lines and well separated words. If the script, however, is characterised by gaps of different sizes, methods specialised on differentiating between inter-character gaps and inter-word gaps have been found successfully [5,4]. In old church registers, connections between adjacent words may occur. Therefore we must look for potential word gaps within text objects as well.

1.1 Date Types

The possible number and position of boundaries between date components can be restricted if the different date constituents are known a-priori. We examined a large number of entries in church registers and found that the date in all entries consisted of the elements ciphers (C), artefacts (A), and month names (M) with the following combinations being possible: *C-C-A-M, C-A-M, C-C-M, C-M.*

The artefacts after the ciphers are "te" or "ten" and indicate the date. Names of the months may be abbreviated.

1.2 Data Base

The date in a church register is user identified by marking the begin and end of the date entry. We created a database with a size of 298 different date entries from church registers of the county of Wegenstedt for development, training and test of our method. The entries contain 674 word boundaries and were from chronicles between 1719 and 1813. The following information is generated for each selected date from our pre-processing step:

- Skeletons of stroke segments (between stroke crossings or ends) that are certain or potential parts of the text in this line.
- Connectivity information between different segments.
- Line width of segments.
- Course of text lines (baseline and midline, baseline of the text line above and midline of the text line below).

The following information was added interactively to serve for training and test purposes:

- Day, month and year of the date (the year is not part of the date entry)
- Date type (such as, e. g., C-A-M).
- Position of boundaries between date elements.

2 Preprocessing

Script objects are identified based on the knowledge about the baseline and midline paths as well as the position of the left and right date boundaries. There

Fig. 1. A marked date (C-C-A-M) with left and right boundaries (solid line) and found word boundaries (dashed line), certainly (black) and potentially (grey) parts of the date

are two classes of objects: one class containing all objects which are *certainly* part of the date and one class containing all objects which are *potentially* part of the date [1]. Subsequently, by using objects only, which are certainly part of the date, interferences from adjacent lines or words are avoided.

In order to find potential word boundaries, preprocessing steps like slant correction or base line adjustment have to be performed. In the following, boundaries between all date elements (words or ciphers) are called word boundaries.

2.1 Slant Correction

There is a number of methods for slant correction which determine the best angle by searching for the most vertical strokes such as [11] but in our case the simple procedure, described in the following, corrects slants effectively.

We estimate the slant of the script by considering the single line segments as vectors. The average direction of all vectors, weighted by their length, is calculated. The average direction determines the slant angle. Every skeleton point is displaced vertically depending on the slant angle and the distance to the base line. Due to the calculation on the bases of discrete coordinate values, a gap is likely to appear between two adjacent skeleton points. These gaps will be closed again. Additionally, the skeleton segments are smoothed in order to eliminate artefacts which were caused by the correction.

2.2 Base Line Adjustment

The vertical distances of script objects and centre line are determined relatively to the baseline in order to improve the examination of the script object arrangement.

2.3 Removal of Punctuation Marks

Small objects between midline and baseline, potentially representing punctuation marks, are removed prior to searching word boundaries. An object is small if the vertical and horizontal extent of its skeleton is smaller than the stroke width.

3   Potential Boundary Search

In the following, objects are connected continua within the date zone. A date
entity is either of the three classes cipher, month, or artefact (see Sect. 1.1).

A list of potential word boundaries between slant-corrected objects is generated. Boundaries may exist at horizontal gaps between objects as well as within
an object. The latter is true when two date entities touch each other.

A height of the date $y_{max}^{high}(x)$ is computed for each location x as the maximum
height of the object at this location. A second measure $y_{max}^{low}(x)$ is computed as
the maximum height of strokes at location x which are below the midline.

Two types of potential word boundaries (pWB) are computed. A pWB of
type I is generated at each gap in the text line main area between baseline and
midline. This finds all potential boundaries between non-connected text parts as
well as between those that are connected above the midline (such as touching
capital letters and/or ciphers). A pWB of type II is generated at position x if
there is only one line segment and $y_{max}^{low}(x)$ has a local minimum. In order to find
only relevant local minima, a vertical search window is used. The width of the
window is two times the stroke width of the single segment.

4   Assessing Potential Word Boundaries

There exist eight different kinds of boundaries $g = 1 \ldots 8$ for the four types
of date entries (see Sect. 1.1). Date entries of our data base have between 5
and 25 potential boundaries (e. g. see Fig. 2). In the following, these boundaries are assessed regarding their positions and local attributes in order to derive
hypotheses about the positioning of the word boundaries. For every word boundary, probability values are calculated for every kind of boundary by determining
the average value of a probability distribution curve p_g^{DC} (see Sect. 4.1) and the
normalized output value of a neural network p^{NN} (see Sect. 4.2).

4.1   Probability Distribution Curves

For every kind of boundary g, a probability distribution curve is generated.
The position of a training boundary is normalized related to the date width
and it ranges therefore in the interval $[0, 1]$. The probability distribution curve
which results from the samples is smoothed by a gaussian function. The variance

Fig. 2. Adjusted skeleton of the date entry with marked position of potential word
boundaries.

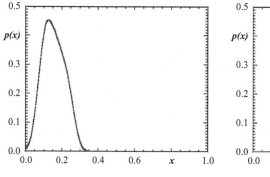

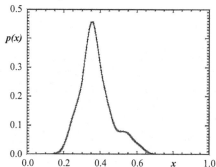

(a) Boundary between cipher and artefact.

(b) Boundary between artefact and month.

Fig. 3. Probability distribution curves for the date type C-A-M.

decreases with an increasing number of samples (see (2)). An appropriate value for k was found experimentally at 0.04. The probability value $p_g^{DC}(x_i)$ of a potential boundary with position $x_i \in [0, 1]$ for boundary type g is calculated by

$$p_g^{DC}(x_i) = \frac{1}{N_g} \cdot \sum_{j=1}^{N_g} \exp\left(\frac{(x_i - x_{g,j})^2}{-2\sigma_g^2}\right) \tag{1}$$

$$\sigma_g^2 = k \cdot \frac{1}{N_g} \tag{2}$$

where N_g denotes the number of training boundaries $x_{g,j}$ for boundary type g and $j = 1 \ldots N_g$. The probability distribution curves of the two word boundaries of date type C-A-M is shown in Fig. 3.

4.2   Local Features

Four features are extracted and propagated by a neural network in order to further examine a potential boundary. We used a multi-layer perceptron with four input neurons, eight hidden layer neurons and one output neuron. It was trained in a way that a value of 0.2 is expected at the output neuron for a wrong boundary and a value of 0.8 for a correct boundary.

Due to the sigmoid transfer functions of the neurons, values of 0 and 1 are inappropriate [6]. For further processing, the output o of the network is normalised to $p^{NN}(x_i) \in [0, 1]$:

$$p^{NN}(x_i) = \begin{cases} 0 & o < 0.2 \\ (o - 0.2)/0.6 & 0.2 \leq o \leq 0.8 \\ 1 & o > 0.8 \end{cases} \tag{3}$$

The four features we used are boundary width, number of crossings respectively touchings with script objects, height of the script left to the boundary, height of the script right to the boundary.

Boundary Width. We estimate the beginning $x_{\min}(b_i)$ and the end $x_{\max}(b_i)$ of the interval which contains the boundary b_i. In case of boundaries of type I, $x_{\min}(b_i)$ is the beginning and $x_{\max}(b_i)$ the end of the gap in the main area of line. In case of type II, $x_{\min}(b_i)$ is the position of the next local maximum of $y_{\max}^{\text{low}}(x)$ left to the boundary and $x_{\max}(b_i)$ the position of the next local maximum right to the boundary. In order to minimise the influence of the script width, we normalise the boundary width related to the date width w_{total} and the number of potential boundaries N_{pb}. The boundary width $w(b_i)$ is therefore

$$w(b_i) = \frac{(x_{\max}(b_i) - x_{\min}(b_i)) \cdot N_{\text{pb}}}{w_{\text{total}}} \tag{4}$$

Number of Object Touchings. The more often a potential object boundary touches a script line, the less likely it is a true object boundary. This relation is implemented by counting the number of cuts.

Height of the Script Next to a Boundary. Inter-word boundaries and inter-character boundaries differ also by the shape of adjacent characters. For this reason, the height of the characters left and right to the boundary is included as a feature.

The width of a character is about two times the distance of two potential boundaries. Thus, we calculate the width w_a of the interval to be examined by

$$w_a = \frac{2N_{\text{pb}}}{w_{\text{total}}} \tag{5}$$

The left interval has a range of $\max(0, x_{min} - w_a)$ to w_a and the right interval has a range of x_{max} to $\min(w_{\text{total}}, x_{max} + w_a)$.

In each of those intervals, the maximum height of the script objects $y_{\max}^{\text{high}}(x)$ is calculated and normalised by dividing by the distance $y_{ml}(x)$ between baseline and midline.

5   Generating Hypotheses

Since the type of a date is unknown, for each of the four possible types, containing $k = 1 \ldots 3$ word boundaries, $\binom{N_{\text{pb}}}{k}$ hypotheses are generated from the combination of the N_{pb} potential boundaries.

The probability $\mathrm{P}(h_i)$ of hypothesis h_i is calculated by the average of probabilities $\mathrm{P}(b_x)$, $\mathrm{P}(b_y)$, $\mathrm{P}(b_z)$ of word boundaries b_x, b_y, b_z with $1 \leq x < y < z \leq N_{\text{pb}}$.

$$\mathrm{p}(h_i) = \frac{\mathrm{P}(b_x)[+\mathrm{P}(b_y)[+\mathrm{P}(b_z)]]}{k_i} \tag{6}$$

Finally, a list with all hypotheses is created and sorted according to their probability $\mathrm{P}(h_i)$.

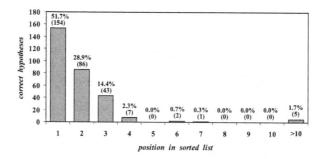

Fig. 4. Positions of 298 correct hypotheses in sorted list related to their probability.

6   Results

We extracted 298 date entries and manually defined the correct word boundaries from church registers of the 18th and 19th century. Because of the insufficient size of the data base, we performed several runs where we used 90% (268) as training data and 10% (30) as test data. After 10 runs with different training and test sets, 97% of the correct word boundary combinations are included in the best four hypotheses (see Fig. 4). In case of using the local features only, we obtain 88%, while the processing of the distribution curve without the local features results in 69%. This shows the advantage of combining the two kinds of property – position and local features.

A fast automatic evaluation of the tests was possible since information about the correct word boundaries was also available for the test data.

Wrongly assessed hypotheses may have different reasons. In many cases, mistakes are due to the fragmentation of actually connected word segments caused by bleached ink. These segments could thus not be classified as certain part of the date. Since only the certain script objects were considered in the method described above, the shape of the script was changed. An additional source of error was punctuation which was not removed due to it's size. A more elaborated removal technique such as the one applied in [10] might solve this problem.

7   Conclusions

In this paper, we presented a method which delivers hypotheses about the position of word boundaries. We considered scripts whose word boundaries are not characterised by obvious gaps as well as scripts containing word touchings. This was achieved by using additional information about the word sequence to be examined as shown exemplarily for date entries from old church registers.

We plan to improve the segmentation by reducing sources of error such as incomplete removal of punctuation marks. The output of the algorithm are hypotheses about the number and positioning of word boundaries. These hypotheses about date components will then serve as prior information for a date recogniser.

References

1. M. Feldbach and K. D. Tönnies. Line Detection and Segmentation in Historical Church Registers. In *Sixth International Conference on Document Analysis and Recognition*, pages 743–747, Seattle, USA, September 2001. IEEE Computer Society.
2. M. Feldbach and K. D. Tönnies. Robust Line Detection in Historical Church Registers. In *Pattern Recognition, 23rd DAGM Symposium*, pages 140–147, Munich, Germany, September 2001. Springer-Verlag.
3. D. Kazakov and S. Manandhar. A hybrid approach to word segmentation. In D. Page, editor, *Proceedings of the 8th International Conference on Inductive Logic Programming*, volume 1446, pages 125–134. Springer-Verlag, 1998.
4. G. Kim and V. Govindaraju. Handwritten Phrase Recognition as Applied to Street Name Images. *Pattern Recognition*, 31(1):41–51, January 1998.
5. S. H. Kim, S. Jeong, G.-S. Lee, and C.Y.Suen. Word Segmentation in Handwritten Korean Text Lines Based on Gap Clustering Techniques. In *Sixth International Conference on Document Analysis and Recognition – ICDAR 2001*, pages 189–193. IEEE Computer Society, September 2001.
6. H. Kruse, R. Mangold, B. Mechler, and 0. Pengler. *Programmierung Neuronaler Netze: Eine Turbo Pascal Toolbox*. Addison-Wesley, 1991.
7. U. Mahadevan and R. C. Nagabushnam. Gap Metrics for Word Separation in Handwritten Lines. In *International Conference on Document Analysis and Recognition*, pages 124–127, Montreal, Canada, 1995.
8. R. Manmatha and N. Srimal. Scale space technique for word segmentation in handwritten documents. In *Scale-Space Theories in Computer Vision*, pages 22–33, 1999.
9. U. Marti and H. Bunke. Text line segmentation and word recognition in a system for general writer independent handwriting recognition. In *Sixth International Conference on Document Analysis and Recognition*, pages 159–163, Seattle, USA, September 2001. IEEE Computer Society.
10. G. Seni and E. Cohen. External word segmentation of off-line handwritten text lines. *Pattern Recognition*, 27(1):41–52, January 1994.
11. A. Vinciarelli and J. Luettin. A new normalization technique for cursive handwritten words. *Pattern Recognition Letters*, 22(9):1043–1050, 2001.

Approach to Object Recognition
by Learning Mobile Robots

Minh-Chinh Nguyen and Bernd Radig

Tachnical University Munich, Department of Informatics, 85748 Garching Germany,
{Nguyen,Radig}@in.tum.de, http://www9.in.tum.de/

Abstract. An approach to object recognition by visual mobile robots is
introduced. It eliminates the need for a calibration of the robot and of the
vision system; it uses no world coordinates, and compensates perspective
distortion in the image by a depth-dependent image transformation. The
approach allows the robot to learn and to recognize objects that may
appear in unpredictable and widely varying distances. The key point of
the approach is a subsampling of the image with the interval between
subsampling points in each small region of the image being inversely
proportional to the local depth.

The approach was realized and evaluated in real-world experiments on
different calibration-free vision-guided mobile robots for recognizing objects in an office environment.

Keywords: Calibration-Free Visual Mobile Robots, Distance-Invariant
Object Recognition, Object Recognition, Robot Vision, Sampling, Vision-
Guided Mobile Robots. . . .

1 Introduction

Future service robots will have to interact closely with humans and, specifically,
with humans who are not robotics experts and often not even interested in
robotics and other technical matters. Moreover, if such robots are to be deployed
in massive numbers, e.g., in unstructured and continuously changing household
environments or construction sites, it is clearly impossible to have professional
experts spend much time for setting up each individual robot and adjusting it to
the characteristics of its particular environment. In recent years there has been,
thus, great interest in the realization of calibration-free vision-guided robots,
i.e., robots depend neither on inbuilt quantitative models nor on pre-defined
numerical values of any parameter [1].

This contribution presents an approach to object recognition that may lead
to realize such calibration-free vision-guided mobile robots.

The objects to be recognized by an autonomous mobile robot navigating in
an office environment include objects that might constitute a collision hazard,
objects that should be manipulated in some way, or, generally speaking, all
static or moving objects that could be relevant for the behavior of the robot.
Among them are, for instance, corridors, junctions, doors, work places (e.g.,
tables, chairs, etc), humans and information signs (e.g., door plates), etc.

L. Van Gool (Ed.): DAGM 2002, LNCS 2449, pp. 411–420, 2002.

Such objects may have arbitrary appearance in terms of shape, texture and rigidity, and may be detected with some basic assumptions about the appearance of the background when it is obstacle-free (see [3]). The problem is that such objects may sometimes be close to the robot, at other times the same objects may be far away, and in some situations they must be recognized even while their distance is changing rapidly. The great variability of distance in which objects may be seen by a robot is one of the factors making object recognition difficult.

To overcome such a difficulty for vision-guided mobile robots working in office environments is the goal of this contribution.

The paper is organized as follows: In the next section we will briefly represent effects of the distance to object recognition. The third section will present our approach to distance-invariant object recognition. It includes not only the concept and the method for learning the distance-invariant object representation, but also the object representation in the robot's object knowledge base, and methods for object recognition. We will describe several experiments performed to validate the concepts and the obtained results in the fourth section. A summary and some conclusions are given in the fifth section.

2   Distance Effects to Object Recognition

If vision is the sensing modality used for mobile robots the perspective distortion in the image affects the appearance of an object in the following ways:

- The visual appearance of an object depends strongly on the distance, D, from which it is seen. For a given camera and object, the size of the object's image is inversely proportional to the square of the distance, i.e., to D^{-2}
- The linear size of the image is inversely proportional to the distance, i.e., to D^{-1}
- The contrast of an object to its surroundings in the image decreases as the distance D increases,
- If an object moves relative to the camera and parallel to the image plane the resulting displacement of its image relative to the image frame, and thus the resulting motion blur, is inversely proportional to the distance, i.e., to D^{-1}.

The combination of these effects makes it difficult for a vision system to determine, for instance, whether two images, both showing an object, but in different distances, show the same object or not. It also makes it difficult to determine if distances, e.g., d_1, between nearby doors and distances, d_2, d_3, between distant doors (Fig. 1) in an image are the same or different . Generally speaking, images of distant objects tend to look small and have low contrast, while images of nearby objects are usually large, clear, and have sharp contrast, etc. For human beings these difficulties apparently do not exist. We can easily recognize an object when we see it more or less, regardless of its distance. This phenomenon has been studied and stated by psychologists, e.g., [1], [8].

Especially, the study of certain optical illustrations has led to the assumption that the human visual system estimates the distance from objects that are being

Fig. 1. A corridor scene with the doors seen from different distances. The size of the doors and the distance between them in the image look different.

seen and uses this information for modeling external objects with their supposedly true size, regardless of the distance from which they are imaged. The human visual system performs a distant-dependent transformation on the elements of an image as one of the first steps of object recognition.

Such lacks of technical vision systems may be overcome by an approach presented in sequel. With it, a machine vision system may similarly transform distant-dependent image data into an approximately distance-invariant form in order to model physical objects regardless of the distance from which they are seen.

3   Distance-Invariant Object Recognition

3.1   Concept

Conventional approaches for recognizing objects that could appear in widely varying distant were the use of different models. For instance, to recognize obstacles on highway [6], [7] have used two separate models for their appearances, one for the near range and one for the far range. In the similar manner, in the object manipulation domain [5] have introduced different object models to recognize a variety of differently shaped objects used for manipulating objects by uncalibrated vision-guided manipulators.

Although such solutions proved successful, but it may be raised the question which one of the models should be chosen in any specific situation. Nevertheless, using distinct models for specific distance ranges may not be the best possible solution.

A novel approach that may be assumed to exist in a similar form in organic vision system [1], [8] is, therefore, investigated to recognize objects in an office environment by learning mobile robots. Key points of this approach are:

- Compensating the effects of perspective distortions in the image to the appearance of an object by a distance-invariant transformation. The transfor-

mation is performed on that section of the image, which contains the object candidate. Thus, in the transformed image section the object's image have a standard size independent of distance from which it is seen.
- The image transformation is performed by subsampling the image in a distance-dependent way.
- Representing the visual appearances of the detected objects in the robot's object knowledge base by data, e.g., a name, information about its visual appearance, and gray-levels at subsampled points contained in the object.

A priori it is unknown in which distance, in which environment, and under which illumination an object will be seen at the time when it should be recognized. Ideally, the object representation should, therefore, be invariant relative to such conditions. Moreover, the actual recognition of objects must occur fast, and the introduction of new objects into the database should be simple. To meet these requirements we decided to base the recognition upon 2-D images of objects, rather than upon a 3-D representation of their shapes.

3.2   Learning for Distance-Invariant Representation

In order to create a distant-invariant representation of an object from its image we have developed an approach of distance-dependent subsampling.

For the facilitation it is supposed that a camera is mounted in a mobile robot navigating in an office environment. The camera's optical axis is parallel to the corridor's floor plane. The robot's task is to recognize objects appearing in the front of the camera without knowledge of the vision system.

The first subtask is to detect the corridor's floor edges in the image. The image region corresponding to the corridor's floor is then searched for objects (It is supposed these tasks were performed by the module of the object detector that is not described here). In reality, the corridor's floor normally has the same width. Due to perspective distortion, distant sections of the corridor's floor appear, however, narrower in the image than nearby sections (Fig. 1). In order to compensate this distortion of the apparent corridor's floor width the image is subsampled in the horizontal row within the image of the corridor's floor into n equidistant subsegments. The distance, d, between the subsampled points (Fig. 2) in each line is given by:

$$d = \frac{W}{n-1} \tag{1}$$

Where W is the width of the corridor's floor in that specific image row (Fig. 2). The maximum distance up to which this transformation may be performed is reached when the number of pixels on the corridor's floor image in that row.

The horizontal density of subsampled points, and thus n, should be sufficiently high to guarantee that even the narrowest objects that is to be recognized is covered by a sufficient number of such points.

The vertical density of subsampled points, too, depends on the goal. In practice, it is noted that not all of the various parts of the object to be recognized

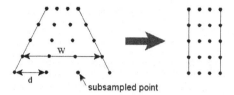

Fig. 2. Concept for transforming the image of the corridor's floor into an image of distance-invariant width by horizontal sub-sampling.

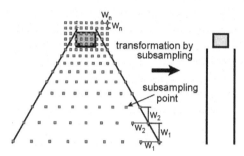

Fig. 3. The subsampling interval on the image of the floor plane varies with distance. The subsampling grid in the image region of the expected object is a square continuation of the grid used on the image of the floor plane.

have the same distance from the camera, but these differences are small in comparison with the distance between the object and the camera. Therefore, it is a permissible simplification to consider all visible parts of the object to be located within a common object plane that is parallel to the image plane.

Object detection is typically the first step of object recognition. If in a search of the floor all physical objects of a certain vertical extent and located on the floor plane are to be detected, regardless of their distance, the vertical subsampling ratio should everywhere in the image of the floor plane be proportional or, for instance, equal to the horizontal one. The vertical subsampling interval in the image corresponds then in the 3-D world to a fixed vertical length above the floor plane, regardless of depth (Fig. 3).

Once an object candidate has been found by searching the subsampled image of the corridor's floor, a different kind of subsampling is used for analyzing the object candidate. We assume the object is flat and contained in an object plane parallel to the image plane. Thus, the subsampling points covering the expected object are arranged in a square grid with a horizontal and vertical period equal to the horizontal subsampling period that is applicable to the floor plane where the object plane intersects with the floor plane (Fig. 3). In this way it is assured that the sampling interval in the object plane has a fixed value (a certain fraction of the corridor's floor width), independent of the distance between the object plane and the camera. Consequently, the image of a given object always comprises the same number of subsampled points, regardless of the object's distance from the camera.

3.3   Knowledge Base for Object Representations

The learned objects should be stored in the robot's object knowledge base in a representation in such a way that it may be easily accessed and processed.

It might be cumbersome for a person to generate representation of numerous objects and to insert them into a knowledge base himself. Therefore, we have developed an approach for unsupervised machine learning, i.e., knowledge acquisition is carried out without interaction with a teacher [4]. Once an object is detected, it is automatically introduced to the knowledge base, at which an operator will search if such an object has already existed in the knowledge base. Criteria for recognizing if the new object is identical to available ones are, e.g., gray-levels, size, etc. (more details will be described in Section 3.5). If it is not the case, the object will be automatically stored into the knowledge base. Such an action is characterized as static, i.e., a new object entry in the knowledge base do not lead, in our case, to changing or overwriting the available knowledge base contents. In the object knowledge base each object is represented by the following data:

- A name
- A 2D-representation of the object's visual appearance, e.g., the number of horizontal and vertical subsampled points covered by the object, and
- A gray-level at each subsampled point

Several ways may be used for representing an object's appearance, and it depends on the requirements of the recognition phase which characteristics of an object should be represented and in which way. For real-time systems, like our system it is required that the object recognition must occur fast, and the introduction of new objects into the knowledge base should be simple. Therefore, we decided to base the representation upon a 2-D image of the objects, rather than upon a 3-D representation of their shapes

3.4   Distance Estimation

Although we would like to develop calibration-free mobile robots, it is nevertheless supposed that a quantitative estimation of the distance between the camera and objects in the scene is required. The width of the corridor in the image may be used for estimating depth. The width of a corridor is usually constant over long distances; the width of its image is then inversely proportional to depth if the viewing direction of the camera is parallel to the floor. In a different way of looking at it, the width of the corridor may be used as a reference for constructing a local sampling grid that has a fixed period on the (vertical) surface of a physical object, regardless of depth.

If a calibrated camera is available the distance from an unknown object resting on the floor plane may be calculated from the vertical image coordinate of its lower edge. If the camera is only partially calibrated the vertical image coordinate of an object's lower edge still gives information on relative depth; in combination with other clues this may allow an estimation of its distance. If the true size of an object and the imaging scale factor of the camera are known depth may be computed from the size of the object's image. Motion stereo or parallax stereo may also be used for depth measurement, and if the robot carries some distance measuring equipment its data may be used, provided that the correspondence between distance data and objects in the camera image can be established.

3.5   Object Recognition

To determine whether an object that is being seen by a mobile robot is one of the object that the robot knows and of which a representation exists in the robot's object knowledge base. Two methods are developed: one based on gray-levels, and the other one based on a correlation function.

The Gray-Level Based Method: Once an object detected the gray-level of its subsampled image are compared to the gray-level of the corresponding reference image in the knowledge base. The comparison is performed by computing a similarity function:

$$\Phi(i,j) = - \sum_k \sum_l |I(i+k, j+l) - R(k,l)| \tag{2}$$

where (i, j) is the coordinate of the upper left corner of the image section to be compared, I(x, y) is the gray-value at location (x, y), and R is the reference image of the object stored in the object knowledge base, with R(k, l) being the gray-value at position (k, l) within the reference image. A large negative value indicates a low degree of similarity.

The method works well if both images were obtained under similar conditions. However, if an object is seen from a large distance the contrast in its image is diminished, and the gray-levels of all pixels tend towards a medium gray. If the images to be compared were taken from greatly different distances the results are much poorer. For overcoming such shortcomings, a second method that uses a correlation function is developed.

2-D Correlation Function: The key point of this method is to use the discrete 2-D correlation function Ω for comparing the stored object image with the actual object image. It is defined by:

$$\Omega(i,j) = \frac{\sum_k \sum_l I(i+k, j+l) * R(k,l)}{\sqrt{\sum_k \sum_l I^2(i+k, j+l) * \sum_k \sum_l R^2(k,l)}} \tag{3}$$

Actually this is a comparison based on cross correlation. Thus, it has the advantage of being independent of transformations of the type a∗x + b, where a and b are real numbers, a $\neq$ 0. Consequently a change in illumination level has no effect.

4   Experiments

Since we want to develop an approach to object recognition for realizing calibration-free visual mobile robots, the above presented approach is implemented on a real-time vision system and initially tested in real-world office environments by two different mobile robots B21r and Pioneer (the left and right one respectively in Fig. 4) with quite different physical characteristics and configurations. Without custom or optional attachments, the Pioneer measures only 18 inches (45 cm) from stem to stem, 14.3 inches (36 cm) across the wheels, and nine inches (22.5 cm) to the top of the console (Fig. 4). While the robot B21r has, e.g., diameter = 52.5 cm, height = 106 cm and weight = 122.5 kg.

Because the corridor's floor edge recognition is difficult in our office environment, the subsampling is not based on the floor edges, but on the edges of the skirting board with the wall. That means the subsampling is actually performed on the plane about 10 cm above the floor plane (Fig. 5). The object recognition is, therefore, transformed and performed in this plane, too. Boxes with distinct dimensions have been used for learning and recognizing. The object was located in different distances (nearby, middle and far) in the corridor for learning, and then in other distances for recognizing by the two methods introduced in section 3.5 above. For objects in the nearby and middle distances both methods give the same results, about 96%. But, for object in the far distances the 2-D cross correlation method can achieve to 93%, while only 88% can be obtained by the grey-level based method.

Fig. 4. The stereo visual B21r (left) and monocular visual Pioneer (right) robots used for experiments.

Fig. 5. The subsampling is not based on the corridor's floor edges, i.e., not on the floor plane, but on the skirting board edges, i.e., on a plane about 10 cm from the floor plane.

5 Summary and Conclusions

A novel approach for compensating perspective distortion by a depth-dependent image transformation has been introduced. Its effectiveness in recognizing objects that may appear in unpredictable and widely varying distances has been demonstrated by implementing it on a real-time vision system and testing it in real-world scenes.

Distance-dependent subsampling may be used for learning of distance-independent representations of various objects occurring in office environments. They may be, then, used to recognize those objects at other times.

The key point of the approach is a subsampling of the image where the interval between subsampling points in each small region of the image is inversely proportional to the local depth. Subsampling is not the theoretically best method for performing the desired image transformation. It has, however, proved its usefulness in applications, and it is fast and simple. Thus, it is suitable for real-time systems.

While the described method of image subsampling has its merits it has obviously some shortcomings, too. One is a loss of image resolution, and another one is the violation of the sampling theorem.

The described subsampling converts the rather large and clear image of a nearby object into a much smaller image with much fewer visible details. At first sight this seems to entail an undesirable loss of valuable information. The objective is, however, to provide standardized object images whose characteristics are largely independent of the distance from which they were taken. Obviously it is impossible to construct a clear image with rich details from a somewhat hazy image that has been taken from a long distance and, therefore, lacks details. It is, thus, by necessity that an image standardization can be accomplished only by removing details and clarity from images of nearby objects, and not by adding them to images of far away objects.

Actually, a higher degree of similarity between the distant image and the reduced near image would result if the effects of distance on light propagation and optical imaging were modeled by a carefully designed nonlinear low-pass filter with distance-dependent characteristics, and if that filter were applied to the nearby image before subsampling. The reason why we did not realize such an approach was that designing a filter that models the effects of distance on light propagation and optical imaging with some degree of accuracy would be difficult, and that with available vision systems the computing time for applying such a filter would be prohibitive for real-time applications.

References

1. Gibson, J. J.: The Perception Of The Visual World. Houghton Mifflin, Boston, MA, (1950)
2. Graefe, V.: Calibration-Free Robots. 9th Intelligent System Symposium. Japan Society of Mechanical Engineers, Japan (1999), pp. 27-35.
3. Horswill, I.: Visual Collision Avoidance, Proc. of IEEE/RSJ/GI International Conference on Intelligent Robots and Systems, IROS'94, Munich (1994), pp. 902-909
4. Nguyen,M.-Ch.: Object Manipulation by Calibration-Free Vision-Guided Robots, Dissertation, Bundeswehr University Munich (2000).
5. Nguyen,M.-C., Graefe, V.: Visual Recognition of Objects for Manipulating by Calibration-Free Robots, In Kenneth, V. T., et al. (eds.): Machine Vision Applications in Industrial Inspection VIII. Proc. of IST/SPIE, Vol. 3966, San Jose (1999), ISBN 1-902856-02-3, pp. 290-298.
6. Regensburger, U.: Zur Erkennung von Hindernissen in der Bahn eines autonomen Strassenfahrzeugs durch maschinelles Echzeitsehen. Dissertation, Bundeswehr University Munich (1994).
7. Regensburger, U., Graefe, V.: Visual Recognition of Obstacles on Roads. In V. Graefe (ed.): Intelligent Robots and Systems, Amsterdam: Elsevier (1994), pp. 73-86
8. Rock, I.: Wahnemung: vom visuellen Reiz zum Sehen und Erkennen. Spektrum der Wissenschaft Verlagsgesselschaft, Heidenberg (1985).

Ultrasonic Image Formation Using Wide Angle Sensor Arrays and Cross-Echo Evaluation

Ariel Di Miro, Bernhard Wirnitzer, Christian Zott, and Roland Klinnert

Institute of Digital Signal Processing, University of Applied Sciences Mannheim,
Windeckstr. 110, D-68163 Mannheim, Germany
Robert Bosch GmbH, FV/FLI, Postfach 106050, D-70049 Stuttgart, Germany
aadimiro@ieee.org, b.wirnitzer@fh-mannheim.de

Abstract. Ultrasonic range sensor arrays (URSA) are widely used in robotics in order to explore the environment. A novel concept for near field sonar (< 2m) is presented which comprises the following features: 1) Sensors with wide angle ultrasonic coils are used in order to cover the field of view with only few sensors. 2) All sensors of the array work simultaneously, because stochastic coding is applied. 3) Cross talk (intra-system interference) between the individual sensors of the array is compensated and evaluated in order to get an improved image formation. An additional object tracking algorithm allows further noise reduction. 4) Automatic calibration of the sensor positions. Experimental results are presented, which show that image formation is possible at a rate of 10 frames per second.

Introduction

Most of the URSA systems use narrow angle ultrasonic coils in order to avoid cross talk within the array (intra-system interference). Though this makes it possible to construct real-world maps based on occupancy grids [1][2][3], it is necessary to make a great number of measurements from multiple viewpoints, because only direct echoes are used.

In this paper, we present a new method which takes advantage of cross talk to gain more information about the obstacle at a single measurement (cross talk evaluation). For this purpose wide angle ultrasonic coils are needed and a system identification scheme by means of stochastic coding is used in order to properly classify the received echoes.

If cross talk is available, it is possible to make some classification of an obstacle. In [6][7] it is shown that by evaluation of direct and cross-echoes a planar object can be distinguished from a point-like one.

Nevertheless, before a reliable measurement can be performed it is necessary to know the physical parameters of the sensor array, i.e. the distance between all sensors, relative installation depth between them, etc. An automatic calibration of the array is therefore desired and, as will be shown, can be performed using the estimated direct and cross talk channels and the a-priori information that a wall is being detected.

Finally, the ultrasonic map of the environment is constructed using a vector oriented procedure. The basic cells for the reconstruction are lines and points, whose positions and orientations are calculated by evaluation of the received echoes.

L. Van Gool (Ed.): DAGM 2002, LNCS 2449, pp. 421–428, 2002.

Stochastic Coding

System identification is used to estimate the unknown impulse response g[k] (Fig. 1). For this purpose statistical independent random time signals are used to allow the sensors to work simultaneously [4] [5].

Wide angle ultrasonic coils are used to cover the field of view with only few sensors.

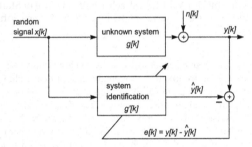

Fig. 1. Adaptive System for ultrasonic distance measurement by stochastic coding and decoding with adaptive filtering.

In our system, the transmitted signal x[k] can be written as a sum of randomly shifted discrete impulses. In this case the classical LMS adaptation algorithm can be simplified considerably, leading to so-called Run-Length Coded LMS algorithm (RLC-LMS). This can be interpreted as a time-varying histogram of the run-lengths of the received echoes and reduces considerably the computational costs [8].

Cross-Echo Compensation and Object Tracking

When an array has N sensors, each transmitted random code signal can propagate to n different receivers. The propagation is described by n impulse responses *gij[k]* from transmitter i to receiver j.

The parallel adaptation scheme showed in Fig. 2 has two advantages: 1) It allows a Decision Feedback Cross-Echo Compensation and 2) Cross talk is estimated. This additional information is very valuable for the identification of obstacles and when ultrasonic maps of environment are to be calculated.

Decision Feedback Cross-Echo Compensation (DFCCC)

DFCCC means that the a-priori information is used, that a detected pulse has propagated either in the direct channel or in one of the cross channels. The decision is based on the received echo (y_j) and the estimated direct (g'_{ii}) and cross (g'_{ij}) estimated impulse responses. For this purpose various criteria can be used. Based on the RLC-LMS a simple method is described by the following update formula:

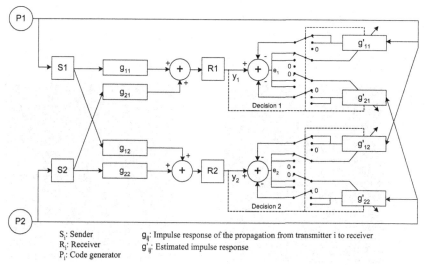

S$_i$: Sender   g$_{ij}$: Impulse response of the propagation from transmitter i to receiver
R$_i$: Receiver   g'$_{ij}$: Estimated impulse response
P$_i$: Code generator

Fig. 2. Simultaneous estimation and compensation of cross talk in adaptive array system identification. The switches are moved simultaneously according to each decision.

$$g_{ij}^{new}[l] = g_{ij}^{old}[l] + \mu.T_{ij}[l] \qquad \text{, with :} \qquad (1)$$

$$H_{ij} : \sum_{k=l-Delta}^{l+Delta} \left| g_{ij}^{old}[k] \right|^2 > Tolerace$$

$$T_{ij}[l] = \begin{cases} 1 & , \left[(H_{ij}\text{true}) \vee (H_{ik}\text{false}, \forall k : 1 < k < N) \right] \wedge (l \in L) \\ -1 & \qquad\qquad other \end{cases}$$

Where L is the set of run-lengths from the time of detection at R$_i$ to the time of transmission at S$_j$ (See fig. 2), H_{ij} a defined hypothesis, N is the number of sensors, and *Delta* and *Tolerance* are adjustable parameters.

As a result a better rate of convergence is achieved and the steady state value of the averaged squared error is improved considerably (Fig. 3).

Object Tracking

The estimated impulse responses can be severely affected if many sensor arrays operate in the same area (additive interference). To meat this an object tracking algorithm (OTA) was developed, which achieves an additional noise reduction. Experimental results can be seen in fig. 4.

The OTA keep a "status" structure for each detected object which contains in principle information about position and velocity. At each adaptation cycle this "a-priori" information of the previous cycle is used to keep track of the object.

DFCCC without object tracking
position [cm]

DFCCC and object tracking
position [cm]

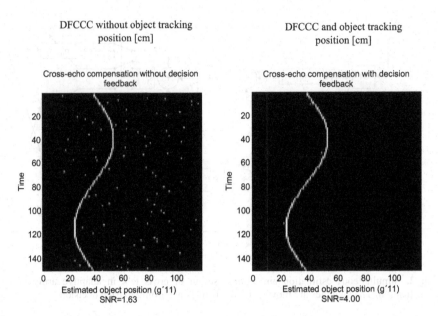

Fig. 3. Improvement of the Signal to Noise Ratio (SNR) using decision feedback based on the most probable channel. Simulations of an array with two sensors without additive interference of a foreigner array. The figures show the estimated impulse response of the direct channel (g'_{11}) in function of the time.

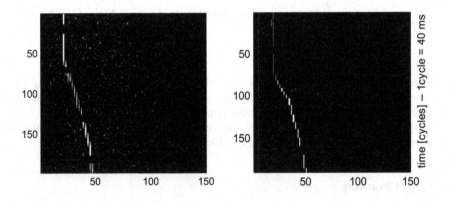

Fig. 4. Improvement of the Signal to Noise Ratio (SNR) using an object tracking algorithm. Experiments with an array of two sensors and the additive interference of a foreigner sensor array. The figures show the estimated impulse response of the direct channel (g'_{11}) in function of the time.

The result of the OTA is in addition used to update the estimated impulse responses in the adaptation algorithm. As a consequence moving targets are tracked better, because spread of the estimated impulse response is reduced (see fig. 5).

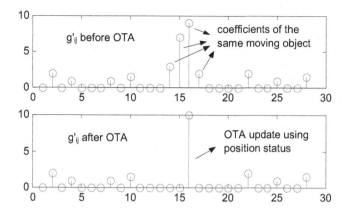

Fig. 5. Impulse response update after the OTA.

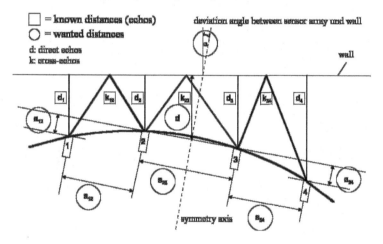

Fig. 6. Computation of the physical parameters of an URSA by means of the measured direct and cross-echoes.

Automatic Calibration of URSA

Automatic calibration means that the URSA must be able to measure its own physical parameters. With the a-priori information that a wall is detected it is possible to estimate these parameters using the direct and cross-echoes (See fig. 6).

With some geometry the wanted distances can be obtained as a function of only d_1, d_2, d_3, d_4, k_{12}, k_{23}, and k_{34}. For example, for S_{23} holds:

$$S_{23} = \sqrt{k_{23}^2 - 4.d_2 d_3} \qquad (2)$$

However, in practice, accuracy problems occur when computing these parameters due to the quantification and the nonlinear relations with the measured distances. If the URSA works with a normal resolution of 1 cm for the measured distances (d_3, d_4 and k_{23}), then the inaccuracy for S_{23} can reach about 10 cm in a typical scenario.

To meet this, a great number of measurements are taken while the URSA is being moved slowly relative to the wall and each measured value is used to calculate the physical parameters. After that, the set of calculated values is analysed with a moving window in order to remove that which differ much from the local mean (see fig. 7). Finally the average of the remaining sets are calculated and an accuracy better than 1 cm is achieved (See table 1).

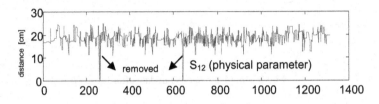

Fig. 7. Experimental data set of a measured physical parameter. During the approximately 1300 measurements the URSA is being moved slowly (about 10 cm/s) relative to a wall.

Table 1. Experimental results of the automatic calibration of URSA. The measured parameters apart less than 1 cm from the real ones.

Physical parameters	S_{12} (cm)	a_{12} (cm)	S_{23} (cm)	S_{34} (cm)	a_{34} (cm)
real	18.3	3.4	20.2	18.3	3.5
measured	18.48	2.90	20.70	18.51	3.41

Image Formation

Once the physical parameters of the URSA are known, it is possible to make some classification of an obstacle. Fig. 8 illustrates the principle of using cross talk in order to achieve this. If the distance k_{12} (cross talk) is equal to the sum of the direct distances (d_1 and d_2), then the object is probably point-like one. In contrast, a similar condition for k_{12}, d_1 and d_2 can be obtained to evaluate the probability of a planar object [6],[7]. Following, two features can be defined in order to distinguish between planar (line) and point-like objects:

$$M_{point} = k_{12} - d_1 - d_2 \quad , \quad |M_{point}| < \Delta M_{point} \qquad (3)$$

$$M_{line} = \sqrt{k_{12} - 4d_1 d_2} - S_{12} \quad , \quad |M_{line}| < \Delta M_{line}$$

The tolerance values ΔM_{point} and ΔM_{line} can be computed using the mean squared error of the two features. Assuming a normal distribution of the measured echoes:

$$\Delta M = \sqrt{\left(\frac{\partial M}{\partial d_1}\Delta d_1\right)^2 + \left(\frac{\partial M}{\partial d_2}\Delta d_2\right)^2 + \left(\frac{\partial M}{\partial k_{12}}\Delta k_{12}\right)^2} \tag{4}$$

Based on this classification the ultrasonic map of the environment is constructed using lines and points as basic cells. The first experiments show that the image formation is possible at a rate of 10 frames per second (see fig.9).

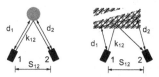

Fig. 8. Classification of planar and point-like objects.

It is important to notice that in addition to the classification it is possible to determine theoretically the exact position of the obstacles. If direct echoes are only available, the certainty of the position of an object is uniformly distributed along an arc [1][3].

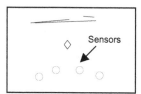

Fig. 9. First experimental results: Image formation based on a vector oriented procedure. The circles represent the four sensors of the array which work simultaneously and whose positions were determined by the automatic calibration algorithm. The lines represent a detected wall and the rhomb a detected point-like object. Each line and rhomb is the result of evaluating direct and cross-echoes between two sensors.

Conclusions

Wide angle URSA in combination with cross-echo evaluation and an early classification scheme are of great benefit for fast and computational effective ultrasonic mapping.

References

[1] Alberto Elfes. Sonar-Based Real-World Mapping and Navigation. IEEE Journal of Robotics and Automation, vol RA-3, NO. 3, June 1987.
[2] J. Borenstein. Histogramic In-Motion Mapping For Mobile Robot Obstacle Avoidance. IEEE Journal of Robotics and Automation, vol 7, NO. 4, 1991, pp. 535-539.

[3] Solomon E. Shimony and Ami Berler. Bayes networks for sensor fusion in occupancy grids. Technical Report FC-96-01, Department of Math. and Computer Science, Ben-Gurion University, 1996.

[4] Wirnitzer, B., H. Schmitt, W. Grimm, and R. Klinnert,   Interference Cancellation in Ultrasonic Sensor Arrays by Stochastic Coding and Adaptive Filtering, Proceedings of the IEEE International Conference on Intelligent Vehicles 1998 , Stuttgart 1998.

[5] Schmitt, H., B. Wirnitzer, W. Grimm, and R. Klinnert,   Arbeitsraumüberwachung mit Ultraschall- Sensorarrays, in Levi, R.J. Ahlers, F. May, M. Schanz: "Mustererkennung 1998", Springer, Berlin, 1998.

[6] Wirnitzer, B., H. Schmitt, W. Grimm, R. Klinnert,Ultrasonic Ranging Devices, International Patent, DE 198 02 724.

[7] Wirnitzer, B., S. Schluff, H. Schmitt, R. Klinnert, Ch. Zott: Selbstkalibirierende Überwachungseinheit für Signal-Echo-Sensoren, Deutsche und internationale Patentanmeldung 2001.

[8] Wirnitzer, B., "Run-length coded LMS-Adaptation", Labornotiz, Institut für digitale Signalverarbeitung, FH-Mannheim, 1999.

Segmenting Microorganisms in Multi-modal Volumetric Datasets Using a Modified Watershed Transform

Steven Bergner[1], Regina Pohle[1], Stephan Al-Zubi[1], Klaus Tönnies[1],
Annett Eitner[2], and Thomas R. Neu[2]

[1] Department of Computing Science, Otto-von-Guericke-University Magdeburg, Germany
sbergner@cs.uni-magdeburg.de,
{regina,alzubi,klaus}@isg.cs.uni-magdeburg.de
http://isgwww.cs.uni-magdeburg.de/bv
[2] Department of Inland Water Research Magdeburg, UFZ Centre for Environmental Research,
Leipzig-Halle, Germany
{eitner,neu}@gm.ufz.de

Abstract. Aquatic interfaces in the environment are colonized by a large variety of pro- and eucaryotic microorganisms, which may be examined by confocal laser scanning microscopy. We describe an algorithm to identify and count the organisms in multi-channel volumetric datasets. Our approach is an intermediate-level segmentation combining a voxel-based classification with low-level shape characteristics (convexity). Local intensity maxima are used as seed points for a watershed transform. Subsequently, we solve the problem of over-segmentation by merging regions. The merge criterion is taking the depth of the 'valley' between adjacent segments into account. The method allows to make correct segmentation decisions without the use of additional shape information. Also this method provides a good basis for further analysis steps, e.g. to recognize organisms that consist of multiple parts.

1 Introduction

In nature microorganisms are mainly associated with interfaces. These interfacial communities are referred to as microbial biofilms consisting of procaryotic and eucaryotic microorganisms [1]. The organisms in these films are important for the sorption and/or degradation of a wide range of anorganic and organic contaminants. Biofilms have a cellular and a polymeric component and may be ideally examined fully hydrated by using confocal laser scanning microscopy [2].

The samples used for this study were lotic biofilms exposed to light. The distribution of bacteria was determined after staining with a nucleic acid specific fluorochrome (SYTO9). The emission signal of SYTO9 was recorded in the green channel. The lectin specific extra-cellular polymeric substances (EPS) were imaged after staining with *Phaseolus vulgaris*-TRITC lectin and recorded in the red channel. Green algae were visualized due to their chlorophyll autofluorescence recorded in the farred channel. Cyanobacteria were distinguished due to their pigments (chlorophyll and

L. Van Gool (Ed.): DAGM 2002, LNCS 2449, pp. 429–437, 2002.

phycocyanin/phycoerythrin) resulting in a double signal recorded in the red and far-red channel.

In order to quantify the 4 signals recorded in the 3 channels it is necessary to find the border of the objects and split them correctly. Thresholding, which is usually employed in quantification procedures, is not suitable as it is not able to handle the large variation in signal intensity. For a satisfactory classification it would be necessary to take size and shape characteristics of the objects into account. But because of the immense diversity of shape in the world of microorganisms, it is difficult to include such information as a-priori knowledge. Additional problems for shape-based methods arise from different scaling and blurring along z-axis, which is due to the acquisition method.

There are a number of algorithms for automatically detecting cells in images of laser-scanning microscopy. They usually rely on a multi-level approach. In the first stage a coarse, purely voxel-based segmentation is performed. For that task it is possible to utilize threshold methods [4, 5, 7] or trained neural networks [6]. As a result some objects are correctly segmented and others are still clustered. Those clusters can be divided using higher-level a-priory knowledge. The type of knowledge used in this second step can be categorized in two groups:

1.   Shape Based Methods

Approaches used here include the use of neural networks, trained to recognize convex shapes [6], or high-level Markov random-fields [8], or fitting hyper-quadrics to previously extracted, polygonal shapes [5]. All methods assume that the cells that have to be divided have a similar shape, which is known in advance.

2.   Intensity Based Methods

This group includes the searching for an optimal path, which minimizes a cost function [9], and the watershed transform (WST), which is either used as morphological WST [7] or as marker based WST [3,4], to divide clustered nuclei. Problems for these methods are caused by noise and an inhomogeneous intensity distribution in the cells, which lead to over segmentation and result in higher number of cells than actually contained in the sample. Also, some of these approaches have only been investigated for 2D images.

In our application we need to analyse the entire volume. Counting organisms in separate layers is only of limited use for the analysis. Hence, a 3D version of the algorithm is required or a way to connect results from 2D analyses. Due to the versatile structure of organisms or pollution, several local intensity maxima are found in each object. That makes the assumption of unique markers hard to fulfil. Thus, a method is required that makes use of the entire information and is robust against local disturbance.

The remainder of this paper is organized as follows: We first describe the problem that we are going to solve. Then we present an algorithm based on the watershed transform. By introducing a new merge criterion the results are made more robust against misleading seed points and locally varying brightness and contrast. Tests on several data sets are presented and discussed. Finally, conclusions are given.

2   Segmentation of Microorganisms in Laser Scanning Microscopy

2.1   Problem Description

The images show a large diversity of shapes among the procaryotic and eucaryotic microorganisms. The autofluorescence signals and fluorochrome stains have been selected in order to record their emission signals in different channels. However, correlation between channels is possible and sometimes characteristic for some object classes. The concentration of the fluorochromes varies within the microorganisms and among different datasets. Furthermore, densely packed structures such as clusters of algae or bacteria lead to a signal increase due to the partial volume effect (see Fig. 1). Thus, intensity thresholding will not be applicable and using shape-based segmentation will be difficult because of the large variety of shapes. We developed a low-level method for segmentation that estimates object boundaries based on intensity and local contrast.

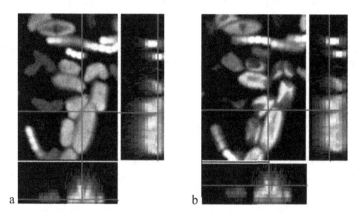

Fig. 1. A cluster of algae shown in two different layers a) Algae are not well separated b) Borders can be clearly distinguished. The gray cross indicates position of horizontal (bottom) and vertical slices (right)

The algorithm was developed based on the following assumptions. The type and concentration of fluorochromes indicate important structural constituents of the biofilms. The intensity is often highest inside of the organisms and decreasing to the outside. This holds for different kinds of organisms at different levels of contrast and brightness. Each of the three classes of organisms can be found in one of the three channels. In the case of cyanobacteria, the co-occurrence in two different channels (chlorophyll and polymer) is characteristic. Due to vertical blurring it can happen that organisms that have a clear shape in one channel are disturbed by other organisms that are visible at almost the same position in a different channel. To avoid the influence of other channels at this early stage of analysis the initial segmentation is carried out in each channel separately.

2.2   Segmentation

Organisms that give a signal in different channels are later classified by correlating segmentation results from the respective channels. In each channel, boundaries between organisms as well as between organism and background are found applying a modified watershed transform with markers [3,4]. The watershed transform (WST) [7] can separate segments based on local maxima thus avoiding segmentation errors due to intensity variations. Applied without markers, it will lead to over-segmentation, which can be overcome by applying a hierarchical WST [10]. However, the hierarchical WST does not use knowledge about possible locations of segments and may accidentally merge different organisms. We chose a marker-based WST with markers being placed into the segments in order to avoid this.

Boundaries between organisms are characterised by local minima whereas those to the background are characterised by an intensity threshold. Thus, we applied a marker-based WST to the data with local intensity minima being the watersheds and included a threshold component to account for the boundary to the background. The main challenge is to find marker positions. We applied a strategy where almost every local maximum in regions above a given intensity threshold is treated as marker. We accept that an organism may have initially several markers set. The only assumption made is that the initial segments are covering at most one object. Regions are then merged based on their characteristics and features of their common boundary. The algorithm consists of three steps:

1. Initial marker placement.
2. Application of the marker based WST.
3. Merging of regions that belong to the same organism.

Markers are placed at local maxima in a 3x3x3 neighbourhood. Markers in regions of constant value are placed only if the region is not adjacent to pixels of higher intensity value. In this case a distance transform is carried out in the region and the marker is placed at the point, which has the highest distance to the boundary.

Markers are not placed if their absolute intensity is below a threshold t_{org} that differentiates organism intensities from background. The threshold is chosen high enough as to securely exclude any background voxels for being selected as marker but lower than the lowest local maximum of the object voxels. It was found experimentally and was set to t_{org}=70 (of 255) for all data sets.

After having determined the markers, the watershed transform is carried out. A local threshold t_{seg} is determined for each marker in order to pre-define a watershed, which prevents water flowing into the background. It was set to 30% of the local maximum value at the marker position. The advantage of using a ratio instead of a fixed threshold is that the cut-off will adapt to the differences in the partial volume effect at different brightness of segments.

Due to local maxima from noise or varying fluorescence signals in the organisms, the initial result is massively over-segmented. In the original watershed transform this is reduced by thresholding gradient magnitudes. Since we are working in the intensity domain this is smoothing, which would just reduce, but not solve the problem of over-segmentation. Smoothing also blurs shape details, which might be necessary to distinguish objects.

We decided against smoothing and merged segments based on characteristics of segments. After applying the WST to each channel independently, segments from corresponding channels are merged, if they overlap and belong to the same class of organism (this is the case, e.g. for cyanobacteria). Two segments in two channels are merged if their spatial overlap is greater than *33%* of their volume. This does not necessarily merge segment of the same channel. It can happen, though, that a segment of another channel is working as a 'bridge'.

The major work of removal of over-segmentations happens in the next part of this step. Two segments are joined, if they have a common boundary and if for their two intensity maxima m_1 and m_2 with $m_1{\leq}m_2$ and the highest intensity value m_a of their boundary the following holds (see Fig. 2):

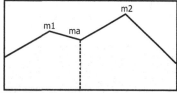

Fig. 2. Adjacency maximum is used as merge criterion

$$\frac{m_a}{w \cdot m_1 + (1-w) \cdot m_2} > t_{bnd}$$
(Eq. 1)

The parameter $0<w<1$ describes a weighting between the higher and the lower maximum. The threshold ratio $0<t_{bnd}<1$ defines the maximum depth of the valley between segments that can be merged. Values for w and t_{bnd} were 0.6 and 0.75, respectively. They were found experimentally and applied to all data sets. The merging is done stepwise iterating through all segments, beginning with the highest maxima. This is repeated until no further changes occur.

After all merging is done each segment covers one unique object. Sometimes the region merging joins segments over the border of the objects, appending lower intensity blur around the organisms. This effect is reduced, but not avoided by the valley criterion. To subsequently refine the shape of objects it is possible to cut off lower intensities. The cutoff threshold is a certain ratio of the maximum value. This works independent from the overall brightness of the segment and produces a clear run of shape. Nevertheless, this step is problematic because it can also discard darker parts of objects, which are not necessarily background.

2.3   Classification

The result of the previous steps are segments of potential interest. An additional classification is needed to finally discard segments that do not match any organism description. The major criterion to distinguish object classes are the channels of fluorescence. This includes looking for co-occurance of signals in multiple channels, which has already been done before merging the fragments. Additional criteria are the volume of the objects and the maximum intensity. For certain object classes, such as algae it is possible to specify a volume threshold. The intensity threshold is useful to find segments caused by background noise. Segments that can not be associated with any class are treated as background, so they do not affect the statistics. All class characteristics and also the important segmentation parameters are taken from an external description file and remain configurable to the user. This makes the framework usable for new types of organisms, or allows the use of additional fluorescence channels.

3   Applying the Algorithm to the Segmentation of Water Samples

The algorithm is used to count bacteria, algae, and cyanobacteria in water samples. The following examples are taken from two different datasets, which have been acquired using a confocal laser-scanning microscope at different resolutions. Fig. 3a shows a slice of the chlorophyll channel with the corresponding segmentation in Fig. 3b. The elongated objects

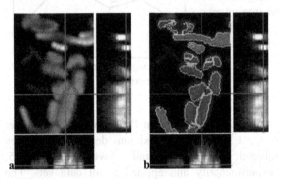

are cyanobacteria, which can be distinguished due to co-occurrence in the polymer channel (not shown). The apparent over-segmentation of algae in the upper middle is actually correct because in upper layers they divide to separate objects. The 3D watershed transform inherently uses information from other layers of the dataset. Therefore the diffuse border be-

Fig. 3. Algae colony, a) shown in chlorophyll channel b) segmented algae

tween the clustered algae can be handled properly.

For the tests the segmentation parameters t_{org}, t_{seg}, and t_{bnd} are the same for all datasets. The dependency of the algorithm on the internal parameters is shown in Fig. 4. The more algae, the less merge test are positive. The chosen value is a compromise between merging all connected segments and separating them all. It fits best with the observed most correct segmentation.

The datasets are taken at different resolution and also at varying brightness. To evaluate the robustness of the method the data has been modified by adding normal distributed noise (of different standard deviation σ) and by reducing the contrast (scaling intensity). The quantification of algae in two different datasets is shown in Fig. 5. The thick black line represents the

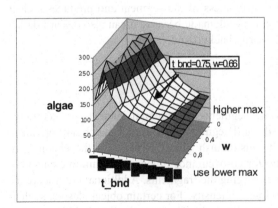

Fig. 4. Detected number of algae depending on t_{bnd} and w from Eq. 1 (dataset of Fig.5a)

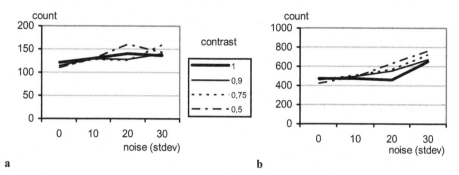

Fig. 5. Detected number of algae in two datasets at different level of noise and contrast, resolution: a) 512x512x29 at 0.09 μm³/voxel b) 512x512x40 at 4.7 μm³/voxel

detected number of algae at original contrast with respect to different level of noise (abscissa). The standard deviation σ for added noise ranged between 0 and 30 of a total intensity range of 0 to 255. The increasing number of objects results from additional local maxima introduced by the noise. This leads to an increased number of initial fragments, which are partly eliminated during the merging step. This also explains the longer runtime of the algorithm with increased noise, going up from 15s ($\sigma=0$) to 90s ($\sigma=30$) for the dataset used in Fig. 5a.

The number of bacteria for the same datasets is shown in Fig. 6. The important difference is that bacteria are much smaller than algae. They are very similar to the size of small maxima introduced by the noise. Therefore their number is hugely increasing at $\sigma=30$ in both datasets. Fig. 6a shows a decreasing number of bacteria as the contrast is reduced. A reason for that could be the low intensity of some bacteria, which falls below the given intensity threshold during classification. Nevertheless, the constant quantity until $\sigma=20$ indicates quite stable results against noise. A possible improvement could be to connect long, thin clusters of bacteria to form filaments. This could be done in a more sophisticated classification step after the initial segmentation and merging is done.

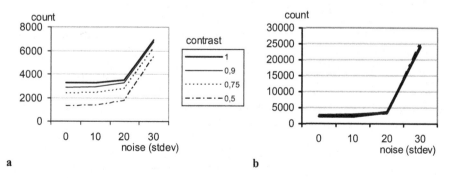

Fig. 6. Detected bacteria in two different datasets at varying level of noise and contrast, resolution: a) 512x512x29 at 0.09 μm³/voxel b) 512x512x40 at 4.7 μm³/voxel

Cyanobacteria are segmented correctly in 85% of all cases. The number of bacteria is only an estimation in addition to a volume analysis. The segmentation of algae is problematic because some of them consist of two or more chloroplasts. Thus, in some cases the result is more the number of chloroplasts than the number of algae.

4 Discussion and Future Work

Some organisms consist of several parts in different channels. Thus, a more sophisticated analysis will require information on shape and object structure. Further investigation needs to be done on grouping characteristic constellations of segments to form higher order composite objects. For those approaches the output of our method could be used as initial dissection of organisms into functional parts.

Because of versatility of microorganisms the algorithm has been developed without using shape information. Within these restrictions the method provides satisfactory results only using simple object descriptions. The merge criterion is used to make the watershed transform more robust against noise and pollution. The resulting method provides a useful basis to the analysis of three-dimensional datasets from laser-scanning microscopy.

References

[1] Lawrence, J.R., Korber, D.R., Wolfaardt, G.M., Caldwell, D.E., Neu, T.R.: Analytical imaging and microscopy techniques. In: Hurst, C.J., Crawford, R.L., Knudsen, G.R., McInerney, M.J., Stetzenbach, L.D. (eds): Manual of environmental microbiology. American Society for Microbiology, Washington (2002) 39-61

[2] Lawrence, J.R., Neu, T.R., Marshall, K.C.: Colonization, adhesion, aggregation and biofilms. In: Hurst, C.J., Crawford, R.L., Knudsen, G.R., McInerney, M.J., Stetzenbach, L.D. (eds): Manual of environmental microbiology. American Society for Microbiology, Washington (2002) 466-477

[3] Malpica, N., de Solórzano, C.O., Vaquero, J.J., Santos, A., Vallcorba, I., Garcýa-Sagredo, J.M., del Pozo, F.: Applying Watershed Algorithms to the Segmentation of Clustered Nuclei. Cytometry, Vol. 28. Wiley-Liss, Inc. (1997) 289-297

[4] Sarti, A., de Solórzano, C.O., Lockett, S., Malladi, R.: A Geometric Model for 3D Confocal Microscope Image Analysis. IEEE Transactions on Biomedical Engineering, Vol. 47, No. 12 (2000) 1600-1609

[5] Cong, G., Parvin, B.: Model Based Segmentation of Nuclei. Journal of Pattern Recognition, Vol. 33, No. 8 (2000) 1383-1393

[6] Nattkemper, T.W., Wersing, H., Schubert, W., Ritter, H.: A Neuronal Network Architecture for Automatic Segmentation of Fluorescence Micrographs. Proc. Of the ESANN, Bruges (2000) 177-182

[7] Rodenacker, K., Brühl, A., Hausner, M., Kühn, M., Liebscher, V., Wagner, M., Winkler, G., Wuertz, S.: Quantification of biofilms in multi-spectral digital volumes from confocal laser-scanning microscopes. Image Anal Stereol; Vol. 19, No. 2 (2000) 151-156

[8] Hurn, M., Rue, H.: High-level image priors in confocal microscopy applications. In: Mardia, K.V., Gill, C.A., Aykroyd, R.G. (eds.): The Art and Science of Bayesian Image Analysis. Leeds University Press (1997) 36-43

[9] Ong, S., Yeow, H., Sinniah, R.: Decomposition of digital clumps into convex parts by contour tracing and labelling. Pattern Recognition Letters, Vol. 13 (1992) 789-795

[10] Wegner, S.: Die Wasserscheidentransformation als Segmentierungsverfahren in der medizinischen Bildverarbeitung, Fortschritt-Berichte, R.10, Nr. 612, VDI Verlag, Düsseldorf 1999

Bayesian Kernel Tracking

Dorin Comaniciu

Real-Time Vision and Modeling Department, Siemens Corporate Research,
755 College Road East, Princeton, NJ 08540, USA,
comanici@scr.siemens.com

Abstract. We present a Bayesian approach to real-time object tracking using nonparametric density estimation. The target model and candidates are represented by probability densities in the joint spatial-intensity
domain. The new location and appearance of the target are jointly derived by computing the maximum likelihood estimate of the parameter
vector that characterizes the transformation from the candidate to the
model. This probabilistic formulation accommodates variations in the
target appearance, while being robust to outliers represented by partial
occlusions. In this paper we analyze the simplest parameterization represented by translation in both domains and present a gradient-based
iterative solution. Various tracking sequences demonstrate the superior
behavior of the method.

Keywords: Real-Time Tracking; Maximum Likelihood Parameter Estimation; Joint Domain Density; Appearance Change.

1 Introduction

Visual object tracking is a task required by various applications such as perceptual user interfaces [4], surveillance [6], augmented reality [11], smart rooms
[18], intelligent video compression [5], and driver assistance [13,1]. In the general
case, a visual tracker involves both *bottom-up* and *top-down* components. The
former are represented by the target representation and localization, appearance
change, and measurement model, while that latter regard the object dynamics,
learning of scene priors, and hypothesis testing and verification.

Common techniques to model the target dynamics are the (extended) Kalman
filter [2] and particle filters [15,10]. The problem of target representation and
localization is related to registration techniques [23,20,19]. The difference is that
tracking assumes small changes in the location and appearance of the target
in two consecutive frames. This property can be exploited to develop efficient,
gradient based localization schemes, using the normalized correlation criterion
[3]. Since the correlation is sensitive to illumination, Hager and Belhumeur [12]
model explicitly geometry and illumination changes. The method is robustified
by Sclaroff and Isidoro [21] by using M-estimators [14]. Learning of appearance
models is discussed in [16] by employing a mixture of stable image structure,
motion information and an outlier process. To efficiently accommodate non-rigid

L. Van Gool (Ed.): DAGM 2002, LNCS 2449, pp. 438–445, 2002.

transformations, Comaniciu *et al.* [8] develop histogram-based tracking. Spatial gradient optimization becomes possible due to a spatially-smooth cost function produced by masking the target with an isotropic kernel.

In this paper we present a new approach for target representation and localization. Our motivation is to develop a framework that is optimal, efficient, robust to outliers, and that can be easily customized. We formulate the problem of *target localization* as a *classification* problem. Assuming that the probability density of the target model is known, we search for target candidates whose probability density under a parameterized transformation matches the density of the target. The matching criterion is derived by minimizing the probability of error in choosing the wrong candidate. Bayesian statistics are used to obtain the maximum likelihood estimates of the best target candidate and parameter vector. As another novelty, the probability densities characterizing the target and candidates are estimated in the *joint spatial-intensity* domain. This implies that location and target appearance are optimized simultaneously.

The organization of the paper is as follows. Section 2 describes the Bayesian alignment of probability densities under a general parameterized transformation. An explicit solution for the translation case is derived in Section 3. Section 4 formulates the density estimation in the spatial-intensity domain. Tracking experiments on different sequences are presented in Section 5.

2   Bayesian Alignment of Densities

Assume that the target model is specified by the d-dimensional sample $Q = \{\mathbf{x}_r, r = 1 \ldots N\}$ drawn i.i.d. from the probability density q. We hypothesize the existence of U target candidates generated by transforming a random variable $\mathbf{X}$ of density p under the parameterized transformation $T(\mathbf{X}; \boldsymbol{\theta}_u)$ where $u = 1 \ldots U$ and $\boldsymbol{\theta}_u$ is the parameter vector. In other words, starting from the sample $\{\mathbf{x}_i, i = 1 \ldots n\}$ drawn from p we obtain samples of the form $\{T(\mathbf{x}_i; \boldsymbol{\theta}_u), i = 1 \ldots n\}$, characterized by the density p_u, with $u = 1 \ldots \mathbf{U}$.

We want to determine a parameter vector $\boldsymbol{\theta}_v$ with $1 \leq v \leq U$ such that the probability that the model sample $Q = \{\mathbf{x}_r, r = 1 \ldots N\}$ and the candidate sample $\{T(\mathbf{x}_i; \boldsymbol{\theta}_v), i = 1 \ldots n\}$ belong to the same density source (i.e., $q = p_v$) is maximized (or, equivalently, the probability of error is minimized). This can be written as

$$v = \underset{u}{arg\,max}\ P(q = p_u | Q) = \underset{u}{arg\,max}\ P(Q | q = p_u) P(p_u) \qquad (1)$$

where the last equality is obtain by applying the Bayes rule. The term $P(p_u)$ represents a priori information on the presence of candidate u. Depending on the tracking formulation $P(p_u)$ is obtained either by learning the motion dynamics or/and the appearance changes. This is a natural way to integrate priors on motion and appearance.

At this moment, we consider all the hypotheses equally probable, which is equivalent to maximizing the likelihood $P(Q | q = p_u)$. By taking into account that Q is drawn i.i.d. and applying the log function, it results that

$$v = arg\overset{u}{max}\ L_u = arg\overset{u}{max} \sum_{r=1}^{N} \log p_u(\mathbf{x}_r) \tag{2}$$

where L_u is the log-likelihood. [1] The kernel estimate of the density p_u computed at location $\mathbf{x}$ is given by

$$p_u(\mathbf{x}) = \frac{1}{nh^d} \sum_{i=1}^{n} K\left(\frac{\mathbf{x} - T(\mathbf{x}_i; \boldsymbol{\theta}_u)}{h}\right) \tag{3}$$

where h is the bandwidth of kernel K [22]. Hence, the log-likelihood is expressed by

$$L_u = \sum_{r=1}^{N} \log \frac{1}{nh^d} \sum_{i=1}^{n} K\left(\frac{\mathbf{x}_r - T(\mathbf{x}_i; \boldsymbol{\theta}_u)}{h}\right) \tag{4}$$

The best target candidate is obtained by maximizing expression (4) as a function of $\boldsymbol{\theta}_u$. Note the optimality of the above formulation.

3   Translation Case

The transformation T is application dependent and related to the expected transformation of the target during tracking. We will show in this section how to maximize the log-likelihood for the translation case. The following computations are similar in strategy to those shown Section 4.2 of [8]. However, their significance is different: we deal here with the maximum likelihood alignment of densities, while in [8] the task was to maximize the Bhattacharyya coefficient between histograms.

The transformation $T(\mathbf{x}_i; \boldsymbol{\theta}_u)$ is replaced by $(\mathbf{x}_i - \mathbf{y})$ and the density p_u is now denoted by $p(\mathbf{x} + \mathbf{y})$, being expressed by

$$p(\mathbf{x} + \mathbf{y}) = \frac{1}{nh^d} \sum_{i=1}^{n} K\left(\frac{\mathbf{x} + \mathbf{y} - \mathbf{x}_i}{h}\right) \tag{5}$$

For the convenience of notation, we introduce the profile of the kernel K as the function $k : [0, \infty) \to R$ such that $K(\mathbf{x}) = k(\|\mathbf{x}\|^2)$. Employing the profile notation we have

$$p(\mathbf{x} + \mathbf{y}) = \frac{1}{nh^d} \sum_{i=1}^{n} k\left(\left\|\frac{\mathbf{x} + \mathbf{y} - \mathbf{x}_i}{h}\right\|^2\right) \tag{6}$$

---

[1] By applying the law of large numbers [9, p.286] it can be easily shown that condition (2) is equivalent to minimizing the Kullback-Leibler distance $D(q\|p_u)$. This is not required by our derivation. Note, however, that the other divergence, $D(p_u\|q)$, is not appropriate for the task.

while log-likelihood (4) becomes

$$L_{\mathbf{y}} = \sum_{r=1}^{N} \log p(\mathbf{x}_r + \mathbf{y}) = \sum_{r=1}^{N} \log \frac{1}{nh^d} \sum_{i=1}^{n} k\left(\left\|\frac{\mathbf{x}_r + \mathbf{y} - \mathbf{x}_i}{h}\right\|^2\right) \quad (7)$$

Assume that the optimization is started with an initial value $\mathbf{y} = \mathbf{y}_0$. Using Taylor expansion around the values $p(\mathbf{x}_r + \mathbf{y}_0)$ the log-likelihood is approximated as

$$L_{\mathbf{y}} \approx \sum_{r=1}^{N} \log p(\mathbf{x}_r + \mathbf{y}_0) - N + \sum_{r=1}^{N} \frac{1}{p(\mathbf{x}_r + \mathbf{y}_0)} \frac{1}{nh^d} \sum_{i=1}^{n} k\left(\left\|\frac{\mathbf{x}_r + \mathbf{y} - \mathbf{x}_i}{h}\right\|^2\right) \quad (8)$$

The last term in (8) represents a weighted sum of density estimates computed at locations $\mathbf{x}_r + \mathbf{y}$. It is natural to employ the mean shift procedure [7] to maximize this term. By taking the gradient of this term with respect to $\mathbf{y}$, after some algebra the new value of $\mathbf{y}$ is obtained as

$$\mathbf{y}_1 = \frac{\sum_{r=1}^{N} \frac{1}{p(\mathbf{x}_r + \mathbf{y}_0)} \sum_{i=1}^{n} (\mathbf{x}_i - \mathbf{x}_r) g\left(\left\|\frac{\mathbf{x}_r + \mathbf{y}_0 - \mathbf{x}_i}{h}\right\|^2\right)}{\sum_{r=1}^{N} \frac{1}{p(\mathbf{x}_r + \mathbf{y}_0)} \sum_{i=1}^{n} g\left(\left\|\frac{\mathbf{x}_r + \mathbf{y}_0 - \mathbf{x}_i}{h}\right\|^2\right)} \quad (9)$$

where $g(x) = -k'(x)$ for the definition domain. At $\mathbf{y}_1$ the log-likelihood function is larger than that at $\mathbf{y}_0$. Expression (9) is computed iteratively until convergence. The new position is determined by weighted sums of local point differences. Since the measurements are local (due to the kernel weighting), the algorithm is robust to outliers in the data.

A more intuitive expression is obtained by replacing k and g by the normal profile and its derivative. The normal profile is

$$k(x) = (2\pi)^{-d/2} \exp\left(-\frac{1}{2} x\right). \quad (10)$$

hence, $g(x) = k(x)/2$. Since k is identical to g up to a constant, expression (9) simplifies to

$$\mathbf{y}_1 = \frac{1}{N} \sum_{r=1}^{N} \frac{\sum_{i=1}^{n} (\mathbf{x}_i - \mathbf{x}_r) k\left(\left\|\frac{\mathbf{x}_r + \mathbf{y}_0 - \mathbf{x}_i}{h}\right\|^2\right)}{\sum_{i=1}^{n} k\left(\left\|\frac{\mathbf{x}_r + \mathbf{y}_0 - \mathbf{x}_i}{h}\right\|^2\right)} \quad (11)$$

This shows that the log-likelihood is maximized by computing weighted sums of local differences.

4 Density Estimation in the Joint Domain

The idea of density estimation in the joint domain is detailed in [7]. Each image pixel $\mathbf{z}$ is characterized by a location $\mathbf{x} = (x_1, x_2)^\top$ and a range vector $\mathbf{c}$.

The range vector is one dimensional in the case of gray level images or three dimensional in the case of color images. In other words, an input image of n pixels is represented as a collection of d-dimensional points $\mathbf{z}_i = (\mathbf{x}_i^\top, \mathbf{c}_i^\top)^\top$ with $i = 1 \ldots n$. The space constructed as above is called the *joint spatial-intensity* domain or spatial-color domain. The concept can be extended by adding a temporal component. To estimate the probability density in the joint space we use a product kernel with bandwidth σ_s for the spatial components and σ_r for the range.[2]

Due to the use of product kernel, different transformations can be accommodated in the two spaces. For example one can define an affine transformation in the spatial domain and a translation in the range. The optimization, however, is performed jointly for both spaces, i.e., for both location and appearance.

5   Experiments

We tested the new tracking framework for various sequences and the results are very promising. Although only translation in the joint domain (spatial/intensity or spatial/color) has been considered, the algorithm proved to be robust to illumination variations and high percentage of occlusions. For all the sequences we used $\sigma_s = 3$ and $\sigma_r = 20$. A three level pyramid was used for efficient implementation of the optimization. The tracker runs in real-time (30fps) on a 1GHz PC.

A gray level tracking sequence is shown in Figure 1. The optimization is performed in a three dimensional space (two spatial dimensions and one intensity dimension). The model is captured in the first frame. We tested the behavior of the algorithm with respect to outliers generated by hand occlusion. As one can see, a large amount of occlusion is tolerated. We also tested the adaptation of the algorithm to illumination changes. The changes were induced by applying the back-light correction of the camera. The model adapted gracefully to the new condition while the tracking continued unperturbed. We again tested the robustness to outliers within the new conditions. Finally, the back-light correction was stopped determining the model to adapt again.

We also tested two color sequences with natural illumination. The optimization is performed in a five dimensional space (two spatial dimensions and three color dimensions). In the first sequence we track a person walking in a garden (Figure 2). Partial occlusion is present from various flowers. In the second sequence we track a car at the exit from the tunnel (Figure 3). The camera gain adapts due to the change in illumination. In both sequences the tracker adapted correctly.

---

[2] The normal kernel is separable, so the idea of product kernel is implicit when a normal kernel is used.

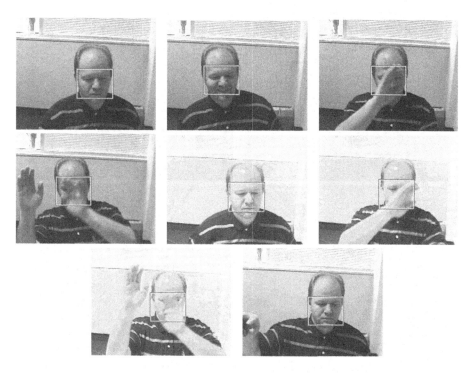

Fig. 1. *Face* sequence. 750 frames.

Fig. 2. *Walking* sequence. 540 frames.

Fig. 3. *Pursuit* sequence. 300 frames.

6   Discussion

This paper presented a Bayesian approach to real-time tracking. Using a new formulation of the target representation and localization problem, we have developed a tracking framework that is both efficient and effective. It can naturally tolerate outliers and changes in the illumination. Results regarding optimization for other type of transformations such as similarity, affine and homography, will be reported in subsequent papers. Techniques that gradually introduce more complex transformation models can be employed [17].

Acknowledgments

I thank Visvanathan Ramesh and Huseyin Tek from Siemens Corporate Research for stimulating discussions on the subject.

References

1. S. Avidan. Support vector tracking. In *Proc. IEEE Conf. on Computer Vision and Pattern Recognition,* Kauai, Hawaii, volume I, pages 184–191, 2001.
2. Y. Bar-Shalom and T. Fortmann. *Tracking and Data Association.* Academic Press, 1988.

3. B. Bascle and R. Deriche. Region tracking through image sequences. In *Proc. 5th Intl. Conf. on Computer Vision,* Cambridge, MA, pages 302–307, 1995.

4. G. R. Bradski. Computer vision face tracking as a component of a perceptual user interface. In *Proc. IEEE Workshop on Applications of Computer Vision,* Princeton, NJ, pages 214–219, October 1998.

5. A. D. Bue, D. Comaniciu, V. Ramesh, and C. Regazzoni. Smart cameras with real-time video object generation. In *Proc. IEEE Intl. Conf. on Image Processing,* Rochester, NY, page to appear, 2002.

6. R. Collins, A. Lipton, H. Fujiyoshi, and T. Kanade. Algorithms for cooperative multisensor surveillance. *Proceedings of the IEEE,* 89(10):1456–1477, 2001.

7. D. Comaniciu and P. Meer. Mean shift: A robust approach toward feature space analysis. *IEEE Trans. Pattern Anal. Machine Intell.,* 24(5):603–619, 2002.

8. D. Comaniciu, V. Ramesh, and P. Meer. Real-time tracking of non-rigid objects using mean shift. In *Proc. IEEE Conf. on Computer Vision and Pattern Recognition,* Hilton Head, SC, volume II, pages 142–149, June 2000.

9. T. Cover and J. Thomas. *Elements of Information Theory.* John Wiley & Sons, New York, 1991.

10. A. Doucet, S. Godsill, and C. Andrieu. On sequential Monte Carlo sampling methods for Bayesian filtering. *Statistics and Computing,* 10(3):197–208, 2000.

11. V. Ferrari, T. Tuytelaars, and L. V. Gool. Real-time affine region tracking and coplanar grouping. In *Proc. IEEE Conf. on Computer Vision and Pattern Recognition,* Kauai, Hawaii, volume II, pages 226–233, 2001.

12. G. Hager and P. Belhumeur. Real-time tracking of image regions with changes in geometry and illumination. In *Proc. IEEE Conf. on Computer Vision and Pattern Recognition,* San Francisco, CA, pages 403–410, 1996.

13. U. Handmann, T. Kalinke, C. Tzomakas, M. Werner, and W. von Seelen. Computer vision for driver assistance systems. In *Proceedings SPIE,* volume 3364, pages 136–147, 1998.

14. P. J. Huber. *Robust Statistical Procedures.* SIAM, second edition, 1996.

15. M. Isard and A. Blake. Condensation - Conditional density propagation for visual tracking. *Intl. J. of Computer Vision,* 29(1), 1998.

16. A. Jepson, D. Fleet, and T. El-Maraghi. Robust online appearance models for visual tracking. In *Proc. IEEE Conf. on Computer Vision and Pattern Recognition,* Hawaii, volume I, pages 415–422, 2001.

17. K. Kanatani. Image mosaicing by stratified matching. In *Proc. Statistical Methods in Video Processing Workshop,* Copenhagen, Denmark, 2002.

18. J. Krumm, S. Harris, B. Meyers, B. Brumitt, M. Hale, and S. Shafer. Multi-camera multi-person tracking for EasyLiving. In *Proc. IEEE Intl. Workshop on Visual Surveillance,* Dublin, Ireland, pages 3–10, 2000.

19. C. Olson. Image registration by aligning entropies. In *Proc. IEEE Conf. on Computer Vision and Pattern Recognition,* Kauai, Hawaii, volume II, pages 331–336, 2001.

20. A. Roche, G. Malandain, and N. Ayache. Unifying maximum likelihood approaches in medical image registration. Technical Report 3741, INRIA, 1999.

21. S. Sclaroff and J. Isidoro. Active blobs. In *Proc. 6th Intl. Conf. on Computer Vision,* Bombay, India, pages 1146–1153, 1998.

22. D. W. Scott. *Multivariate Density Estimation.* Wiley, 1992.

23. P. Viola and W. Wells. Alignment by maximization of mutual information. *Intl. J. of Computer Vision,* 24(2):137–154, 1997.

Nonlinear Matrix Diffusion
for Optic Flow Estimation

Thomas Brox and Joachim Weickert

Faculty of Mathematics and Computer Science, Saarland University,
Building 27.1, P. O. Box 15 11 50, 66041 Saarbrücken, Germany,
{brox,weickert}@mia.uni-saarland.de

Abstract. In this paper we present a method for nonlinear diffusion of matrix-valued data. We adapt this technique to the well-known linear structure tensor in order to develop a new nonlinear structure tensor. It is then used to improve the optic flow estimation methods of Lucas and Kanade and its spatio-temporal variant of Bigün et al.. Our experiments show that the nonlinear structure tensor leads to a better preservation of discontinuities in the optic flow field.

1 Introduction

Nonlinear diffusion techniques have proved to be very useful for discontinuity-preserving denoising of scalar and vector-valued data. Apart from very recent work [10,12], however, not many attempts have been made to design diffusion filters for matrix-valued data. One important representative of matrix-valued data fields is the *structure tensor (ST)*, a frequently used tool for corner detection [3], texture [9] and image sequence analysis [2,5]. The conventional formulation of the structure tensor uses Gaussian smoothing which is equivalent to linear diffusion filtering. This is well-known to blur across data discontinuities.

The goal of the present paper is to formulate a *nonlinear* structure tensor that respects discontinuities in the data. The nonlinear ST can be used in any application working with the conventional linear ST. In our paper we focus on its evaluation for estimating optic flow fields. The well-known optic flow method of Lucas and Kanade [6] or its spatio-temporal counterpart by Bigün et al. [2] use a linear ST that integrates across a neighborhood of a fixed size. The novel nonlinear ST adapts this neighborhood to the data, preserving discontinuities in the optic flow field.

Addressing these issues is the goal of the present paper. It is organized as follows. In Section 2 we present our nonlinear diffusion method for the ST. In Section 3 first the optic flow estimation method of Lucas and Kanade is briefly reviewed. We then apply the nonlinear ST and present experimental results in Section 4. The paper is concluded by a summary in Section 5.

Related Work. The approach of Tschumperlé and Deriche [10] uses space-variant diffusion with a scalar-valued diffusivity. In contrast to our method with

L. Van Gool (Ed.): DAGM 2002, LNCS 2449, pp. 446–453, 2002.

a diffusion tensor, it may be classified as isotropic. Furthermore it is not focusing on the ST, but on diffusion tensor MRI. In the work of Weickert and Brox [12] a general method for diffusing or regularizing matrix-valued data is proposed. The present model differs from this work not only by the fact that the process is specifically adapted to the ST, but also by its application to optic flow estimation. In this sense our work is close in spirit to the interesting papers of Nagel and Gehrke [8] and Middendorf and Nagel [7]. These authors use shape-adapted Gaussians for designing structure tensors that average over regions with similar grey values. While *homogeneous* Gaussian convolution and *linear* diffusion are equivalent, it should be noted that this is no longer the case with *space-variant* Gaussian smoothing and *nonlinear* diffusion. Since scalar-valued nonlinear diffusion filters offer a sound mathematical underpinning, it appears promising to investigate also a nonlinear diffusion formulation of the structure tensor.

2 Matrix-Valued Diffusion

Let us first illustrate the limitations of the conventional linear ST by an example. Figure 1a shows a synthetic test image f which is distorted by Gaussian noise with $\sigma = 30$. Figure 1b depicts the matrix product $J_0 = \nabla f \nabla f^\top$ as a colored orientation plot. The direction of the eigenvector to the largest eigenvalue of J_0 is mapped to the hue value and the largest eigenvalue to the intensity value in the HSI color model. The saturation value is set to its maximum.[1]

The linear ST J_ρ can be seen in Figure 1c. It is derived from J_0 by smoothing each component by a Gaussian kernel with standard deviation ρ. This technique closes structures of a certain scale very well. It also removes the noise appropriately. On the first glance surprising for a linear technique is the preservation of orientation discontinuities. However, discontinuities in the magnitude are not preserved causing object boundaries to dislocate.

This problem can be addressed by replacing the convolution with a Gaussian kernel by a discontinuity preserving diffusion method. However, all capabilities of the linear ST should remain. Therefore, we keep the diffusivity at its maximum except at locations where discontinuities in the magnitude exist. This is done by regarding J_0 as initial matrix field that is evolved under the diffusion equation

$$\partial_t u_{ij} = \mathrm{div}\left(D\left(\left(\nabla_\sigma \sqrt[4]{\sum_{k,l} u_{kl}^2}\right)\left(\nabla_\sigma \sqrt[4]{\sum_{k,l} u_{kl}^2}\right)^\top \right)\nabla u_{ij}\right) \qquad \forall i,j \quad (1)$$

where the evolving matrix field $u_{ij}(x,t)$ uses $J_0(x)$ as initial condition for $t = 0$. The matrix $D(A) = T(g(\lambda_i))T^\top$ is the diffusion tensor for $A = T(\lambda_i)T^\top$ where the last-mentioned expression denotes a principal axis transformation of A with the eigenvalues λ_i as the elements of a diagonal matrix (λ_i) and the normalized eigenvectors as the columns of the orthogonal matrix T.

---

[1] A color version of this paper will be provided in the internet.

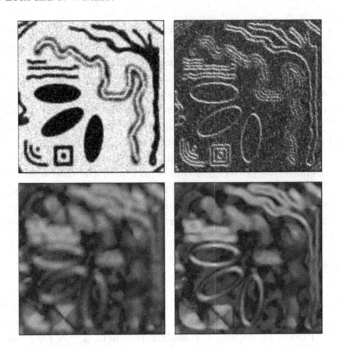

Fig. 1. (a) TOP LEFT: Synthetic image with Gaussian noise. (b) TOP RIGHT: $J_0 = \nabla f \nabla f^\top$. (c) BOTTOM LEFT: Linear structure tensor J_ρ with $\rho = 3$. (d) BOTTOM RIGHT: Nonlinear structure tensor J_t with $t = 12.5$.

The diffusivity $g(s^2)$ is a decreasing function such as $g(s^2) = 1 - e^{-\frac{3.31488\lambda^8}{s^8}}$ with a contrast parameter λ. By ∇_σ we denote the nabla operator where Gaussian derivatives with standard deviation σ are used. For more detailed information about diffusion equations in general we refer to [11].

On the first glance the fourth root in Eq. 1 seems to be quite arbitrary, but there is a good motivation for it: For diffusion time $t = 0$ the structure tensor is

$$J_0 = \begin{pmatrix} f_x^2 & f_x f_y \\ f_x f_y & f_y^2 \end{pmatrix} \tag{2}$$

where subscripts denote partial derivatives. In this case we have

$$\sqrt[4]{\sum_{k,l} u_{kl}^2} = \sqrt[4]{f_x^4 + 2f_x^2 f_y^2 + f_y^4} = \sqrt[4]{(f_x^2 + f_y^2)^2} = \sqrt{f_x^2 + f_y^2} = |\nabla f|. \tag{3}$$

This leads to the interpretation that the image gradient ∇f drives the diffusion. Precisely speaking, this is only exactly the case for $t = 0$: The diffusivity is adapted to the new structure tensor after each time step, therefore resulting in a nonlinear diffusion process.

The nonlinear ST obtained by Equation 1 is depicted in Figure 1d. The result is exactly what we expect from a nonlinear ST: While object boundaries are no longer dislocated, all positive properties of the linear ST remain valid. Noise is removed, structures of a certain scale are closed and orientation discontinuities are preserved. Although there are some additional parameters for the nonlinear ST, they are not really a problem. The diffusion time t simply replaces the scale parameter ρ of the linear ST. The other parameters, namely the diffusivity function $g(s^2)$, its constrast parameter λ as well as the presmoothing parameter σ, are very robust against variations and can be fixed, still yielding good results for a whole set of input data.

3 Optic Flow Estimation

Before we test the performance of the new nonlinear structure tensor by applying it to optic flow estimation, the classic estimation method of Lucas and Kanade [6] using the linear ST is briefly reviewed.

Assuming that image structures do not alter their grey values during their movement can be expressed by the optic flow constraint

$$f_x u + f_y v + f_z = 0. \tag{4}$$

where subscripts denote partial derivatives. As this is only one equation for two flow components the optic flow is not uniquely determined by this constraint (aperture problem). A second assumption has to be made. Lucas and Kanade proposed to assume the optic flow vector to be constant within some neighborhood B_ρ of size ρ. The optic flow in some point (x_0, y_0) can then be estimated by the minimizer of the local energy function

$$E(u,v) = \frac{1}{2} \int_{B_\rho(x_0,y_0)} (f_x u + f_y v + f_z)^2 dxdy. \tag{5}$$

A minimum (u,v) of E satisfies $\partial_u E = 0$ and $\partial_v E = 0$, leading to the linear system

$$\begin{pmatrix} \int_{B_\rho} f_x^2 dxdy & \int_{B_\rho} f_x f_y dxdy \\ \int_{B_\rho} f_x f_y dxdy & \int_{B_\rho} f_y^2 dxdy \end{pmatrix} \begin{pmatrix} u \\ v \end{pmatrix} = \begin{pmatrix} -\int_{B_\rho} f_x f_z dxdy \\ -\int_{B_\rho} f_y f_z dxdy \end{pmatrix}. \tag{6}$$

Instead of the sharp window B_ρ often a convolution with a Gaussian kernel K_ρ is used yielding

$$\begin{pmatrix} K_\rho * f_x^2 & K_\rho * f_x f_y \\ K_\rho * f_x f_y & K_\rho * f_y^2 \end{pmatrix} \begin{pmatrix} u \\ v \end{pmatrix} = \begin{pmatrix} -K_\rho * f_x f_z \\ -K_\rho * f_y f_z \end{pmatrix} \tag{7}$$

where the entries of the linear system are five of the components of the linear ST J_ρ. The linear system can be solved provided the system matrix is not singular. Such singular matrices appear in regions where the image gradient vanishes. They also appear in regions where the aperture problem remains present, leading to the smaller eigenvalue of the system matrix being close to 0. In this case one may only compute the so-called normal flow (the optic flow component parallel to the image gradient). Using sufficiently broad Gaussian filters, however, will greatly reduce such singular situations. In these cases, one may obtain results with densities close to 100 %. In order to improve the quality of the estimated optic flow field, the density can be reduced by using the smaller eigenvalue of the system matrix as confidence measure [1],

By replacing all spatial integrations in Equations 5–7 by spatio-temporal integrations, one ends up with a method that is equivalent to the structure tensor approach of Bigün et al. [2]. The spatio-temporal approach in general yields better results than the spatial one.

The Gaussian convolution in the structure tensor methods of Lucas–Kanade and Bigün is well known to be equivalent to linear diffusion filtering. With our knowledge from Section 2 we may now introduce corresponding *nonlinear* versions of both techniques by replacing the linear ST in equation 7 by the nonlinear one. As mentioned above only the diffusion time is a critical parameter. All results presented in the next section have been achieved with the diffusivity function $g(s^2) = 1 - e^{-\frac{3.31488\lambda^8}{s^8}}$, a contrast parameter $\lambda = 0.1$ and a regularization parameter $\sigma = 1.5$. Only for the noise experiments in Table 2, we adapted σ to the noise.

4   Results

A good image sequence to demonstrate the discontinuity preserving property of the new technique is the Hamburg taxi sequence. In this scene there are four moving objects: a taxi turning around the corner, a car moving to the right, a van moving to the left and a pedestrian in the upper left[2]. Figure 2 shows that using the linear structure tensor in the Lucas–Kanade method causes the flow fields of moving objects to dislocate, whereas the nonlinear structure tensor ensures that object boundaries are preserved in a better way. Like in Barron et al. [1] the sequence was presmoothed along the time axis by a Gaussian kernel with $\sigma = 1$.

In another experiment we used a synthetic street sequence[3]. For this sequence created by Galvin et al. [4] the ground truth flow field is available. This enables the computation of the average angular error between the estimated flow and the ground truth flow field as a quantitative measure [1]. Table 1 shows the angular errors of some algorithms from the literature as well as the linear and nonlinear ST methods. A direct comparison between the angular errors of the method using the linear ST and nonlinear ST respectively, quantifies the improvement achieved with our new technique. It should be noted that the discontinuity locations constitute only a small subset of the entire image. This explains an effect that can be observed for all discontinuity preserving optic flow methods: Visually significant improvements at edges can only lead to moderate improvements for a global measure such as the average angular error.

---

[2] The sequence is available from `ftp://csd.uwo.ca` under the directory `pub/vision`

[3] The sequence can be obtained from `www.cs.otago.ac.nz/research/vision`

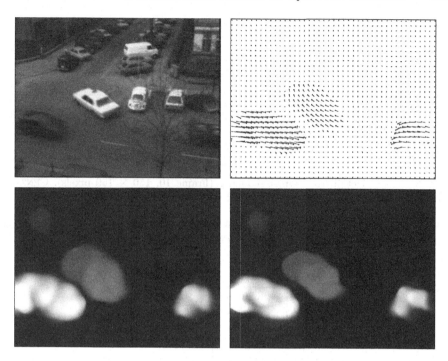

Fig. 2. TOP LEFT: Hamburg Taxi Sequence (Frame 9). TOP RIGHT: Optic flow field with the nonlinear ST. BOTTOM LEFT: Flow magnitude with the linear ST. BOTTOM RIGHT: Flow magnitude with the nonlinear ST.

Table 1. Street sequence. Comparison between the best results from the literature and our results. AAE = average angular error.

Technique	AAE	Density
Camus [4]	13.69°	100%
Proesman et al. [4]	7.41°	100%
Weickert-Schnörr 2D [13]	6.62°	100%
Lucas-Kanade (2D) Linear	**6.29°**	**100%**
Lucas-Kanade (2D) Nonlinear	**5.88°**	**100%**
Bigün (3D) Linear	**5.28°**	**100%**
Bigün (3D) Nonlinear	**5.14°**	**100%**
Weickert-Schnörr 3D [13]	4.85°	100%
Uras et al. [4]	6.93°	54%
Horn-Schunck [4]	6.62°	46%
Singh [4]	6.18°	78%
Lucas-Kanade (2D) Linear	**4.82°**	**52%**
Lucas-Kanade (2D) Nonlinear	**4.51°**	**53%**
Bigün (3D) Linear	**3.49°**	**58%**
Bigün (3D) Nonlinear	**3.30°**	**57%**

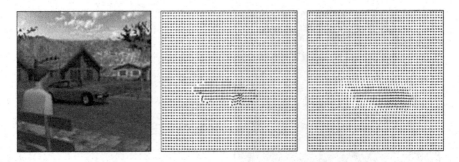

Fig. 3. LEFT: Detail from Street sequence (Frame 10, 150 × 150 pixels). CENTER: Ground truth flow field. RIGHT: Flow field with the nonlinear ST (3D).

Table 2. Street Sequence. Average angular errors for different noise levels (2D version, 100% density). σ_n denotes the standard deviation of the Gaussian noise.

σ_n	linear ST	nonlinear ST
0	6.29°	5.88°
5	7.63°	7.33°
10	10.93°	10.36°
20	15.87°	14.79°

Since the classic Lucas and Kanade technique using the linear ST is known to be very robust against noise, we degraded the Street sequence by Gaussian noise to test whether the nonlinear ST yields any drawbacks in this respect. Table 2 demonstrates that our technique is superior to the original one even in the presence of severe noise.

5   Conclusions

In this paper it was shown how new diffusion methods for matrix-valued data can be used to construct a nonlinear structure tensor. We presented a special diffusion method which keeps all the benefits of the conventional linear ST, but tackles its problem of object delocalizations. Afterwards it was shown that the nonlinear ST could serve to improve the classic optic flow estimation techniques of Lucas and Kanade and of Bigün et al.. Our experiments revealed the superiority of the nonlinear ST to the conventional linear one. Moreover, also in comparison to other estimation techniques our method performed competitive. This supports the expectation that the nonlinear ST can also improve the results of other methods where a linear ST is used.

Acknowledgements

Our research on matrix-valued smoothing methods is partly funded by the projects WE 2602/1-1 and SO 363/9-1 of the *Deutsche Forschungsgemeinschaft (DFG)*. This is gratefully acknowledged.

References

1. J. L. Barron, D. J. Fleet, and S. S. Beauchemin. Performance of optical flow techniques. *International Journal of Computer Vision*, 12(1):43–77, Feb. 1994.
2. J. Bigün, G. H. Granlund, and J. Wiklund. Multidimensional orientation estimation with applications to texture analysis and optical flow. *IEEE Transactions on Pattern Analysis and Machine Intelligence*, 13(8):775–790, Aug. 1991.
3. W. Förstner and E. Gülch. A fast operator for detection and precise location of distinct points, corners and centres of circular features. In *Proc. ISPRS Intercommission Conference on Fast Processing of Photogrammetric Data*, pages 281–305, Interlaken, Switzerland, June 1987.
4. B. Galvin, B. McCane, K. Novins, D. Mason, and S. Mills. Recovering motion fields: an analysis of eight optical flow algorithms. In *Proc. 1998 British Machine Vision Conference*, Southampton, England, Sept. 1998.
5. B. Jähne. *Spatio-Temporal Image Processing*, volume 751 of *Lecture Notes in Computer Science*. Springer, Berlin, 1993.
6. B. Lucas and T. Kanade. An iterative image registration technique with an application to stereo vision. In *Proc. Seventh International Joint Conference on Artificial Intelligence*, pages 674–679, Vancouver, Canada, Aug. 1981.
7. M. Middendorf and H.-H. Nagel. Estimation and interpretation of discontinuities in optical flow fields. In *Proc. Eighth International Conference on Computer Vision*, volume 1, pages 178–183, Vancouver, Canada, July 1995. IEEE Computer Society Press.
8. H.-H. Nagel and A. Gehrke. Spatiotemporally adaptive estimation and segmentation of OF-fields. In H. Burkhardt and B. Neumann, editors, *Computer Vision – ECCV '98*, volume 1407 of *Lecture Notes in Computer Science*, pages 86–102. Springer, Berlin, 1998.
9. A. R. Rao and B. G. Schunck. Computing oriented texture fields. *CVGIP: Graphical Models and Image Processing*, 53:157–185, 1991.
10. D. Tschumperlé and R. Deriche. Diffusion tensor regularization with contraints preservation. In *Proc. 2001 IEEE Computer Society Conference on Computer Vision and Pattern Recognition*, volume 1, pages 948–953, Kauai, HI, Dec. 2001. IEEE Computer Society Press.
11. J. Weickert. *Anisotropic Diffusion in Image Processing*. Teubner, Stuttgart, 1998.
12. J. Weickert and T. Brox. Diffusion and regularization of vector- and matrix-valued images. Technical Report 58, Department of Mathematics, Saarland University, Saarbrücken, Germany, Mar. 2002.
13. J. Weickert and C. Schnörr. Variational optic flow computation with a spatio-temporal smoothness constraint. *Journal of Mathematical Imaging and Vision*, 14(3):245–255, May 2001.

Combining the Advantages of Local and Global Optic Flow Methods

Andrés Bruhn[1], Joachim Weickert[1], and Christoph Schnörr[2]

[1] Mathematical Image Analysis Group,
Faculty of Mathematics and Computer Science,
Building 27.1, Saarland University, 66041 Saarbrücken, Germany,
{bruhn,weickert}@mia.uni-saarland.de
[2] Computer Vision, Graphics, and Pattern Recognition Group,
Department of Mathematics and Computer Science,
University of Mannheim, 68131 Mannheim, Germany,
{schnoerr}@uni-mannheim.de

Abstract. Differential methods are frequently used techniques for optic flow computations. They can be classified into local methods such as the Lucas–Kanade technique or Bigün's structure tensor method, and into global methods such as the Horn–Schunck approach and its modifications. Local methods are known to be more robust under noise, while global techniques yield 100% dense flow fields. No clear attempts to combine the advantages of these two classes of methods have been made in the literature so far.
This problem is addressed in our paper. First we juxtapose the role of smoothing processes that are required in local and global differential methods for optic flow computation. This discussion motivates us to introduce and evaluate a novel method that combines the advantages of local and global approaches: It yields dense flow fields that are robust against noise. Finally experiments with different sequences are performed demonstrating its excellent results.

Keywords: visual motion, differential techniques, variational methods, structure tensor, partial differential equations.

1 Introduction

Differential methods belong to the most widely used techniques for optic flow estimation in image sequences. They are based on the computation of spatial and temporal image derivatives. Differential techniques can be classified into *local* methods that may optimize some local energy-like expression, and *global* strategies which attempt to minimize a global energy functional. Examples of the first category include the Lucas–Kanade method [9], the structure tensor approach of Bigün et al. [3] and its space–variant version by Nagel and Gehrke [12], but also techniques using second order derivatives such as [16]. Global approaches comprise the classic method of Horn and Schunck [6] and discontinuity-preserving

L. Van Gool (Ed.): DAGM 2002, LNCS 2449, pp. 454–462, 2002.

variants such as [10]. Together with phase-based methods [4], differential methods belong to the techniques with the best performance [2,5]. Local methods may offer relatively high robustness under noise, but do not give dense flow fields. Global methods, on the other hand, yield flow fields with 100 % density, but are experimentally known to be more sensitive to noise [2,5].

Almost all differential optic flow methods make use of smoothing techniques and smoothness assumptions: The actual role and the difference between these smoothing strategies, however, has hardly been addressed in the literature so far. In a first step of this paper we juxtapose the role of the different smoothing steps of these methods. We shall see that each smoothing process offers certain advantages that cannot be found in other cases. Consequently, it would be desirable to combine the different smoothing effects of local and global methods in order to design novel approaches that combine the high robustness of local methods with the high density of global techniques. One of the goals of the present paper is to propose and analyse such an embedding of local methods into global approaches. This results in a technique that is robust under noise and gives flow fields with 100 % density. Hence, there is no need for a postprocessing step where sparse data have to be interpolated.

Our paper is organized as follows. In Section 2 we discuss the role of the different smoothing processes that are involved in local and global optic flow approaches. Based on these results we propose two *combined local-global (CLG) methods* in Section 3, one with spatial, the other one with spatiotemporal smoothing. Section 4 is devoted to performance evaluations of the CLG method. Our paper is concluded with a summary in Section 5.

Related Work. Schnörr et al. [14] sketched a framework for supplementing global energy functionals with multiple equations that provide local data constraints. The local method in their experiments used the output of Gaussian filters shifted in frequency space [4]. Methods of Lucas–Kanade or Bigün type have not been considered in this context.

Our proposed technique differs from the majority of global regularization methods by the fact that we also use spatiotemporal regularizers instead of spatial ones. This relates our method to earlier work with spatiotemporal regularizers such as [11,17].

While the noise sensitivity of local differential methods has been studied intensively in recent years [1,7,8,13,15], the noise sensitivity of global differential methods has been analysed to a significantly smaller extent. In this context, Galvin et al. [5] have compared a number of classical methods where small amounts of Gaussian noise had been added. Their conclusion was similar to the findings of Barron et al. [2]: the global approach of Horn and Schunck is more sensitive to noise than the local Lucas–Kanade method.

2   Role of the Smoothing Processes

In this section we discuss the role of smoothing techniques in differential optic flow methods. For simplicity we focus on spatial smoothing. All spatial smoothing strategies can easily be extended into the temporal domain. This will usually lead to improved results.

Let us consider some image sequence $g(x, y, t)$, where (x, y) denotes the location within a rectangular image domain Ω, and $t \in [0, T]$ denotes time. It is common to smooth the image sequence prior to differentiation [2,8], e.g. by convolving each frame with some Gaussian $K_\sigma(x, y)$ of standard deviation σ:

$$f(x, y, t) := (K_\sigma * g)(x, y, t), \tag{1}$$

The low-pass effect of Gaussian convolution removes noise and other destabilizing high frequencies. In a subsequent optic flow method, we may thus call σ the *noise scale*. While some moderate presmoothing improves the results, great care should be taken not to apply too much presmoothing, since this would severely destroy important image structure.

Many differential methods for optic flow are based on the assumption that the grey values of image objects in subsequent frames do not change over time. For small displacements this yields the *optic flow constraint*

$$f_x u + f_y v + f_t = 0, \tag{2}$$

where the displacement field $(u, v)^\top (x, y, t)$ is called *optic flow* and subscripts denote partial derivatives. Evidently, this single equation is not sufficient to uniquely compute the two unknowns u and v *(aperture problem)*: For nonvanishing image gradients, it is only possible to determine the flow component parallel to $\nabla f := (f_x, f_y)^\top$, i.e. normal to image edges, the so-called *normal flow*. In order to cope with the aperture problem, Lucas and Kanade [9] proposed to assume that the unknown optic flow vector is constant within some neighbourhood of size ρ. In this case it is possible to determine the two *constants* u and v at some location (x, y, t) from a weighted least square fit by minimizing the function

$$E_{LK}(u, v) := K_\rho * \left((f_x u + f_y v + f_t)^2 \right). \tag{3}$$

Here the standard deviation ρ of the Gaussian serves as an *integration scale* over which the main contribution of the least square fit is computed. Therefore the effect to the neighborhood is limited by the value of ρ. As a result structures of the same order do occur. In particular, a sufficiently large value for ρ is very successful in rendering the Lucas–Kanade method robust under noise.

A minimum (u, v) of E_{LK} satisfies $\partial_u E_{LK} = 0$ and $\partial_v E_{LK} = 0$. This gives the linear system

$$\begin{pmatrix} K_\rho * (f_x^2) & K_\rho * (f_x f_y) \\ K_\rho * (f_x f_y) & K_\rho * (f_y^2) \end{pmatrix} \begin{pmatrix} u \\ v \end{pmatrix} = \begin{pmatrix} -K_\rho * (f_x f_t) \\ -K_\rho * (f_y f_t) \end{pmatrix} \tag{4}$$

which can be solved provided that its system matrix is invertible. This is not the case in flat regions where the image gradient vanishes. In some other regions, the smaller eigenvalue of the system matrix may be close to 0, such that the aperture problem remains present and the data do not allow a reliable determination of the full optic flow. All this results in nondense flow fields. They constitute the most severe drawback of local gradient methods: Since many computer vision applications require dense flow estimates, subsequent interpolation steps are required.

In order to end up with dense flow estimates one may embed the optic flow constraint into a regularization framework. Horn and Schunck [6] have pioneered this class of global differential methods. They determine the unknown *functions* $u(x, y, t)$ and $v(x, y, t)$ as the minimizers of the global energy functional

$$E_{HS}(u, v) = \int_\Omega \left((f_x u + f_y v + f_t)^2 + \alpha \left(|\nabla u|^2 + |\nabla v|^2\right)\right) dx\,dy \qquad (5)$$

where the smoothness weight $\alpha > 0$ serves as *regularization parameter:* Larger values for α result in a stronger penalization of large flow gradients and lead to smoother flow fields. The unique minimizer of this convex functional benefits from the *filling-in effect:* At locations with $|\nabla f| \approx 0$, no reliable local flow estimate is possible, but the regularizer $|\nabla u|^2 + |\nabla v|^2$ fills in information from the neighbourhood. This results in dense flow fields and makes subsequent interpolation steps obsolete. This is a clear advantage over local methods.

It has been observed that global methods may be more sensitive to noise than local differential methods [2,5]. An explanation for this behaviour can be given as follows. Noise results in high image gradients. They serve as weights in the data term of the regularization functional (5). Since the smoothness term has a constant weight α, smoothness is relatively less important at locations with high image gradients than elsewhere. As a consequence, *flow fields are less regularized at noisy image structures.* This sensitivity under noise is therefore nothing else but a side-effect of the desired filling-in effect. Increasing the regularization parameter α will finally also smooth the flow field at noisy structures, but at this stage, it might already be too blurred in flatter image regions.

3   A Combined Local–Global Method

We have seen that both local and global differential methods have complementary advantages and shortcomings. Hence it would be interesting to construct a hybrid technique that constitutes the best of two worlds: It should combine the robustness of local methods with the density of global approaches. This shall be done next. We start with spatial formulations before we extend the approach to the spatiotemporal domain. In order to design a *combined local–global (CLG) method*, let us first reformulate the previous approaches. Using the notations

$$\begin{aligned} w &:= (u, v, 1)^\top, & |\nabla w|^2 &:= |\nabla u|^2 + |\nabla v|^2, \\ \nabla_3 f &:= (f_x, f_y, f_t)^\top, & J_\rho(\nabla_3 f) &:= K_\rho * (\nabla_3 f\,\nabla_3 f^\top) \end{aligned}$$

it becomes evident that the Lucas–Kanade method minimizes the quadratic form

$$E_{LK}(w) = w^\top J_\rho(\nabla_3 f)\,w, \qquad (6)$$

while the Horn–Schunck technique minimizes the functional

$$E_{HS}(w) = \int_{\Omega} \left(w^{\top} J_0(\nabla_3 f)\, w + \alpha |\nabla w|^2 \right) dx\, dy. \tag{7}$$

This terminology suggests a natural way to extend the Horn–Schunck functional to the desired CLG functional. We simply replace the matrix $J_0(\nabla_3 f)$ by the structure tensor $J_\rho(\nabla_3 f)$ with some integration scale $\rho > 0$. Thus, we propose to minimize the functional

$$E_{CLG}(w) = \int_{\Omega} \left(w^{\top} J_\rho(\nabla_3 f)\, w + \alpha |\nabla w|^2 \right) dx\, dy. \tag{8}$$

Its minimizing flow field (u, v) satisfies the Euler–Lagrange equations

$$\Delta u - \tfrac{1}{\alpha} \left(K_\rho * (f_x^2)\, u + K_\rho * (f_x f_y)\, v + K_\rho * (f_x f_t) \right) = 0, \tag{9}$$

$$\Delta v - \tfrac{1}{\alpha} \left(K_\rho * (f_x f_y)\, u + K_\rho * (f_y^2)\, v + K_\rho * (f_y f_t) \right) = 0, \tag{10}$$

where Δ denotes the Laplacean.

A spatiotemporal variant of the Lucas–Kanade approach is due to Bigün et al. [3]. It replaces convolution with 2-D Gaussians by spatiotemporal convolution with 3-D Gaussians. This still leads to a 2×2 linear system of equations for the two unknowns u and v.

A spatiotemporal version of our CLG functional is given by

$$E_{CLG3}(w) = \int_{\Omega \times [0,T]} \left(w^{\top} J_\rho(\nabla_3 f)\, w + \alpha |\nabla_3 w|^2 \right) dx\, dy\, dt \tag{11}$$

The Euler–Lagrange equations in the spatiotemporal setting have the same structure as (9)–(10), apart from the fact that spatiotemporal Gaussian convolution is used, and that the spatial Laplacean is replaced by the spatiotemporal one due to $|\nabla_3 w|^2$. In general, the spatiotemporal Gaussians may have different standard deviations in space and time.

4   Experiments

For our experiments a standard finite difference discretization of the Euler–Lagrange equations (9)–(10) is used. The resulting sparse linear system of equations is solved iteratively by an SOR scheme. Apart from the first iteration, where additional convolutions with K_ρ are computed, the CLG method is as fast as the Horn and Schunck algorithm.

Figure 1 shows our first experiment. It depicts a flight through to the Yosemite National Park where divergent motion is dominating. The original synthetic sequence was created by Lynn Quam. A modified variant without clouds is available from http://www.cs.brown.edu/people/black/images.html.

We have added Gaussian noise with zero mean and different standard deviation to this sequence, and we used the 3-D CLG method for computing the

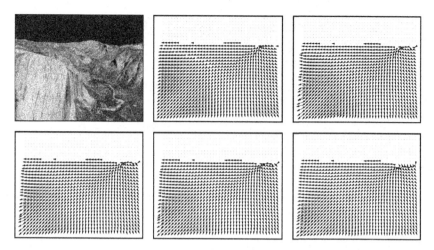

Fig. 1. *(a) Top left:* Frame 8 of the Yosemite sequence severely degraded by Gaussian noise with $\sigma_n = 40$. *(b) Top middle:* Ground truth flow field. *(c) Top right:* Computed flow field for $\sigma_n = 0$. *(d) Bottom left:* Ditto for $\sigma_n = 10$. *(e) Bottom middle:* $\sigma_n = 20$. *(f) Bottom right:* $\sigma_n = 40$.

flow field. Figure 1(c) shows that the recovered flow field is not very sensitive to Gaussian noise and that it coincides well with the ground truth flow field in Figure 1(b). These qualitative results are confirmed by the quantitative evaluations in Table 1, where we have studied the effect of replacing spatial smoothing steps by spatiotemporal ones. As one may expect, both the quality of the optic flow estimates and their robustness under Gaussian noise improve when temporal coherence is taken into account. The angular error has been computed as proposed in [2].

Another example demonstrating the excellent results of our CLG technique with spatiotemporal regularization is the Marble sequence. This non-synthetical sequence created by Nagel and Otte is available at the following internet adress: http://i21www.ira.uka.de/image_sequences

In Figure 2 (b) the ground truth flow field is shown, whereby the grey value at a pixel is related to the length of its displacement vector. As one can see the flow field estimated by our 3-D CLG technique in Figure 2 (c) matches the ground truth very well. This impression is confirmed by an average angular error

Table 1. Results for the 2-D and 3-D CLG method using the *Yosemite* sequence without clouds. Gaussian noise with varying standard deviations σ_n was added, and the average angular errors and their standard deviations were computed.

	$\sigma_n{=}0$	$\sigma_n{=}10$	$\sigma_n{=}20$	$\sigma_n{=}40$
2-D CLG	$2.64° \pm 2.27°$	$4.45° \pm 2.94°$	$6.93° \pm 4.31°$	$11.30° \pm 7.41°$
3-D CLG	$1.79° \pm 2.34°$	$2.53° \pm 2.75°$	$3.47° \pm 3.37°$	$5.34° \pm 3.81°$

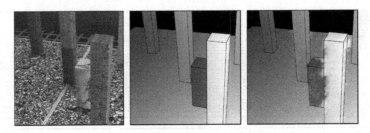

Fig. 2. *From left to right:* (a) Frame 16 of the Marble sequence. (b) Ground truth flow field (length). (c) Computed flow field (length).

Table 2. Stability of the 2-D CLG method under parameter variations. The data refer to the *marble* sequence without noise. AAE = average angular error.

σ	ρ	α	AAE	σ	ρ	α	AAE	σ	ρ	α	AAE
1.30	1.8	1000	5.70°	2.60	0.9	1700	5.31°	2.60	1.8	500	5.40°
1.73	"	"	5.45°	"	1.2	"	5.30°	"	"	666	5.34°
2.60	"	"	5.30°	"	1.8	"	5.30°	"	"	1000	5.30°
3.90	"	"	5.52°	"	2.7	"	5.30°	"	"	1500	5.33°
5.20	"	"	6.05°	"	3.6	"	5.31°	"	"	2000	5.39°

of 2.06°. A comparison to our result for the 2-D variant of 5.30° demonstrates a strong improvement by spatiotemporal regularization one more time.

Let us now investigate the sensitivity of the CLG method with respect to parameter variations. This is done in Table 2 for the *marble* sequence. We observe that the average angular error does hardly deteriorate when two parameters are fixed, while the other one varies by a factor 4. This stability under parameter variations may be regarded as another experimental confirmation of the well-posedness of the CLG approach. Moreover, this also indicates that the method performs sufficiently robust in practice even if non-optimized default parameter settings are used.

5   Summary and Conclusions

In this paper we have analysed the smoothing effects in local and global differential methods for optic flow computation. As prototypes of local methods we used the spatial least-square fit of Lucas and Kanade [9] and the spatiotemporal structure tensor method of Bigün et al. [3], while the Horn and Schunck approach [6] was our representative for a global method. We saw that the smoothing steps in each of these methods serve different purposes and have different advantages and shortcomings. As a consequence, we proposed a combined local-global (CLG) approach that incorporates the advantages of both paradigms: It is highly robust under Gaussian noise while giving dense flow fields. Experiments have also shown that the CLG method is not very sensitive under parameter variations. Nonlinear CLG techniques will be described in forthcoming papers.

Acknowledgements

Our research has been partly funded by the *Deutsche Forschungsgemeinschaft (DFG)* under the project SCHN 457/4-1.

References

1. A. Bainbridge–Smith and R. G. Lane. Determining optical flow using a differential method. *Image and Vision Computing*, 15(1):11–22, Jan. 1997.
2. J. L. Barron, D. J. Fleet, and S. S. Beauchemin. Performance of optical flow techniques. *International Journal of Computer Vision*, 12(1):43–77, Feb. 1994.
3. J. Bigün, G. H. Granlund, and J. Wiklund. Multidimensional orientation estimation with applications to texture analysis and optical flow. *IEEE Transactions on Pattern Analysis and Machine Intelligence*, 13(8):775–790, Aug. 1991.
4. D. J. Fleet and A. D. Jepson. Computation of component image velocity from local phase information. *International Journal of Computer Vision*, 5(1):77–104, Aug. 1990.
5. B. Galvin, B. McCane, K. Novins, D. Mason, and S. Mills. Recovering motion fields: an analysis of eight optical flow algorithms. In *Proc. 1998 British Machine Vision Conference*, Southampton, England, Sept. 1998.
6. B. Horn and B. Schunck. Determining optical flow. *Artificial Intelligence*, 17:185–203, 1981.
7. B. Jähne. *Digital Image Processing*. Springer, Berlin, 1997.
8. J. K. Kearney, W. B. Thompson, and D. L. Boley. Optical flow estimation: an error analysis of gradient-based methods with local optimization. *IEEE Transactions on Pattern Analysis and Machine Intelligence*, 9(2):229–244, Mar. 1987.
9. B. Lucas and T. Kanade. An iterative image registration technique with an application to stereo vision. In *Proc. Seventh International Joint Conference on Artificial Intelligence*, pages 674–679, Vancouver, Canada, Aug. 1981.
10. H.-H. Nagel. Constraints for the estimation of displacement vector fields from image sequences. In *Proc. Eighth International Joint Conference on Artificial Intelligence*, volume 2, pages 945–951, Karlsruhe, West Germany, August 1983.
11. H.-H. Nagel. Extending the 'oriented smoothness constraint' into the temporal domain and the estimation of derivatives of optical flow. In O. Faugeras, editor, *Computer Vision – ECCV '90*, volume 427 of *Lecture Notes in Computer Science*, pages 139–148. Springer, Berlin, 1990.
12. H.-H. Nagel and A. Gehrke. Spatiotemporally adaptive estimation and segmentation of OF-fields. In H. Burkhardt and B. Neumann, editors, *Computer Vision – ECCV '98*, volume 1407 of *Lecture Notes in Computer Science*, pages 86–102. Springer, Berlin, 1998.
13. N. Ohta. Uncertainty models of the gradient constraint for optical flow computation. *IEICE Transactions on Information and Systems*, E79-D(7):958–962, July 1996.
14. C. Schnörr, R. Sprengel, and B. Neumann. A variational approach to the design of early vision algorithms. *Computing Suppl.*, 11:149–165, 1996.
15. E. P. Simoncelli, E. H. Adelson, and D. J. Heeger. Probability distributions of optical flow. In *Proc. 1991 IEEE Computer Society Conference on Computer Vision and Pattern Recognition*, pages 310–315, Maui, HI, June 1991. IEEE Computer Society Press.

16. O. Tretiak and L. Pastor. Velocity estimation from image sequences with second order differential operators. In *Proc. Seventh International Conference on Pattern Recognition*, pages 16–19, Montreal, Canada, July 1984.
17. J. Weickert and C. Schnörr. Variational optic flow computation with a spatiotemporal smoothness constraint. *Journal of Mathematical Imaging and Vision*, 14(3):245–255, May 2001.

Mixed OLS-TLS for the Estimation of Dynamic Processes with a Linear Source Term*

Christoph S. Garbe[1], Hagen Spies[2], and Bernd Jähne[1]

[1] Interdisciplinary Center for Scientific Computing, INF 368, D-69120 Heidelberg, Germany
[2] ICG-III (Phytosphere) Forschungszentrum Jülich GmbH, D-52425 Jülich, Germany,
Christoph.Garbe@iwr.uni-heidelberg.de

Abstract. We present a novel technique to eliminate strong biases in parameter estimation were part of the data matrix is not corrupted by errors. Problems of this type occur in the simultaneous estimation of optical flow and the parameter of linear brightness change as well as in range flow estimation. For attaining highly accurate optical flow estimations under real world situations as required by a number of scientific applications, the standard brightness change constraint equation is violated. Very often the brightness change has to be modelled by a linear source term. In this problem as well as in range flow estimation, part of the data term consists of an exactly known constant. Total least squares (TLS) assumes the error in the data terms to be identically distributed, thus leading to strong biases in the equations at hand. The approach presented in this paper is based on a mixture of ordinary least squares (OLS) and total least squares, thus resolving the bias encountered in TLS alone. Apart from a thorough performance analysis of the novel estimator, a number of applications are presented.

Keywords. *parameter estimation, least squares, dynamic processes, brightness change, optical flow.*

1 Introduction

Many different methods to recover the optical flow exist [3]. In the context of this paper a gradient based technique for optical flow estimation is used. Here motion computations are motivated by scientific applications. As such they were extended to parameterize the underlying physical processes [6,12,13].

In most gradient based techniques the optical flow estimates are obtained by pooling local constraints over a small spatio-temporal neighborhood in a least squares sense. This approach does of course assume the parameters of the constraint equations to be constant throughout the region of support. This assumption can be violated at motion discontinuities, thus leading astray the estimator presented in this paper. To overcome

* We gratefully acknowledge financial support of this research by the German Science Foundation (DFG) through the research unit "Image Sequence Processing to Investigate Dynamic Processes".

L. Van Gool (Ed.): DAGM 2002, LNCS 2449, pp. 463–471, 2002.

this limitation the estimator can readily be extended to robust statistic by means of M- or LMSOD estimation [1,6,8,11].

Using ordinary least squares (OLS) techniques the temporal derivatives are treated as erroneous observations and the spatial gradients as error free. This approach will lead to biases in the estimates, as all gradients are generally obscured by noise [14]. Under these circumstances the use of a total least squares (TLS) method [20] is the estimator of choice [16]. The local constraints of gradient based optical flow techniques do generally not incorporate brightness changes. This can of course only be a first approximation, as brightness changes due to inhomogeneous or fluctuating illumination prevail in real world scenes. Moreover, in scientific applications these brightness changes may be induced by physical processes. Hence the parameters of brightness change might be equally important as the actual optical flow [13]. A number of physically induced brightness changes as well as those caused by inhomogeneous illumination can be modelled quite accurately by a source term in the constraint equation. Additionally does the computation of surface motion from range data lead to the same type of constraints [19]. This type of equations can be thought of as multivariate intercept models. The data matrix of such a model for the TLS estimator contains a column of exactly known elements thus inducing a strong bias in the estimation. This bias can be efficiently eliminated by mixing the OLS and TLS estimator as outlined in the next section.

2 Mixing Ordinary Least Squares and Total Least Squares

In TLS estimates the parameter vector p^{est} converges to the true vector p only for independently and identically distributed errors in the observations [5,9,20]. This means that all observations should have the same standard deviation σ, which can be achieved by scaling the data accordingly, an approach also known as equilibration [10,15,17]. However, there are instances when one column in the data matrix is known *exactly*, that is it is not subject to any errors. This is the case in intercept models of the form

$$c + a_1 x_1 + \cdots + a_m x_m = b, \tag{1}$$

which will be used in a number of applications introduced in Section 4. Such a model gives rise to an overdetermined set of equations of the form

$$(1_N; A) \begin{pmatrix} c \\ x \end{pmatrix} = b, \tag{2}$$

where $1_N = (1, \ldots, 1)^\top$ is the first column of the data matrix and thus exactly known.

The accuracy of the estimated parameters can be maximized by requiring that the exactly known columns in the data matrix be unperturbed [4,20]. This can be achieved by reformulating the TLS problem in a more general form by mixing OLS and TLS:

Definition 1 *Given a set of n linear equations with p unknown parameters x*

$$(A_1, A_2) x = b, \quad \text{with} \quad A_1 \in \mathbb{R}^{n \times p_1}, A_2 \in \mathbb{R}^{n \times p_2}, x \in \mathbb{R}^p, b \in \mathbb{R}^n, \tag{3}$$

and $p_1 + p_2 = p$. The mixed OLS-TLS problem then seeks to minimize

$$\min \ \left[(A_2, b) \, p_2 \right]^2 \tag{4}$$
$$\text{subject to} \ \ (A_1, A_2) \, x = A_1 x_1 + A_2 x_2 = b,$$

where $p = \left(x^\top, -1 \right)^\top$, $p_2 = \left(x_2^\top, -1 \right)^\top$ and $x = \left(x_1^\top, x_2^\top \right)^\top$.

In the specific example of Equation (1) $p_1 = 1$ and $p_2 = m$. Equation (4) can thus be depicted as first finding a TLS solution on the reduced subspace of erroneous observations and than choosing from this set the one solution that solves the equations of unperturbed data exactly.

In the event of all observations A being known exactly, the OLS-TLS solution reduces to the OLS solution, while at the other extreme of only erroneous data the problem reduces to the TLS problem.

2.1   Implementation of Mixed OLS-TLS Estimator

The implementation of the mixed OLS-TLS estimator is straightforward. The columns of the data matrix A are permuted by a permutation matrix P in such a way, that the submatrix A_1 contains the p_1 exactly known observations, that is

$$A \cdot P = (A_1, A_2), \ \text{where} \ A \in \mathbb{R}^{n \times p}, A_1 \in \mathbb{R}^{n \times p_1}, A_2 \in \mathbb{R}^{n \times p_2}, P \in \mathbb{R}^{p \times p}. \tag{5}$$

In a next step a QR factorization of the matrix (A_1, A_2, b) is performed, thus

$$(A_1, A_2, b) = Q \begin{pmatrix} R_{11} & R_{12} \\ 0 & R_{22} \end{pmatrix}, \tag{6}$$

with Q being orthogonal and R_{11} upper triangular. The QR factorization is justified because the singular vectors and singular values of a matrix are not changed by multiplying it by an orthogonal matrix [10].

The solution for the sub system of equations $R_{22} p_2 = 0$ is computed in a TLS sense, which boils down to an singular value analysis of the data matrix R_{22} [20].

With the known estimate of p_2 the system of equations $R_{11} p_1 + R_{12} p_2 = 0$ is solved for p_1 by back-substitution. The parameter vector $p = \left(p_1^\top, p_2^\top \right)^\top$ has then to be transformed back reversing the initial permutations of the columns by $p \leftarrow P^{-1} p$. The step of permuting the data and parameters can of course be omitted by formulating the problem in such a way that the constant terms are in the first columns of the data matrix, as will be done in the remainder of this paper.

3   Comparison of OLS-TLS and TLS

In this section the properties of both the mixed OLS-TLS and standard TLS estimator shall be analyzed. We make use of the Generalized Brightness Change Constraint Equation (GBCCE) with constant linear motion and the brightness change modelled with a

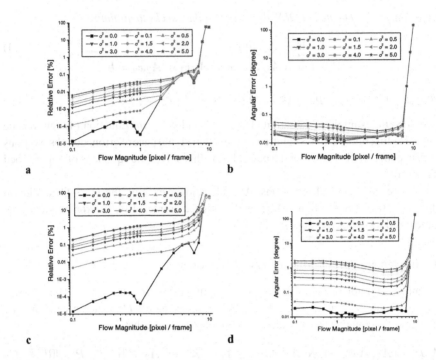

Fig. 1. Comparison of the relative error E_r of the flow magnitude and corresponding angular errors E_ϕ. In **a** the relative Error E_r of the mixed OLS-TLS estimator is shown and in **b** the corresponding angular Error. Respectively, in **c** and **d** both E_r and E_ϕ are shown for the TLS estimator.

source term, that is

$$\begin{pmatrix} -1 & g_{x,1} & g_{y,1} & g_{t,1} \\ -1 & g_{x,2} & g_{y,2} & g_{t,2} \\ \vdots & \vdots & \vdots & \vdots \\ -1 & g_{x,n} & g_{y,n} & g_{t,n} \end{pmatrix} \cdot \begin{pmatrix} c \\ \delta x \\ \delta y \\ \delta t \end{pmatrix} = D \cdot p = 0, \quad \text{with} \quad D \in \mathbb{R}^{n \times 4}, \; p \in \mathbb{R}^4. \quad (7)$$

Here n represents the size of the spatio-temporal neighborhood and $g_{i,j}$ the partial derivative of the grey value g with respect to the coordinate i at pixel location j.

Following [2] the algorithms were tested on a sinusoidal test sequence. For optical flow computation it is interesting to study the dependence of the computed optical flow $f = (u,v)^\top = (dx/dt, dy/dt)^\top$ on the noise added to the synthetic sequence. In the present context it is of equal importance to know how accurate the intensity change present in the sequence can be detected. To address these issues first a constant intensity change was uniformly added to the sequence. The magnitude of the flow was varied from no movement ($v_{\text{corr}} = 0$ pixel / frame) up to $v_{\text{corr}} = 10$ pixel / frame in 20 steps, with the direction of the velocity vector along one coordinate axis. Although this is not a common situation encountered in real world situations, most gradient filters

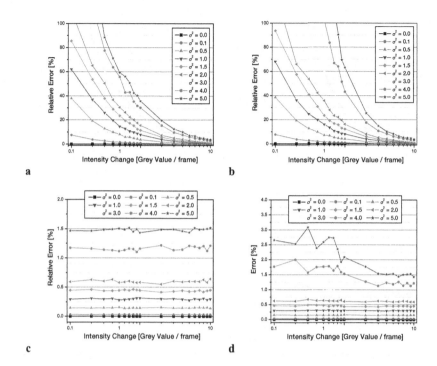

Fig. 2. Comparison of the relative errors in estimating an intensity change at fixed flow magnitude. In **a** the intensity change is computed from the mixed OLS-TLS estimator and in **b** with the TLS estimator. Shown in **c** and **d** are the relative errors in computing the magnitude of the optical flow $|f_{est}|$ for an increasing level of intensity change for both the mixed (**c**) and the TLS (**d**) estimators.

possess optimum properties along this direction [18]. Hence results presented here give a lower bound for movement along other directions. The reason for choosing this specific direction is that the performance of the optical flow computation was to be analyzed independent of the actual optimization of the gradient filter used. Along other directions the actual performance of gradient filters can vary significantly and is subject to filter optimization [18]. The results of this analysis are shown in Figure 1.

The accuracy of establishing an estimate for the parameter c of brightness change in Equation (7) was examined with the three alternative techniques, namely the mixed OLS-TLS, the scaled TLS and the plain TLS estimator. Also the accuracy of detecting the optical flow $f_{est} = (u_{est}, v_{est})^\top$ under different flow magnitudes and different intensity changes was inspected. Not all the resulting plots are presented in this paper. In Figure 2 the relative errors of the intensity changes are shown. It can be seen that the OLS-TLS estimator presents the most accurate results, while the scaled TLS estimate is prone to slightly larger errors. The unscaled TLS technique proves to be quite inaccurate, most notably on higher noise levels. Generally all estimators exhibit the highest accuracy on large intensity changes. The accuracy of recovering the flow magnitude proved to be

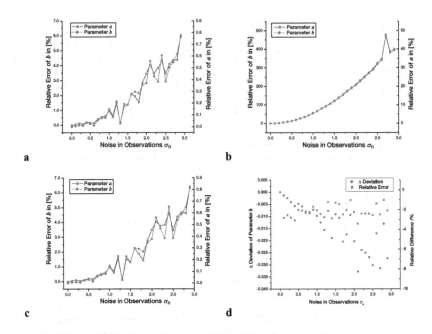

Fig. 3. The relative error measure E_r for the OLS-TLS and unscaled TLS estimators is shown in **a** and **b** respectively. The same for the scaled TLS estimate in **c** . The relative difference between the two OLS-TLS and scaled TLS estimator is shown in **d** , indicating that the OLS-TLS estimator still has a better performance than the scaled TLS estimator by roughly 2%.

independent of the intensity change in the OLS-TLS estimator and depends linearly on the noise level σ. The TLS estimate is biased towards higher intensity changes.

In Figure 3 the performance of OLS-TLS, scaled TLS and TLS are shown in fitting a line with intersect, where parameter a represents the slope of the line and parameter b the offset. The slope is of course equivalent to the optical flow and the offset to the source term of intensity change. The great reduction of error of the OLS-TLS estimator with respect to the TLS can be seen quite nicely. Albeit reducing the bias, the scaled TLS estimator is still less acurate than the OLS-TLS by roughly 2%.

4 Applications

The mixed OLS-TLS estimator was tested on synthetic data in the previous section. In this section its performance is analyzed on real data. It is difficult to obtain ground truth data for optical flow with intensity change. To this end ground truth data was recorded with a range sensor and a structured light system. Correct movement of two objects (crumbled paper and a toy tiger, see Figure 4) was established by placing them on a system of linear positioners. Range flow can be estimated by employing the range flow constraint equation [21], were the depth velocity can be treated as a source term [19].

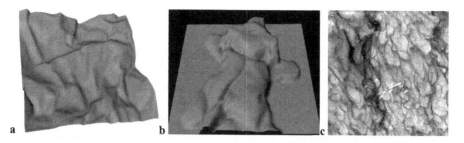

Fig. 4. Real test sequences: **a** crumpled sheet of paper **b** toy tiger **c** thermographic image of ocean surface.

The relative error of the flow can thus be estimated. Comparing the mixed OLS-TLS and TLS estimators we obtain:

method	$E_{\text{paper}}[\%]$	density$_{\text{paper}}[\%]$	$E_{\text{tiger}}[\%]$	density$_{\text{tiger}}[\%]$
TLS	0.29 ± 2.88	12.3	6.0 ± 6.5	16.1
Mixed	0.18 ± 0.13	22.1	2.1 ± 2.9	10.0

These findings underline the superior performance of the mixed OLS-TLS estimator. It is evident that the mixed estimator can under some circumstances help to increase the density of the estimate. As it turns out, choosing correct thresholds for correct estimates is less dependent of the specific image sequences at hand, greatly simplifying the use of this estimator in image processing applications. The reduction of the bias, evident in the smaller relative Error E is remarkable. Only with this reduced bias is it possible to employ the presented estimator on a number of scientific applications, where the source term might be an important parameter in the underlying physical processes.

One such process of interest is the heat transfer at the sea surface. It can be shown that this source term of linear intensity change is equivalent to the total derivative of the temperature structures recorded from infrared sequences[8]. Such a thermographic image is shown in Figure 4. From this total derivative with respect to time the net heat flux at the sea interface can be estimated. Due to this use of thermography coupled with the estimator presented in this paper both spatially and temporally highly resolved heat flux estimates at the sea surface could be attained for the first time[7]. Without the reduction of the bias by the mixed estimator presented in this paper a sufficiently accurate estimate of the net heat flux would not be feasible.

5   Conclusion

In this paper a mixed OLS-TLS estimator was presented that allows to significantly reduce the bias in the estimation of the parameters in differential equations with a linear source term. This type of equation can be used to estimate the optical flow subject to linear intensity changes in the scene or optical flow from range data. The standard TLS estimator proved to be too inaccurate for this type of problem. It was shown that it exhibits a strong bias and thus depends highly on the noise level and intensity change present in the imagery. By performing a column scaling of the data matrix D_{noise}, this bias could be lessened somewhat. The virtual deviation of the exactly known first column of the data matrix has to be scaled with a variance of at least four orders of magnitude smaller than that found in the other columns. Numerically more attractive and also providing the most accurate results is the mixed OLS-TLS estimator presented in this paper, which is an unbiased estimator under iid Gaussian noise. This results was verified both on synthetic and real data. These findings emphasize the importance of this mixed estimator for accurate estimation of optical flow with linear intensity change or range flow based on range data.

References

1. A. Bab-Hadiashar and D. Suter. Robust optic flow computation. *IJCV*, 29(1):59–77, 1998.
2. J. L. Barron, D. J. Fleet, and S. Beauchemin. Performance of optical flow techniques. *International Journal of Computer Vision*, 12(1):43–77, 1994.
3. S. S. Beauchemin and J. L. Barron. The computation of optical flow. *ACM Computing Surveys*, 27(3):433–467, 1995.
4. A Björck. Least squares methods. In P. G. Ciarlet and J. L. Lions, editors, *Finite Difference Methods (Part 1)*, volume 1 of *Handbook of Numerical Analysis*, pages 465–652. Elesvier Science Publishers, North-Holland, 1990.
5. P. P. Gallo. Consistency of regression estimates when some variables are subject to error. *Communications in statistics / Theory and methods*, 11:973–983, 1982.
6. C. S. Garbe. *Measuring Heat Exchange Processes at the Air-Water Interface from Thermographic Image Sequence Analysis*. PhD thesis, University of Heidelberg, Heidelberg, Germany, 2001.
7. C. S. Garbe, H. Haußecker, and B. Jähne. Measuring the sea surface heat flux and probability distribution of surface renewal events. In E. Saltzman, M. Donelan, W. Drennan, and R. Wanninkhof, editors, *Gas Transfer at Water Surfaces*, Geophysical Monograph. American Geophysical Union, 2001.
8. C. S. Garbe and B. Jähne. Reliable estimates of the sea surface heat flux from image sequences. In *Proc. of the 23rd DAGM Symposium*, Lecture Notes in Computer Science, LNCS 2191, pages 194–201, Munich, Germany, 2001. Springer-Verlag.
9. L. J. Gleser. Estimation in a multivariate "error in variables" regression model: Large sample results. *Annals of Statistics*, 9:24–44, 1981.
10. G. H. Golub and C. F. van Loan. *Matrix Computations*. The Johns Hopkins University Press, Baltimore and London, 3 edition, 1996.
11. F. R. Hampel, E. M. Ronchetti, P. J. Rousseeuw, and W. A. Stahel. *Robust Statistics: The Approach Based on Influence Functions*. John Wiley and Sons, New York, 1986.
12. H. Haußecker and D. J. Fleet. Computing optical flow with physical models of brightness variation. *PAMI*, 23(6):661–673, June 2001.
13. H. Haußecker, C. S. Garbe, H. Spies, and B. Jähne. A total least squares for low-level analysis of dynamic scenes and processes. In *DAGM*, pages 240–249, Bonn, Germany, 1999. Springer.
14. H. Haußecker and H. Spies. Motion. In B. Jähne, H. Haußecker, and P. Geißler, editors, *Handbook of Computer Vision and Applications*, volume 2, chapter 13, pages 309–396. Academic Press, San Diego, 1999.

15. R. Mester and M. Mühlich. Improving motion and orientation estimation using an equilibrated total least squares approach. In *ICIP*, Greece, October 2001.
16. M. Mühlich and R. Mester. The role of total least squares in motion analysis. In *ECCV*, pages 305–321, Freiburg, Germany, 1998.
17. M. Mühlich and R. Mester. Subspace methods and equilibration in computer vision. Technical Report XP-TR-C-21, Institute for Applied Physics, Goethe-Universitaet, Frankfurt, Germany, November 1999.
18. H. Scharr. *Optimale Operatoren in der Digitalen Bildverarbeitung.* PhD thesis, University of Heidelberg, Heidelberg, Germany, 2000.
19. H. Spies, H. Haußecker, B. Jähne, and J. L. Barron. Differential range flow estimation. In *DAGM*, pages 309–316, Bonn, Germany, September 1999.
20. S. Van Huffel and J. Vandewalle. *The Total Least Squares Problem: Computational Aspects and Analysis.* Society for Industrial and Applied Mathematics, Philadelphia, 1991.
21. M. Yamamoto, P. Boulanger, J. Beraldin, and M. Rioux. Direct estimation of range flow on deformable shape from a video rate range camera. *PAMI*, 15(1):82–89, January 1993.

Motion Competition: Variational Integration of Motion Segmentation and Shape Regularization

Daniel Cremers and Christoph Schnörr

Computer Vision, Graphics and Pattern Recognition Group,
Department of Mathematics and Computer Science, University of Mannheim,
D–68131 Mannheim, Germany,
{cremers,schnoerr}@uni-mannheim.de, http://www.cvgpr.uni-mannheim.de

Abstract. We present a variational method for the segmentation of piecewise affine flow fields. Compared to other approaches to motion segmentation, we minimize a *single* energy functional both with respect to the affine motion models in the separate regions and with respect to the shape of the separating contour. In the manner of region competition, the evolution of the segmenting contour is driven by a force which aims at maximizing a homogeneity measure with respect to the estimated motion in the adjoining regions.

We compare segmentations obtained for the models of piecewise affine motion, piecewise constant motion, and piecewise constant intensity. For objects which cannot be discriminated from the background by their appearance, the desired motion segmentation is obtained, although the corresponding segmentation based on image intensities fails. The region–based formulation facilitates convergence of the contour from its initialization over fairly large distances, and the estimated discontinuous flow field is progressively improved during the gradient descent minimization. By including in the variational method a statistical shape prior, the contour evolution is restricted to a subspace of familiar shapes, such that a robust estimation of irregularly moving shapes becomes feasible.

Keywords: Region Competition, Motion segmentation, piecewise affine motion, variational methods, statistical shape prior.

1 Related Work

Discontinuity–preserving motion estimation by variational methods and related partial differential equations have a long tradition in computer vision. In some approaches the motion discontinuities are modeled implicitly in terms of appropriate (non–quadratic) regularizers [14,2,12,11,17]. Other approaches pursue separate steps of variational motion estimation on disjoint sets with a shape optimization procedure [16,4,15,8]. For the case of grey value segmentation, there exist some region–based variational approaches with explicit discontinuities (cf. [13]) and extensions to color and texture segmentation [18].

In this paper, we present a variational method for motion segmentation with an explicit contour description. The problems of segmentation and motion estimation are jointly solved by gradient descent on a *single* energy functional. In

L. Van Gool (Ed.): DAGM 2002, LNCS 2449, pp. 472–480, 2002.

contrast to implicit level set based shape representations (cf. [4]), the *explicit* representation of the contour does not permit topological changes. However, it facilitates the incorporation of a statistical prior on the shape of the segmenting contour. Furthermore, in many applications it is known that topological changes of shapes do not occur, in which case a fixed topology is preferable.

Deformable shape models are combined with motion segmentation in [10]. However, there the authors do not propose a variational integration of motion segmentation and shape prior. Rather they optimize a small number of shape parameters by simulated annealing, which — unlike our approach — cannot be applied to more general shape priors.

2   Variational Motion Segmentation

Let $f(x, t)$ be an image sequence which is assumed to be differentiable. If the intensity of a moving point is constant throughout time, we obtain a continuity equation given by the classical optic flow constraint:

$$\frac{d}{dt} f(x, t) = \frac{\partial}{\partial t} f + w^t \nabla f = 0,$$

where $w = \frac{dx}{dt}$ denotes the local velocity. Given two consecutive images f_1 and f_2 from this sequence, we can approximate $\frac{\partial}{\partial t} f \approx (f_2 - f_1)$ and $\nabla f \approx \frac{1}{2} \nabla (f_1 + f_2)$.

We propose to segment the image plane into areas R_i of parametric motion $w_i = w(\alpha_i)$ by minimizing the energy functional

$$E(\alpha, C) = \sum_i \int_{R_i} \left(f_2 - f_1 + \frac{w_i^t}{2} \nabla (f_1 + f_2) \right)^2 dx + \nu \, E_c(C) \tag{1}$$

simultaneously with respect to both the contour C which separates the regions R_i, and the motion parameters $\alpha = \{\alpha_i\}$. The term E_c represents an *internal shape energy*, such as the length of the contour or a more elaborate shape dissimilarity measure, which will be detailed in Section 5.

With the extended velocity vector $v = \binom{w}{1}$ and the spatio–temporal structure tensor [1]

$$S = (\nabla_3 f)(\nabla_3 f)^t, \quad \text{with } \nabla_3 f = \begin{pmatrix} \nabla f \\ \frac{\partial}{\partial t} f \end{pmatrix},$$

the energy (1) can be rewritten as

$$E(\alpha, C) = \sum_i \int_{R_i} \left(v_i^t \, S \, v_i \right) dx + \nu \, E_c(C). \tag{2}$$

In practice, the homogeneity term shows a bias towards velocity vectors of large magnitude. As proposed in [7], we therefore perform an isotropy compensation of the structure tensor by replacing S with $S - \lambda_3 I$, where λ_3 is the smallest eigenvalue of S and I is the 3×3 unit matrix.

3   Piecewise Homogeneous Motion

The proposed *motion energy* (2) can be interpreted as an extension of the Mumford–Shah model [13,6] to the problem of motion segmentation. Rather than measuring the grey value homogeneity, it measures the homogeneity with respect to parametric motion models in the respective regions. In the following we will focus on the two cases of constant motion and affine motion, but depending on the application other motion models can be used, as long as the extended velocity vector is linear in the parameters.

For the model of **piecewise constant motion**, the extended velocity vector for region R_i is given by:

$$v_i = T\alpha_i = \begin{pmatrix} 1 & 0 & 0 \\ 0 & 1 & 0 \\ 0 & 0 & 1 \end{pmatrix} (a_i \; b_i \; 1)^t, \tag{3}$$

where a_i and b_i denote the velocity in x– and y–direction. For the model of **piecewise affine motion**, we have:

$$v_i = T\alpha_i = \begin{pmatrix} x & y & 1 & 0 & 0 & 0 & 0 \\ 0 & 0 & 0 & x & y & 1 & 0 \\ 0 & 0 & 0 & 0 & 0 & 0 & 1 \end{pmatrix} (a_i \; b_i \; c_i \; d_i \; e_i \; f_i \; 1)^t, \tag{4}$$

with 6 parameters defining the motion in region R_i.

Inserting the respective parametric motion model into the motion energy (2), we get:

$$E(\alpha, C) = \sum_i \alpha_i^t Q_i \alpha_i + \nu \, E_c(C), \tag{5}$$

where

$$Q_i = \int_{R_i} T^t S T \, dx = \begin{pmatrix} \bar{Q}_i & q_i \\ q_i^t & \gamma_i \end{pmatrix}.$$

Depending on the model, the submatrix $\bar{Q}_i$ and the vector q_i have the dimension 2 for the constant motion model or 6 for the affine model.

4   Energy Minimization

The motion energy (5) must be simultaneously minimized both with respect to the evolving contour and with respect to the motion parameters $\{\bar{\alpha}_i\}$, where $\alpha_i = \begin{pmatrix} \bar{\alpha}_i \\ 1 \end{pmatrix}$ is defined with respect to the chosen motion model — see equations (3) and (4).

Minimization with respect to $\bar{\alpha}_i$ results in the linear equation $\bar{Q}_i \, \bar{\alpha}_i = -q_i$. Due to the well–known *aperture problem*, the symmetric square matrix $\bar{Q}_i$ may not be invertible. In this case, we impose an additional constraint by choosing the solution of minimal length. This amounts to applying the pseudo–inverse (cf. [7]):

$$\bar{\alpha}_i = -\bar{Q}_i^\dagger \, q_i. \tag{6}$$

Using Green's theorem (cf. [18]), minimization of (2) with respect to the contour C results in the gradient descent evolution equation

$$\frac{dC}{d\tau} = -\frac{dE}{dC} = \left(e^- - e^+\right) n - \nu \frac{dE_c}{dC} \tag{7}$$

The last term minimizes the internal shape energy which will be treated in the next section. The superscripts $j = +/-$ denote the two regions to the left and to the right of the respective contour point (in the sense of the contour parameterization), and n is the normal on the contour pointing out of the region R_+.

The adjacent regions compete for the contour in terms of the associated energy densities[1]

$$e^j = v_j^t S v_j. \tag{8}$$

This *motion competition* enforces regions of homogeneous optic flow, thus separating regions moving at different velocities w_j.

Following the argumentation in [7], we normalize the cost function in (8) by replacing $v_j^t S v_j$ with $\frac{v_j^t S v_j}{||v_j||^2 trS}$. Although this modification is not strictly derived by minimizing energy (5), it tends to slightly improve the contour evolution.

5   Internal Shape Energy

In the following, we will present two possible models for the internal shape energy E_c in (5). We will restrict the space of possible motion contours to closed spline curves of the form $C : [0,1] \to \Omega$, $C(s) = \sum_{n=1}^N p_n B_n(s)$, with spline control points $p_n = (x_n, y_n)^t$ and periodic quadratic basis functions B_n [3]. This permits a relatively fast numerical optimization. Moreover, it facilitates the incorporation of a statistical shape prior on the control point vector $z = (x_1, y_1, \ldots, x_N, y_N)^t$.

The first and fairly general internal energy is given by a measure of the contour length:

$$E_c(C) := \frac{1}{2} \int_0^1 \left(\frac{dC}{ds}\right)^2 ds. \tag{9}$$

In the case of quadratic B-spline basis functions, the corresponding Euler–Lagrange equation is equivalent to an equidistant spacing of control points. The term $-\nu \frac{dE_c}{dC}$ in the evolution equation (7) simply pulls each control point towards the center of its respective neighbors.

For the second choice of internal energy, we construct a *shape dissimilarity measure* which encodes statistically the silhouettes of a set of sample shapes [6]. To this end, the images of training objects are binarized, a spline contour is

---

[1] In the equivalent probabilistic interpretation, this energy density represents the *log likelihood* for the probability that a given location is part of one or the other motion hypothesis.

fitted to the boundary, and the set of training contours is aligned with respect to similarity transformations [9] and cyclic permutation of the control points.

The distribution of control point vectors $z \in \mathbb{R}^{2N}$ is assumed to be Gaussian: $\mathcal{P}(z) \propto \exp\left(-\frac{1}{2}(z - z_0)^t \Sigma^{-1} (z - z_0)\right)$. The mean control point vector z_0 and sample covariance matrix Σ are determined for the training set.[2] The negative logarithm of the Gaussian probability can be interpreted as a shape energy of Mahalanobis type:

$$E_{shape}(z) = \frac{1}{2}(z - z_0)^t \Sigma^{-1}(z - z_0). \tag{10}$$

By construction, this energy is not invariant with respect to transformations such as translation or rotation of the shape. As shown in [5], there is a closed–form solution for incorporating such invariances in the variational approach. One simply applies the function (10) to the argument after alignment of the respective contour with respect to the mean shape z_0:

$$E_c(z) := E_{shape}\left(\frac{R(z - z_c)}{|R(z - z_c)|}\right), \tag{11}$$

where z_c denotes the centered version of z and R denotes the optimal rotation with respect to the mean z_0. The resulting expression can be differentiated with respect to the control point vector z (cf. [5]). This incorporates similarity invariance on the basis of the control point polygons without any additional parameters to encode rotation angle, scale and translation.

6   Evolution of the Motion Boundary

Equation (7) can be converted to an evolution equation for the spline control points by inserting the spline representation of the contour. The equation is discretized with a set of nodes s_i along the contour, where s_i is chosen as the point where the respective spline basis function B_i attains its maximum. Including the contribution of the internal shape energy, we obtain for the x–coordinate of control point m:

$$\frac{dx_m(t)}{d\tau} = \sum_k \left(\mathbf{B}^{-1}\right)_{mk}\left(e_{s_k}^+ - e_{s_k}^-\right)n_x(s_k) - \nu\left(\frac{dE_c}{dz}\right)_{2m-1}, \tag{12}$$

where n_x denotes the x–coordinate of the normal vector and the index $2m-1$ refers to the component of the given vector which is associated with the x–coordinate of control point m. The cyclic tridiagonal matrix $\mathbf{B}$ contains the spline basis functions evaluated at the nodes: $B_{ij} = B_i(s_j)$. A similar expression holds for the y–coordinates.

---

[2] If the dimension of the subspace spanned by the training vectors is smaller than the dimension $2N$ of the underlying vector space, the sample covariance matrix Σ is regularized by replacing the non–zero eigenvalues by a constant $\sigma_\perp = 0.5\,\sigma_r$, where σ_r is the smallest non–vanishing eigenvalue. For a justification we refer to [6].

The two terms in (12) can be interpreted as follows: The first term forces the contour towards the boundaries of the two motion fields by minimizing the motion inhomogeneity in the adjoining regions, measured by the energy density (8). The last term minimizes the internal shape energy — in our case the length of the contour (9), a shape dissimilarity measure of the form (11) or a linear combination of both. The total energy (5) is minimized by iterating the contour evolution (12) in alternation with the update (6) of the motion estimates.

7   Experimental Results

Model Comparison. Figure 1 shows a comparison of segmentation results obtained for the model (5) of **piecewise affine motion** (4), **piecewise constant motion** (3) and the corresponding model of **piecewise constant intensity** [6]. With the affine model the object is correctly segmented and the rotational motion is correctly estimated. In particular, the estimated center of rotation converges towards the correct one (not shown here) during the minimization. The model of piecewise constant motion only segments a small region of the object which complies with the hypothesis of constant motion. The last image shows that the hypothesis of constant intensity (i.e. average grey value) is obviously not applicable here due to clutter and difficult lighting conditions.

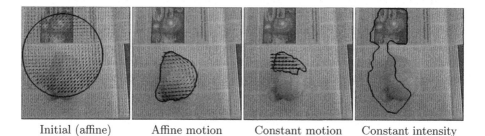

Initial (affine)   Affine motion   Constant motion   Constant intensity

Fig. 1. Model comparison: Initial contour and final segmentation obtained by minimizing the functional (5) with the piecewise affine motion model (4), and final segmentations (with the same initialization) for the model (3) of piecewise constant motion, and the corresponding model of piecewise constant intensity [6]. The input images show a duck figure rotated on a newspaper. The affine motion model captures the rotation and thereby correctly segments the duck. The model of constant motion only captures those parts which show approximately constant motion, whereas the model of constant intensity is mislead by background clutter and the difficult lighting conditions.

Moving Background. Figure 2 shows an example of two differently moving regions. We took a snapshot of a section of wallpaper and artificially rotated a circular region in the center, the remaining area was rotated in the opposite sense (see ground truth on the right). The contour evolution shows how the two affine motion fields are progressively separated during the energy minimization.

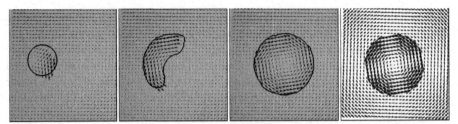

Contour evolution for the model of piecewise affine motion   True motion field

Fig. 2. Separating two affine motion fields: Gradient descent evolution for the functional (5) with the piecewise affine motion model (4). The input sequence shows a wallpaper with a circular area in the center rotated in one sense, and the background rotated in the opposite sense, as indicated by the true motion field on the right. During energy minimization the estimated motion fields are continuously improved, the two motion fields are separated, and the circular area is correctly segmented. Note that the circular area cannot be detected based on grey value information.

The final segmentation cannot be visually distinguished from the rotated circular area.

Motion Segmentation with a Statistical Shape Prior. Figure 3 shows a contour evolution with a statistical prior favoring hands which was automatically generated from a set of 10 binary training images [6]. The evolving contour is effectively restricted to the submanifold of familiar shapes. While the two estimated affine flow fields are initially fairly similar, they are progressively improved during the energy minimization. In particular, the rotatory motion of the hand and the static background are correctly determined in the final segmentation.

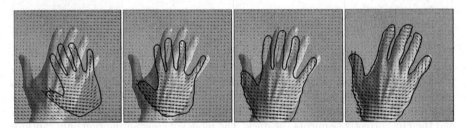

Fig. 3. Knowledge–driven motion segmentation: Gradient descent on the functional (5) with the piecewise affine motion model (4) and a statistical prior (11) favoring hand shapes. The input sequence is a rotating hand in front of a static background. During the contour evolution the estimated motion fields are continuously improved, while the statistical prior restricts the contour to the submanifold of familiar shapes.

8   Conclusion

We presented a variational method for the segmentation of piecewise affine flow fields. In the manner of region competition, the evolution of the segmenting contour is driven by a force which aims at maximizing a homogeneity measure with respect to the estimated motion in the adjoining regions. By minimizing a *single* functional, we jointly solve the problems of segmentation and motion estimation. Experimental results demonstrate that objects which are not discernible by their appearance can be segmented according to their relative motion. The region–based formulation permits a convergence of the contour over large distances. Moreover, by the variational integration of a *statistical shape prior*, the evolving contour can be effectively restricted to a subspace of familiar shapes, which facilitates the robust segmentation of more complex moving shapes.

References

1. J. Bigün, G. H. Granlund, and J. Wiklund. Multidimensional orientation estimation with applications to texture analysis and optical flow. *IEEE Trans. on Patt. Anal. and Mach. Intell.*, 13(8):775–790, 1991.
2. M. J. Black and P. Anandan. The robust estimation of multiple motions: Parametric and piecewise–smooth flow fields. *Comp. Vis. Graph. Image Proc.: IU*, 63(1):75–104, 1996.
3. A. Blake and M. Isard. *Active Contours*. Springer, London, 1998.
4. V. Caselles and B. Coll. Snakes in movement. *SIAM J. Numer. Anal.*, 33:2445–2456, 1996.
5. D. Cremers, T. Kohlberger, and C. Schnörr. Nonlinear shape statistics in Mumford–Shah based segmentation. In A. Heyden et al., editors, *Proc. of the Europ. Conf. on Comp. Vis.*, volume 2351 of *LNCS*, pages 93–108, Copenhagen, May, 28–31 2002. Springer, Berlin.
6. D. Cremers, F. Tischhäuser, J. Weickert, and C. Schnörr. Diffusion–snakes: Introducing statistical shape knowledge into the Mumford–Shah functional. *Int. J. of Comp. Vis.* Accepted for publication.
7. G. Farnebäck. *Spatial Domain Methods for Orientation and Velocity Estimation*. PhD thesis, Dept. of Electrical Engineering, Linköpings universitet, 1999.
8. G. Farnebäck. Very high accuracy velocity estimation using orientation tensors, parametric motion, and segmentation of the motion field. In *Proc. 8th Int. Conf. on Computer Vision*, volume 1, pages 171–177, 2001.
9. C. Goodall. Procrustes methods in the statistical analysis of shape. *J. Roy. Statist. Soc., Ser. B.*, 53(2):285–339, 1991.
10. C. Kervrann and F. Heitz. Statistical deformable model-based segmentation of image motion. *IEEE Trans. on Image Processing*, 8:583–588, 1999.
11. P. Kornprobst, R. Dériche, and G. Aubert. Image sequence analysis via partial differential equations. *J. Math. Imag. Vision*, 11(1):5–26, 1999.
12. E. Mémin and P. Pérez. Dense estimation and object–based segmentation of the optical flow with robust techniques. *IEEE Trans. on Im. Proc.*, 7(5):703–719, 1998.
13. D. Mumford and J. Shah. Optimal approximations by piecewise smooth functions and associated variational problems. *Comm. Pure Appl. Math.*, 42:577–685, 1989.

14. P. Nesi. Variational approach to optical flow estimation managing discontinuities. *Image and Vis. Comp.*, 11(7):419–439, 1993.
15. J.-M. Odobez and P. Bouthemy. Direct incremental model–based image motion segmentation for video analysis. *Signal Proc.*, 66:143–155, 1998.
16. C. Schnörr. Computation of discontinuous optical flow by domain decomposition and shape optimization. *Int. J. of Comp. Vis.*, 8(2):153–165, 1992.
17. J. Weickert and C. Schnörr. A theoretical framework for convex regularizers in PDE–based computation of image motion. *Int. J. of Comp. Vis.*, 45(3):245–264, 2001.
18. S. C. Zhu and A. Yuille. Region competition: Unifying snakes, region growing, and Bayes/MDL for multiband image segmentation. *IEEE Trans. on Patt. Anal. and Mach. Intell.*, 18(9):884–900, 1996.

Fisher Light-Fields for Face Recognition across Pose and Illumination

Ralph Gross, Iain Matthews, and Simon Baker

The Robotics Institute, Carnegie Mellon University,
5000 Forbes Avenue, Pittsburgh, PA 15213,
{rgross,iainm,simonb}@cs.cmu.edu

Abstract. In many face recognition tasks the pose and illumination conditions of the probe and gallery images are different. In other cases multiple gallery or probe images may be available, each captured from a different pose and under a different illumination. We propose a face recognition algorithm which can use any number of gallery images per subject captured at arbitrary poses and under arbitrary illumination, and any number of probe images, again captured at arbitrary poses and under arbitrary illumination. The algorithm operates by estimating the *Fisher light-field* of the subject's head from the input gallery or probe images. Matching between the probe and gallery is then performed using the Fisher light-fields.

1 Introduction

In many face recognition scenarios the pose of the probe and gallery images are different. The gallery contains the images used during training of the algorithm. The algorithms are tested with the images in the probe sets. For example, the gallery image might be a frontal "mug-shot" and the probe image might be a 3/4 view captured from a camera in the corner of the room. The number of gallery and probe images can also vary. For example, the gallery may consist of a pair of images for each subject, a frontal mug-shot and full profile view (like the images typically captured by police departments). The probe may be a similar pair of images, a single 3/4 view, or even a collection of views from random poses.

Face recognition across pose, i.e. face recognition where the gallery and probe images do not have the same poses, has received very little attention. Algorithms have been proposed which can recognize faces [1] (or more general objects [2]) at a variety of poses. However, most of these algorithms require gallery images at every pose. Algorithms have been proposed which do generalize across pose, for example [3], but this algorithm computes 3D head models using a gallery containing a large number of images per subject captured using controlled illumination variation. It cannot be used with arbitrary gallery and probe sets.

After pose variation, the next most significant factor affecting the appearance of faces is illumination. A number of algorithms have been developed for face recognition across illumination, but they typically only deal with frontal faces [4,5]. Only a few approaches have been proposed to handle both pose and

L. Van Gool (Ed.): DAGM 2002, LNCS 2449, pp. 481–489, 2002.

illumination variation at the same time. For example, [3] computes a 3D head model requiring a large number of gallery images, and [6] fits a previously constructed morphable 3D model to single images. This last algorithm works well across pose and illumination, however, the computational cost is very high.

We propose an algorithm for face recognition across pose and illumination. Our algorithm can use any number of gallery images captured at arbitrary poses and under arbitrary illuminations, and any number of probe images also captured with arbitrary poses and illuminations. A minimum of 1 gallery and 1 probe image are needed, but if more images are available the performance of our algorithm generally gets better.

Our algorithm operates by estimating a representation of the light-field [7] of the subject's head. First, generic training data is used to compute a linear subspace of head light-fields, similar to the construction of Fisher-faces [4]. Light-fields are simply used rather than images. Given a collection of gallery or probe images, the projection into the subspace is performed by setting up a least-squares problem and solving for the projection coefficients similarly to approaches used to deal with occlusions in the eigenspace approach [8,9]. This simple linear algorithm can be applied to any number of images, captured from any poses under any illumination. Finally, matching is performed by comparing the probe and gallery Fisher light-fields using a nearest-neighbor algorithm.

2   Light-Fields Theory

The *plenoptic function* [10] or *light-field* [7] is a function which specifies the radiance of light in free space. It is a 5D function of position (3D) and orientation (2D). In addition, it is also sometimes modeled as a function of time, wavelength, and polarization, depending on the application in mind. In 2D, the light-field of a 2D object is actually 2D rather, than the 3D that might be expected. See Figure 1 for an illustration.

2.1   Eigen Light-Fields

Suppose we are given a collection of light-fields $L_i(\theta, \phi)$ of objects O_i (here faces of different subjects) where $i = 1, \ldots, N$. See Figure 1 for the definition of this notation. If we perform an eigen-decomposition of these vectors using Principal Component Analysis (PCA), we obtain $d \leq N$ eigen light-fields $E_i(\theta, \phi)$ where $i = 1, \ldots, d$. Then, assuming that the eigen-space of light-fields is a good representation of the set of light-fields under consideration, we can approximate any light-field $L(\theta, \phi)$ as:

$$L(\theta, \phi) \approx \sum_{i=1}^{d} \lambda_i E_i(\theta, \phi) \qquad (1)$$

where $\lambda_i = \langle L(\theta, \phi), E_i(\theta, \phi) \rangle$ is the inner (or dot) product between $L(\theta, \phi)$ and $E_i(\theta, \phi)$. This decomposition is analogous to that used in face and object

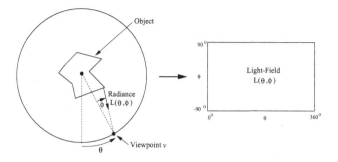

Fig. 1. The object is conceptually placed within a circle. The angle to the viewpoint v around the circle is measured by the angle θ, and the direction that the viewing ray makes with the radius of the circle is denoted ϕ. For each pair of angles θ and ϕ, the radiance of light reaching the viewpoint from the object is then denoted by $L(\theta, \phi)$, the *light-field*. Although the light-field of a 3D object is actually 4D, we will continue to use the 2D notation of this figure in this paper for ease of explanation.

recognition [11,2]; The mean light-field could also be estimated and subtracted from all of the light-fields.

Capturing the complete light-field of an object is a difficult task, primarily because it requires a huge number of images [12,7]. In most object recognition scenarios it is unreasonable to expect more than a few images of the object; often just one. However, any image of the object corresponds to a curve (for 3D objects, a surface) in the light-field. One way to look at this curve is as a highly occluded light-field; only a very small part of the light-field is visible. Can the eigen coefficients λ_i be estimated from this highly occluded view? Although this may seem hopeless, consider that light-fields are highly redundant, especially for objects with simple reflectance properties such as Lambertian. An algorithm is presented in [8] to solve for the unknown λ_i for eigen-*images*. A similar algorithm was implicitly used in [9]. Rather than using the inner product $\lambda_i = \langle L(\theta, \phi), E_i(\theta, \phi) \rangle$, Leonardis and Bischof [8] solve for λ_i as the least squares solution of:

$$L(\theta, \phi) - \sum_{i=1}^{d} \lambda_i E_i(\theta, \phi) \; = \; 0 \qquad (2)$$

where there is one such equation for each pair of θ and ϕ that are un-occluded in $L(\theta, \phi)$. Assuming that $L(\theta, \phi)$ lies *completely within the eigen-space* and that enough pixels are un-occluded, then the solution of Equation (2) will be exactly the same as that obtained using the inner product [13]. Since there are d unknowns $(\lambda_1 \ldots \lambda_d)$ in Equation (2), at least d un-occluded light-field pixels are needed to over-constrain the problem, but more may be required due to linear dependencies between the equations. In practice, $2 - 3$ times as many equations as unknowns are typically required to get a reasonable solution [8]. Given an image $I(m, n)$, the following is then an algorithm for estimating the eigen light-field coefficients λ_i:

1. For each pixel (m, n) in $I(m, n)$ compute the corresponding light-field angles $\theta_{m,n}$ and $\phi_{m,n}$. (This step assumes that the camera intrinsics are known, as well as the relative orientation of the camera to the object.)
2. Find the least-squares solution (for $\lambda_1 \ldots \lambda_d$) to the set of equations:

$$I(m, n) - \sum_{i=1}^{d} \lambda_i E_i(\theta_{m,n}, \phi_{m,n}) = 0 \tag{3}$$

where m and n range over their allowed values. (In general, the eigen light-fields E_i need to be interpolated to estimate $E_i(\theta_{m,n}, \phi_{m,n})$. Also, all of the equations for which the pixel $I(m, n)$ does not image the object should be excluded from the computation.)

Although we have described this algorithm for a single image $I(m, n)$, any number of images can obviously be used (so long as the camera intrinsics and relative orientation to the object are known for each image). The extra pixels from the other images are simply added in as additional constraints on the unknown coefficients λ_i in Equation (3). The algorithm can be used to estimate a light-field from a collection of images. Once the light-field has been estimated, it can then be used to render new images of the same object under different poses. (See [14] for a related algorithm.) In [13] we show that the algorithm correctly re-renders a given object assuming a Lambertian reflectance model.

2.2 Fisher Light-Fields

Suppose now we are given a set of light-fields $L_{i,j}(\theta, \phi)$, $i = 1, \ldots, N, j = 1, \ldots, M$ where each of N objects O_i is imaged under M different illumination conditions. We could proceed as described above and perform Principal Component Analysis on the whole set of $N \times M$ light-fields. An alternative approach is Fisher's Linear Discriminant (FLD) [15], also known as Linear Discriminant Analysis (LDA) [16], which uses the available class information to compute a projection better suited for discrimination tasks. Analogous to the algorithm above, we now find the least squares solution to the set of equations:

$$L(\theta, \phi) - \sum_{i=1}^{m} \lambda_i W_i(\theta, \phi) = 0 \tag{4}$$

where $W_i, i = 1, \ldots, m$ are the generalized eigenvectors computed by the LDA. The extension of eigen light-fields to Fisher light-fields mirrors the step from eigenfaces to Fisher-faces in face recognition as proposed in [4].

3   Face Recognition across Pose and Illumination

We will evaluate our algorithm on a subset of the CMU PIE database [17]. In the PIE database 68 subjects are imaged under 13 different poses and 21 different illumination conditions (see Figure 2). Many of the illumination directions

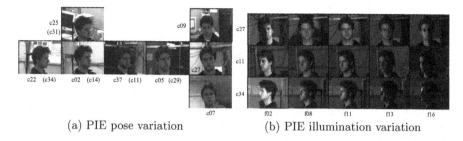

(a) PIE pose variation   (b) PIE illumination variation

Fig. 2. The pose and illumination variation in the PIE database [17].(a) The pose varies from full right profile (c22) to full left profile (c34). (b) The illumination part shows 5 of the 12 illumination conditions used in the experiments here.

introduce fairly subtle variations in appearance so we selected 12 of the 21 illumination conditions which span the set of variation widely. In total we use 10,608 images in the experiments.

3.1   Gallery, Probe, and Generic Training Data

There are 68 subjects in the PIE database. We randomly select $N = 34$ of these subjects and use the images spanning all pose and illumination conditions as generic training data to construct the Fisher light-fields. Of the remaining 34 subjects, the images are divided into *completely disjoint* gallery and probe sets based on the pose and illumination condition they are captured in.

We determined the x-y positions of both eyes (pupils) and the tip of the nose in all 10,608 images we use in the experiments. Within each pose separately the face images are normalized for rotation, translation, and scale. The face region is then tightly cropped using the normalized feature point distances. See [13] for more details of this step.

3.2   Constructing the Light-Field Subspace

Suppose $Training \subset \{1, 2, \ldots, 68\}$ denotes the set of generic training subjects, $Gallery_P$ and $Probe_P$ are the gallery and probe poses and $Gallery_I$ and $Probe_I$ are the gallery and probe illumination conditions. Note that $Gallery_P \cap Probe_P = \oslash$ and $Gallery_I \cap Probe_I = \oslash$ holds. We then assemble the set of images $I_{Train} =$

$$\{Im_{s,p,i} \mid s \in Training, p \in Gallery_P \cup Probe_P, i \in Gallery_I \cup Probe_I\}$$

The images are raster-scanned and concatenated. Between 7,000 and 14,000 pixels are extracted from each image depending on the pose. PCA and LDA is performed on these 408 vectors (34 subjects under 12 illumination conditions) to form the vectors W_i.

3.3   Processing the Gallery and Probe Images

Although the derivation in Section 2 is in terms of the entire light-field, the results also clearly hold for any subset of rays (θ, ϕ) in the light-field. We therefore do not need to densely sample the entire light-field to be able to use the algorithm. For each W_i $(i = 1, \ldots, m$, the dimension of the light-field subspace) we extract the elements corresponding to the gallery and probe images and form shorter vectors W_i^G and W_i^P. For each non-training subject id $\notin Training$ we raster-scan the set of images:

$$\{Im_{id,p,i} \mid p \in Gallery_P, i \in Gallery_I\}, \{Im_{id,p,i} \mid p \in Probe_P, i \in Probe_I\}$$

to form a set of vectors of the same length. We solve Equation (4) for these shortened vectors resulting in λ_i^{id} for the gallery images and μ_i^{id} for the probe images.

3.4   The Classification Algorithm

In order to determine the closest gallery vector for each probe vector we perform nearest neighbor classification using the L_2 and Mahalanobis distance metrics on the PCA and the FLD subspaces. For each probe subject id we determine $id_{\min}$ as

$$id_{\min} = \arg\min_{id^*} d(\mu^{id}, \lambda^{id*}), d \in \{d_{L_2}, d_{Mahal}\} \tag{5}$$

If $id_{\min}$ = id the algorithm has correctly recognized the subject.

4   Experimental Results

We previously showed [13] that our algorithm outperforms eigenfaces [11] and FaceIt, the commercial face recognition system from Visionics. In Figure 3(a) we compare the recognition rate of the three algorithms for the gallery $E^G = \{27\}$ (frontal view). On average our algorithm achieves a recognition accuracy of 73% vs. 59% for FaceIt and 29% for eigenfaces. All images involved in the test were recorded with the same constant illumination. We also showed in [13] that the performance of our algorithm improves with the number of gallery images and that the role of the gallery and probe sets are approximately interchangeable. The average recognition accuracies are summarized in Table 1.

In Figure 3(b) we show a comparison between two light-field variants, FaceIt and eigenfaces for the gallery $E^G = \{27\}$ with frontal illumination. Here the recognition accuracies for the probe camera poses are obtained by averaging the results of testing the gallery illumination condition against a set of probe illumination conditions. Overall the Fisher light-field performs better (47% accuracy) than the eigen light-field (41% accuracy). The average accuracy for FaceIt is 38%. Eigenfaces perform poorly across most probe poses with an average accuracy of 6%. Figure 4 visualizes the differences in performance for eigenfaces and

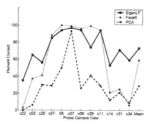 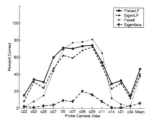

(a) Across pose (same illumination)   (b) Across pose and illumination

Fig. 3. (a) A comparison of our algorithm with eigenfaces [11] and FaceIt on the gallery $E^G = \{27\}$. The recognition rate of the eigen light-fields and FaceIt is similar for the cameras $\{05, 07, 09\}$ closest to the gallery. For the profile views $\{02, 22, 25, 31, 34\}$ our algorithm outperforms FaceIt by far. (b) A comparison of two light-field variants with FaceIt and eigenfaces across pose and illumination with gallery $E^G = \{27\}$ and frontal gallery illumination. For each probe pose the accuracy is averaged over a set of probe illumination conditions.

Table 1. Comparison of FaceIt, eigenfaces, eigen light-fields and Fisher light-fields over all three conditions. Due to the time constraints given for the preparation of this paper, complete FaceIt results are not presented. They will be made available at [18].

Condition	FaceIt	Eigenface	Eigen LF	Fisher LF
Varying pose, same illumination	–	0.24	0.73	–
Varying pose, varying illumination	0.16	0.08	0.22	0.36
Same pose, varying illumination	–	0.60	0.60	0.81

(a) Eigenfaces   (b) Eigen LF   (c) Fisher LF

Fig. 4. Comparison of eigenfaces with two light-field variants across all illumination conditions with gallery pose $E^G = \{27\}$ (frontal view) and probe pose $E^P = \{37\}$ (3/4 view). The gallery illumination conditions are shown along the x-axis, the probe illumination conditions along the y-axis.

two light-field variants across all possible gallery and probe illumination conditions for the gallery $E^G = \{27\}$ (frontal view) and probe $E^P = \{37\}$ (3/4 view). The eigen light-field performs well close to the diagonal of the confusion matrix, whereas the Fisher light-field performs well across a broader range of conditions. Eigenfaces perform poorly in all tests. The average recognition accuracies are summarized in Table 1.

In the case of identical gallery and probe poses, Fisher light-fields are identical to Fisherfaces [4]. As a baseline experiment we compare the recognition accuracies for identical gallery and probe poses across all illumination conditions. The results in Table 1 show that Fisher light-fields/Fisherfaces outperform eigen light-fields and eigenfaces by a large margin.

5   Discussion

In this paper we proposed an algorithm to recognize faces across pose and illumination. We have simplified this task in several ways: (1) the poses of the cameras are known and fixed, (2) the locations of the eyes and the nose used to extract the face region are marked by hand, and (3) the generic training data is captured with the same cameras that are used to capture the gallery and probe images. All of these factors make face recognition easier and are limitations on the current algorithm. We are continuing to develop our algorithm to remove these limitations, while retaining the desirable properties of the algorithm.

To address part (3) we recently conducted preliminary experiments using PIE images as generic training data and FERET images as gallery and probe images. Our algorithm achieves a recognition accuracy of 81.3%, which compares very well to the performance of FaceIt over the same dataset (84.4%).

Acknowledgements

The research described in this paper was supported by U.S. Office of Naval Research contract N00014-00-1-0915. Portions of the research in this paper use the FERET database of facial images collected under the FERET program.

References

1. Pentland, A., Moghaddam, B., Starner, T.: View-based and modular eigenspaces for face recognition. In: Proc. of CVPR. (1994)
2. Murase, H., Nayar, S.: Visual learning and recognition of 3-D objects from appearance. IJCV **14** (1995) 5–24
3. Georghiades, A., Belhumeur, P., Kriegman, D.: From few to many: Generative models for recognition under variable pose and illumination. In: Proc. of the 4th Conf. on Face and Gesture Recognition. (2000)
4. Belhumeur, P., Hespanha, J., Kriegman, D.: Eigenfaces vs. Fisherfaces: Recognition using class specific linear projection. IEEE PAMI **19** (1997) 711–720
5. Batur, A., Hayes, M.: Linear subspaces for illumination robust face recognition. In: Proc. of the 2001 CVPR,. (2001)
6. Blanz, V., Romdhani, S., Vetter, T.: Face identification across different poses and illumination with a 3d morphable model. In: Proc. of the 5th Conf. on Face and Gesture Recognition. (2002)
7. Levoy, M., Hanrahan, M.: Light field rendering. In: Proc. of SIGGRAPH. (1996)
8. Leonardis, A., Bischof, H.: Dealing with occlusions in the eigenspace approach. In: Proc. of CVPR. (1996)

9. Black, M., Jepson, A.: Eigen-tracking: Robust matching and tracking of articulated objects using a view-based representation. IJCV **36** (1998) 101–130
10. Adelson, E., Bergen, J.: The plenoptic function and elements of early vision. In Landy, Movshon, eds.: Computational Models of Visual Processing. MIT Press (1991)
11. Turk, M., Pentland, A.: Face recognition using eigenfaces. In: CVPR. (1991)
12. Gortler, S., Grzeszczuk, R., Szeliski, R., Cohen, M.: The lumigraph. In: SIG-GRAPH. (1996)
13. Gross, R., Baker, S., Matthews, I.: Eigen light-fields and face recognition across pose. In: Proc. of the 5th Conf. on Face and Gesture Recognition. (2002)
14. Vetter, T., Poggio, T.: Linear object classes and image synthesis from a single example image. IEEE Trans. on PAMI **19** (1997) 733–741
15. Fukunaga, K.: Introduction to statistical pattern recognition. Academic Press (1990)
16. Zhao, W., Krishnaswamy, A., Chellappa, R., Swets, D., Weng, J.: Discriminant Analysis of Principal Components for Face Recognition. In: Face Recognition: From Theory to Applications. Springer Verlag (1998)
17. Sim, T., Baker, S., Bsat, M.: The CMU pose, illumination, and expression (PIE) database. In: Proc. of the 5th Conf. on Face and Gesture Recognition. (2002)
18. http://www.hid.ri.cmu.edu/FisherLF.

A Multimodal System for Object Learning*

Frank Lömker and Gerhard Sagerer

Applied Computer Science, Technical Faculty, Bielefeld University,
P. O. Box 10 01 31, 33501 Bielefeld,
floemker@techfak.uni-bielefeld.de

Abstract. A multimodal system for acquiring new objects, updating already known ones, and searching for them is presented. The system is able to learn objects and associate them to speech received from a speech recogniser in a natural and convenient fashion. The learning and retrieval process takes into account information gained from multiple attributes calculated from an image recorded by a standard video camera, from deictic gestures, and from information of a dialog based conversation. Histogram intersection and subgraph matching on segmented color regions are used as attributes.

1 Introduction

Denominating objects is a common task in every day communication. Numberless different objects with a large set of names can be referenced. Sometimes the used names are very generic, e.g. if a word like 'bin' for a complete class of objects is used. On the other hand names can be very specific and adapted to one person, e.g. if he refers to his favourite cup he got from his grandmother 20 years ago. This might happen with a term like 'my favourite cup' or with a nickname normally not directly involved with cups.

This clearly shows that a service robot, which should act in a scenario not strongly restricted, can not be limited to a previously known set of objects or object names. The robot should be able to adapt itself to the environment including relevant objects and to humans communicating with him to allow a robust man machine interaction. A typical scenario is a service robot at home. The human should be able to simply buy a new robot and show and describe it any new objects, which are encountered during normal use of the robot, in a natural and convenient way. In order to allow this the system must be able to cope with completely unknown percepts, symbols, and mappings between them.

Different references exist to research in the field of language learning. In [Roy99] a system is presented which learns new words, new visual concepts, and the correspondence between them based on a low level clustering process. This is a very fundamental approach which tries to bootstrap the complete system with minimal prior knowledge. In [SK01] a system for social learning of language is described. It is shown that a strong interaction with a mediator helps a lot in learning new objects. Taking this into account using multiple modalities in a dialog based environment helps to acquire new and updated objects.

---

* This work is supported within the Graduate Program "Task Oriented Communication" by the German Research Foundation (DFG).

The system described in this paper is a first step towards such a system. The human can use deictic gestures and speech to refer to objects. The system analyses the scenario recorded by a standard video camera and extracts different visual attributes for the object recognition and learning task and hand trajectories for the gestures recognition task. By combining this information the system tries to find an already known object, to update a known object, or to learn a new one. To get more details the system can request further information from the user via a spoken dialog.

In the next section an overview of the system is given. After that the different parts of the system are described in more detail. In section 4 the process of acquiring a new view of an object is presented and section 5 gives the results of two experiments performed with the system.

2   System Overview

Fig. 1 shows the architecture of the system. A speech module and a hand tracking module continuously analyse the utterances and the hand movements made by the user. If the control module receives a semantically parsed utterance with an object specification it grabs a new image and tries to find a corresponding object in the surrounding of a deictic gesture received from the tracking module. For this the different modules for the calculation of visual attributes are triggered to generate hypotheses taking into account the restriction of the tracking module. Currently the attributes *histogram intersection* and *subgraph matching*, which performs subgraph matching on region segmented images, are integrated into the system. The control module does not have any further knowledge about the attributes besides the order in which they should be called, which makes it easy to integrate new attribute modules.

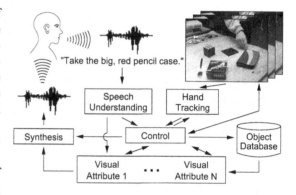

Fig. 1. Architecture of the object localisation and learning system. The human can use speech and gestures to refer to objects. The system learns new objects by combining these information with visual attributes.

The attribute modules fetch attribute features describing the intended object from the database and search for the object in the image. On success one or more judged hypotheses are generated and passed to the control module, where hypotheses of different attribute modules are merged. If the judgement of the best judged hypothesis is above a threshold it is accepted as a found object and announced to the user by the speech synthesis module. Otherwise the object is learned in a dialog with the user. During this a new view with attribute features describing the object is generated and stored in the database. The database holds an unrestricted number of objects with an unrestricted number of views for every object and thus provides mappings between percepts and all symbols learned so far.

3   Modules

Speech. The speech module uses the HMM-based ESMERALDA speech recogniser [Fin99]. The syntactical analysis, based on an LR1 parser, is directly integrated into the recogniser, which enables us to exploit grammar restrictions in much the same way as scores provided by a statistical model [WFS98]. Following the technique from [BFWS99] a flat semantic analysis is carried out getting objects, object attributes, and actions. As an example, for the sentence from Fig. 1 a semantically parsed utterance of the following form is retrieved:

```
(Action: take (Object 0:
                    ('pencil case' (Color: red) (Size: big)))))
```

Gesture Recognition. Gesture recognition is based on the tracking of skin colored regions. Motion information obtained from difference images is used to further judge these regions. A Kalman filter is applied to track the regions and obtain the hand trajectories (for details see [FLWS00]).

Synchronisation between speech and vision is done by looking at the derivative of the trajectory f around the occurrence of definite determiners in time (t). A pointing gesture is assumed if the minimum gradient magnitude $|\Delta f_{min}|$ of f in an interval around t is smaller than a threshold $T1$ and the difference of the average gradient magnitude $|\overline{\Delta f}|$ in this interval and $|\Delta f_{min}|$ is above a second threshold $T2$. $|\Delta f_{min}|$ specifies the position in time and space of the gesture.

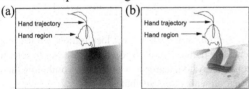

The direction of the pointing gesture is determined using the direction of the trajectory f. By using the singular value decomposition a line is optimally fitted into some points in the history of f. The pointing direction results from the direction of the line. The number of points is chosen such that the distance between the points and the

Fig. 2. (a) An attention map calculated based on the gesture trajectory and the hand region. (b) A hand trajectory and its restriction on the input image.

number of the points is above a threshold. Based on the pointing direction and the position of the segmented hand region an attention map is calculated. The map specifies for every position the probability that this point is in the focus of the pointing gesture. It has the shape of a truncated cone with blurred borders and slowly decreasing probability in the distance.

Fig. 2 (a) shows an example for an attention map for the gesture performed in Fig. 1. The hand trajectory and the hand region at its pointing position corresponding to $|\Delta f_{min}|$ are displayed. In Fig. 2 (b) the attention map from Fig. 2 (a) is applied to the image from Fig. 1 as an alpha mask. All parts of the image which are faded out are assumed to be not relevant for the pointing gesture.

Attribute Histogram Intersection. The *histogram* attribute uses the histogram intersection method introduced by Swain and Ballard [SB91], which compares an object histogram with a histogram obtained from the current image. The histograms are calculated in the perceptually uniform CIE L*u*v* color space [CIE86] with a coarser partitioning of the luminance channel. During the learning phase a histogram of the region an object consumes must be calculated and stored in the database. To speed up the calculation of intersections a rectangular region is preferred. By using only a rectangle of the middle width and height of the region placed around its center of mass and thus removing most of the background pixels the bounding box of the region would contain, the comparison becomes less dependent on the exact placement of the object. Fig. 3 (a) shows an example. Only the part inside the rectangle is used for the histogram calculation.

To find an object, a window of the size of the object histogram obtained from the database is shifted over the complete image. For every position the histogram I at that position is compared with the object histogram O by using the histogram intersection H.

$$H(I, O) = \frac{\sum_{j=1}^{n} \min(I_j, O_j)}{\sum_{j=1}^{n} O_j}$$

For a speedup of the search phase it can be utilised that a histogram at one position and the histograms of adjacent positions are mostly identical. So an estimation for histogram intersections in the neighbourhood of one pixel can be calculated. This positions can be skipped for the histogram calculation and comparison if the estimation shows that the object histogram and the histogram of the image part can not be similar enough. This

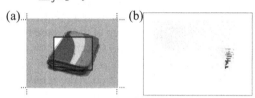

Fig. 3. The attribute histogram intersection: (a) Part of the image from which a histogram is calculated. (b) Result of an active search histogram intersection.

active search called algorithm was introduced by Vinod and Murase [VM97]. Further significant speedups are achieved by calculating the estimates not for every pixel but in an interval of currently 8 pixels around the current point. The size of the surrounding the estimates are calculated is identified based on the value of the intersection at the current point. Histogram intersections of neighbouring pixels are calculated together.

Fig. 3 (b) shows the result of an active search for the image from Fig. 1. Gesture information is integrated in a probabilistic fashion by multiplying this image with the attention map obtained from gesture recognition as shown in Fig. 2 (a).

Attribute Subgraph Matching. The *subgraph matching* attribute locates objects by comparing graphs build from region segmented images. For region segmentation the *mean shift* algorithm as described in [CM97] is used. This is a global technique which clusters the image in the L*u*v* color space into different color classes and enhances the clustering result in the image domain. In contrast to [CM97] for clustering a constant threshold independent of the color covariance matrix is used to be less dependent on the complete image. Fig. 4 shows the regions obtained from the image of Fig. 1 with its center of mass marked as crosses. Based on the region segmentation the *subgraph* *matching* module approximates the regions by polygons, tries to merge further regions, and calculates the features (a) middle color in the YUV color space, (b) size, (c) eccentricity, (d) compactness, and (e) adjacent regions of the region. Moreover during the learning phase a judgement for all regions is calculated which tries to identify regions which do not belong to the object, e.g. because of shadows. A region from color class C has a low judgement, if

- all pixels of the same class C are near the border of the object,
- only few pixels of regions colored differently are located between pixels of color class C and the object border,
- other regions of color classes $\neq C$ are judged good according to these criteria,
- and the region is small.

Learned objects are represented by graphs, where nodes represent regions and edges specify the neighbourhood between the regions. Attached to the nodes are the region features and the judgement. The edges are labeled by the product of the judgement of the two adjacent regions. Locating objects is based on error tolerant subgraph isomorphism [MB98]. The object graphs from the database are matched against a graph representing the segmented image. The region features as well as the attention map of the gesture recognition influence the deletion, insertion, and substitution of nodes. Deletion and insertion of nodes and edges can happen with a small cost if their judgement is small and the corresponding position in the attention map has a high value. Substitution costs are based on the comparison of the region features weighted with the value of the attention map at the position of the region.

Fig. 4. Region segmented input image.

Combination. Every attribute module passes hypotheses containing the used view from the database, a judgement, and features specifying estimates for the size and location of the objects to the control module. Based on the size and location features the control module is able to fuse hypotheses from different attribute modules. Two hypotheses are fused if they descent from different attributes, represent the same object, and have at least an overlap of 40% with the larger hypothesis and 60% with the smaller hypothesis. As a new judgement the sum of the previous judgements is used.

Every attribute of every view in the database has a judgement about its relevance for the object. The judgement of a hypothesis is weighted with all judgements from all attributes used for the hypothesis. If the best judged hypothesis is above a threshold it is accepted as a found object. If this hypothesis is accepted by the user the judgement of all used attributes from the views used for the hypothesis are increased. If the hypothesis is rejected by the user the judgements are decreased. Thus a simple but effective relevance feedback is performed.

4   Learning

If an object could not be found, the learning process is started. As at least the incarnation of the object in the current image is unknown the dimensions of the object are unknown, too. To get them the user is asked to remove the object and to announce the completion of this task. Again utilising maximal information the hand trajectory as well as the images before and after the scene change are used to gather information about the object. The difference image D of the two images $I^{(1)}$ and $I^{(2)}$ gives information about possible object positions and sizes:

$$D'(x,y) = 0.5 * (|I_u^{(2)}(x,y) - I_u^{(1)}(x,y)| + |I_v^{(2)}(x,y) - I_v^{(1)}(x,y)|)$$

$$D(x,y) = \begin{cases} 255 & , D'(x,y) > T \\ 0 & , D'(x,y) \leq T \end{cases}$$

$I_u(x,y)$ specifies the value of the channel U from image I at position x,y. T is a threshold. The difference image is smoothed and cleaned by applying a median filter and a closing operation. Fig. 5 (b) shows an example of the resulting image if the difference image D is applied as a mask to the input image $I^{(1)}$ shown in Fig. 5 (a). It can be seen that not only the desired object is segmented as other changes occurred in the scene.

Usually, the user does not know the exact part of the scene the system sees. Thus instead of removing the object completely from the scene sometimes he only moves it to another position and changes the scene further by moving his hands. To overcome these problems the hand trajectory between the request to the user to remove the object and his answer on completion is used. Using the assumption that he moved forward to grasp the object and then retracted, the point of his segmented hand farthest away from the start and end points of the trajectory is used as the most probable object location. Points nearer to him are assumed to be less likely then points far away. Points behind the start of the trajectory are completely rejected. Fig. 5 (c) shows an example where points with a high probability for the object location are darker then points with a low probability.

The region from the masked image $I^{(1)}$ whose center of mass has the highest probability according to the trajectory analysis and is big enough compared to the biggest regions of this image is used as the region which contains the object to learn. On this region the attribute modules are triggered to calculate the attributes of the new object. During this the attribute modules can request further information from the user by asking questions. E.g. the region attribute module may ask if the regions of objects of this type have always the colors red, yellow, and green (if the user meant a special incarnation of an object), or if the colors can vary (perhaps if the object "pencil case" denotes a more general object). After the control module receives the attributes, it stores the new view of the object, consisting of the attributes and a judgement about their relevance for the object, in the database.

Fig. 5. Learning a new object: (a) Original image. (b) Object segmentation based only on a smoothed difference image. (c) Attention map calculated from the hand trajectory and the segmented hand region.

Fig. 6. Three scenes from the two experiments. (a) and (b) show all used objects in different positions. (c) is an example for a successful gesture evaluation in this scenario.

5   Results

The region tracking is done on a DEC Personal Workstation 433au (SPECInt95 13.9) at a frame rate of 20 Hz using an image size of 189x139 pixel. The remaining system is running on a COMPAQ Professional Workstation XP1000 (SPECInt95 37.5) and uses an image size of 378x278 pixel. Searching the complete database consisting of five objects with thirteen views took 1600 ms. 750 ms were needed for the mean shift region segmentation. The histogram intersection needed 540 ms. About 260 ms took the subgraph matching. This was quite fast as the different views of the objects had only zero to four regions. Learning a new view of an object took about 330 ms. Fig. 6 shows three example scenes with the five objects used during the experiments.

The complete system was tested with two initial experiments with in total 131 queries, both utilising the scene shown exemplarily in Fig. 6. The first one started with an empty database. The system was queried for the five objects, e.g. with 'Take the disk box.'. As the object to search was known an object localisation task had to be performed. If the system could not find an object or made a mistake a new view for the object was learned. If an error of the speech recogniser occurred the query was repeated. Table 1 shows the results. As the database was initially empty, the first query for every objects failed. The cup and the milk box could be recognised without any further errors. The three other objects had very promising result, too. The selection of the correct learning region was always correct, hence it is not specified further in the table.

The second experiment started with the database build in the first experiment. Here the query 'Take the item.' was placed in combination with a pointing gesture on an object. Fig. 6 (c) shows an example for an analysed gesture. As this is a query with

Table 1. Experimental results. Experiment 1 started with an empty database, so errors for every object had to occur as initially the system did know nothing about the intended object. In Experiment 2 the database from Experiment 1 was used.

	Experiment 1					Experiment 2			
	recognised /total	no obj. found	wrong object	speech error	num views	recognised /total	gesture error	wrong object	speech error
Disk Box	15/18	1	1	1	2	5/9	1	2	1
Pencil Case	14/17	3	-	-	3	6/9	2	-	1
Magic Cube	11/18	4	2	1	6	6/9	2	-	1
Cup	16/17	1	-	-	1	7/9	1	-	1
Milk Box	16/17	1	-	-	1	8/8	-	-	-
sum	72/87	10	3	2	13	32/44	6	2	4

an unspecified object, the complete database had to be searched in an area around the pointing gesture. Thus instead of an object localisation task an object identification and gesture evaluation task was performed. The results are shown in Table 1.

6 Conclusion

A system for learning and retrieving unknown objects was presented. To enhance the learning capabilities multiple modalities are used. The user can talk to the system, his hand movements are analysed based on an image from a video camera and visual object attributes are calculated from this image. Histogram intersection and subgraph matching on segmented color regions are currently used as attributes.

Although the system works quite well in many cases, various things still remain to be done. E.g. for an improved handling of objects more attributes would be useful, especially a texture attribute is missing. If more objects and views come into the database the performance of the system drops significantly as the database is searched in a linear fashion. A clustering of the database could help to speed up the search process.

References

BFWS99.   H. Brandt-Pook, G. A. Fink, S. Wachsmuth, and G. Sagerer. Integrated recognition and interpretation of speech for a construction task domain. In H.-J. Bullinger and J. Ziegler, editors, *Proc. 8th Int. Conf. on Human-Computer Interaction*, volume 1, pages 550–554, München, 1999.

CIE86.   CIE. CIE colorimetry specifications. No. 15.2, Central Bureau of the CIE, Vienna, Austria, 1986.

CM97.   D. Comaniciu and P. Meer. Robust analysis of feature space: Color image segmentation. In *Proc. IEEE Conf. on Computer Vision and Pattern Recognition*, pages 750–755, Puerto Rico, 1997.

Fin99.   G. A. Fink. Developing HMM-based recognizers with ESMERALDA. In V. Matoušek, P. Mautner, J. Ocelíková, and P. Sojka, editors, *Lecture Notes in Artificial Intelligence*, volume 1692, pages 229–234, Berlin Heidelberg, 1999. Springer.

FLWS00.   J. Fritsch, F. Lömker, M. Wienecke, and G. Sagerer. Detecting assembly actions by scene observation. In *Proc. Int. Conf. on Image Processing*, volume I, pages 212–215, Vancouver, CA, 2000. IEEE.

MB98.   B. T. Messmer and H. Bunke. A new algorithm for error-tolerant subgraph isomorphism detection. *IEEE Trans. PAMI*, 20:493–505, 1998.

Roy99.   D. K. Roy. *Learning Words from Sights and Sounds: A Computational Model*. PhD thesis, Massachusetts Institute of Technology, 1999.

SB91.   M. J. Swain and D. H. Ballard. Color indexing. *International Journal of Computer Vision*, 7(1):11–32, 1991.

SK01.   L. Steels and F. Kaplan. Aibo's first words : The social learning of language and meaning. *Evolution of Communication*, 4(1), 2001.

VM97.   V. V. Vinod and H. Murase. Focused color intersection with efficient searching for object extraction. *Pattern Recognition*, 30(10):1787–1797, 1997.

WFS98.   S. Wachsmuth, G. A. Fink, and G. Sagerer. Integration of parsing and incremental speech recognition. In *Proc. of the European Signal Processing Conf.*, volume 1, pages 371–375, Rhodes, September 1998.

Maximum Entropy and Gaussian Models
for Image Object Recognition

Daniel Keysers, Franz Josef Och, and Hermann Ney

Lehrstuhl für Informatik VI, Computer Science Department,
RWTH Aachen – University of Technology, D-52056 Aachen, Germany,
{keysers,och,ney}@informatik.rwth-aachen.de

Abstract. The principle of maximum entropy is a powerful framework
that can be used to estimate class posterior probabilities for pattern
recognition tasks. In this paper, we show how this principle is related
to the discriminative training of Gaussian mixture densities using the
maximum mutual information criterion. This leads to a relaxation of the
constraints on the covariance matrices to be positive (semi-) definite.
Thus, we arrive at a conceptually simple model that allows to estimate
a large number of free parameters reliably. We compare the proposed
method with other state-of-the-art approaches in experiments with the
well known US Postal Service handwritten digits recognition task.

1 Introduction

The maximum entropy framework is based on principles applied in the natural
sciences. It has been applied to the estimation of probability distributions [6]
and to classification tasks such as natural language processing [1] and text classification [8].

The contributions of this paper are

- to show the relation between maximum entropy and Gaussian models,
- to present a framework that allows to estimate a large number of parameters
  reliably, e.g. the entries of full class specific covariance matrices, and
- to show the applicability of the maximum entropy framework to image object
  recognition.

2 Gaussian Models for Classification

To classify an observation $x \in \mathbb{R}^D$, we use the Bayesian decision rule

$$x \quad \longmapsto \quad r(x) = \operatorname*{argmax}_{k} \left\{ p(k|x) \right\}$$

$$= \operatorname*{argmax}_{k} \left\{ p(k) \cdot p(x|k) \right\}.$$

Here, $p(k|x)$ is the class posterior probability of class $k \in \{1, \dots, K\}$ given the
observation x, $p(k)$ is the a priori probability, $p(x|k)$ is the class conditional

L. Van Gool (Ed.): DAGM 2002, LNCS 2449, pp. 498–506, 2002.

probability for the observation x given class k and $r(x)$ is the decision of the classifier. This decision rule is known to be optimal with respect to the number of decision errors, if the correct distributions are known. This is generally not the case in practical situations, which means that we need to choose appropriate models for the distributions. In the training phase, the parameters of the distribution are estimated from a set of training data $\{(x_n, k_n)\}$, $n = 1, \ldots, N$, $k_n \in 1, \ldots, K$. If we denote by Λ the set of free parameters of the distribution, the maximum likelihood approach consists in choosing the parameters $\hat{\Lambda}$ maximizing the log-likelihood on the training data:

$$\hat{\Lambda} = \operatorname*{argmax}_{\Lambda} \sum_n \log p_\Lambda(x_n|k_n) \tag{1}$$

Alternatively, we can maximize the log-probability of the class posteriors,

$$\hat{\Lambda} = \operatorname*{argmax}_{\Lambda} \sum_n \log p_\Lambda(k_n|x_n) \, , \tag{2}$$

which is also called discriminative training, since the information of out-of-class data is used. This criterion is often referred to as mutual information criterion in speech recognition, information theory and image object recognition [3,9].

We will regard Gaussian models for the class conditional distributions:

$$
\begin{aligned}
p(x|k) &= \mathcal{N}(x|\mu_k, \Sigma_k) \\
&= \det(2\pi\Sigma_k)^{-\frac{1}{2}} \cdot \exp\left[-\tfrac{1}{2}(x - \mu_k)^T \Sigma_k^{-1}(x - \mu_k)\right]
\end{aligned} \tag{3}
$$

The free parameters of these models are the class means μ_k and the class specific covariance matrices Σ_k. The conventional method for estimating these parameters is to maximize the log-likelihood (1) on the training data, which yields the empirical mean and the empirical covariance matrix as solutions. Problems with this approach arise if the feature dimensionality is large with respect to the number of training samples. This is common e.g. in appearance based image object recognition tasks, where each pixel value is considered a feature. The problems are that the large number of $K \cdot D \cdot (D + 1)/2$ parameters of the covariance matrices often cannot be estimated reliably using the usually small amount of training data available. Common methods for coping with this problem are to constrain the covariance matrices, e.g. to use diagonal covariance matrices, or to use pooling, i.e. to estimate only one covariance matrix Σ instead of K matrices.

3   Maximum Entropy Modeling

The principle of maximum entropy has origins in statistical thermodynamics, is related to information theory and has been applied to pattern recognition tasks such as language modeling and text classification. Applied to classification, the basic idea is the following: We are given information about a probability distribution by samples from that distribution (training data). Now, we choose the distribution such that it fulfills all the constraints given by that information, but otherwise has the highest possible entropy. (This inherently serves as regularization to avoid overfitting.) It can be shown that this approach leads to so-called log-linear models for the distribution to be estimated.

Consider a set of so-called feature functions $\{f_i\}, i = 1, \ldots, I$ that are supposed to compute 'useful' information for classification:

$$f_i \quad : \quad \mathbb{R}^D \times \{1, \ldots, K\} \longrightarrow \mathbb{R} \quad : \quad (x, k) \longmapsto f_i(x, k)$$

From the information in the training set, we can compute the numbers

$$F_i := \sum_n f_i(x_n, k_n) \ .$$

Now, the maximum entropy principle consists in maximizing

$$\max_{p(k|x)} \left\{ - \sum_n \sum_k p(k|x_n) \log p(k|x_n) \right\}$$

over all possible distributions with the requirements:

- normalization constraint for each observation x:

$$\sum_k p(k|x) = 1$$

- feature constraint for each feature i:

$$\sum_n \sum_k p(k|x_n) f_i(x_n, k) = F_i$$

It can be shown that the resulting distribution has the following log-linear or exponential functional form:

$$p_\Lambda(k|x) = \frac{\exp\left[\sum_i \lambda_i f_i(x, k)\right]}{\sum_{k'} \exp\left[\sum_i \lambda_i f_i(x, k')\right]}, \quad \Lambda = \{\lambda_i\}. \tag{4}$$

Interestingly, it can also be shown that the stated optimization problem is convex and has a unique global maximum. Furthermore, this unique solution is also the solution to the following dual problem: Maximize the log probability (2) on the training data using the model (4). In this formulation of the problem, it is easier to see that there exists exactly one maximum, because (2) is a sum of convex functions and therefore also convex. A second desirable property of the discussed model is that effective algorithms are known that compute the global maximum of the log probability (2) given a training set. These algorithms fall into two categories: On the one hand, we have an algorithm known as generalized iterative scaling [4] and related algorithms that can be proven to converge to the global maximum. On the other hand, due to the convex nature of the criterion (2), we can also use general optimization strategies as e.g. conjugate gradient methods [10, pp. 420ff.]. The crucial problem in maximum entropy modeling is the choice of the appropriate feature functions $\{f_i\}$.

4   Maximum Entropy and Discriminative Training for Gaussian Models

Consider first-order feature functions for maximum entropy classification

$$f_{k,i}(x, k') = \delta(k, k')\, x_i \,,$$
$$f_k(x, k') = \delta(k, k') \,,$$

where $\delta(k, k') := 1$ if $k = k'$, and 0 otherwise denotes the Kronecker delta function. In the context of image recognition, we may call the functions $f_{k,i}$ appearance based image features, as they represent the image pixel values. The duplication of the features for each class is necessary to distinguish the hypothesized classes. The functions f_k allow for a log-linear offset in the posterior probabilities. Now, using the properties of the Kronecker delta, the structure of the posterior probabilities becomes

$$
\begin{aligned}
p_\Lambda(k|x) &= \frac{\exp\left[\alpha_k + \sum \lambda_{k,i} x_i\right]}{\sum_{k'} \exp\left[\alpha_{k'} + \sum \lambda_{k',i} x_i\right]} \\
&= \frac{\exp\left[\alpha_k + \lambda_k^T x\right]}{\sum_{k'} \exp\left[\alpha_{k'} + \lambda_{k'}^T x\right]} \qquad \Lambda = \{\lambda_{k,i}, \alpha_k\} \,,
\end{aligned}
\tag{5}
$$

where α_k denotes the coefficient for the feature function f_k.

Now, consider a Gaussian model (3) for $p(x|k)$ with pooled covariance matrix $\Sigma_k = \Sigma$. Using Bayes' rule, and the relation

$$
\begin{aligned}
\log \mathcal{N}(x|\mu_k, \Sigma_k) &= -\tfrac{1}{2}\log\det(2\pi\Sigma_k) - \tfrac{1}{2}(x - \mu_k)^T \Sigma_k^{-1}(x - \mu_k) \\
&= -\tfrac{1}{2}\log\det(2\pi\Sigma_k) - \tfrac{1}{2}x^T \Sigma_k^{-1} x + \mu_k^T \Sigma_k^{-1} x - \tfrac{1}{2}\mu_k^T \Sigma_k^{-1}\mu_k \,,
\end{aligned}
$$

we can rewrite the class posterior probability (note that the terms that do not depend on the class k cancel in the fraction):

$$
\begin{aligned}
p(k|x) &= \frac{p(k)\, \mathcal{N}(x|\mu_k, \Sigma)}{\sum_{k'} p(k')\, \mathcal{N}(x|\mu_{k'} \Sigma)} \\
&= \frac{\exp\left[(\log p(k) - \tfrac{1}{2}\mu_k^T \Sigma^{-1}\mu_k) + (\mu_k^T \Sigma^{-1})x\right]}{\sum_{k'} \exp\left[(\log p(k') - \tfrac{1}{2}\mu_{k'}^T \Sigma^{-1}\mu_{k'}) + (\mu_{k'}^T \Sigma^{-1})x\right]} \\
&= \frac{\exp\left[\alpha_k + \lambda_k^T x\right]}{\sum_{k'} \exp\left[\alpha_{k'} + \lambda_{k'}^T x\right]}
\end{aligned}
\tag{6}
$$

As result, we see that for unknown class priors $p(k)$ the resulting model (6) is identical to the maximum entropy model (5). We can conclude that the discriminative training criterion (2) for the Gaussian model (3) with pooled covariance matrices results in exactly the same functional form as the maximum entropy model for first-order features. This allows to use the well understood algorithms for maximum entropy estimation to estimate the parameters of a Gaussian model discriminatively.

If we repeat the same argument as above for the case of Gaussian densities without pooling of the covariance matrices, we find that we can again establish a correspondence to a maximum entropy model:

$$p(k|x) = \frac{p(k)\,\mathcal{N}(x|\mu_k, \Sigma_k)}{\sum_{k'} p(k')\,\mathcal{N}(x|\mu_{k'}\Sigma_k)}$$

$$= \frac{\exp\left[\alpha_k + \lambda_k^T x + x^T S_k x\right]}{\sum_{k'} \exp\left[\alpha_{k'} + \lambda_{k'}^T x + x^T S_{k'} x\right]}$$

Here, the square matrix S_k corresponds to the negative of the inverse of the covariance matrix Σ_k. These parameters can be estimated using a maximum entropy model with the second-order feature functions

$$f_{k,i,j}(x,k') = \delta(k,k')\,x_i x_j\,, \quad i \geq j\,,$$
$$f_{k,i}(x,k') = \delta(k,k')\,x_i\,,$$
$$f_k(x,k') = \delta(k,k')\,.$$

One interesting consequence of using the corresponding maximum entropy model and estimation is that we implicitly relax the constraints on the covariance matrices to be positive (semi-) definite. Therefore, the resulting model is not exactly equivalent to a Gaussian model.

This result is in contrast to the approach taken in [5], where the authors derive discriminative models for Gaussian densities based on priors of the parameters and the minimum relative entropy principle. Their solution results in discriminatively trained weights for the training data and therefore preserves the mentioned constraints.

5   Experiments and Results

We performed experiments on the well known US Postal Service handwritten digit recognition task (USPS). It contains normalized greyscale images of handwritten digits taken from US zip codes of size 16×16 pixels. The corpus is divided into a training set of 7,291 images and a test set of 2,007 images. Reported recognition error rates for this database are summarized in Table 1.

In most of the experiments performed we obtained better results using 'feature normalization'. This means that we enforced for each observation during training and testing that the sum of all feature values is equal to one by scaling the feature values appropriately. Thus, we obtain new feature functions $\{\tilde{f}_i\}$:

$$\forall x, k, i:\ \tilde{f}_i(x,k) = \left(\sum_{i'} f_{i'}(x,k)\right)^{-1}\cdot f_i(x,k)$$

In the following, we only report result obtained using feature normalization. The parameters were trained using generalized iterative scaling [4].

Table 2 shows the main results obtained in comparison to other approaches along with the number of free parameters of the respective models. The error

Table 1. Summary of results for the USPS corpus (error rates, [%]). *: training set extended with 2,400 machine-printed digits

method		ER[%]
human performance	[SIMARD et al. 1993] [14]	2.5
relevance vector machine	[TIPPING et al. 2000] [15]	5.1
neural net (LeNet1)	[LeCun et al. 1990] [13]	4.2
support vectors	[SCHÖLKOPF 1997] [11]	4.0
invariant support vectors	[SCHÖLKOPF et al. 1998] [12]	3.0
neural net + boosting	[DRUCKER et al. 1993] [13]	*2.6
tangent distance	[SIMARD et al. 1993] [14]	*2.5
nearest neighbor classifier	[7]	5.6
mixture densities	[2] baseline	7.2
	+ LDA + virtual data	3.4
kernel densities	[7] baseline	5.5
	+ tangent vectors + virtual data	2.4

Table 2. Overview of the results obtained on the USPS corpus using maximum entropy modeling in comparison to other models (error rates, [%]). ML: maximum likelihood, MMI: maximum mutual information, *: with pooled diagonal covariance matrix.

model	training criterion	# parameters	ER[%]
Gaussian model*	ML	2 816	18.6
	Σ: MMI, μ_k: ML	2 816	14.2
maximum entropy, first-order features	MMI	2 570	8.2
second-order features	MMI	331 530	5.7
nearest neighbor classifier		1 866 496	5.6

rates show that we can already gain recognition accuracy by using the maximum entropy framework to only estimate the pooled covariance matrix of a Gaussian model, while fixing the mean vectors to their maximum likelihood values. Taking into account the class information in training using the maximum entropy framework increases the recognition accuracy for first-order features from 18.6% to 8.2% error rate using less parameters.

Furthermore, it can be observed that the maximum entropy models perform better for second-order features than for first-order features. This is in contrast to the experience gained with maximum likelihood estimation of Gaussian densities, where best results were obtained using pooled diagonal covariance matrices [2]. Note for example that the maximum likelihood estimation of class specific diagonal covariance matrices already imposes problems for the USPS data, because in some of the classes some of the dimensions have zero variance in the training data. This can be overcome e.g. by using interpolation with the identity matrix, but the maximum entropy framework offers an effective way to overcome these problems.

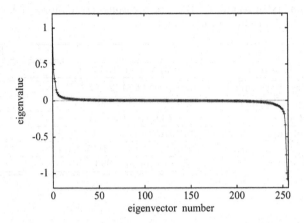

Fig. 1. Eigenvalue distribution for the 'covariance matrix' of the class '5', estimated using the maximum entropy approach.

Using the equivalent of a full class specific covariance matrix, i.e. second-order features, the error rate of a 'pseudo Gaussian' model with 5.7% error rate approaches that of a nearest neighbor classifier, which has more than five times as many parameters.

Fig. 1 shows the eigenvalues of the 'covariance matrix' of this 'pseudo Gaussian' model for the class '5' ordered by size. It can be observed that about half of the eigenvalues are positive, while the other half is negative. The distribution of the negative eigenvalues seems to match the distribution of the positive eigenvalues. We can conclude that besides the typical important eigenvectors with large positive eigenvalues there are also important eigenvectors with large negative eigenvalues in this discriminative context. This means that the relaxation of the constraint on the covariance matrix to be positive (semi-) definite leads to discriminative models that are not Gaussian any more.

6   Conclusion

We presented the connection between the following classification models: (a) discriminative training using the maximum mutual information criterion of Gaussian models for the class conditional probability and (b) models for the class posterior probability based on the principle of maximum entropy. We showed that these models lead to identical functional forms for the correct choice of feature functions for the maximum entropy model. One of the main differences is that the maximum entropy model implicitly relaxes the constraint on the co-variance matrices to be positive (semi-) definite. This leads to a conceptually simpler model with well understood estimation algorithms. A further advantage of the maximum entropy approach is that it is easily possible to include new feature functions into the classifier.

We evaluated the approach for image object recognition using the US Postal Service handwritten digits recognition task, obtaining significant improvements with respect to maximum likelihood based training. The best result of 5.7% error rate using second-order features is competitive with other results reported on this dataset, although approaches with significantly better performance exist. (Note that the latter are highly tuned to the specific task at hand while the maximum entropy approach is of very general nature.) The accuracy of the resulting model shows that the maximum entropy approach allows robust estimation of the equivalent of full covariance matrices even on this small training set, which may be a problem for approaches based on maximum likelihood.

References

1. A.L. Berger, S.A. Della Pietra, V.J. Della Pietra: A Maximum Entropy Approach to Natural Language Processing. *Computational Linguistics*, 22(1):39–72, March 1996.
2. J. Dahmen, D. Keysers, H. Ney, M.O. Güld: Statistical Image Object Recognition using Mixture Densities. *J. Mathematical Imaging and Vision*, 14(3):285–296, May 2001.
3. J. Dahmen, R. Schlüter, H. Ney: Discriminative Training of Gaussian Mixture Densities for Image Object Recognition. In *21. DAGM Symposium Mustererkennung*, Bonn, Germany, pp. 205–212, September 1999.
4. J.N. Darroch, D. Ratcliff: Generalized Iterative Scaling for Log-Linear Models. *Annals of Mathematical Statistics*, 43(5):1470–1480, 1972.
5. T. Jaakkola, M. Meila, T. Jebara: Maximum Entropy Discrimination. In *Advances in Neural Information Processing Systems 12*, MIT Press, Cambridge, MA, pp. 470–476, 2000.
6. E.T. Jaynes: On the Rationale of Maximum Entropy Models. *Proc. of the IEEE*, 70(9):939–952, September 1982.
7. D. Keysers, J. Dahmen, T. Theiner, H. Ney: Experiments with an Extended Tangent Distance. In *Proc. 15th IEEE Int. Conf. on Pattern Recognition*, volume 2, Barcelona, Spain, pp. 38–42, September 2000.
8. K. Nigam, J. Lafferty, A. McCallum: Using Maximum Entropy for Text Classification. In *IJCAI-99 Workshop on Machine Learning for Information Filtering*, Stockholm, Sweden, pp. 61–67, August 1999.
9. Y. Normandin: Maximum Mutual Information Estimation of Hidden Markov Models. In C.H. Lee, F.K. Soong, K.K. Paliwal (Eds.): *Automatic Speech and Speaker Recognition*, Kluwer Academic Publishers, Norwell, MA, pp. 57–81, 1996.
10. W.H. Press, S.A. Teukolsky, W.T. Vetterling, B.P. Flannery: *Numerical Recipes in C*. Cambridge University Press, Cambridge, second edition, 1992.
11. B. Schölkopf: *Support Vector Learning*. Oldenbourg Verlag, Munich, 1997.
12. B. Schölkopf, P. Simard, A. Smola, V. Vapnik: Prior Knowledge in Support Vector Kernels. In *Advances in Neural Information Processing Systems 10*. MIT Press, pp. 640–646, 1998.
13. P. Simard, Y. Le Cun, J. Denker, B. Victorri: Transformation Invariance in Pattern Recognition — Tangent Distance and Tangent Propagation. In G. Orr, K.R. Müller (Eds.): *Neural Networks: Tricks of the Trade*, volume 1524 of *Lecture Notes in Computer Science*, Springer, Heidelberg, pp. 239–274, 1998.

14. P. Simard, Y. Le Cun, J. Denker: Efficient Pattern Recognition Using a New Transformation Distance. In *Advances in Neural Information Processing Systems 5*, Morgan Kaufmann, San Mateo, CA, pp. 50–58, 1993.
15. M.E. Tipping: The Relevance Vector Machine. In *Advances in Neural Information Processing Systems 12*. MIT Press, pp. 332–388, 2000.

Evaluation of Confidence Measures for On-Line Handwriting Recognition

Anja Brakensiek[1], Andreas Kosmala[1], and Gerhard Rigoll[2]

[1] Dept. of Computer Science, Faculty of Electrical Engineering,
Gerhard-Mercator-University Duisburg, D-47057 Duisburg,
{anja,kosmala}@fb9-ti.uni-duisburg.de
[2] Inst. for Human-Machine Communication,
Technical University of Munich, D-80290 Munich, rigoll@ei.tum.de

Abstract. In this paper a writer-independent on-line handwriting recognition system is described comparing the effectiveness of several confidence measures. Our recognition system for single German words is based on Hidden Markov Models (HMMs) using a dictionary. We compare the ratio of rejected words to misrecognized words using four different confidence measures: One depends on the frame-normalized likelihood, the second on a garbage model, the third on a two-best list and the fourth on an unconstrained character recognition. The rating of recognition results is necessary for an unsupervised retraining or adaptation of recognition systems as well as for a user friendly human-computer interaction avoiding excessive call backs.

1 Introduction

Automatic recognition systems for unconstrained on-line handwritten words become more and more important, especially with respect to the use of pen based computers or electronic address books (PDA, compare also [6, 7]). In this field of research, HMM-based techniques (for a detailed introduction see [8]), which are well known in speech recognition, have been established because of their segmentation-free recognition approach and their automatic training capabilities.

Although the performance of recognition systems increases, the error rate of writer independent recognizers is still quite high. By computing confidence measures for recognition, a reliability assessment of the results becomes feasible. Thus, using these measures it is possible to decide whether the recognition result is uncertain or not. The goal is to reject most of the misrecognized words and as few as possible of the correct results. This problem seems to be easy, regarding the recognition of single characters (or pre-segmented words) using e.g. neural networks or distance measures (e.g. KNN-classifier) to prototypes. In general these techniques automatically compute a kind of posterior probability which can be used as a confidence measure. In contrast to this the HMM-based technique yields a likelihood, which has to be transformed resp. normalized, as it is described in Section 3. Here, just that word of a dictionary, which is the

L. Van Gool (Ed.): DAGM 2002, LNCS 2449, pp. 507–514, 2002.
© Springer-Verlag Berlin Heidelberg 2002

most probable, is selected. And this probability cannot be regarded offhand for confidence.

A rating of correctness of a result is helpful in several applications for speech and handwriting recognition systems. The (re-) training of a system can be done in an unsupervised mode using automatically generated labels with a high confidence score. So the large amount of training data does not need to be labeled manually. The same applies to an unsupervised adaptation to a certain writer or speaker (compare [1, 10]). Another application is the detection of out-of-vocabulary (OOV) words (see [11]) or a more user friendly dialog between humans and automatic recognition systems (e.g. call backs in information systems).

In the following sections our baseline recognition system (Sec. 2), the theory (Sec. 3) and some results (Sec. 4) which are obtained by four investigated confidence measures are described.

2   System Architecture

Our handwriting recognition system (compare also [1]) consists of about 90 different linear HMMs, one for each character (upper- and lower-case letters, numbers and punctuation marks). In general the continuous density HMMs consist of 12 states (with up to 15 Gaussian mixtures per state depending on the amount of training data per HMM) for characters and numbers and fewer states for some special characters depending on their width. The presented results refer to a single word recognition rate using a dictionary of about 2200 German words (no out of vocabulary).

For our experiments we use a large on-line handwriting database of several writers (compare Fig.1), which is described in the following. The database consists of cursive script samples of 166 different writers, all writing several words or sentences on a digitizing surface. The training of the writer independent system is performed using about 24400 words of 145 writers. Testing is carried out with 2071 words of 21 different writers (about 100 words per writer).

After the resampling of the pen trajectory in order to compensate different writing speeds the script samples are normalized. Normalization of the input-

Fig. 1. Some examples of the handwritten database (7 different writers)

data implies the correction of slant and height. Slant normalization is performed by shearing the pen trajectory according to an entropy-criterion (see also [2]).

Then the following features are derived from the trajectory of the pen input:

- the angle of the spatially resampled strokes ($\sin \alpha$, $\cos \alpha$)
- the difference angles ($\sin \Delta\alpha$, $\cos \Delta\alpha$)
- the pen pressure (binary)
- a sub-sampled bitmap slid along the pen trajectory (9-dimensional vector), containing the current image information in a 30×30 window

The baseline system and the feature extraction method is described in [1] in greater detail. To train the HMMs we use the Baum-Welch algorithm, whereas for recognition the Viterbi algorithm is used always presenting these 14-dimensional feature vectors $\underline{x}$ in one single stream.

The recognition problem using HMMs can be described by the following Eq. 1 using Bayes' rule (with X is the sequence of feature vectors and W represents the class resp. word):

$$P(W|X) = \frac{P(X|W) \cdot P(W)}{P(X)} \tag{1}$$

Here $P(W|X)$ is the posterior probability, $P(X|W)$ represents the feature model (the likelihood, which is computed by the HMM), $P(W)$ describes the a priori probability of the word W (e.g. grammar or language model) and $P(X)$ represents the a priori probability of the feature vectors. The recognition of a single word W^*, which is defined in a dictionary (the same a priori probability for each entry) , leads to this equation

$$W^* \approx \underset{W}{\operatorname{argmax}}\ P(X|W) \cdot P(W) \approx \underset{W}{\operatorname{argmax}}\ P(X|W) \tag{2}$$

because $P(X)$ and $P(W)$ are the same for all classes W ($P(X)$ is independent of W and $P(W)$ is nonrelevant per definition). Disregarding these probabilities the relative order of the best recognition results will not change. Thus for recognition only, this simplification is permitted. However, the probability $P(X)$ is important to compute the probability of correctness – the confidence – of the recognition result (see Sec. 3).

3   Confidence Measures

The likelihood $P(X|W)$, which is used for recognition according to Eq. 2 is not an absolute measure of probability, but rather a relative measure. Thus, we just know which word of a given closed dictionary is the most likely, but we do not know the certainty of correctness of this recognition result. This certainty is described by confidence measures. If the confidence measure $Conf$ of a recognition result is below a threshold τ, this data image resp. test-word is rejected. The consequence of that is a manual labeling or a call back in a human-machine interface, for example.

For our handwriting recognition problem of single words (no OOV) we compare four different confidence measures:

1. the frame normalized likelihood $P(X|W)$ (as a reference)
2. the posterior probability $P(W|X)$ by approximating $P(X)$ using a garbage-model W_{garb}
3. the posterior probability $P(W|X)$ by approximating $P(X)$ using a two-best recognition
4. the likelihood $P(X|W)$, which is normalized by the likelihood $P(X|C)$ obtained by a character decoding without dictionary

As first investigated measure, the likelihood $P(X|W)$, which is normalized by the number of frames (resp. corresponding feature vectors) is used as confidence measure (see e.g. [3]). Here the computational costs are very low, because this measure exists in any case. Because of the dynamic of the HMM-based decoding procedure, in general these measures are computed as log likelihoods. The higher the normalized likelihood, the higher the reliability.

The following confidence measures take Eq. 1 into account. The posterior probability $P(W|X)$ will be an optimal confidence measure, if it was possible to estimate $P(X)$:

$$Conf := \frac{P(X|W)}{P(X)} \qquad Conf \begin{cases} < \tau \to reject & (N_r) \\ \geq \tau \to classify & (N_c + N_e) \end{cases} \qquad (3)$$

Thus, the second confidence measure, we tested, is based on a garbage- or filler-model (compare [9, 4]). The garbage-model W_{garb} is trained on all features of the training-set (independent of the character-label), which leads to an unspecific average model. Often, such a garbage-model is used for OOV detection in speech recognition. The confidence measure can be calculated using the garbage-model as an approximation of $P(X)$:

$$P(X) \approx P(X|W_{garb}) \qquad (4)$$

If this ratio of word and garbage dependent likelihood is large, the correctness is more likely. To determine $P(X|W_{garb})$ the decoding procedure has to be expanded, as it is shown in Fig. 2.

The third evaluated confidence measure depends on a two-best recognition according to Eq. 5 (see also [3, 4]):

$$P(X) \approx \sum_{k=1}^{N} P(X|W_k) \cdot P(W_k) \quad \Rightarrow \quad P(X) \approx P(X|W_{1st}) + P(X|W_{2nd}) \quad (5)$$

This measure contains the difference of the log likelihoods between the best and the second best hypothesis for the same sequence of feature vectors. The approximation in Eq. 5 is valid under the assumption, that the likelihoods of the best and second best class are much higher than those of the other $(N-2)$ classes of the dictionary. Transforming this equation because of the dynamic range of

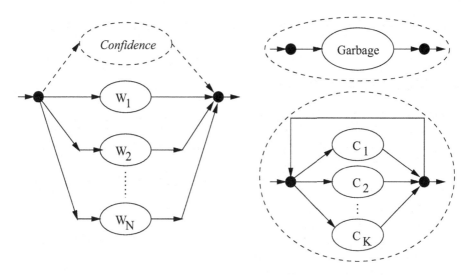

Fig. 2. Decoding configuration to obtain confidence measures: for recognition using a dictionary with the classes W a further path to compute the confidence (garbage model or recognition of characters c) can be added

the values, the new confidence measure $Conf^* = \frac{Conf}{1-Conf}$ can be defined as follows:

$$Conf = \frac{P(X|W_{1st})}{P(X|W_{1st}) + P(X|W_{2nd})} \quad \Rightarrow \quad Conf^* = \frac{P(X|W_{1st})}{P(X|W_{2nd})} \quad (6)$$

Again, for rejection the rule of Eq. 3 is applied (only the domain of τ has been changed).

The fourth method to obtain confidence measures is based on a character decoding without dictionary (compare e.g. [11, 5]), as it is shown in Fig. 2. The character-based likelihood $P(X|C)$ is used for normalization:

$$P(X|C) = P(X|c_1, ...c_k) = \prod P(X_{f_i}|c_i) \quad \Rightarrow \quad Conf := \frac{P(X|W)}{P(X|C)} \quad (7)$$

A recognition without vocabulary leads to an arbitrary sequence of characters $c_i : 1 \le i \le K$ (K is the number of different character HMMs) which is the most likely without respect to the lexicon. In general $P(X|C)$ will be greater (or equal) than $P(X|W)$.

Additionally to this character-based likelihood, also the character-sequence itself can be regarded by calculating the Levenshtein-distance between W and C. The Levenshtein-distance describes how many changes are necessary to transform one string into the other.

These confidence measures differ significantly regarding the computational costs, the effectiveness and the application. In the literature, there are described much more confidence measures especially for continuous speech recognition.

But often, they take the grammar $P(W)$ of a sentence into account, which is not possible for single word recognition (such as in our experiments).

4   Experimental Results

In the presented experiments we examine the influence of four different confidence measures for on-line handwriting recognition of single words (no OOV).

The recognition results, which are shown in Fig. 3, are determined using an increasing threshold τ (which differs using different confidence measures). Using the baseline system without rejection (N_r =0, r =0%) a word recognition rate of 87.0% (N_c =1801 words are recognized correctly) is achieved testing the entire test-set of N_a= 2071 words. For testing of confidence measures always the ratio of error rate e and rejection rate r is calculated using the following definition (N_r is the number of rejected examples, N_e is the number of errors within the not rejected set). The term f denotes the quota of false classified examples, which are not rejected.

$$r = \frac{N_r}{N_a} \ , \quad e = \frac{N_e}{N_a} \ , \quad f = \frac{N_e}{N_a - N_r} \qquad \text{with:} \quad N_r + N_e + N_c = N_a \quad (8)$$

As can be seen in Fig. 3 the frame-based likelihood (1) is the worst confidence measure. Even if 52.1% of the test words are rejected, the error rate decreases only from 13.0% to 3.3% (Tab. 1). That implies 7.0% false classified words (referring to the number of words, which are not rejected). The confidence measures

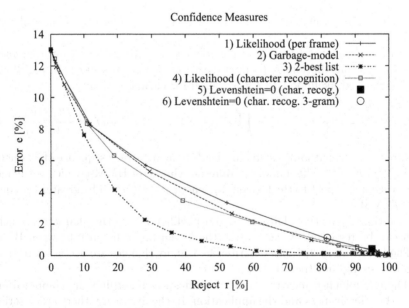

Fig. 3. Recognition results for 21 writers using different confidence measures

Table 1. Selected values of word recognition results (%) for 21 writers

confidence measure	reject word (r)	error word (e)	false classified word (f)	char	FAR word	FRR word
baseline system	0.0	13.0	13.0	6.4	100	0.0
(1) likelihood (per frame)	52.1	3.3	7.0	2.4	25.6	48.8
(3) 2-best list	44.8	0.9	1.7	0.6	7.0	37.5

based on the garbage model (2) or the character decoding (4) are only slightly more effective. The best method relies on the two-best list (3). For example, rejecting 44.8% of the data, the error is reduced by about 93% relative and the quota of false classified words decreases to 1.7% (Tab. 1: last row).

Additionally, in Fig. 3 two significant points (5,6) are marked depending on the Levenshtein-distance. For this a character recognition without dictionary is implemented (compare confidence measure (4)) and the Levenshtein-distance between the dictionary-based word recognition and the recognized character sequence is computed. In contrast to (4) and (5), in (6) this character recognition is performed using a statistical language model (backoff 3-gram) to enhance the recognition performance. (5) and (6) denote the ratio of rejected and error when the dictionary-based recognition and the character-based recognition leads to the same word-class (Levenshtein-distance=0). Regarding (6) the word error rate is not smaller than using the frame-normalized likelihood, but here most of the errors are caused by a substitution of a single character only ('wo' – 'Wo', 'der' – 'dar') depending on the lexicon.

The recognition rate is highly dependent on the underlying vocabulary. Here, not only the size of the dictionary but also the similarity between distinct entries is essential. This fact is considered by the two-best confidence measure. If the best and second-best hypothesis are quite similar (small Levenshtein-distance), because they differ only in one character, the corresponding likelihoods will be quite similar, too. Thus, such an uncertain recognition result will be rejected. Using another dictionary the ratio of rejection to error could be completely different. The other evaluated confidence measures are independent of the dictionary, and so just these errors cannot be avoided (compare confidence (5,6)).

Some results using selected confidence thresholds are described in Tab. 1 in greater detail. For comparison, the usual false acceptance rate FAR and the false rejection rate FRR are computed.

For recognition purpose with high certainty (e.g. human-computer interface without enquiry call or address recognition for postal automation as an off-line application) the confidence measure based on the two-best list will be reasonable. For a retraining of a recognition system or an unsupervised writer adaptation the other confidence measures can be sufficient, too. In this application the character error rate (see Tab. 1) is much more important than the word error rate and, in general, the amoun t of unlabeled training data is such high that the rejection rate can be disregarded. These aspects will be evaluated in the future work.

5   Summary and Conclusions

In this paper we presented the comparison of four different confidence measures for an on-line handwriting recognition system for single words, which is based on HMMs. It has been shown that a confidence measure depending on a two-best list performs significant better than those which are based on the frame-normalized likelihood, a garbage model or an unconstrained character recognition. Some extensions to this work, we want to examine in the future, are the combination of different confidence measures and the usage for unsupervised writer adaptation.

References

[1] A. Brakensiek, A. Kosmala, and G. Rigoll. Writer Adaptation for On-Line Handwriting Recognition. In *23. DAGM-Symposium, Tagungsband Springer-Verlag*, pages 32–37, Munich, Germany, Sept. 2001.

[2] A. Brakensiek, A. Kosmala, and G. Rigoll. Comparing Normalization and Adaptation Techniques for On-Line Handwriting Recognition. In *16th Int. Conference on Pattern Recognition (ICPR), to appear*, Quebec, Canada, Aug. 2002.

[3] J. Dolfing and A. Wendemuth. Combination of Confidence Measures in Isolated Word Recognition. In *5th Int. Conference on Spoken Language Processsing (IC-SLP)*, pages 3237–3240, Sydney, Australia, Dec. 1998.

[4] S. Eickeler, M. Jabs, and G. Rigoll. Comparison of Confidence Measures for Face Recognition. In *IEEE Int. Conference on Automatic Face and Gesture Recognition*, pages 257–262, Grenoble, France, Mar. 2000.

[5] T. Hazen and I. Bazzi. A Comparison and Combination of Methods for OOV Word Detection and Word Confidence Scoring. In *IEEE Int. Conference on Acoustics, Speech, and Signal Processing (ICASSP)*, Salt Lake City, Utah, May 2001.

[6] J. Hu, S. Lim, and M. Brown. HMM Based Writer Independent On-line Handwritten Character and Word Recognition. In *6th Int. Workshop on Frontiers in Handwriting Recognition (IWFHR)*, pages 143–155, Taejon, Korea, 1998.

[7] R. Plamondon and S. Srihari. On-Line and Off-Line Handwriting Recognition: A Comprehensive Survey. *IEEE Transactions on Pattern Analysis and Machine Intelligence (PAMI)*, 22(1):63–84, Jan. 2000.

[8] L. Rabiner and B. Juang. An Introduction to Hidden Markov Models. *IEEE ASSP Magazine*, pages 4–16, 1986.

[9] R. Rose and D. Paul. A Hidden Markov Model based Keyword Recognition System. In *IEEE Int. Conference on Acoustics, Speech, and Signal Processing (ICASSP)*, pages 129–132, Albuquerque, New Mexico, 1990.

[10] F. Wallhoff, D. Willett, and G. Rigoll. Frame Discriminative and Confidence-Driven Adaptation for LVCSR. In *IEEE Int. Conference on Acoustics, Speech, and Signal Processing (ICASSP)*, pages 1835–1838, Istanbul, Turkey, June 2000.

[11] S. Young. Detecting Misrecognitions and Out-Of Vocabulary Words. In *IEEE Int. Conference on Acoustics, Speech, and Signal Processing (ICASSP)*, pages 21–24, Adelaide, Australia, Apr. 1994.

ViRoom – Low Cost Synchronized Multicamera System and Its Self-calibration

Tomáš Svoboda, Hanspeter Hug, and Luc Van Gool

Computer Vision Laboratory,
Department of Information Technology and Electrical Engineering,
Swiss Federal Institute of Technology,
Gloriastrasse 35, 8092 Zürich, Switzerland,
svoboda@vision.ee.ethz.ch, http://www.vision.ee.ethz.ch/

Abstract. This paper presents a multicamera Visual Room (ViRoom). It is constructed from low-cost digital cameras and standard computers running on Linux. Software based synchronized image capture is introduced. A fully automatic self-calibration method for multiple cameras and without any known calibration object is proposed and verified by 3D reconstruction experiments. This handy calibration allows an easy reconfiguration of the setup. Aside from the computers which are usually already available, such a synchronized multicamera setup with six or seven cameras costs less than 1000 USD.

1 Introduction

With decreasing prices of powerful computers and cameras smart multicamera systems start to emerge. Some of them were developed for creating realistic 3D models or mixing real humans with artificial data, (virtualized reality [5]). In late 1990's, new kinds of multicamera setups appeared. The main goal was not so much reconstruction but action recognition and interpretation. Cameras were often combined with microphone arrays for voice recognition and/or navigation. The EasyLiving project from Microsoft Research is developing an intelligent room that will be able to unobtrusively interact with a user [1]. The AVIARY project uses cameras and a microphone array for finding moving and/or speaking person. The detected speaker is then tracked and the best camera is chosen. A limited number of basic events are recognized [12]. The monitoring of a person's activities in the Intelligent meeting room, is the second part of that project. Detected activities are annotated and stored in a database for future browsing [8]. However, as stated in the overview [9], the interpretation of the activities is only at an early stage of development. Only a small subset of the rich variety of human gestures can be recognized.

Our work is similar to the AVIARY project. However, the cameras used in most of the previous projects are expensive, with external synchronization. Such a multicamera setup requires additional hardware, is restricted to one room and is hard to reconfigure. We wanted to build an easily reconfigurable and scalable environment without unnecessary cabling. We use simple digital cameras with an

L. Van Gool (Ed.): DAGM 2002, LNCS 2449, pp. 515–522, 2002.

IEEE1394 (Firewire) interface. The current IEEE1394 standard has 400 Mbit/s bandwidth but a higher bandwidth is expected in the near future[1]. The simple cameras do not allow external synchronization. We propose a software based synchronized capture.

A multicamera system can be efficiently used even without calibration, as shown e.g. in recent multicamera tracking work [6]. Nevertheless, a calibrated system has many advantages, like for 3D human motion analysis, inserting virtual objects into video streams, or aligning of the camera system with a previously reconstructed scene.

The proposed self-calibration method utilizes state of the art methods. It is mainly based on the self-calibration scheme proposed by Pollefeys et al. [10]. It requires no calibration object. A person waves a standard laser pointer which is dimmed down by a piece of paper while captured by cameras. The positions of the laser are detected in each image with subpixel precision. As the laser is moved around and visits several points, these positions make up the projection of a virtual object (3D point cloud) with unknown 3D position. This merged image is the input of the self-calibration procedure.

2   Setup and Synchronization of Cameras

The main underlying ideas of the setup can be characterized as follows:

- Use of many simple and *cheap cameras* rather than a few complicated and expensive pan and tilt devices.
- The system should allow easy and frequent *reconfiguration*, like adding, removing or replacing cameras.
- It should *adapt* its functionality to the number of available cameras and their arrangement. A slight mobile version with few cameras is also foreseen.

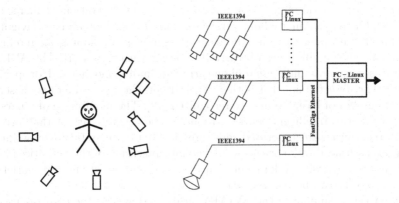

Fig. 1. Cameras may be placed relatively arbitrary, but a significant overlap of their fields of view is necessary. Cameras are connected to PCs by Firewire cables.

---

[1] http://www.1394ta.org/Technology/About/1394b.htm

– Synchronized, or at least almost synchronized, capture is essential for consistent multicamera analysis.

2.1 Camera Setup

We decided to use digital cameras with IEEE1394 (Firewire) interface and PCs running on Linux. Up to three cameras can be connected with a Linux machine and processed simultaneously. The Linux programming environment offers standards for network computing.

One overhead camera with very wide field of view gives an overview of the scene. It helps to resolve ambiguities, especially in arrangements with few cameras and many occlusions. The purchased cameras can be seen in Fig 2.

Fig. 2. Left: PYRO 1394 WebCam from ADS Technologies is a simple, cheap (around 100 USD) color digital camera. Right: SONY DFW-V500 is a more advanced digital camera with C-mount. The photo shows it with a fish-eye lens. Both cameras have a resolution of 640 × 480 pixels and allow progressive scan (non-interlaced) at 30 fps.

2.2 Software Based Synchronization

The simple cheap cameras do not allow synchronization through external triggering. More advanced digital cameras, like the one we use with the fish-eye lens, allow this however, cost approximately 15 or 20 times more. Moreover, external triggering would require additional hardware and cabling which might be acceptable for a fixed environment but would be obtrusive for a mobile version. Therefore, we propose a software based synchronization.

The *CameraD*[2] system consists of two parts. The camera server and various clients. The camera server runs on each computer that has one or more cameras attached to it. The clients can run on any machine with a network connection.

The *Camerad* server is a rather simple internet server. After startup it waits for client connections. When a connection arrives, *Camerad* stops listening for further connections in favor of servicing the one already established. As a consequence only one client can connect to any given camera server at any point in

---

[2] From CAMERA Daemon.

time. This "one client only" rule is rather unusual for internet servers but it is no particular disadvantage in our application. It simplifies the camera server in two ways. First, there is no need for the camera server to sequentialize simultaneous access to the hardware (the cameras) by multiple clients. Second, the camera server does not need to service a network connection while it accesses the hardware. Capturing is controlled by a single client. The client opens a connection to each camera server and then sends a "trigger" signal simultaneously to all servers. After receiving this signal, the servers will immediately start capturing an image. The timing accuracy depends on:

- How fast the client can send signals to multiple camera servers. With an unloaded ethernet connection the time between the signal to the first server and the signal to the last server is reasonably short ($\leq$ 1ms). However, if the network is loaded or if a different type of network is used (e.g. a dialup modem connection) this delay might be unpredictably long.
- How fast the servers can react to a received signal. This response time is dictated by the Linux scheduler. On a normal Linux system time slices are 10 ms long which means that the response time will be $(10n + m)$ [ms] where n is a non-negative integer and $0.0 \leq m \leq 10.0$. As system load goes up n will increase and the expected value for m will approach 5.0. Running the camera server with realtime priority should reduces n to zero and m close to it. (e.g. through the use of the low latency patch which is expected to become part of standard Linux). This version has not been tested yet.
- The camera drivers and hardware, these aspects are not controlled by the camera server. Currently it is assumed that the delays introduced by the camera drivers and hardware are the same on all systems involved.

Our current implementation of the *CameraD* package contains a client called "cdcap"[3] which captures synchronously images from different cameras on different computers and stores them on local disks. The implementation and the firewire library are not mature yet, hence, only up to 10 n-tuple synchronized images can be captured per second. Still, it is enough for first self-calibration, motion segmentation and tracking experiments.

3   Self-calibration

3.1   Theory

Let us consider n cameras and m object points $\mathbf{X}_j = [X_j, Y_j, Z_j, 1]^T, j = 1, \ldots, m$. We assume the pinhole camera model is valid, see [4] for details. The points $\mathbf{X}_j$ are projected to image points $\mathbf{u}_{ij}$ as

$$\lambda_{ij} \begin{bmatrix} u_{ij} \\ v_{ij} \\ 1 \end{bmatrix} = \lambda_{ij}\mathbf{u}_{ij} = P_i\mathbf{X}_j, \qquad \lambda_{ij} \in \mathbb{R}^+ \tag{1}$$

---

[3] CameraD CAPture

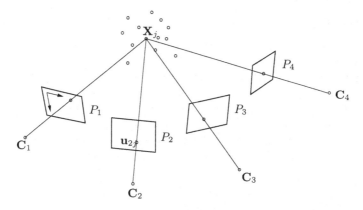

Fig. 3. Multicamera setup with 4 cameras.

where each P_i is a 3×4 matrix that contains 11 camera parameters. They depend on the six DOF that describe camera position and orientation and on the five internal parameters. The $\mathbf{u}_{ij}$ are observed pixel coordinates. The goal of the calibration is to estimate scales λ_{ij} and the camera projection matrices P_i. We can put all (1) into one matrix W_s:

$$W_s = \hat{P}\hat{X}, \tag{2}$$

where W_s is called the *scaled measurement matrix*, $\hat{P} = [P_1 \cdots P_n]^\top$ and $\hat{X} = [\mathbf{X}_1 \cdots \mathbf{X}_m]$. $\hat{P}$ and $\hat{X}$ are referred to as the *projective motion* and the *projective shape*. If we collect enough noiseless points (u_{ij}, v_{ij}) and the λ_{ij} are known, then W_s has rank 4 and can be factorized into $\hat{P}$ and $\hat{X}$. The factorization (2) recovers the motion and shape up to a 4×4 linear projective transformation H:

$$W_s = \hat{P}\hat{X} = \hat{P}HH^{-1}\hat{X} = PX, \tag{3}$$

where $P = \hat{P}H$ and $X = H^{-1}\hat{X}$. Any non-singular 4×4 matrix may be inserted between $\hat{P}$ and $\hat{X}$ to get another compatible motion and shape pair P, X. The self-calibration process computes such a matrix H that P and X become Euclidean. The task of finding the appropriate H can only be achieved by imposing certain geometrical constraints. The most general constraint is the assumption of orthogonal rows and columns of the CCD chips in cameras. Alternatively, we can assume that some internal parameters of the cameras are the same, which would be more useful for a monocular camera sequence. The minimal number of cameras for successful self-calibration depends on the number of known camera parameters or the number of fixed parameters. For instance, 8 cameras are needed when the orthogonality of rows and columns is the only constraint and three cameras are sufficient if all principal points are known or if the internal camera parameters are completely unknown but the same for all cameras. See [4] for a more detailed treatment of self-calibration theory.

3.2   Practical Implementation

The main problem in the self-calibration is usually establishing a set of correspondences $\mathbf{u}_{ij}$. We exploit the synchronized capture. A person moves a standard
laser pointer around, which is dimmed down by a piece of paper and is seen by
the cameras. The very bright projections of the laser can be detected in each
image with subpixel precision by fitting an appropriate point spread function.
These particular positions are then merged together over time, creating thus
projections of a virtual 3D object. Our proposed self-calibration scheme can be
outline as follows:

1. Find the projections of the laser pointer in the images.
2. Discard wrongly detected points or incorrect matches made due to imperfect
   synchronization by pairwise RANSAC analysis [2].
3. Estimate projective depths λ_{ij} from (2) by using the approach proposed
   in [11].
4. Perform the rank 4 factorization of the matrix W_s to get projective shape
   and motion [4].
5. Upgrade the projective structures to Euclidean [10,3].

Our current implementation of the factorization method requires to have correspondences across all images. This would be a significant constraint for future
installations of the Visual Room. However, we plan to use a new method proposed in [7] which was successfully tested on image sets where a significant
portion of correspondences was missing.

4   Experiments

Our first Visual Room consists of four computers and four cameras, one camera
attached to one computer. Its arrangement and an example of the 4 camera
views is shown in Fig 4.

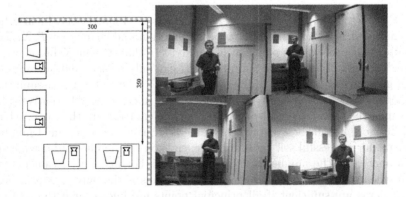

Fig. 4. Left: A sketch of our first ViRoom. Right: Images captured by our first prototype of Visual Room.

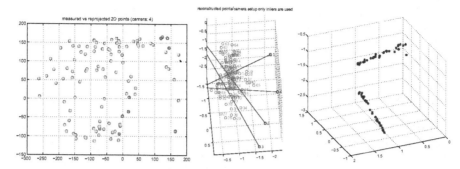

Fig. 5. Calibration results. Left: Positions of the laser pointer are denoted by small circles. Green asterisks denote reprojected good points and red crosses reprojection of points which did not come through the RANSAC validation. Middle: Reconstructed points, positions of cameras and orientations of optical axes. Right: Reconstructed virtual wall points.

We performed several self-calibration experiments. We put the principal points of the cameras in the center of the images and assume orthogonality of CCD rows and columns. No other information about the cameras is used. We evaluate the reliability and precision of the self-calibration by measuring 2D reprojection errors and by performing 3D reconstruction of points on the two visible walls. A person waved a laser pointer and about 150 image 4-tuples were captured. From these data, 97 4-correspondences survived the RANSAC validation step. Calibration results can be seen in Fig 5. The average reprojection error is 0.69 pixels with a standard deviation of 0.41 pixels. It is difficult to directly evaluate the self-calibration results – the camera matrices P_i. We can do it by reconstructing a known 3D object. We pointed the laser pointer to two visible walls to generate virtual points. Correspondences were established by the same method as for the self-calibration. The camera matrices P_i were inserted into a linear triangulation method which minimizes the algebraic error [4] of 3D reconstruction. The reconstructed points are shown in 5. A linear method was used to find the parameters of the two planes. The angle between the planes is 92°. We did several calibration experiments and the angle between the reconstructed walls varied in the range $90 \pm 5°$.

5   Conclusion

The ViRoom, a low cost synchronized multicamera system, was introduced. It consists of standard PCs running on Linux and simple digital cameras with firewire interfaces. No other special hardware is required. A software package for synchronized capturing based on the TCP/IP communication protocol was developed. The proposed self-calibration method does not require a special calibration object. The only input in this calibration is a sequence of images with easily detectable bright spots.

We are currently working on the synchronized image capture, with a larger set of cameras, on self-calibration with occlusions to some of the cameras and on the integration of this multicamera system with our body modeling and gesture analysis software.

Acknowledgment

Support from the ETH project "Blue-C" is gratefully acknowledged. We thank Ondřej Chum from CMP at CTU Prague for his implementation of the RANSAC.

References

1. Barry Brumitt, Brian Meyers, John Krumm, Amanda Kern, and Steven Shafer. Easyliving: Technologies for intelligent environments. In *Proceedings of the 2nd International Symposium on Hanheld and Ubiquitos Computing*, pages 12–29, September 2000.
2. M.A. Fischler and R.C. Bolles. Random sample consensus: A paradigm for model fitting with applications to image analysis and automated cartography. *Communications of the ACM*, 24(6):381–395, June 1981.
3. Mei Han and Takeo Kanade. Creating 3D models with uncalibrated cameras. In *Proceeding of IEEE Computer Society Workshop on the Application of Computer Vision (WACV2000)*, December 2000.
4. R. Hartley and A. Zisserman. *Multiple View Geometry in Computer Vision*. Cambridge University Press, Cambridge, UK, 2000.
5. Takeo Kanade, P.J. Narayanan, and Peter W. Rander. Virtualized reality: Concepts and early results. In *IEEE Workshop on the Representation of Visual Scenes*, pages 69–76, June 1995.
6. Sohaib Khan, Omar Javed, Zeeshan Rasheed, and mubarak Shah. Human tracking in multiple cameras. In *International Conference on Computer Vision*, July 2001.
7. Daniel Martinec and Tomáš Pajdla. Structure from many perspective images with occlusions. In *European Conference on Computer Vision*. Springer-Verlag, May 2002. To appear.
8. Ivana Mikic, Koshia Huang, and Mohan Trivedi. Activity monitoring and summarization for an intelligent room. In *IEEE Workshop on Human Motion*, pages 107–112, December 2000.
9. Alex Pentland. Looking at people: Sensing for ubiquitous and wearable computing. *IEEE Transactions on Pattern Analysis and Machine Intelligence*, 22(1):107–119, January 2000.
10. Mark Pollefeys, Reinhard Koch, and Luc Van Gool. Self-calibration and metric reconstruction inspite of varying and unknown intrinsic camera parameters. *International Journal of Computer Vision*, 32(1):7–25, August 1999.
11. Peter Sturm and Bill Triggs. A factorization based algorithm for multi-image projective structure and motion. In *European Conference on Computer Vision*, pages 709–720. Springer - Verlag, 1996.
12. Mohan M. Trivedi, Ivana Mikic, and Sailendra K. Bhonsle. Active camera networks and semantic event databases for intelligent environments. In *IEEE Workshop on Human Modeling, Analysis and Synthesis (in conjunction with CVPR)*, June 2000.

Real-Time Tracking
Using Wavelet Representation

Thierry Chateau[1], Frederic Jurie[1], Michel Dhome, and Xavier Clady

Lasmea, CNRS UMR 6602, Blaise Pascal Univ., 63177 Aubière, France,
{thierry.chateau,...,}@lasmea.univ-bpclermont.fr,
http://wwwlasmea.univ-bpclermont.fr

Abstract. We have recently developed an original tracking framework allowing to track textured templates in real time [3]. This framework is based on the use of *difference images*, the difference between the target template and the template included in predicted area of interest. For efficiency purposes, the difference image was limited to a few points belonging to the area of interest. The measurements were therefore very punctual. In this article a wavelet representation of the area of interest is used as a substitute for this punctual measurement. In this case, the difference image is a difference of wavelet parameters (difference between the wavelet representation of the target and the wavelet representation of the template included in the current position of the region of interest). This algorithm is a part of a real-time system aiming at automatically detecting and tracking vehicles in video sequences.

1   Introduction

This paper is focussed on the real-time tracking of 2D templates in video sequences. The method presented here is an extension of our works [3,2]. We have recently proposed an efficient method for tracking 2D and 3D objects, in real time using difference images.

The tracking problem is posed as the problem of finding the best (in least squares sense) set of parameter values describing the target motion $\delta\mu$ through a video sequence. Parameter variations $\delta\mu$ are written as a linear function of a *difference image* (the difference between the target template and the template included in the predicted region of interest), as illustrated Figure 1. This approach is very efficient as motion can be easily deduced from difference image.

Basically, the parameter variations $\delta\mu$ are computed using the relation $\delta\mu = \mathbf{A}\delta\mathbf{i}$ where $\mathbf{A}$ is a matrix called *interaction matrix* and $\delta\mathbf{i}$ is a vector denoting the difference image. Matrix $\mathbf{A}$ is learnt during an off-line stage. The time required to compute $\mathbf{A}$ is a function of the cube of the number of pixel in the difference image. This is why only a few number (several hundred) of pixels were used in $\delta\mathbf{i}$. Therefore the difference image was computed from very punctual measurements, making it sensitive to noise.

In this paper we try to substitute a wavelet representation of difference images for this punctual representation. The main idea is that with the same number

L. Van Gool (Ed.): DAGM 2002, LNCS 2449, pp. 523–530, 2002.

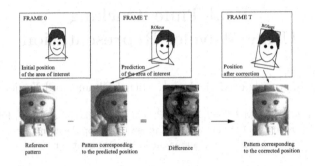

Fig. 1. Principle of the difference image based approach.

of measurements a more global representation will be obtained. We therefore evaluate the consequences of using a Haar wavelets based description of the image instead of the classical gray levels one.

Moreover, we propose to use this algorithm to track vehicles in road video sequences. The initial detection is performed with the help of a recognition method which is also using a Haar wavelet representation of objects. Since real time is crucial for tracking applications, we propose to use a fast method to compute Haar parameters.

The paper is organized as follows: in section 2 we explain the tracking principles and we also explain how Haar wavelets based descriptions can be used instead of the previously proposed punctual approach. Section three is a study on the convergence area of the tracker using static images. Finally, in section four, we explain how this tracking algorithm has been used together with a detection algorithm, in order to detect and track vehicles.

2   Tracking Templates from Their Haar Wavelets Description

2.1   Tracking from Differences

The algorithm proposed here is based on the *difference image scheme*, that we described in [3].

Let us call the pattern to be tracked the *reference pattern*. Let us also suppose that the *region of interest* (ROI) is centered on the pattern in the first image of the sequence. Tracking the reference pattern can be seen as finding the position of the ROI in the subsequent images of the sequence, or finding its relative displacement $\delta\mu$, between two consecutive frames. In this paper, the displacement considered is modeled by rotations, scaling and 2D translations of the ROI into the image. $\delta\mu$ is therefore a four dimensional vector. Tracking the reference pattern can be done by computing the relative motion $\delta\mu$ between the current ROI and the correct position of the template.

Let us describe the image included in a ROI using a Haar wavelets representation. We call *reference vector* the Haar parameters associated with the reference pattern, denoted **Ir**. The *current vector* is the Haar representation of the image included in the current ROI, denoted **Ic**. If the ROI is correctly located, the current vector and the reference vector are the same. Otherwise, if the ROI location is not correct, the difference between the two vectors $\delta \mathbf{i} = \mathbf{Ir} - \mathbf{Ic}$ is not null, and this difference can be used to correct it, as it is representative of the localization error.

This correction is done using a linear relationship between the difference image $\delta \mathbf{i}$ and the variations of the ROI position:

$$\delta \mu = \mathbf{A} \delta \mathbf{i}$$

In this relation, matrix **A** is called the *interaction matrix* which is computed off line. The multiplication of this matrix by the difference image vector gives the correction to be applied to the ROI to bring it to the right position, in the current image.

To learn matrix **A**, we suppose that the current position μ of the region of interest in the first image is known. If this position is disturbed such that $\mu'_0 = \mu_0 + \delta \mu$, the template is moved and the vector $\delta \mathbf{i}$ can be computed. This "disturbance" procedure is repeated N_p times, with $N_p > N$ (N is the size of $\delta \mathbf{i}$). At the end, we have collected N_p pairs $(\delta \mathbf{i}^k, \delta \mu^k)$. It is then possible to obtain the matrix **A** such $\sum_{k=1}^{k=N_p}(\delta \mu^k - \mathbf{A} \delta \mathbf{i}^k)^2$ is minimal. By writing $\mathbf{H} = (\delta \mathbf{i}^1, \ldots \delta \mathbf{i}^{N_P})$ and $\mathbf{Y} = (\delta \mu^1, \ldots, \delta \mu^{N_P})$, **A** can be obtained by computing

$$\mathbf{A} = (\mathbf{H}^T \mathbf{H})^{-1} \mathbf{H}^T \mathbf{Y}.$$

The ROI is arbitrary chosen to be rectangular. It is characterized by a vector of four parameters corresponding to the position of its upper left (px_{ul}, py_{ul}) and lower right (px_{lr}, py_{lr}) corner, into the reference system of the image. These parameters define a local reference system in which the Haar parameters are computed.

2.2 A Haar Wavelets Based Description of Images

The parameters used by the tracker are computed from the Haar basis functions which have been used by Papageorgiou et al. [1]. Figure 2 shows the three kinds of wavelets that are used. A parameter is computed subtracting the sum of the pixels within black regions from those belonging to white regions.

The ROI is recursively divided into four sub-windows (up left, up right, down left an down right), and, for each sub-window, we compute three parameters (called "*horizontal parameter*", "*vertical parameter*", and "*corner parameter*".

Fig. 2. Example of rectangle features.

So, the *pattern vector* is continued by $4^l \times 3$ where l is the number of level of this quad-tree representation.

As the final application must be run in real time, we have to use fast processing methods in order to compute Haar parameters. Viola et al. [5] proposed to build Haar parameters from an integral 2D pseudo-image of the initial image. If $I(x, y)$ denotes the gray level corresponding to the pixel of coordinates (x, y), the integral image I_i is computed by :

$$I_i(x, y) = \sum_{j=1}^{y} \sum_{i=1}^{x} I(i, j) \tag{1}$$

In can be build in a recursive way. The area of a rectangular window of the image delimited by $P_{ul} = (x_{ul}, y_{ul})$ (up left), $P_{dr} = (x_{dr}, y_{dr})$ (down right) is then computed using the following equation :

$$Area = I_i(x_{dr}, y_{dr}) + I_i(x_{ul}, y_{ul}) - (I_i(x_{dr}, y_{ul}) + I_i(x_{ul}, y_{dr})) \tag{2}$$

3   Evaluation of the Haar Based Tracker

Let measure how much the interaction matrix provides good estimations of corrections, *ie* corrections that brings the ROI to the right template position in the image. In these experiments, we manually select a target region in an image, and learn the interaction matrix corresponding to that template. In a second time, we move the region from this target position and use the tracking algorithm to retrieve the target position. We are then able to compare the real motion (or shift) with the one given by the tracker.

The image used during these test is presented Figure 3(a). The rectangle shows the ROI and the reference pattern. The *pattern vector* is composed by the 12 features presented in the previous section. We set l to 1, as our goal is to show that we can track complex features from only a few parameters. The relative displacement of the ROI is modeled by a vector $\delta\mu = (t_x, t_y, s)$ representing the horizontal translation, the vertical translation and the scale factor of the ROI between the initial position and the correct position. In these experiments, rotations are not taken into account. A set of 100 random perturbations of the ROI ($txmax = 20\%$ of ROI width, $tymax = 20\%$ of the ROI height, $smax = 0.05$)

Fig. 3. (a) Image used for the tests. The rectangle represents the ROI. (b) Positions of the disturbed ROIs in the image

is used to compute the interaction matrix **A**. Figure 3(b) shows the positions of the disturbed ROIs on the image.

After learning the interaction matrix, we move the region of interest from the initial position. Images (a), (b) and (c) in Figure 4 show the positions of the ROI obtained by various horizontal translations, vertical translations, and scale transformations. For each one of these position we can compare the real shift with the shift obtained by computing $\delta\mu = \mathbf{A}\delta\mathbf{i}$.

Figure 5 shows the estimation of the correction as a function of the real error. If the estimation was a perfect straight line with the equation $y = x$ (represented by the continues line curve on the graphs) would have been obtained.

Two distinct areas can be distinguished in these graphics. The first area is located between the two values corresponding to the amplitude used to learn the interaction matrix. In this case, the parameter estimation is near the ideal

Fig. 4. Positions of the ROI after displacement. (a): horizontal translation, (b): vertical translation, (c): scale transformation.

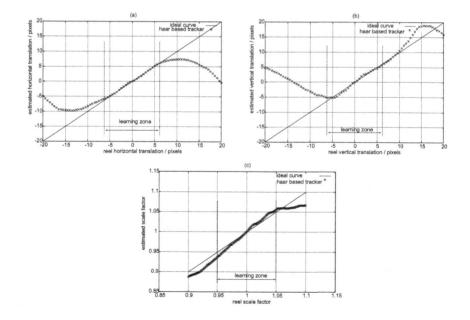

Fig. 5. Estimation of the displacement as a function of the real displacement. (a): horizontal translation, (b): vertical translation, (c): scale transformation

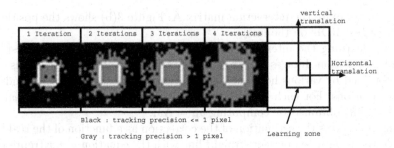

Fig. 6. Evolution of the tracking precision according to the number of iterations of the tracker.

curve and the tracker is working fine. The second area is located outside the two values corresponding to the amplitude used for the learning of the interaction matrix. In that case, several iterations of the tracker are necessary to reach the solution. Figure 6 shows the evolution of the tracker precision according to the number of iterations. The area of the gray zone (precision less or egal to 1 pixel) increases with the number of iterations. For the 1 iteration tracker, three black points appears inside the learning zone. The system needs a second iteration in order to provide good corrections everywhere within the learning zone.

4   Application to Vehicles Tracking

Recent works on object detection can be classified into two main approaches. On one hand, the features based object detection uses explicit knowledge of the object (model of the object). It is based on two stages: features extraction, and matching. This approach can often be exploited in real time systems. For a complete discussion about feature methods used to recognize vehicles, we refer the reader to [9].

On the other hand, detection from appearance provides a pixel classification using appearance based representations of objects. In this category, several recent approaches, often derived from pattern recognition, are very robust. Papageorgiou *et al.* [1] propose a complete method for vehicle detection. However, since these methods required a multi-resolution scanning, they are highly time consuming.

The vehicle detection method proposed in this application combines the efficiency of feature based approaches and the robustness of appearance based approaches: the first one produces hypotheses that are verified by the second.

We use the localization of the vehicle shadow on the road and a 3D road model, in order to produce regions of interest from which Papageorgious et al. algorithm can be applied. The road detection algorithm that we use is described in [6]. Once a vehicle is detected, a tracking process is started.

4.1 Vehicle Detection

Shadows areas are areas that are darker than the road. Therefore, the shadow detection algorithm needs a grey level model of a roads, as described in [4,8,7]. However, these methods are highly time consuming.

We propose a simpler approach, consisting in thresholding the image and filtering the thresholded image. The threshold is computed by analyzing the bottom of the image (see images below), where the probability of the presence of a vehicle is very low. Filters used on the binary image remove shadows outside of the road as well as noisy pixels, and keep only the shadows within a given range of scale, according to the 3D road model and the mean size of vehicles.

From the result of the shadow detection, we can define ROI from which Haar-like parameters are computed. As we use the work of Papageorgiou et al. in order to detect the presence of vehicles, we refer the readers to [1] for further details on the method.

4.2 Tracking

Once the vehicle is detected, it is tracked. The ROI is resized to a image of 32×32 pixels and the learning stage is performed on this ROI. The advantage of the tracker is that the learning stage is very fast because the size of the *pattern vector* is only 12 and can be done with real time constraints. Figure 7 shows the results obtained with the tracking algorithm described in this paper, on a video sequence. Very reliable results have been obtained.

(a)   (b)   (c)   (d)

Fig. 7. Result of the tracker for a video sequence. (a): image 0. (b): image 100. (c): image 200. (d): image 300.

5 Conclusion

We have presented an approach for tracking 2D templates in video sequences, using Haar-like features to describes templates. The main idea of this paper is to propose an algorithm allowing to track efficiently complex real templates using only a few number of parameters. It overcomes the limitation of our previous approaches by reducing the time required to learn the interaction matrix. Since computing time is crucial for tracking algorithms, we have used a fast method to compute Haar parameters.

We have tested the convergence of the proposed tracker on static images and show that the convergence area is compatible with our applications.

We have also presented an application of this algorithm to the tracking of vehicles.

More works can be done in order to use all the characteristics of the Haar-like parameters within our tracking framework. For example, it is possible to take into account Haar features from different scales. Since the number of parameters increases a lot with scale, it will be necessary to select the most relevant features.

References

1. C. Papageorgiou, M. Oren, and T. Poggio. A general framework for object detection. In *IEEE Conference on Computer Vision*, pp 555-562, 1998.
2. F. Jurie and M. Dhome. Real time 3d template matching. In *Computer Vision and Pattern Recongition*, pages (I)791–797, Hawai, December 2001.
3. F. Jurie and M. Dhome. Real time template matching. In *Proc. IEEE International Conference on Computer vision*, pages 544–549, Vancouver, Canada, July 2001.
4. N.D. Matthews, P.E. An, D. Charnley, and C.J. Harris. Vehicle detection and recognition in greyscale imagery. In *2nd Int. Workshop on Intelligent Autonomous Vehicles*, pages 1–6, Helsinki, 1995. IFAC.
5. P. Viola and M. Jones. Robust Real-time Object Detection. In *Second International Workshop on statistical and computational theories of vision-modeling, learning, computing, and sampling*, Vancouver, Canada, 13 July 2001.
6. R. Aufrere, R. Chapuis, F. Chausse, and J. Alizon. A fast and robust visionbased road following algorithm. In *IV'2001 (IEEE Int. Conf. on Intelligent Vehicles*, pages 13–18, May 2001. Tokio, Japan.
7. P. Sayd, R. Chapuis, R. Aufrere, and F. Chausse. A dynamic vision algorithm to recover the 3d shape of a non-structured road. In *Proceedings of the IEEE International Conference on Intelligent Vehicles*, pp 80-86, Stuttgart, Germany, October 1998.
8. C. Tzomakas and W. von Seelen. Vehicle detection in traffic scenes using shadows. Technical report, IRINI 98-06, Institut fur Neuroinformatik, Ruhr-Universitat Bochum, D-44780 Bochum, Germany, August 1998.
9. Marinus B. van Leeuwen and Frans C.A. Groen. Vehicle detection with a mobile camera. Technical report, Computer Science Institute, University of Amsterdam, The Netherlands, October 2001.

Hands Tracking from Frontal View
for Vision-Based Gesture Recognition

Jörg Zieren, Nils Unger, and Suat Akyol

Chair of Technical Computer Science, Aachen University (RWTH),
Ahornst. 55, 52074 Aachen, Germany,
{zieren,unger,akyol}@techinfo.rwth-aachen.de,
http://www.techinfo.rwth-aachen.de

Abstract. We present a system for tracking the hands of a user in a
frontal camera view for gesture recognition purposes. The system uses
multiple cues, incorporates tracing and prediction algorithms, and applies probabilistic inference to determine the trajectories of the hands
reliably even in case of hand-face overlap. A method for assessing tracking quality is also introduced. Tests were performed with image sequences
of 152 signs from German Sign Language, which have been segmented
manually beforehand to offer a basis for quantitative evaluation. A hit
rate of 81.1% was achieved on this material.

1 Introduction

Vision-based hand gesture recognition is a popular research topic for human-
machine interaction. A common problem when working with monocular frontal
view image sequences is the localization of the user's hands. This problem is usually ignored or simplified by special restrictions. For example in [2,7,10] recognition is based on properties that are computed for the whole input image rather
than for hand regions only. This is disadvantageous when gestures merely differ
in details of hand shape, since these constitute only a fraction of the image. In [5]
the number and properties of all moving connected regions (motion blobs) are
considered. This approach is intrinsically sensitive to motion originating from
other objects and is therefore only applicable with static backgrounds. The system described in [12] performs explicit localization, but was not designed to yield
correct positions in the case of hand and face overlap. In sign language applications, however, overlap is actually frequent. In summary we regard explicit hand
localization as a *prerequisite* when:

- signs only differ in details of hand shape,
- the system has to be independent from the image background,
- overlap is likely to occur.

Hand localization is primarily a tracking problem. Tracking algorithms which
have been shown to work for faces fail because hand motion is fast and discontinuous and often disturbed by overlap. E.g. the mean shift tracker is unable to
handle motion exceeding its maximum search extent [4].

L. Van Gool (Ed.): DAGM 2002, LNCS 2449, pp. 531–539, 2002.
© Springer-Verlag Berlin Heidelberg 2002

Currently, the most promising research directions with regard to tracking hands for gesture recognition are probabilistic reasoning and multiple hypothesis testing [11,9]. Additional stability can be gained from consideration of multiple visual cues [16,6] and body models [3,15]. Quantitative statements about the tracking quality are rarely found, although an immediate influence on recognition results must be expected.

We developed a tracking system that combines multiple visual cues, incorporates a mean shift tracker and a Kalman filter and applies probabilistic reasoning for final inference. For testing purposes we recorded a total of 152 signs from German Sign Language in several variations. The image sequences (2–3 seconds, 25 fps, 384×288×24bpp) were segmented manually to have a basis for quantitative evaluation. Results were rated by a special tracking quality assessment method. At the above resolution the system runs approximately in real time on an 800MHz PC.

2   Experimental Setup and Basic Assumptions

In our setup the framing dimensions are chosen to capture the signer's upper body. At the start and the end of each sign, both hands are outside or at the lower border of the image. The permanent presence of the face is essential, although it may be completely occluded by the hands. We regard the user's face position as given, since powerful face detection [13,17] and face tracking methods are available [4]. We also presume that a user specific skin color distribution can be estimated from the face and a general skin color model [1] as source.

The only restriction for the user is to wear non-skin-colored clothes with long sleeves, which is a commonly stated requirement [11,16,6,3]. This allows to extract the skin regions which represent the hands and the face of the user in arbitrary environments as long as there is no other content similar in color and as long as illumination conditions are reasonable. Figure 1 shows an example view. It should be noted that a uniform white background and uniform black

Fig. 1. *Left:* Example view of experimental setup with manually segmented regions and hand trajectories (384×288 pixel). *Right:* Corresponding skin probability map

clothing were used here for convenience, but are not necessary if the previously stated requirements are met.

3   Tracking Concept

The basic idea of our tracker is to extract connected skin colored regions (blobs) from the image and assign the labels F (face), LH (left hand), and RH (right hand) to them. More than one label may be assigned to one blob, since overlapping objects form a single blob. Under the given conditions there can be at most three blobs, depending on whether the hands overlap the face, overlap each other, or are simply not inside the image. Since the face remains in the image, there is at least one blob. A "virtual" blob is placed below the lower border of the image, where the hands can enter and leave. Assigning a label to this virtual blob is equivalent to assuming a hand to be out of the image.

Since a blob set is never unique, there are always multiple possible assignments. Each assignment is a *hypothesis* claiming a certain configuration of face and hands to be the source of the current blob set (see Fig. 2). There are always multiple hypotheses, the most likely of which is selected for further processing.

In order to find the most likely one, all hypotheses are evaluated using the available information, and rated with a *total score* $s \in \mathbb{R}_0^-$. The total score is composed of several scores s_i computed by distinct modules, each representing visual cues or high level knowledge about the tracking task. If a hypothesis is in complete agreement with the information considered in a module, it receives a

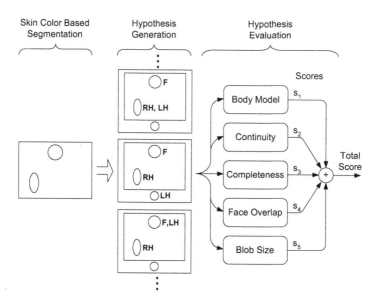

Fig. 2. Generation and evaluation of hypotheses for extracted skin color blobs

score of 0 (which is thus the maximum). With increasing deviation or disagreement, the score decreases accordingly.

The subsequent sections describe these scoring modules. A module's score may consist of multiple subscores. Weights w_i permit a variation of each module's influence on the total score. Distances (measured between the objects' centers of gravity (COG)) and areas are normalized by the width and the area of the face bounding box, respecitvely, for independence of image resolution.

3.1 Body Model

This module consists of two subcomponents that both aim at preventing a confusion of left and right hand. The first one represents the assumption that the left (right) hand is typically found to the left (right) of the face. If a hypothesis violates this assumption, it receives a negative subscore which is proportional to the x coordinate difference between the face and the hand, Δx_{LH} (Δx_{RH}). The second subcomponent contributes a negative subscore if the right hand is positioned left to the left hand, at a distance of Δx. The module's score s_1 is given by (1).

$$s_1 = -w_{1a}\Delta x_{LH} - w_{1a}\Delta x_{RH} - w_{1b}\Delta x \qquad (1)$$

3.2 Continuity

This module rates the continuity of motion, considering initialization and dynamic conditions. Its score s_2 is the sum of two subscores s_{2a} and s_{2b} described below.

Initialization Conditions. In the initial frame, hands may not overlap with the face (see Sect. 2); hypotheses violating this condition are disqualified by a subscore of $-\infty$. In all subsequent frames, the (dis)appearance of a hand is assumed most likely at the bottom border of the image. Thus, for every hand (dis)appearing at a distance of Δy from the bottom border (which is equivalent to a "jump" from (to) the virtual blob), a subscore $s_{2a} = -w_{2a}\Delta y$ is added.

Dynamic Conditions. As soon as a hand has appeared in the image, a Kalman filter is initialized, using a 6-dimensional system state X consisting of position, velocity, and acceleration in both x and y direction (see (2)). A motion model of constant acceleration is assumed. The filter state is initialized to the detected hand's position, with velocity and acceleration set to zero.

$$X = (x, \dot{x}, \ddot{x}, y, \dot{y}, \ddot{y})^T \qquad (2)$$

In subsequent frames, the Kalman filter yields position predictions and receives the actual measurements for state updates (see Sect. 4). Depending on the distance d between the prediction and the position indicated by the hypothesis, a subscore s_{2b} is computed according to (3). d_{min} can be set to allow for a deviation from the above motion model. If the hypothesis states that the hand has left the image, d is set to the prediction's distance from the lower border.

$$s_{2b} = \begin{cases} -w_{2b}d & \text{if } d > d_{min} \\ 0 & \text{otherwise} \end{cases} \tag{3}$$

3.3 Completeness

The assumptions described in Sect. 2 ensure that the only skin colored objects in the image are the signer's face and hands. This means that each blob must be assigned at least one object. It is therefore an error if a hypothesis leaves a blob unassigned. In such a case, the output of the Completeness module is a score $s_3 = -\infty$; otherwise, $s_3 = 0$.

3.4 Face Overlap

The area of the face blob does not change significantly in the given setup. A sudden increase can only be caused by an overlap; likewise, a sudden decrease is related to the cessation of an overlap. Therefore, unless the face is already overlapped, an observed face size change should be matched by the hypothesis in that it states the start/end of an overlap accordingly. Hence this module computes a score reflecting the degree of match between observation and hypothesis as follows:

$$s_4 = \begin{cases} -w_4 & \text{hypothesis expects size incr./decr., but none observed} \\ -w_4 & \text{size incr./decr. observed, but none expected by hypothesis} \\ -2w_4 & \text{hypothesis expects size incr./decr., but opposite observed} \\ 0 & \text{otherwise} \end{cases} \tag{4}$$

3.5 Blob Size

Since the size of both hand blobs may change quickly, the above scheme can only be applied to a face-hand-overlap, but not to a hand-hand-overlap. However, the size of a hand blob usually does not change more than 20% from one frame to another, making size a suitable property for telling hands apart. To this end, the Blob Size module computes the relative increase in area Δa from a hand's size in the previous and current frame (a_{n-1} and a_n, respectively) as

$$\Delta a = \left| \frac{a_n}{a_{n-1}} - 1 \right| . \tag{5}$$

This is only possible if the hand is visible and not overlapping in both the previous and the current frame, for in case of overlapping neither object's area can be determined accurately. The module's score s_5 is given by (6).

$$s_5 = \begin{cases} -w_5(\Delta a - 0.2) & \text{if } \Delta a > 0.2 \\ 0 & \text{otherwise} \end{cases} \tag{6}$$

4   Determination of Hand Position

The hypothesis which received the highest score by the process described in
Sect. 3 is considered correct and is processed further to yield measurements and
estimations for the next frame (see e.g. Sect. 3.2).

Normally a hand's position is determined as the corresponding blob's COG.
In case of overlap, however, this is inaccurate because the blob's border includes
multiple objects. To obtain a more accurate position, the skin probability map
is merged with a motion map to yield a combined map [1]. The CAMSHIFT
algorithm [4] is then applied to this new map, with a search window of fixed
size and an initial position according to the Kalman prediction. The mean shift
centers the search window on the nearest peak, which represents a skin colored
and moving object. This technique is applied in case of hand-face overlap, since
the hand is generally moving more than the face. It is less suitable for hand-hand
overlaps, which show no reliable correlation between peaks and hand centers.

Before processing the measurement, the Kalman filter's measurement noise
matrix is set to reflect the accuracy of the method used to determine the hand's
position (high accuracy for skin color blob based segmentation (i.e. no overlap),
low accuracy in case of the CAMSHIFT method (i.e. overlap)).

The following figure shows the result of the described tracking scheme for
the sign "Evening" from German Sign Language.

 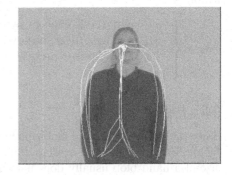

Fig. 3. Tracking example. *Left:* Target trajectories for 10 variations (from manual
segmentation). *Right:* Tracker output for 3 variations

5   Evaluation of Tracking Quality

The tracker's output can be qualified as hit or miss using the reference target in
the manually segmented data. Sensible definitions of a hit are (see Fig. 4):

1. Estimation lies inside a limited region around the target center.
2. Estimation lies within the border of the target object.

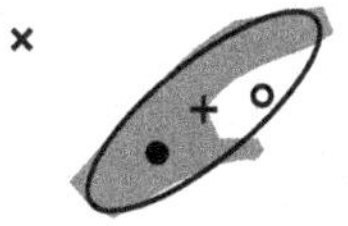

+ target center
● hit on object
○ hit near center
× miss

Fig. 4. Definition of tracker hit and miss with regard to target object (*grey area*). The ellipse shows a line of constant distance for quantifying tracker accuracy

Both definitions are valid, since subsequent processing steps might either require seed points which must be inside the object (e.g. region growing), or might be satisfied with points near the target center, regardless of whether the point is actually part of the object or not (e.g. active shape models).

When the tracker misses the object, the displacement is quantified by the Euclidean distance to the target center. In case of a hit, a Mahalanobis distance with regard to the object's main axes and their extent is used instead, resulting in elliptic lines of equal distance. This reflects the fact that displacement in direction of the elongated axis is less severe than along the shorter axis.

The main axes are defined as the eigenvectors of the 2D shape and their extent is proportional to the square root of the eigenvalues λ_1 and λ_2. Considering these axes as origin for the coordinate system with the coordinates x' and y' allows to compute the Mahalanobis distance by

$$d_{hit} = \left(\frac{x'}{c \cdot \sqrt{\lambda_1}}\right)^2 + \left(\frac{y'}{c \cdot \sqrt{\lambda_2}}\right)^2 \quad c \in \mathbb{R} \ . \tag{7}$$

Table 1 shows a selection of results for five two-handed signs, one of which is free from overlap ("Car"), as well as the overall performance on the complete set of 152 signs. Here $c = 2$ was chosen and hits near center were limited to distances below or equal to 1. Only the right (dominant) hand was considered. (Note that "on object" and "near center" are independent properties of a hit, so the corresponding columns need not add up to the percentage of total hits.)

An analysis of the complete results identifies two main causes for errors:

1. In case of hand-face overlap, the CAMSHIFT algorithm does not converge on the hand due to lack of motion, but rather on the face.

Table 1. Hit statistics including Mahalanobis distance (for hits) and Euclidian distance (for misses; unit: pixels). *Cells contain:* Percentage; min/mean/max distance

Sign	Total Hits	Hits on Object	Hits Near Center	Missed
Evening	90.8; 0.0/0.5/2.2	83.7; 0.0/0.5/2.2	76.5; 0.0/0.4/1.0	9.2; 16.2/22.3/30.4
Work	91.1; 0.0/0.2/1.0	88.1; 0.0/0.2/1.0	89.1; 0.0/0.2/0.9	8.9; 18.0/47.9/60.1
Banana	65.7; 0.0/0.4/1.7	48.8; 0.0/0.3/1.7	59.2; 0.0/0.3/1.0	34.3; 17.5/42.7/75.0
Computer	61.4; 0.0/0.7/2.1	55.4; 0.0/0.7/2.1	42.6; 0.0/0.4/1.0	38.6; 13.0/27.4/66.4
Car	100; 0.0/0.0/0.1	100; 0.0/0.0/0.1	100; 0.0/0.0/0.1	0.0; 0.0/0.0/0.0
(all)	81.1; 0.0/0.2/3.1	78.4; 0.0/0.2/3.1	78.8; 0.0/0.1/1.0	18.9; 7.3/45.9/175.9

2. When hands overlap each other, the tracker uses for both hands the position given by the corresponding blob's COG, which deviates from each hand's individual center.

Results for "Evening"and "Work" are already very satisfactory, while "Banana" and "Computer" show a need for improvement. The complete hit statistics clearly identify overlap as the main problem. Sequences without overlap (e.g. "Car") are almost always handled without error.

6   Outlook

We expect to improve the system's performance by exploiting additional image cues, e.g. by template matching. Multiple hypothesis tracking and the handling of distractors are obvious but complex steps towards independence from the image background. This would also suggest a more sophisticated body model. Putting the system to use by extracting features and performing recognition tests will be the subject of further research.

References

1. Akyol, S., Alvarado, P.: Finding Relevant Image Content for mobile Sign Language Recognition. In: Hamza, M.H. (ed.): IASTED International Conference- Signal Processing, Pattern Recognition and Applications (SPPRA), Rhodes (2001) 48-52
2. Bobick, A.-F., Davis, J.-W.: The Representation and Recognition of Action Using Temporal Templates. IEEE PAMI 3:23 (2001) 257–267
3. Bowden, R., Mitchell, T.A., Sahadi, M.: Non-linear statistical models for the 3D reconstruction of human pose and motion from monocular image sequences. Image and Vision Computing Journal 18 (2000) 729–737
4. Bradski, G.R.: Computer vision face tracking for use in a perceptual user interface. Intel Technology Journal Q2 (1998)
5. Cutler, R., Turk, M.: View-based Interpretation of Real-time Optical Flow for Gesture Recognition. Proc. IEEE Conf. Face and Gesture Recognition (1998) 416–421
6. Imagawa, K., Lu, S., Igi, S.: Color-Based Hands Tracking System for Sign Language Recognition. Proc. IEEE Conf. Face and Gesture Recognition (1998) 462–467
7. Nagaya, S., Seki, S., Oka, R.: A Theoretical Consideration of Pattern Space Trajectory for Gesture Spotting Recognition. Proc. IEEE Conf. Face and Gesture Recognition (1996) 72–77
8. Oliver, N., Pentland, A.: Lafter: Lips and face real-time tracker. Proc. IEEE Conf. Computer Vision Pattern Recognition (1997) 123–129
9. Rasmussen, C., Hager, G.D.: Joint Probabilistic Techniques for Tracking Objects Using Visual Cues. Intl. Conf. Intelligent Robotic Systems (1998) no pagenumbers
10. Rigoll, G., Kosmala, A., Eickeler, S.: High Performance Real-Time Gesture Recognition Using Hidden Markov Models. In: Wachsmut, I., Fröhlich, M. (eds.): Gesture and Sign Language in Human-Computer Interaction. Springer (1998) 69–80

11. Sherrah, J., Gong, S.: Tracking Discontinuous Motion Using Bayesian Inference. Proc. European Conf. on Computer Vision (2000) 150–166
12. Starner, T., Pentland, A.: Visual Recognition of American Sign language Using Hidden Markov Models. Proc. IEEE Workshop Face and Gesture Recognition (1995) 189–194
13. Viola, P., Jones, M.J.: Robust Real-time Object Detection. Technical Report CRL 2001/01, Cambridge Research Laboratory (2001)
14. Welch, G., Bishop, G.: An introduction to the Kalman Filter. Technical Report 95-041, Dept. of Computer Science, University of Chapel Hill (2001)
15. Wren, C., Azarbayejani, A., Darrell, T., Pentland, A.: Pfinder: Real-time tracking of the human body. IEEE PAMI 7:19 (1997) 780–785
16. Yang, M., Ahuja, N.: Extraction and Classification of Visual Motion Patterns for Hand Gesture Recognition. Proc. IEEE Conf. CVPR (1998) 892–897
17. Yang, M., Kriegman, D.J., Ahuja, N.: Detecting faces in images: a survey. IEEE PAMI 1:24 (2002) 34–58

Automatic Annotation
of Tennis Video Sequences

Corrado Calvo[1], Alessandro Micarelli[2], and Enver Sangineto[1]

[1] Centro di Ricerca in Matematica Pura e Applicata (CRMPA),
Sezione "Roma Tre", Via della Vasca Navale 79, 00146 Roma, Italia
[2] Dipartimento di Informatica e Automazione (DIA), AI Lab,
Università degli Studi "Roma Tre", Via della Vasca Navale 79, 00146 Roma, Italia,
{calvo,micarel,sanginet}@dia.uniroma3.it

Abstract. In this paper we propose a complete system for automatic annotation of tennis video sequences. The method is completely automatic and computationally efficient. The court lines are detected by means of the Hough Transform while the players' positions are extracted looking for those edge pixels whose orientation is different from the lines of the court. Finally, we show some experimental results remarking the system efficiency and classification skills.

1   Motivations and Goals

In the last few years there has been a consistent increasing of the amount of video information in different fields such as academic education, training courses, video surveillance, etc. In such fields content-based indexing and retrieval can play an important role to speed up the browsing. Annotation of a video sequence concerns the extraction of high level semantics from its visual content.

Traditional approaches to content-based retrieval have focused the attention on visual features such as color, shape, texture and motion. The main advantage of such approaches is that they can be applied to a wide variety of videos, but the very limiting drawback is that visual features just represent low level information. When retrieving specific kind of video segments, most users need to access to high level information which cannot be easily extracted from low level features. On the other hand, the manual generation of high level annotation is a time consuming and expensive process. These considerations lead to the need of algorithms for automatic generation of high level annotation from visual features.

Automatic video annotation is a very hard task in a domain independent perspective. Indeed automatic interpretation of a still image is an open and difficult research problem, and video annotation adds the time variable to this task. The common solution of the state of the art research in video annotation is to focus the analysis on a specific domain and successively try to adapt the found techniques to different fields. We chose the sport video domain realizing an automatic system for tennis video annotation. Nevertheless, most of the proposed

L. Van Gool (Ed.): DAGM 2002, LNCS 2449, pp. 540–547, 2002.

techniques (such as the significant frame selection, the court lines' detection, the player localization and so on) can be used in different sports.

Sudhir, Lee and Jain [4] proposed in 1998 a system for automatic tennis video annotation. The system performs a color-based selection of the video sequence frames. A frame is considered *significant* only if the number of pixels with the same color of the court is above a prefixed threshold. Then, they extract three basic segments from the image which are used to reconstruct the whole court exploiting the perspective camera projection and the known court geometric structure. Initial players' positions are represented by the centroids of the largest connected areas in the smoothed *residue image* (defined as the difference of two consecutive frames) inside two rectangular search windows. After the detection of the initial locations, two templates of suitable sizes are generated for the two players and located on the corresponding centroids. Then a common template matching technique is used to track the players' positions over the following frames. The last module determines the game action type taking into account the initial and final positions of the players with respect to the court lines.

In Miyamori and Iisaku's system [2], proposed in 2000, there is no module for the selection of the frames containing the court. Indeed, they assume to work only with significant frames. The court lines extraction is based on the Hough Transform [1]. Initial positions of the lines have to be given as input to the system; afterwards each line is transformed onto the Hough plane. Hence, the line detection is done by means of a semi-automatic system. Successively tracking of the court lines is computed over all the frames of the sequence. Players' tracking is then performed with an approach very similar to the previous mentioned work. The initial players' positions are detected searching for the largest connected areas in the residue images. The search is restricted to two previous computed rectangular search windows. Once the players' centroids representing their initial positions in the video sequence are known, two templates of suitable sizes are positioned on them. Finally, template matching is used to track the players' positions in the successive sequence frames. Template matching is also used to track the ball and to compare the extracted players' silhouettes with pre-defined human silhouettes representing peculiar player behaviours.

These two sketched approaches summarize some of the most common techniques used (with minor differences) in tennis video annotations, such as the significant frame selection, the residue images, the search window selection and the players' tracking by means of an *adaptive* template matching technique. In our proposed approach, we perform the significant frame selection phase and we utilize suitably computed search windows but we do not use any residue image; moreover, we do not perform players' tracking nor adaptive template matching to find them. Indeed, we search for players' locations looking for pixel regions with an edge gradient orientation different from the court lines', and we found this approach more robust than the simple template matching. Furthermore, we reconstruct the court structure using an Hough Transform technique to detect the straight lines but our detection is completely automatic and does not need an initial positioning. Finally, high level annotation is generated by means of a statistic analysis of the players' positions in the whole sequence.

In the next section we show the details of our proposal, while in Section 3 the implementation features and its experimental results are presented. Section 4 concludes the paper sketching some remarkable notes.

2   Description of the Method

Figure 1 shows the scheme of the proposed system. The first module performs a color-based frame selection. In this way we discard all those sequence frames not representing a game action, such as player zooming, audience shot or commercials. The *significant* frame selection is realized taking into account only the pixels belonging to a central 100×100 pixel window. A frame is significant if more than the 60% of such pixels have a hue value inside a (pre-fixed) *court color interval*. Not significant frames are discarded and not taken into account in successive processing phases. It is worth to note that in tennis video there are just two kind of perspective views of the action: top rear overview and bottom rear zoom-like view. Since the top rear overview is definitely more common and with a richer information content, we utilize the mentioned approach to select frames belonging to it. This is a common assumption in video tennis annotation [4] but it does not mean that the camera is fixed.

Also the second module utilizes a color-based filter. The objective is to discard the audience area possibly present on the sides and/or on the top of the current (significant) frame. We analyze the pixels near the borders of the current frame looking for those pixels whose hue value is not belonging to the court color interval (red) nor to the court line color interval (white). Such pixels are eliminated (marked as *not interesting*) in order to avoid noise in the successive edge detection phase. Both the first and the second modules are based on an a initial image conversion from the RGB to the HSB representation.

The third module applies some standard edge detection algorithms. We chose to use the Canny edge detector with 3×3 Sobel masks [1]. The output of this step is the *edge map*, in which each image's interesting pixel is represented as 0 (for background pixels) or 1 (lines and players and, often, noise). Figure 2 shows an example of significant frame and of its resulting edge map. Finally, each edge pixel p is associated with its edge orientation $\varphi(p)$, extracted using Sobel masks.

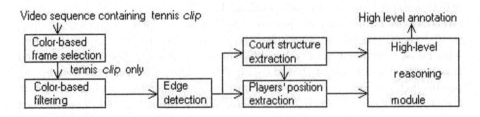

Fig. 1. System overview.

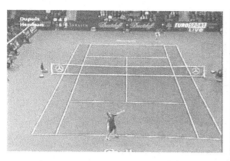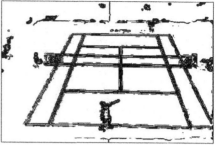

Fig. 2. An example of color-based filtering and edge detection.

The fourth module concerns the detection of both the court (straight) lines and their adjacency relationships. Straight line detection is realized using the standard Hough Transform (HT) [1]. We adopt the (ρ, θ) representation of the Hough parameters. This allows us to efficiently index the Hough accumulator (H) by using information about the edge orientation [1]. More in details, for each edge pixel $p = (x, y)$, we increment $H(\rho, \theta)$, where $\theta = \varphi(p)$ and:

$$\rho = y sin(\varphi(p)) + x cos(\varphi(p)). \tag{1}$$

The Hough accumulator is analyzed first of all searching for horizontal lines. Hence, we scan H taking into account only the columns with $\theta \in [90 - th_1, 90 + th_1]$ (presently, $th_1 = 16.875$). We use a one dimensional vector V to collect all those votes belonging to this strip of H:

$$V(\rho) = \sum_{\theta \in [90 - th_1, 90 + th_1]} H(\rho, \theta). \tag{2}$$

Horizontal court lines are local maxima in V. To distinguish them, we select a central window (V_c) in V, composed of the elements of V belonging to the range: $\rho \in [th_2, th_3]$ (presently, $th_2 = 0.27 \times h$, $th_3 = 0.66 \times h$, h being the height of the whole image). The most voted local maximum in V_c is one of the two *Net-lines*. The other Net-line is the second voted local maximum in V_c. *Top Base-line* and *Top Service-line* are the two most voted local maxima in V above the *Top Net-line*, while *Bottom Base-line* and *Bottom Service-line* are the two most voted local maxima below *Bottom Net-line*.

This algorithm is based on two assumptions. The first is that the range defining V_c is always enough large to include both the Service-Lines. The second concerns the fact that a Service-line is always much smaller then any Net-line, thus, also if one of the Service-lines belongs to V_c, it can not be neither the first nor the second most voted local maximum in V_c.

After horizontal lines, we scan H searching for vertical lines. The *Central Vertical line* is the absolute maximum in $H(\rho, \theta)$ with $\theta \in [-th_4, th_4]$ (presently, $th_4 = 5.72$). Finally, we extract the two absolute maxima with $\theta \in [th_5, th_6]$

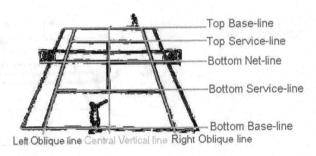

Fig. 3. The main court lines.

(presently, $th_5 = -33.7$, $th_6 = 11.2$) for *Left Oblique lines* and the two absolute maxima with $\theta \in [th_7, th_8]$ ($th_7 = 11.2$, $th_8 = 33.7$) for *Right Oblique lines*. The last (trivial) step concerns the selection, from the Left Oblique lines and the Right Oblique lines the two most internal ones as the court bounding lines.

Once all the court lines have been extracted, we compute the intersections among the 5 horizontal lines (Top and Bottom Base-line, Top and Bottom Service-line and Bottom Net-line) with the 3 vertical lines (Central Vertical line, Left Oblique line and Right Oblique line). These 8 court lines and their intersections give us a complete structure of the whole game court (Figure 3).

The fifth module of Figure 1 concerns the players' localization. Exploiting the knowledge of the game court we select two *search regions*, above and below the Net-lines. For players' localization we do not compute any residue image but we observe the edge map and the edge orientations. We define as a *candidate edge* an edge pixel p s.t. $\varphi(p)$ does not belong to the court lines' orientations (see the previously defined orientation ranges). Then, we scan the Top and the Bottom search regions by means of two rectangular windows of different dimensions in order to take into account perspective issues. For each pixel p, if the *Bottom window* (W_B) is centered in p, we count the number of candidate pixels in $W_B(p)$. Then we select max_B, the centroid of the bottom player, as the position which maximizes W_B (with an analogous reasoning for the top one). Finally, we obtain the *bottom player position* (its feet position) P_B subtracting an half of W_B height from max_B (see Figure 4).

The candidate pixel counting phase can be computationally optimized computing, for each column of the search region, only the first window and then deriving the others by the last one just computed with a dynamic programming technique. Indeed, we observe that, if x is not the first column of the search region, then:

$$W(x,y) = W(x-1,y) - W_1(x-1,y) + W_l(x,y), \qquad (3)$$

where $W_1(p)$ is the first column of the window $W(p)$ and $W_l(p)$ is the last column of the window $W(p)$.

The last module, inheriting information about the game court structure and the players' positions, is now able to perform the sequence annotation. First of

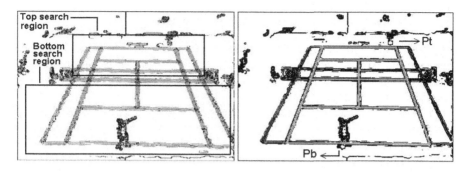

Fig. 4. The image on the left shows the search regions and the candidate edge pixels (black pixels). The image on the right is an example of court game structure (gray lines) and players' positions.

all, we compare the distance between the top player position and the 3 horizontal lines Top Base-line, Top Service-line and Bottom Net-line, choosing the closest one. We do the same with the 3 vertical lines (Central Vertical line, Oblique Left and Right line). We will assign to the top player a *position label* given by the two chosen lines (for instance, "BL-C" for Base Line and Central point). The labeling process for the bottom player is analogous.

All the shown processing phases are applied to all the frames of the sequence. Finally, the system classifies different kinds of game actions from the initial and final position of the two players (Table 1). *Initial player position* corresponds to the position label with the highest occurrence in the first half of the sequence, final player position corresponds to the position label with the highest occurrence in the second half of the sequence. We use this method in order to get the system more robust to possible recognition errors made in a single frame.

Table 1. Annotation of different game actions through the initial (I) and the final (F) players' positions.

Top Plr I	Top Plr F	Bottom Plr I	Bottom Plr F	Annotation
BL	BL	BL	BL	Base-line rally
BL	SL	BL	BL	Bottom Plr Passing shot
BL	BL	BL	SL	Top Plr Passing shot
BL	BL	BL-C	SL-C	Bottom Plr Serve-Volley
BL-C	SL-C	BL	BL	Top Plr Serve-Volley
BL-L	BL-L	BL-C	BL-C	Bottom Plr Serve (left side)
BL-R	BL-R	BL-C	BL-C	Bottom Plr Serve (right side)
BL-C	BL-C	BL-L	BL-L	Top Plr Serve (left side)
BL-C	BL-C	BL-R	BL-R	Top Plr Serve (right side)
SL	NL	SL	NL	Net-game

3   Efficiency and Experimental Results

The first three modules of the proposed system (frame selection, color-based filtering and edge detection) are based on low-level *local* filters applying small masks on each original image pixel, thus having a computational complexity linear with the number of pixels.

The court structure extraction is composed of a series of steps. The HT voting phase is proportional to the number of edge pixel. Indeed we adopt a (ρ, θ) representation of the lines and a voting mechanism which exploits each pixel's edge orientation to map it in H solving the equation (1) in constant time. The local maxima detection is linear with the number of elements of H. The other operations of this module (line intersection computation) are computed on a very small (and fix) set of elements (8) to be considered computationally constant.

Finally, also the players' position localization is done in an efficient way. We do not need to compute a residue image at each significant frame. We only need to explore the two search regions. On each element (pixel) of such regions we center a rectangular window (presently, W_T dimension is 16×24 and W_B is 28×50) and we count the candidate edge pixels looking for the maxima. This operation is optimized exploiting (3) with a computational cost of $O(Nl)$, where l is the vertical side of W (24 or 50) and N the number of elements of the two search regions. Sub-sampling N we are able to perform the players'localization in 0.32 seconds as average time (with a Pentium IV).

It is worth to note that the choice to utilize candidate pixels' searching instead of (traditional) residue image computation followed by template matching is based not only on computational efficiency issues. Indeed the main advantage of our proposed approach is its stronger robustness to errors. This because a template matching technique leads to errors if the first localization phase makes an error (all the remaining trajectory will be falsely classified). Conversely, in our proposed approach, the localization phase is (efficiently) repeated for each significant frame, and the final annotation depends on statistical considerations on the whole trajectory (see Section 2).

The overall computational complexity of the system is given by the sum of all the modules (sequentially run), but we can assume it is equal to the most time-consuming operation (the only not linear one): $O(Nl)$.

Experimental tests have been done on a set of 57 sequences extracted from a tennis indoor match. Video sequences consist of 4 seconds' actions sampled 6 frames per second. Each frame is 384×288 pixels wide. The system has been implemented in JAVA and the experimentation realized using a 1.7 GHz Pentium IV, 256 MB RAM. The average execution time of all the system modules is 0.578 seconds per image and 13.8 seconds for a sequence of 24 significant frames. Table 2 summarizes the results obtained with the proposed system.

4   Conclusions

In this paper we have presented an automatic system for tennis video annotation, whose objective is to facilitate content-based retrieval based on high-level infor-

Table 2. Classification results obtained with 57 sequences.

Action type	Tested actions	Correct	False	Missed	Precision	Recall
Base-line rally	28	22	2	6	0.92	0.79
Bottom Passing shot	4	2	0	2	1	0.5
Top Passing shot	3	2	0	1	1	0.66
Bottom Serve-& -volley	2	2	2	0	0.5	1
Top Serve-& -volley	1	0	1	1	0	0
Bottom Serve (left side)	3	2	1	1	0.66	0.66
Bottom Serve (right side)	6	6	0	0	1	1
Top Serve (left side)	3	3	0	0	1	1
Top Serve (right side)	2	1	0	1	1	0.5
Net-game	5	3	0	2	1	0.6
Tot	57	43	6	14	0.88	0.75

mation. The system is completely automatic: lines' detection, players' detection and all the other phases are completely automatic and do not need any human positioning. The approach is quite robust and does not need residue image computation and template matching. Players' localization based on candidate pixels is an easy and very robust technique. Moreover, players' localization frame by frame allows to classify the whole player trajectory with a statistical consideration on the whole sequence, reducing dependence on first frame classification.

We have presented some preliminary experimental results showing precision and recall rates respectively of 88% and 75% and very poor time consuming executions. We believe our results are already encouraging, nevertheless we have planned a more extensive testing with a greater number of sequences and different videos.

References

1. Ballard and Brown, *Computer Vision*, Prentice Hall, 1982.
2. H. Miyamori and S. Iisaku, *Video Annotation for Content-based retreival using Human Behaviour Analisys and Domain Knowledge*, Proceedings of the Fourth IEEE International Conference on Automatic Face and Gesture Recognition 2000.
3. G.S. Pingali, Y.J. and I. Carlbom, *Real-time tracking for enhanced tennis broadcasts*, Visual Communication Research Department, Bell Laboratories, Lucent Technologies, Murray Hill, NJ 07974.
4. G. Sudhir, J.C.M. Lee and A.K. Jain, *Automatic classification of tennis video for high-level content-based retreival*, Proc. of the 1998 Int. Workshop on Content-based Access of Image and Video Databases, January 3, 1998, Bombay, India.
5. D. Zhong and S.H. Chang, *Structure parsing and event detection for sports video*, Dep. of Electrical Engineering, Columbia University - Technical report, December 27, 2000, USA.

Fitting of Parametric Space Curves and Surfaces by Using the Geometric Error Measure

Sung Joon Ahn, Wolfgang Rauh, and Engelbert Westkämper

Fraunhofer IPA, Nobelstr. 12, 70569 Stuttgart, Germany,
{sja,wor,wke}@ipa.fraunhofer.de,
http://www.ipa.fraunhofer.de/Arbeitsgebiete/BereichE/620/

Abstract. For pattern recognition and computer vision, fitting of curves and surfaces to a set of given data points in space is a relevant subject. In this paper, we review the current orthogonal distance fitting algorithms for parametric model features, and, present two new algorithms in a well organized and easily understandable manner. Each of these algorithms estimates the model parameters which minimize the square sum of the shortest error distances between the model feature and the given data points. The model parameters are grouped and simultaneously estimated in terms of form, position, and rotation parameters. We give various examples of fitting curves and surfaces to a point set in space.

1 Introduction

The least squares fitting of curves and surfaces is a relevant subject in pattern recognition, computer vision, computer aided geometric design, and coordinate metrology. Among the various fitting methods, the *orthogonal distance fitting* is of topical interest because of the used error definition [5], namely the shortest distance (frequently referred to as geometric distance or Euclidean distance in the literature) from the given point to the model feature. Really, the use of the geometric distance as the error measure to be minimized is prescribed in a recently ratified international standard for testing the data processing softwares for coordinate metrology [7]. While there are orthogonal distance fitting algorithms for *explicit* [3], and *implicit* model features [2,9] in the literature, we intend to describe and compare in this paper the fitting algorithms for *parametric* model features [4,6,8,10] (Fig. 1).

The ultimate goal of the orthogonal distance fitting of a model feature to a set of m given points in space is the estimation of the model parameters **a** which minimize the performance index

$$\sigma_0^2 = (\mathbf{X} - \mathbf{X}')^{\mathrm{T}} \mathbf{P}^{\mathrm{T}} \mathbf{P} (\mathbf{X} - \mathbf{X}') \tag{1}$$

or

$$\sigma_0^2 = \mathbf{d}^{\mathrm{T}} \mathbf{P}^{\mathrm{T}} \mathbf{P} \mathbf{d} , \tag{2}$$

where $\mathbf{X}^{\mathrm{T}} = (\mathbf{X}_1^{\mathrm{T}}, \ldots, \mathbf{X}_m^{\mathrm{T}})$ and $\mathbf{X}'^{\mathrm{T}} = (\mathbf{X}_1'^{\mathrm{T}}, \ldots, \mathbf{X}_m'^{\mathrm{T}})$ are the coordinate column vectors of the m given points and of the m corresponding points on the model feature, respectively. And, $\mathbf{d}^{\mathrm{T}} = (d_1, \ldots, d_m)$ is the distance column vector with $d_i = \|\mathbf{X}_i - \mathbf{X}_i'\|$,

L. Van Gool (Ed.): DAGM 2002, LNCS 2449, pp. 548–556, 2002.

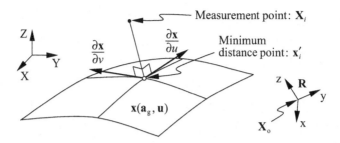

Fig. 1. Parametric surface and, the minimum distance point $\mathbf{x}'_i$ in model frame xyz from the given point $\mathbf{X}_i$ in reference frame XYZ

$\mathbf{P}^{\mathrm{T}}\mathbf{P}$ is the weighting or error covariance matrix. We call the fitting algorithms minimizing the performance indexes (1) and (2), respectively, *coordinate-based algorithm* and *distance-based algorithm*.

In particular of parametric model features, a subproblem of the orthogonal distance fitting is the finding the location parameters $\{\mathbf{u}_i\}_{i=1}^m$ which represent the minimum distance points $\{\mathbf{X}'_i\}_{i=1}^m$ on the model feature from each given point $\{\mathbf{X}_i\}_{i=1}^m$. The model parameters a and the location parameters $\{\mathbf{u}_i\}_{i=1}^m$ will generally be estimated through iteration. By the *total method* [6,8], a and $\{\mathbf{u}_i\}_{i=1}^m$ will be simultaneously determined, while they are to be separately estimated by the *variable-separation method* [4,10] in a nested iteration scheme. There could be four combinations for algorithmic approaches as shown in Table 1. One of them results in an obviously underdetermined linear system for iteration, thus, has no practical application.

A model fitting algorithm will be very helpful to applications, e.g., object recognition, robot vision, motion analysis, and coordinate metrology, if the model parameters a are grouped and simultaneously estimated in terms of form, position, and rotation parameters as $\mathbf{a}^{\mathrm{T}} = (\mathbf{a}_{\mathrm{g}}^{\mathrm{T}}, \mathbf{a}_{\mathrm{p}}^{\mathrm{T}}, \mathbf{a}_{\mathrm{r}}^{\mathrm{T}})$. The *form parameters* $\mathbf{a}_{\mathrm{g}}$ (e.g., three axis lengths a, b, c of an ellipsoid) describe the shape and size of the standard model feature defined in model coordinate system xyz (Fig. 1)

$$\mathbf{x} = \mathbf{x}(\mathbf{a}_{\mathrm{g}}, \mathbf{u}) \qquad \text{with} \qquad \mathbf{a}_{\mathrm{g}} = (a_1, \ldots, a_l)^{\mathrm{T}} . \tag{3}$$

The form parameters are invariant to the rigid body motion of the model feature. The *position parameters* $\mathbf{a}_{\mathrm{p}}$ and the *rotation parameters* $\mathbf{a}_{\mathrm{r}}$ describe the rigid body motion

Table 1. Orthogonal distance fitting algorithms for parametric model features

Algorithmic approach	Distance-based algorithm	Coordinate-based algorithm
Total method	Underdetermined system	Algorithm I (ETH)
Variable-separation method	Algorithm II (NPL, FhG)	Algorithm III (FhG)

of the model feature in machine coordinate system XYZ

$$X = R^{-1}x + X_o \quad \text{or} \quad x = R(X - X_o) \ , \qquad \text{where} \qquad (4)$$
$$R = R_\kappa R_\varphi R_\omega = (r_1 \ r_2 \ r_3)^T \ , \qquad R^{-1} = R^T \ ,$$
$$a_p = X_o = (X_o, Y_o, Z_o)^T \ , \qquad \text{and} \qquad a_r = (\omega, \varphi, \kappa)^T \ .$$

In the following sections, we describe and compare the three approaches for orthogonal distance fitting of *parametric* model features (Table 1), with which the model parameters a are estimated in the three groups of $a^T = (a_g^T, a_p^T, a_r^T)$. For the orthogonal distance fitting of *implicit* model features, interested readers are referred to [2].

2   Algorithm I (ETH)

The algorithm I (ETH) [6,8] is based on the performance index (1) and, simultaneously estimates the model parameters a and the location parameters $\{u_i\}_{i=1}^m$. We define the new estimation parameter vector b consisting of a and $\{u_i\}_{i=1}^m$ as below:

$$b^T = (a_g^T, a_p^T, a_r^T, u_1^T, \ldots, u_m^T) = (a_1, \ldots, a_q, u_1, v_1, \ldots, u_m, v_m) \ .$$

The parameter vector b minimizing (1) can be determined by the Gauss-Newton method

$$P \frac{\partial X'}{\partial b}\bigg|_k \Delta b = P(X - X')|_k \ , \qquad b_{k+1} = b_k + \alpha \Delta b \ , \qquad (5)$$

with the Jacobian matrices of each point X_i' on the model feature, from (3) and (4),

$$J_{X_i',b} = \frac{\partial X}{\partial b}\bigg|_{X=X_i'} = \left(R^{-1}\frac{\partial x}{\partial b} + \frac{\partial R^{-1}}{\partial b}x + \frac{\partial X_o}{\partial b} \right)\bigg|_{u=u_i}$$
$$= \left(R^{-1}\frac{\partial x}{\partial a_g} \bigg| \quad I \quad \bigg| \frac{\partial R^{-1}}{\partial a_r}x \bigg| 0_1, \cdots, 0_{i-1}, \ R^{-1}\frac{\partial x}{\partial u}, \ 0_{i+1}, \cdots, 0_m \right)\bigg|_{u=u_i} .$$

A disadvantage of the algorithm I is that the storage space and the computing time cost increase very rapidly with the number of the data points, if the sparse linear system (5) is not beforehand handled by a sparse matrix algorithm (assuming $m \gg q$ and the use of SVD for solving (5), they are approximatley proportional to m^2 and m^3, respectively).

3   Algorithm II (NPL, FhG)

The algorithm II, the initial NPL algorithm [4,10] without the parameter grouping of $a^T = (a_g^T, a_p^T, a_r^T)$ yet, is based on the performance index (2) and, separately estimates the parameters a and $\{u_i\}_{i=1}^m$ in a *nested iteration* scheme

$$\min_a \ \min_{\{u_i\}_{i=1}^m} \ \sigma_0^2 \left(\{X_i'(a, u)\}_{i=1}^m \right) \ .$$

The inner iteration determines the location parameters $\{u_i'\}_{i=1}^m$ for the minimum distance points $\{X_i'\}_{i=1}^m$ on the current model feature from each given point $\{X_i\}_{i=1}^m$, and, the outer iteration updates the model parameters a. In this paper, in order to implement the parameters grouping of $a^T = (a_g^T, a_p^T, a_r^T)$, a very desirable algorithmic feature for applications, we have modified the initial NPL algorithm into a new algorithm.

3.1 Minimum Distance Point

For each given point $\mathbf{x}_i = \mathbf{R}(\mathbf{X}_i - \mathbf{X}_o)$ in frame xyz, we determine the minimum distance point $\mathbf{x}'_i$ on the standard model feature (3). Then, the minimum distance point $\mathbf{X}'_i$ in frame XYZ to the given point $\mathbf{X}_i$ will be obtained through a backward transformation of $\mathbf{x}'_i$ into XYZ. Our aim in this subsection is to find the location parameter values $\mathbf{u}$ which minimize the error distance d_i between the given point $\mathbf{x}_i$ and the corresponding point $\mathbf{x}$ on the model feature (3)

$$d_i^2 = \|\mathbf{x}_i - \mathbf{x}(\mathbf{a}_g, \mathbf{u})\|^2 = (\mathbf{x}_i - \mathbf{x}(\mathbf{a}_g, \mathbf{u}))^{\mathrm{T}}(\mathbf{x}_i - \mathbf{x}(\mathbf{a}_g, \mathbf{u})) \ . \tag{6}$$

The first order necessary condition for a minimum of (6) as a function of $\mathbf{u}$ is

$$\mathbf{f}(\mathbf{x}_i, \mathbf{x}(\mathbf{a}_g, \mathbf{u})) = \frac{1}{2}\begin{pmatrix} \partial d_i^2/\partial u \\ \partial d_i^2/\partial v \end{pmatrix} = -\begin{pmatrix} (\mathbf{x}_i - \mathbf{x}(\mathbf{a}_g, \mathbf{u}))^{\mathrm{T}}\mathbf{x}_u \\ (\mathbf{x}_i - \mathbf{x}(\mathbf{a}_g, \mathbf{u}))^{\mathrm{T}}\mathbf{x}_v \end{pmatrix} = \mathbf{0} \ . \tag{7}$$

Equation (7) means that the error vector $(\mathbf{x}_i - \mathbf{x})$ and the feature tangent vectors $\partial\mathbf{x}/\partial\mathbf{u}$ at $\mathbf{x}$ should be orthogonal (orthogonal contacting equation, Fig. 1). We solve (7) for $\mathbf{u}$ by using the generalized Newton method (How to derive the matrix $\partial\mathbf{f}/\partial\mathbf{u}$ is shown in Section 4.)

$$\left.\frac{\partial\mathbf{f}}{\partial\mathbf{u}}\right|_k \Delta\mathbf{u} = -\mathbf{f}(\mathbf{u})|_k \ , \qquad \mathbf{u}_{k+1} = \mathbf{u}_k + \alpha\Delta\mathbf{u} \ . \tag{8}$$

3.2 Orthogonal Distance Fitting

We update the model parameters $\mathbf{a}$ minimizing the performance index (2) by using the Gauss-Newton method (outer iteration)

$$\left.\mathbf{P}\frac{\partial\mathbf{d}}{\partial\mathbf{a}}\right|_k \Delta\mathbf{a} = -\mathbf{Pd}|_k \ , \qquad \mathbf{a}_{k+1} = \mathbf{a}_k + \alpha\Delta\mathbf{a} \ . \tag{9}$$

From $d_i = \|\mathbf{X}_i - \mathbf{X}'_i\|$, and equations (3) and (4), we derive the Jacobian matrices of each *minimum distance* d_i as below:

$$\mathbf{J}_{d_i,\mathbf{a}} = \frac{\partial d_i}{\partial\mathbf{a}} = -\frac{(\mathbf{X}_i - \mathbf{X}'_i)^{\mathrm{T}}}{\|\mathbf{X}_i - \mathbf{X}'_i\|}\left.\frac{\partial\mathbf{X}}{\partial\mathbf{a}}\right|_{\mathbf{u}=\mathbf{u}'_i}$$

$$= -\frac{(\mathbf{X}_i - \mathbf{X}'_i)^{\mathrm{T}}}{\|\mathbf{X}_i - \mathbf{X}'_i\|}\left.\left(\mathbf{R}^{-1}\left(\frac{\partial\mathbf{x}}{\partial\mathbf{a}} + \frac{\partial\mathbf{x}}{\partial\mathbf{u}}\frac{\partial\mathbf{u}}{\partial\mathbf{a}}\right) + \frac{\partial\mathbf{R}^{-1}}{\partial\mathbf{a}}\mathbf{x} + \frac{\partial\mathbf{X}_o}{\partial\mathbf{a}}\right)\right|_{\mathbf{u}=\mathbf{u}'_i} \ .$$

With (4), and (7) at $\mathbf{u} = \mathbf{u}'_i$, the Jacobian matrix $\mathbf{J}_{d_i,\mathbf{a}}$ can be simplified as follows:

$$(\mathbf{X}_i - \mathbf{X}'_i)^{\mathrm{T}}\mathbf{R}^{-1}\left.\frac{\partial\mathbf{x}}{\partial\mathbf{u}}\right|_{\mathbf{u}=\mathbf{u}'_i} = (\mathbf{x}_i - \mathbf{x}'_i)^{\mathrm{T}}\left.\frac{\partial\mathbf{x}}{\partial\mathbf{u}}\right|_{\mathbf{u}=\mathbf{u}'_i} = \mathbf{0}^{\mathrm{T}} \ , \qquad \text{thus}$$

$$\mathbf{J}_{d_i,\mathbf{a}} = -\frac{(\mathbf{X}_i - \mathbf{X}'_i)^{\mathrm{T}}}{\|\mathbf{X}_i - \mathbf{X}'_i\|}\left(\mathbf{R}^{-1}\left.\frac{\partial\mathbf{x}}{\partial\mathbf{a}_g}\right|_{\mathbf{u}=\mathbf{u}'_i} \ \left| \ \mathbf{I} \ \right| \ \frac{\partial\mathbf{R}^{-1}}{\partial\mathbf{a}_r}\mathbf{x}'_i\right) \ .$$

A drawback of the algorithm II is that the convergence and the accuracy of 3D-curve fitting (e.g., fitting a circle in space) are relatively poor [10]. 2D-curve fitting or surface fitting with the algorithm II do not suffer from such problem.

4   Algorithm III (FhG)

At the Fraunhofer IPA (FhG-IPA), a new orthogonal distance fitting algorithm for parametric model features is developed, which minimizes the performance index (1) in a nested iteration scheme (variable-separation method). The new algorithm is a generalized extension of an orthogonal distance fitting algorithm for implicit plane curves [1]. The location parameter values $\{u_i'\}_{i=1}^m$ for the minimum distance points $\{X_i'\}_{i=1}^m$ on the current model feature from each given point $\{X_i\}_{i=1}^m$ are to have been found by the algorithm described in Section 3.1 (inner iteration). In this section, we intend to describe the outer iteration which updates the model parameters a minimizing the performance index (1) by using the Gauss-Newton method

$$\mathbf{P}\frac{\partial \mathbf{X}'}{\partial \mathbf{a}}\bigg|_k \Delta\mathbf{a} = \mathbf{P}(\mathbf{X} - \mathbf{X}')|_k \ , \qquad \mathbf{a}_{k+1} = \mathbf{a}_k + \alpha\Delta\mathbf{a} \ , \tag{10}$$

with the Jacobian matrices of each *minimum distance point* $\mathbf{X}_i'$, from (3) and (4),

$$\mathbf{J}_{\mathbf{X}_i',\mathbf{a}} = \frac{\partial \mathbf{X}}{\partial \mathbf{a}}\bigg|_{\mathbf{X}=\mathbf{X}_i'} = \left(\mathbf{R}^{-1}\left(\frac{\partial \mathbf{x}}{\partial \mathbf{a}} + \frac{\partial \mathbf{x}}{\partial \mathbf{u}}\frac{\partial \mathbf{u}}{\partial \mathbf{a}}\right) + \frac{\partial \mathbf{R}^{-1}}{\partial \mathbf{a}}\mathbf{x} + \frac{\partial \mathbf{X}_o}{\partial \mathbf{a}}\right)\bigg|_{\mathbf{u}=\mathbf{u}_i'}$$

$$= \mathbf{R}^{-1}\frac{\partial \mathbf{x}}{\partial \mathbf{u}}\frac{\partial \mathbf{u}}{\partial \mathbf{a}}\bigg|_{\mathbf{u}=\mathbf{u}_i'} + \left(\mathbf{R}^{-1}\frac{\partial \mathbf{x}}{\partial \mathbf{a}_g}\bigg|_{\mathbf{u}=\mathbf{u}_i'} \bigg| \mathbf{I} \bigg| \frac{\partial \mathbf{R}^{-1}}{\partial \mathbf{a}_r}\mathbf{x}_i'\right) \ . \tag{11}$$

The derivative matrix $\partial \mathbf{u}/\partial \mathbf{a}$ at $\mathbf{u} = \mathbf{u}_i'$ in (11) describes the variational behavior of the location parameters $\mathbf{u}_i'$ for the minimum distance point $\mathbf{x}_i'$ in frame xyz relative to the differential changes of $\mathbf{a}$. Purposefully, we derive $\partial \mathbf{u}/\partial \mathbf{a}$ from the orthogonal contacting equation (7). Because (7) has an implicit form, its derivatives lead to

$$\frac{\partial \mathbf{f}}{\partial \mathbf{u}}\frac{\partial \mathbf{u}}{\partial \mathbf{a}} + \frac{\partial \mathbf{f}}{\partial \mathbf{x}_i}\frac{\partial \mathbf{x}_i}{\partial \mathbf{a}} + \frac{\partial \mathbf{f}}{\partial \mathbf{a}} = \mathbf{0} \quad \text{or} \quad \frac{\partial \mathbf{f}}{\partial \mathbf{u}}\frac{\partial \mathbf{u}}{\partial \mathbf{a}} = -\left(\frac{\partial \mathbf{f}}{\partial \mathbf{x}_i}\frac{\partial \mathbf{x}_i}{\partial \mathbf{a}} + \frac{\partial \mathbf{f}}{\partial \mathbf{a}}\right) \ , \tag{12}$$

where $\partial \mathbf{x}_i/\partial \mathbf{a}$ is, from $\mathbf{x}_i = \mathbf{R}(\mathbf{X}_i - \mathbf{X}_o)$,

$$\frac{\partial \mathbf{x}_i}{\partial \mathbf{a}} = \frac{\partial \mathbf{R}}{\partial \mathbf{a}}(\mathbf{X}_i - \mathbf{X}_o) - \mathbf{R}\frac{\partial \mathbf{X}_o}{\partial \mathbf{a}} = \left(\mathbf{0} \bigg| -\mathbf{R} \bigg| \frac{\partial \mathbf{R}}{\partial \mathbf{a}_r}(\mathbf{X}_i - \mathbf{X}_o)\right) \ .$$

The other three matrices $\partial \mathbf{f}/\partial \mathbf{u}$, $\partial \mathbf{f}/\partial \mathbf{x}_i$, and $\partial \mathbf{f}/\partial \mathbf{a}$ in (8) and (12) are to be directly derived from (7). The elements of these three matrices are composed of simple linear combinations of components of the error vector $(\mathbf{x}_i - \mathbf{x})$ with elements of the following three vector/matrices $\partial \mathbf{x}/\partial \mathbf{u}$, $\mathbf{H}$, and $\mathbf{G}$ (XHG matrix):

$$\frac{\partial \mathbf{x}}{\partial \mathbf{u}} = (\mathbf{x}_u \ \mathbf{x}_v) \ , \quad \mathbf{H} = \begin{pmatrix} \mathbf{x}_{uu} & \mathbf{x}_{uv} \\ \mathbf{x}_{vu} & \mathbf{x}_{vv} \end{pmatrix} \ , \quad \mathbf{G} = \begin{pmatrix} \mathbf{G}_0 \\ \mathbf{G}_1 \\ \mathbf{G}_2 \end{pmatrix} = \frac{\partial}{\partial \mathbf{a}_g}\begin{pmatrix} \mathbf{x} \\ \mathbf{x}_u \\ \mathbf{x}_v \end{pmatrix} \ , \tag{13}$$

$$\frac{\partial \mathbf{f}}{\partial \mathbf{u}} = (\mathbf{x}_u \ \mathbf{x}_v)^{\mathrm{T}}(\mathbf{x}_u \ \mathbf{x}_v) - \begin{pmatrix} (\mathbf{x}_i - \mathbf{x})^{\mathrm{T}}\mathbf{x}_{uu} & (\mathbf{x}_i - \mathbf{x})^{\mathrm{T}}\mathbf{x}_{uv} \\ (\mathbf{x}_i - \mathbf{x})^{\mathrm{T}}\mathbf{x}_{vu} & (\mathbf{x}_i - \mathbf{x})^{\mathrm{T}}\mathbf{x}_{vv} \end{pmatrix} \ ,$$

$$\frac{\partial \mathbf{f}}{\partial \mathbf{x}_i} = -(\mathbf{x}_u \ \mathbf{x}_v)^{\mathrm{T}} \ , \quad \frac{\partial \mathbf{f}}{\partial \mathbf{a}} = \begin{pmatrix} \mathbf{x}_u^{\mathrm{T}}\mathbf{G}_0 - (\mathbf{x}_i - \mathbf{x})^{\mathrm{T}}\mathbf{G}_1 \\ \mathbf{x}_v^{\mathrm{T}}\mathbf{G}_0 - (\mathbf{x}_i - \mathbf{x})^{\mathrm{T}}\mathbf{G}_2 \end{pmatrix} \bigg| \mathbf{0} \bigg| \mathbf{0} \ .$$

Now, equation (12) can be solved for $\partial \mathbf{u}/\partial \mathbf{a}$ at $\mathbf{u} = \mathbf{u}'_i$, then, the Jacobian matrix (11) and the linear system (10) can be completed and solved for the parameter update $\Delta \mathbf{a}$. We would like to stress that only the standard model equation (3), without involvement of the position/rotation parameters, is required in (13). The overall structure of the algorithm III remains unchanged for all fitting problems for parametric model features (Fig. 2). All that is necessary for a new parametric model feature is to derive the XHG matrix of (13) from (3) of the new model feature, and to supply a proper set of initial parameter values $\mathbf{a}_0$ for iteration (10). The algorithm III shows robust and fast convergence for 2D/3D-curve and surface fitting. The storage space and the computing time cost are proportional to the number of the data points.

As a fitting example, we show the orthogonal distance fitting of a helix. The standard model feature (3) of a helix in frame xyz can be described as follows:

$$\mathbf{x}(\mathbf{a}_g, u) = \mathbf{x}(r, h, u) = (r \cos u, \ r \sin u, \ hu/2\pi)^{\mathrm{T}} \ ,$$

with a constraint between the position and the axis orientation of the helix

$$f_c(\mathbf{a}_p, \mathbf{a}_r) = (\mathbf{X}_o - \overline{\mathbf{X}})^{\mathrm{T}} \mathbf{r}_3(\omega, \varphi) = 0 \ ,$$

where r and h are the radius and elevation of a helix, respectively. $\overline{\mathbf{X}}$ is the gravitational center of the given point set, and, $\mathbf{r}_3$ (see (4)) is the direction cosines vector of the z-axis. We obtain the initial parameter values from a 3D-circle fitting, and a cylinder fitting, successively. The helix fitting to the point set in Table 2 with the initial parameter values of $h = 5$ and $\kappa = \pi/2$ terminated after 7 iteration cycles 0.07 s for $\|\Delta \mathbf{a}\| = 9.2 \times 10^{-7}$ with a Pentium 133 MHz PC (Table 3, Fig. 3). They were 10 iteration cycles 0.16 s for $\|\Delta \mathbf{a}\| = 4.7 \times 10^{-7}$ by the algorithm I, and, 128 iteration cycles 2.21 s for $\|\Delta \mathbf{a}\| =$

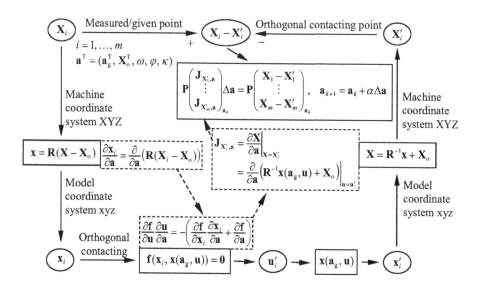

Fig. 2. Information flow with the algorithm III (FhG)

Table 2. Ten coordinate triples representing a helix

X	7	5	3	1	−1	−3	−4	−5	−5	−5
Y	1	3	4	4	4	4	2	1	−1	−3
Z	3	4	4	4	3	2	1	0	−1	−1

Table 3. Results of the orthogonal distance fitting to the point set in Table 2

	$\hat{a}$	σ_0	r	h	X_o	Y_o	Z_o	ω	φ	κ
Circle	1.2264	6.6484	−−	1.3055	−1.5365	0.6629	0.4707	−0.2235	−−	
$\sigma(\hat{a})$	−−	0.4262	−−	0.3662	0.5513	0.4289	0.0854	0.0544	−−	
Cylinder	0.4696	7.0495	−−	1.9752	0.0669	−1.8749	1.1132	0.0086	−−	
$\sigma(\hat{a})$	−−	0.4841	−−	0.3381	0.7822	1.1540	0.2390	0.0963	−−	
Helix	0.8736	5.8695	12.2904	0.8919	−0.9342	1.0216	0.6774	−0.6012	2.1575	
$\sigma(\hat{a})$	−−	0.7900	5.2913	0.5218	0.7419	0.5099	0.1516	0.1986	0.2848	

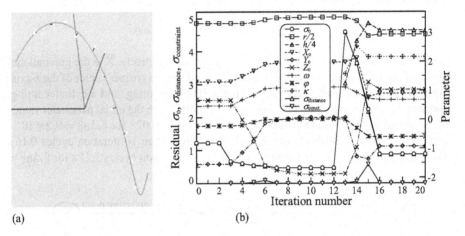

(a)   (b)

Fig. 3. Orthogonal distance fitting to the point set in Table 2: (a) Helix fit; (b) Convergence of the fit. Iteration number 0–2: 3D-circle, 3–12: circular cylinder, and 13–: helix fit with the initial values of $h = 5$ and $\kappa = \pi/2$

6.2×10^{-6} by the algorithm II. The algorithm II showed relatively slow convergence for the 3D-circle and the helix fitting (3D-curve fitting).

To compare the convergence and the computing time cost of the three algorithms, we fit an ellipsoid of $\mathbf{x}(\mathbf{a}_g, \mathbf{u}) = (a \cos u \cos v, \ b \sin u \cos v, \ c \sin v)^T$ to the point sets of 10 to 100 points (Fig. 4). There is no significant difference of the convergence behavior between the algorithm II and III (Fig. 4b). The algorithm I shows bad convergence behavior, if the initial parameter values are not close to the final estimation values. The computing cost by the algorithm I increases very rapidly with the number of the data points (for $m = 100$, it is 140 times higher than that of the algorithm II or III (Fig. 4c)). The algorithm III demands a little higher computing cost than the algorithm II does, because the linear system (10) is three times larger than (9).

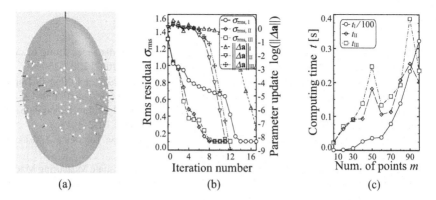

Fig. 4. Comparison of the convergence and the computing cost between the three algorithms: (a) Ellipsoid fit to the 100 points randomly distributed on $-1.0 \leq u \leq 3.0$ and $-0.5 \leq v \leq 0.5$ with an rms error distance of 0.1 for $\mathbf{a}_g \approx (10, 15, 20)^T$, $\mathbf{a}_p \approx (10, -10, 10)^T$, $\mathbf{a}_r \approx (0.5, -0.5, 0.5)^T$. Distance error bars are 10 times elongated; (b) Convergence of the ellipsoid fit to the 100 points; (c) Computing time cost with a Pentium 866 MHz PC.

5 Summary

In this paper, we have reviewed the current orthogonal distance fitting algorithms for parametric curves and surfaces and, presented two new algorithms in a well organized and easily understandable manner. By each of the algorithms the model parameters are grouped and simultaneously estimated in terms of form/position/rotation parameters. The algorithm I demands large amount of storage space and high computing cost, and, the algorithm II shows relatively poor performance on 3D-curve fitting. The algorithm III has no such drawbacks of the algorithm I and II. A disadvantage of the algorithm III is that it requires the second derivatives $\partial^2 \mathbf{x} / \partial \mathbf{a}_g \partial \mathbf{u}$ demanding an additional implementation cost. The algorithm III does not require a necessarily good initial parameter values set. The initial values could also be internally supplied as demonstrated with the fitting examples, through which the parameter values experience no abrupt changes with the model transition (seamless model transition), thus, a stable convergence could be guaranteed. For implementation and application to a new model feature, we merely need the standard model equation (3) of the new model feature, which has only a few form parameters. The functional interpretation and treatment of the position/rotation parameters are basically identical for all parametric model features. The storage space and the computing cost are proportional to the number of the given points. Together with other fitting algorithms for implicit features [2], the algorithm III is certified by the German federal authority PTB [5,7], with a certification grade that the parameter estimation accuracy is higher than $0.1\,\mu$m for length unit, and $0.1\,\mu$rad for angle unit for all parameters of all tested model features with all test data sets.

References

1. Ahn, S.J., Rauh, W., Warnecke, H.-J.: Least-squares orthogonal distances fitting of circle, sphere, ellipse, hyperbola, and parabola. Pattern Recognition **34** (2001) 2283–2303
2. Ahn, S.J., Rauh, W., Cho, H.S., Warnecke, H.-J.: Orthogonal Distance Fitting of Implicit Curves and Surfaces. IEEE Trans. Pattern Analy. Mach. Intell. **24** (2002) 620–638
3. Boggs, P.T., Byrd, R.H., Schnabel, R.B.: A stable and efficient algorithm for nonlinear orthogonal distance regression. SIAM J. Sci. Stat. Comput. **8** (1987) 1052–1078
4. Butler, B.P., Forbes, A.B., Harris, P.M.: Algorithms for Geometric Tolerance Assessment. Report No. DITC 228/94. NPL, Teddington, UK (1994)
5. Drieschner, R., Bittner, B., Elligsen, R., Wäldele, F.: Testing Coordinate Measuring Machine Algorithms: Phase II. BCR Report, EUR 13417 EN. Commission of the European Communities, Luxemburg (1991)
6. Gander, W., Golub, G.H., Strebel, R.: Least-squares fitting of circles and ellipses. BIT **34** (1994) 558–578
7. ISO 10360-6: Geometrical Product Specifications (GPS) - Acceptance and reverification test for coordinate measuring machines (CMM) - Part 6: Estimation of errors in computing Gaussian associated features. ISO, Geneva, Switzerland (2001)
8. Sourlier, D.: Three Dimensional Feature Independent Bestfit in Coordinate Metrology. Ph.D. Thesis, ETH Zurich, Switzerland (1995)
9. Sullivan, S., Sandford, L., Ponce, J.: Using Geometric Distance Fits for 3-D Object Modeling and Recognition. IEEE Trans. Pattern Analy. Mach. Intell. **16** (1994) 1183–1196
10. Turner, D.A.: The approximation of Cartesian coordinate data by parametric orthogonal distance regression. Ph.D. Thesis, University of Huddersfield, UK (1999)

Efficient, Active 3D Acquisition, Based on a Pattern-Specific Snake

T.P. Koninckx and L. Van Gool

[1] Katholieke Universiteit Leuven, ESAT/VISICS,
Kasteelpark Arenberg 10, 3001 Heverlee, Belgium,
{thomas.koninckx,luc.vangool}@esat.kuleuven.ac.be,
http://www.esat.kuleuven.ac.be/psi/visics/
[2] Swiss Federal Institute of Technology, ETH/BIWI,
Gloriastrasse 35, 8092 Zurich, Switzerland,
vangool@vision.ee.ethz.ch, http://www.vision.ee.ethz.ch

Abstract. The paper discusses a structured light setup for fast, one-shot 3D acquisition. The projection pattern consists of equidistant, vertical stripes. The main problem is the determination of the stripe-boundaries. They are extracted with sub-pixel accuracy by a pattern-specific snake. An initialization procedure yields the rough contours. Sub-pixel accuracy is reached through an iterative relaxation process. The labeling problem is automatically solved if all boundaries are located. Interpolation guarantees that the correct number of boundaries is initialized.

1 Introduction

The problem of recovering depth information using images has been studied for years. A wide variety of methods has been developed. Stereo-vision (e.g. [1]), structured light systems (e.g. [3,4]), and shape from shading (e.g. [5]), are among the most often used techniques. They share an important drawback in that they all rely on off-line computations.

This paper proposes a 3D structured light approach, that is amenable to real-time implementation. Real-time, structured light techniques have been demonstrated recently [7,8]. These systems still use a series of subsequent projections, which complicates projection and reduces the speed with which objects may move while being captured. On the other hand, the possibility of one-shot acquisition is corroborated by other results [6]. The 3D extraction by the latter system was still largely off-line. It is our goal to achieve real-time, one-shot acquisition. The paper discusses the approach we are implementing to this end. This combination of features opens new opportunities in areas such as virtual and augmented reality, motion capture, image assisted surgery, robot navigation, etc.

The organisation of the paper is as follows. Section 2 describes the outline of the system, section 3 explains how the boundaries of the projected stripes are located. Section 4 shows some results and section 5 concludes the paper.

L. Van Gool (Ed.): DAGM 2002, LNCS 2449, pp. 557–565, 2002.

2   Background and Problem-Statement

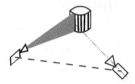

Fig. 1. *System Setup*

Our system consists of a single camera and a single LCD projector. The projected pattern consists of a series of vertical, equidistant black stripes on a white background, where each stripe has the same width and where this width equals the distance between the stripes. Each boundary of each stripe delimits a plane in 3D-space. These planes are assumed to be more or less parallel, i.e. pseudo-orthographic projection of the stripes is assumed. A similar model is used for the image projection. The intersection of the planes with the lines of sight of the boundary pixels, observed by the camera, gives the locations of the points in space. This setup is sketched in figure 1. The system is assumed to be calibrated, i.e. the orientations of the planes with respect to the camera and their relative distances, as well as the intrinsic camera parameters are assumed to be known. Within the orthographic projection context, the absolute position of the planes is not important, but their relative position has to be determined correctly. The shape can then be extracted up a to a translation.

There are multiple reasons to consider stripes with their two edges rather than thin lines. the latter are more difficult to extract robustly. They also only yield a single plane. The fact that black-white and white-black transitions should follow on eachother is a constraint that helps to eliminate false boundary detections.

The main problem now boils down to identifying the stripe boundaries, with sub-pixel precision, and to labeling them correctly. This localization and labeling problem should be done fast, so that real-time 3D acquisition is not jeopardized.

3   Method: Stripe-Boundary Localization

In this section the stripe boundary detection process is sketched. It is implemented as a two step procedure:

 - a rough initialization: mostly with pixel accuracy, sometimes worse
 - a refinement step: the wrong parts of the previous step are corrected, and the stripe boundaries are trimmed to their correct sub-pixel location.

For continuous processing, only the second step will be re-executed.

3.1   A Four-Step Initialization Procedure

This is the most time consuming step in the stripe boundary detection pipeline. The knowledge of the repetitivity in the pattern can be used to speed up the detection process, at the risk of making an early fault and letting it propagate from one line to another. A careful balance between a global approach, with enough redundancy for error detection and a more local approach, with quick local decisions is essential.

Step 1: Preprocessing. First the input image is convolved with a Sobel kernel By computing the mean distance between consecutive local minima and maxima, we get an accurate estimate of the average inter-stripe distance. Based on this, we adjust, if necessary, the size of the kernel and reiterate the convolution. After this, a suitable threshold is chosen, based on the distribution of the output of the Sobel filter.

The image is separated in pixels which are local maxima, local minima and non-extrema. Only the extrema will be important. Finally only sequential extrema which have a horizontal spacing within a tolerance interval around the average spacing (or average inter-stripe distance, as computed in the first step) are withheld. Isolated extrema are removed. This last step gives an accurate indication of the region in which stripes are detectable. This process is illustrated in figure 2 Figure 3 shows the intermediate images in this stage.

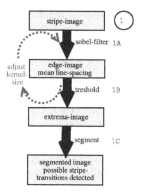

Fig. 2. *Preprocessing*

The applications we have in mind require the 3D shape acquisition for a single object. Stripes not falling on the object, but on the background, can automatically be removed by putting the object sufficiently far in front. Lines projected on e.g. a back wall will then fall outside of the region corresponding to the depth-of-field of the camera and will go undetected.

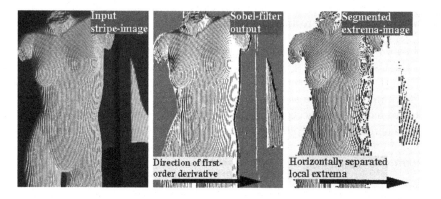

Fig. 3. *First stage of the detection pipeline illustrated on a foam mannequin.*

Step 2: Line-Propagation.

Forward Propagation: Within the region of interest, detected in the previous step, we pick a suitable starting point. We concatenate the extrema in vertical direction into a 'line segment'. This concatenation is stopped as soon as a gap is encountered.

Given this first segment, we set out to construct the nearest segment on the next stripe boundary. To this end, we choose a set of 'seed points' on the initial segment. These points are moved horizontally, until they reach the next extrema with opposite sign. If the next-boundary candidate is detected too close or too far, regarding the average inter-stripe distance, this seed point is discarded. If the process reaches a good extremum, this will serve as a starting point for concatenation. Segments to the right of the first one get increasingly higher numbers. A similar concatenation wave is going to the left from the first segment onwards, and decreasing segment numbers are assigned during this process.

The whole process is repeated from each seed point. If two segments with the same line number reach eachother through concatenation, they are merged. In case they reach the same height but at a different horizontal position, the most logical solution is chosen. This is the one that best approaches the (local) inter-stripe distance and that yields the smoothest continuation in terms of position and orientation. As vertical stripes are projected, there also is a preference for vertical orientations.

This process is continued for the whole image. Segment after segment is detected, with each segment generating new seeds for the next segment. The wave of segment detection starts locally, but spreads out over the entire, striped region. A segment always belongs to a single stripe boundary. Of course, the complete boundary can be composed of several segments. It is very helpful that we can predict almost always the position of the next segment. On the other hand, once a segment is detected or numbered incorrectly, all the following numbers will also be incorrect. Because of this risk, and because we can not reach all segments out of the initial seeds, we restart the process in reverse.

Backward Propagation: Identically the same process as described above is started from the last line detected in the forward propagation mode. The seeds are now grown in the opposite direction. All segments which are detected in both forward *and* backward mode are stored. A segment that is only detected in forward *or* backward mode is also accepted, unless a conflict between the numbering of these modes emerges. Such segment is removed from the solution.

$$
segments_{result-set} = \begin{pmatrix} \{segments_{forward} \cap segments_{backward}\} \cup \\ \{segments_{backward} \setminus segments_{forward}\} \cup \\ \{segments_{forward} \setminus segments_{backward}\} \end{pmatrix} \quad (1)
$$

The result, shown in figure 4 together with the process-outline, is a line image of individual segments. Where the stripes were salient, most of the boundaries are identified. In the other regions, missing out on segments is preferred over finding spurious ones. This said, the system increases its chances to find segments through the built-in redundancy. The two-way process and the use of multiple seed points are cases in point.

Step 3: Linking and Inconsistency Removal. The 3rd step starts off with a check for the occurrence of the same image pixels on two segments with a

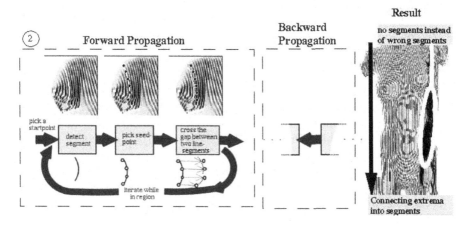

Fig. 4. *Line-propagation illustrated, each direction uses local decisions, the intersection makes the strategy more global*

different line number. The result is a set of line segments with a numbering that is most of the time correct, and always consistent. This means that, given segments $S_{k,i}$ and $S_{l,j}$, with $i \leq j \implies i_d \leq j_d$ and $|i{-}i_d| \leq i$ and $|j{-}j_d| \leq j$ where $S_{k,i}$ is the 'real segment', with line-number i, on which this is the k'th vertical segment. SD_{k_d,i_d} is the detected segment, to which we have assigned line number i_d, on which this is the $k'_d th$ segment. The same applies to $S_{l,j}$ vs. SD_{l_d,j_d}. This means that the order is never inverted, and that the fault in the numbering is limited by the actual line number.

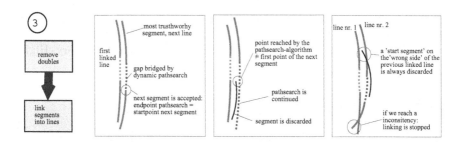

Fig. 5. *Linking left: gap bridged, middle: gap bridged but next segment discarded, right: inconsistent*

Now we link the individual segments of a stripe boundary into a continuous line. Figure 5 shows the different characteristic situations encountered when we bridge a gap. The following box summarizes this part of the algorithm:

choose of all segments SD_{k_d,i_d} the one with the lowest detection uncertainty: $SD_{k_{ds},i_{ds}}$
for$\{i_d=i_{ds}$; $i_d \leq$ max(line-number); i_d++$\}$ && for$\{i_d=i_{ds}$; $i_d \geq 0$; i_d- -$\}$
$\{$(for all boundaries)

- search for fixed i_d (the group of segments which lie above or below each other on the same stripe-boundary) the segment SD_{l_d,i_d} with the lowest detection uncertainty.
- determine the gap-length between SD_{l_d,i_d} and $SD_{l_d\pm1,i_d}$, the next segment above or below
- start a dynamic path-search algorithm to bridge this gap
- if the point reached belongs to the next segment: accept the whole segment, else: discard this segment, and continue the path-search $\}$

Fig. 6. *An initialized mesh*

Step 4: Mesh Initialization. Lines which are too short (e.g. because we reached an inconsistent case in step 3), are extended until the median length of their immediate environment is reached. Now that the stripe boundaries have been detected, the lines are sampled into a mesh. See figure 6. Each column corresponds to a line in the input-image. The rows are generated by the vertical sampling. The parts of the lines which are still missing are interpolated, based on the line distance and the location of their neighbors. The result is a crude, pixel accurate mesh.

In the case were the lines were very badly visible the result even doesn't reach pixel accuracy. As the next section will show, this isn't a real problem. As long as most of the lines are less or more correct and we have initialized the correct number of lines, the outcome is satisfactory. Higher accuracy would cost too much time.

3.2   Sub-pixel Refinement

In order to refine the initialized mesh to sub-pixel accuracy, we propose a generalized active contour. In contrast to a snake, our shape is a 2D mesh. Moreover, the mesh is composed of open contours and has no fixed point or other kinds of pinpoints. The contour is completely free to move. Each node has a weight and an activity. A node is connected to its four neighbors by four (linear) springs, with the average line spacing as their length at rest.

The mesh energy is minimized iteratively. In order to pull it towards the stripe boundaries, external force are applied. These depend on the gradient given by the Sobel operator. This is illustrated in figure 7. If a node is near its correct position, tension is small. Only tiny steps towards the boundary result. Soon external and internal forces are in equilibrium and the node is fixated. On the other hand, a node in a completely wrong position (e.g see the right side of belly in figure 6) experiences a big force from the springs. These will pull the node easily over the local extremum of the gradient. Once in its correct environment, the boundary homes in on a sub-pixel precise position.

$$F_{intern,hor} = \alpha * k_x * \big((L - (x_i - x_{i-1})) * W_{x_{i-1,y}} + ((x_{i+1} - x_i) - L) * W_{x_{i+1,y}}\big) \tag{2}$$

$$F_{intern,vert} = \beta * k_y * \big((L' - (y_i - y_{i-1})) * W_{x_{i,y-1}} + ((y_{i+1} - x_i) - L) * W_{x_{i,y+1}}\big) \tag{3}$$

$$F_{spring} = (F_{intern,vert} + F_{intern,hor}) * W_{x_{i,y}} \tag{4}$$

$$F_{extern} = \gamma * \frac{grad_{x,y}}{\|max(grad_{im})\|} \tag{5}$$

With k the spring-constant, L the length at rest, and W the weight of the node. The latter expresses the confidence in this node. An interpolated node is given only half the average weight of its neighbors, multiplied by its connectivity number, devided by four. A detected node, on the other hand, is assigned a unit weight multiplied by the difference between the mean line distance of the local neighborhood and the distance between this node and his neighbors. The parameters α, β and γ control the influence of each force. As the problem is 2D, not only elasticity but also bending is implicitly taken into account.

Fig. 7. *A Node between its Four Neighbors*

The behavior of the mesh is that of a 'dynamic sponge'. If one applies a force a continuous deformation is propagated trough the structure. The weights of the nodes determine their own mobility and their influence on their neighbors. Nodes which are detected during initialization with a very low certainty are given a low weight: they influence their neighbors less, but are themselves more mobile. In this way, salient (correct) nodes will try to move the dubious ones in a more correct position, and not v.v.

The level of activity of a node determines if its position should still be updated in the current iteration. As about 75% of the nodes are in their correct position after a couple of iterations, this can speed up iterations considerably. The activity update-mechanism is based on the local spring-energy around the node.

The step size also influences the rate of convergence. The energy of the active part of the mesh determines the current step width. As long as the energy in the mesh decreases sufficiently, the steps can be made bigger. Otherwise they should be decreased. This causes the step to very soon reach its ideal width.

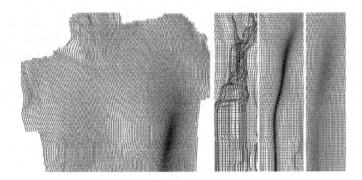

Fig. 8. *Close-up of the mannequin after relaxation, this should be compared to the initialization. The figures right show the right side of the belly at intermediate stages.*

4   Results

Fig. 9. reconstruction

Figure 8 shows the result of 50 iterations on the (quite badly initialized) left side of the mannequin belly. The result is a smooth, regular mesh, which is sub-pixel precise in regions with salient lines. Figure 9 shows a reconstruction. In regions with faint stripes, lines were initialized by interpolation. The number of lines to be interpolated is determined exactly if the gap is completely surrounded by detected lines. In other cases, we could estimate the correct number through a locally adapted average line spacing. This interpolation strategy, almost completely removed any spatial continuity assumptions about the object shape. The position of the interpolated lines will be at least acceptable. When compared with the input image, their position is most of the time very close to the real boundary positions. The whole initialization/relaxation step took less than 1 sec on a pentIII @700Mhz. One of the targeted applications is the acquisition of deformable surfaces. As the system is one-shot, it suffices to take images with a video camera and to produce a 3D reconstruction from every frame. Such continuous operation will allow us to speed up the system further. For the detection of the stripe boundaries in the next frame, the initialization step of the previous image can be used. This relaxation process can run in real-time. Work on an optimal implementation aiming at this real-time adaptation is underway.

5   Conclusion

We have demonstrated the use of a generalized 2D active mesh, for the detection of stripe boundaries by a structured light system. The mesh is first roughly initialized, after which it is iteratively trimmed to a sub-pixel precise position. Results showed that even with a very bad initialization, the mesh still converges to its correct position. During the initialization phase speed, a correct number of lines, and their correct numbering were the most important issues. Precision was less important. The use of both global and quick local decisions was essential.

Very fast 3D reconstructions are possible. A modification of the iterative relaxation algorithm, such that it can adapt after initialization to its correct position in all subsequent frames is possible. This makes real-time range scanning in dynamic environments possible.

Acknowledgements

The authors gratefully acknowledge financial support by the Research Council of the Kath. Un. Leuven through the GOA project 'Variability in Human Shape and Speech' (VHS+).

References

1. J.Gluckman, and S.K.Nayar, Handling Occlusions in Dense Multi-view Stereo, IEEE Comp. Soc. Conf. on Computer Vision and Pattern Recognition I-103-117, 2002.
2. Z.Zhang, R.Deriche, O.Faugeras, and Q.Luong A Robust Technique for Matching Two Uncalibrated Images through the Recovery of the Unknown Epipolar Geometry, Artificial Intelligence Journal 78, 1995.
3. D.Caspi, N.Kyriati,and J.Shamir Range Imaging With Adaptive Color Structured Light, IEEE Transact. on Pat. Anal. and Machine Intelligence vol 20, nr.5, 1998.
4. J.Batlle, E.Mouaddib and J.Salvi Recent Pogress in Coded Structured Light as a Technique to Solve the Correspondence Prob: Survey, Pat. Recog. vol 31, nr.7, 1998.
5. A.J.Stewartand M.S.Langer Towards Accurate Recovery of Shape from Shading under Diffuse Lighting, IEEE Pat. Anal. and Machine Intel. 1020-1025, 1997
6. M.Proesmans & L.Van Gool 1-Shot Act. 3D Im. Capt., Proc. SPIE p 50-61, 1997
7. O.Hall-Holt and S.Rusinkiewicz Stripe Boundary Codes for Real-Time Struct.-Light, Proc. ICCV 2001.
8. S.Rusinkiewicz and M.Levoy Efficient Variants of the ICP Algo., Proc. ICCV 2001.

Appearance-Based 3-D Face Recognition from Video

Volker Krüger[1], Ralph Gross[2], and Simon Baker[2]

[1] University of Maryland, Center for Automation Research,
A.V. Williams Building, College Park, MD 20742
[2] The Robotics Institute, Carnegie Mellon University,
5000 Forbes Avenue, Pittsburgh, PA 15213

Abstract. In this work we present an appearance-based 3-D Face Recognition approach that is able to recognize faces in video sequences, independent from face pose. For this we combine *eigen light-fields* with probabilistic propagation over time for evidence integration. Eigen light-fields allow us to build an appearance based 3-D model of an object; probabilistic methods for evidence integration are attractive in this context as they allow a systematic handling of uncertainty and an elegant way for fusing temporal information. Experiments demonstrate the effectiveness of our approach. We tested this approach successfully on more than 20 testing sequences, with 74 different individuals.

1 Introduction

Face recognition has been a major research topic in recent years. Among the most successful approaches are [21,12,22]. The techniques have been thoroughly evaluated in the FERET-Protocol [15] and produce acceptable recognition rates in ideal conditions. However, if ideal conditions are not met, e.g., in case of out-of-plane rotation, recognition rates drop drastically. The major reason is, that the above recognition approaches use the *still-to-still* technique: gallery and probe sets contain still face images (mug-shots), and recognition rates are high only if geometrical and photometrical conditions of the test images in the probe set match those in the gallery set. To solve these problems a *video-to-video* technique has been proposed [8]. In this setting, gallery and probe sets consist of videos, instead of mug-shots, i.e., each individual is represented by a video ideally showing a variety of views, and the individual is to be recognized from a video where he/she also shows a wide variety of views. In this approach, exemplars are learned that summarize the visible 3-D variations of the face in the video, their priors as well as their dynamics. Matching is done by evidence integration over time; a particle method is used to analytically estimate the probability density function over the set of known individuals.

The set of exemplars that are learned from the training videos represent an appearance-based 3-D representation of the face. This representation is built incrementally and depends heavily on the training video: slight variations in the video lead to completely different representations. This hinders a common representation of the face space; the consequence is that one needs to test each single face as a hypothesis. A more systematic way of building an appearance-based 3-D model is therefore important. In this paper we propose to use *eigen*

L. Van Gool (Ed.): DAGM 2002, LNCS 2449, pp. 566–574, 2002.
© Springer-Verlag Berlin Heidelberg 2002

light-fields (ELFs) [4], which were previously used to build a view-independent *still-to-still* face representation. In this paper we combine the advantages of the ELFs with the probabilistic evidence integration over time of [8]. The challenge is to use ELFs for low resolution video data instead of high resolution still images.

The remainder of this paper is organized as follows: Sec. 2 introduces some preliminaries. In Sec. 3 we introduce eigen light-fields. The recognition method is discussed in Sec. 4. We conclude with experimental results in Sec. 5 and final remarks are in Sec. 6.

2   Preliminaries

Before delving into details about ELFs and evidence integration, we will introduce some terminology borrowed from the FERET evaluation protocol [15]. A *Gallery* $\mathcal{V} = \{V_1, V_2, \ldots, V_N\}$ is a set of image sets. Each V_i is associated with a single individual, i.e., N individuals $\mathcal{N} = \{1, 2, \ldots, N\}$, are represented in the Gallery $\mathcal{V}$. The gallery contains the exemplars against which the probe set is matched. A *Probe set* $\mathcal{P} = \{P_1, P_2, \ldots, P_M\}$ is a set of M probe videos which are used for testing.

2.1   Geometric and Photometric Transformations

An image Z may undergo a geometrical or photometrical transformation

$$\tilde{Z} = \mathcal{T}_\alpha\{Z\} \tag{1}$$

for $\alpha \in \mathcal{A}$, where $\mathcal{A}$ is the set of possible transformations. The set of possible transformations $\mathcal{A}$ has to be pre-defined in our framework.

2.2   Likelihood Measure

Let $F = \{f_1, f_2 \ldots, f_N\}$ be a set of face images, with $\mathcal{N} = \{1, 2, \ldots, N\}$. Let further $X \in \mathcal{A} \times \mathcal{N}$ be a random variable. This random variable defines the transformation $\mathcal{T}_\alpha$ and the number i of a face $f_i \in F$. Thus, having observed a video image Z, the observation likelihood for a hypothesis $X = (\alpha, i)$, is given by

$$p(Z|X) \equiv p(Z|\alpha, i)$$
$$\propto z \exp -\frac{1}{2\sigma^2} d(Z, \mathcal{T}_\alpha\{f_i\}) \ , \tag{2}$$

Eq. (2) computes the probability that the observation Z shows the face of an individual i, while the face f_i undergoes the transformation α. Here, $d(\cdot, \cdot)$ is a suitable distance function. In face recognition, one usually deals with the inner face region of the subject, rather than the entire image. We therefore interpret Eq. (2) such that $\mathcal{T}_\alpha\{f_i\}$ is compared to a subimage of Z where the position and scale of the subimage is specified by α. If $\mathcal{A}$ is the set of affine deformation, our-of-plane rotation cannot be modeled adequately. Such transformations have to be coped with in a different manner. To do so, we use as the distance function d the eigen light-fields, that will be introduced in the next section.

3   Appearance-Based 3-D Representation with Eigen Light-Fields

3.1   Object Light-Fields

The *plenoptic function* [1] or *light-field* [10] is a function which specifies the radiance of light in free space. It is a 5D function of position (3D) and orientation (2D). In addition, it is also sometimes modeled as a function of time, wavelength, and polarization, depending on the application in mind. Assuming that there is no absorption or scattering of light through the air [14], the light-field is actually only a 4D function, a 2D function of position defined over a 2D surface, and a 2D function of direction [3,10]. In 2D, the light-field of a 2D object is actually 2D rather, than the 3D that might be expected. See Figure 1,left, for an illustration.

3.2   Eigen Light-Fields

Suppose we are given a collection of light-fields $L_i(\theta, \phi)$ where $i = 1, \ldots, N$. See Figure 1,left, for the definition of this notation. If we perform an eigen-decomposition of these vectors using Principal Components Analysis (PCA), we obtain $d \leq N$ eigen light-fields $E_i(\theta, \phi)$ where $i = 1, \ldots, d$. Then, assuming that the eigen-space of light-fields is a good representation of the set of light-fields under consideration, we can approximate any light-field $L(\theta, \phi)$ as:

$$L(\theta, \phi) \approx \sum_{i=1}^{d} \lambda_i E_i(\theta, \phi) \tag{3}$$

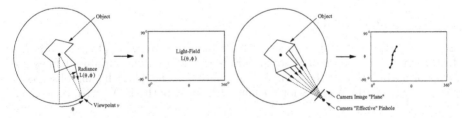

Fig. 1. Left image: An illustration of the 2D light-field of a 2D object [10]. The object is conceptually placed within a circle. The angle to the viewpoint v around the circle is measured by the angle θ, and the direction that the viewing ray makes with the radius of the circle is denoted ϕ. For each pair of angles θ and ϕ, the radiance of light reaching the viewpoint from the object is then denoted by $L(\theta, \phi)$, the *light-field*. Although the light-field of a 3D object is actually 4D, we will continue to use the 2D notation of this figure in this paper for ease of explanation. **Right image:** The 1D image of a 2D object corresponds to a curve (surface for a 2D image of a 3D object) in the light-field. Each pixel in the image corresponds to a ray in space through the camera pinhole and the location of the pixel on the image plane. In general this ray intersects the light-field circle at a different point for each pixel. As the pixel considered "moves" in the image plane, the point on the light-field circle therefore traces out a curve in θ-ϕ space. This curve is a straight vertical line iff the "effective pinhole" of the camera lies on the circle used to define the light-field.

where $\lambda_i = \langle L(\theta,\phi), E_i(\theta,\phi) \rangle$ is the inner (or dot) product between $L(\theta,\phi)$ and $E_i(\theta,\phi)$. This decomposition is analogous to that used in face and object recognition [19, 13]; it is just performed on the entire light-field rather than on images.

3.3   Estimating Light-Fields from Images

Capturing the complete light-field of an object is a difficult task, primarily because it requires a huge number of images [3, 10]. In most object recognition scenarios it is unreasonable to expect more than a few images of the object; often just one. As shown in Figure 1, right, however, any image of the object corresponds to a curve (for 3D objects, a surface) in the light-field. One way to look at this curve is as a highly occluded light-field; only a very small part of the light-field is visible.

It was argued in [4] that the eigen coefficients λ_i can be estimated from such an occluded view. An algorithm used in [4] solves for λ_i as the least squares solution of:

$$L(\theta,\phi) - \sum_{i=1}^{d} \lambda_i E_i(\theta,\phi) = 0 \qquad (4)$$

where there is one such equation for each pair of θ and ϕ that are un-occluded in $L(\theta,\phi)$. Assuming that $L(\theta,\phi)$ lies *completely within the eigen-space* and that enough pixels are un-occluded, then the solution of Equation (4) will be exactly the same as that obtained using the inner product [4].

Since there are d unknowns $(\lambda_1 \ldots \lambda_d)$ in Equation (4), at least d un-occluded light-field pixels are needed to over-constrain the problem, but more may be required due to linear dependencies between the equations. In practice, $2 - 3$ times as many equations as unknowns are typically required to get a reasonable solution [9]. Given an image $I(m,n)$, the following is then an algorithm for estimating the eigen light-field coefficients λ_i:

Algorithm 1: Eigen Light-Field Estimation.

1. For each pixel (m,n) in $I(m,n)$ compute the corresponding light-field angles $\theta_{m,n}$ and $\phi_{m,n}$.
2. Find the least-squares solution (for $\lambda_1 \ldots \lambda_d$) to the set of equations:

$$I(m,n) - \sum_{i=1}^{d} \lambda_i E_i(\theta_{m,n}, \phi_{m,n}) = 0 \qquad (5)$$

where m and n range over their allowed values.

Although we have described this algorithm for a single image $I(m,n)$, any number of images can obviously be used. The extra pixels from the other images are simply added in as additional constraints on the unknown coefficients λ_i in Equation (5). Algorithm 1 can be used to estimate a light-field from a collection of images. Once the light-field has been estimated, it can then be used to render new images of the same object under different poses (See also [20]). It was shown in [4] that the algorithm correctly re-renders a given object assuming a Lambertian reflectance model.

4   Tracking and Recognizing in Video

In this section we discuss the recognition of individuals in videos. After the generation of ELFs from the image sets $\mathcal{V}_i$ in the previous section, we have a vector of eigen values for each individual $i \in \mathcal{N}$ in the Gallery $\mathcal{V}$.

4.1   Tracking and Recognition in the Bayesian Framework

We can now compute the observation likelihoods as in Eq. 2 and we can track and identify individuals in the video: Let $X_t = (\alpha_t, i_t) \in \mathcal{A} \times \mathcal{N}$ be a random variable. We want to find X_t such that the joint distribution

$$p(X_t|Z_1, \ldots, Z_t) \tag{6}$$

is maximal. Using the classical Bayesian propagation over time, we get

$$
\begin{aligned}
p(X_t|Z_1, Z_2, \ldots, Z_t) &\equiv p_t(\alpha_t, i_t) \\
&= \sum_{i_{t-1}} \int_{\alpha_{t-1}} p(Z_t|\alpha_t, i_t) p(\alpha_t, i_t|\alpha_{t-1}, i_{t-1}) p_{t-1}(\alpha_{t-1}, i_{t-1}) \,.
\end{aligned}
\tag{7}
$$

Marginalizing the posterior over the possible transformations $\alpha \in \mathcal{A}$ we get a probability mass function for the identity:

$$p(i_t|Z_1, \ldots, Z_t) = \int_{\alpha_t} p(\alpha_t, i_t|Z_1, \ldots, Z_t) \,. \tag{8}$$

Maximizing (8) leads to the desired identity.
In Eq. (7)

$$p(X_t|X_{t-1}) \equiv p(\alpha_t, i_t|\alpha_{t-1}, i_{t-1})$$

defines the probability of the state variable to change from X_{t-1} to X_t. The transformation α_t may change according to a dynamic model. The identity i, however, is assumed to be constant over time, i.e., it is assumed that the identity of the tracked person does not change over time. Learning of a dynamic model has been discussed in [18].

We have used a particle method to efficiently compute $p_t(i_t, \alpha_t|Z_t)$ [23, 2, 6, 7, 11], where i_t, α_t depicts the hypothesised identity and transformation of the individual in the video. In [6] only the transformation α_t was estimated, in [23] the special case was discussed where each individual is presented by only a single exemplar. In [8] this was generalized to the case of several exemplars for each individual. Since the ELFs offer a common 3-D representation for each face, we use the more efficient particle method of [23].

5   Experiments

We used the CMU PIE database [16] as the training set to build eigen light-fields for our experiments and as part of the gallery. The database consists of 68 subjects. The images were preprocessed as explained in [4] and were then

Fig. 2. The pose variation in the PIE database [17]. The pose varies from full left profile (c34) to full frontal (c27) and on to full right profile (c22). The 9 cameras in the horizontal sweep are each separated by about 22.5°. The 4 other cameras include 1 above (c09) and 1 below (c07) the central camera, and 2 in the corners of the room (c25 and c31), typical locations for surveillance cameras.

downsampled to a height of 38 pixels. In Fig. 2 the set of available views in the training set is shown. For testing we have used CMU Mobo Database [5]. We needed to select a subset of 6 individuals and 20 videos as the facial views in the remaining videos were not consistent with the 3-D model as defined by the eigen light-fields: in those videos, the individuals looked either up or down, a pose which was not modeled by our ELFs (see Fig. 2 for the possible views). We therefore extracted manually the inner face regions from the selected 20 videos of the individuals for additional training. The complete Gallery therefore consisted of 74 individuals (6 from the MoBo database and 68 from the PIE database). Between two and four face images were extracted from the videos of each of the 6 individuals. The face images had a height of between 30 and 38 pixels. Smaller images were scaled to a consistent hight of 38 pixels. Using a small number of low-resolution video images results in quite noisy eigenvectors that can hardly be used for recognition based on still images (see below).

The video sequences in the MoBo database show the individuals walking on a tread-mill. Different walking styles were used to assure a variety of conditions that are likely to appear in real life: *slow walk, fast walk, incline walk* and *walking while carrying a ball*. Therefore, four videos per person are available. During the recording of the videos the illumination conditions were not altered. Each video consists of 300 frames (480 × 640 pixels per frame) captured at 30 Hz.

Some example images of the videos (*slowWalk*) are shown in Fig. 3.

The inner face regions in these videos are between 30×30 and 40×40 pixels.

During testing, the ELFs were used to compute, over time, the posteriori probabilities $p_t(i_t|Z_t)$. It is interesting to see, how the posteriori probabilities develop over time. Examples for this can be seen in Fig. 4. The dashed line refers to the correct hypothesized identity, the other five curves refer to the probabilities of the top matching identities other than the true one. One can see, that the dashed line (true hypothesis) increases quickly to one.

Of the 20 videos tested, recognition was successful in 13 cases, i.e. the true hypothesis had maximal probability after convergence. In 4 cases, the true hypothesis was the second highest probability during the evidence integration process, i.e. in 17 cases the true hypothesis was among the top two matches. In the remaining three videos, recognition failed. After an average time of 15 frames the particle method had converged.

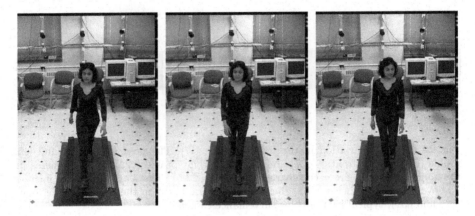

Fig. 3. The figure shows example images of one of the videos (*slow Walk*).

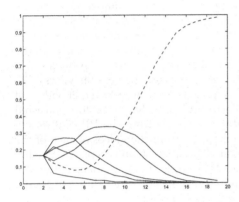

Fig. 4. The figure shows how the posterior probabilities $p_t(i_t|Z_t)$ develop over time. The dashed curve refers to the correct hypothesis. The y-axis refers to the believe that at a given time t a given hypothesis is the correct one.

We also tested the recognition without evidence integration: Testing on all single images of the videos, recognition only succeeded in two cases. This shows the importance of evidence integration for recognition when dealing with noisy observations.

Video images from our test data were converted from color to gray value images, but no further processing was done. The set of deformations $\mathcal{A}$ included scale and translation. Shear and rotation were not considered.

Top matches	13 (out of 20)
Second best matches	4 (out of 20)
still-to-still	2 (out of 1500)

Table 1. The Table summarizes the recognition results: In 13 out of twenty videos the individuals were correctly identified. In four out of twenty, the correct match was only the second best match. Applying the ELF approach without evidence integration lead to 2 correct matches on all images of the videos.

6   Conclusion

In this paper we presented a novel approach for appearance based face recognition across pose. We used eigen light-fields to build a 3-D model of faces. The advantage of ELFs is that once a 3-D model is built from a generic training set, one only needs two to four views of a new and before unseen face to be able to recognize this face from a new and previously unseen view.

This property has been shown in [4] with a large number of experiments. In [4], however, the face sets consisted of high resolution images and the faces did not show any facial expressions. In this paper we examined how this method scales to face images as small as 30×38 pixels with strong variations in appearance due to facial expressions. The resulting noisy feature vectors could not have been used for *still-to-still* recognition. We solved this problem by integrating the evidence of identity over time by applying Bayesian propagation [8]. Using this approach, experiments showed more stable recognition results.

As it is difficult to draw general conclusions from a database of only 20 videos, we currently evaluate our approach on 40 newly recorded sequences.

References

1. E.H. Adelson and J. Bergen. The plenoptic function and elements of early vision. In Landy and Movshon, editors, *Computational Models of Visual Processing*. MIT Press, 1991.
2. A. Doucet, S. Godsill, and C. Andrieu. On sequential monte carlo sampling methods for bayesian filtering. *Statistics and Computing*, 10:197–209, 2000.
3. S. Gortler, R. Grzeszczuk, R. Szeliski, and M. Cohen. The lumigraph. In *SIG-GRAPH*, 1996.
4. R. Gross, I. Matthews, and S. Baker. Eigen light-fields and face recognition across pose. In *Proc. Int. Conf. on Automatic Face and Gesture Recognition*, Washington, DC, USA, May 21-22, 2002.
5. Ralph Gross and Jianbo Shi. The cmu motion of body (mobo) database. Technical Report CMU-RI-TR-01-18, Robotics Institute, Carnegie Mellon University, Pittsburgh, PA, June 2001.
6. M. Isard and A. Blake. Condensation – conditional density propagation for visual tracking. *Int. J. of Computer Vision*, 1998.
7. G. Kitagawa. Monta carlo filter and smoother for non-gaussian nonlinear state space models. *J. Computational and Graphical Statistics*, 5:1–25, 1996.
8. V. Krueger and S. Zhou. Exemplar-based face recognition from video. In *Proc. European Conf. on Computer Vision*, Copenhagen, Denmark, June 27-31, 2002.
9. A. Leonardis and H. Bischof. Dealing with occlusions in the eigenspace approach. In *Proceedings of CVPR*, 1996.
10. M. Levoy and M. Hanrahan. Light field rendering. In *Proc. of SIGGRAPH*, 1996.
11. J.S. Liu and R. Chen. Sequential monte carlo for dynamic systems. *Journal of the American Statistical Association*, 93:1031–1041, 1998.
12. B. Moghaddam and A. Pentland. Probabilistic visual learning for object detection. *IEEE Trans. Pattern Analysis and Machine Intelligence*, 17:696–710, 1997.
13. H. Murase and S.K. Nayar. Visual learning and recognition of 3-D objects from appearance. *Int. J. of Computer Vision*, 14:5–24, 1995.
14. S.K. Nayar and S. Narasimhan. Vision in bad weather. In *Korfu, Greece*, 1999.
15. P. Phillips, H. Moon, S. Rizvi, and P. Rauss. The feret evaluation methodology for face-recognition algorithms. *IEEE Trans. Pattern Analysis and Machine Intelligence*, 22:1090–1103, 2000.

16. T. Sim, S. Baker, and M. Bsat. The CMU Pose, Illumination, and Expression (pie) database. In *Proc. Int. Conf. on Automatic Face and Gesture Recognition*, Washington, DC, USA, May 21-22, 2002.
17. T. Sim, S. Baker, and M. Bsat. The CMU pose, illumination, and expression (PIE) database. In *Proc. of the 5th IEEE International Conference on Automatic Face and Gesture Recognition*, 2002.
18. K. Toyama and A. Blake. Probabilistic tracking in a metric space. In *Proc. Int. Conf. on Computer Vision*, volume 2, pages 50–59, Vancouver, Canada, 9-12 July, 2001.
19. M. Turk and A. Pentland. Face recognition using eigenfaces. In *Proc. of CVPR*, 1991.
20. T. Vetter and T. Poggio. Linear object classes and image synthesis from a single example image. *IEEE Trans. on PAMI*, 19(7):733–741, 1997.
21. L. Wiskott, J. M. Fellous, N. Krüger, and C. v. d. Malsburg. Face recognition and gender determination. In *Proc. Int. Workshop on Automatic Face and Gesture Recognition*, Zurich, Switzerland, June 26-28, 1995.
22. W. Zhao, R. Chellappa, and N. Nandhakumar. Discriminant analysis fo principal components for face recognition. In *Nara, Japan, April 14-16*, pages 336–341, 1998.
23. S. Zhou, V. Krüger, and R. Chellappa. Face recognition from video: A CONDEN-SATION approach. In *Proc. Int. Conf. on Automatic Face and Gesture Recognition*, Washington, DC, USA, May 21-22, 2002.

Direct Method for Motion Estimation: An Alternative to Decomposition of Planar Transformation Matrices

Nassir Navab, Yakup Genc, Ali Khamene, and Matthias Mitschke

Siemens Corporate Research, 755 College Road East, Princeton, NJ 08540, USA,
{Nassir.Navab,Yakup.Genc,Ali.Khamene,Matthias.Mitschke}@scr.siemens.com

Abstract. *Recently, we have seen a proliferation in research addressing the motion estimation problem and its practical applications based on
coplanar point configurations [10,14,12,9,6,7,13]. This paper introduces a
new approach where following an estimation of the full projection matrix
from non-coplanar points in one reference frame, the system provides better motion estimation results based on coplanar point configurations without estimating the camera intrinsic parameters. The new mathematical
framework allows us to directly estimate the rigid transformation between
a full projection matrix and a homography. Experimental results compare
the accuracy of this and the homography decomposition approach, proposed in [14], in the context of an augmented reality application where
three cameras are calibrated for real-time image augmentation.*

1 Introduction

A variety of computer vision applications require accurate estimation of motion
of a camera observing a set of 3D features. The complexity of these features,
e.g., points, limits the use of many sophisticated algorithms. Coplanar points,
on the other hand, are easier to generate and configure in the scene and simpler
to localize and track in images.

Recently, we have seen a proliferation in research addressing the motion estimation problem based on coplanar 3D point configurations. Notable ones include
Sturm [10], Zhang [14], Wexler and Shashua [12], Simon *et al.* [9], Rekimoto [7],
and Kato and Bilinghurst [6] the latter of which is mostly application oriented.

[14] and [10] proposed a simple and practical solution for decomposition of
homography matrix using two or more images to calibrate a camera observing
a set of coplanar features. The homography is a 3×3 matrix that defines the
mapping from the plane formed by the scene points and the image plane and
can be computed using four or more points and their images. If the camera
is internally calibrated, this allows the recovery of the motion from a single
view. Alternatively, the algorithm can recover both intrinsic and extrinsic camera
parameters from three or more images. However, [13] showed that the estimation
of intrinsic parameters this way can be quite noise sensitive.

For sequences taken by the same camera, we can often suppose that the intrinsic parameters remain constant between consecutive frames. This suggests a

L. Van Gool (Ed.): DAGM 2002, LNCS 2449, pp. 575–582, 2002.
© Springer-Verlag Berlin Heidelberg 2002

pre-calibration step. Most calibration processes, however, involve decomposition of the *projection* matrix. The 3×4 projection matrix captures the relation of the 3D points and their 2D projections.

Here, we propose an alternative method that does not decompose the projection matrix. Instead, the new method uses the projection matrix for the reference frame and the homography for any other frame to estimate the relative or inter-frame motion between the two frames. This is a compromise between using only all coplanar or all non-coplanar points. It requires that in the pre-calibration step a non-coplanar set of points is available to estimate a projection matrix. For any other frame only a set of coplanar points is needed.

Another advantage of the new method becomes more visible in augmented reality (AR) applications. In a typical AR system, three cameras are attached rigidly where one camera is used to estimate the motion of the other two [8]. In this case, our method offers a simple solution where the inter-frame motion estimated for the first camera is propagated to the other two cameras in order to estimate the projection matrices using the reference projection matrices obtained in the preparation step. This way, by avoiding the estimation of the rigid motion between the first and the other two cameras, potential errors that might be introduced by this process is eliminated.

This paper is organized as follows: After reviewing the basic formulation of the problem in the following section, Section 3 lays the foundations of the proposed method. Section 4 experimentally compares the different alternatives and our method. We follow the following notation throughout the paper unless noted otherwise: For a matrix M, $\boldsymbol{m}_i$ is the ith column vector, $\boldsymbol{m}_j^T$ is the jth row vector and M_{13} is the sub-matrix formed by the first three columns of M. Furthermore, m_{ij} represents the entry at the ith row and jth column of the matrix.

2   Mathematical Formulation

We define the inter-frame motion estimation problem as follows: Two pinhole cameras are observing a rigid scene with their centers of projections placed at $O_C^{(1)}$ and $O_C^{(2)}$ with extrinsic camera parameters represented by the rotations $R^{(1)}$ and $R^{(2)}$ and translation $\boldsymbol{t}^{(1)}$ and $\boldsymbol{t}^{(2)}$ respectively. The inter-frame motion is represented by R and $\boldsymbol{t}$. Finally, the pinhole cameras are simply represented by the intrinsic parameters:

$$A = \begin{pmatrix} \alpha_u & s & u_0 \\ 0 & \alpha_v & v_0 \\ 0 & 0 & 1 \end{pmatrix},$$

where α_u and α_v are the scale in horizontal and vertical directions, s is the skew, and u_0 and v_0 are the coordinates of the principal point [2].

The relation between each 3D point defined in the world and the position of its projection in an image can be captured by a 3×4 projection matrix P: $\boldsymbol{u}_i = \lambda_i P \boldsymbol{x}_i$, where $\boldsymbol{u}_i = (u_i, v_i, 1)^T$ is the projection of point $\boldsymbol{x}_i = (x_i, y_i, z_i, 1)^T$

for the ith point with $i = 1, ..., n$. λ_i is the point and image dependent scale often known as projective depth [2]. The projection matrices can be described in terms of intrinsic and extrinsic camera parameters: $P = \lambda A [R \quad t]$. From $n \geq 6$ pairs of 3D to 2D correspondences, the projection matrix can be computed easily via least squares methods [4,1].

When a set of coplanar points are observed, the relation between these points and their projections in the image plane can be described by a planar transformation or homography $H \in \mathbb{R}^{3 \times 3}$. This transformation is defined by $\boldsymbol{u}_i = \lambda_i H \boldsymbol{x}'_i$, where $\boldsymbol{x}'_i = (x'_i, y'_i, 1)^T$ are the scene points on $z = 0$ plane. Similar to the projection matrices, for $n \geq 4$ pairs of corresponding points $\boldsymbol{u}_i$ and $\boldsymbol{x}'_i$, the resulting homogeneous system can be solved via a least squares methods [3,14,10].

3   Direct Estimation of Inter-frame Motion

Here we present a method which assumes that a projection matrix for the first frame, i.e., the reference frame, is available. This method computes the inter-frame motion for any successive frames observing a set of coplanar points. In essence, the homography is computed for each frame, and the relative motion with respect to the reference frame is computed from the homography and reference projection matrix. Avoiding an explicit calibration makes this method simple to implement and accurate.

The rigid motion $[R \quad t]$ between two frames, where the first is represented by a projection matrix P and the second by a homography H is described as

$$\lambda H = P \begin{pmatrix} R & t \\ \mathbf{0}^T & 1 \end{pmatrix} \begin{pmatrix} 1 & 0 & 0 \\ 0 & 1 & 0 \\ 0 & 0 & 0 \\ 0 & 0 & 1 \end{pmatrix}. \tag{1}$$

Rotation − To recover the rotation from (1), we need to solve the following system of equation for the first two column vectors of R, i.e., $\boldsymbol{r}_1$ and $\boldsymbol{r}_2$:

$$\lambda H_{12} = P_{13} [\boldsymbol{r}_1 \, \boldsymbol{r}_2], \tag{2}$$

taking their orthogonality constraint into account.

By taking the orthogonality of $\boldsymbol{r}_1$ and $\boldsymbol{r}_2$ into account, we can provide an explicit solution to (2). This equation can be considered as an orthographic projection of $\boldsymbol{p}_1$, $\boldsymbol{p}_2$, and $\boldsymbol{p}_3$, the three rows of P_{13}, onto $\boldsymbol{h}_1$, $\boldsymbol{h}_2$, and $\boldsymbol{h}_3$, the three rows of the matrix H_{12}:

$$\lambda \boldsymbol{h}_i = [\boldsymbol{r}_1 \, \boldsymbol{r}_2]^T \boldsymbol{p}_i, \quad \text{for} \quad i = 1, ..., 3. \tag{3}$$

This is analogous to having three 3D to 2D point correspondences. We choose the coordinate systems such that $\boldsymbol{h}_1$ and $\boldsymbol{p}_1$ define the origin, x-axes point towards $\boldsymbol{h}_2$ and $\boldsymbol{p}_2$, and y-axes perpendicular to x-axes lie on the plane formed by the three points for $\boldsymbol{h}_i$ and $\boldsymbol{p}_i$ respectively. We have:

$$\lambda \boldsymbol{h}'_i = [\boldsymbol{r}_1 \, \boldsymbol{r}_2]^T \boldsymbol{p}'_i, \quad \text{for} \quad i = 1, ..., 2, \tag{4}$$

where $h_i' = (h_i - h_1)$ and $p_i' = (p_i - p_1)$. The above transformations are accomplished with R' and R'' for 2D and 3D cases respectively:

$$R' = [r_1', r_2'] \quad \text{and} \quad R'' = [r_1'', r_1'', r_1'' \times r_2''].$$

with $r_1' = \frac{h_2'}{\|h_2'\|}$, $r_2' = \frac{h_3' - (r_1'^T h_3')r_1'}{\|h_3' - (r_1'^T h_3')r_1'\|}$, $r_1'' = \frac{p_2'}{\|p_2'\|}$, and $r_2'' = \frac{p_3' - (r_1''^T p_3')r_1''}{\|p_3' - (r_1''^T p_3')r_1''\|}$.
Applying these transformations to (3), we get the following system:

$$\lambda' \begin{bmatrix} 1 & \alpha \\ 0 & \beta \end{bmatrix} = [\tilde{r}_1 \, \tilde{r}_2]^T \begin{bmatrix} 1 & a \\ 0 & b \\ 0 & 0 \end{bmatrix},$$

where the only unknowns are the scale factor λ' and $[\tilde{r}_1 \tilde{r}_2]^T = R'[r_1 r_2]^T R''$. This results in $\tilde{r}_{1,2} = \frac{\alpha - a}{b} \tilde{r}_{1,1}$ and $\tilde{r}_{2,2} = \frac{\beta}{b} \tilde{r}_{1,1}$. Taking the orthogonality constraints of the rotation matrix, i.e. $\|\tilde{r}_2\| = \|\tilde{r}_1\| = 1$ and $\tilde{r}_1^T \tilde{r}_2 = 0$, into account, an explicit solution to the problem can be found by solving the following equation for $\tilde{r}_{1,1}$:

$$\frac{\beta^2}{b^2}\tilde{r}_{1,1}^4 - (1 + \frac{\beta^2 + (\alpha - a)^2}{b^2})\tilde{r}_{1,1}^2 + 1 = 0. \tag{5}$$

It is easy to show that the roots of this quadratic equations in $\tilde{r}_{1,1}^2$ are all positive and the two roots lie on the opposite site of 1 in the number line. Since, $\tilde{r}_{1,1}$ is an entry in a rotation matrix, it's square should be in the interval $[0, 1]$. Thus we can obtain an unambiguous solution to $\tilde{r}_{1,1}^2$ which in turn yields two solutions. The right solution can be easily chosen using Cheirality invariants [5].

Scale – The matrix equation $\lambda H_{12} = P_{13}R_{12}$ results in six equations for the unknown λ which can be computed via least squares methods.

Translation – The decoupled translation equation out of (1) is $\lambda h_3 = P_{13}t + p_4$. The translation is then directly computed with $t = P_{13}^{-1}(\lambda h_3 - p_4)$.

4   Experiments

In this section we present experiments conducted using an Augmented Reality (AR) setup (see Figure 1) to compare the direct method introduced in the previous chapter against Zhang's [14] and Tsai's [11] methods.

A typical video see-through AR system with a vision-based tracker device consists of a head-mounted display (HMD) and three rigidly attached cameras. Two of the cameras, with narrow field-of-view (FOV), provide the images to the user, and the third camera, with larger FOV, tracks a set of features to estimate in real-time the position and orientation of the HMD in the world.

For high accuracy and robustness, these systems are calibrated off-line. The calibration usually entails the estimation of a set of parameters in some form for each camera assuming they are rigidly attached. For the large FOV camera some

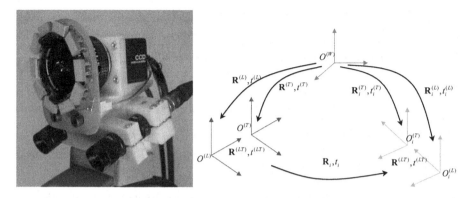

Fig. 1. The setup for the experiments using a tracker camera and two other cameras from an augmented reality system.

radial distortion correction may also be needed. Off-line calibration can be best realized using a large set of non-coplanar calibration points. While the relative motion between the different cameras are fixed, their intrinsic parameters can be assumed fixed as well.

Once the calibration is achieved, the system estimates the relative position of the HMD in real-time. For this, a smaller set of features are tracked by the tracker camera. The markers need to be carefully calibrated and at the same time they should be relocatable. In this respect, planar markers are better and used frequently [8,6,9].

We have used the direct pose estimation algorithm (Table 1) described in this paper to estimate the pose of an HMD in this setting. We have also applied Zhang's [14] method to the same problem for comparison purposes. The methods are tested by using the following estimated projection matrices to compare the back projection results on the left camera:

Table 1. Direct method for inter-frame motion estimation (superscripts $^{(T)}$, $^{(R)}$ and $^{(L)}$ stand for the tracker, right and left cameras respectively and $^{(LT)}$ stands for the transformation from the left to the right cameras).

Off-line:

– Estimate reference projection matrices ($P^{(T)}$, $P^{(R)}$ and $P^{(L)}$) from points well distributed in 3D.

On-line (for ith frame):

– Determine the homography $H_i^{(T)}$ from a planar set of points.
– Using $H_i^{(T)}$, estimate the rotation R_i and translation t_i relative to reference frame.
– Apply the motion $[R_i \ t_i]$ to the reference projection matrices $P_i^{(T)}$, $P_i^{(R)}$ and $P_i^{(L)}$ to get the corresponding projection matrices for the ith frame.

DI (Direct Method): First estimates the inter-frame motion between the reference frame and the ith frame directly for the tracker camera, and then applies this transformation to the augmentation camera as follows: $P_i^{(L)} = P^{(L)} \begin{pmatrix} R_i & t_i \\ 0 & 1 \end{pmatrix}$

TS1 and TS2 (Tsai Calibration): Calibrates each camera off-line and for ith image estimates the projection matrix using the transformation obtained for the tracker camera as follows: $P_i^{(L)} = A^{(L)} \begin{pmatrix} R_i^{(LT)} & t_i^{(LT)} \\ 0 & 1 \end{pmatrix} \begin{pmatrix} R_i^{(T)} & t_i^{(T)} \\ 0 & 1 \end{pmatrix}$. TS1 uses a full optimization for external calibration whereas TS2 only uses the linear estimate of the motion for Tsai's algorithm.

Z1a and Z1b (Zhang's Method Using Tsai Calibration): First estimates the rigid transformation from the tracker camera to the augmentation camera, and then uses Zhang's algorithm to estimate the absolute pose for the ith tracker frame, finally computing the projection matrix for the augmentation camera as follows (with two versions with a) internal parameters are fixed, b) internal parameters are allowed to vary for pose estimation): $P_i^{(L)} = A^{(L)} \begin{pmatrix} R_i^{(LT)} & t_i^{(LT)} \\ 0 & 1 \end{pmatrix} \begin{pmatrix} R_i^{(T)} & t_i^{(T)} \\ 0 & 1 \end{pmatrix}$.

Z2a and Z2b (Zhang's Method Backprojection): Estimates the absolute pose for the tracker camera (the same as Z1a and Z1b) and obtains the projection matrix for the augmentation camera with: $P_i^{(L)} = P^{(L)} \begin{pmatrix} R^{(T)} & t^{(T)} \\ 0 & 1 \end{pmatrix}^{-1} \begin{pmatrix} R_i^{(T)} & t_i^{(T)} \\ 0 & 1 \end{pmatrix}$.
Augmentation methods of Z1a and Z2a are different, but they both compute the same pose from the same observations (similarly Z1b and Z2b).

Fig. 2 summarizes the results of these experiments. In each experiment, we have used the same reference frames and three different set of markers (including 4, 7, and 17 points) to estimate the pose of six different views. The statistics of the error, as the distance between the observed location of a point feature and the projection of the corresponding 3D point, is plotted for each method. The height of the bar represents the mean error and the standard deviation is plotted on top of the bar. The order of the bars representing the different methods is from left to right 1) TS1, 2)TS2, 3) DI, 4) Z1a, 5) Z1b, 6) Z2a, and 7) Z2b.

Tsai calibration with full optimization uses all of the 17 available points, hence giving the smallest error. We displayed results from Tsai calibration to establish a ground truth for comparison. Note that this calibration involves a nonlinear optimization whereas the others are all linear. As shown in the figure, when no optimization is used, the linear Tsai algorithm yields increased error even though still using all of the 17 available points. The reader should also note that Tsai method is not the preferred method for estimating the planar transformations because it needs at least 6 points to work whereas the other methods can estimate the pose with as low as 4 points.

As can be seen from the results, the method of decomposing homography (i.e., Zhang) performs well as long as we make the intrinsic values of the camera constant while using the projection matrix at the reference frame to generate

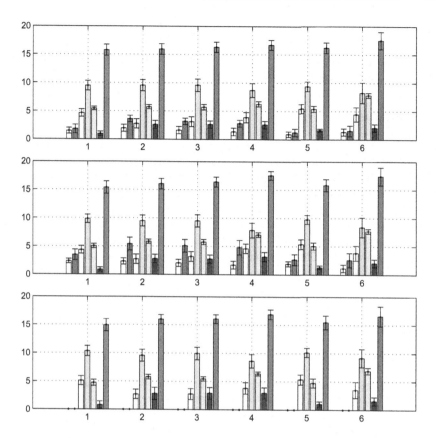

Fig. 2. Comparison of the five methods for the first frame as the reference when all 17 (top), 7 (middle) and 4 (bottom) planar points are used for homography estimation. For each of the six frames, the bars from left to right represents the results for the methods TS1, TS2, DI, Z1a, Z1b, Z2a and Z2b. Note that TS1 and TS2 are depicted here for reference purposes only and need at least 6 points.

the full projection matrix at the ith frame. By doing this we get the error plots with the lowest level for the Zhang. However, it should be noted that the same motion while coupled with homogeneous transformation yields the worst results as shown in the figure. The latter shows that although the lumped full projection matrix performs better, the decomposed motion is not accurate enough. By letting the re-computation of the internal parameters in the Zhang's method we get less severe of this effect as depicted in the figure.

The direct method performs quite well even with a minimum number of available points. In particular, when compared to Zhang the performance suggests that the inter-frame motion estimation for the tracker camera in direct estimation is most precise in all cases.

For comparison, we should note that in the backprojection error of the planar points, Z2a gives the best results. However, it's counterpart, i.e., Z1a, which is based on the same computation but backprojects the pre-transformed 3D planar points, does not give as good results. This suggests that metric pose as estimated from Zhang's algorithm is not as good. Whereas, DI gives consistently better estimation on the metric transformation.

5 Conclusion

This paper present a new motion estimation method based on off-line estimation of a reference projection matrix and on-line (real-time) estimation of planar transformations. This new method combines the advantages of easy, robust and practical estimation of planar transformations, e.g., in real-time applications such as augmented reality and the complete information of a projection matrix estimated only for one reference frame. The proposed mathematical formulation allows robust estimation of inter-frame motion with no need for recovery of the intrinsic parameters. The method makes the reasonable assumption that the intrinsic parameters remain constant. The method is successfully implemented within the context of an augmented reality application.

References

1. O. D. Faugeras and G. Toscani. The calibration problem for stereo. In *Proc. CVPR*, 1996.
2. O.D. Faugeras. *Three-Dimensional Computer Vision*. MIT Press, 1993.
3. O.D. Faugeras and F. Lustman. Motion and structure from motion in a piecewise-planar environment. *J. of Pattern Rec. and Art. Int.*, 2(3):485–508, 1988.
4. S. Ganapathy. Decomposition of transformation matrices for robot vision. In *Proc. Int. Conf. on Robotics and Automation*, pages 130–139, 1984.
5. R.I. Hartley Cheirality invariants In *Proc. DARPA Image Understanding Workshop*, 745-753, Washington, D.C., 1993.
6. H. Kato and M. Billinghurst. Marker tracking and hmd calibration for a video-based augmented reality conferencing system. In *IWAR*, San Francisco, CA, 1999.
7. J. Rekimoto and Y. Ayatsuka. Cybercode: Designing augmented reality environments with visual tags. In Proc. Designing AR Environments, 2000.
8. F. Sauer, F. Wenzel, S. Vogt, Y. Tao, Y. Genc, and A. Bani-Hashemi. Augmented workspace: Designing an AR testbed. In *ISAR*, Germany, 2000.
9. G. Simon, A. W. Fitzgibbon, and A. Zisserman. Markerless tracking using planar structures in the scene. In *ISAR*, Germany, 2000.
10. P. Sturm. Algorithms for plane-based pose estimation. In *CVPR*, Hilton Head Island, SC, 2000.
11. R.Y. Tsai. A versatile camera calibration technique for high-accuracy 3D machine vision metrology using off-the-shelf TV cameras. *IEEE J. of Robotics and Automation*, RA-3(4):323–344, 1987.
12. Y. Wexler and A. Shashua. On the sysnthesis of dynamic scenes from reference views In *CVPR*, Hilton Head Island, SC, 2000.
13. X. Zhang and N. Navab. Tracking and pose estimation for computer assisted localization in industrial environments. In *WACV*, Palm Springs, CA, 2000.
14. Z. Zhang. A flexible new technique for camera calibration. *PAMI*, 41(11):1330–1334, 2000.

A Feature-Driven Attention Module
for an Active Vision System

Kyungjoo Cheoi and Yillbyung Lee

Dept. of Computer Science and Industrial Systems Engineering, Yonsei University 134,
Sinchon-dong, Seodaemoon-gu, Seoul, 120-749, Korea
{kjcheoi,yblee}@csai.yonsei.ac.kr

Abstract. An approach of using an attention module for an active vision system to elicit a fixation point, and some examples in its application of locating candidate regions of interest on various images, are presented. Many evidences show that biological system appear to employ a serial strategy by which an attentional spotlight rapidly selects circumscribed regions in the scene, rather than attempting to fully interpret visual scenes in a parallel manner for further analysis. Based on this mechanism, our proposed system helps in selecting the most interesting region. The results are reported various color images taken from a variety of different domains.

1 Introduction

One of the main difficulties in trying to build active vision systems is to deal with the time-scale problem. Due to the computational complexity problem of the processing, which is followed by enlarging images reached to the image acquisition system, treating the visual information is so difficult. Active vision emphasizes the importance of an active approach to visual perception, which seeks regions of interest in an image in order to reduce the computational complexity associated with time-consuming process, by dynamically changing the parameters of image acquisition system. A major feature of active vision is gaze control for the generation of saccades, allowing acquisition of relevant visual information from a large image without scanning the whole field of view. The gaze control of robot head is usually modeled after the human visual system. It consists of many low level control units which interact to direct the attention of the system to a desired location.

As seen, the importance of selecting the relevant information from the image is highly recognized in computer vision or active vision. Previous works have employed various filtering techniques. Such methods usually process the information contained within a field of view centered at a focal point. However such methods are rather inefficient in aspect of computational complexity if one has to process lots of focal points in an image. Many studies of visual attention and eye movements [17] have shown that humans generally only attend to a few areas in an image rather than scan the whole image, and visual attention models provide a general approach to control

L. Van Gool (Ed.): DAGM 2002, LNCS 2449, pp. 583–590, 2002.

the activities of active vision systems. A large number of visual attention models have been presented in the past. See [3,5,9,10,13,14,15] for review on psychological computational models, [7,8,12] for computer vision models, and [2,6,11,16] for active vision models. And see [1,4] for a neuropsyhological review on visual attention.

High level feature can be very useful in determining region's importance in situations where a template of a target is known a priori, viewer's eye movements can be modeled with high accuracy. However in the general case, little is known about the contents of the scene, thus such high level information cannot be used. In our approach, we used only bottom-up component of visual attention, and we can easily extend the system to various applications.

Our proposed attention module is presented in Section 2. Section 3 describes experiments and the results, and concluding remarks are made in Section 4.

2   A Feature-Driven Attention Module

In this chapter, we will describe our feature-driven attention module in detail. The basic operation of our attention module is shown in Fig.1. As shown, it uses RGB color image as an input and extracts three early visual feature maps in parallel. Then, each map is reorganized in order to extract orientations and to enhance the regions of pixels which are largely different from their surroundings'. The resulting feature maps are then integrated into a saliency map. This saliency map can be used to control the pan and tilt parameters of the camera in active vision systems.

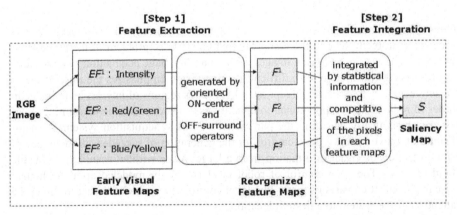

Fig. 1. Detailed view of the attention module where input image is processed through two steps, feature extraction and integration. In first step, the input image is separated into three early visual feature maps, EF^1 for intensity contrast, EF^2 for red/blue opponency, and EF^3 for green/yellow opponency. Then, three early visual feature maps are reorganized into F^1, F^2, and F^3, respectively. Each map has one more feature, orientation, than early visual feature maps, and also has enhanced pixel values which are largely different from their surroundings'. These reorganized feature maps are propagated to the next step and integrated into a saliency map by statistical information and competitive relations of the pixels in each reorganized feature map. Through saliency map, the most interesting regions are selected.

2.1 Step 1: Feature Extraction

Early Visual Feature Maps. Given input image is separated into three early visual feature maps in parallel. As an early visual feature, intensity contrast(EF^1) and two color-opponency(red/blue: EF^2, green/yellow: EF^3) are extracted.

EF^1 is generated by intensity information of input image. First, red, green and blue components of original input image are first extracted as R, G, B, and then EF^1 is computed as Eq. 1

$$EF^1 = (R + G + B)/3 \tag{1}$$

EF^2 and EF^3 are modeled with the two types of color opponency exhibited by the cells with homogeneous type of receptive fields in visual cortex, which respond very strong to color contrast. First, broadly tuned color channels are extracted as r, g, b, and y by $r = R - (G+B)/2$, $g = G - (R+B)/2$, $b = B - (R+G)/2$, $y = R+G - 2(|R-G|+2)$. Each of which indicates red, green, blue, and yellow channels respectively, and each yields maximal response for pure hue to which it is tuned. And then, EF^2 is generated to account for red/green color opponency by Eq. 2, and EF^3 for blue/yellow color opponency by Eq. 3.

$$EF^2 = r - g \tag{2}$$

$$EF^3 = b - y \tag{3}$$

Reorganized Feature Maps. All generated three independent early visual feature maps are then processed by

$$F^k_{x,y} = \sum_{\theta} \left(\sum_{m,n} EF^k_{m,n} \cdot h_{x-m,y-n}(\theta) \right)^2 \tag{4}$$

where

$$h_{x,y}(\theta) = \left| K_1 \cdot G_{x,y}(\sigma, r_1 \cdot \sigma, \theta) - K_2 \cdot G_{x,y}(r_2 \cdot \sigma, r_1 \cdot r_2 \cdot \sigma, \theta) \right| \tag{5}$$

Through this process, reorganized feature map F^k extracts additional feature, orientation, and enhances the regions of pixels which are largely different from their surroundings'.

As expressed in Eq. 4, reorganizing process of the feature map can be explained as following three steps. First, each of the early visual feature maps EF^k (k=1,2,3) is first normalized in the range [0,1] in order to eliminate across-modality differences due to dissimilar feature extraction mechanisms. Second, each of the normalized feature map is convolved with the bank of $h(\theta)$ filter at orientations($\theta \in \{0, \pi/8, 2\pi/8, \cdots, 7\pi/8\}$). The bank of $h(\theta)$ filter is an oriented ON-center, OFF-surround operator, and is generated by Eq. 5. In Eq. 5, two $G_{x,y}(\cdot, \cdot, \cdot)$ indicate 2-D oriented Gaussian functions as expressed in Eq. 6, K_1, K_2, positive constants, r_1, the eccentricities of the two Gaussians, and r_2, the ratio between the widths of the ON and OFF Gaussians.

$$G_{x,y}(\sigma, r_1 \cdot \sigma, \theta) = e^{\frac{(x\cos\theta + y\sin\theta)^2}{2\sigma_x^2}} \cdot e^{\frac{(-x\sin\theta + y\cos\theta)^2}{2\sigma_y^2}} \tag{6}$$

where σ_x, σ_y denote widths of two Gaussians. Finally, the results are squared to enhance the contrast, and are summarized to eliminate orientation parameter θ.

2.2 Step 2 : Feature Integration

Considerations for Integrating Multiple Features. Although many features which influence visual attention have been identified, little quantitative data exists regarding the exact weighting of the different features and their relationship. Some factors are clearly very high importance, but it is difficult to define exactly how much more important one feature is than another[Osn98]. A particular feature may be more important than another in one image, while in another image the opposite may be true.

Saliency Map. We integrated multiple feature maps into one by statistical information and competitive relations of the pixels in each feature map. The operation of our integration method can be described as following three steps.

First, each computed feature map is convolved with the large size of the *LoG* filter, and the result is added with the original one by

$$\hat{F}_{x,y}^k = \sum_{m,n} \left(F_{m,n}^k \cdot LoG_{x-m,y-n} \right) + F_{x,y}^k \tag{7}$$

This operation is iterated, so it causes the effect of short-range cooperation and long-range competition among neighboring values of the map, and reduces noises. As for the resulting feature maps, the notation $\hat{F}^k$ will be dropped, and the symbol F^k will be kept for the processed feature maps.

Second, the processed map is processed by

$$S_{x,y}^k = \frac{SF_{x,y}^k - MinSF}{MaxSF - MinSF} \tag{8}$$

where

$$SF_{x,y}^k = F_{x,y}^k \times \left(MaxF^k - AveF^k \right)^2,$$

$$MaxF^k = \max(F_{x,y}^k), \quad AveF^k = \text{average}(F_{x,y}^k), \tag{9}$$

$$MaxSF = \max\left(SF_{x,y}^1, SF_{x,y}^2, SF_{x,y}^3 \right), \quad MinSF = \min\left(SF_{x,y}^1, SF_{x,y}^2, SF_{x,y}^3 \right)$$

This operation enhances the values associated with strong peak activities in the map while suppressing uniform peak activities, by the statistical information of the pixels in the map. If we compare the maximum value in the entire map to the average over all pixels in the map, we can know that how different the most activation location is from the average. When this difference is large, the most active location stands out. Otherwise, the map contains nothing unique. Also, comparing the map with other maps enables to retain relative importance of a feature map with respect to other ones. And irrelevant information extracted from ineffective feature map would be suppressed.

Finally, three SF^k maps are just simply summed into a single saliency map S by

$$S_{x,y} = \sum_{k=1}^{3} SF_{x,y}^k \qquad (10)$$

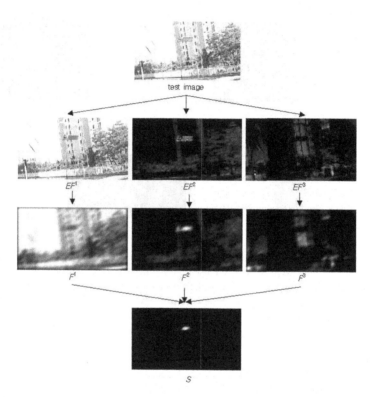

Fig. 2. An example of overall working of our attention module. Three early visual feature maps, EF^1 for intensity contrast, EF^2 for red/blue opponency, and EF^3 for green/yellow opponency, are extracted in parallel and directly from the input test image, and reorganized into enhanced feature maps, F^1, F^2, and F^3. Each reorganized map has orientation features addition to pre-computed features, and also has enhanced pixel values which are largely different from their surroundings'. These enhanced feature maps are integrated into a saliency map by statistical information and competitive relations of the pixels in each enhanced feature map. In upper test image, the attention region is yellow traffic sign. We've tested this image psychological, i.e. we compared the output of our system to the maximum measured behaviors of 40 normal human subjects, and the result is that most of subjects selected the yellow traffic sign as a most attended region. Integrated saliency map shows that the most salient region is yellow traffic sign.

3   Experiments and the Results

Various types of images were used in testing our attention module(See Fig. 2 ~ Fig. 4 for examples). Fig. 2 shows overall working of our system. Fig 3 shows results with color images of natural environments. Three typed test images shown in Fig. 3 ranged in degree of complexity, and the quality of the image. And Fig. 4 shows the results with simple artificial images.

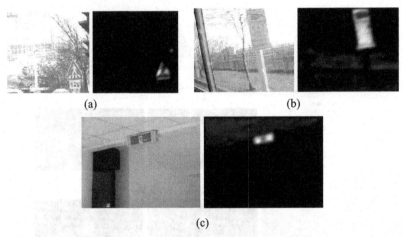

(a)   (b)

(c)

Fig. 3. Some test images(left image) which was applied to various target detection tasks, and the results(right image) are presented. We used three types of color images of natural environment, which differ in complexity degree of their backgrounds and the quality of the image. (a) shows an experimental result with an image in which very complex background and strong local variations in illumination are contained. Attention region in this image is a blue traffic sign. (b) shows an experimental result with an image whose complexity of background is simpler than that of an image in (a), and the image was photographed in running car. Attention region in this image is a yellow banner. (c) shows an experimental result with an image in which relatively simple background is contained, and the image was photographed inside the building. Attention region in this image is a green emergency lamp.

4   Concluding Remarks

This paper suggests active vision system to employ attention module in controlling the parameters of image acquisition system. This module identifies the regions of an image that contain the most "interesting" features with only bottom-up features. As our modeling approach is bottom-up, we cannot account for top-down effects as a matter of course. However, there are many potential ways to extend our module. Modifying the feature maps with the simulated top-down knowledge which is trained by neural processing, and presented in the feature extraction process, might be the one way.

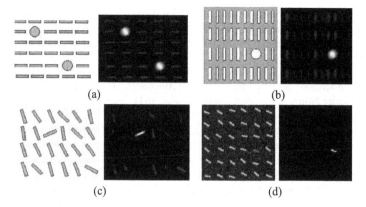

Fig. 4. Some test images(left image) of simple artificial images, and the results(right image) are presented. (a)~(b) shows the results of shape pop-out task. The input image in (a) has background of lighter contrast than the those of the foreground and the test image in (b) has the opposite kind of background.(c) shows the results of orientation pop-out task, and (d) shows color pop-out task.

The results of our module are very useful to active vision system. For example, the location of the most interesting region can be used to change the gaze of an image acquisition system. When attention regions are extracted by the attention module, the camera can zoom onto them, and can obtain a more detailed image of the corresponding regions. More over, the use of attention module is not restricted to active vision problems, but can be generalized to any system for which efficiency is especially important.

References

1. Bear, M., Connors, B., Paradiso, M.: Neuroscience exploring the brain. Williams and Wilkins, USA (1996)
2. Burt, P.J.:Smart sensing within a pyramid vision machine, Proc. IEEE, 76 (1988) 1006-1015
3. Cave, K., Wolfe, J.: Modeling the Role of Parallel Processing in Visual Search. Cognitive Psychology 22 (1990) 225-271
4. Colby:The neuroanatomy and neurophysiology of attention. Journal of Child Neurology 6 (1991) 90-118
5. Duncan, J., Humphreys, J.: Visual search and stimulus similarity. Psychological Reviews 96 (1989) 433-458
6. Giefing, G., Mallot, H.: Saccadic Object Recognition with an Active Vision System., 10th European Conf. on Artificial Intelligence (1992) 803-805
7. Itti, L., Koch, C.,: A saliency-based search mechanism for overt and covert shifts of visual attention. Vision Research 40(10-12) (2000) 1489-1506
8. Itti, L., Koch, C., Niebur, E.: Model of saliency-based visual attention for rapid scene analysis. IEEE Transactions on Pattern Analysis and Machine Intelligence (1998) 1254-1259

9. Koch, C., Ullman, S.: Shifts in Selective Visual Attention : Towards the Underlying Neural Circuitry. Human Neurobiology 4 (1985) 219-227

10. Mozer, M.: The Perception of Multiple Objects : a Connectionist Approach. MIT Press, Cambridge, MA (1991)

11. Olivier, S., Yasuo, K., Gordon, C.:Development of a Biologically Inspired Real-Time Visual Attention System. In:Lee, S.-W.,Buelthoff, H.-H., Poggio, T.(eds.):BMCV 2000.Lecture Notes in Computer Science, Vol. 1811. Springer-Verlag, Berlin Heidelberg New York (2000) 150–159

12. Osberger, W., Maeder, A.J.:Automatic identification of Perceptually important regions in an image. Proc. of Fourteenth Intl. Conf. On Pattern Recognition 1 (1998) 701-704

13. Treisman, A.-M., Gelade, G.-A.: A Feature-integration Theory of Attention. Cognitive Psychology 12 (1980) 97-136

14. Tsotsos, J., Culhane, S., Winky, Y., Yuzhong, L., Davis, N., Nuflo, F.: Modeling Visual Attention via Selective Tuning. Artificial Intelligence 78 (1995) 507-545

15. Wolfe, J., Cave, K.: Guided Search : An Alternative to Feature Integration Model of Visual Search. Journal of Experimental Psychology : Human Perception and Performance 15 (1989) 419-433

16. Yagi, T., Asano, N., Makita, S., Uchikawa, Y.:Active vision inspired by mammalian fixation mechanism. Intelligent Robots and Systems (1995) 39-47

17. Yarbus, A.L.: Eye Movements and Vision. Premium Press, New York (1967)

Analytic Reduction of the Kruppa Equations

Nikos Canterakis

Albert-Ludwigs-Universität Freiburg, Computer Science Department,
Institute for Pattern Recognition and Image Processing, D-79110 Freiburg, Germany,
`canterakis@informatik.uni-freiburg.de`

Abstract. Given the fundamental matrix between a pair of images taken by a nonstationary projective camera with constant internal parameters, we show how to use the two independent Kruppa equations in order to explicitly cut down the number of parameters of the Kruppa matrix $\mathbf{KK}^T$ by exactly two. Thus, we derive a procedure which results in a closed formula for the Kruppa matrix that depends on exactly three remaining parameters. This formula allows an easy incorporation of the positivity constraint and admits of an interpretation in terms of the image of the horopter. We focus on the general case where the camera motion is unknown and not restricted to some special type. Solutions of the Kruppa equations given three fundamental matrices have been attempted in the past by iterative numerical methods that are searching in multidimensional spaces. As an application of the reduced Kruppa matrix mentioned above we also outline how this problem can be analytically reduced to the determination of the real, positive roots of a polynomial of 14-th degree in one variable.

1 Introduction

The possibility of calibrating a moving projective camera on-the-fly has been indicated about ten years ago in the seminal papers [2] and [11]. The resulted technique referred to as self-calibration greatly increases the flexibility in using a camera for computer vision purposes because there is no need any more to tediously precalibrate the camera using special calibration objects. Self-calibration is performed only on the basis of image measurements and despite unknown camera motion. The basic observation was that there is a relation connecting the fundamental matrix between two views and the calibration matrix of the camera which contains the internal parameters. This relation is given in terms of the Kruppa equations [6] dating back to 1913. Since the fundamental matrix can be computed from image measurements, this gives conditions for the calibration matrix from image measurements alone. However, barring special restricted cases, the solution of the Kruppa equations turned out to be extremely difficult due to the nonlinear nature of the problem. Although there have been designed numerical methods ([9], [16]) for their solution, many problems like high computational cost motivated researchers to look for alternatives of self-calibration. These efforts produced several techniques like the formulation in terms of the

L. Van Gool (Ed.): DAGM 2002, LNCS 2449, pp. 591–599, 2002.

absolute quadric [15], combinations of scene and auto-calibration constraints [7], or stratified approaches by first computing the plane at infinity [12].

In this paper we investigate in some detail the space of the solutions of the Kruppa equations between two views and derive an intricate relation with the image of the horopter. According to this relation, there is a one dimensional infinity of well specified point pairs on the image of the horopter, each generating, in a sense to be explained below, a different three-dimensional subspace of the six-dimensional space of symmetrical 3×3 matrices. We show that every point on any of those subspaces solves the Kruppa equations and that conversely any solution of the Kruppa equations must lie in some of those subspaces. The parameter of the point pair above and the projective position within the 3D subspace it generates, are the new three parameters of the Kruppa matrix which can even be given in closed form and in dependence of these three parameters. The incorporation of the positivity constraint is easily accomplished.

As an application of the derived parameterisation of the reduced Kruppa matrix we show how to use it in order to reduce the six Kruppa equations, given three fundamental matrices, to a single polynomial equation of 14-th degree in one variable.

2   Self-calibration from the Infinity Homography

Considering two projective cameras $\mathbf{P}_I$ and $\mathbf{P}_J$ with the same calibration matrix $\mathbf{K}$ we can choose the world coordinate system aligned with the camera $\mathbf{P}_I$, such that the two cameras described by homogeneous 3×4 matrices will read: $\mathbf{P}_I \sim \mathbf{K}(\mathbf{I}; \mathbf{0})$ and $\mathbf{P}_J \sim \mathbf{K}\mathbf{R}_J(\mathbf{I}; -\mathbf{c}_J)$ where $\mathbf{K}$ denotes the common upper right triangular matrix that contains the internal parameters of the cameras, $\mathbf{R}_J$ denotes the 3×3 rotation matrix describing the orientation of the camera $\mathbf{P}_J$ with respect to $\mathbf{P}_I$, and $\mathbf{c}_J$ is the camera center of the camera $\mathbf{P}_J$. Of course, $\mathbf{P}_I$ and $\mathbf{P}_J$ may and in general will denote two instances of the same camera in two different positions. It is easy to see that between the images of points at infinity will lie the so called infinity homography $\mathbf{H}_{JI}^{\infty} = \mathbf{K}\mathbf{R}_J\mathbf{K}^{-1}$ with determinant normalised to one. Now it is also easy to eliminate the unknown rotation $\mathbf{R}_J$ from this equation giving

$$\mathbf{H}_{JI}^{\infty}\mathbf{K}\mathbf{K}^T\mathbf{H}_{JI}^{\infty T} = \mathbf{K}\mathbf{K}^T . \tag{1}$$

The positive definite symmetric matrix $\mathbf{K}\mathbf{K}^T$ also called Kruppa matrix [1] contains the same information as the calibration matrix $\mathbf{K}$ since we can derive $\mathbf{K}$ from $\mathbf{K}\mathbf{K}^T$ by a Cholesky factorisation. The geometrical meaning of the Kruppa matrix is very well known to be the description of the dual image of the absolute conic. The algebraic structure of equation (1) is that of an eigenvector one: The 6-dimensional vector containing all elements in the upper right half of $\mathbf{K}\mathbf{K}^T$ is an eigenvector of a certain 6×6 matrix $\mathbf{H}_{JI}^{\infty[2]}$, depending homomorphically on $\mathbf{H}_{JI}^{\infty}$, to the eigenvalue 1. However, since the eigenvalues of $\mathbf{H}_{JI}^{\infty}$ are the same as the eigenvalues of $\mathbf{R}_J$ they are given by the set $\{e^{j\phi}, e^{-j\phi}, 1\}$ where ϕ denotes the angle of rotation of $\mathbf{R}_J$. In turn, the eigenvalues of $\mathbf{H}_{JI}^{\infty[2]}$ will be all six products of the three eigenvalues above taken two at a time (including repetitions) which gives the set $\{e^{j2\phi}, 1, e^{j\phi}, e^{-j2\phi}, e^{-j\phi}, 1\}$. We observe that $\mathbf{H}_{JI}^{\infty[2]}$ will possess a double eigenvalue 1 which means that $\mathbf{KK}^T$ has to be sought in a two dimensional eigenspace. Indeed, with $\mathbf{a}_J$ denoting the axis of rotation of $\mathbf{R}_J$ it is well known that we also will have $\mathbf{H}_{JI}^{\infty} \mathbf{Ka}_J = \mathbf{KR}_J \mathbf{a}_J = \mathbf{Ka}_J$ and consequently also $\mathbf{H}_{JI}^{\infty} \mathbf{Ka}_J \mathbf{a}_J^T \mathbf{K}^T \mathbf{H}_{JI}^{\infty T} = \mathbf{Ka}_J \mathbf{a}_J^T \mathbf{K}^T$. Thus, any linear combination of $\mathbf{KK}^T$ and $\mathbf{Ka}_J \mathbf{a}_J^T \mathbf{K}^T$ will solve equation (1). Therefore, a single image pair won't be enough for self-calibration from the infinity homography in the general case. To resolve the ambiguity, a second image pair and the associated infinity homography is necessary.

Obtaining the infinity homography or the plane at infinity is known to be usually very hard to achieve if no special scene structure or restricted camera motion like for example a stationary rotating camera [3] can be assumed. In contrast, the fundamental matrix is far easier to obtain but the resulting Kruppa equations are considerably weaker allowing therefore a richer solution space that complicates the problem. In the next section we formulate the Kruppa equations and start with the investigation of their solution space for one image pair.

3   The Kruppa Equations

Algebraically, the Kruppa equations are immediately obtained from equation (1). Denoting with $\mathbf{e}_{JI}$ the epipole on image J and with $[\mathbf{e}_{JI}]_\times$ the 3×3 rank two skew symmetrical matrix that computes the cross product with $\mathbf{e}_{JI}$ and multiplying (1) from both sides with $[\mathbf{e}_{JI}]_\times$ one gets $[\mathbf{e}_{JI}]_\times \mathbf{H}_{JI}^{\infty} \mathbf{KK}^T \mathbf{H}_{JI}^{\infty T} [\mathbf{e}_{JI}]_\times \sim [\mathbf{e}_{JI}]_\times \mathbf{KK}^T [\mathbf{e}_{JI}]_\times$. Since the product $[\mathbf{e}_{JI}]_\times \mathbf{H}_{JI}^{\infty}$ is recognised to be the fundamental matrix $\mathbf{F}_{JI}$ assigning to points on image I epipolar lines on image J, the derived Kruppa equations read in matrix form

$$\mathbf{F}_{JI} \mathbf{KK}^T \mathbf{F}_{JI}^T \sim [\mathbf{e}_{JI}]_\times \mathbf{KK}^T [\mathbf{e}_{JI}]_\times \ . \tag{2}$$

Note that since the fundamental matrix as well as the matrix $[\mathbf{e}_{JI}]_\times$ is singular, we cannot normalise with respect to the determinant any more.

It is well known that the Kruppa equations for a single image pair are equivalent to only two independent scalar equations. This fact can be shown in a number of ways as for example using the singular value decomposition of the fundamental matrix ([4], [8]). Initially, we will follow a different approach starting from the analysis of the solution space of equation (1) given in the previous section.

We first mention the well known observation that any solution of equations (1) will a fortiori also solve the Kruppa equations (2). But the space of possible solutions $\mathbf{X}$ of the Kruppa equations $\mathbf{F}_{JI} \mathbf{XF}_{JI}^T \sim [\mathbf{e}_{JI}]_\times \mathbf{X}[\mathbf{e}_{JI}]_\times$, where $\mathbf{X}$ is a symmetric 3×3 matrix, is now much richer, mainly due to the singularity of $\mathbf{F}_{JI}$ and $[\mathbf{e}_{JI}]_\times$. Consider $\mathbf{X}_0 \sim \mathbf{e}_{JI} \mathbf{e}_{IJ}^T + \mathbf{e}_{IJ} \mathbf{e}_{JI}^T$. It is easy to see that $\mathbf{F}_{JI} \mathbf{X}_0 \mathbf{F}_{JI}^T = \mathbf{0} = [\mathbf{e}_{JI}]_\times \mathbf{X}_0 [\mathbf{e}_{JI}]_\times$. Since adding an arbitrary multiple of $\mathbf{X}_0$ to any solution $\mathbf{X}$ of (2) would only add the zero matrix to both sides of the equation, the sum $\mathbf{X} + \lambda \mathbf{X}_0$ would be a solution of (2) as well for all λ.

The linear subspace $\langle \mathbf{KK}^T, \mathbf{Ka}_J \mathbf{a}_J^T \mathbf{K}^T, \mathbf{X}_0 \rangle$ spanned by these three symmetric matrices is therefore already a 3-dimensional linear solutions-subspace within the six-dimensional space of symmetric 3×3 matrices that contains the sought solution $\mathbf{KK}^T$. We will show: There is an infinity of such 3-dimensional linear subspaces, all points $\mathbf{X}$ of which solve $\mathbf{F}_{JI} \mathbf{X} \mathbf{F}_{JI}^T \sim [\mathbf{e}_{JI}]_\times \mathbf{X} [\mathbf{e}_{JI}]_\times$. Each one of these subspaces is generated by a point pair on the image of the horopter.

For the further description we need some basic and well known facts concerning the horopter and its image (cf. [5]) as well as a suitably normalised canonical parametric equation [13] of the latter which we introduce in the subsection 4.1.

4   The Horopter and Its Image

The horopter is defined as a curve in space, all points of which map onto identical positions on the image planes I and J, i.e. we have $\mathbf{P}_I \mathbf{X} \sim \mathbf{P}_J \mathbf{X} \sim \mathbf{x}$ if and only if the space point $\mathbf{X}$ is on the horopter. Since the image $\mathbf{x}$ is self corresponding it must fulfil the epipolar condition $\mathbf{x}^T \mathbf{F}_{JI} \mathbf{x} = 0$. This shows that with $\mathbf{F}_{JI}^s$ being the symmetric part of the fundamental matrix, $\mathbf{F}_{JI}^s \sim \mathbf{F}_{JI} + \mathbf{F}_{JI}^T$, we will have $\mathbf{x}^T \mathbf{F}_{JI}^s \mathbf{x} = 0$ which means that the image point $\mathbf{x}$ must lie on the conic that is described by the symmetric and generally regular matrix $\mathbf{F}_{JI}^s$. Consequently, this conic is the image of the horopter. One easily verifies that both epipoles $\mathbf{e}_{IJ}$ and $\mathbf{e}_{JI}$ are lying on the image of the horopter. Furthermore, even the antisymmetric part $\mathbf{F}_{JI}^a \sim \mathbf{F}_{JI}^T - \mathbf{F}_{JI}$ of $\mathbf{F}_{JI}$ admits of an important geometrical interpretation. Since it is a singular, skew-symmetric 3×3 matrix we can express it with the aid of its null vector $\mathbf{f}_{JI}$ as $\mathbf{F}_{JI}^a \sim [\mathbf{f}_{JI}]_\times$. The point $\mathbf{f}_{JI}$ will then be the intersection of the two tangential lines at the epipoles (cf. Fig. 1).

4.1   Canonical Parametric Equation

To develop the theory further we introduce a suitably normalised canonical parametric representation of the image of the horopter through the following steps:

- Define the vector $\mathbf{f}_{JI}$ (with the resulting scale) through $[\mathbf{f}_{JI}]_\times := \mathbf{F}_{JI}^T - \mathbf{F}_{JI}$.
- Compute $\mathbf{f}_{JI}^T \mathbf{F}_{JI} \mathbf{f}_{JI} =: a$ and normalise $\mathbf{F}_{JI}$ and $\mathbf{f}_{JI}$ by the real third root of $-a$, i.e. set $\mathbf{F}_{JI} \to \mathbf{F}_{JI}/(-a)^{1/3}$ and $\mathbf{f}_{JI} \to \mathbf{f}_{JI}/(-a)^{1/3}$. We will then have $\mathbf{f}_{JI}^T \mathbf{F}_{JI} \mathbf{f}_{JI} = -1$ and $[\mathbf{f}_{JI}]_\times = \mathbf{F}_{JI}^T - \mathbf{F}_{JI}$ as before.

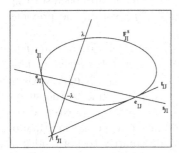

Fig. 1. The image of the horopter is in the general case a conic that is expressed by the symmetric part $\mathbf{F}_{JI}^s = \mathbf{F}_{JI} + \mathbf{F}_{JI}^T$ of the fundamental matrix and contains the epipoles. The antisymmetric part $\mathbf{F}_{JI}^a = \mathbf{F}_{JI}^T - \mathbf{F}_{JI} = [\mathbf{f}_{JI}]_\times$ of the fundamental matrix is expressed by the point $\mathbf{f}_{JI}$. Lines through the point $\mathbf{f}_{JI}$ intersect the image of the horopter in points parameterised by λ and $-\lambda$ if the canonical parametric equation introduced below is used.

- Define $\mathbf{F}^s_{JI}$ through $\mathbf{F}^s_{JI} := \mathbf{F}_{JI} + \mathbf{F}^T_{JI}$.
- Normalise $\|\mathbf{e}_{JI}\|$ to unity and compute the scale of $\mathbf{e}_{IJ}$ such that the equation $\mathbf{e}^T_{IJ}\mathbf{F}_{JI}\mathbf{e}_{JI} = 1$ is valid.
- Define the matrix $\mathbf{H}_{JI}$ through $\mathbf{H}_{JI} := (\mathbf{e}_{JI}; \mathbf{f}_{JI}; \mathbf{e}_{IJ})$.

It is then easy to show that the following relations will be valid:

$$\mathbf{H}^T_{JI}\mathbf{F}^s_{JI}\mathbf{H}_{JI} = \begin{pmatrix} 0 & 0 & 1 \\ 0 & -2 & 0 \\ 1 & 0 & 0 \end{pmatrix} =: \mathbf{G}, \quad \mathbf{F}_{JI}\mathbf{e}_{JI} = \mathbf{e}_{JI} \times \mathbf{f}_{JI}, \quad \mathbf{F}_{JI}\mathbf{f}_{JI} = \mathbf{e}_{JI} \times \mathbf{e}_{IJ}.$$

All these relations are easy to verify. The defined matrix $\mathbf{H}_{JI}$ offers an easy to handle parametric representation of the image of the horopter as well as a transformation of the Kruppa equations to a very simple new normal form. To see the first property consider with any real number λ the vector $\boldsymbol{\lambda} := (\lambda^2, \lambda, 1)^T$. From the equation $\boldsymbol{\lambda}^T\mathbf{G}\boldsymbol{\lambda} = 0 \; \forall\lambda$ we deduce the relation $\boldsymbol{\lambda}^T\mathbf{H}^T_{JI}\mathbf{F}^s_{JI}\mathbf{H}_{JI}\boldsymbol{\lambda} = 0$ which expresses the fact that points on the image of the horopter are given by $\mathbf{H}_{JI}\boldsymbol{\lambda}$. In other words, the number λ is a projective parameter for the points on the image of the horopter. The epipole $\mathbf{e}_{IJ}$ is parameterised by $\lambda = 0$ and the epipole $\mathbf{e}_{JI}$ by $\lambda \to \infty$. Furthermore, since the vectors $(\lambda^2, \lambda, 1)$, $(\lambda^2, -\lambda, 1)$ and $(0, 1, 0)$ are linearly dependent, the points parameterised by λ and $-\lambda$ must be collinear with the point $\mathbf{f}_{JI}$ (see Fig. 1).

5   Simplifying the Kruppa Equations

Now we come to the most important property of the matrix $\mathbf{H}_{JI}$ in simplifying the Kruppa equations. We reconsider these equations in the form $\mathbf{F}_{JI}\mathbf{X}\mathbf{F}^T_{JI} \sim [\mathbf{e}_{JI}]_\times\mathbf{X}[\mathbf{e}_{JI}]_\times$ and introduce the following transformation of the unknown matrix $\mathbf{X}$ to another symmetric matrix $\mathbf{Y}$: $\mathbf{X} = \mathbf{H}_{JI}\mathbf{Y}\mathbf{H}^T_{JI}$. Since $\mathbf{H}_{JI}$ is in the general case regular this transformation is one to one. From the normalisations defined above we will have: $\mathbf{F}_{JI}\mathbf{H}_{JI} = (\mathbf{e}_{JI} \times \mathbf{f}_{JI}; \mathbf{e}_{JI} \times \mathbf{e}_{IJ}; \mathbf{0}) =: (\mathbf{t}_{JI}; \mathbf{s}_{JI}; \mathbf{0})$ and $[\mathbf{e}_{JI}]_\times\mathbf{H}_{JI} = (\mathbf{0}; \mathbf{e}_{JI} \times \mathbf{f}_{JI}; \mathbf{e}_{JI} \times \mathbf{e}_{IJ}) = (\mathbf{0}; \mathbf{t}_{JI}; \mathbf{s}_{JI})$ with $\mathbf{t}_{JI}$ denoting the tangent at the epipole $\mathbf{e}_{JI}$ and $\mathbf{s}_{JI}$ the line connecting the two epipoles. We observe that the products $\mathbf{F}_{JI}\mathbf{H}_{JI}$ and $[\mathbf{e}_{JI}]_\times\mathbf{H}_{JI}$ differ only in a cyclical shift of the columns. $\mathbf{Y}$ must now solve the transformed Kruppa equations $(\mathbf{t}_{JI}; \mathbf{s}_{JI}; \mathbf{0})\mathbf{Y}(\mathbf{t}_{JI}; \mathbf{s}_{JI}; \mathbf{0})^T \sim (\mathbf{0}; \mathbf{t}_{JI}; \mathbf{s}_{JI})\mathbf{Y}(\mathbf{0}; \mathbf{t}_{JI}; \mathbf{s}_{JI})^T$. With $\mathbf{Y} \sim \begin{pmatrix} a & b & c \\ b & d & e \\ c & e & f \end{pmatrix}$ symmetric, the equations above translate to

$a\mathbf{t}_{JI}\mathbf{t}^T_{JI} + b(\mathbf{t}_{JI}\mathbf{s}^T_{JI} + \mathbf{s}_{JI}\mathbf{t}^T_{JI}) + d\mathbf{s}_{JI}\mathbf{s}^T_{JI} = \lambda(d\mathbf{t}_{JI}\mathbf{t}^T_{JI} + e(\mathbf{t}_{JI}\mathbf{s}^T_{JI} + \mathbf{s}_{JI}\mathbf{t}^T_{JI}) + f\mathbf{s}_{JI}\mathbf{s}^T_{JI})$ whence since the three matrices $\mathbf{t}_{JI}\mathbf{t}^T_{JI}$, $(\mathbf{t}_{JI}\mathbf{s}^T_{JI} + \mathbf{s}_{JI}\mathbf{t}^T_{JI})$ and $\mathbf{s}_{JI}\mathbf{s}^T_{JI}$ are linearly independent we obtain: $a = \lambda d = \lambda^2 f$, $b = \lambda e$ and $d = \lambda f$. Renaming the parameters above we deduce that the matrix $\mathbf{Y}$ must be of the form

$$\mathbf{Y} \sim \begin{pmatrix} a\lambda^2 & b\lambda & c \\ b\lambda & a\lambda & b \\ c & b & a \end{pmatrix} .$$

5.1   Incorporating the Positivity Constraint

An important property that must have a solution $\mathbf{X}$ of the Kruppa equations we are interested in is that of being positive definite. Otherwise, the Cholesky factorisation will fail to yield a real upper triangular calibration matrix $\mathbf{K}$ with $\mathbf{K}\mathbf{K}^T = \mathbf{X}$. This property must be shared by the transformed solution $\mathbf{Y}$ as well and is usually very difficult to incorporate into numerical schemes that are searching in a multidimensional space for solutions of the Kruppa equations. Positive definitness means that all eigenvalues of $\mathbf{Y}$ must be positive. An easy analysis of these eigenvalues (for example using Hurwitz criteria) first reveals that necessary conditions for all eigenvalues of $\mathbf{Y}$ to be positive are: $\lambda > 0$ and $a > 0$. Using this and again renaming parameters, we arrive at

$$\mathbf{Y} \sim diag(\lambda, \sqrt{\lambda}, 1) \underbrace{\begin{pmatrix} 1 & a & b \\ a & 1 & a \\ b & a & 1 \end{pmatrix}}_{=:\mathbf{Z}} diag(\lambda, \sqrt{\lambda}, 1).$$ From this we deduce that any so-

lution $\mathbf{X}$ of the Kruppa equations that could be factored like $\mathbf{K}\mathbf{K}^T$ should read as follows:

$$\mathbf{X} \sim \mathbf{K}\mathbf{K}^T \sim \mathbf{H}_{JI} diag(\lambda, \sqrt{\lambda}, 1) \mathbf{Z} diag(\lambda, \sqrt{\lambda}, 1) \mathbf{H}_{JI}^T . \qquad (3)$$

Now positivity of $\mathbf{X}$ is tantamount to positivity of the matrix $\mathbf{Z}$ with the eigenvalues $x_1 = 1 - b$, $x_{2/3} = (2 + b \mp \sqrt{8a^2 + b^2})/2$. By demanding $x_1 > 0$ and $x_2 > 0$ we thus arrive at the following remarkably simple result:

Proposition 1 (Region of Positivity). *The matrix $\mathbf{Z}$ and consequently also a solution $\mathbf{X} \sim \mathbf{H}_{JI} diag(\lambda, \sqrt{\lambda}, 1) \mathbf{Z} diag(\lambda, \sqrt{\lambda}, 1) \mathbf{H}_{JI}^T$ of the Kruppa equations will be positive definite if and only if $2a^2 - 1 < b < 1$.*

Eq. (3) describes the Kruppa matrix $\mathbf{K}\mathbf{K}^T$ with only three parameters, namely λ, a and b. That means, two parameters out of the five have been eliminated by using the two independent Kruppa equations. Moreover, besides $\lambda > 0$ the parameters a and b have to lie in a closed convex region of the $a - b$ space limited from above by the line $b = 1$ and from below by the parabola $b = 2a^2 - 1$.

5.2   The 3-D Solution Subspaces

Multiplying out the matrix $\mathbf{Y}$ and again absorbing the factor $\sqrt{\lambda}$ in a and the factor λ in b we also have the expression

$$\mathbf{K}\mathbf{K}^T \sim \mathbf{H}_{JI} \left[\begin{pmatrix} \lambda^2 & & \\ & \lambda & \\ & & 1 \end{pmatrix} + a \begin{pmatrix} & \lambda & \\ \lambda & & 1 \\ & 1 & \end{pmatrix} + b \begin{pmatrix} & & 1 \\ & & \\ 1 & & \end{pmatrix} \right] \mathbf{H}_{JI}^T . \qquad (4)$$

This expression clearly indicates that the Kruppa matrix $\mathbf{K}\mathbf{K}^T$ is contained in a three-dimensional linear subspace. The parameter λ specifies the linear subspace and the vector $(1, a, b)^T$ specifies projective position within the subspace. As already mentioned, the parameter λ can also be given a geometric interpretation in terms of the image of the horopter. Indeed, it is not hard to see that the 3-d subspace above is also spanned by the matrices $\mathbf{p}_+(\lambda)\mathbf{p}_+(\lambda)^T$, $\mathbf{p}_-(\lambda)\mathbf{p}_-(\lambda)^T$ and $\mathbf{X}_0$ where $\mathbf{p}_\pm(\lambda) = \mathbf{H}_{JI}(\lambda, \pm\sqrt{\lambda}, 1)^T$ is a generating point pair on the image of the horopter parameterised by λ.

In the next section we introduce a second and a third image pair and outline how the new four Kruppa equations can be used in order to solve for the three parameters λ, a and b.

6   Solving the Kruppa Equations from Three Image Pairs

We now consider the Kruppa equations (2) arising from the second image pair IK using at the same time the SVD of the corresponding fundamental matrix $\mathbf{F}_{KI}$: $\mathbf{F}_{KI} \sim \mathbf{U}_{KI} diag(s_{IK}, 1, 0)\mathbf{U}_{IK}^T$ where $\mathbf{U}_{KI}$ and $\mathbf{U}_{IK}$ are orthogonal matrices, s_{IK} is the ratio of the two nonzero singular values of $\mathbf{F}_{KI}$ and the epipole $\mathbf{e}_{KI}$ is given by the third column $\mathbf{u}_{KI}^3$ of $\mathbf{U}_{KI}$ (cf. [4], [8]). It is then easy to show that the Kruppa equations take the form $(\mathbf{u}_{IK}^1 s_{IK}; \mathbf{u}_{IK}^2)^T \mathbf{KK}^T (\mathbf{u}_{IK}^1 s_{IK}; \mathbf{u}_{IK}^2) \sim (\mathbf{u}_{KI}^2; -\mathbf{u}_{KI}^1)^T \mathbf{KK}^T (\mathbf{u}_{KI}^2; -\mathbf{u}_{KI}^1)$. This is a homogeneous, two by two symmetrical matrix equation that is obviously equivalent to two scalar equations. Now upon substituting for $\mathbf{KK}^T$ the reduced Kruppa matrix derived in (4) and elaborating, we arrive at an eigenvector equation of the following form: $\mathbf{P}(\lambda)\mathbf{a} \sim \mathbf{a}$. Here denotes $\mathbf{a}$ the vector $(1, a, b)^T$ and $\mathbf{P}(\lambda)$ is a 3×3 matrix whose entries are polynomials in λ with known coefficients. The degrees of the polynomials in the first row are 3, 2 and 1, in the second row 4, 3 and 2 and in the third row 5, 4 and 3. Similarly, the third image pair JK yields in the same way an eigenvector equation $\mathbf{Q}(\lambda)\mathbf{a} \sim \mathbf{a}$ and the problem of determining the parameter λ boils down to the condition for the two matrices $\mathbf{P}(\lambda)$ and $\mathbf{Q}(\lambda)$ to possess a common eigenvector. A necessary condition for that is the vanishing of the determinant of the commutator between $\mathbf{P}$ and $\mathbf{Q}$: $det(\mathbf{PQ} - \mathbf{QP}) = 0$. For three by three matrices the determinant of the commutator may be given by the expression $vec(\mathbf{Q})^T(\mathbf{P}^T \otimes \mathbf{P}^* - \mathbf{P}^{*T} \otimes \mathbf{P})vec(\mathbf{Q}^{*T})$ where vec denotes the row-wise conversion of a matrix to a column vector, $\otimes$ is the Kronecker product and $\mathbf{P}^*$ and $\mathbf{Q}^*$ are the adjoints of $\mathbf{P}$ and $\mathbf{Q}$. Fortunately, we could show that in each polynomial entry of the adjoints, as computed from the entries of $\mathbf{P}(\lambda)$ and $\mathbf{Q}(\lambda)$, the first and the last coefficient vanishes. That gives the following degrees of the entries of the adjoints: First row: 4, 3, 2; second row: 5, 4, 3; and third row: 6, 5, 4. Therefore, the expression for the determinant of the commutator given above results in a polynomial of 14-th degree in λ. Numerical experiments indicate that generally there will be at most only a few (four or six) real, positive roots of this polynomial. For each one of them we have to check whether $\mathbf{P}(\lambda)$ and $\mathbf{Q}(\lambda)$ possess common eigenvectors. Generally, this will be the case for only one root. The common eigenvector $\mathbf{a}$ will then contain the parameters a and b and eq. (4) will give the Kruppa matrix.

7   Conclusion and Outlook

In this paper we have studied in some detail the space of solutions of the Kruppa equations arising from a single image pair. We have revealed a very interesting connection with the image of the horopter and used them to considerably simplify the equations resulting in a closed formula for the Kruppa matrix depending on only three parameters. As a potential application of this simplification, we have reduced the six nonlinear Kruppa equations given three fundamental matrices to a polynomial of 14-th degree in one variable. Generally, all multiple solutions up to one are discarded from consistency conditions. It is of course needless to say that all previously reported ambiguous or degenerate situations (cf. [14], [10]) remain valid. Such situations will manifest themselves in the framework of the present paper for example in giving a degenerate image of the horopter ($\mathbf{H}_{JI}$ singular). Currently we are investigating the possibility of factorising analytically the obtained polynomial of 14-th degree. That would reduce its degree even more and increase the stability of the resulting solutions.

References

1. O.D. Faugeras and Q-T. Luong. *The Geometry of Multiple Images*. MIT Press, 2001.
2. O.D. Faugeras, Q.-T. Luong, and S.J. Maybank. Camera Self-Calibration: Theory and Experiments. In G. Sandini, editor, *Proceedings of the 2nd European Conference on Computer Vision, Santa Margherita Ligure, Italy, volume 588 of Lecture Notes in Computer Science*, pages 321-334. Springer-Verlag, 1992.
3. R.I. Hartley. Self-Calibration from Multiple Views with a Rotating Camera. In J.-O. Eklundh, editor, *Proceedings of the 3rd European Conference on Computer Vision, Stockholm, Sweden, volume 800 of Lecture Notes in Computer Science*, pages 471-478. Springer-Verlag, 1994.
4. R.I. Hartley. Kruppa's Equations Derived from the Fundamental Matrix. *IEEE Transactions on Pattern Analysis and Machine Intelligence*, 19(2):133-135, 1997.
5. R.I. Hartley and A. Zisserman. *Multiple View Geometry in Computer Vision*. Cambridge University Press, 2000.
6. E. Kruppa. Zur Ermittlung eines Objektes aus zwei Perspektiven mit innerer Orientierung. *Sitz.-Ber. Akad. Wiss., Wien, math. naturw. Abt. IIa., vol. 122*, pages 1939-1948, 1913.
7. D. Liebowitz and A. Zisserman. Combining Scene and Auto-calibration Constraints. In *Proceedings of the 7th International Conference on Computer Vision, Kerkyra, Greece*, pages 293-300. IEEE Computer Society Press, 1999.
8. M.I. Lourakis and R. Deriche. Camera Self-Calibration Using the Singular Value Decomposition of the Fundamental Matrix. In Proceedings of the 4th Asian Conference on Computer Vision, volume I, pages 403-408, 2000.
9. Q.-T. Luong and O.D. Faugeras. Self-Calibration of a Moving Camera from point Correspondences and Fundamental Matrices. *International Journal of Computer Vision*, 22(3):261-289, 1997.
10. Y. Ma, R. Vidal, J. Kosecka, and S. Sastry. Kruppa Equation Revisited: Its Renormalization and Degeneracy. In D. Vernon, editor, *Proceedings of the 6th European Conference on Computer Vision, Dublin, Ireland, volume 1843 of Lecture Notes in Computer Science*, pages II.562-II.577. Springer-Verlag, 2000.

11. S.J. Maybank and O.D. Faugeras. A Theory of Self Calibration of a Moving Camera. *International Journal of Computer Vision*, 8(2):123-151, 1992.
12. M. Pollefeys and L. Van Gool. Stratified Self-Calibration with the Modulus Constraint. *IEEE Transactions on Pattern Analysis and Machine Intelligence*, 21(8):707-724, 1999.
13. J.G. Semple and G.T. Kneebone. *Algebraic Projective Geometry*. Oxford University Press, 1952.
14. P. Sturm. A Case Against Kruppa's Equations for Camera Self-Calibration. *IEEE Transactions on Pattern Analysis and Machine Intelligence*, 22(10):1199-1204, 2000.
15. B. Triggs *The Absolute Quadric* In *Proceedings of the IEEE Conference on Computer Vision and Pattern Recognition*, pages 609-614, 1997.
16. C. Zeller and O. D. Faugeras. *Camera Self-Calibration from Video Sequences: The Kruppa Equations Revisited* Research Report 2793, INRIA, 1996.

Query-Dependent Performance Optimization for Vocabulary-Supported Image Retrieval

Julia Vogel and Bernt Schiele

Perceptual Computing and Computer Vision Group, ETH Zurich, Switzerland,
{vogel,schiele}@inf.ethz.ch, http://www.vision.ethz.ch/pccv

Abstract. In [1], we proposed a two-stage retrieval framework which makes not only performance characterization but also performance optimization manageable. There, the performance optimization focused on the second stage of the retrieval framework. In this paper, we extend the method to a full two-stage performance characterization and optimization. In our retrieval framework, the user specifies a high-level concept to be searched for, the size of the image region to be covered by the concept (e.g. "Search images with 30-50% of sky") and an optimization option (e.g. "maximum recall", "maximum precision" or "joint maximization of precision and recall"). For the detection of each concept such as "sky", a multitude of concept detectors exist that perform differently. In order to reach optimum retrieval performance, the detector best satisfying the user query is selected and the information of the corresponding concept detector is processed and optimized.

Besides the optimization procedure itself the paper discusses the generation of multiple detectors per semantic concept. In experiments, the advantage of joint compared to individual optimization of first and second stage is shown.

1 Introduction

Performance characterization in the area of computer vision [1,2] and especially in the area of content-based image retrieval (CBIR) [3,4] has long been recognized as being essential. It is indispensable for the comparison of different algorithms and it allows to integrate different CBIR algorithms into larger systems. Nonetheless, performance characterization of CBIR systems is especially challenging since it is difficult to obtain ground truth. The desired output of the retrieval varies greatly between users, tasks, applications and even sessions of the same user.

From the user's perspective, the database is queried with high-level vocabulary such as "sky", "buildings", "water", etc. A possible user query might be: *'Search images with 10-30% of water'*. Thus, a user query consists of the concept being searched for (here: 'water') and a user interval $U = [U_{low}\%, U_{up}\%]$ (here: $U = [10\%, 30\%]$) that specifies the amount of the image to be covered by the concept. This query mode is semantically close to the human description of images.

L. Van Gool (Ed.): DAGM 2002, LNCS 2449, pp. 600–608, 2002.

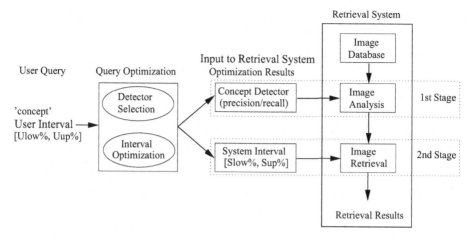

Fig. 1. Two-Stage Retrieval Framework with Performance Optimization

The image retrieval proceeds in two stages (Fig. 1). In the first stage, the images are analyzed through so-called concept detectors. In the current implementation, each image is subdivided into a regular grid of patches each comprising 1% of the image. The concept detectors classify the image patches. The result is a binary decision whether the patch contains the particular concept. A main benefit of this framework is that for those concepts ground truth is more easily available. The performance of the concept detectors is modeled through the respective detector precision and detector recall (Table 1). In the second stage, the information of the concept detector is processed according to the user interval in order to actually retrieve a set of images. The system returns all images in which the amount of positive patches lies inside the user interval $U = [U_{low}\%, U_{up}\%]$.

The general goal of the query-dependent performance optimization is to increase the retrieval performance, that is precision and recall of the *retrieval*, depending on the desired concept, depending on the user interval and depending on the optimization option ("maximum precision", "maximum recall", "joint maximization of precision and recall"). This special form of image retrieval might be used as a pre-filtering stage for succeeding retrievals. In [5], the performance optimization is limited to the second stage of the framework. In this paper, we propose a complete two-stage query-dependent performance optimization that has an impact at *both* retrieval stages. In the first stage, one of the available

Table 1. Possible outcomes of the concept detection per patch

DETECTOR	Concept present	Concept not present	Precision/Recall
Detected	True Positive: p	False Positive: $1 - q$	$prec_{det} = \frac{p}{p+1-q}$
Not Detected	False Negative: $1 - p$	True Negative: q	$recall_{det} = p$

concept detectors has to be selected that will maximize the retrieval performance. Since the concept detectors are not perfect (Table 1), the overall retrieval performance will change if the system is queried internally using an interval $S = [S_{low}\%, S_{up}\%]$ that differs from the user interval $U = [U_{low}\%, U_{up}\%]$. Thus, in the second stage, the performance optimization searches for a system interval $S = [S_{low}\%, S_{up}\%]$ that maximizes the retrieval performance given the concept detector selected in the first stage.

In this paper, we propose the generation and selection of the concept detectors in the first stage of the performance optimization and the joint combination of first and second stage performance optimization. Using AutoClass [6], we learn multiple detectors per semantic concept that perform differently. During the two-stage query optimization, the selection of the best concept detector in the first stage is interlinked with the optimization of the system interval in the second stage. The advantage of this architecture is that any concept detector can be used as long as its performance can be characterized. Hereby, the best concept detector for the optimization of the retrieval recall is usually not the same as for example for the optimization of the retrieval precision. The performance optimization is completely query-dependent. It depends not only on the concept the user is looking for, but also on the size of the region to be covered by the concept and on the optimization option. Thus, the strength of concept detectors that perform only well in special situations can be exploited.

The following section presents the generation of the concept detectors located in the first stage of the retrieval framework. Here, especially the performance optimization of the concept detectors is discussed. Section 3 explains theoretical and practical aspects of the two-stage performance optimization. The main difficulty is that the two optimization stages are interlinked and that they cannot be performed independently from each other.

2   Concept Detectors

The concept detectors are located at the first stage of the retrieval framework. Their task is to decide independently per patch whether the respective concept is present in the patch. The advantage of the performance optimization in the first retrieval stage is that depending on the user query the most suitable detector from a multitude of concept detectors will be selected. Prerequisite is solely that all concept detectors can be characterized in terms of precision and recall.

Our goal is to learn multiple concept detectors that have varying performance characteristics depending on the concept and the feature set. AutoClass [6], an unsupervised Bayesian classification system that includes the search for the optimal number of classes, is especially well suited for that goal. In addition, other classifiers with known performance characteristics can be added such as for example the semantic classifiers of Town and Sinclair [7]. They obtain good classification rates in labeling image regions semantically by using neural network classifiers.

Training and Performance of the Concept Detectors. The training of the concept detectors is performed off-line. For the generation of the various concept detectors, 4000 patches hand-labeled with "sky", "water", "grass" and "buildings" are used. Hereby, the classes can be very diverse. For example, a "sky"-patch might comprise cloudy, rainy or sunny sky regions as well as sky regions during sunset. The patches are represented by 4^3-bin RGB-color histograms (col64), 4^3-bin histograms of third-order MR-SAR texture features (tex64) [8] and $(2 * 4^3)$-bin histograms (coltex128) that are combined of the 4^3-bin RGB-color histogram and the 4^3-bin texture histograms.

Depending on the feature set, AutoClass finds between 100 and 130 clusters in the data. Each cluster contains multiple classes resulting in class probabilities for each cluster. Depending on the feature set, the *highest* class probability in each cluster ranges from 25% to 100%. The availability of the class probabilities for each cluster provides us with three methods to obtain multiple classifiers. Firstly, in order to improve the precision of the concept detectors, only clusters with a class probability higher than a certain threshold are accepted. Obviously, this leads to a loss in recall. However, precision and recall of the concept detectors can thus be precisely controlled. Secondly, the classification using one feature set often performs much better for one class than for another. Thus, it is advantageous to use multiple feature sets. Thirdly, the classifications of two feature sets can be combined by means of the cluster precision: all cases are classified twice and the vote of the cluster with the higher precision counts.

The performance of various "sky"- and "grass"-detectors for different feature sets and feature combinations is shown in Fig. 2. Here, "col64+coltex128" denotes the combination of the col64- and the coltex128-feature set according to the class probabilities per cluster. As expected, the feature sets and combinations perform differently for different classes. For the "sky"-detector, the color feature is not discriminant which lies in the fact, that the "sky" class is very diverse in color. For the "grass"-detector, the texture feature fails. This indicates that the employed texture feature catches primarily very small structure

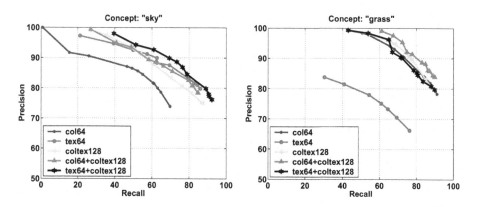

Fig. 2. Precision vs. Recall for various "sky" (left) and "grass" (right) detectors

and not the larger structure that exists in grass patches. The combination of two classifications as described above leads to an improvement in performance. In summary, the "tex64+coltex128"-detector performs best for "sky"-patches, whereas "grass"-patches are detected best with the "col64+coltex128"-detector. In order to obtain maximum performance, the best detection method for the desired precision/recall-value can be selected on the fly by the optimization procedure described in the following section.

3   Two-Stage Performance Optimization

The input to the optimization stage is a user query that consists of the concept being searched for, the user interval $U = [U_{low}\%, U_{up}\%]$ and possibly a minimum value for precision and recall (Fig. 1)). Based on this information, the performance optimization returns a system interval $S = [S_{low}\%, S_{up}\%]$ for internal use and the selection of the appropriate concept detector that will optimize the performance according to the user's option.

The search for the system interval is carried out in the second stage of the retrieval framework. Assuming a fixed performance of the concept detectors, it is possible to derive a closed-form expression for the probability of precision and recall of the retrieval [5]:

$$P_{precision} = \frac{P_{true\_positive}(U, S)}{P_{retrieved}(S)} = \frac{\sum_{N_P=U_{low}}^{U_{up}} P(N_{retrieved} \in S|N_P)P(N_P)}{\sum_{N_P=0}^{N} P(N_{retrieved} \in S|N_P)P(N_P)} \quad (1)$$

$$P_{recall} = \frac{P_{true\_positive}(U, S)}{P_{relevant}(U)} = \frac{\sum_{N_P=U_{low}}^{U_{up}} P(N_{retrieved} \in S|N_P)P(N_P)}{\sum_{N_P=U_{low}}^{U_{up}} P(N_P)} \quad (2)$$

where

$$P(N_{retrieved} \in S|N_P) = \sum_{i=S_{low}}^{S_{up}} \sum_{j=0}^{i} p_{true}(i-j) \cdot p_{false}(j) \quad (3)$$

$$p_{true}(k) = \binom{N_P}{k} p^k (1-p)^{N_P-k} \quad (4)$$

$$p_{false}(k) = \binom{N-N_P}{k} (1-q)^k q^{N-N_P-k}. \quad (5)$$

N_P denotes the number of positive patches in an image. $p_{true}(k)$ is the probability that k positive patches are correctly returned for an image that in fact has N_P positive patches. Respectively, $p_{false}(k)$ is the probability that k out of $(N - N_P)$ negative patches are retrieved (incorrectly). p and q model the performance of the concept detectors (Table 1).

Eqs. 1 and 2 can recursively be optimized in order to maximize precision and/or recall [5]. The search space is depicted in Fig. 5 for the user interval [20%, 40%] of "sky" and a fixed $p = q = 0.90$. Each point in the graph corresponds to a different system interval $S = [S_{low}\%, S_{up}\%]$. Depending on the

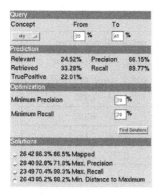

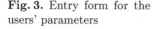

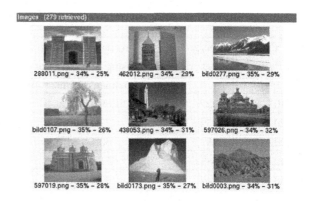

Fig. 3. Entry form for the users' parameters

Fig. 4. Retrieval results for [20%,40%] of "sky", $p = q = 0.90$

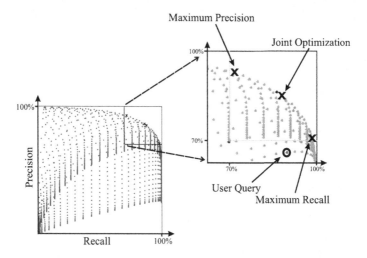

Fig. 5. Predicted search space for [20%,40%] of "sky", $p = q = 0.90$

user's option (see Fig. 3), one of the solutions that are marked by black crosses in the enlarged part of Fig. 5 is selected and the corresponding system interval is used internally for the retrieval. Possible optimization options are "maximum recall", "maximum precision" or "joint maximization of precision and recall".

In Fig. 4, the retrieval result is depicted. The user selected the 'Min. Distance to Maximum' option, that is joint optimization of precision and recall. Only the first nine retrieved images are displayed. Note the visual difference of the retrieved images that is due to the use of *concept* detectors.

Up to this point, a fixed performance p and q of the concept detectors has been assumed for the performance optimization in the second stage of the retrieval framework. On the other hand, it has been shown in Section 2 that also the performance of the concept detectors can be controlled. Using the envelopes of

Table 2. Comparison of retrieval optimization for "grass" queries

Query "grass"	$prec_{det}/rec_{det}$ of best detector		retrieval $prec/rec$ using best detector two-stage optimization	retrieval $prec/rec$ using best detector NO second stage optimization	
10 − 30%	99%	61%	89% 88%	85%	63%
20 − 40%	95%	72%	77% 79%	71%	65%
20 − 50%	95%	72%	82% 84%	75%	71%
40 − 60%	88%	85%	71% 86%	67%	90%
50 − 90%	84%	90%	89% 89%	62%	99%

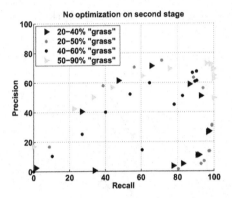

Fig. 6. Retrieval prec/rec with various 'grass'-detectors: no optimization of system interval on second stage

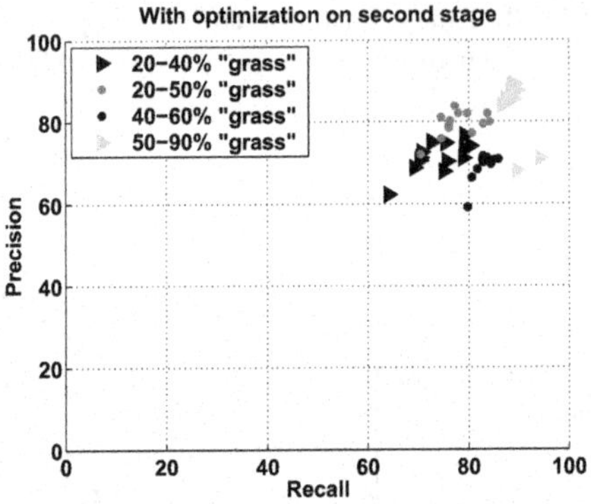

Fig. 7. Retrieval prec/rec with various 'grass'-detectors: complete two-stage optimization (joint optimization)

the curves in Fig. 2, about thirteen discrete precision/recall pairs that correspond to different concept detectors can be obtained. The performance optimization and detector selection is extended to the first stage of the retrieval framework by evaluating Eqs. 1 and 2 for all those detector precision/recall pairs.

The result of this two-stage query-dependent performance optimization is summarized in Table 2 and in Figs. 6 and 7. The queries all concern the detection of different amounts of "grass" in the database images. From the second column in Table 2 it can be seen that the best "grass"-detector is different for all queries. This underlines the fact, that we should have multiple detectors for the same concept at hand. It also shows, that it is not possible to first select the concept detector in the first stage and then to perform the interval optimization in the second stage. Instead, the two optimization stages have to be interlinked as described above. The third column lists the performance after complete two-stage optimization, whereas in column four only the best detector was selected, but no second-stage optimization was carried out. Here it can be seen that the optimization according to the user's option is carried out in the second stage. The user's option was to *jointly* optimize precision and recall. Thus, for example a high recall coupled with low precision does not satisfy the user query. The overall performance is higher when both first and second stage optimization took place. This can also be observed in Figs. 6 and 7 which show the retrieval performances for all queries and for all "grass"-detectors. In Fig. 6 the optimization of the system interval in stage two has been left out whereas in Fig. 7 the second stage performance optimization has been carried out for all detectors. The figures show that only the combination of both optimization steps leads to maximum retrieval performance. Note, that the best detector for a certain query in Fig. 6 does not necessarily correspond to the best performance in Fig. 7.

4   Conclusion

In this paper, we presented a full query-dependent performance optimization that affects jointly both stages of our two-stage image retrieval framework. The input of the optimization is a semantic concept the user is looking for, the amount of the image to be covered by the concept and the user's option for the optimization. Depending on this input, the optimization system selects a set of internal parameters that maximize the performance of the image retrieval. The selection of the concept detector that is suited best for the respective query guarantees constant quality of the performance optimization. We also presented a method to generate multiple detectors per concept that have differing performances.

Acknowledgements

This research is funded in part by the Comission of the European Union under contract IST-2000-29375, and the Swiss Federal Office for Education and Science (BBW 00.0617).

References

1. Clark, A., Courtney, P., eds.: Workshop on Performance Characterisation and Benchmarking of Vision Systems, Las Palmas, Spain (1999)
2. Haralick, R., Klette, R., Stiehl, S., Viergever, M.: Evaluation and validation of computer vision algorithms. http://www.dagstuhl.de/data/seminars/98/, Dagstuhl Seminar No. 98111 (1998)
3. Smith, J.R.: Image retrieval evaluation. In: IEEE Workshop on Content-based Access of Image and Video Libraries, Santa Barbara, California (1998)
4. Müller, H., Müller, W., Squire, D., Marchand-Maillet, S., Pun, T.: Performance evaluation in content-based image retrieval: overview and proposals. Pattern Recognition Letters **22** (2001) 593–601
5. Vogel, J., Schiele, B.: On performance categorization and optimization for image retrieval. In: European Conference on Computer Vision ECCV. Volume IV., Copenhagen, Denmark (2002) 49–63
6. Cheeseman, P., Kelly, J., Self, M., Stutz, J., Taylor, W., Freeman, D.: AutoClass: A bayesian classification system. In: International Conference on Machine Learning, Ann Arbor, MI (1988) 54–64

7. Town, C., Sinclair, D.: Content based image retrieval using semantic visual categories. Technical Report 2000.14, AT&T Laboratories Cambridge (2000)
8. Mao, J., Jain, A.: Texture classification and segmentation using multiresolution simultaneous autoregressive models. In: Pattern Recognition. Volume 25. (1992) 173–188

Multiscale Image Processing on the Sphere*

Thomas Bülow

Computer Science Division, University of California, Berkeley,
485 Soda Hall # 1776, Berkeley, CA 94720-1776, USA,
thomasbl@cs.berkeley.edu,
Phone: +1 (510) 642 5029, Fax: +1 (510) 643 1534

Abstract. We present linear filters for image processing in the case that
the image data is given on the sphere rather than on a plane. Such spherical images occur in various situations in computer vision and computer
graphics. The class of filters we present is derived from the spherical
Gaussian kernel defined as the Green's function of the spherical diffusion
equation. The derived filters include Laplacian of Gaussian, directional
Gaussian derivatives, and their Hilbert transform. All computations are
directly performed on the sphere without ever switching to a planar domain. These filters allow spherical image processing on multiple scales.
We present results on images obtained from an omnidirectional camera.

Keywords: Spherical Images, Omnidirectional Images, Spherical Gaussian, Linear Diffusion, LSI Filters.

1 Introduction

Images defined on a spherical surface rather than in the image plane arise in
various situations in computer vision and computer graphics. Some examples
are **environment maps** which are used as global light sources in computer
graphics. **3D object surfaces** for certain classes of objects can be defined as
functions on the sphere. **Omnidirectional images** representing a large subset
of the viewing sphere (e.g. one hemisphere as shown in Fig. 1) appear distorted
in the image plane and are naturally defined on the sphere. A sketch of the
catadioptric camera used for taking the picture in Fig. 1(a) is shown in Fig. 2.
For more details on omnidirectional imaging see [4] Working with this kind of
images, the need arises to define image processing operators for spherical images.
These should be conceptually similar to the ones which are used for planar
images in low-level computer vision. Linear shift-invariant filters derived from
the Gaussian kernel are probably the single class of filters with most applications
in computer vision. These include Gaussian scale space, which has turned into
a research area on its own right [10].

---

* This work was supported by the German Research Association (Deutsche
Forschungsgemeinschaft – DFG) under the grant Bu 1259/2-1.

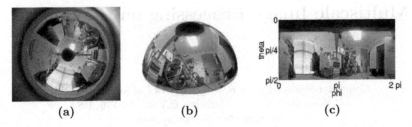

Fig. 1. (a) An image taken with a catadioptric camera (The geometry of this device is sketched in Fig. 2). The hemispherical field of view is mapped to a disk-shaped region in the catadioptric image plane. (b) The same image, back-projected to the hemisphere. (c) The image in the spherical coordinate plane.

The range of areas in which Gaussian filters have been used is by far too large to be covered here appropriately. Let us just mention that basic edge detectors like the Canny and the Marr-Hildreth edge detectors are based on Gaussian derivatives [8]. Together with their Hilbert transforms these directional derivatives of the Gaussian can be used for the phase-independent detection of directional features. Convolution with Gaussian derivatives is equivalent to the computation of "blurred" image derivatives [9].

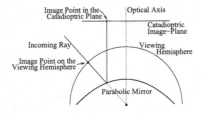

Fig. 2. A sketch of the catadioptric device composed of a parabolic mirror and an orthographic camera.

In this paper we derive the corresponding class of linear shift invariant (LSI) filters for application on the sphere. These filters facilitate multiscale approaches to spherical image processing with potential application in all of the abovementioned areas.

1.1 Failing Approaches

The most immediate attempt to filter spherical images might be to map the spherical image to a plane, to apply an LSI-filter in that domain and map the result back to the sphere. Figure 3 shows a Gaussian function at two different positions in the (φ, ϑ)-plane, exemplifying shift-invariant filtering in the plane. It can be seen that the filter is space-variant if mapped to the sphere. Thus, it is necessary to apply filters in a way which is shift invariant on the sphere itself.

The second important question to be answered is how scale should be defined on the sphere. In planar image processing a filter (e.g. the Gaussian) can be simply dilated to change scale: $g(\boldsymbol{x}) \mapsto a^{-2}g(a^{-1}\boldsymbol{x})$. In the spherical case a direct approach would be to dilate a spherical function by applying a scaling factor to the polar angle ϑ: $g(\varphi, \vartheta) \mapsto N(a)g(\varphi, a\vartheta)$. This kind of dilation does not map the spherical domain to itself: Either it is not injective ($0 < a < 1$) or

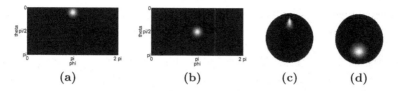

(a)   (b)   (c)   (d)

Fig. 3. A filter which is shift invariant on the spherical coordinate plane ((**a**) and (**b**)) is space variant on the sphere itself ((**c**) and (**d**)). (a) corresponds to (c) and (b) to (d).

it is not surjective ($a > 1$). Dilating a function around the north-pole leads to an overlapping conflict at the south-pole.

1.2   Related Work

A lot of work has been done on the analysis of data on the sphere, the review of which is outside the scope of this paper. We merely mention the approach most closely related to ours here. Demanet et al. [5] presented a way to construct directional filters on the sphere. The approach is to define the filter in the plane and map it by inverse stereographic projection to the sphere. This approach is based on work by Antoine et al. [1] who derive a continuous wavelet transform on the sphere. This involves the definition of dilation on the sphere by (1) stereographically projecting a function from the sphere to the plane (2) dilating the function in the plane and (3) projecting the result back to the sphere. This approach is clearly superior to the naïve dilation mentioned in Sect. 1.1 since it establishes a one to one mapping of the sphere to itself. However, it suffers from the fact that at large scales the neighborhood of the south-pole is highly squeezed which leads to undesirable effects like components of increasing frequency at increasing scales (see Fig. 4).

Fig. 4. A large scale planar Gabor filter mapped to the sphere. High frequency components emerge around the south-pole.

1.3   Contribution and Structure of This Paper

Due to the abovementioned problems with dilation on the sphere, we abandon this approach. Another way to generate the Gauss function at different scales is to let Dirac's δ-function evolve under the diffusion PDE $k\Delta u = \partial_t u$. Following this construction principle we define the spherical Gaussian function as the solution of the diffusion equation on the sphere, with a Dirac-impulse as initial condition. The diffusion equation is solved in the domain of the expansion coefficients of functions into sums of spherical harmonics (i.e. in the spherical frequency domain). We will show how the Gaussian derivatives and Hilbert transforms are readily defined in terms of the expansion coefficients of the spherical Gaussian.

To the best of our knowledge this is the first time that isotropic and directional filters for multiscale analysis of spherical images have been defined consistently and directly on the sphere.

2 Mathematical Tools

We will use the standard spherical coordinates to parametrize the unit sphere

$$\mathbb{S}^2 = \left\{ \eta(\varphi, \vartheta) := \begin{pmatrix} \cos(\varphi)\sin(\vartheta) \\ \sin(\varphi)\sin(\vartheta) \\ \cos(\vartheta) \end{pmatrix}, \quad \varphi \in [0, 2\pi), \vartheta \in [0, \pi] \right\}. \tag{1}$$

The spherical harmonic functions $Y_{lm} : \mathbb{S}^2 \to \mathbb{C}$ constitute a complete orthonormal system of the space of square integrable functions on the sphere $L^2(\mathbb{S}^2)$. In spherical coordinates the Y_{lm} are given by

$$Y_{lm}(\eta) = \sqrt{\frac{2l+1}{4\pi} \frac{(l-m)!}{(l+m)!}} P_l^m(\cos(\vartheta))e^{im\varphi}, \tag{2}$$

with $l \in \mathbb{N}$ and $|m| \leq l$. Here P_l^m denote the associated Legendre polynomials [3]. Any $f \in L^2(\mathbb{S}^2)$ can be expanded into spherical harmonics:

$$f = \sum_{l \in \mathbb{N}} \sum_{|m| \leq l} \hat{f}_{lm} Y_{lm} \quad \text{with} \quad \hat{f}_{lm} = \int_{\mathbb{S}^2} f(\eta) Y_{lm}^*(\eta) \, d\eta, \tag{3}$$

where $\cdot^*$ denotes complex conjugation. For the surface element on the sphere we use the shorthand notation $d\eta := \sin(\vartheta) \, d\vartheta \, d\varphi$. The set of coefficients $\hat{f}_{lm}$ is called the *spherical Fourier transform* or the *spectrum* of f. A rotated spherical harmonic function can be expressed by

$$Y_{lm}(g^{-1}\eta) = \sum_{|n| \leq l} e^{-im\gamma} P_{mn}^l(\cos(\beta))e^{-in\alpha}Y_{ln}(\eta), \tag{4}$$

if the rotation $g \in SO(3)$ is parameterized in Euler angles $g = R_z(\alpha)R_y(\beta)R_z(\gamma)$. The explicit form of the generalized associated Legendre polynomials P_{mn}^l can be found in [3]. Spherical harmonics are eigenfunctions of the Laplace operator restricted to the sphere $\Delta_{\mathbb{S}^2}$ as well as of the derivative operator with respect to the azimuthal angle φ:

$$\Delta_{\mathbb{S}^2} Y_{lm} = -l(l+1)Y_{lm}, \quad \partial_\varphi Y_{lm} = im Y_{lm}. \tag{5}$$

A spherical filter h is applied to the spherical image f by correlation

$$(f * h)(g) = \int_{\eta \in S^2} f(\eta)h(g\eta) \, d\eta, \quad g \in SO(3) \tag{6}$$

as used by Wandelt et al. [11]. Note, that the correlation result is defined on $SO(3)$ opposed to the image and the filter which are defined on the sphere.[1] A fast algorithm for the computation of the discrete version of (6) has been given by Wandelt et al. [11]. For *rotationally symmetric filters* h it is sufficient to place the center of the filter mask at each possible position on the sphere and neglect the rotation of the filter about its center. To distinguish this definition from (6) we denote it by $f \star h$. The result of this correlation is defined on the sphere which is at the same time the domain of the image and the filter themselves. We state the following correlation theorem without proof here: For functions $f, h \in L^2(\mathbb{S}^2)$ with $\hat{h}_{lm} = 0$ for $m \neq 0$ the spectrum of the correlation is a pointwise product of the spectra of f and h

$$(\widehat{f \star h})_{lm} = \sqrt{\frac{4\pi}{2l+1}} \hat{f}_{lm} \hat{h}_{l0}. \tag{7}$$

A similar result starting from another definition of convolution has been proven by Driscoll and Healy [6].

3   The Spherical Gaussian and Its Derivatives

Using (3) and (5) it can be easily verified that the spherical function G given by its spectrum as

$$\widehat{G(\cdot; t)}_{lm} = \begin{cases} \sqrt{\frac{2l+1}{4\pi}} e^{-l(l+1)t} & \text{if } m = 0 \\ 0 & \text{else} . \end{cases} \tag{8}$$

solves the spherical diffusion equation $\Delta_{\mathbb{S}^2} u = \partial_t u$. We call G the spherical Gaussian function. The derivation of this result has been given in [2]. Examples of the filters to be derived in this section are shown in Fig. 5.

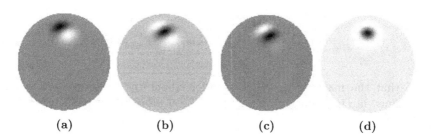

(a)   (b)   (c)   (d)

Fig. 5. **(a)** 1st derivative of a spherical Gaussian. **(b)** 2nd derivative of a spherical Gaussian. **(c)** Spherical Hilbert transform of (b). **(d)** Laplace of a spherical Gaussian.

---

[1] This property shows that filter kernels cannot be interpreted as impulse responses. Consequently, it is justified to apply the filters through correlation rather than convolution.

3.1   Laplacian of Gaussian on the Sphere

Starting from the spherical Gaussian function (8) we can enrich our set of filters by including derivatives of the Gaussian. For the derivation of the Laplacian of the spherical Gaussian (LoG) we make use of the fact that spherical harmonics are eigenfunctions of the spherical Laplace operator (5). For any function f on the sphere it follows from (3) and (5) that $(\widehat{\Delta_{\mathbb{S}^2} f})_{lm} = -l(l+1)\hat{f}_{lm}$. Applying this to the spherical Gaussian (8) we find

$$\widehat{LoG(\cdot;t)}_{lm} = \begin{cases} -l(l+1)\sqrt{\frac{2l+1}{4\pi}}e^{-l(l+1)t} & \text{if } m = 0 \\ 0 & \text{else .} \end{cases} \qquad (9)$$

3.2   Directional Gaussian Derivatives on the Sphere

It follows from (3) and (5) that taking the derivative with respect to the azimuthal angle φ of any function $f \in L^2(\mathbb{S}^2)$ can be expressed in the spectral domain as $(\widehat{\partial_\varphi f})_{lm} = im\,\hat{f}_{lm}$. Since the spectrum of the spherical Gaussian (8) contains nonzero coefficients only for $m = 0$ it follows immediately that $\partial_\varphi G(\varphi, \vartheta; t) = 0$. This is a direct consequence of the spherical Gaussian being invariant with respect to rotations about the z-axes.

We would like to apply no other operations than the ones which are easily expressible in the spectral domain. These are rotation (4), taking the derivative with respect to the azimuthal angle φ and application of the Laplacian (5). In order take the kth derivative across the center of the spherical Gaussian, we thus (I) apply a rotation about the y-axis by $\pi/2$ (which moves the center of the Gaussian to the equator of the sphere, (II) differentiate k times with respect to φ (i.e. along the equator) and (III) rotate the result by $-\pi/2$ about the y-axis (which transports the center of the filter back to the north-pole). We denote the such defined $k^t h$ derivative by G^k and find the expression

$$\widehat{G^k(\cdot;t)}_{lm} = \sqrt{\frac{2l+1}{4\pi}} \exp(-l(l+1)t) \sum_{n=-l}^{l} P_{mn}^l(0)(in)^k P_{0n}^l(0) \qquad (10)$$

Note, that the matrix $P_{nm}^l(0)$ for rotation about the y-axis by $\pi/2$ is unitary. Thus, in (10) rotation by $-\pi/2$ has been achieved by replacing $P_{nm}^l(0)$ by $P_{mn}^l(0)$.

3.3   Hilbert Transform of Directional Functions on the Sphere

The Hilbert transform of a real function $f \in L^2(\mathbb{R})$ is obtained from f by suppressing the DC-component and multiplying the frequency components by $-i$ and i for positive and negative frequencies, respectively. For background on the Hilbert transform see e.g. [7]. Observing that the φ-dependency of spherical harmonics has the same form as the 1D Fourier transform, we define the equatorial

Hilbert transform in the analogous way:

$$(\widehat{f_H})_{lm} = \begin{cases} -i\hat{f}_{lm} & \text{if } m > 0 \\ 0 & \text{if } m = 0 \\ i\hat{f}_{lm} & \text{if } m < 0. \end{cases} \quad \cdot \quad (11)$$

This applies the 1D Hilbert transform along the equator. If we are interested in the Hilbert transform of a directional Gaussian derivative we need to apply (11) between steps (II) and (III) as defined in Sect. 3.2. This introduces an extra factor $\text{sign}(n)$ under the sum in (10).

4   Experiments

Figure 6 demonstrates the effects of smoothing in different domains on synthetic data. We generate a texture which is homogeneously distributed on the sphere. Gaussian smoothing is applied in three different domains. The texture in Fig. 6(a) was generated as a sum of spherical Gaussian who's centers are at the vertices of a icosahedron which has been subdivided twice. Smoothing in the catadioptric plane as well as smoothing in the (φ, ϑ)-plane is space-variant on the sphere. Application of a spherical Gaussian leads to space-invariant smoothing. Note, that Fig. 6(d) exhibits the coarse scale structure of the texture shown in Fig. 6(a): The vertex positions of the original icosahedron stand out much more clearly on a coarse scale. Figure 7 shows some filter results for the catadioptric image shown in Fig. 1. Simple edge features are ridges of the norm of the gradient (Fig. 7(b)) or zero-crossings of the LoG filter, possibly weighted with the norm of the gradient (Figs. 7(c) and (d)). These are just some examples of possible applications. The purpose of this paper is rather to provide a generic toolbox of filters which can be applied to spherical images just like Gaussians and their derivatives are used in planar images.

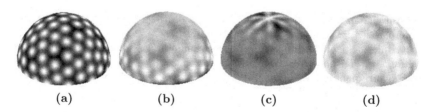

(a)   (b)   (c)   (d)

Fig. 6. (a) A synthetic texture on the upper hemisphere. (b) After Gaussian smoothing in the catadioptric plane. The smoothing effect is stronger near the pole. (c) After Gaussian smoothing in the (φ, ϑ)-plane. The smoothing effect is stronger close to the equator. (d) After spherical Gaussian smoothing.

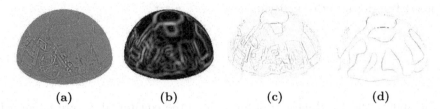

(a)   (b)   (c)   (d)

Fig. 7. All results are obtained from the input image shown in Fig. 1. **(a)** Difference of the original the smoothed image (with $t = 0.0001$). **(b)** Norm of the gradient obtained the first derivative of a spherical Gaussian with $t = 0.0002$. **(c)** Zero-crossings of the filter response of a LoG with $t = 0.0002$ weighted with the norm of the gradient. (dark = large gradient.) **(d)** Like (c). $t = 0.05$.

5   Conclusion

We have presented the construction and application of image processing filters for images defined on the sphere. These filters are derived from the Green's function of the spherical diffusion equation. They are mathematically well founded and closed expressions in the spherical frequency domain exist. The existence of fast algorithms for the computation of the spherical Fourier transform [6] and convolution on the sphere [11] make these filters a practical tool for a wide range of applications in computer vision.

Acknowledgments

This work was initiated while I worked at the University of Pennsylvania with Kostas Daniilidis whos interest and comments are highly acknowledged. The catadiopric images were supplied by Ameesh Makadia and Kostas Daniilidis. Furthermore I would like to thank Berthold Horn for discussions on this subject.

References

1. J. Antoine and P. Vandergheynst. Wavelets on the 2-sphere: A group-theoretical approach. *Appl. Comput. Harmon. Anal.*, 7, 1999.
2. Th. Bülow. Spherical diffusion for surface smoothing. In *First International Symposium on 3D Data Processing, Visualization, and Transmission*, 2002.
3. G.S. Chirikjian and A.B. Kyatkin. *Engineering Applications of Noncommutative Harmonic Analysis*. CRC Press, 2001.
4. K. Daniilidis, editor. *IEEE Workshop on Omnidirectional Vision, Hilton Head Island, SC, June 12*, 2000.
5. L. Demanet and P. P. Vandergheynst. Directional wavelets on the sphere. Technical Report R-2001-2, Signal Processing Laboratory (LTS), EPFL, Lausanne, 2001.
6. J.R. Driscoll and D.M. Healy. Computing fourier transforms and convolutions on the 2-sphere. *Advances in Applied Mathematics*, 15:202–250, 1994.
7. G.H.Granlund and H. Knutsson. *Signal Processing for Computer Vision*. Kluwer Academic Publishers, 1995.

8. B.K.P. Horn. *Robot Vision*. MIT Press, 1986.
9. J.J. Koenderink and A. von Dorn. Representation of local geometry in the visual system. *Biological Cybernetics*, 55(6):367–375, 198u.
10. J. et al. Sporring, editor. *Gaussian scale-space theory*. Kluwer, Dordrecht, 1997.
11. B.D. Wandelt and K.M. Gorski. Fast convolution on the sphere. *Phys Rev D63, 123002/1-6*, 2001.

Polydioptric Cameras:
New Eyes for Structure from Motion

Jan Neumann, Cornelia Fermüller, and Yiannis Aloimonos

Center for Automation Research, University of Maryland, College Park, MD 20742-3275, USA,
{jneumann,fer, yiannis}@cfar.umd.edu

Abstract. We examine the influence of camera design on the estimation of the motion and structure of a scene from video data. Every camera captures a subset of the light rays passing though some volume in space. By relating the differential structure of the time varying space of light rays to different known and new camera designs, we can establish a hierarchy of cameras. This hierarchy is based upon the stability and complexity of the computations necessary to estimate structure and motion. At the low end of this hierarchy is the standard planar pinhole camera for which the structure from motion problem is non-linear and ill-posed. At the high end is a camera, which we call the *full field of view polydioptric* camera, for which the problem is linear and stable. We develop design suggestions for the polydioptric camera, and based upon this new design we propose a linear algorithm for structure-from-motion estimation, which combines differential motion estimation with differential stereo.

1 Introduction

When we think about vision, we usually think of interpreting the images taken by (two) eyes, such as our own, that is images acquired by planar eyes. These are the so-called camera-type eyes based on the pinhole principle on which commercially available cameras are founded. But these are clearly not the only eyes that exist; the biological world reveals a large variety of designs. It has been estimated that eyes have evolved no fewer than forty times, independently, in diverse parts of the animal kingdom. The developed designs range from primitive eyes such as the nautilus' pinhole eye or the marine snail eye to the different types of compound eyes of insects, camera-like eyes of land vertebrates and fish eyes that are all highly evolved.

Evolutionary considerations tell us that the design of a system's eye is related to the visual tasks the system has to solve. The way images are acquired determines how difficult it is to perform a task and since systems have to cope with limited resources, their eyes should be designed to optimize subsequent image processing as it relates to particular tasks. As such a task we chose the recovery of descriptions of space-time models from image sequences – a large and significant part of the vision problem itself. By "space-time models" we mean descriptions of shape and descriptions of actions (Action is defined as the change of shape over time). More specifically, we want to determine how we ought to collect images of a (dynamic) scene to best recover the scene's shapes and actions from video sequences or in other words: "What camera should we use, for collecting video, so that we can subsequently facilitate the structure

L. Van Gool (Ed.): DAGM 2002, LNCS 2449, pp. 618–625, 2002.

from motion problem in the best possible way?" This problem has wide implications for a variety of applications not only in vision and recognition, but also in navigation, virtual reality, tele-immersion, and graphics.

To classify cameras, we will study the most complete visual representation of the scene, namely the plenoptic function as it changes differentially over time [1]. Any imaging device captures a subset of the plenoptic function. We would like to know how, by considering different subsets of the plenoptic function, the problem of structure from motion becomes easier or harder. A theoretical model for a camera that captures the plenoptic function in some part of the space is a surface S that has at every point a pinhole camera. We call this camera a *polydioptric* camera[1]. With such a camera we observe the scene in view from many different viewpoints (theoretically, from every point on S). A polydioptric camera can be obtained if we arrange ordinary cameras very close to each other (Fig. 2). This camera has an additional property arising from the proximity of the individual cameras: it can form a very large number of orthographic images, in addition to the perspective ones. Indeed, consider a direction r in space and then consider in each individual camera the captured ray parallel to r. All these rays together, one from each camera, form an image with rays that are parallel. Furthermore, for different directions r a different orthographic image can be formed. For example, Fig. 3 shows that we can select one appropriate pixel in each camera to form an orthographic image that looks to one side (blue rays) or another (red rays). Fig. 4 shows all the captured rays, thus illustrating that each individual camera collects conventional pinhole images. In short, a polydioptric camera has the unique property that it captures, simultaneously, a large number of perspective and affine images (projections). We will demonstrate later that this property also makes the structure from motion problem linear. In contrast, standard single-pinhole cameras capture only one ray from each point in space, and from this ray at different times the structure and motion must be estimated. This makes estimation of the viewing geometry a non-linear problem.

There is another factor that affects the estimation, namely the surface S on which light is captured. It has long been known that there is an ambiguity in the estimation of the motion parameters for small field of view cameras, but only recently has it been noticed that this ambiguity disappears for a full field of view camera. For a planar camera, which by construction has a limited field of view, the problem is nonlinear and ill-posed. If, however, the field of view approaches 360°, that is, the pencil of light rays is cut by a sphere, then the problem becomes well-posed and stable [7], although still nonlinear. The basic understanding of the influence of the field of view has attracted a few investigators over the years. In this paper we will not study this question in more detail and only refer to the literature for more information [3,6,10].

Thus, in conclusion, there are two principles relating camera design to performance in structure from motion – the field of view and the linearity of the estimation. These principles are summarized in Fig. 1.

---

[1] The term "plenoptic camera" had been proposed in [2], but since no physical device can capture the true time-varying plenoptic function, we prefer the term "polydioptric" to emphasize the difference between the continuous concept and the discrete implementation.

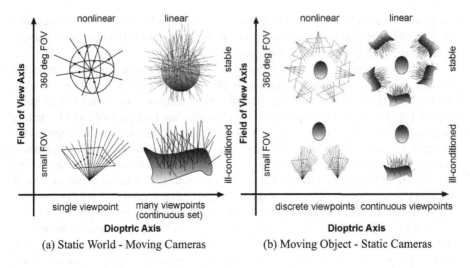

<table>
</table>

    (a) Static World - Moving Cameras   (b) Moving Object - Static Cameras

Fig. 1. Hierarchy of Cameras. We classify the different camera models according to the field of view (FOV) and the number and proximity of the different viewpoints that are captured (Dioptric Axis). This in turn determines if structure from motion estimation is a well-posed or an ill-posed problem, and if the motion parameters are related linearly or non-linearly to the image measurements. The camera models are clockwise from the lower left: small FOV pinhole camera, spherical pinhole camera, spherical pol ydioptric camera, and small FOV polydioptric camera.

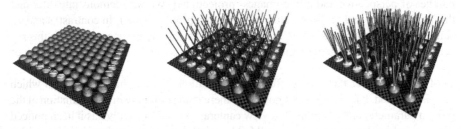

Fig. 2. Design of a polydioptric camera   **Fig. 3.** capturing parallel rays   **Fig. 4.** and capturing pencils of rays.

A polydioptric spherical camera is therefore the ultimate camera since it combines stability of full field of view motion estimation with a linear formulation of the structure-from-motion problem.

The outline of this paper is as follows. We will use the framework of plenoptic video geometry (Section 2) to show how a polydioptric camera makes structure from motion estimation a linear problem and how the image information captured by a polydioptric camera relates to the image information of a conventional pinhole cameras. Based on the insights gained, we propose a linear algorithm to accurately compute the structure and motion using all the plenoptic derivatives, and we conclude with suggestions about applications of these new cameras and how to implement and construct polydioptric cameras.

2   Plenoptic Video Geometry:
The Differential Structure of the Space of Light Rays

At each location x in free space the light intensity or color of the light ray coming from a given direction r at time t can be measured by the plenoptic function $E(x; r; t)$; $E :$ $\mathbb{R}^3 \times \mathbb{S}^2 \times \mathbb{R}_+ \rightarrow \mathbb{R}^d$, where $d = 1$ for intensity, $d = 3$ for color images, and $\mathbb{S}^2$ is the unit sphere of directions in $\mathbb{R}^3$ [1]. Since a transparent medium such as air does not change the color of the light, we have a constant intensity or color along the view direction r: $E(x; r; t) = E(x + \lambda r; r; t)$ as long as $\lambda \in \mathbb{R}$ is chosen such that $(x + \lambda r)$ is in free space. Therefore, the plenoptic function in free space reduces to five dimensions – the time-varying space of directed lines for which many representations have been presented (for an overview see Camahort and Fussel [5]). We will choose the two-plane parameterization that was introduced by [8,12] in computer graphics. All the lines passing through some space of interest can be parameterized by surrounding this space (that could contain either a camera or an object) with two nested cubes and then recording the intersection of the light rays entering the camera or leaving the object with the planar faces of the two cubes. We only describe the parameterization of the rays passing through one side of the cube, the extension to the other sides is straight forward. Without loss of generality we choose both planes to be perpendicular to the z-axis and seperated by a distance of f. We denote the inner plane as *focal plane* Π_f indexed by coordinates (x, y) and the outer plane as *image plane* Π_i indexed by (u, v), where (u, v) is defined in a local coordinate sytem with respect to (x, y) (see Fig. 5a). Both (x, y) and (u, v) are aligned with the (X, Y)-axes of the world coordinates and Π_f is at a distance of Z_Π from the origin of the world coordinate system.

This enables us now to parameterize the light rays that pass through both planes at any time t using the five tupels (x, y, u, v, t) and we can record their intensity in the time-varying lightfield $L(x, y, u, v, t)$. For fixed location (x, y) in the focal plane,

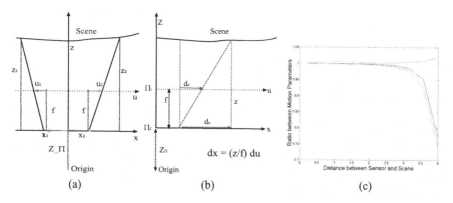

Fig. 5. (a) Lightfield Parameterization (here shown only for x and u) (b) Relationship between Perspective and Orthographic Derivatives (c) Accuracy of Plenoptic Motion Estimation. The plot shows the ratio of the true and estimated motion parameters (vertical axis) in dependence of the distance between the sensor surface and the scene (horizontal axis) for $f = 60$ and spheres of unit radius. The scene is shown in Fig. 6a.

$L(x, y, \cdot, \cdot, t)$ corresponds to the image captured by a perspective camera. If instead we fix the view direction (u, v), we capture an orthographic image $L(\cdot, \cdot, u, v, t)$ of the scene.

A sensor element on the imaging surface S captures a light ray ϕ indexed by (x, y, u, v, t). If in the neighbourhood of the ray ϕ the radiance is varying continuously (e.g., smoothly varying reflectance and albedo, and ϕ is not tangent to a scene surface), then we can develop the lightfield in the neighborhood of ray ϕ, that is $L(x, y, u, v, t)$, into a Taylor series

$$L(x + dx, y + dy, u + du, v + dv, t + dt) = L(x, y, u, v, t) + \quad (1)$$
$$L_x dx + L_y dy + L_u du + L_v dv + L_t dt + \mathcal{O}(\|dx, dy, du, dv, dt\|^2)$$

where $L_x = \partial L/\partial x, \ldots, L_t = \partial L/\partial t$ are the partial derivatives of lightfield. Disregarding the higher-order terms, we have a linear function which relates a local change in view ray position and direction to the differential brightness structure of the plenoptic function at the sensor element.

The camera moves in a static world, therefore, we assume that the intensity of a light ray in the scene remains constant over consecutive time instants. This allows us to use the spatio-temporal brightness derivatives of the light rays captured by an imaging surface to constrain the *lightfield flow* $[dx/dt, dy/dt, du/dt, dv/dt]^T$, that is the difference between the index tupels that correspond to the same physical light ray at consecutive time instants ($dt = 1$). We generalize the well-known *Image Brightness Constancy Constraint* to the *Lightfield Brightness Constancy Constraint*:

$$\frac{d}{dt} L(x, y, u, v, t) = L_t + L_x \frac{dx}{dt} + L_y \frac{dy}{dt} + L_u \frac{du}{dt} + L_v \frac{dv}{dt} = 0. \quad (2)$$

It is to note, that this formalism can also be applied if we observe a rigidly moving object with a set of static cameras (as seen in Fig. 1b). In this case, we attach the world coordinate system to the moving object and we can relate the relative motion of the image sensors with respect to the object to the spatio-temporal derivatives of the light rays that leave the object.

3   Plenoptic Motion Equations

Assuming that the imaging sensor undergoes a rigid motion with instantaneous translation t and rotation ω around the origin of the world coordinate system, then the motion of a point in the world in the coordinate frame of a camera located at position (x, y) on the plane Π_f is given by $\dot{P} = -\omega \times (P - [x, y, Z_\Pi]^T) - t$. Using the well-known equations relating the motion parameters to the motion flow in perspective and orthographic images [9], we can define the lighfield ray flow for the ray indexed by (x, y, u, v, t) as ($[\cdot; \cdot]$ denotes the vertical stacking of vectors):

$$\begin{pmatrix} dx/dt \\ dy/dt \\ du/dt \\ dv/dt \end{pmatrix} = \begin{pmatrix} 1 & 0 & -\frac{u}{f} & -\frac{uy}{f} & \frac{ux}{f} + Z_\Pi & -y \\ 0 & 1 & -\frac{v}{f} & -(\frac{vy}{f} + Z_\Pi) & \frac{vx}{f} & x \\ 0 & 0 & 0 & -\frac{uv}{f} & f + \frac{u^2}{f} & -v \\ 0 & 0 & 0 & -(f + \frac{v^2}{f}) & \frac{uv}{f} & u \end{pmatrix} \begin{pmatrix} t \\ \omega \end{pmatrix} = M[t; \omega]. \quad (3)$$

Combining Eqs. 2 and 3 leads to the *lightfield motion constraint*

$$-L_t = [L_x, L_y \, L_u, L_v] M[t; \boldsymbol{\omega}] \qquad (4)$$

which is a linear constraint in the motion parameters and relates them to all the differential image information that an imaging sensor can capture. Thus, by combining the constraints across all the lightfield, we can form a highly over-determined linear system and solve for the rigid motion parameters. To our knowledge, this is the first time that the temporal properties of the lightfield have been related to the structure from motion problem. In previous work, only four-dimensional static lightfields have been studied in the context of image-based rendering in computer graphics [8,12].

It is important to realize that the lightfield derivatives $L_x, \ldots L_t$ can be obtained directly from the image information captured by a polydioptric camera. Recall that a polydioptric camera can be envisioned as a surface where every point corresponds to a pinhole camera (see Fig. 4). To convert the image information captured by these pinhole cameras into a lightfield, for each camera we simply have to intersect the rays from its optical center through each pixel with the two planes Π_f and Π_i and set the corresponding lightfield value to the pixel intensity. Since our measurements are in general scattered, we have to use appropriate interpolation schemes to compute a continuous lightfield function (for an example see [8]). The lightfield derivatives can then easily be obtained by applying standard image derivative operators. The lightfield motion constraint is extended to the other faces of the nested cube by premultiplying t and ω with the appropriate rotation matrices to rotate the motion vectors into local lightfield coordinates.

The relationship between the structure from motion formulation for conventional single viewpoint cameras and the formulation for polydioptric cameras can easily be established. If we assume that the surface has slowly varying reflectance, we can apply a simple triangulation argument to get the following identity (du is the change in view direction and dx the corresponding change in view position as illustrated in Fig. 5b. In the illustration we set $u = 0$):

$$L(x, y, u + du, v + dv, t) = L(x, y, u + \frac{f}{z}dx, v + \frac{f}{z}dy, t) = L(x + dx, y + dy, u, v, t)$$
$$(5)$$

where z denotes the depth of the scene measured from the location (x, y) on plane Π_f in the direction indicated by (u, v). From Eq. 5, we can deduce now that we can replace any flow in the view direction variables (u, v) that is inversely proportional to the depth of the scene such as the projection of the translational flow by flow in the view points (x, y) that is independent of the scene. This enables us to formulate the structure from motion problem independent of the scene in view as a linear problem. We also see that the depth z is encoded as a scaled ratio between the positional and directional derivatives $z/f = L_u/L_x = L_v/L_y$ which is identical to the relation between depth and differential image measurements used in differential stereo and in the epipolar-plane image analysis [4]. Thus, we can interpret plenoptic motion estimation as the integration of differential motion estimation with differential stereo.

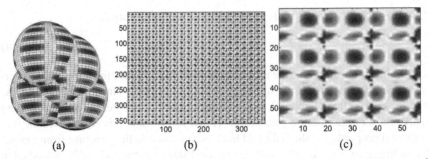

Fig. 6. (a) Subset of an Example Scene, (b) the corresponding unfolded lightfield of size 19^4 and (c) a detailed view of the upper left corner ($u, v = 1, \ldots, 19, x, y = 1, 2, 3$).

4   Experiments

To examine the performance of an algorithm using the lightfield motion constraint, we did experiments with synthetic data. We distributed spheres, textured with a smoothly varying pattern, randomly in the scene so that they filled the horizon of the camera (see Fig. 6a). We then computed the lightfields for all the faces of the nested cube surrounding the camera through raytracing (Fig. 6b-6c), computed the derivatives, stacked the linear equations (Eq. 4) to form a linear system, and solved for the motion parameters. Even using derivatives only at one scale, we find that the motion is recovered very accurately as seen in Fig. 5c. As long as the relative scales of the derivatives are similar enough (scene distance matches the filter widths of the derivative operators) the error in the motion parameters varies between 1% and 3%. This accurate egomotion estimate could then be used to compute depth from differential measurements using the following four formulas (M_i denotes the ith row of the coefficient matrix M in Eq. 3):

$$z = \frac{L_u}{fL_x} = \frac{L_v}{fL_y} = -\frac{[L_uM_1; L_vM_2][t;\omega]}{f(L_t + [L_uM_3; L_vM_4][t;\omega])} = -\frac{L_t + [L_xM_1, L_yM_2][t;\omega]}{f[L_xM_3, L_yM_4][t;\omega]}$$

These differential depth measurements can finally be refined using the large baseline stereo information from widely seperated views along the path of the camera to construct accurate three-dimensional descriptions or image-based representations (e.g. [11]) of the scene.

5   Conclusion

According to ancient Greek mythology Argus, the hundred-eyed guardian of Hera, the goddess of Olympus, alone defeated a whole army of Cyclopes, one-eyed giants. The mythological power of many eyes became real in this paper, which proposed a mathematical analysis of new cameras. Using the two principles relating camera design to the performance of structure from motion algorithms, the field of view, and the linearity of the estimation, we defined a hierarchy of camera designs. In this paper, based upon the two design principles that we have formulated, we have introduced a new family of cameras we called polydioptric cameras. Polydioptric cameras are constructed by placing a large number of individual cameras very close to each other. Polydioptric cameras capture all the rays falling on a surface and allow estimation of the plenoptic ray flow of any light ray under any rigid movement. This provides polydioptric cameras with the capability of solving for ego-motion and scene models in a linear manner, opening new avenues for a variety of applications. For example, polydioptric domes open new avenues for 3D video development. This linear formulation is based upon the study of the plenoptic video geometry that is the relation between the local differential structure of the time-varying lightfield and the rigid motion of an imaging sensor which was introduced in this paper.

Perhaps the biggest challenge in making a polydioptric camera is to make sure that neighboring cameras are at a distance that allows estimation of the "orthographic" derivatives of rays, i.e., the change in ray intensity when the ray is moved parallel to itself. By using special pixel readout from an array of tightly spaced cameras we can obtain a polydioptric camera. For scenes that are not too close to the cameras it is not necessary to have the individual cameras very tightly packed; therefore, miniature cameras may be sufficient.

Currently, we are developing different physical implementations of polydioptric eyes as suggested, and we will evaluate the proposed plenoptic structure from motion algorithm on a benchmark set of image sequences captured by these new cameras.

References

1. E. H. Adelson and J. R. Bergen. The plenoptic function and the elements of early vision. In M. Landy and J. A. Movshon, editors, *Computational Models of Visual Processing*, pages 3–20. MIT Press, Cambridge, MA, 1991.
2. E. H. Adelson and J. Y. A. Wang. Single lens stereo with a plenoptic camera. *IEEE Trans. PAMI*, 14:99–106, 1992.
3. G. Adiv. Inherent ambiguities in recovering 3D motion and structure from a noisy flow field. In *Proc. IEEE Conference on Computer Vision and Pattern Recognition*, pages 70–77, 1985.
4. R. C. Bolles, H. H. Baker, and D. H. Marimont. Epipolar-plane image analysis: An approach to determining structure from motion. *International Journal of Computer Vision*, 1:7–55, 1987.
5. E. Camahort and D. Fussell. A geometric study of light field representations. Technical Report TR99-35, Dept. of Computer Sciences, The University of Texas at Austin, 1999.
6. K. Daniilidis. *On the Error Sensitivity in the Recovery of Object Descriptions*. PhD thesis, Department of Informatics, University of Karlsruhe, Germany, 1992. In German.
7. C. Fermüller and Y. Aloimonos. Observability of 3D motion. *International Journal of Computer Vision*, 37:43–63, 2000.
8. S. Gortler, R. Grzeszczuk, R. Szeliski, and M. Cohen. The lumigraph. In *Proc. of ACM SIGGRAPH*, 1996.
9. B. K. P. Horn. *Robot Vision*. McGraw Hill, New York, 1986.
10. A. D. Jepson and D. J. Heeger. Subspace methods for recovering rigid motion II: Theory. Technical Report RBCV-TR-90-36, University of Toronto, 1990.
11. R. Koch, M. Pollefeys, B. Heigl, L. VanGool, and H. Niemann. Calibration of hand-held camera sequences for plenoptic modeling. In *ICCV99*, pages 585–591, 1999.
12. M. Levoy and P. Hanrahan. Light field rendering. In *Proc. of ACM SIGGRAPH*, 1996.
13. J. C. Yang and L. McMillan. A lumigraph camera for image based rendering. Technical report, MIT Graphics Lab, 2001.

Author Index

Lecture Notes in Computer Science

For information about Vols. 1–2380
please contact your bookseller or Springer-Verlag

Vol. 2417: M. Ishizuka, A. Sattar (Eds.), PRICAI 2002: Trends in Artificial Intelligence. Proceedings, 2002. XX, 623 pages. 2002. (Subseries LNAI).

Vol. 2418: D. Wells, L. Williams (Eds.), Extreme Programming and Agile Methods – XP/Agile Universe 2002. Proceedings, 2002. XII, 292 pages. 2002.

Vol. 2419: X. Meng, J. Su, Y. Wang (Eds.), Advances in Web-Age Information Management. Proceedings, 2002. XV, 446 pages. 2002.

Vol. 2420: K. Diks, W. Rytter (Eds.), Mathematical Foundations of Computer Science 2002. Proceedings, 2002. XII, 652 pages. 2002.

Vol. 2421: L. Brim, P. Jančar, M. Křetínský, A. Kučera (Eds.), CONCUR 2002 – Concurrency Theory. Proceedings, 2002. XII, 611 pages. 2002.

Vol. 2422: H. Kirchner, Ch. Ringeissen (Eds.), Algebraic Methodology and Software Technology. Proceedings, 2002. XI, 503 pages. 2002.

Vol. 2423: D. Lopresti, J. Hu, R. Kashi (Eds.), Document Analysis Systems V. Proceedings, 2002. XIII, 570 pages. 2002.

Vol. 2425: Z. Bellahsène, D. Patel, C. Rolland (Eds.), Object-Oriented Information Systems. Proceedings, 2002. XIII, 550 pages. 2002.

Vol. 2426: J.-M. Bruel, Z. Bellahsène (Eds.), Advances in Object-Oriented Information Systems.Procedings, 2002. IX, 314 pages. 2002.

Vol. 2430: T. Elomaa, H. Mannila, H. Toivonen (Eds.), Machine Learning: ECML 2002. Proceedings, 2002. XIII, 532 pages. 2002. (Subseries LNAI).

Vol. 2431: T. Elomaa, H. Mannila, H. Toivonen (Eds.), Principles of Data Mining and Knowledge Discovery. Proceedings, 2002. XIV, 514 pages. 2002. (Subseries LNAI).

Vol. 2432: R. Bergmann, Experience Management. XXI, 393 pages. 2002. (Subseries LNAI).

Vol. 2434: S. Anderson, S. Bologna, M. Felici (Eds.), Computer Safety, Reliability and Security. Proceedings, 2002. XX, 347 pages. 2002.

Vol. 2435: Y. Manolopoulos, P. Návrat (Eds.), Advances in Databases and Information Systems. Proceedings, 2002. XIII, 415 pages. 2002.

Vol. 2436: J. Fong, C.T. Cheung, H.V. Leong, Q. Li (Eds.), Advances in Web-Based Learning. Proceedings, 2002. XIII, 434 pages. 2002.

Vol. 2438: M. Glesner, P. Zipf, M. Renovell (Eds.), Field-Programmable Logic and Applications. Proceedings, 2002. XXII, 1187 pages. 2002.

Vol. 2439: J.J. Merelo Guervós, P. Adamidis, H.-G. Beyer, J.-L. Fernández-Villacañas, H.-P. Schwefel (Eds.), Parallel Problem Solving from Nature – PPSN VII. Proceedings, 2002. XXII, 947 pages. 2002.

Vol. 2440: J.M. Haake, J.A. Pino (Eds.), Groupware: Design, Implementation and Use. Proceedings, 2002. XII, 285 pages. 2002.

Vol. 2442: M. Yung (Ed.), Advances in Cryptology – CRYPTO 2002. Proceedings, 2002. XIV, 627 pages. 2002.

Vol. 2443: D. Scott (Ed.), Artificial Intelligence: Methodology, Systems, and Applications. Proceedings, 2002. X, 279 pages. 2002. (Subseries LNAI).

Vol. 2444: A. Buchmann, F. Casati, L. Fiege, M.-C. Hsu, M.-C. Shan (Eds.), Technologies for E-Services. Proceedings, 2002. X, 171 pages. 2002.

Vol. 2445: C. Anagnostopoulou, M. Ferrand, A. Smaill (Eds.), Music and Artificial Intelligence. Proceedings, 2002. VIII, 207 pages. 2002. (Subseries LNAI).

Vol. 2446: M. Klusch, S. Ossowski, O. Shehory (Eds.), Cooperative Information Agents VI. Proceedings, 2002. XI, 321 pages. 2002. (Subseries LNAI).

Vol. 2447: D.J. Hand, N.M. Adams, R.J. Bolton (Eds.), Pattern Detection and Discovery. Proceedings, 2002. XII, 227 pages. 2002. (Subseries LNAI).

Vol. 2448: P. Sojka, I. Kopeček, K. Pala (Eds.), Text, Speech and Dialogue. Proceedings, 2002. XII, 481 pages. 2002. (Subseries LNAI).

Vol. 2449: L. Van Gool (Ed.), Pattern Recognotion. Proceedings, 2002. XVI, 628 pages. 2002.

Vol. 2451: B. Hochet, A.J. Acosta, M.J. Bellido (Eds.), Integrated Circuit Design. Proceedings, 2002. XVI, 496 pages. 2002.

Vol. 2452: R. Guigó, D. Gusfield (Eds.), Algorithms in Bioinformatics. Proceedings, 2002. X, 554 pages. 2002.

Vol. 2453: A. Hameurlain, R. Cicchetti, R. Traunmüller (Eds.), Database and Expert Systems Applications. Proceedings, 2002. XVIII, 951 pages. 2002.

Vol. 2454: Y. Kambayashi, W. Winiwarter, M. Arikawa (Eds.), Data Warehousing and Knowledge Discovery. Proceedings, 2002. XIII, 339 pages. 2002.

Vol. 2455: K. Bauknecht, A M. Tjoa, G. Quirchmayr (Eds.), E-Commerce and Web Technologies. Proceedings, 2002. XIV, 414 pages. 2002.

Vol. 2456: R. Traunmüller, K. Lenk (Eds.), Electronic Government. Proceedings, 2002. XIII, 486 pages. 2002.

Vol. 2458: M. Agosti, C. Thanos (Eds.), Research and Advanced Technology for Digital Libraries. Proceedings, 2002. XVI, 664 pages. 2002.

Vol. 2462: K. Jansen, S. Leonardi, V. Vazirani (Eds.), Approximation Algorithms for Combinatorial Optimization. Proceedings, 2002. VIII, 271 pages. 2002.

Vol. 2463: M. Dorigo, G. Di Caro, M. Sampels (Eds.), Ant Algorithms. Proceedings, 2002. XIII, 305 pages. 2002.

Vol. 2464: M. O'Neill, R.F.E. Sutcliffe, C. Ryan, M. Eaton, N. Griffith (Eds.), Artificial Intelligence and Cognitive Science. Proceedings, 2002. XI, 247 pages. 2002. (Subseries LNAI).

Vol. 2469: W. Damm, E.-R. Olderog (Eds.), Formal Techniques in Real-Time and Fault-Tolerant Systems. Proceedings, 2002. X, 455 pages. 2002.

Vol. 2470: P. Van Hentenryck (Ed.), Principles and Practice of Constraint Programming – CP 2002. Proceedings, 2002. XVI, 794 pages. 2002.

Vol. 2479: M. Jarke, J. Koehler, G. Lakemeyer (Eds.), KI 2002: Advances in Artificial Intelligence. Proceedings, 2002. XIII, 327 pages. (Subseries LNAI).

Vol. 2483: J.D.P. Rolim, S. Vadhan (Eds.), Randomization and Approximation Techniques in Computer Science. Proceedings, 2002. VIII, 275 pages. 2002.